DATE DUE

Psychology at Work

AN INTRODUCTION TO INDUSTRIAL/ORGANIZATIONAL PSYCHOLOGY

Diane Krumm
College of Lake County

Worth Publishers

Psychology at Work

ISBN: 1-57259-659-7
Printing: 5 4 3 2 1
Year: 04 03 02 01 00

Acquisitions Editor: Marjorie Byers
Development Editor: Marian Wood
Marketing Manager: Renée Altier
Art Director: Barbara Reingold
Project Editor: Margaret Comaskey
Production Manager: Barbara Anne Seixas
Cover Art: by José Ortega. *Building a Business*
Cover and Text Designer: Lissi Sigillo
Photo Editor: Karen Barr
Photo Researchers: Kathy Bendo, Vikii Wong
Line Art: Alan Reingold
Composition: TSI Graphics, Inc.
Printing and Binding: R.R. Donnelley & Sons Company

Library of Congress Cataloging-in-Publication Data

Krumm, Diane J.
  Psychology at work: an introduction to industrial/organizational psychology / Diane J. Krumm.
     p. cm.
  Includes bibliographical references and index.
  ISBN 1-57259-659-7
    1. Industrial psychology. 2. Organizational behavior. I. Title: Introduction to
industrial/organizational psychology. II. Title.

HF5548.8 .K79 2000
158.7--dc21

00-046281

Worth Publishers
41 Madison Avenue
New York, New York 10010
www.worthpublishers.com

To my family

B r i e f   C o n t e n t s

Preface XXI

Student Preface XXV

1 Introduction
chapter 1 Introduction to Industrial/Organizational Psychology 1

chapter 2 Research Methods in Industrial/Organizational Psychology 38

2 Organizational Psychology
chapter 3 Organizational Structure 79

chapter 4 The Changing Structure of the Organization: Diversity and Development 114

chapter 5 Communication and Group Processes 152

chapter 6 Motivation and Job Satisfaction 192

chapter 7 Leadership 235

3 Personnel Psychology
chapter 8 Personnel Selection and Placement 279

chapter 9 Employee and Organizational Testing 321

chapter 10 Performance Appraisal 366

chapter 11 Employee Training and Development 409

4 The Work Environment
chapter 12 Job and Work Design 453

chapter 13 Employee Stress, Safety, and Health 492

Statistical Appendix 534

Glossary G-1

References R-1

Answers to Review Questions A-1

Name Index NI-1

Subject Index SI-1

Contents

Preface XXI
Student Preface XXV

PART 1 INTRODUCTION
Chapter 1 Introduction to Industrial/Organizational Psychology 1
LEARNING OBJECTIVES 2
WHAT IS INDUSTRIAL/ORGANIZATIONAL PSYCHOLOGY? 2
THE DEVELOPMENT OF INDUSTRIAL/ORGANIZATIONAL PSYCHOLOGY 5
>   *The Beginnings of Industrial/Organizational Psychology 5*
>   Case Study *Scientific Management at Work 8*
>   *World War I 9*
>   *Industrial/Organizational Psychology between the Wars 11*
>   *The Hawthorne Studies 12*
>   *World War II 16*
>   *The 1960s to 1980s: Legislation and Organizational Psychology 18*
>   *Current Industrial/Organizational Psychology 20*
>   *Critical Forces in the Future 23*

THE FIELD OF INDUSTRIAL/ORGANIZATIONAL PSYCHOLOGY 26
>   *Careers in Industrial/Organizational Psychology 26*
>   *Education and Training Requirements 28*
>   *Regulation and Licensing 28*

OVERVIEW OF THE TEXT 30
>   Main Points 32
>   Key Terms 33
>   Historical Figures 33
>   Review Questions 34
>   Web Exercise 37

Chapter 2 Research Methods in Industrial/Organizational Psychology 38
LEARNING OBJECTIVES 39
THE PURPOSE OF RESEARCH 40
THE SCIENTIFIC METHOD 40
>   *Hypotheses 41*
>   *Theories 42*

THE TYPES OF RESEARCH IN I/O PSYCHOLOGY   42

Experiments 42

Quasi Experiments 47

Case Study Research at Work 48

Laboratory versus Field Experiments 48

Realism 49

Correlational Studies 51

Field Studies 57

Simulation Studies 58

Surveys 58

Case Studies 60

THE REQUIREMENTS OF GOOD RESEARCH 60

Validity 60

Generalization 61

Reliability 61

THE ANALYSIS AND PRESENTATION OF RESEARCH DATA 62

The Visual Presentation of Data 63

Understanding Statistics 66

ETHICS IN RESEARCH 67

Main Points 69

Key Terms 71

Review Questions 72

Web Exercise 76

PART 2 ORGANIZATIONAL PSYCHOLOGY

Chapter 3 Organizational Structure 79

LEARNING OBJECTIVES 80

ORGANIZATIONAL STRUCTURE: HISTORY AND THEORIES 80

Bureaucratic Structures 81

Human Relations Structures 85

Systems Theory Structures 87

Sociotechnical Systems Structures 92

ORGANIZATIONAL CLIMATE AND CULTURE 95

Levels of Organizational Culture 96

Measurement of Organizational Culture 98

Person–Organization Fit 99

Creation of Organizational Culture 99

Organizational Culture Change 101

Case Study Organizational Culture Change 102

Measurement of Organizational Climate 104

Use of Climate and Culture in Organizations 106

Organizational Citizenship 106

ORGANIZATIONAL EFFECTIVENESS 107

    Main Points 109

    Key Terms 110

    Review Questions 110

    Web Exercise 113

Chapter 4 The Changing Structure of the Organization: Diversity and Development 114

LEARNING OBJECTIVES 115

THE CHANGING STRUCTURE OF THE WORKPLACE 115

DIVERSITY ISSUES IN THE WORKPLACE 116

    Benefits of Workplace Diversity 117

    Racial and Ethnic Issues 118

    Language Issues 120

    Age Issues 122

    Disability Issues 125

ORGANIZATIONAL DEVELOPMENT 130

    Components of Organizational Development 130

    Resistance to Change 132

    Organizational Change Process: Action Method 133

    Organizational Development Techniques 134

    Case Study Diversity at Work 142

    Organizational Transformation 143

    Evaluating Organizational Development 145

    Main Points 147

    Key Terms 148

    Review Questions 148

    Web Exercise 151

Chapter 5 Communication and Group Processes 152

LEARNING OBJECTIVES 153
COMMUNICATION 153

Conditions of Communication 154
Parts of the Communication Process 154
Problems in the Communication Process 158
Nonverbal Communication 159
Communication Networks 161
Formal Organizational Communication Patterns 163
Informal Organizational Communication Patterns 166
Computer-Based Communication 168
Case Study *Communications at Work 171*

GROUPS IN ORGANIZATIONS 171

Formal Groups 172
Informal Groups 173
Group Decision Making 173
Brainstorming 175
Groupthink 176
Social Loafing 178
Group Polarization 179
Group Cohesion 180
The Bottom Line 180

LABOR UNIONS 182

Reasons for Joining Unions 182
Changes in Union Membership 182
Comparisons with Nonunion Employees 183
Lack of Involvement with I/O Psychology 183
Ways to Use I/O Psychology to Rebuild Unions 183

Main Points 185
Key Terms 186
Review Questions 187
Web Exercise 191

Chapter 6 Motivation and Job Satisfaction 192

LEARNING OBJECTIVES 193
DEFINING MOTIVATION 193

THEORIES OF MOTIVATION 195

Need Theories 195

Job Design Theories 199

Cognitive Theories 203

Case Study *Delivering Psychology at Work 212*

Behavioral Theories 214

Emerging Theories 217

JOB SATISFACTION 218

Job Outcomes 218

Personal Factors in Job Satisfaction 222

Measurement of Job Satisfaction 223

Increasing Job Satisfaction 225

Main Points 227
Key Terms 228
Review Questions 229
Web Exercise 234

Chapter 7 Leadership 235

LEARNING OBJECTIVES 236
DEFINITIONS OF LEADERSHIP 237
THEORIES OF LEADERSHIP 238

Trait Theories 238

Behavioral Theory 241

Contingency Theories 243

Transformational and Charismatic Leadership 253

SUBSTITUTES FOR LEADERSHIP AND EMPLOYEE EMPOWERMENT THEORIES 256

Case Study *Leadership at Work 258*

POWER AND LEADERSHIP 259

Position and Personal Power 259

Bases of Power 259

Use of Influence 261

Power of Followers 263

PERSONAL VARIABLES IN LEADERSHIP 264

Gender Roles in Leadership 264

Racial Issues in Leadership 266
Cross-Cultural Management 269

BEING AN EFFECTIVE LEADER 269
  Main Points 271
  Key Terms 272
  Review Questions 272
  Web Exercise 276

PART 3 PERSONNEL PSYCHOLOGY
Chapter 8 Personnel Selection and Placement 279
LEARNING OBJECTIVES 280
THE IMPORTANCE OF PERSONNEL SELECTION 280
JOB ANALYSIS, DESCRIPTION, AND SPECIFICATION 281
RECRUITMENT 283
  Recruitment Methods 283
  Case Study *Psychology in Personnel Selection 286*
  Factors that Influence Recruitment 287

METHODS OF PERSONNEL SELECTION 288
  Application Blanks, Résumés and Biodata 289
  Interviews 292
  Physical Examinations 297
  Background and Reference Checks 301
  Graphology and Miscellaneous Selection Methods 303
  Assessment Centers 303

SELECTION DECISIONS 307
  Diversity Issues and the Selection Ratio 307
  Simple Regression Model 308
  Multiple Regression Model 310
  Multiple Cutoff Model 310
  Multiple Hurdle Model 311
  Utility Decisions 313

  Main Points 313
  Key Terms 315
  Review Questions 315
  Web Exercise 320

Chapter 9 Employee and Organizational Testing 321

LEARNING OBJECTIVES 322
PURPOSE AND HISTORY OF EMPLOYMENT TESTING 322
LEGAL REQUIREMENTS OF TESTING 324
ETHICS AND TESTING 327
TYPES OF COMMONLY USED TESTS 329

Mental Ability Tests 329

Interest Inventories 331

Personality Tests 332

Aptitude and Achievement Tests 334

Integrity (Honesty) Tests 336

WHAT MAKES A GOOD PSYCHOLOGICAL TEST? 339

Reliability 339

Validity 341

Item Analysis 346

Norms 346

Standardization 347

CLASSIFICATION OF TESTS 347

Power versus Speed 347

Individual versus Group 348

Paper and Pencil versus Performance 348

Objective versus Subjective 348

Language versus Nonlanguage 349

Computerized Testing 349

Case Study *Selection Testing with Computers 350*

CHOOSING THE RIGHT TEST 354
ADVANTAGES AND DISADVANTAGES OF USING TESTS 355

Advantages 355

Disadvantages 356

THE FUTURE OF TESTING 357

Main Points 358
Key Terms 359
Legal Rulings and Legislation Influencing Personnel Selection Decisions 360
Review Questions 361
Web Exercise 365

Chapter 10 Performance Appraisal 366

LEARNING OBJECTIVES 367
PURPOSE OF PERFORMANCE APPRAISALS 368
  Individual Purposes 368
  Organizational Purposes 369

WHAT MAKES A PERFORMANCE APPRAISAL FAIR? 370
JOB ANALYSIS 371
  Methods of Job Analysis 371
  Job Evaluation and Comparable Worth 376

METHODS OF PERFORMANCE APPRAISAL 378
  Outcome-Based Methods 378
  Absolute Standards Methods 381
  Relative Comparisons Methods 387

ERRORS IN PERFORMANCE APPRAISAL 388
  Halo Errors 388
  Leniency and Severity Errors 389
  Central Tendency Errors 389
  Contrast and Similarity Errors 390
  Recency Error 390
  Frame of Reference Errors 390

WHO DOES THE PERFORMANCE APPRAISAL? 392
  Immediate Supervisor 392
  Subordinate Appraisal 393
  Peer Evaluation 393
  Self-Evaluation 394
  Human Resources Department and Assessment Centers 394
  Multiple Raters 395
  Case Study *Appraisals at Work 396*

PERFORMANCE APPRAISAL INTERVIEWS 396
IMPROVING PERFORMANCE APPRAISALS 399
EVALUATING PERFORMANCE APPRAISAL PROGRAMS 400
  Main Points 402
  Key Terms 403
  Review Questions 403
  Web Exercise 408

Chapter 11 Employee Training and Development 409

LEARNING OBJECTIVES 410

INDIVIDUAL AND ORGANIZATIONAL TRAINING PURPOSES 411

Workplace Literacy 412

New-Employee Orientation 413

Continuing Education and Career Development 414

Retirement Planning 416

ASSESSMENT OF TRAINING NEEDS 416

Organizational Needs Analysis 417

Task Needs Analysis 417

Person Needs Analysis 418

TRAINING OBJECTIVES 419

PRINCIPLES OF LEARNING 420

Classical and Operant Conditioning 420

Schedules of Reinforcement 421

Transfer of Training 421

Other Principles of Learning 422

Cognitive Learning 423

Readiness and Motivation 423

Role of the Trainer 424

TRAINING METHODS AND TECHNIQUES 426

Training at the Job Site 426

Off-the-Job-Site Training 430

EVALUATION OF TRAINING PROGRAMS 439

Training Evaluation Criteria 439

Design of Training Evaluation Models 442

Cost of Training Evaluation 444

Case Study Training Works On-Line 444

Main Points 445

Key Terms 446

Review Questions 447

Web Exercise 450

PART 4 THE WORK ENVIRONMENT

Chapter 12 Job and Work Design 453

LEARNING OBJECTIVES 454

INTRODUCTION TO HUMAN FACTORS PSYCHOLOGY 455
EQUIPMENT DESIGN 456
  Role of the Human Factors Psychologist 456
  Roles of People and Machines 458
  Displays 459
  Controls 461

WORKSPACE DESIGN 465
  Psychological Factors in Workspace Design 465
  Workplace Envelope 465

COMPUTERS AND HUMAN FACTORS 467
  Ergonomic Computer Workspace Design 468
  Problems in the Computer Workspace 468
  Computer Hardware and Software 469
  Attitudes toward Computer Use 471
  Virtual Reality 471

ROBOTS AND HUMANS 472
NONTRADITIONAL WORK SCHEDULES 475
  Shift Work 475
  Compressed Work Week 476
  Flextime 477
  Job Sharing 478

WORKPLACE DESIGN 478
  Open Offices 479
  Telecommuting 480
  Case Study *Telecommuting Works 481*

QUALITY OF WORK LIFE 484
  Main Points 486
  Key Terms 487
  Review Questions 487
  Web Exercise 491

Chapter 13 Employee Stress, Safety, and Health 492
LEARNING OBJECTIVES 493
STRESS IN THE WORKPLACE 493
  Stress and Productivity 494

Consequences of Stress 496

Contributors to Stress 498

Stress Management at Work 509

SAFETY IN THE WORKPLACE 511

Accidents, Injuries, and Illnesses at Work 512

Reducing and Preventing Accidents and Injuries at Work 517

Workplace Violence 522

Case Study *Preventing Violence at Work 525*

Main Points 527
Key Terms 528
Review Questions 529
Web Exercise 533

Statistical Appendix 534

LEARNING OBJECTIVES 535
DESCRIPTIVE STATISTICS 535

Measures of Central Tendency 535

Normal and Skewed Distributions 536

Measures of Variability 540

INFERENTIAL STATISTICS 544

Point Estimation 544

Hypothesis Testing 545

Meta-Analysis 546

Main Points 546
Key Terms 547
Review Questions 547

Glossary G-1
References R-1
Answers to Review Questions A-1
Name Index NI-1
Subject Index SI-1

Like many of you, I have spent a number of years searching for textbooks that meet my teaching needs as well as the learning needs of the students. This text has been carefully designed to blend the best of traditional and current approaches to teaching I/O psychology, with an innovative topic order, unique new features, and a firm foundation of pedagogical soundness.

As in economics classes, where many instructors have strong beliefs about the best sequence for teaching macro and microeconomics, I/O psychology instructors often have strong feelings about the best sequence for teaching the industrial and organizational topics of the course. Traditionally, the industrial topics have been presented first in this course, because they were the initial focus of I/O psychology. Since those early years, the organizational side of I/O psychology has become increasingly important, emphasizing the interaction between these fields. The name change from Industrial Psychology to Industrial/Organizational Psychology in the 1970s reflected this interaction and interdependence. When I started teaching 28 years ago, industrial topics were still receiving the greatest attention in this course. Many texts and course outlines added organizational material as it became more significant, but it was typically added at the end of the text and the course.

Yet in course evaluations and conversations, students often told me that they wished the organizational material had been covered first, because these topics gave them a better overall perspective of organizations and I/O psychology. Many colleagues agreed that these student comments made sense. I tried teaching the organizational topics before the industrial topics for several semesters and I found better student understanding and a better flow of topics. These are some of the reasons that I structured this text to cover the organizational topics directly after the introductory and research methods chapters. I hope you will try this sequence and let me know if you have the same success I have had.

Of course, if you prefer the traditional sequence, the chapters on industrial topics can easily be presented to satisfy that choice. While topics from each chapter do form a foundation for later chapters, there is enough independence so that after the first two foundational chapters, sequencing is more of a preference than a requirement.

Given the importance of integrating research and theory, pedagogical soundness and currency are vital underlying elements of this text. This book has been a wonderful opportunity for me to read and incorporate original and historical source material as well as the most current materials from sources such as *The Industrial/Organizational Psychologist* newsletter site on the World Wide Web and other Internet sources.

I have also put special emphasis on presenting the material in an accessible, logical way so students can get the most out of each chapter's concepts, applications, and features. Each chapter starts with learning objective questions. The question format makes these objectives more interactive for students. The objectives could easily be used as the basis for essay exam questions. At the end of each chapter a list of important points gives students a way to check that they have covered the material in the chapter.

The review questions at the end of each chapter interactively reinforce student learning of the chapter material. Instead of waiting for a classroom test to assess comprehension, students can receive feedback and go back to material that has not been mastered before they take the classroom test. I have found that questions like this also leads to students asking more questions in class. Instead of saying that they don't understand Locke's goal setting theory, for example, it is often easier for them to ask, "Could you explain Question 13?"

The marginal glossary defines important terms as they are encountered in the text. Since students often come to this course with a variety of academic and psychology backgrounds, less-critical terms are italicized and defined in a glossary at the end of the text. Students who have more knowledge of psychology will probably not need to look up the italicized terms. Students with less background will not be left behind as they can quickly locate definitions.

To encourage more personal applications as well as the use of Internet resources, each chapter includes an exercise using the World Wide Web. My students have been using similar exercises for several semesters, and I have received very positive feedback from them. They have even suggested additional sites and exercises! Although all links mentioned are active as this book went to press, it is possible some may change during the life of this edition. If you find an inactive or changed link, please check the book's companion website (http://www.worthpublishers.com) for information.

One of the other concerns I often hear from students is the problem of relating abstract concepts to the frame of reference in their workplace. Only a small number of introductory I/O psychology students are going to become industrial/organizational psychologists, work in human resources departments, or become executives; most have worked and will work in very diverse jobs and settings. Therefore, throughout this text, I have discussed a broad sample of jobs and settings, from the traditional to the very nontraditional, including volunteers and students. I have also, at every opportunity, illustrated concepts and theories with a variety of real-life examples, because such concrete examples are often the difference between students just memorizing a concept and really understanding the material. In addition, each chapter includes a *Psychology at Work* case study highlighting a concept or theory from the chapter with a real-world application. The case study also shows students that the concepts and theories discussed in the text can actually be applied in real-life settings.

Recent research shows that many of the principles and concepts of I/O psychology fit much broader applications than we have traditionally used. This text helps students see that work can mean many different jobs and settings, from CEO of a large organization to the volunteer who works at the local library. My hope is that students will find a greater carryover to the different jobs in their work world.

Each semester I have tried to improve my teaching and the materials I use — and I continued my quest for the I/O psychology book that has everything I wanted as well as being interesting to my students. Each semester I added more material from other sources and developed more of my own material. I wrote a study guide for the students based on the text I was using. All these efforts and encouragement from my colleagues and students led to this text, bringing together the best of the traditional and the most recent developments to make a comprehensive yet highly readable text that will enhance the learning process for students and instructors alike.

In addition to helping students to be successful in this course, Worth Publishers and I also want you to be successful as instructors in this course. As well as the supplementary material such as the Internet exercises and the case studies, we have also prepared a text-specific Web site (http://www.worthpublishers.com/), a test item file and instructor's manual, and a student study guide

Writing this text has truly been a labor of love for me, but it would not have been possible without the wonderful help and support of many people:

Catherine Woods, publisher, for her initial interest and belief in this project, and continuing support for making my dreams into reality. I continue to be in awe at how many projects and roles she juggles at the same time without dropping the balls.

Marge Byers, sponsoring editor, and Mark Cajigao, project director, for unending patience, answers to all my fears and problems, creative solutions, calmness in the middle of many storms, and for their friendship.

Marian Wood, developmental editor, for her ability to focus on the end result and skillfully help me to get there.

Tracey Kuehn, associate managing editor, for her careful and thorough work shepherding this book and me through the publication process.

Margaret Comaskey, project editor, for her attention to details and quest for perfection, and her friendly voice on the phone.

Barbara Reingold, for a design and layout that is exactly what I wanted if I had been good enough to do it.

Barbara Seixas and Stacey Alexander, production managers for the book and the supplements, for keeping everything on schedule.

Connie Meinholdt, who wrote the instructor's manual and test bank, Katherine Demitrakis, who prepared the study guide, and Graig Donini, the supplements and media editor.

John F. Binning, Illinois State University; Richard D. Goffin, University of Western Ontario; Jane A. Halpert, DePaul University, Jack Hartnett, Virginia Commonwealth University; Jo Ann Lee, University of North Carolina at Charlotte; James B. Meyer, Florida State University; Michael McCall, Ithaca College; Steven G. Rogelberg , Bowling Green State University; N. Clayton Silver, University of Nevada, Las Vegas; and Marie Waung, University of Michigan-Dearborn; who reviewed the manuscript and provided invaluable advice.

Peggy, Sandy, Joan, Karen, John and Wendy at the College of Lake County for their tireless support of and interest in this project.

My students, past, present and future. They continue to be a source of intellectual stimulation and challenge. My high scores on job satisfaction and job involvement are in large measure generated by them.

My daughter, Kayde. Not only does she provide relief from work, but she brings joy and a whole different perspective to my work and life. She has shared my deadlines and goals from watching me type on my laptop computer while she took tae kwon do lessons to helping me choose cover designs for the book.

Most of all, to my mentor and friend, Bob Daugherty of Southern Illinois University at Edwardsville. Although his untimely death prevents him from seeing the completion of the path he started me on, his influence remains as strong as ever.

This text is designed as a firm foundation for helping students reach their goals. Whether you are teaching this class for the first time or the 200th time, I hope that this text will interest you and your students and assist both of you in reaching your goals for the class. I believe this is the text many of you have been looking for. I look forward to hearing from you.

Diane Krumm
College of Lake County
Grayslake, IL 60030
DJKPSY@aol.com

Dear Student,

This textbook was created especially for you. I know your instructor has chosen this text, but you will be spending a lot of time using it during the course.

Many of you are currently working as well as taking classes. For this reason, I have written about a wide variety of work settings from the traditional office to my workspace at home and your jobs as well. Today, research and applications are leading to new and exciting definitions of work. If you go to school full-time and you are getting good grades, is this considered work? If you go to school and work full-time, is school your part-time job? If you are a parent and also work full-time outside the home, do you have, in effect, more than one full-time job?

I have tried, through text material and specific examples, to show you different facets of the changing nature of work. You will find that many of the examples, drawn from actual organizations, may relate to you as a student, but they could equally apply to many other jobs as well. All these examples were carefully chosen to spark insights and ideas about your role in the world of work.

Another way this text brings industrial and organizational psychology to life is by showing how theories and concepts can be applied to everyday work situations. For example, the *Psychology at Work* case study in each chapter provides you with an application of one or more of that chapter's concepts. Students often tell me that applications help them to understand abstract concepts or theories. The case studies also demonstrate that these theories and concepts really work in organizational settings.

Many of the features in this book are the result of feedback from students like you. During my many years of teaching at the college level, I listened carefully as students told me what was good and bad about the course and the text. Many students said they benefited from activities that required them to be actively involved rather than just passively reading the text. That's why each chapter in this text begins with learning objective questions to direct your reading. After you complete a section, you will be able to look back and answer the learning objective questions for that section. In fact, many of the questions may be similar to the essay exam questions used by your instructor.

Another valuable feature, included in response to student feedback, is the margin glossary. With this feature, the most important terms from each chapter are defined in the margin on the page where the term is first used, so you can review definitions without losing your place or interrupting your reading. Other important terms you may need to know are defined in the glossary at the end of the text.

Each chapter ends with a summary of the important points covered in the chapter and a number of review questions on the chapter material. These questions may be similar to exam questions used by your instructor. They are also a good learning check for you to make sure you have mastered the material in the chapter.

One of the most rewarding experiences for me occurs when students return after finishing this course (sometimes after several years) and tell me how all or part of what they learned in the course really applied to them, no matter how diverse the work setting. I learn so much from my students each semester and they often provide me with wonderful examples and applications. I hope you will get in touch with me, share any comments you have, and let me know where you are in the world of work.

Diane Krumm
College of Lake County
Grayslake, IL
DJKPSY@aol.com

Introduction

Introduction to Industrial/Organizational Psychology

1

Chapter Outline

LEARNING OBJECTIVES

WHAT IS INDUSTRIAL/ORGANIZATIONAL PSYCHOLOGY?

THE DEVELOPMENT OF INDUSTRIAL/ORGANIZATIONAL PSYCHOLOGY

The Beginnings of Industrial/Organizational Psychology

Case Study Scientific Management at Work

World War I

Industrial/Organizational Psychology between the Wars

The Hawthorne Studies

World War II

The 1960s to 1980s: Legislation and Organizational Psychology

Current Industrial/Organizational Psychology

Critical Forces in the Future

THE FIELD OF INDUSTRIAL/ORGANIZATIONAL PSYCHOLOGY

Careers in Industrial/Organizational Psychology

Education and Training Requirements

Regulation and Licensing

OVERVIEW OF THE TEXT

Learning Objectives

After reading this chapter, you should be able to answer the following questions:
- What is industrial/organizational (I/O) psychology, and what are its three major specialty areas?
- How did the following people and time periods contribute to the development of I/O psychology: Scott, Münsterberg, Bingham, and Taylor (early 1900s); Yerkes (World War I); the Hawthorne Studies (1920s); Cattell, Gilbreth, and Bills (1930s); World War II; and the 1960s to 1980s?
- What are the current trends in I/O psychology?
- What are the seven critical forces that are likely to influence I/O psychology in the future?
- What are the requirements for becoming an I/O psychologist?

"Hi! I'm Diane Krumm. I teach psychology at a college in Illinois": my name, my job, and where I work. How many times have you described yourself to someone by using similar words? Where you work and what you do are central to who you are as a person. The years you spend at work may make up the longest period of continuing activity in your adult life. Even when you leave work at the end of the day, your job and your workplace continue to influence you. The stress of a merger at work may keep you from getting enough sleep at night. When you decide which computer to buy for your personal use, you may choose the model you use at work. If your company gives you a bonus for exercising three times a week, you may join a health club with your spouse. Since work is so important in everyday life, it makes sense to learn how to make your work experience beneficial for you and the organization for which you work.

WHAT IS INDUSTRIAL/ORGANIZATIONAL PSYCHOLOGY?

In this textbook you will discover the field of industrial/organizational (I/O) psychology, which focuses on understanding work from the perspective of psychology. Most people are familiar with psychology from courses they have taken or from popular literature but do not understand how influential I/O psychology is until they take a course and read a textbook such as this one. One reason people are not familiar with the work of I/O psychologists is that these psychologists often work in the background and sometimes do not have much contact with employees.

Evidence for the influence of I/O psychology can be seen in virtually every aspect of the work experience, however. From the employment tests you took when applying for your job, to the training you received at various points in your career, to the design of your job, to your preparation for retirement, I/O psychologists have affected you and your company. One of the two goals of this book is to increase your awareness of the role of I/O psychology in work life; the other goal is to familiarize you with the major topics, theories, and principles of I/O psychology as they relate to everyday life. While most of you will not become I/O psychologists, you will be consumers of the research and work of I/O psychologists; at the end of this course, you should be better consumers.

Before studying I/O psychology, it is important to understand how it relates to the entire field of psychology. Industrial/organizational psychology is an area of specialization within the field of psychology. Although many people associate psychology primarily with the study of abnormal behavior, it includes specialization areas that study everything from perception and sensation to brain functions. Figure 1.1 shows some of those areas. **Psychology** is the scientific study of behavior and mental processes. It is a research-based science. This means that when psychologists study behavior and mental processes, they must use systematic, exacting research methods. This reliance on a rigorous, meticulous research

Psychology The scientific study of behavior and mental processes.

F i g u r e   1 . 1

Specialization areas in psychology and the percentage of people working in each area.

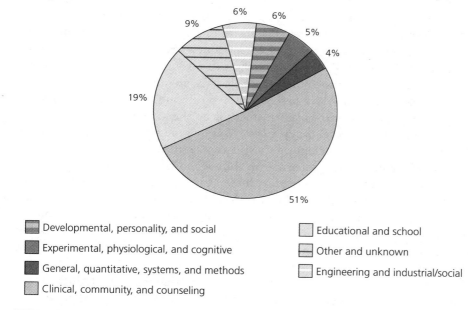

- Developmental, personality, and social
- Experimental, physiological, and cognitive
- General, quantitative, systems, and methods
- Clinical, community, and counseling
- Educational and school
- Other and unknown
- Engineering and industrial/social

methodology is part of I/O psychology just as it is part of every other specialty area in the field.

Industrial/organizational psychology refers to the application of psychological theory and methodology to the problems of organizations and the problems of groups and individuals in organizational settings (American Psychological Association, 1981). Over the last several decades I/O psychology has expanded to include many organizational settings other than traditional businesses. The principles of I/O psychology apply as much to hospitals, schools, the military, and volunteer organizations as they do to factories and stores. (Sometimes it is difficult to think of a student or a library volunteer as having a job, but most people agree that taking classes or shelving books involves doing work.) Expanding the field of I/O psychology beyond traditional settings has brought beneficial information and new areas of understanding to the entire field.

Although the traditional topics associated with I/O psychology, such as productivity and the selection of new employees, continue to be important areas of research and application, new areas develop in response to the needs of and changes in society. The study of employee fitness and health has become an important field (Gebhardt & Crump, 1990), as has the balance between family life and work life as the number of dual-career couples continues to increase (Zedeck & Mosier, 1990). Even investment in stocks and bonds has become an area of psychological study (Dreman, 1995).

Within I/O psychology, there are three major specialty areas. **Personnel psychology** is the area of I/O psychology that deals with employee recruitment and selection, training and development, performance appraisal, and job analysis. Many of you will have the greatest amount of contact with this specialty. Psychologists in this area often work in human resources departments. In other departments of organizations they may help develop programs to increase motivation and job satisfaction and to reduce stress. Although the whole organization may benefit from these programs, the focus is on the individual employee.

In **organizational psychology,** the focus is on group influences on individual employees. The individual employee is still a concern, but the primary subject of study is the influence the group has on the individual employee. I/O psychologists in this area may be concerned with the structure of the organization, communication patterns in the organization, the effect of diversity among employees, the organizational climate and culture, and group decision making. A psychologist working in this area is often a consultant who joins an organization for a particular project, rather than a permanent employee such as a member of the human resources department.

The third specialty area is **human factors** or **engineering psychology,** which focuses on the interaction between people and machines in the workplace. This may include workplace and equipment design as well as safety programs. The increased use of technology, such as computers, has increased the need for I/O psychologists trained in human factors. Psychologists who work in this area often have a background in engineering as well as psychology.

Each of these specialty areas is represented in the chapters of this textbook. While I/O psychology was not originally so influential, the role of I/O psychologists has expanded greatly with the development of the field. The next section shows how the field grew and changed in the twentieth century.

THE DEVELOPMENT OF INDUSTRIAL/ ORGANIZATIONAL PSYCHOLOGY

One way to understand the work I/O psychologists do today is to look at what they did in the past. From the beginnings of I/O psychology in the early 1900s to the present, the field has expanded and added work and research areas in response to the needs expressed by society, business, and government.

The Beginnings of Industrial/Organizational Psychology

The field of psychology is only a little over a hundred years old. One person who often is given credit as a founder of the field is **Wilhelm Wundt,** who was responsible for the development of the first psychological laboratory at Leipzig University in Germany in 1879 (Lindsley, 1988). Many of the early psychologists, some of whom became I/O psychologists, studied in Germany with Wundt. Psychology as a formal field of study is generally regarded as having begun in the United States in 1892 with the founding of the American Psychological Association (APA), which is still the largest professional organization for psychologists.

I/O psychology as a specialty field dates back to the early 1900s, when psychologists began to study problems related to work and work behavior. Their studies dealt with topics such as how telegraph operators acquired their skills (Bryan & Harter, 1897) and the potential use of psychological principles in advertising (Scott, 1903). At that time the field was referred to as industrial psychology because the focus was on the individual employee at work.

Two men often are cited as the founders of I/O psychology. In 1901 **Walter Dill Scott,** then a professor at Northwestern University, was asked to give a speech to a businessmen's club in Chicago (Landy, 1993). He was somewhat hesitant to accept the invitation. He had studied with Wundt in Germany, where he had been trained in using measurements and observable data. At that time psychologists were supposed to be concerned only with pure research. Many of them did not view the application of psychological principles to business concerns as an acceptable practice. Scott stated that he kept his interest in advertising a secret from his colleagues at Northwestern because he thought they would ridicule him (Baritz, 1960). Although the conflict between application and research thus started many years ago, it is still an active concern in I/O psychology (Farr, 1997).

After some thought Scott did give the speech, which was well received and led to several articles and books on the use of psychological principles in advertising. He then became prominent in the business community. In addition to applying psychological principles to advertising, Scott introduced the notion of incentive pay to motivate employees. He was concerned with employees' attitudes as well. Scott also worked on methods of employee selection and persuaded several companies to use psychological tests as part of the selection process for new employees. He started a private consulting firm, the Scott Company, in 1919, beginning a long tradition of I/O psychologists serving as consultants to the business community.

The other contender for the honor of being the founder of I/O psychology was **Hugo Münsterberg,** who emigrated from Germany after studying with Wundt and receiving a doctorate. Münsterberg spent time back in Germany during the years when he taught at Harvard. This led to the introduction of industrial psychology in Germany.

Münsterberg was a proponent of selection testing. He developed tests for traveling salesmen at the American Tobacco Company and for motormen with the Dallas street railway system. After the sinking of the *Titanic*, he publicized his earlier studies on personnel selection tests for ship captains (Van De Water, 1997). He also announced the development of the first "lie detector," or polygraph. (Landy, 1993).

It has been estimated that as late as 1917 there were only ten I/O psychologists in the United States (Katzell & Austin, 1992). Even with so few practitioners, conflict developed. Münsterberg, who was described as a man "people loved to hate" because of his very strong personality (Landy, 1993), was at the center of many conflicts. Those disputes involved his working outside the academic community, taking too much credit for the development of psychology at Harvard University, and supporting Germany in World War I.

He wrote what many people consider the first industrial psychology textbook, *Psychology and Industrial Efficiency* (1913), which examined the possibilities of psychology in industry. The writing of that textbook marked the beginning of formal training in industrial psychology. In 1915, at the Carnegie Institute of Technology, **Walter V. Bingham** started the Division of Applied Psychology, the first academic program in I/O psychology. Bingham often is regarded as being responsible for the emphasis on basic research in the early years of I/O psychology. In 1916 he persuaded Walter Scott to come to Carnegie and become the first professor of applied psychology.

Although most people would credit either Scott or Münsterberg, or both, as the founder(s) of I/O psychology, another person had a profound effect on the developing field. **Frederick W. Taylor** was an engineer who believed that scientific principles could be applied to redesign the work environment. Taylor thought that this would result in greater productivity, benefiting the organization and leading to higher wages for the employees. When you think of "efficiency experts," you are thinking of a field that dates back to Taylor. Taylor developed the theory of **scientific management,** the first widely accepted management theory: It was based on using the most efficient tools and motions to do a job. His *Principles of Scientific Management* (1911) described the basic principles of the theory. Taylor was the first person to recognize the importance of considering the employees in work situations (Greenberg & Baron, 1993). Until that time concern for the worker was not a factor in developing work methods and work environments. The four fundamental principles of scientific management are shown in Table 1.1.

Scientific management
The first widely accepted theory of management. Developed by Frederick W. Taylor, it was based on using the most efficient tools and motions to do a job.

Table 1.1

FUNDAMENTAL PRINCIPLES OF TAYLOR'S SCIENTIFIC MANAGEMENT THEORY

1. Work methods can be scientifically designed for efficiency, which results in the "one best method" for doing a job.
2. The best workers should be selected and trained in the new "one best method."
3. There should be a spirit of cooperation between management and workers; management and workers must share responsibility for the design and conduct of work.
4. Motivation results from monetary gain.

Today many of those principles seem like common sense. The major belief of scientific management was that production processes should be standardized to increase workers' productivity. At that time, however, Taylor's theory was so different from the popular view that it met with resistance from both management and workers. In a time when craft workers still made entire products, it was difficult to believe that a single most efficient method could be defined for each job. That method was determined by dividing a job into the smallest possible units of time and motion and looking for the movements and methods that would lead to the least waste of time and motion.

In one of his early applications of scientific management Taylor studied the work of a group of coal shovelers. Before his study each worker typically brought his own shovel to work. As Taylor studied the movements made by the shovelers, he found that different shovels worked better for different types of loads. By changing the movement patterns of the shovelers and then having them use different company-supplied shovels for different types of loads, he dramatically increased the shovelers' output.

Taylor was able to show that he could improve the efficiency of many jobs. Some of those changes now seem simplistic, such as giving tall workers shovels with longer handles. Many managers found his theory appealing because it had a direct effect on financial gain for the organization and provided an objective system for evaluating workers and allocating pay. However, many workers believed that scientific management was a scheme to get them to do more work for the same money or less.

The emphasis of scientific management on efficiency and productivity led to charges of exploiting workers. Because of high unemployment and the fear that more efficient workers would mean fewer jobs, the attacks became so hostile that Taylor was investigated by the U.S. House of Representatives (Van De Water, 1997). Some of his principles eventually were shown to be wrong. Taylor intended his theory to apply only to manual jobs where workers were regarded as no more than pieces of machinery to be used in the most efficient way possible. A number of Taylor's principles have, however, been updated and applied in the field of human factors, or engineering, psychology. The case study "Scientific Management at Work" shows how some organizations are making use of Taylor's work today.

[Case Study] SCIENTIFIC MANAGEMENT AT WORK

The time-and-motion studies of scientific management have been updated by human factors specialists in I/O psychology to include making work better for the employee as well as for the organization. When Dan Bishop founded Maids International, a franchised housecleaning service, he carefully studied how workers cleaned homes. Then he found ways to simplify and speed up each movement. For instance, he showed workers how to wind a vacuum cord in three seconds instead of eight and revised the order of tasks so that workers would bend over thirty times, not seventy-two times, during a cleaning session. Thanks to human factors, housecleaning is more efficient and less tiring, reducing worker turnover and boredom.

Since the 1920s time-and-motion studies have helped United Parcel Service (UPS) identify the best and fastest ways to accomplish specific tasks. Shaving just a few seconds off the handling of each of the twelve million packages delivered daily can make a big difference in the efficiency of UPS's 331,000 employees. In the delivery end of the business UPS managers have measured how much time a driver needs to walk up to a customer's door and deliver a package. Based on the results of those studies, the company settled on the optimal methods and timing for delivery. Now UPS drivers are trained to ignore the doorbell and knock when delivering a package to most homes. UPS also has applied scientific management to its back-office operations. As a result, back-office workers are expected to sort 1,124 packages an hour with fewer than one mistake every two hours. Employees who load the delivery trucks are expected to handle five hundred or more packages every hour. These standards help UPS balance speed and accuracy in getting packages to the right destination at the right time and have helped employees improve their job performance ratings.

From UPS revolves around you. United Parcel Service jobs employment page, http://www.upsjobs.com (April 6, 1999); Why the maids. Maids International home page, http://www.maids.com/future/whymaids.htm (April 6, 1999); The tightest ship in the shipping business. In Gregory Moorhead & Ricky W. Griffin. (1998). *Organizational behavior.* Boston: Houghton-Mifflin, p. 9; Courtland L. Boveé, John V. Thill, Marian Burk Wood, & George P. Dovel. (1993). *Management.* New York: McGraw-Hill, p. 44.

The last important event in the early period of I/O psychology occurred in 1917, when the *Journal of Applied Psychology* started to report research in this field. The publication also became a platform for establishing scientific standards for research in I/O psychology. It is still one of the major sources for published research in the field. Although many articles explore basic research issues, there are also a number of applied studies. Students often use this journal for reports; they are able to understand the applied research because it relates directly to their own work experience. For example, later in this text you will read about the use of equity theory, which can predict whether employees will steal from work if they have their pay lowered without receiving an explanation for the decrease.

After the establishment of I/O psychology early in the twentieth century, the outbreak of World War I led to rapid and extensive growth in the field.

World War I

Scientific advances often seem to happen much faster during wars, perhaps because of the necessity of doing things quickly and the urgent need to solve problems. Some psychologists believe that industrial psychology really began on April 6, 1917—the day the United States entered World War I—based on the enormous growth of the field during and shortly after the war (Dunnette & Borman, 1979).

The U.S. Army was confronted with the problem of classifying millions of recruits. It had never faced that problem before because the machinery of war had never included sophisticated weapons such as tanks and planes. Who should become an infantryman, who should be sent to officers candidate school, and who should receive technical training? In 1916 a group of psychologists headed by **Robert M. Yerkes,** working under the surgeon general of the United States, reviewed hundreds of intelligence tests. From that review they drew up a series of tests, which they tried out on four groups of military personnel. Eventually, those tests were given to almost two million men by more than four hundred officers and enlisted men who were specially trained to administer them (Figure 1.2).

Figure 1.2

World War I led to the use of psychological tests to classify recruits
or reject them from military service.

Corbis/Bettmann

When the results of the first test, the Army Alpha, were analyzed, it was discovered that over a quarter of the recruits were illiterate and unable to take the
test. Another test, the Army Beta, was developed to test illiterate recruits. The
main purpose of those early intelligence tests was to identify "officer material"
and men with such low mental ability that they should be dismissed from the military. Before the war military officers had identified these two groups through
trial and error or from experience. After the entry into the war time was at a premium, and trial-and-error methods were too slow to meet personnel needs.

Classifying recruits according to intelligence test scores was only a first step
toward the goal of classifying recruits for job training in the military. A group of
psychologists that included Walter Dill Scott and Walter Bingham turned their attention to rating men in the army according to their abilities, education, and
prior experience in order to place them in jobs that would make the best use of
their skills. The psychologists also developed methods to rate officers for ap-
pointment and promotions. After the war ended, the surgeon general's office and
the U.S. Army were flooded with requests for information about the testing programs. Many psychologists agree that the Army Alpha and Army Beta demonstrated that large-scale group testing works and that they led to the growth of
psychological testing after the war (Hale, 1982; Sokal, 1987).

Industrial/Organizational Psychology between the Wars

After the war I/O psychology continued to develop. The first doctorate in industrial psychology was awarded in 1921 (Katzell & Austin, 1992). The subfield of personnel testing grew quickly but contracted somewhat when the results did not meet managers' expectations. One writer estimated that up to 90 percent of organizations that started using psychological tests at the end of the war later abandoned them (Baritz, 1960).

New types of tests, such as those on vocational interests, were developed during this period. Organizations began to add personnel departments, and companies turned to industrial psychologists to help increase efficiency and workers' well-being. However, not all organizations sought to improve workers' well-being from purely unselfish motives; managers thought that improving morale would make employees less vulnerable to the appeals of labor unions, which were starting to grow in the postwar period (Baritz, 1960).

To help with these and other problems, organizations sought out newly formed consulting firms.

In addition to Walter Scott's consulting company, there was **James Cattell's** firm, the Psychological Corporation. Cattell hoped to find a way to conduct psychological research without depending on public institutions such as universities or the government, by providing consulting services for a fee. The money received would be split between the corporation and the psychologists, with the corporation's funds being used for research. The Psychological Corporation is still in business and is a major developer of psychological tests that earn millions of dollars in revenue—even though the corporation made a profit of only $51 in its first two years (Landy, 1993). The Psychological Corporation's board of directors has often been a who's who of psychologists, including John Watson and Edward Thorndike, the fathers of operant conditioning; Edward Titchener, often called the father of American psychology; Lewis Terman, who originated the concept of the intelligence quotient (IQ) and developed the first successful American intelligence test; and Walter Dill Scott.

You may have noticed that all the early I/O psychologists discussed so far were men. As in other sciences in the early 1900s, psychology included only a small number of women. In 1917 Cattell found that males constituted 90 percent of all psychologists (Cattell, 1917). However, the 9.8 percent female representation in psychology was much higher than the 2.1 percent in chemistry or the 1.3 percent in physics and geology. Whereas men held the majority of psychology positions at universities and colleges, women held the majority of positions in applied psychology in the early years, although I/O psychology had the lowest percentage of women of any of the applied areas (Koppes, 1997). For many years the applied areas of psychology were viewed as having less prestige than the academic areas, and this may have allowed more women to enter the applied areas.

Among the early female psychologists who influenced the development of I/O psychology were **Marion Bills** and **Lillian Gilbreth.** After completing her studies and holding other positions, Bills worked at Aetna Life Insurance Company for almost thirty years. While there, she published articles in a number of journals. She also developed a wage incentive system, a job classification system, and a job evaluation program (Austin & Waung, 1994). Gilbreth is best known for the time-and-motion studies she did as a consultant with her husband, Frank Gilbreth (Koppes, 1997). After her husband died in 1924, she continued their consulting business for forty years. One of her goals was to humanize scientific management. She published many books and articles, including "The Present State of Industrial Psychology" (Gilbreth, 1925).

These women, along with the men already discussed, established the field of I/O psychology as an important part of both psychology and the work environment. They set the stage for the expansion of research, as will be described in the next section.

The Hawthorne Studies

One of the foundations of the development of I/O psychology between the world wars was the **Hawthorne Studies** (Mayo, 1933). The I/O psychologist most often associated with these studies is **Elton Mayo,** but many others were involved in different aspects of the research. The Hawthorne Studies are important for three reasons. First, while it may not have been planned, they represent an effort to understand employees rather than approaching problems solely from the point of view of increasing workers' efficiency. The Hawthorne Studies also used more rigorous experimental methods than did many of the other early field experiments. Second, they were the first studies to show how employees' attitudes and interpersonal relationships affect productivity (Roethlisberger & Dickson, 1939). Third, they led to one of the most important movements in industrial psychology: the human relations movement.

Hawthorne Studies
A landmark series of research studies that changed the focus of early I/O psychology from scientific management to human relations.

The Hawthorne Studies began in the late 1920s as a joint effort between researchers at Harvard University and the Western Electric Company of Chicago. The studies initially were concerned with topics such as the effects of different levels of illumination, wage incentives, ventilation, and rest pauses. These topics relate to Taylor's theory of scientific management. The studies started by changing the level of illumination in three selected departments. At that time the electrical industry was promoting the use of artificial light in places of work instead of inconsistent natural light. Representatives of the industry claimed that good artificial light would reduce accidents, save workers' sight, and improve production rates as much as 25 percent (Gillespie, 1991).

One of the reasons three departments were selected was that each one had a different pay system, which the researchers believed might affect the lighting study results. From the start the researchers were aware that the workers would talk with one another and that such "people factors" could influence the results. Thus, from the start, in an attempt to minimize the people factors, the researchers told the workers about the study. They changed the lighting on weekends when the workers were not present, but interviews showed that the workers were aware of the changed lighting levels. Some employees were interviewed about their personal reactions to the lighting changes. During the experimental period, performance improved in all three departments. The problem for the researchers was that there was no relationship between the periods of lighting levels and the productivity levels. Improved lighting could not be clearly identified as the cause of the improved productivity.

After the researchers concluded that the lighting changes were not the major reason for the productivity changes, they started looking for other explanations. One possibility was greater supervision during the test periods. The extensive measurements and interviews meant that the supervisors spent more time with the workers. The groups also appeared to have started a production competition among themselves. The researchers decided to try to eliminate these possible reasons for the productivity changes.

A second series of experiments tried to control more variables and use different experimental situations. The experimental and control groups were put in different buildings to reduce group competition. A control group of relay assemblers was given the same supervision as the experimental group, but without the lighting changes. The results were so erratic that "no increase in production levels could be credited to the illumination increases" (Gillespie, 1991). After a third test with similar results the experimenters began to concentrate on the human factors rather than trying to eliminate them as they had in the earlier experiments.

At that point the researchers established a relay assembly test room and developed a list of questions. Lighting was no longer the focus of the research; the questions instead dealt with worker fatigue and attitudes. Relay assembly was chosen because it was a repetitive task that often was associated with fatigue. The test room was set up for six workers and equipped to record individual production automatically. The women chosen to work in the test room were all young, single women from the ethnic communities of Chicago. Production was monitored carefully for each individual and for the group. The women were examined each month at a local hospital to obtain health information. Production increased in over two-thirds of the twenty-four experimental test periods.

The women were active participants in the research. They were told in advance about changes, and discussions were held about what effect the changes could have on production. For example, when rest periods were introduced, the

■ Workers at the Hawthorne Western Electric plant about the time of the Hawthorne Studies. My grandfather is the blond-haired man in the front row, third from the right.

Courtesy of Diane Krumm

women were told that these periods could contribute to increased production. The women were allowed to check the monitoring equipment and get reports about their output several times each day. They did not like the hospital checkups, and so the checkups were turned into party events with refreshments and entertainment; they began to call the man in charge of the test room by a nickname. In general, the atmosphere was very easygoing and social. The social status of the women in the test room soared above that of the other relay assemblers in the plant. The women clearly saw the testing room as an opportunity to achieve social status levels in the company that otherwise would not have been available to them. They had the opportunity to control their work situation to an extent not available to any other workers in the plant. Since they valued their positions in the test room and believed that those positions depended on their being good producers, they organized a system that allowed them to work cooperatively to keep up the group rate so that they could hold on to their positions.

Production rates increased greatly, but the researchers were unable to pin down the cause. At that point Elton Mayo and another psychology professor, **Clair Turner,** were asked to help interpret the data. They also added more data by requesting information about the women's diets, blood pressure, recreation, hours of sleep, and menstrual cycles, as well as about room temperature and humidity. Even with the additional data, a clear cause for the production increases was not found. Later tests used different jobs and different pay systems without finding the causes of the results. Although no single cause for the production increases was found, the result of the Hawthorne Studies was a shift from Taylor's belief that workers are motivated only by money to the position of the human relations movement that worker satisfaction increases productivity.

Among the findings commonly attributed to the Hawthorne Studies are the following:

1. Employees' productivity is affected by their relationships with coworkers; the work environment is also a social environment.

2. A supervisor's leadership style and the amount of attention directed toward subordinates affect workers' productivity.
3. Workers set their own standards or norms for acceptable behavior and output.

These findings of the Hawthorne Studies may now seem only common sense; for example, it may seem obvious that a supervisor's leadership style has an effect on productivity. Before the Hawthorne Studies, however, leadership style was regarded as unrelated to workers' productivity: If you dislike your supervisor, you can still do your job; the job will not be as pleasant, but there is no reason why you cannot do it at the same level you would achieve if you liked and respected your supervisor. However, you may quit as soon as you can, and that would lead to replacement costs. A similar belief was held about association with coworkers; because employees were viewed as another type of machinery, it was thought that whether workers liked their coworkers had no significant effect on productivity.

One of the findings of the Hawthorne Studies that directly opposed the theory of scientific management is that groups set their own norms for the amount of work each employee produces. Scientific management assumed that groups would not set standards of what is acceptable output or productivity if they were paid by piece rate, where an individual employee can make more money by producing more. Piece rate involves paying an employee for every unit produced. For example, a drill-press operator may be paid two dollars for every piece produced correctly. The concept of incentive and piece-rate pay was introduced by Scott (Landy, 1993).

The Hawthorne Studies showed, on the contrary, that the group decides over time what is acceptable productivity and what is not. For example, assume that the average drill-press operator can produce twelve pieces per hour. If one person with exceptional skill can produce twenty pieces per hour, there will be considerable pressure on that person not to work as hard as he or she can but to cut back and produce perhaps fifteen or sixteen pieces per hour. The average employee in this situation will be concerned that management will lower the pay rate per piece: If one person can do twenty pieces per hour, why can't everyone? Employees also are concerned about appearing to be less competent than the exceptional employee and how that will affect their jobs. The superior employees in these situations often feel pressure to lower their productivity. They often are excluded from the social relationships within the group. If that does not work, they may be threatened or even physically abused.

One of the major results of the Hawthorne Studies was the **human relations movement** (Bass & Barrett, 1981), which was concerned with studying employees' attitudes, interpersonal relationships, and leadership styles in order to achieve better production. The focus of this movement was an increased sensitivity toward workers and the conditions of work. Workers could no longer be

Human relations movement A movement that studies employees' attitudes, interpersonal relationships, and leadership styles to achieve better production.

viewed as passive. Employees set their own norms of behavior, work more productively under certain types of supervision, and often are more concerned with what their peers believe than with what the supervisor believes. The social factors in an organization have to be taken into account. Many people believe that this began the transition from industrial psychology to industrial/organizational psychology, even though the formal change did not take place for almost forty years.

Scientific management was criticized for looking at only one dimension of employees, physical efficiency; a similar criticism could have been applied to the human relations movement, the slogan of which might have been "A happy worker is a productive worker." Earlier in this section the example was used of the person who liked his supervisor and worked very hard. The opposite example was used of the worker who disliked his supervisor but still worked very hard. Getting good performance involves more than providing monetary rewards or being kind to employees. Some scientists and employees view human relations techniques as a way to manipulate employees to work harder for less pay. Throughout the years, the methodology of the Hawthorne Studies has often been criticized (Bramel & Friend, 1981; York & Whitsett, 1985). However, their profound effect on the field of industrial psychology cannot be questioned (Sonnenfeld, 1982). The Hawthorne effect (the influence of observation on behavior) has found its way into all areas of psychology.

World War II

World War II, like World War I, was a major catalyst in the development of I/O psychology. Hundreds of psychologists worked in the armed forces, including Bingham and Yerkes, who had been involved in testing armed forces personnel during World War I. A major difference was that this time the military approached the psychologists instead of the other way around.

A major development was the Army General Classification Test, which was developed to place recruits in separate categories on the basis of their ability to learn different military duties and responsibilities. The assessment center method of appraisal (see Chapter 10) was developed by the Office of Strategic Services (OSS) (Murry & Mackinnon, 1946). The purpose of this program was to test a candidate's ability to work in stressful situations before his assignment to a military intelligence unit. As an example, a candidate was instructed to perform a certain task and was given helpers. However, the "helpers" were psychologists who tried to obstruct the work or sat by passively. The candidates were assessed for the appropriateness of their responses to the stressful situation created by the helpers.

One of the major areas of development during the war was equipment design. As a result of the tremendous advances in technology, equipment needed to be made easier to use correctly. An example is the aircraft used in the war. Training times for pilots had to be decreased drastically from prewar standards to meet wartime demands. (Before this time, planes made by different manufacturers had different controls in different places.) Airplane instruments were now made easier to use, and controls were standardized. For all practical purposes, every aspect of the war effort became a topic for industrial psychology: Selection and placement, training, performance appraisal, morale and attitude change, and the design of equipment were all areas of study for I/O psychologists (Figure 1.3).

Figure 1.3

The sophisticated equipment used by the military in World War II led psychologists to become involved in designing equipment that was easier to use.

Northrop Grumman/Index Stock

Corbis

Industrial psychology also became a factor in civilian life. The workforce and the country faced several unique challenges. The economy had to move from peacetime production to accelerated war production. Workers, many of whom had no previous work experience, flooded into the expanding defense industry. This problem was magnified by the shortage of qualified instructors. The wartime economy also saw an influx of women into the workforce. Millions of men were serving in the military, creating a shortage of workers; women were encouraged to join the workforce to replace the men. Before the war the concern had been fitting people to jobs. World War II saw the addition of an organizational aspect to industrial psychology as the focus shifted to fitting work to people at the level of the organization and the work group, not only at the level of the specific job (Katzell & Austin, 1992). Human factors psychology became more important in achieving those goals.

Division of Industrial and Organizational Psychology
A division of the American Psychological Association group that later was incorporated as the Society for Industrial/Organizational Psychology.

The enormous expansion of I/O psychology and a restructuring of the American Psychological Association led to the establishment in 1945 of a separate division in the APA, Division 14, the Division of Industrial and Business Psychology. In 1960 "Business" was dropped from the title, and in 1970 the name became the **Division of Industrial and Organization Psychology**. In 1982 the division was incorporated as the Society for Industrial and Organizational Psychology, Inc. (SIOP). The next section looks at some of the changes in the field that influenced those changes.

The 1960s to 1980s: Legislation and Organizational Psychology

After World War II, industry and the public sector in the United States adopted many of the findings of industrial psychology. Unlike the situation after World War I, the military did not suddenly lose interest in research; instead, each branch of the military created its own research center (Katzell & Austin, 1992). With the change from a manufacturing-based to a service-based economy, in the late 1950s, for the first time, the number of workers providing services increased to more than 50 percent of the workforce (Bass, 1965). Work became more specialized. Equipment became more technologically advanced with the later advent of computers and robotics. Unions were a major force in industry at this time due to the increasing number of collective bargaining agreements.

One of the major influences on I/O psychology was government regulation, which directly affected I/O psychologists, workers, and employers. In the 1950s various states and the APA began suggesting or legislating standards for the use of the title "psychologist." By the mid-1960s an unprecedented growth in government regulations and laws began to affect employees directly. Some of the most influential legislative acts are listed in Table 1.2.

Organizations had to be concerned not only with specific federal and state laws but with the agencies established by those laws, which often have the authority to set guidelines and make laws, issue executive orders, and influence court rulings. One of the major effects of this legislation on I/O psychology was to focus concern on the validity and fairness of tests used in employment settings. As organizations were required to show the legal fairness of their tests, they increasingly called on I/O psychologists for proof of fairness or the development of new tests that would be fair.

The scope of topics studies by I/O psychologists grew tremendously during the 1960–1980 period. Like society as a whole, I/O psychology has become diversified since the 1960s as its focus has widened to include new areas. These changes led to the name change to industrial/organizational psychology and the incorporation of Division 14 of the APA, which was mentioned in the last section.

Table 1.2

LEGISLATION AND ORGANIZATIONS THAT HAVE INFLUENCED THE FIELD OF
I/O PSYCHOLOGY SINCE WORLD WAR II

Legislation	Purpose
Civil Rights Act of 1964 and Civil Rights Act of 1991	Outlaw discrimination against many groups of employees
Equal Employment Opportunity Commission (EEOC), established by Title VII of the Civil Rights Act of 1964	Investigate charges of discrimination and develop selection and hiring guidelines for employees
Occupational Safety and Health Act of 1970 (OSHA)	Regulate workplace safety for employees
Family and Medical Leave Act of 1993	Allow covered employees up to twelve weeks of unpaid leave during a twelve-month period after a birth or adoption; to care for a seriously ill parent, spouse, or child; or to receive medical treatment for a serious illness
Age Discrimination in Employment Acts of 1976 and 1978	Prevent unfair treatment of workers age forty to seventy in the workplace
Pregnancy Sex-Discrimination Prohibition Act of 1978	Require that pregnancy-related medical conditions be treated in the same way as any other medical disability
Americans with Disabilities Act (ADA) of 1990	Protect the rights of disabled employees in the workplace

As people began to work in increasingly diverse settings, I/O psychologists found that the theories and research findings of I/O psychology also applied to settings other than industrial organizations. Organizations not traditionally associated with industrial psychology began to be involved in research and applications. Hospitals, charities, and schools are all concerned with and profit from I/O psychology.

Also, industrial psychologists began to study organizations as a whole with regard to their influence on individual employees. Some attention shifted from individual workers and jobs to the characteristics of organizations and their relationship to employees' attitudes and behavior (Katzell & Austin, 1992). Factors such as organizational culture, organizational change, and organizational development became substantive issues. How the organization as a whole affects satisfaction, commitment, goal setting, and productivity became an important concern. Motivational approaches such as expectancy theory and goal setting (see Chapter 6) reflected this new concern with organizational issues. Organizational behavior modification echoed the interest of society in behaviorism and the work of B. F. Skinner.

Current Industrial/Organizational Psychology

Many of these newer trends and issues are represented in the current major areas of interest in I/O psychology.

In addition, there are areas being researched today that were rarely considered twenty years ago. As the importance of personnel health and stress management was recognized, I/O psychologists began to study the contribution of work to individual wellness and disease (Ilgen, 1990). With a more affluent and educated workforce and increasing costs of replacing dismissed or fired employees, job satisfaction and motivation became more important. I/O psychologists now study the off-the-job life of workers (Zedeck & Mosier, 1990) as it affects their life at work. Decreases in organizational loyalty among employees have led to research on organizational commitment. Among the main topics of study for I/O psychology today are the following:

1. Legal and social issues such as court rulings, safety standards, and fair employment
2. Employee recruitment and retention, along with the study of future human resource needs
3. The analysis of training needs and the evaluation of training programs
4. Organizational culture (the "personality" of the organization)
5. Fitness, health, and stress
6. The effect of new technology on the workplace and employees
7. Future needs of and challenges faced by organizations
8. The internationalization and increasing diversity of the workplace (Offerman & Gowing, 1990; Schmidt, Ones, & Hunter, 1992; Schmidt & Robertson, 1990: Tannenbaum & Yukl, 1992)

In terms of work, a survey of members of SIOP showed that the most active areas were organizational development, personnel selection, attitude surveys, and performance appraisals (Borman & Cox, 1996). Some of this work is being done by academic I/O psychologists who work part time in organizations or by external consultants. In 1998 SIOP developed a statement to answer the question "What is an I/O psychologist?" The preliminary draft stated that

> Industrial/Organizational (I/O) Psychologists use scientific methods, theory and data to understand and influence behavior and experiences in organizations. They are committed to doing research that is relevant to solving real-world problems and to practice that is firmly grounded in research and data. They have training, supervised experience and competencies in most or all of these areas: (1) the design and analysis of research, (2) the analysis and evaluation of jobs and work systems, (3) performance measurement, (4) assessing individual differences, (5) personnel recruitment, selection and placement,

(6) training and structured learning, (7) career development, (8) job attitudes and work motivation, (9) development and management of work teams, (10) leadership and supervision, (11) organizational theory and organizational development, (12) health and stress in organizations (*TIP*, 1998)

I/O psychology will have to continue to change and grow in order to survive and thrive in the future. The scope of human resource planning is changing as organizations now are forced to compete with organizations around the world as well as with those nearby (Jackson & Schuler, 1990). As the global economy has become more competitive, organizations have laid off employees in the process of downsizing in order to improve their competitive position. Increased displacement of employees has led to another relatively new area of study as I/O psychologists attempt to help employees make an easier transition from one career to another and attempt to find new placements for dismissed employees (Cameron, Freeman, & Mishra, 1991). As employees become more concerned with issues such as career choice, development, and adjustment, I/O psychology is developing new models and treatments to meet those concerns (Osipow, 1991).

Another trend that had its beginnings in the human relations movement is the concern with leisure time. Employees are less willing to give up time for recreation and family, but the distinction between work time and family time is becoming blurred. Technological advances such as laptop computers, cellular telephones, pagers, and fax machines can keep employees in contact with their employers and on the job anywhere and at any time.

The composition of the American workforce is changing demographically. As American society becomes older, the age of the average worker is expected to increase significantly in the next several decades. Thus, health care concerns are becoming more important, leading to research on staffing, productivity, and management development in the health care field (Metzger, 1991). The gender, ethnic, and racial compositions of the workforce are also changing. For example, the majority of married women now work outside the home, a major change from the situation twenty years ago. Workforce diversity and training for a diverse workplace (a workplace that doesn't follow the strict 9–5 structure in many ways) have become major concerns in I/O psychology.

New technological developments will influence I/O psychology, as they will society as a whole. I/O psychology typically has been concerned with helping make new technologies easier to use and more likely to increase workers' productivity. Thus, human factors specialists look, for example, for ways to design computer monitors to reduce glare and computer keyboards to reduce the incidence of carpal tunnel syndrome. I/O psychologists realize that new technology alone will not lead to increased productivity (Turnage, 1990); correct selection and training of personnel will also be needed. Anyone who has watched and waited while a

Figure 1.4

The increasing use of technology in modern businesses has involved I/O psychologists in the design of equipment and in training employees to use it.

Crandall/The Image Works

salesperson entered endless numbers and codes before taking a customer's money and offering a receipt knows that technology that is used incorrectly often makes things harder. When improved technology leads to higher productivity and better work, everyone benefits; but when it results in lower productivity, many people blame the technology rather than human factors. Training can be too brief or too superficial. Employees may lack the experience and training to deal with unusual situations. I/O psychologists have increased their presence in these situations to improve the interactions between technology and employees (Figure 1.4).

Technology will also influence how the field of I/O psychology itself functions. Personal computers and the Internet allow quick access to sources and data that were not easily available in the past. Current issues of *TIP* (*The Industrial Psychologist*) on the SIOP Web site can communicate information before it reaches print media. Statistical analyses that years ago would never have been considered are now done by computer programs. Technology may also be used in new methods of data collection and other areas, such as training, communication, and employee safety and health.

State, local, and federal legislation will continue to affect I/O psychology. Sometimes the role of the I/O psychologist is that of an interpreter for the purpose of applying legislation in everyday work settings. For example, the Occupational Safety and Health Administration (OSHA) has 140 rules concerning the use of wooden ladders, and its regulations for the selling of cabbage are over 29,000 words long (Howard, 1994). Most organizations want to meet legal standards, but the overwhelming number of legislative acts and rules may make it difficult for them to comply. The Small Business Administration (SBA) estimates that small businesses spend a billion hours a year filling out government forms. Organizations must react to changes in laws and court rulings even when regulations are eliminated. The mid-1990s saw many court rulings limiting the use of affirmative action. Organizations were forced to change their policies in order to follow the new rulings, some of which have the power of law.

Critical Forces in the Future

One reason for looking so closely at the development of I/O psychology is to find hints about what the field will be like in the future. In the development of I/O psychology, different skills and knowledge were emphasized at different times. In each new era skills and knowledge were added, but for the most part very few requirements or jobs for I/O psychologists have been eliminated. The future most likely will involve an expansion of the role of I/O psychology. In *Future Work*, Coates, Jarratt, and Mahaffie (1990) look at seven critical forces that are changing the workforce and the job of the I/O psychologist.

The first critical force is increasing diversity in the workforce. Older Americans are increasing in numbers and influence. They are remaining in the workforce longer and present challenges to I/O psychologists to keep them productive. Hispanic Americans are the fastest-growing minority in the United States today. The increasing numbers of members of racial and ethnic minorities in the workplace require organizations to look at a human resource pool that is focused on job performance rather than stereotypes of perfect employees. After the year 2000 women will make up 50 percent or more of the workforce. Since most women, in addition to working outside the home, still have the primary responsibility for child and family care, I/O psychology has become involved in ways to help them—and all employees—integrate multiple roles and responsibilities to achieve the best outcomes for themselves and the organization.

Gender and sexuality issues have blurred the line between work issues and away-from-work issues because the changing makeup of the workforce has made these social concerns relevant to the workplace, for example, in cases of sexual harassment. Legislation has required organizations to make reasonable accommodations for disabled employees who are able to do the job, leading to a need for evaluating the tasks essential for each job. In some cases this means a complete job analysis and new job description for a number of positions that currently are not open to some disabled workers.

The second critical force is a reintegration of home life and work life. Before the Industrial Revolution, a large percentage of work was home based. For the blacksmith who worked in a barn next to his house and the inn owners who lived on the top floor of the inn, home life and work life were one. An inn owner would not close the doors at eight in the evening and tell people looking for a place to stay that it was family time and she was not working anymore that day. The Industrial Revolution of the mid-1800s brought people to central work locations that often were some distance from their homes. Work life and home life became distinct. Employees might stay long hours at work, but they would not bring the assembly line home with them.

Modern technology has made the blurring of work life and home life an issue again. It has allowed a new type of home-based work called telecommuting in which the employee works at home several days a week but stays connected to the office by means of a computer, modem, telephone, fax machine, and other technology. For employees who spend very little time at a central office, hotel-type arrangements allow them to reserve an office on a given day and are reducing real estate costs for organizations. Even for an employee who works primarily at the organization site, technology has allowed her to bring work home more easily. Pagers and cellular telephones allow her to stay in touch with the office twenty-four hours a day. Work arrangements such as job sharing and flextime also make better use of human resources. But the blurring of work life and family life has also led to increased employee stress, and thus to I/O psychologists paying greater attention to stress management.

The third force changing I/O psychology is globalization. Multinational organizations and customers present new opportunities but new challenges as well. I/O psychologists often facilitate the development of a world focus in balance with a national focus. It is becoming more difficult to define a country of origin for a number of products. If parts for a car come from four different countries before final assembly in the United States, it is only partially correct to identify it as an American-made car. Organizational ownership may consist of a group of foreign investors who want to bring new methods from their country as well as to adopt American methods in their own country. Preparing to work and live in a multicultural workplace can be less stressful with careful planning and the help of I/O psychologists. Within the field of cross-cultural psychology, researchers are beginning to look at cultural differences and similarities in areas such as negotiation, motivation, and work behavior (Bond & Smith, 1996).

The fourth force is expanding human resources planning. The head of the human resources department in an organization is becoming as much of a strategic planner as is the chief financial officer; planning and supplying human resource needs are becoming as critical as planning and supplying financial needs. When employees and their skills are seen as company assets rather than costs, it becomes important to develop those assets. As organizations continue to down-size, the human resources department becomes critical in retraining personnel and developing clear rewards for performance. As workers become more directly accountable for performance, they desire greater control over their jobs; success-ful implementation of employee empowerment programs usually requires the as-sistance of I/O psychologists.

The fifth force is the change from a manufacturing-based to a knowledge-based workforce. In 1998, 80 percent of U.S. employees worked in the service sec-tor and only 20 percent worked in the manufacturing sector (*Newsweek*, 1999). The American Society for Training and Development has said that by the year 2000, 75 percent of all employees will need to be retrained in new jobs or taught new skills for their current jobs. For I/O psychology, this means developing se-lection methods that assess current skills and retraining workers in new skills.

As work teams become more prominent in the workplace, training in group dynamics and social interaction skills becomes more important. Because they are unable to find enough applicants who have high-school-level reading and mathe-matics skills, some organizations have begun to offer basic literacy programs to bring the skills of applicants up to the standards required for entry-level jobs. Other organizations are requiring computer literacy for all management person-nel and are providing training to reach that goal. Organizations are continuing to increase their technology expenditures, which will require training in the new technology to make those purchases cost-effective.

The sixth force affecting I/O psychology is rising employee expectations and the need to balance the costs and demands of those expectations. The increased costs of health care have led organizations to focus on programs that promote employee wellness in order to reduce medical expenses. I/O psychologists are in-volved in designing programs that will get employees to change unhealthful be-haviors and practice new healthful behaviors. Just as many workers are being given greater control over their jobs, organizations are shifting greater responsi-bility for health care to their employees. On the other side of the issue, employ-ees are demanding healthier workplaces. This means greater attention to the physical requirements of the workplace by I/O psychologists who specialize in human factors. Increasing fears about violence in the workplace are leading orga-nizations to develop programs to prevent such violence and crisis management programs to deal with it when it does occur. Prevention programs include more careful screening of applicants and better assessment of employee behaviors that may lead to violence.

The seventh force critical in the development of I/O psychology is a renewal of corporate social responsibility. As the federal government looks to shift more responsibilities to state and local governments, companies are seen as having more responsibility for societal problems that affect the workplace. In some cases it is financially beneficial for organizations to deal with problems such as substance abuse and family needs. In other cases laws such as the Family and Medical Leave Act and the Americans with Disabilities Act (ADA) are requiring organizations to act in socially responsible ways. Developing and administering programs and policies with respect to these issues often can be done more effectively with the help of an I/O psychologist.

Where will you be working in 2010? What kind of job will you have in 2020? Although people may be unsure about where they will work or what kind of jobs they will do, it is likely that work will continue to be one of the major influences in people's lives. Therefore, it is likely that the role of I/O psychologists will also be important. A number of business forecasters have predicted that the need for I/O psychologists will increase steadily in the future. Each of the trends discussed in *Future Work* (Coates, Jarratt, & Mahaffie, 1990) confirms an expanded role for I/O psychologists in the workplace. The next section looks at the requirements for becoming an I/O psychologist and some issues for people who work in the field.

THE FIELD OF INDUSTRIAL/ORGANIZATIONAL PSYCHOLOGY

As the last section explained, I/O psychology has grown in many different directions. The field also has increased in importance since the early years. If all I/O psychologists were eliminated, many organizations would continue to function, but not as well. Many employees would still be able to do their jobs, but not as effectively. Some employees and organizations would stop functioning altogether. The growth of I/O psychology in applications and importance over the years is an indication of the value of this field in the work environment.

Careers in Industrial/Organizational Psychology

Opportunities in I/O psychology are abundant, and the scope of employment in the field is predicted to increase in the future. As you have seen throughout this chapter, I/O psychology is involved in many areas of organizational and work situations. Figure 1.5 shows where I/O psychologists are employed and the types of work they do. Many I/O psychologists are employed in private industry, where they are involved with real-life situations. I/O psychologists sometimes work as coordinators, bringing together a number of specialists to solve a work-related problem. Other I/O psychologists are employed at colleges or universities, where they consult with organizations; they may work independently or be sponsored by the college or university where they teach. In a survey, about 75 percent of academic-based SIOP members said they did professional work in organizations (Farr, 1997).

Figure 1.5

(a) Employment settings of I/O psychologists. Data from A. Howard (1990). *The Multiple Facets of Industrial/Organizational Psychology: Membership Survey Results.* (b) Work areas for I/O psychologists. From P. R. Jeanneret (1991). Growth trends in I/O psychology. *Industrial-Organizational Psychologist, 29*(2), 51.

WHERE I/O PSYCHOLOGISTS WORK AND WHAT THEY DO.

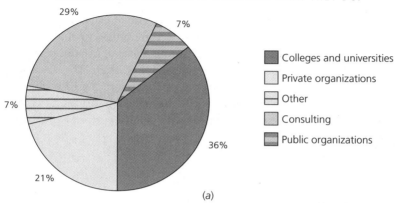

Colleges and universities
Private organizations
Other
Consulting
Public organizations

(a)

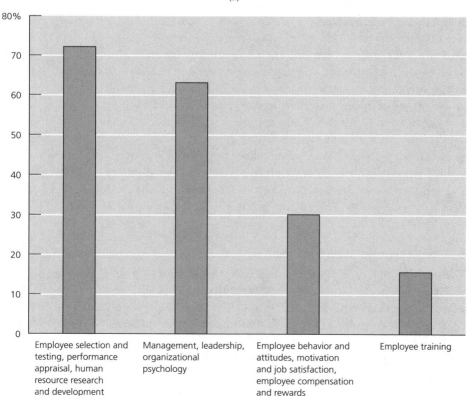

(b)

I/O psychology is involved with so many areas that there are career opportunities for people with a wide range of educational backgrounds and degrees who may not be I/O psychologists but are concerned with some aspect of the field. They often work with I/O psychologists in a variety of settings. For example, a physical or occupational therapist may be involved with exercise or stress management programs in an organization. Engineers may work with I/O psychologists to help develop equipment that is more efficient and easier to use. People trained as teachers often make excellent trainers and may become involved in training programs in industry. Communications and English majors may become involved in writing instruction manuals, employee handbooks, and press releases and in translating materials into other languages for workers who are not native speakers. People with a background in mathematics are employed to do in-depth statistical analyses of data. Even people with educational backgrounds that seem far from business related are needed and sought—such as art majors to illustrate technical manuals.

Education and Training Requirements

For an I/O psychologist, the minimum level of education is a master's degree; a doctoral degree is becoming more common as more colleges and universities develop these programs. A master's degree usually involves thirty to forty credits of graduate work; a thesis (an original research project) must also be developed and completed. In addition to the requirements for a master's degree, a doctorate involves several more years of course work, a dissertation (similar to a thesis but usually based on more extensive original research), and a series of comprehensive examinations. I/O psychologists are fairly well paid, and unemployment in the field is low (Erffmeyer & Mendel, 1990; Lowe, 1993). Many psychologists do not go directly to graduate school after college but go to work first, both for the money and for the experience. In addition to a good undergraduate grade point average and good scores on the Graduate Record Examination (the graduate school equivalent of the SAT or ACT), graduate schools value experience in the field.

Regulation and Licensing

The purpose of licensing or regulating certain occupations is to ensure that the public receives goods and services from qualified people and that unqualified people are prevented from deceiving or endangering the public (Fretz & Mills, 1980). Psychology, like other fields, has had its share of fakes and impostors; the training and licensing requirements in the field of I/O psychology are designed to make it less likely that such people will be able to present themselves as qualified psychologists. Psychology is just one of the over eight hundred occupations that according to government regulations must license their practitioners (Shimberg, 1981).

Permission to practice psychology is regulated in all states. The problem in describing these regulations is that every state has its own laws and regulations. While all states require clinical psychologists to be licensed, this is not true for I/O psychologists. Generally, to be licensed requires having a certain level of education or training and passing an examination. SIOP has recommended that where licensing for I/O psychologists is required, candidates be allowed to fulfill the requirements by completing a doctoral program with training in specific I/O fields and completing a supervised practice experience similar to an internship. Some psychologists view the licensing of I/O psychologists as desirable; others do not.

In addition to the conflict over licensing, there is continuing conflict between psychologists who practice in the field (practitioners) and academics (scientists) who do research and teach. The conflict has a long history. In the early years of psychology, in the late 1800s and early 1900s, leaders in the field promoted a view that using psychology outside the laboratory was contrary to the objective of developing psychology as a science (Benjamin, 1997). It was not until the overwhelming applied use of I/O psychology during World War II that the APA included practitioners as full members. The increased use of psychological tests in business illustrates how applied psychology has grown. In 1939 only 14 percent of businesses were using psychological tests. In 1947, 50 percent were using psychological tests, and by 1952, the proportion had increased to 75 percent (Napoli, 1981).

The president of SIOP discussed this continuing conflict in his presidential address in April 1997, indicating this was still a current issue (Farr, 1997). Some of the tension comes from the assignment of I/O psychology to the applied side of the field, which sometimes is seen as a less worthy type of psychology. In the applied areas of psychology, information is gathered and research is done for the purpose of solving an immediate problem or need. Also, nonpsychologists often do some of the actual, hands-on work, such as training and interviewing. Earlier in this chapter it was mentioned that Walter Dill Scott hid the work he was doing in advertising and other applications because he felt his teaching colleagues would be critical of him.

The need to answer a specific question quickly is seen as removing some of the objectivity of a good scientist. The basic research areas of psychology may deal with the same questions as the applied areas, but the concern is with larger issues and research for its own sake; such research may lead to applications in the future, but that is not a concern at the time of the original research. Basic research often is thought of as research conducted at colleges and universities and at associated research centers, but this distinction is not as clear as it once was; this chapter has indicated that a large number of academic psychologists now also work in industry.

The best I/O psychologist is often someone who fits the scientist/practitioner model, that is, who is able to bridge the gap between basic or academic psychology and applied psychology. Someone who can work in an organizational setting to improve the organization and its employees is regarded as a practitioner. Someone who can go back to the basic principles of psychology to investigate organizational and employee needs is successfully integrating the scientist and practitioner roles.

A recent article in *TIP* suggested that the best way to resolve this conflict may be to ask, "Who are the customers of I/O psychology?" (Hoffman, 2000). The article answers that the customers of I/O research include other researchers, practitioners, managers, employees, the media, and the public. This leads to a greater sharing of the work of both the scientist and the practitioner.

OVERVIEW OF THE TEXT

The purpose of this text is to provide an introduction to the field of industrial/organizational psychology as it relates to your everyday life. You will find many real-life examples in this text. Each chapter features a case study of a person or organization that illustrates one or more of the concepts in the chapter. When you read the chapters, apply those examples to your own experience. This will help make the theories and concepts more understandable.

Each chapter begins with learning objectives whose purpose is to give you an overview of the chapter topics at the start and to make sure you cover all the main points in your reading. At the end of each chapter there is a summary of the main points and questions that review the material. If you cannot answer the questions correctly after reading the chapter, go back and reread it. Definitions of new terms are printed in the margin, and the terms are printed in boldface type in the text in order to aid your review. They also appear in a Glossary at the end of the text, along with other terms that you may not be familiar with.

The book is divided into four sections. Part 1 provides an introduction to the field of industrial/organizational psychology (Chapter 1) and discusses the methods used in research by I/O psychologists (Chapter 2). The material in those chapters forms the basis for all the other chapters, and does not require any previous knowledge of research methods or statistics.

Part 2 is concerned with organizational psychology, which, in general, studies the nature of organizations, their structure, how members of organizations communicate, how organizations affect their members, and how organizations differ. The study of organizations as a whole is one of the newer areas of I/O psychology. Chapter 3 examines organizations as entities that change and grow, and it deals with the effects organizations have on their members. This includes the concepts of organizational structure, culture, and effectiveness. In Chapter 4 you will learn about the way the diversity movement is changing the structure of the workplace and using organizational development to change the structure of organizations. Chapter 5 discusses group processes, communication within organizations, and decision making. Chapter 6 deals with the major theories of motivation and job satisfaction, concluding with a discussion of the quality of work life, an area that is becoming increasingly important. Chapter 7 discusses types of leadership styles and how and when different styles are effective, the use of power, and the satisfactions and problems of being a leader. (Leadership was one of the earliest areas of study in I/O psychology.)

Part 3 of the text is concerned with personnel psychology, an area that dates back to the beginning of I/O psychology and the one that many students think of first when they think of I/O psychology. Chapter 8 is concerned with employee recruitment, the steps in the selection process, and legal factors in employment. Employee and organizational testing is closely related to recruitment and selection but is not limited to those areas. Chapter 9 discusses what is involved in a good test, how organizations use tests, and the tests commonly used. Performance appraisal, which is a part of almost everyone's work career, is covered in Chapter 10. Topics here include the different types of performance appraisals, problems with those methods, and the rewarding of performance. Employee training and development are examined in Chapter 11. Different training methods are covered, along with the advantages and disadvantages of each one and principles of learning that apply to specific training situations.

Part 4 covers the work environment, an area of increasing importance as a result of the concerns about safety, maintaining productivity, and new technology. Chapter 12 is concerned with job design and evaluation. It discusses the design of equipment to make it easier for workers to use, the redesign of work environments, and the increasing use of computers and robots. Chapter 13 examines another rapidly growing area: employee health and stress. This chapter looks at the psychological conditions of work, conflict in organizations, and stress management.

As you read the book, remember that all the areas interact with and affect one another. In addition, I/O psychology is a multidisciplinary science that employs the findings, methods, and techniques not just of other areas of psychology but of other disciplines as well. Work is one of the major activities in all people's lives. In this text you will find concepts and applications that you can use right now and for the rest of your life. You will also learn about the interactions between work life and life outside work and how to improve both through a knowledge of I/O psychology.

MAIN POINTS

- Industrial/organization (I/O) psychology is the area of psychology that deals with the study of human behavior and mental processes and the application of psychological principles to the problems of individuals, groups, and organizations in organizational settings.

- The three major specialty areas in I/O psychology are personnel psychology, organizational psychology, and human factors or engineering psychology.

- Walter Dill Scott is considered a founder of I/O psychology because of his application of psychological principles to advertising.

- Hugo Münsterberg, also considered a founder of I/O psychology, wrote the first industrial psychology textbook.

- Frederick W. Taylor developed the theory of scientific management, the first widely accepted theory of management, which focused on finding the most efficient way to do jobs.

- World War I saw the growth of group testing. Marion Bills and Lillian Gilbreth were among the earliest female I/O psychologists.

- The Hawthorne Studies were the first I/O research studies to consider factors such as employees' attitudes, group norms, and leadership styles.

- The human relations movement, which assumes that social factors lead to job satisfaction and higher productivity, was an outgrowth of the Hawthorne Studies.

- World War II saw further developments in testing, training, and performance appraisal. Advances in equipment design and attempts to make equipment easier to use were major developments.

- Government regulations have been a driving force in I/O psychology since the mid-1960s, leading to changes in psychological tests and personnel practices.

- Current concerns in I/O psychology include areas developed in the earliest years of the field, such as organizational psychology, as well as areas such as those dealing with the use of computers and contemporary technology.

- Seven critical forces in the workplace in the future that will continue to influence the field of I/O psychology are (1) increasing workforce diversity, (2) reintegration of work life and home life, (3) globalization, (4) expanding human resources planning, (5) the shift to a knowledge-based workforce, (6) rising employee expectations, and (7) a renewal of corporate social responsibility.

- Career opportunities in I/O psychology are increasing and involve a wide variety of settings and job choices.

■ The minimum educational requirement for a professional I/O psychologist is usually a master's degree. Regulations and licensing laws for I/O psychologists vary by state but generally require a minimum level of education and passing a licensing test.

■ I/O psychology has reacted to and been driven by the needs of society from its beginning; this has led to increasing job opportunities for I/O psychologists.

■ I/O psychology is concerned with more than efficiency and productivity. Employee health, stress reduction, and the quality of work life are becoming increasingly important.

KEY TERMS

Division of Industrial and
   Organizational Psychology
Hawthorne Studies
Human factors or engineering
   psychology
Human relations movement

Industrial/organizational psychology
Organizational psychology
Personnel psychology
Psychology
Scientific management

HISTORICAL FIGURES

Bills, Marion. An early female I/O psychologist known for applied work in the field.

Bingham, Walter V. An early psychologist who started the first college program in I/O psychology.

Cattell, James. An early psychologist who started the Psychological Corporation for research and testing early in the 1900s.

Gilbreth, Lillian. An early female I/O psychologist known for time and motion studies.

Mayo, Elton. An early I/O psychologist who worked on and reported the findings of the Hawthorne Studies.

Münsterberg, Hugo. A founder of I/O psychology who wrote the first I/O psychology textbook.

Scott, Walter Dill. A founder of I/O psychology who applied psychological principles to advertising.

Taylor, Frederick W. An engineer who developed the theory of scientific management.

Turner, Clair. An early researcher who worked on the Hawthorne Studies.

Wundt, Wilhelm. An early psychologist who influenced many industrial psychologists.

Yerkes, Robert M. An early I/O psychologist who helped develop the first group intelligence tests used by the military in World War I.

REVIEW QUESTIONS

Answers to these questions can be found at the end of the book.

1. Which of the following is true?

   a. I/O psychology began during World War I, when group tests were developed.

   b. Frederick W. Taylor is considered the father of I/O psychology because he developed the first theory of management, the theory of scientific management.

   c. I/O psychology is concerned only with industries and businesses, organizations that attempt to make a profit.

   d. From the beginning, I/O psychology has been concerned with solving current, practical problems.

2. One of the two people considered the founders of I/O psychology was _____ _____, who wrote the first textbook of I/O psychology. The other person considered a founder was _____ _____, who wrote a book applying psychological principles to advertising.

3. Which of the following is *not* a principel of Taylor's theory of scientific management?

   a. There is often one best method for doing a job.

   b. There should be cooperation between management and workers.

   c. Employees' attitudes and group norms must be considered in dealing with employees.

   d. Motivation results from monetary gain.

4. Which of the following specialty areas of I/O psychology focuses on equipment design and safety issues?

   a. Personnel psychology

   b. Organizational psychology

   c. Human factors psychology

   d. Engineering psychology

   e. c and d

5. One of the major journals that publishes research in the field of I/O psychology is the

   a. *American Psychologist.*

   b. *Journal of Applied Psychology.*

   c. *Journal of Organizational Research.*

   d. *Journal of Applicational Studies.*

6. The Hawthorne Studies

   a. led to the human relations movement.

   b. demonstrated the importance of employees' attitudes and work groups.

   c. demonstrated that people will work as hard as they can when they are paid for every unit they produce.

   d. a and b

   e. all of the above

7. At the end of the Hawthorne Studies the researchers found that strict experimental requirements could control for the influence of social factors.

   a. True

   b. False

8. The major influence on I/O psychology in the last several decades has been

   a. increased competition from overseas.

   b. free trade agreements with other countries.

   c. an increase in the number of part-time workers.

   d. government regulations.

9. The name change from industrial psychology to industrial/organizational psychology occurred because of which of the following factors?

   a. The principles of I/O psychology apply to all organizations, not just traditional business or industrial organizations, and organizations now are studied in their totality, including structure or communication patterns.

   b. The trends in employee demographics that started in the mid-1960s led I/O psychologists to study organizationwide employee traits rather than just perform individual testing.

   c. Government regulations forced the name change as a result of the application of organizationwide rules and laws.

d. It was required by the APA.

e. a, b, and c

10. Which of the following is *not* a current influence on I/O psychology?

a. Legal requirements in the workplace

b. Changes in technology in the workplace

c. A return to an interest in scientific management principles of reducing the human element in the workplace

d. Greater diversity in the workplace

11. Which of the following are employees' expectations for the workplace of the future?

a. Greater personal responsibility for health

b. The need for protection from workplace violence

c. The requirement to purchase computers for the home

d. a and b

e. All of the above

12. Which of the following is true in regard to the licensing of I/O psychologists?

a. There are federal regulations that cover licensing in all states.

b. Licensing is a way to make it less likely that fakes or impostors will be able to work in the field.

c. The minimum educational requirement for a psychologist is a bachelor's degree.

d. a and b

e. All of the above

13. I/O psychologists can be either scientists or practitioners, but they cannot be both because they cannot work for management and employees at the same time.

a. True

b. False

14. The greater the needs and problems of society and work,

a. the slower the growth of I/O psychology because of its failure to help fix those needs and problems.

b. the faster the growth of I/O psychology.

c. the more I/O psychology has drifted toward pure research and away from practical everyday problems.

d. the more government regulations have required I/O psychologists to try to fix those problems.

15. In the last several years, there has been a trend toward

a. becoming less concerned with employees' health and more concerned with productivity, as a result of increased international competition.

b. becoming more concerned with efficiency, since most I/O psychologists are now employed by management rather than universities.

c. researching and improving employees' health and the quality of work life.

d. I/O psychologists refusing to share their work, since that might help a competitor.

Use your browser to go to the home page for the Society for Industrial and Organizational Psychology (http://www.siop.org). Find the link to the on-line SIOP news journal and read an article from a recent issue. Write a one-page report discussing how the research and findings in that article relate to one or more of the seven critical forces discussed in this chapter.

WEB EXERCISE

Research Methods in Industrial/Organizational Psychology

LEARNING OBJECTIVES

THE PURPOSE OF RESEARCH

THE SCIENTIFIC METHOD
Hypotheses
Theories

THE TYPES OF RESEARCH IN I/O PSYCHOLOGY
Experiments
Quasi Experiments
Case Study Research at Work
Laboratory versus Field Experiments
Realism
Correlational Studies
Field Studies
Simulation Studies
Surveys
Case Studies

THE REQUIREMENTS OF GOOD RESEARCH
Validity
Generalization
Reliability

THE ANALYSIS AND PRESENTATION OF RESEARCH DATA
The Visual Presentation of Data
Understanding Statistics

ETHICS IN RESEARCH

Chapter Outline

Whether you work as an industrial/organizational (I/O) psychologist or choose another field, you are going to be exposed to many different types of research in your work. Sometimes an I/O psychologist may have done the research, and sometimes you yourself may be involved in doing research. For example, your supervisor may ask you to choose among several training programs to teach employees how to operate a new computer system. You may listen to sales presentations from different companies and choose a particular training program. If you want to find out which method might actually be the best for your company, you may be able to find research study results that can help you make the decision. If those studies show that two different methods may work well at your company, the managers may want to do a research study of their own before committing the entire organization to a training method. One training method may involve having employees watch a video showing how to operate the new computer system correctly. The other method may involve having trainees use a manual while they try the new system. Both may lead to similar performance levels; a research study can help your company choose the best method.

Depending on the organization and its goals, managers use many different types of research, ranging from the placement of dashboard gauges in cars so that they are easier to read to evaluating employee health and fitness programs. When you read the newspaper or watch television you are exposed to a wide array of research findings, such as surveys on political candidates and studies of new medications. How can you tell the difference between good and poor research? By

Applied research Research
conducted to solve current,
practical real-world problems.

Basic research Research
conducted to find basic
principles on which other
research can build.

understanding the basics of research and statistical methods, you will be able to spot poorly designed or executed experiments and know which studies you can rely on (Blackburn, 1987).

THE PURPOSE OF RESEARCH

In Chapter 1 I/O psychology was examined with regard to the difference between basic and applied psychology. Research studies also can be divided into applied and basic research. **Applied research** is research conducted to solve the practical problems that affect an organization. Most research in organizations is conducted to answer a question and solve a problem. In an organizational setting these questions and problems are practical everyday matters that often adversely affect the organization, its employees, or its members. Applied research problems can involve determining the efficiency of new training programs and procedures, deciding what type of test or application procedure will ensure that the best job applicants are hired, attempting to increase job satisfaction among an organization's employees, and determining which type of solicitation method increases donations to a charitable organization. All these problems have several factors in common: (1) They require the systematic gathering of data and the objective analysis of the data; (2) the results must be presented in a way that is understandable to the person who will be using the results, who often is not a psychologist acquainted with the technical language common to all sciences; and (3) there must be a statement detailing how the results should be used to help solve the problem.

The other category under which research can be classified is **basic research,** which is conducted to find principles on which other research, such as applied research, can build. Large corporations such as ITT and IBM often engage in basic research, as do almost all large universities. Basic research does not try to solve a current real-life problem as applied research does; its goal instead is to find basic underlying principles, the building blocks of science. Many of the great scientific findings, such as the transistor and the microchip, were made in the course of basic research. These findings often have tremendous technological and social applications.

THE SCIENTIFIC METHOD

The rules, procedures, and principles covered in this section apply both to the most formal basic research done at universities and corporate research centers and to the informal applied research that managers do when they decide to investigate problems such as which training method to use. Regardless of the type of research, the rules are the same.

Different problems require different research methods. However, regardless of the research method used, certain principles are common to all good research (Kaplan, 1964).

1. The research must be objective. Data collection and analysis must be done in a manner that ensures that biases, intentional or not, do not influence the research.

2. Variables have to be controlled as much as possible to have confidence that the results are due to experimental manipulations, not to chance, as well as to explain the results accurately.

3. Measurements, manipulations, and definitions must be precise, not vague and ambiguous.

4. The approach must be systematic and cumulative so that future research can build on the results.

5. The findings must be replicable. The research must be designed so that it can be repeated to determine whether the same results occur in different situations with different populations.

When these principles are used to conduct research, researchers are applying the **scientific method.** The scientific method is a general approach for gathering research information and answering questions in a way that minimizes errors in the research (McCormick & Tiffin, 1974). The next sections consider the steps used in the scientific method.

Scientific method The rules, procedures, and principles that guide scientific research.

Hypothesis A statement that predicts the results of an experiment.

Hypotheses

The first step in conducting research is to form a **hypothesis,** the statement the researcher makes to predict the outcome of an experiment. Earlier in this chapter an example was used of an employer who decided to introduce a new computer training system. The company was considering two different training methods.

If you were asked to do a research study to find the best training method, you would start with a hypothesis stating which method you predicted would be the most effective. You also should be able to explain why the predicted outcome is going to occur. A hypothesis often is referred to as an educated guess. When a researcher can explain the reasons for the results of an experiment, an educated guess becomes less of a guess and more of a hypothesis.

Good hypotheses must meet three basic requirements. First, the hypothesis must predict the outcome of the study. Second, the hypothesis should be as clear and simple as possible. Third, the hypothesis should be capable of being tested by research.

Operational definition
A precise, measurable explanation of the variables present in an experiment, including how the variables are manipulated and observed.

Theory A set of basic principles that explain and integrate a group of facts. Theories explain, interpret, and predict events.

Experiment A research study in which the researcher manipulates the independent variable and measures the dependent variable.

To meet these requirements, researchers use a specific type of language that is common to all sciences. This means using operational definitions to write hypotheses. An **operational definition** is a precise, specific explanation of the variables in an experiment. The experimenter must specify as precisely as possible what manipulations are going to be made and how the measurements will be done. Operational definitions must be measurable, observable, and objective. This means taking variables that cannot be observed directly, such as memory, and defining them in a measurable way. An operational definition of "memory" might be "the number of words recalled by a subject after a two-minute exposure to a list of ten words."

In an applied field such as I/O psychology, operational definitions can prevent confusion when managers try to apply research results in a work setting. If a manager reads a study that indicates that if supervisors are nice to subordinates, the subordinates will have higher job satisfaction, she may interpret "nice" to mean offering extra pay for overtime work. Another manager may interpret it as a lenient policy on lateness. The original researcher might have defined "nice" as smiling three times a day at each subordinate. When the manager used this definition, she might have been discouraged when she found that her subordinates did not respond as she hoped. She then might have concluded that it was not worth being nice to her subordinates, much to her subordinates' dismay. A good way to check a hypothesis for operational definitions is to ask yourself how you would measure or count each part of the hypothesis. To make hypotheses as clear and simple as possible, researchers are required to use operational definitions when they state them.

Theories

In science, a **theory** is a set of principles that explain and integrate facts within a framework. Facts can be thought of as statements that are agreed on, such as: "Employees prefer high pay to low pay." A theory should lead to the formation of specific hypotheses to test the theory or a particular aspect of it. Like a hypothesis, a theory has to be testable to be valid. The purpose of theories is to take a group of facts and integrate them into a set of basic principles that explain, predict, and interpret events. Theories must help advance science and build on previous research. To do this, they must be able to be tested scientifically. Theories must be able to be translated into hypotheses that are based on operational definitions.

THE TYPES OF RESEARCH IN I/O PSYCHOLOGY

Experiments

In an **experiment,** the researcher purposely introduces changes in a situation so that he can observe the effect of the changes on the issue he is studying (Dyer,

1995). For example, a researcher might change the hours employees in the production section of a company work, in order to study the effects of the change on measures such as productivity, the scrap rate, and absenteeism. Before research can be conducted, the variables in the study must be identified. A **variable** is anything that can be manipulated or measured or that can assume different values. The difficulty of a test, how much a person smokes or eats, grades on a test, intelligence, height and weight, and how much money people contribute to a charity are all variables.

An experiment typically involves two types of variables. The first type is the **independent variable,** the variable whose effects the researcher is investigating—such as the length of a training program. The researcher wants to determine what will happen if this variable is changed. In an experiment, the independent variable is the variable that is manipulated or changed by the experimenter. The only time there is a true experiment is when the researcher manipulates the independent variable.

The **dependent variable** is the variable that is measured so that the researcher knows what effect manipulating the independent variable had. If a researcher wants to determine the effects of cigarette smoke on employees' concentration, she will have one group of employees work in a smoke-filled room and another group do the same work in a smoke-free room. After an appropriate period of time, she will compare the job performance of the two groups. What she is investigating is the effect of smoke on employees' concentration. The presence of smoke is the independent variable. To determine whether the smoke has any effects on employees' concentration, she measures performance as her operational definition of concentration. A way to distinguish between the independent variable and the dependent variable is to remember that the dependent variable is called that because it depends on the independent variable for any changes.

The simplest type of experiment exposes one group to the independent variable while the other group is not exposed to it. The group that is exposed to or receives the independent variable is called the **experimental group.** The group that is not exposed to the independent variable is called the **control group.** A key to the success of an experiment is that the experimental and control groups are treated exactly the same way except for the independent variable. In the example on smoke and concentration, the researcher would not have the control group work in an air-conditioned room while the experimental group was working in an overheated, crowded room.

In this experiment it is not enough to compare a smoke-filled room with a smoke-free room. The *amount* of smoke also could have an effect. In an experiment, the independent variable must have a minimum of two *levels* or *treatments.* In the experiment on smoke and concentration, the experimental group was in a room filled with smoke while the control group was in a smoke-free room. The

Variable Anything that can be manipulated or measured.

Independent variable In an experiment, the variable that is manipulated or changed in order to study its effect.

Dependent variable In an experiment, the variable that is measured. The change in the dependent variable should be due to the independent variable.

Experimental group In an experiment, the group that receives or is exposed to the independent variable.

Control group In an experiment, the group that is not exposed to the independent variable. This group is compared to the experimental group to determine whether the independent variable had an effect.

presence of smoke was one level or treatment, and the absence of smoke was the other level or treatment. Adding more treatments or levels would make the experiment more complicated but might result in more information. A variation of this experiment might be to add more levels of cigarette smoke to the room. For example, the researcher could test subjects in rooms with the smoke from 1, 10, 25, 50, 75, and 90 cigarettes. The experiment would have six levels or treatments. She could also have a zero smoke level to check the results of the first experiment. This is called *replication*. In this method, a study is repeated to verify the results. The second experiment would be able to provide much more information than the first experiment did. This is one of the methods commonly used to show the reliability of research. The results would show the effect of the various levels of smoke on concentration, as is illustrated in Figure 2.1.

F i g u r e 2 . 1

Amount of smoke present in a room and job performance scores.

Number of cigarettes used to produce smoke	0	1	5	10	25	50	75
Job performance scores (percent)	88	89	57	56	58	54	55

Instead of merely concluding that cigarette smoke decreases concentration and lowers job performance, the researcher can conclude that it takes the smoke of at least 5 cigarettes to decrease concentration. The next step in the research would be to test the effects that the smoke of 2, 3, and 4 cigarettes would have in order to determine precisely how much smoke must be present before concentration is lowered—as is shown in Figure 2.2.

The data in Figure 2.2 show that smoke from 2 or 3 cigarettes does not seem to lower concentration, whereas the smoke from 4 cigarettes does seem to lower concentration. One reason this experiment is done with groups of employees is to eliminate the problem of one employee reacting very differently from most other

F i g u r e 2 . 2

An example of research building on previous research (see Figure 2.1).

Number of cigarettes used to produce smoke	2	3	4
Job performance scores (percent)	87	88	54

employees and biasing the results. Selecting people for the different groups in the experiment is an important part of good research.

Assigning Subjects to Groups

There are two common ways to assign subjects to groups in experiments. The first method is **random assignment,** where subjects are assigned by chance to the different groups. There are statistical tables of random numbers that make it possible to assign subjects to groups randomly, but pulling names or numbers out of a bowl is also a method of random selection.

Random assignment eliminates an important problem in experiments: extraneous variables. An **extraneous variable** is anything that affects the outcome of a study but is not part of what is being studied in the experiment. There are four types of extraneous variables (Dyer, 1995). The first type is participant, or subject, variables: individual differences among the subjects, such as intelligence and motivation, that are not being studied in the experiment. The second type is treatment variables, that is, the way subjects are assigned to different treatments, such as how many subjects are in more than one treatment group. The third type is task variables, the procedures the subjects are required to follow in the experiment, such as instructions given by the researcher. The last type is situation variables, all the conditions in the experimental environment, such as temperature, humidity, noise, and the number of people in the room.

Random assignment of subjects is important because it causes all the extraneous variables to be distributed evenly among the groups. If there are two hundred subjects to start with and they are randomly assigned either to the control group or the experimental group, the extraneous variables most likely will be evenly distributed between the groups. The average age of each group will be about the same; there will be about the same number of men in each group; and there will be about the same number of new employees in each group. The chance of the experimental group being extremely different from the control group with respect to any of the variables becomes very small once each group contains about thirty or forty people.

The other method used to assign subjects to groups is called matched groups. In **matched groups,** the experimenter tries to make the subject groups equal on the extraneous variables or on characteristics that may influence the results of the study. This method appears to provide better control than random selection does, but it is often difficult to use because the subjects must be matched on all the variables that may affect the outcome of the experiment. In an experiment on exercise and the absentee rate, the researcher would have to match the subjects on more variables than sex, age, and smoking. There are other variables that have an effect on whether a person is absent, such as diet, occupation, and stress. The list of variables on which subjects have to be

Random assignment A method in which subjects are assigned by chance either to the experimental group or the control group in an experiment.

Extraneous variable Any variable that affects the outcome of an experiment but is not part of the experiment and therefore should be controlled.

Matched groups A method in which the subjects in an experiment are made equal or balanced on any variables or characteristics that may influence the outcome of the experiment.

Single-blind control
A research control in which the subjects in an experiment do not know whether they are in the control group or the experimental group.

Placebo effect A change in the behavior of control group subjects resulting from their belief that they have been treated with the independent variable when they actually have been treated with something ineffective.

matched becomes longer and longer, and it becomes harder and harder to find matches. If the subject pool is more limited, so that there are only two hundred subjects to choose from, it is almost impossible to match the subjects on more than three or four variables before the researcher runs out of subjects and ends up doing an experiment with only fifteen or fewer subjects in each group. Depending on the type of research and analysis, a certain minimum number of subjects is required in each group to meet experimental requirements (Morse, 1998).

Preventing Bias

After subjects have been assigned to groups, there are other techniques that can be used to prevent bias. Many experiments are done using a **single-blind control,** in which the subjects do not know what group or level of the experiment they are in. The subjects usually are told they are participating in an experiment and informed of the purpose of the experiment. If they are told they will be a part of a study of the effects of caffeine on alertness, both groups will be given cups of coffee but the subjects do not know which ones got coffee with caffeine and which ones received coffee without caffeine.

The purpose of using a single-blind control is to prevent the **placebo effect.** This effect occurs when subjects receive a treatment and change their behavior based on what they believe to be the effects of the treatment rather than on the actual effects. The single-blind control typically is used when a new medication is tested, because if only the subjects in one group received a pill, they would be the only ones who believed that their symptoms were being treated. Instead, one group gets the pill with the active medication, an the other group gets an identical pill without the active ingredient. If both groups get relief from their symptoms, this is due to the subjects' belief about the medication rather than the effects of the medication. If only the group that receives the active ingredients gets relief, the active ingredient in the medication caused the result.

In workplace experiments, using a single-blind control often involves taking the subjects away from work for the same period of time to make sure that the independent variable is the real cause of the results. If a researcher wants to test a hypothesis about improving subordinates' job satisfaction by having supervisors watch management training films, the control group of supervisors must be away from work the same amount of time as the film-watching supervisors. This protects against extraneous variables and avoids subjects perceiving a difference in treatment. If both groups were not taken away from work and shown films, those who were not shown the management training films might believe they had received no treatment that would cause them to improve. If the supervisors were all very ineffective at the start of the experiment, the researcher would want to make sure that just having the supervisors gone from the workplace was not the cause of the improvement.

Double-blind controls add a further measure to prevent bias. In addition to the subjects not being aware of which group they are in, the person collecting the data does not know which group they are in. This means that when the dependent variable is measured, such as whether the subjects feel better after taking a new medication, the person doing the measuring does not know whether a subject got real medicine or a placebo. The data collector cannot be biased in her expectations because she cannot have any expectations about the subjects' responses. In any situation where experimenter bias might influence the results or measurements, a double-blind procedure should be used. Going back to the example of choosing between different computer training programs, if you had been offered a free vacation by one of the training program publishers, you would not be an appropriate choice to collect the data in the study. The measurement would have to be done by someone who did not know which training program the subjects had gone through and who did not have any bias toward one of the programs.

Quasi Experiments

Sometimes researchers cannot realistically assign subjects to do certain things or have certain characteristics for an experiment, such as smoking, studying more or studying less, being rich or poor, being an education major in college, eating red meat, or working on removing asbestos. In such cases the subjects' behavior or status determines the group to which they are assigned. This is called a **quasi experiment.** In a quasi experiment, the researchers have some control over the research but are not able to meet the strict requirements of true experiments. They observe differences for the effects those differences have on the behavior of the subjects (Campbell & Stanley, 1963).

Certain problems are unique to quasi experiments, such as how the researchers choose the subjects. In many studies, the experimental group is made up of volunteers and the control group consists of "everyone else." This is a very common type of study because organizations already have employees with a certain behavior who can serve as the control group. The experimental group becomes a group that has volunteered or been assigned to try something different. The quasi-experimental approach is seen in the case study "Research at Work." Here, the virtual office group was made up of IBM employees whose traditional office space had been eliminated. They were not randomly assigned to the group; their choice was based on the ability of IBM to take away the traditional office without suffering a financial loss. The virtual office group showed higher productivity and greater flexibility but not a better work–life balance or longer hours of work. The question is what caused the results. The people who were in the experimental and the control groups were different to begin with. In a quasi experiment, the researcher cannot conclude that the differences in the independent

Double-blind control A research procedure in which the subjects and the researcher measuring the dependent variable do not know whether the subjects are in the experimental group or the control group.

Quasi experiment A research technique that is similar to but does not meet the strict requirements for a true experiment.

variable caused the differences in the dependent variable. The results might suggest a cause but cannot prove it (Cook & Campbell, 1976). It is possible that the virtual office caused higher productivity, but it is also possible that the virtual office employees felt that this was a way for IBM to terminate them gradually and worked harder because of that fear.

[Case Study] RESEARCH AT WORK

Like many other organizations in the 1990s, IBM began to allow some of its employees to work at home some or all of the workweek. Since such employees stay connected to the main office by computer modem, telephone, or fax machine, this is referred to as working in a virtual office, or telecommuting.

Like other organizations that used telecommuting, IBM wanted to know if this work arrangement was beneficial to the employees and the company. Three researchers from the Global Employee Research Division designed a research study to compare the telecommuters with a group of typical office employees.

The telecommuters were service and marketing employees from several western states. All marketing and service employees eventually were going to be moved to virtual offices; some of them had already moved from the traditional office because IBM was able to move them when rental leases ended (and thus suffered no financial loss). This group made up the experimental group. The employees in the traditional offices made up the control group. This research was a quasi-experimental study because the subjects in the control and experimental groups were not randomly assigned to the groups. A number of extraneous variables, such as the presence of preschool children in the home and a home office with a door, were controlled for both groups.

The research group analyzed both objective (quantitative) data, such as the number of hours worked, and subjective (qualitative) data, such as employees' perceptions of their work–life balance. The study showed clearly that the telecommuters were higher in productivity, but it failed to confirm the popular belief that telecommuting leads to a better work–life balance or longer work hours. This study was valuable to IBM because it showed the difference between beliefs about telecommuting and the actual results of research.

Adapted from J. E. Hill, B. C. Miller, S. P. Weiner, & J. Colihan. (1998). Influences of the virtual office on aspects of work and work/life balance. *Personnel Psychology, 51*(3), 667–684.

Laboratory versus Field Experiments

Laboratory experiment
An experiment done in a controlled environment.

Field experiment
An experiment done in a real-life environment.

Some researchers make a distinction between a laboratory experiment and a field experiment. The basic difference is that a **laboratory experiment** is done in an artificial situation or environment and a **field experiment** is done in the real world, such as a classroom, a division of an organization, or the parking lot of a stadium. The key is that a field experiment is done in a natural setting and that the subjects may not know they are participating in an experiment. The basic principles are the same whether the experiment is done in a laboratory or in the field. Field experiments, however, are more likely to be quasi experiments, although true experiments are also possible in the field.

Each type of experiment has advantages and disadvantages. The main advantage of a laboratory experiment is that if it is properly designed the entire situation is under the control of the experimenter; thus it should be easier to eliminate or at least manage any extraneous variables that could affect the results. The manipulation of the independent variable and the measurement of the dependent variable are much more precise in laboratory conditions. In experiments, if the researcher produces the only changes between the groups, she is more likely to be able to determine what caused the difference in the dependent variable between the two groups. Another advantage of laboratory experiments is that they are much more easily replicated, a factor that contributes to the reliability of the results. The obvious disadvantage of laboratory experiments is the lack of realism. They often occur in artificial settings. The participants know that the setting is artificial and that they are subjects in an experiment. Another disadvantage is that some variables cannot be studied in a laboratory. For example, studies about factors relating to alcohol consumption and driving behavior often can only be studied in a field situation.

The advantages and disadvantages of field experiments are almost the opposite of those of laboratory experiments. Field experiments are realistic because they take place in the real world, and their results can more easily be applied to other situations. The subjects may not know they are in an experiment, and so their behavior is not affected by such knowledge. The most significant disadvantage of field experiments is that there is often less control: It is much harder to manipulate the independent variable precisely, measure the dependent variable, and control any extraneous variables. In the example cited about choosing different computer system training methods, if some of the employees got a regularly scheduled salary increase during the study, that could influence the outcome of the research.

Realism

Psychologists use the term "realism" in research in two different ways: *mundane realism* and *experimental realism*. Mundane realism involves how closely the experiment resembles real life. If an experiment closely resembles a real-life situation for the subjects, that experiment has high mundane realism. For example, if part of an experiment was to have computer programmers attempt to debug a computer program, that experiment would have high mundane realism. Computer programmers debug programs as part of their jobs, and doing it in an experiment would involve nothing unusual for them.

Experimental realism has two components. One aspect concerns the subjects taking the experiment seriously. Do the subjects try the best they can, follow instructions, and reply honestly to questions? Subjects in experiments sometimes do not do their best, and some may actually try to sabotage the experiment. Subjects in a workplace experiment may be afraid of losing their jobs, or having their pay cut, or they may be unhappy about having to be in an experiment. No matter how much the experimenter tries to convince subjects that the experiment will have no effect on their job security, promotion, or pay, the subjects may not believe that.

The other aspect of experimental realism concerns whether the subjects become involved in the experiment. The goal of a good experiment is to have the subjects do what they would do normally if they were not in an experiment. An example of an experiment having low mundane realism but high experimental realism is a classic study done by Stanley Milgram (1974) that was designed to investigate obedience to authority.

Volunteer subjects were recruited from newspaper advertisements for an experiment on the effects of punishment and learning on memory. The subjects appeared to be randomly assigned to the positions of "learner" and "teacher," but the assignments were actually fixed by Milgram. The learner was a confederate who knew all about the experiment. The learner was taken into a room and strapped into a chair with an electrical battery connection on his finger. The teacher's job was to help Milgram run the memory test, including delivering the punishment, an electric shock, when the learner answered incorrectly. The teacher delivered the shock through what appeared to be a complex control panel that delivered shocks ranging from 15 to 450 volts. The control panel was clearly labeled from "Slight Shock" at 15 volts to "Danger: Severe Shock" at 450 volts. Every time the learner gave a wrong answer, he was to be punished with the electric shock, and each succeeding wrong answer was punished with a stronger shock. At about 75 volts the learner started moaning and grunting; at 300 volts the learner insisted that the experiment be stopped, screamed in pain, and failed to answer any more questions. Giving no answer was treated as being a wrong answer and was punished. There was no visual contact between the teacher and the learner, and so the teacher could not see that the learner was not actually receiving electric shocks.

How far did the teacher subjects go before telling Milgram that they would not continue to do this? Sixty-two percent of the teacher subjects went all the way to the maximum of 450 volts and kept giving 450 volts until they ran out of questions. Among the 38 percent who quit before reaching the maximum, the average quitting point was 370 volts. No one quit before 150 volts.

Besides demonstrating that people have a tendency to follow orders from an authority figure, the Milgram experiment demonstrates several points about psychological research. The first point is that the experiment had low mundane realism. This is not an everyday situation for people, yet the subjects became deeply involved in the experiment. The teacher subjects begged Milgram not to make them deliver the punishment, started crying, and were clearly upset by what they were doing, but they delivered the punishment anyway. The only thing Milgram said to the teacher subjects was that they must go on because the experiment demanded it. The design of the experiment limited him to saying that the experiment demanded that the teacher do his job and that Milgram would take any responsibility for harm to the learner. The second point is that the experiment had very high experimental realism. The subjects were caught up in the experiment.

When students read about this experiment, their first reaction usually is to deny that they would ever behave like the teachers. This is called **pluralistic ignorance** in reference to the belief that the results of scientific studies apply only to other people. Sometimes smokers or people with high cholesterol levels use pluralistic ignorance to defend continuing their unhealthful behaviors. Pluralistic ignorance also refers to people who look for something about themselves that makes them special. The original Milgram experiments involved only male subjects, and so females might say, "Men would do this, not women." Later, the experiment was done with women subjects, with minority subjects, and in countries from Japan to Sweden, but the results were the same. In any study where people do something "bad," people always prefer to be seen as one of the "good" ones.

Another common reaction to research findings is **hindsight bias,** which occurs when a person hears the results of a study and indicates that she always knew that the results would turn out the way they did. Even if this is true, the experiment is still valuable for scientifically confirming commonsense beliefs. If an employer wants to find out whether four 10-hour days would be better for employees and the organization than the traditional five 8-hour days per week, he might do a research study that found that the five-day schedule was best for the organization and employees. While many people might say that they always knew that was true, the research confirmation provides a better platform than intuitive guesses for decision making.

Correlational Studies

The next research method is the **correlational study,** which determines whether two variables are related to each other. In a correlational study the researcher is attempting to determine whether one variable where the scores are moving up or down is related to another variable where the scores are moving up or down. There are several aspects to correlational studies. First, the researcher cannot assume a cause-and-effect relationship between the variables. The reason for this is that in many correlational studies, the independent variable cannot be manipulated and

Pluralistic ignorance The belief that the results of scientific studies apply to other people but not to oneself, that one is somehow special or the exception.

Hindsight bias The tendency of people to overestimate their knowledge or their ability to predict events once the answer is known or the results of a study occur.

Correlational study Research done to determine whether changes in one variable are related to changes in another variable.

subjects are not randomly assigned to groups. This is different from quasi experiments in which the researcher often has some degree of manipulation or control but not as much as true experiments require. Suppose a researcher wanted to study whether intelligence is related to school grades. As IQ (intelligence quotient) scores go up, do grades go up? In this study the researcher cannot change a student's IQ to see what happens to his or her grades, and so she measures the IQ and looks for a relationship to grades.

Correlation Coefficient

Correlation studies are designated by the manner in which the data in the study are analyzed. The method of analysis is the *correlation coefficient*. Researchers look at correlation coefficients to learn three things:

1. Are the variables related? If one changes, does the other one change?
2. The strength of the relationship
3. The direction of the relationship

The following example illustrates each of these points. If a researcher is interested in doing a study to determine whether the number of years of job-related experience is related to current job performance ratings, he might use a correlational study. He will take a random sample of employees at an organization. Although this is a random sample, it does not involve random assignment to groups as is done in an experiment, because the groups are different at the start of the experiment. He will determine the subjects' years of job-related experience (perhaps from their personnel files) and job performance ratings (also perhaps from their personnel files or by measuring their job output).

Figure 2.3 shows the numerical results of the reseacher's study. A graph of the data from a correlational study is called a *scatterplot*. One axis of the graph shows one variable, and the other axis shows the other variable. Figure 2.4 shows how the data from the study on work experience and job performance can be graphed to show that as the years of work experience increase, so does the level of job performance rating. Further, the relationship looks perfect because if the dots on the graph were connected they would all fall on a straight line. If the relationship between two variables

Figure 2.3

A study comparing years of job-related work experience and current job performance. As experience increases, job performance increases.

Years of experience	1	2	3	4	5	6	7	8	9	10
Job performance	0.5	1.0	1.5	2.0	2.5	3.0	3.5	4.0	4.5	5.0

Figure 2.4

A scatterplot showing a perfect positive correlation.

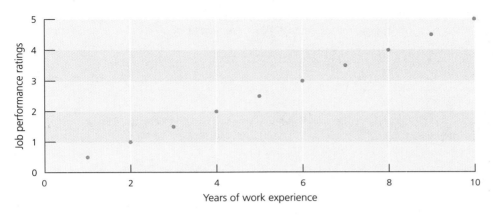

is perfect, all the data points will fall on a straight line. The result is that if the value of one variable is known, the value of the other variable is also known. The data in Figure 2.4 show that when an employee is hired it would be possible to predict his job performance rating from his years of work experience. The relationship would always hold. Every employee with four years of work experience would receive a 2.0 job performance rating. A perfect correlation means perfect prediction.

If the data from Figure 2.4 were used to calculate the correlation coefficient, the correlation would be +1.0. A correlation of +1.0 is a perfect positive correlation. The correlation coefficient figure (the symbol used is r) indicates two things:

1. The strength of the relationship, that is, the numerical part of the correlation
2. The direction of the relationship, that is, the plus or minus part of the correlation.

A correlation of +1.0 is a perfect correlation, the highest one possible. A correlation of 1.0 occurs only when the data points all fall on a straight line. The plus sign shows that the variables move in the same direction. This means that if one variable increases or goes up, the other variable also increases or goes up. In the example, as work experience increases, so does the job performance rating. If the correlation coefficient has a minus sign in front of it, this is referred to as a negative correlation. In a negative correlation the variables move in the opposite direction: As one variable increases, the other variable decreases. If there is a negative correlation between the number of years of work experience and the number of sick days taken per year, that means that as the number of years of work experience increases, the number of sick days each year decreases.

The example of work experience and job performance rating illustrates a perfect relationship, but perfect relationships are not common in the real world. In Figure 2.5 the data points do not all fall on a straight line; therefore, the relationship is not perfect. In general, the more work experience a person has, the better her job performance rating is. However, there are exceptions. In this example, the person with six years of work experience has a performance rating below that of all the employees with four years of work experience.

F i g u r e 2 . 5

A scatterplot in which the variables are related but the relationship is not perfect.

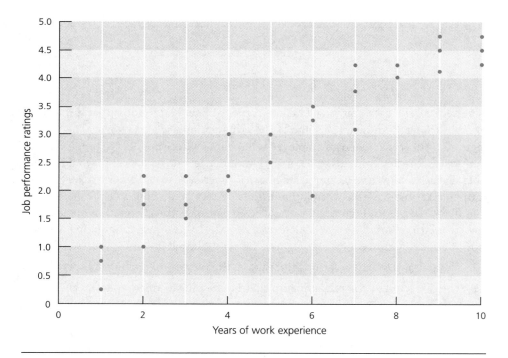

The correlation coefficient can be any number between −1.0 and +1.0. The closer the data are to a straight line, the closer the correlation is to 1.0. The closer the data are to a random pattern, the closer the correlation is to 0. Figure 2.6 illustrates how the correlation changes as the data get farther and farther from a straight line. There are statistical tables that show how large a correlation has to be for it to be significant or meaningful and thus for the researchers to find the results useful.

Some researchers believe that certain statistical techniques should be used in addition to correlation. These techniques determine the magnitude or effects of the

Figure 2.6

Scatterplots representing different correlations.

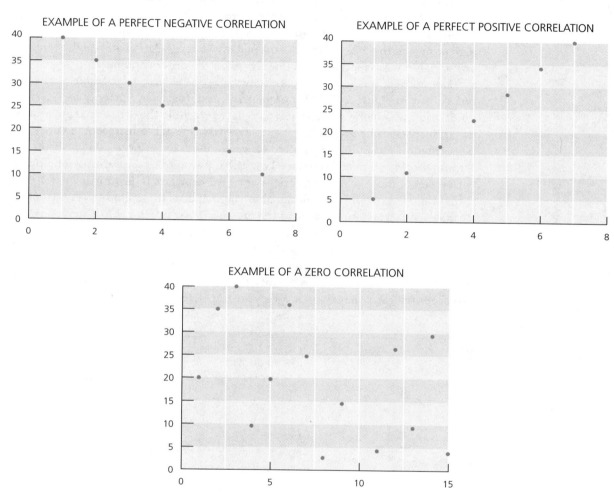

variables independently of their statistical significance (Rosenthal, 1990; Rosnow & Rosenthal, 1989). The data in these techniques are viewed in terms of opposite categories of outcomes, such as increased productivity and no increased productivity. The purpose of these techniques is to determine the practical significance of the results. Regardless of the statistical procedures employed, the decision whether to implement the changes that were explored in the research study is going to be based on the benefits of the change balanced against the costs of the change. These decisions can become more complicated as the data points form less of a straight line.

Linear and Curvilinear Relationships

The examples of correlation discussed so far are all linear relationships. In a positive *linear relationship,* low scores on one variable are associated with low scores on the other variable, average scores on one variable are associated with average scores on the other variable, and high scores on one variable are associated with high scores on the other variable. In a negative linear relationship, high scores on one variable are associated with low scores on the other variable.

Not all relationships are linear, however. A *curvilinear relationship* is like the one shown in Figure 2.7. The variables increase together, but only to a certain point, after which one variable starts to decrease while the other variable continues to increase. The graph shows that as work experience increases, so does job performance, but only so far; after six years of job experience, job performance actually begins to decrease. Note how the data points representing employees with seven or more years of experience move downward, indicating lower job performance. In a curvilinear relationship there is a relationship between the two variables, but it is not as simple as the one in a linear relationship. Curvilinear relationships are one of the reasons figures and graphs are so important. A simple correlation coefficient for the data in Figure 2.7 would have shown a very low correlation because the correlation coefficient assumes that there is a linear relationship, which is most often correct. From the scatterplot in Figure 2.7, however, it is clear that there is a very strong relationship between the two vari-

F i g u r e   2 . 7
A curvilinear relationship.

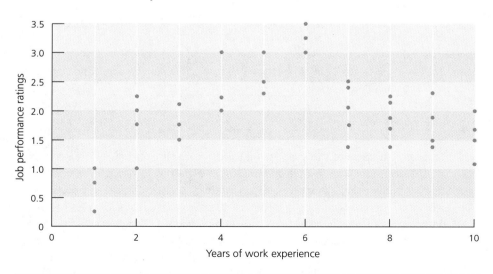

ables—a curvilinear relationship, not a linear relationship. In evaluating research, it is always a good idea to compare graphs with statistics or numbers. If they do not make sense when they are viewed together, different types of analysis may be required.

Field study A research method in which the researcher makes no manipulations but studies only what occurs in the environment naturally.

Field Studies

Field studies are conducted in a natural environment with no manipulation of the variables by the researcher. They are different from the field experiments discussed earlier in this chapter. In field studies, the independent variable is manipulated because of natural events in the environment, not because of something the researcher changes. The researcher measures the dependent variable to see what effects the changes in the independent variable had on it.

Many field studies are conducted because the research cannot be done as experiments. If a researcher were interested in the reactions of people who had lost their homes and possessions to a natural disaster such as a flood, these reactions could not be studied by conducting an experiment in which the researcher caused some of the subjects to be exposed to the disaster and left others unexposed. Concerns about workplace violence have led to a number of field studies investigating the effects of episodes of such violence. If a researcher wants to learn whether more episodes of workplace violence lead to higher turnover rates, he will have to wait for a certain number of episodes of violence to occur; he cannot arrange for them to occur. Thus, one of the problems with field studies is that the researchers have to wait for changes in the independent variable to occur; this can make a study more difficult to conduct and complete.

On the other hand, the major advantage of field studies is that they are done in the real world with real people acting in the way they normally would, since they do not know they are in a research study. These are real-life situations. In addition, the researcher may use unobtrusive measures to avoid letting the subjects know they are being studied. This means that the results of naturalistic observation studies are easier to apply to other real-life situations. If a researcher wanted to find out whether downsizing led to an increase in absenteeism and health insurance claims, she probably would get better results if the employees did not know that she was watching their absences and insurance claims.

Although field studies at first seem a better way to do research than experiments, they have one major flaw: lack of control. In an experiment, particularly in the laboratory, the experimenter can control all the variables. In a field study, the researcher cannot control any of the variables. In the example of workplace violence, many extraneous variables could influence the dependent variable. The location of the company and the ease of getting a new job in the same geographic area could influence turnover rate as much as incidences of workplace violence.

Simulation study
A research method in which the study takes place in an artificial setting designed to look and respond like the real-world setting.

Survey A research method that measures the verbal responses of subjects, usually in response to a series of questions.

Field studies are a useful technique if attention is paid to the influence this lack of control can have on the results. Field studies often are used by researchers as the basis for further research. A researcher might be interested in whether playing computer games at home increases motor skill ability at work, and then will do a field study of this. If the study supports the hypothesis, the researcher may design an experiment to test the hypothesis in a situation in which the different variables can be controlled and cause and effect can be shown.

Simulation Studies

A **simulation study** tries to combine the control and precision of an experiment with as realistic a setting as possible (Landy, 1985), much in the way use of an airplane simulator provides a realistic replication of conditions in an airplane cockpit. Although the situation is clearly artificial, some simulators, such as those used for pilot training, have very realistic movement and tilting, have the same noises and noise level as a real plane, and respond to airplane control input the same way a real airplane does. The use of virtual reality equipment (see Chapter 11) has increased the level of realism in many simulator situations. Although the majority of simulation studies do not have access to equipment as sophisticated as those with virtual reality, most organizations can set aside a room equipped to look like an office or a portion of the production area in a factory. Simulators can be expensive or inexpensive; the more realistic and sophisticated they are, the more expensive they become. Cost savings come, however, when the employees can learn a new production procedure on a simulator and not monopolize production facilities or damage equipment. If a researcher wanted to determine which training method would be more effective in helping pilots overcome a particular emergency, a simulation study probably would be the best method to determine which training system was actually the best. Not using a real airplane would mean saving both the expense of aircraft operation and the expense of an accident in a real aircraft (Landy, 1985).

Surveys

Almost everyone has participated in a number of surveys. A **survey** involves asking people questions about their behavior rather than measuring their actual behavior. Surveys are useful for assessing behavior that is not subject to experimentation. Surveys can collect a large amount of information in a short period of time. The information collected is often easy to analyze statistically.

Although surveys seem simple and have been used for many years, new methods and techniques are being developed (Rosenfield, Edwards, & Thomas, 1993). Recently, methods have been developed to use the World Wide Web for survey research (Schmidt, 1997). ICorp Survey* Net (http://www.survey.net/) conducts

Internet surveys on a variety of subjects, including presidential polls, shopping preferences, and demographics. You can take the surveys and see the results. While there are many different types of surveys—mail, telephone, in-person, and computer-aided (Shangraw, 1986)—they all have one feature in common: The respondent is asked a question or a series of questions and asked to answer. There is both a strength and a weakness to the survey method. Surveys are usually quick and inexpensive methods of collecting data, but they do not measure behavior. Surveys measure only what people say they will do or have done; there is often a big difference between what people say and what they really do. In answering a survey, even with a researcher they have never seen before, there is a tendency for people to want to make themselves appear favorably.

Some common problems with surveys can limit their usefulness. They should not contain leading questions that direct a particular answer, such as: "Would you favor helping underprivileged people?" Almost no one would answer "no" to that question; therefore, the results are known before the survey is done. Another problem occurs when survey participants are allowed to give neutral responses such as "can't say" or "average" to the questions. It is often too easy to choose the neutral answer rather than take a stand. But if the neutral category is eliminated and the respondents are forced to choose one side or the other, they may give any answer or guess in order to please the person taking the survey (Sanchez & Morchio, 1992).

One of the greatest limitations of survey research is that the sort of people who respond to a survey are often different from those who do not respond. The responders may be more interested in the topic, more educated or less educated, or biased. One way to look at people who respond to a survey is to think of them as volunteers. When surveys are based only on the people who voluntarily responded, it is particularly difficult to determine whether the results would have been the same if nonresponders had been included. It is also difficult to apply the findings to other populations (Viswesvaran, Varrick, & Ones, 1993). There are techniques that increase response rates, such as notifying subjects that they will be in a survey and offering a small premium or gift for participating (Chebat & Picard, 1991; Murphy, Daley, & Dalenberg, 1991). A good survey is based on a random sample of the entire population of interest. Even if a researcher starts with a random sample, nonresponders may cause the survey to be based on a biased sample of the population. A study of telephone survey firms found that some firms made up to ten callbacks to nonresponders while other firms made no callbacks (Taylor, 1997).

Another problem with surveys is that different techniques may have to be used with different groups, depending on the subjects being surveyed. For example, someone who is not comfortable with computers may not respond to a computer-aided survey. When sensitive topics, such as employee theft and sexual behavior, are surveyed, telephone surveys may get more honest responses than face-to-face surveys do.

Case studies A research method in which one individual or thing is studied in detail.

Validity Evidence that the results of a research study were caused by the manipulations of the researcher, not by extraneous variables.

Case Studies

Case studies examine one person or thing in detail. For example, an employer may study the best employee in the organization to try to determine why that person is the best; or the employer may look at a successful company similar to hers to determine why it is successful. The object of a case study is to determine what characteristics the person or thing being studied demonstrates that may result in its being different. A common type of case study involves observing a person's behavior, for example, watching the steps the best employee takes to solve problems. Since his behavior may change if he knows he is being observed, observation may be done with or without the person's knowledge.

One problem with case studies is that the people or things chosen are almost never average or typical. Case studies concentrate on the best or the worst; although the purpose often is to find out what makes a person or thing the best or worst, it can be difficult to apply the results to other people or situations. It is risky to apply results based on one person to a whole group of people who may have very little in common with that person. Some researchers (Howard, 1993) consider this type of research superior, in certain circumstances, to research methods such as experiments; other researchers question the usefulness and acceptance of many types of case studies, particularly self-report case studies (Prochaske, 1993).

Case studies are particularly useful for initial research ideas and for developing hypotheses to test later with more controlled methods that may apply to a broader population. Care must be taken in applying the results from a case study to other situations or other people without first doing further research to replicate the findings on additional subjects.

THE REQUIRMENTS OF GOOD RESEARCH

All the research methods discussed in this chapter have advantages and disadvantages. Beyond the need to use each research method appropriately is the requirement that it meet the standards for good research. While there are many research standards, validity, generalization, and reliability are among the ones most commonly cited.

Validity

Validity is concerned with whether an experiment was designed and carried out in such a way that the researcher can be sure that the results were not due to chance, improper selection of subjects, bias, or improper measurements. Two aspects of the validity of research are internal validity and external validity.

Internal validity means that the researcher can rule out any effects that are due to extraneous variables. The researcher can be sure that the results of the experiment are due to the independent variable. Without internal validity, the results of an experiment cannot be interpreted (Drew & Hardman, 1985). If an experiment controls for threats to internal validity, the experiment is valid and the researcher can be confident about the results. In the example of a company doing research to find the best training method for a new computer system, if one type of training was done early in the day and the other type of training was done at the very end of the day, it would be impossible to make a valid comparison of the two training systems.

External validity means that the results of a study can be applied to other situations and populations. If research is done in a way that is almost exactly like the situation to which the results will be applied, the research is likely to have external validity. When researchers read about an experiment done someplace other than their own organizations, they have to look at the different aspects of the situation and determine whether the results can apply to their situations. If subjects in the research study knew they were participating in an experiment, they might not have acted like actual employees in an organization. This could change the results of the experiment.

Generalization

Since very few applications of research take place in exactly the same situation as the research, being able to generalize results from one setting or group to another is critical to the usefulness of research. Generalization refers to the ability to use research findings that are similar but not exactly the same. If each research situation has nothing in common with any other setting, the value of the research is limited. Sometimes it is easy to see that research results cannot apply to different situations, as in studies that try to apply research about crowding among rats in cages to crowding among employees in cubicles. Sometimes it is more difficult to judge whether research studies can be applied to other situations. In the example of an organization trying to determine the better of two computer system training methods, it might be possible to find a study comparing the two methods among employees with no computer experience. If the employees at your company have some computer experience, can the research results apply? They probably can, but that is a judgment of the external validity of the research.

Reliability

Reliability in a research study refers to the stability or constancy of the results. At several points in this chapter replication was described as a way to test for the reliability of the results of a study. If a researcher finds that extra time off is the best motivator for clerical workers, other researchers in a similar situation should

Reliability Stability or constancy of results.

get the same results. If they do not, it may mean that the results of the first study were not reliable or that the situations were not similar enough for comparison. If a company is going to spend a large amount of money on a new training program, it is important that the research on which it bases that choice is reliable or the company may be wasting its money.

THE ANALYSIS AND PRESENTATION OF RESEARCH DATA

It is critical for a researcher to present the results of research in a way that makes the results easy to understand, brings order to the data, and emphasizes the important aspects or findings. Presenting the data is often as important as collecting the data because it focuses the decision makers' attention on key points and helps them make sense of the outcomes.

Although different types of data are put together differently, the first step in organizing any data is to put the items in some kind of order. For example, if a plant manager has 100 employees' hourly performance rates (how much an employee produces each hour), simply listing the scores as they are turned in will not yield very useful information. The first step would be to list the scores from lowest the highest. Figure 2.8 shows this form of organization.

The next step is to organize the data in a way that aids understanding. Instead of making a list of 100 scores, the scores could be grouped by 10-point groups and the number of employees in that range could be indicated next to the grade interval. This is called a *frequency distribution* because it shows how often each score occurs. The data start to have meaning and are much easier to understand (Table 2.1). The size of the interval is up to the researcher; the goal is to use an interval that brings out the important points in the data.

Figure 2.8

Scores of thirty employees on a measure of hourly performance rates.

Employee number	1	2	3	4	5	6	7	8	9	10	11	12	13	14	15
Hourly performance rate	99	97	93	93	90	87	82	81	75	73	73	73	70	67	64

Employee number	16	17	18	19	20	21	22	23	24	25	26	27	28	29	30
Hourly performance rate	63	62	61	60	59	58	56	55	55	54	52	51	50	49	49

Table 2.1

FREQUENCY DISTRIBUTION OF TEST SCORES FROM DATA IN FIGURE 2.8

Score Interval	Frequency of Scores	Score Interval	Frequency of Scores
40–45	0	71–75	4
46–50	3	76–80	0
51–55	5	81–85	2
56–60	4	86–90	2
61–65	4	91–95	2
66–70	2	96–100	2

The Visual Presentation of Data

Some general rules can improve data presentation in a graph format. The first rule is to label the graph carefully. In graphing data, the horizontal axis usually should represent categories of the independent variable and the vertical axis should represent the scores or measures of the dependent variable (Figure 2.9).

Figure 2.9

Example of the use of labels for a graph.

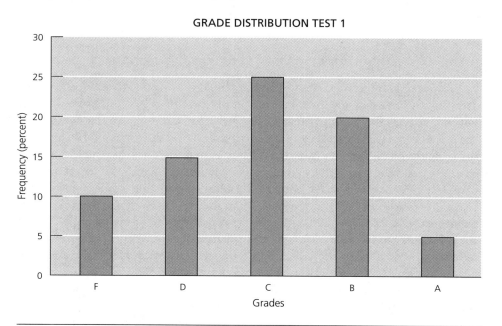

GRADE DISTRIBUTION TEST 1

A graph needs a title and a sentence briefly describing what it shows. A person should be able to get a good idea of what a graph represents without first reading the accompanying text. This text should contain further details about the graph. Two common types of graphs are shown in Figure 2.10: (a) a *frequency polygon* or line graph and (b) a *histogram* or bar graph. The same data can be presented using different kinds of graphs.

Figure 2.10

(a) A frequency polygon and
(b) a histogram presenting the same data.

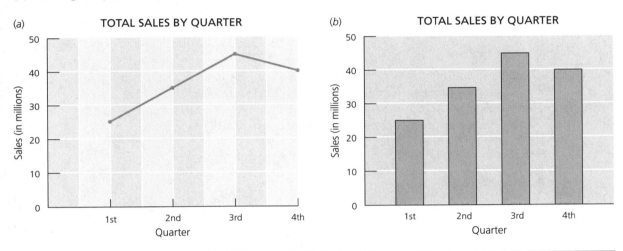

A type of graph sometimes used in psychology is a *cumulative frequency graph,* as in Figure 2.11, showing the total number of tax returns received by the Internal Revenue Service (IRS) from January 1 to April 15. In a cumulative frequency graph the line never goes back to zero. Since this graph shows the total number of tax returns received, the number cannot return to zero until a new graph is started for the next year. The graph shows that returns do not come into the IRS at a steady pace; few returns are received early in the filing period, but this is followed by a sharp increase as April 15 approaches. Cumulative frequency graphs often bring out aspects of data that would be difficult to spot on other types of graphs. The IRS could use this type of information to make plans to have fewer people working during the early months of the year, when fewer tax returns are received, and more people working as the rate of returns received increases.

Another common type of graph is the *pie chart,* useful when researchers want to show how much of a total amount is devoted to a single category (see Figure 2.12). A number of computerized financial programs are designed to make pie charts showing family spending in each of a number of categories throughout the year.

Figure 2.11

A cumulative frequency graph showing the percentage of total tax returns filed with the IRS.

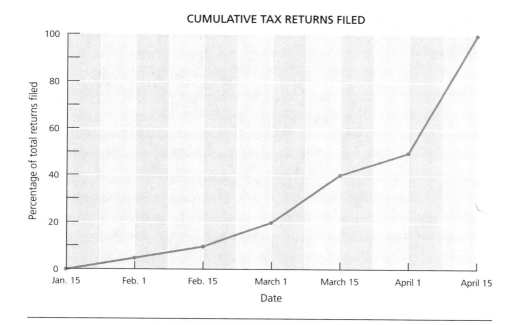

Figure 2.12

A pie chart showing an organization's training expenses.

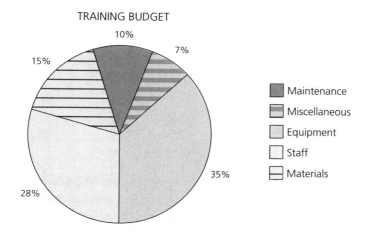

Understanding Statistics

Researchers use a variety of statistical methods to analyze data. Depending on how involved you are in research at work, you may perform some statistical analyses or may be asked to evaluate statistical analyses done by others. If you are required to perform them or want to understand simple statistical calculations, the Statistical Appendix at the end of this book, describing statistical methods, will be helpful.

Even if you do not have to perform statistical calculations, you need to understand how statistics are used in research. Most people have heard the phrase "Statistics lie." Statistics are just numbers. Numbers do not lie, but sometimes statistics are presented in a way that promotes a particular view. People can use the same set of data to reach very different conclusions. Sometimes what people leave out of a statistical presentation gives more information than the material that they include. Knowing who the promoters of a particular research study are can be as useful as understanding statistics in interpreting the results of an experiment. If researchers rely too much on statistical procedures rather than checking the validity, generalization, and reliability of a study, the research conclusions may not be worth the time it took to do the statistics (Rosnow & Rosenthal, 1989).

Statistical Significance

One of the reasons researchers use statistical analyses is to determine whether the results of a study were caused by the actions of the experimenter or by accidental factors. In psychology, researchers must be able to show that there is a chance of 5 percent or less that the results occurred because of an accidental factor. This means that the researchers are at least 95 percent sure that their actions or what they are measuring in the experiment caused the result. While it is never possible to be 100 percent sure that the actions or measurements of the researchers have caused the results of an experiment, the closer the results are to this standard, the safer it is to base conclusions on those results. Significance results are reported as probability (p) values—such as $p < .05$, which means that there is a chance of 5 percent or less that the results of the experiment were caused by accidental factors.

Meta-Analysis

Meta-analysis A statistical technique that allows the results of a number of studies to be combined and analyzed together to provide a single conclusion.

Earlier in this chapter, replication of research was discussed as a way to determine the reliability of a study. While the ideal is to repeat the study exactly, this often is not possible. If many similar studies could be combined for analysis, that would help determine the significance of the variables being studied. The statistical technique of **meta-analysis** (Glass, 1976; Rosnow & Rosenthal, 1989) allows the results of many studies to be considered together. One experiment alone is usually not enough to let the researchers be completely confident about the results. Even if the results of several studies are similar, the size of the effects of the independent variables may be different. For example, fifteen studies may show that the independent variable had a very strong effect, while thirty studies may show that the independent variable had a small effect. The problem is to determine which set of studies more accurately reflects the effect of the independent variable.

Another problem is that different research studies may have very different results. Several studies may show that the independent variable had an effect, while others may show that it had no effect. The problem then becomes a matter of determining what conclusions, if any, can be drawn from the conflicting studies. Meta-analysis has become an increasingly accepted method for combining and analyzing the results of many research studies to reach a single summary conclusion, estimating both the direction and the strength of the effects of the independent variables (Baron, 1995; Wolf, 1986).

The fact that a meta-analysis allows data from many different experiments to be analyzed together means that the probability of increasing the cumulative knowledge in a field is greater than it would be if studies were analyzed individually (Schmidt, 1992). The emphasis traditionally placed on the individual study may be replaced by an emphasis on an analysis of numerous studies. This combined analysis may show underlying regularities and effects that may not be apparent in individual studies as a result of certain statistical procedures (Schmidt, 1992). Meta-analysis has become particularly popular in I/O psychology because it allows the discovery of trends that would not be discernible from a single study. While there is an underlying assumption that the individual studies that are used for the meta-analysis are well done, if some or all of them are not done correctly, the meta-analysis will not be valid (Sohn, 1996).

ETHICS IN RESEARCH

The American Psychological Association (1992) has laid down ethical principles and a code of conduct to guide the profession. An issue that has grown in importance over the last several decades is the use of deception. "Deception" means that the real purpose of an experiment is withheld from subjects until after the experiment is completed. Some researchers (Baumrind, 1985) believe that subjects never should be deceived. Others believe that deception should be used only as a last resort (Oliansky, 1991). Most psychologists believe that many kinds of research could not be done if subjects knew the true purpose of an experiment. The American Psychological Association (1992) states that deception is appropriate if no alternative procedures are feasible. If employees are being tested to see what work situations increase the incidence of theft, the employees cannot be told the purpose of the experiment without destroying the experiment. The organization at which the research is being done must give permission for the research, including the use of deception (American Psychological Association, 1992).

Although experiments are often short and temporary, they may result in the participants feeling stress, anxiety, and lowered self-esteem over the long term. Even the short-term effects on subjects should not be overlooked. In an experiment on employee theft, suppose the researcher were interested in whether an employee would be more inclined to steal a piece of equipment if she had just been treated unfairly by the organization. Unfair treatment might be, for example, receiving a severe reprimand for causing a problem that the employee believed was not her fault. Would the employee then be more likely to steal? Such a reprimand would certainly cause employees to feel angry, raise stress levels, and perhaps even make some employees believe they had been partly responsible for the problem. If an employee did attempt the theft, she might feel a high level of guilt; she could change her perception of herself as an honest person to a dishonest person.

The employees in this situation must be debriefed and told why the deception was necessary. When subjects have been deceived, several points should be made in the debriefing. First, subjects must be told clearly that the deception was necessary because the research would have been useless without it. Second, they should be told about the importance of the research and how that justified the use of deception. Third, the subjects should be reassured that their behavior is not considered deviant, bad, or inappropriate. It should be stressed that the situation was arranged so that the subjects were led to behave in a certain manner. Research has shown that most subjects do not resent being deceived and understand the need for deception (Sharpe, Adair, & Roese, 1992; Smith & Richardson, 1985). Some subjects not only do not mind the use of deception but report that they learned more when deception was used (Christensen, 1988). Other subjects, however, do become angry at being deceived (Oliansky, 1991). The debriefing is important in determining how the subjects reacted to finding out that they were deceived. The American Psychological Association (1992) states that debriefing should occur as soon as possible after the subjects' participation in the experiment. If this will jeopardize the use of other subjects in later parts of the experiment, the debriefing should be done for all the subjects as soon as possible after the conclusion of the research.

The anonymity of employees in research studies is very important. If an employee participating in the study of employee theft does try to steal equipment, she should not be reprimanded or labeled as a potential thief. The organization should not even know which employee tried to steal and which ones did not. The experiment should be devised so that there is no possibility of the individual employee's behavior being identified. Ethical questions have also been raised about the types of people used as experimental subjects. Employees may feel that there is subtle pressure to participate in the experiment. College students often are required to participate in an experiment as part of the requirements for their psychology classes. Dalziel (1996) stresses that the best results come from a research experiment in which both the experimenter and the subjects learn and benefit.

One of the problems that continues to confront psychology is that people without the proper training and experience attempt to conduct research, training, or therapy. This includes people with good intentions who do research at the organizations that employ them but do not have the training to design a study, conduct it, analyze the data, and then debrief the subjects properly. This chapter covers only the basics of psychological research. Psychologists are required to study experimental methods in depth, both in undergraduate and graduate school. After that classroom training, they often spend time in supervised settings to gain more knowledge and experience.

It is an organization's responsibility to determine whether the person doing the research is qualified by his or her training and experience. Any psychological activity such as research or training should be conducted only by someone who has the proper training, education, and experience (American Psychological Association, 1992) to be a psychologist practitioner or researcher as discussed in Chapter 1. Sometimes researchers other than psychologists conduct research, but they must be as well qualified as psychologists to do so. The beginning of this chapter discussed the possibility that you will be asked to do research where you work. It is important that you learn what is necessary to be a qualified researcher or that a qualified researcher supervise you.

MAIN POINTS

- Research can be classified as either applied or basic.
- Applied research is used to solve current practical problems; basic research is used to find basic underlying principles.
- To be valid, research must follow the principles of the scientific method.
- The scientific method requires that research be objective; variables be controlled; and measurements and manipulations of variables be precise, not vague or ambiguous.
- A hypothesis is a statement that predicts the results of an experiment before that experiment is done.
- The variables in an experiment require an operational definition, which is a precise explanation of how the independent variable is going to be manipulated and how the dependent variable is going to be measured.

- Theories lead to hypotheses or other tests.
- An experiment is a research technique in which the independent variable is manipulated by the researchers and the dependent variable is measured.
- In an experiment, the experimental group is exposed to or receives the independent variable, while the control group is treated exactly the same except that it is not exposed to or does not receive the independent variable.
- The two types of assigning subjects to groups are random assignment, in which subjects are assigned to different groups by chance, and matched groups, in which subjects are balanced on any variables that may affect the outcome of the experiment.
- Extraneous variables must be controlled as much as possible to do good research.
- Single-blind and double-blind controls help prevent subject and experimenter bias from influencing the results of experiments.
- Quasi experiments are used when the experimenter cannot meet the rigorous standards necessary for a true experiment. Subjects are assigned to groups on the basis of their behavior.
- Experiments can be classified as laboratory or field experiments. Laboratory experiments are done in an artificial environment; field experiments are done in a natural, real-world setting.
- Experiments are concerned with two kinds of realism: mundane and experimental.
- Mundane realism refers to how closely an experiment resembles real life. Experimental realism refers to how involved the subjects become in an experiment.
- Pluralistic ignorance is the belief that the results of an experiment do not apply to oneself, only to other people.
- Hindsight bias, which occurs once a person knows the results of an experiment, is the feeling that the results are a matter of common sense or could have been predicted easily.
- Correlational studies are concerned with whether two variables are associated with each other. If one changes, does the other change?
- The statistic used to determine whether two variables are related is the correlation coefficient.
- Correlations can show linear or curvilinear relationships.
- Field studies are a research technique in which the researcher studies what occurs naturally in the environment without any manipulation.

- A simulation study uses an artificial environment that looks and reacts like the real-world environment.

- Surveys are concerned with a subject's verbal responses rather than with actual behavior.

- The most common forms of surveys are mail, telephone, computer-aided, and in-person surveys.

- A case study looks at one person or thing in detail to determine what behaviors, attitudes, and experiences differentiate that person or thing from other people or things.

- Good research is valid, generalizable, and reliable.

- The two types of validity are internal and external.

- An important aspect of research is presenting the results in a way that is understandable to the people who use them.

- One of the methods of presenting results is the graphic presentation of data.

- Statistical analyses show whether research results occurred because of manipulation by the experimenter or by chance.

- Meta-analysis is a statistical technique used to combine the results of many studies.

- Among the ethical questions considered by researchers are the use of deception, protecting the anonymity of subjects, and the use of qualified researchers.

KEY TERMS

Applied research
Basic research
Case studies
Control group
Correlational study
Dependent variable
Double-blind control
Experiment
Experimental group
Extraneous variable
Field experiment
Field study
Hindsight bias
Hypothesis
Independent variable
Laboratory experiment

Matched group
Meta-analysis
Operational definition
Placebo effect
Pluralistic ignorance
Quasi experiment
Random assignment
Reliability
Scientific method
Simulation study
Single-blind control
Survey
Theory
Validity
Variable

REVIEW QUESTIONS

Answers to these questions can be found at the end of the book.

1. You are trying to find the best method to decrease absences and tardiness at your workplace. This is an example of _____ research. You are testing to see whether computer chips operate faster at supercool temperatures. This is an example of _____ research.

2. Research that is done in a way that prevents it from being biased by the researcher's beliefs is referred to as _____.

3. Which of the following is *not* an important factor in research?

   a. The data must be gathered systematically and objectively.

   b. Variables have to be controlled as much as possible to ensure that the results are due to the experimental manipulations, not to chance.

   c. The results must be presented only in psychological terminology in order to be precise. It is up to the person reading the results to know enough to understand the terminology.

   d. It is important that the research be done in such a way that it can be repeated to be sure of the results.

4. When an experiment is done again to see whether the same results occur, that is called _____.

5. The rules, procedures, and principles of valid research

   a. apply only to research done in places such as universities and large corporations.

   b. often can be violated as long as the researcher is aware that they are being violated and can compensate for the violations.

   c. differ between basic research and applied research.

   d. are the same regardless of the type of research, where the research is done, and the complexity of the research.

   e. all of the above

6. Which of the following is *not* true about a hypothesis?

   a. A hypothesis should predict what is going to happen in an experiment.

   b. A hypothesis should be as clear and simple as possible.

   c. A hypothesis should not be able to be tested. If a hypothesis can be tested, it becomes a theory.

   d. A hypothesis should be written in operational terms.

7. If you are testing whether a new pay system increases productivity, the new pay system is the _____ variable. Productivity is the _____ variable.

8. In the study in question 7, if one group of employees works under the old pay system and one group of employees works under the new system, the group that works under the old system is the _____ group. The group that works under the new pay system is the _____ group.

9. In a double-blind experiment, which of the following is true?

   a. The dependent variable is measured without the knowledge of the subject.

   b. The subjects in the experimental and control groups do not know which group they are in.

   c. Biases that the researcher measuring the dependent variable may have cannot influence the results of the study.

   d. The independent variable is presented to subjects in the experimental and control groups.

   e. b and c

10. The two ways to assign subjects to groups are _____ _____ and _____ _____.

11. A variable that affects the outcome of an experiment but is not part of the experiment is called a(n) _____ variable.

12. Your teacher tests whether students using this textbook learn more than students using an older, traditional textbook do. Which of the following is *not* true?

    a. The group using the old textbook is the control group.

    b. The group using the new textbook is the experimental group.

    c. The new textbook is the independent variable. How much students learn is the dependent variable.

    d. The experimental group should be told to study more, since the purpose of the experiment is to determine how good the new textbook is and there is no way to do that unless the students in the experimental group use and study the textbook more thoroughly than they normally would.

    e. c and d

13. A precise definition of how the independent variable is going to be manipulated and how the dependent variable is going to be measured is called the _____ _____.

14. In an experiment, which of the following is true?

    a. The independent variable is the variable that is measured; the dependent variable is the variable that is manipulated.

b. The control group is measured on the dependent variable; the experimental group is measured on the independent variable.

c. The control and experimental groups are both measured on the dependent variable; the difference is that the experimental group is exposed to the independent variable and the control group is not.

d. The control and experimental groups are both exposed to the independent variable; however, the control group is not manipulated by the independent variable.

15. One reason a researcher might use a quasi-experimental design is that the standards for a true experiment cannot be met.

a. True

b. False

16. If I believe that I would have been one of the people in the Milgram study who stopped and would not deliver the painful shock, that is an example of _____ _____.

17. Which of the following is true of laboratory and field experiments?

a. In a field experiment the independent variable is not manipulated.

b. In a field experiment the dependent variable cannot be measured but must be estimated by the experimenters.

c. It is much easier to control and measure the variables in a field experiment.

d. A researcher can be more confident about cause and effect in a laboratory experiment because of the control that type of experiment offers.

18. If you look at the answers to this review before doing it and say to yourself that you would have known all the answers, that is an example of _____ _____.

19. Which of the following is an example of experimental realism?

a. The experiment takes place in a laboratory designed to look like a real-world setting such as a classroom.

b. The experiment takes place in a real-world setting such as a classroom.

c. The subjects forget that they are in an experiment and act naturally.

d. The subjects remember they are in an experiment but act the way they think they would act anyway.

20. A correlation coefficient for a perfect positive correlation is _____. The correlation coefficient for a perfect negative relationship is _____.

21. Correlation shows whether two variables are _____, the _____ of the relationship, and the _____ of the relationship.

22. Which of the following is *not* true?

    a. A positive correlation means that as one variable goes up, so does the other variable.

    b. A negative correlation means that as one variable goes up, the other variable goes down.

    c. When a correlation is perfect, if you know the value of one variable you can predict the value of the other variable.

    d. A correlation of +.7 means that 70 percent of the change in one variable is predicted by the other variable.

23. In a curvilinear relationship, which of the following is true?

    a. As one variable goes up, so does the other variable.

    b. As one variable goes up, so does the other variable, but only to a point, after which, as one variable goes up, the other variable goes down.

    c. There is no relationship between the two variables; a scatterplot would show the data points in random pattern.

    d. There is a relationship between the two variables, but there is no pattern to it.

24. The research technique in which a researcher studies the natural environment and makes no manipulations is called a(n) _____ _____.

25. Which of the following is true of a field study?

    a. There is more control that there is in an experiment.

    b. The study can be replicated easily.

    c. The major advantage is that the study is done in the real world with real people.

    d. When both an experiment and a field study can be done, the best technique is to use a field study because it is more controllable.

    e. a and b

26. Case studies

    a. usually examine unique individuals or people who are the best at something; therefore, the results may not apply to the average person.

    b. are useful for initial research and to develop hypotheses to test later in experiments.

    c. must be done in a simulated environment to ensure valid results.

    d. a and b

    e. all of the above

27. A valid experiment is one in which
    a. the independent variable is manipulated and the dependent variable is measured.
    b. subjects do not drop out of the experiment.
    c. the experiment is conducted in such as way that the effects of extraneous variables can be ruled out.
    d. a and b
    e. all of the above

28. Even though research studies may be done in separate locations by different researchers, it may be possible to combine the results for statistical analyses.
    a. True
    b. False

29. The ethical principles of the American Psychological Association
    a. never allow the use of deception.
    b. allow the use of deception if the subjects are over age twenty-one.
    c. allow deception if the subjects are told about it before the experiment.
    d. allow deception if no alternative method is feasible.

WEB EXERCISE

Use your browser to go to the article from *Technical Review*, "How Numbers Are Tricking You" (http://www.techreview.com/articles/oct94/barnett.html). Choose two of the examples of bad research. Describe how you would change the way the research was done in order to improve it. Support your answer by describing the research technique that would correct the problem and make this good research.

part 2

Organizational Psychology

Organizational Structure

3

Chapter Outline

LEARNING OBJECTIVES

ORGANIZATIONAL STRUCTURE: HISTORY AND THEORIES
Bureaucratic Structures
Human Relations Structures
Systems Theory Structures
Sociotechnical Systems Structures

ORGANIZATIONAL CLIMATE AND CULTURE
Levels of Organizational Culture
Measurement of Organizational Culture
Person–Organization Fit
Creation of Organizational Culture
Organizational Culture Change
Case Study Organizational Culture Change
Measurement of Organizational Climate
Use of Climate and Culture in Organizations
Organizational Citizenship

ORGANIZATIONAL EFFECTIVENESS

Learning Objectives

After reading this chapter, you should be able to answer the following questions:

- What are the characteristics of a bureaucracy, and when is a bureaucracy an effective organizational structure?
- What are the characteristics of Theory X and Theory Y human relations structures? When is Theory Y an effective organizational structure?
- What are the contingency models of organizational structure?
- What are the characteristics of open systems and closed systems? What are the advantages of open systems?
- What are the characteristics of sociotechnical systems?
- What are the main features of organizational climate and culture?
- How are organizational culture and climate measured? How can they be changed?
- What are the basic facets of organizational effectiveness, and how can it be measured?

Chapters 1 and 2 provided an overview of industrial/organizational (I/O) psychology and the methods used to research issues and topics in this field. Later chapters will look at topics that will affect you as an individual in an organization, such as personnel selection and training. This chapter starts with the big picture: the organization as a whole.

ORGANIZATIONAL STRUCTURE: HISTORY AND THEORIES

In recent years I/O psychology has broadened its focus from looking only at business organizations to looking at all kinds of organizations in which people work. This includes not only traditional corporate settings but also educational organizations, military organizations, religious organizations, volunteer organizations, and any other place where people work. This broadening of focus has expanded the field greatly, but it has also made the issues and questions more complicated. When one asks the question, "What is the best way to structure an organization?" a number of other questions influence the answer. The easiest answer is, "Whatever structure works best," but that raises a number of new questions about other variables that can influence the answer. The two most obvious variables are the employees and the organization. If you have always worked for a small family-owned business, you may believe that is the best sort of organization in which to get work done. If you have not been happy there, you may believe that kind of structure is the least desirable.

The best organizational structure for an employee also depends on a number of variables. In reading this chapter, as you learn about different organizational structures and how those structures can be changed, it is important to think about what the employee wants from the organization and what the organization wants to accomplish.

Bureaucratic Structures

When workers were individual craftspeople, the question of organizational structure in the work environment had little meaning. Even on a family farm, the family structure provided a pattern for the organization of the work. With the spread of the Industrial Revolution by the mid-1800s, however, the need for organizational structure became apparent. The use of machinery required employees to work cooperatively in a single location. When companies were small, the company founder typically established and controlled the structure of the organization. If the head of the company was dissatisfied or simply wanted a change, he made changes. This sometimes was referred to as management by chaos or management by whim. Although this was clearly undesirable for the employees, so long as the organization was successful, management might not have been concerned about the employees' wants or needs. As more competitors came into the marketplace, the need for better-run organizations became a requirement for survival in many organizations. Max Weber, a German social scientist, analyzed the need for an orderly, efficient organizational structure and introduced the concept of the bureaucracy to meet that need.

When Weber (1947) first described a bureaucracy, he thought of it as an agent for salvation from chaos for both the workers and the managers in organizations. He devised the **bureaucracy** as a rational, legal organizational structure governed by formal rules and procedures. Many people associate the word "bureaucracy" negatively with "red tape," "government," and "post office," and bureaucracies often are viewed as models of inefficiency, but that is the exact opposite of what Weber saw and what the bureaucratic organization can be in the correct setting.

Principles of the Bureaucracy

During the Industrial Revolution of the 1800s the world of work changed in dramatic ways. At the beginning, there were no rules and organizational structure could change weekly or even daily. Bureaucratic structure introduced order into chaos through a number of organizing principles. The first one is **division of labor,** which means that each job is clearly defined in terms of its activities and responsibilities. The goal of division of labor is to make each job simple enough that the worker can master it and do it well. An organizational chart such as the one shown in Figure 3.1 illustrates this clear division of labor. In a

Bureaucracy Weber's rational, legal system of organizational structure with a hierarchical form.

Division of labor A clear definition of jobs in terms of their activities and responsibilities.

bureaucracy that is functioning well, each person is competent, knowledgeable about her job, and aware of the entire organizational picture as it is shown on the organizational chart. One of the reasons for the negative associations with bureaucracies is interaction with employees who have used the principle of the division of labor as an excuse for not getting work done. Have you ever heard someone say, "It's not my job"? While that may technically be true, in a functioning bureaucracy the employees should be able to tell you whose job it is to deal with your problems.

Figure 3.1

Organizational chart of management at an engineering company.

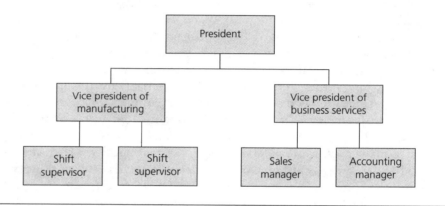

If employees are not doing their best, they have missed one of the other basic principles of the bureaucracy. In the functioning bureaucracy getting a job and holding a job are based solely on merit. **Merit-based employment** means that only qualifications for a job enter into employment decisions. Favoritism, seniority, nepotism, social goals such as affirmative action, and other non-job-related factors are not used. The person who does the job best gets and keeps the job.

An employee who says, "It's not my job," is also missing another principle of the bureaucracy. *Formal rules and procedures*, an essential component of a bureaucracy, are documents that regulate behavior in an organization. Again, each employee should be knowledgeable about these rules and procedures. In a bureaucracy the emphasis is on maintaining written records, a process that can safeguard the employees and the organization. Not only do the rules and procedures protect employees, they direct the employees' behavior in the organization. Before Weber invented the concept of the bureaucracy, there was no consistent structure, and so there was no protection for employees or direction for their behavior. In a correctly functioning bureaucracy, there is a clear path for both the

Merit-based employment
Job hiring based only on job-relevant factors.

employee and the organization to follow in order to reach their goals, and employees are enabled to be more effective (Adler & Borys, 1996).

Organizational clarity results partly from a clear **chain of command**. This is a hierarchical type of structure that is shaped somewhat like a pyramid. The greatest amount of power and authority is found in the few people near the top of the organization, but each person knows who reports to whom. This means that an employee who says, "It's not my job," may be telling the truth, but not the whole truth. She should be able to take the customer to the person who can handle the problem.

A clear chain of command, with each person knowing who is responsible for which tasks, can be extremely beneficial in an emergency situation. Hunt, Carter, and Kelly (1993) show how a well-developed chain of command improved the effectiveness of the Incident Command System, the government organization that is in charge of responding to hazardous materials emergencies such as a crude oil spill. Often, several agencies and jurisdictions are involved in this type of emergency, and quick, correct, coordinated responses are essential. Without the Incident Command System, the result could be confusion, diffusion of authority, poor communication, and lack of direction and coordination.

In a bureaucracy the number of people who report to a single supervisor is referred to as the **span of control**. Although it may seem obvious that the number of people who can be supervised by one person depends on both the manager and the job, Weber felt that there was an ideal number for the span of control, which he tried unsuccessfully to find. Organizations with a large number of people reporting to a single supervisor are called **flat organizations,** and organizations with a small number of people reporting to a single supervisor are called **tall organizations.** Tall organizations typically have many levels from the top to the bottom, and flat organizations typically have few levels between the top and the bottom. Tall organizations provide more opportunities for advancement, but flat organizations typically have more responsibility and authority at the lower levels.

Advantages and Disadvantages of the Bureaucracy

Although the bureaucracy appears to have a number of desirable properties, it may not be the best choice of structure in certain situations. The usefulness of the bureaucracy in the current world of work may be limited. These limitations come from a variety of sources. Although Weber felt there was an ideal shape to the bureaucracy, researchers have been unable to identify a single pattern. Research has shown that this structure may be too simple for most work settings because there are so many variables and different work situations. There may be many "ideal" settings. However, some work settings are still a good fit for the bureaucratic model.

One of the reasons the bureaucracy had a favorable reception when Weber first devised this system relates to the different levels of employees in an

---

Chain of command
Specification of the authority structure and responsibility in an organization.

Span of control The number of subordinates who report to a single supervisor.

Flat organization An organizational structure with few levels between the top and the bottom of the organization and many people reporting to a single supervisor.

Tall organization An organizational structure with many levels between the top and the bottom of the organization and only a few people reporting to a single supervisor.

organization. Research consistently has shown that those at the top levels of an organization are much more satisfied with the bureaucratic structure than those at the lower levels are (Jha, Mishra, & Bhardwaj, 1994; Koberg & Hood, 1991; Myers, 1990). This is not surprising in light of the fact that research confirms that the people who have the most decision-making authority and control in organizations usually have higher job satisfaction. The pyramidal structure of the bureaucracy places the greatest power, authority, and control at the top of the organization. Lower-level employees often mention their dissatisfaction at being "out of the loop." As organizations grow and more levels are added, this becomes a more common problem.

Lower-level employees sometimes attempt to deal with their frustrations with the bureaucracy by working around instead of through the system. Recently I warmly thanked a car rental agent who ignored the company rule that rental cars could not be turned in unless the driver had a copy of the rental agreement. My copy of the agreement had blown into the ocean an hour before I turned in the car. A strict and impersonal application of the rules would have required me to apply to the main office for a duplicate copy that would have taken several hours to arrive. When employees are successful at working outside the system to accomplish goals, such as satisfying customers, people often applaud their strengths and accomplishments. But while an organization can tolerate and afford to ignore a few employees who do not follow the rules, following the rules is one of the major elements that make a bureaucratic organization work. The type of employee who usually is most satisfied and does well in a bureaucracy is a person who likes the backup of written policies and rules, prefers a rule-oriented environment, and prefers not be in charge of decision making (at least at lower bureaucratic levels).

Not only does the bureaucracy have a rule for almost every situation, those rules are typically in written form. Once a policy is committed to writing, it becomes more difficult to change. Changing often requires one or more meetings and perhaps written proposals. The changes then must be communicated through all the organizational levels. This lengthy process slows the pace of change and may encourage personnel to avoid change. College professors typically spend a good amount of time moaning about the demands of the bureaucratic structure at their schools; the very characteristics, such as autonomy and flexibility, that contribute to their success as teachers are usually undesirable characteristics for good bureaucrats.

Although it is easy to be critical about the bureaucratic structure—and many people have negative associations because of personal experience—very few I/O psychologists would suggest totally discarding this type of organizational structure. A bureaucracy may be the best choice in a number of settings, including the military, large ships at sea, and supermarkets. Each of these work settings has many of the elements that make a bureaucratic structure functional. Job specialization, relatively simple products or outputs, and the use of many unskilled or semiskilled people are common aspects of these different work settings. Some organizations are in fact returning to a bureaucratic structure after having tried other systems (Sanders, 1997; Siding, Larsen, Gironda, & Sorensen, 1994).

Human Relations Structures

The development of the bureaucracy shows how historical events such as the Industrial Revolution can affect the organization of the workplace. Later, the combination of increasing dissatisfaction with the bureaucratic structure and the influence of the Hawthorne Studies (see Chapter 1) led to the development of new organizational systems. **Human relations structures** focus on employees as interacting social individuals. The Hawthorne Studies brought an awareness that looking only at the formal structure of an organization leaves an incomplete view of the organization.

Theory X and Theory Y

Two of the best-known examples of a human relations organizational system are the **Theory X** and **Theory Y** concepts developed by Douglas McGregor (1960). McGregor described his dissatisfaction with bureaucratic structures by listing a series of assumptions that he believed were necessary for a bureaucracy. He called these the Theory X assumptions:

1. Most people naturally dislike work and will avoid it in any way they can.

2. Constant threats of punishment and constant offers of rewards are the only way to get people to do the required work. They must be supervised and directed closely by management.

3. People want decisions to be made for them. They want to avoid responsibility and want the security of formal organizational structures although they are not concerned about organizational needs.

4. People are self-centered and resistant to change.

McGregor felt that the evidence for these assumptions was apparent in the ways managers tried to motivate subordinates and in the physical features of the work environment. For example, if a manager required her subordinates to sign out for equipment and supplies because she thought they would steal the supplies or not return the equipment, that would show her belief in Theory X.

Believing that employees' behavior is determined by the way supervisors act toward them, McGregor thought that Theory X structures cause employees to find ways to "beat the system." In the example previously given, McGregor would predict that employees would try to find ways to take the supplies not because

Human relations structures An organizational design based on the assumption that interpersonal relations are the most important factor in an organization.

Theory X McGregor's organizational structure based on the assumption that people dislike work and need close supervision to get work done.

Theory Y McGregor's organizational structure based on the assumption that people naturally look for satisfaction through work.

they wanted or needed them but to show that they could get away with that in spite of the rules. Employees might get so involved in finding ways to get around the rules that even less work was done. Neuliep (1996) found that Theory X managers perceive unethical behavior to be much more effective than Theory Y managers do.

McGregor believed that the way to avoid these problems is to structure the organization on Theory Y assumptions. Those assumptions include the following:

1. Work in terms of physical and mental effort is desirable and actively desired by most people.

2. People are internally directed to achieve the goals they want to reach.

3. Commitment to achieve goals and desire for responsibility come from the individual's ability to satisfy personal needs for growth.

4. Most people are imaginative and creative.

Applying these assumptions would lead to an organization almost the opposite of the bureaucracy. The Theory Y organization would be very flat, and authority would be delegated to the lowest possible level. Delegating authority in this way also would enlarge the jobs of employees and provide greater participation and individual satisfaction as well as greater productivity. In this system employees are encouraged to set their own goals for work. Self-evaluation is the major method of performance appraisal.

At Rosenbluth International travel services, the most basic core value is "Treat the employees well, and everything else will fall into place." At that agency this guiding principle has been translated into success in an extremely competitive market. An example of the practice of Theory Y at Rosenbluth International is the personalized learning plan indicating short- and long-term goals, which each employee develops cooperatively with a supervisor (Walker, 1997).

Advantages and Disadvantages of Human Relations Structures

From the point of view of the individual, human relations structures have great appeal. From the point of view of the organization, these structures may lead to a number of problems. Although greater personal growth and satisfaction may lead to greater productivity, that is not always the case. Human relations structures assume that these factors are causally related, but there is not a perfect correlation between them. As was mentioned previously, some organizations do best with structures such as the bureaucracy.

Theory Y assumes that all employees want opportunities for greater personal growth and participation. This is somewhat similar to the problem of finding the ideal set of conditions for the perfect bureaucratic structure. It is no more correct than the belief that one-size-fits-all clothing actually fits everyone. There is no one-size-fits-all organizational structure. Not only do organizations differ in what they require from the organizational structure, individuals differ in what they bring to the organization and what they desire in the organizational structure. Very few people are entirely or always oriented toward personal growth. Some people do not want more responsibility and enlarged jobs; there are those who like to have decisions made for them and find work desirable only because of the money they earn. McGregor would argue that this is the case only because of bad experiences they have had in Theory X settings, but that argument ignores the reality that individuals are different from one another. Work settings and goals are also different from one another.

It appears that dissatisfaction with the bureaucratic structure led too far in the opposite direction in regard to human relations structures. There is little research showing that human relations structures increase productivity. People who support these types of structures believe, anyway, that production is not the main purpose of organizational structure. But an organization that ignores production and hopes that it will improve as employees seek to satisfy their personal growth needs is not likely to remain competitive very long. The economic bottom line is usually a major factor in organizational success.

Dissatisfaction with the human relations structures led to newer models of organizational structure. Since it and the bureaucratic model seemed to be based on looking only at the formal structure or the social structure, the next major approach to organizational structure tried to bring both points of view into the picture through the use of systems theory.

Systems Theory Structures

Systems theory originated in the field of biology as scientists looked at organisms and saw how they constantly change to meet internal and external demands. If the classroom you are in becomes very cold, your body will shiver in an attempt to keep your temperature at the normal level. If you have eaten a large meal, your digestive system will gear up to handle the increased demands. Both of those actions can take place at the same time as your body adjusts to maintain its normal functioning levels, or **homeostasis**. These are examples of a natural system, the human body.

A system generally refers to a group of integrated parts or elements that work toward one or more goals. Organizations usually are not referred to as natural systems because each part or subsystem has the ability to achieve purposeful action and change. The sales department in an organization can decide that it wants to sell only to clients who will purchase large amounts of its product. This is not true in natural systems such as the human body. Your stomach cannot decide by itself that it wants to digest only oranges, not avocados.

Systems theory The belief that an organism or an organization must be regarded as an integrated whole, with any action in one part influencing all the other parts.

Homeostasis A state of balance, or equilibrium, in the different parts of a system.

Open system
An organizational structure that is responsive to internal and external changes in the environment.

Closed system
An organizational structure that is not responsive to internal and external changes in the environment.

Contingency model
An organizational structure system that suggests that the best organizational structure depends on being responsive to continuing changes in the environment.

Open and Closed Systems

Organizations that can respond to internal and external changes the way your body does in the example above are called **open systems.** Organizations such as the bureaucracy, which ignore changes and search for a stable "ideal" to maintain, are called **closed systems.** The differences between the two systems are shown in Figure 3.2. Systems theory and the sociotechnical systems theory (described on p. 92) often are referred to as contingency models of organizational structure. **Contingency models** suggest that the best organizational structure depends on being responsive to continuing changes in the environment.

Figure 3.2

Comparison of open and closed systems.

CONTRAST BETWEEN OPEN AND CLOSED ORGANIZATIONAL STRUCTURES

	Closed	Open
General nature	Undisturbed	Excited
Predictability	Certain, stable	Uncertain, unstable
Relationship to the outside world	Mostly off limits, limited to a few members, well defined (e. g., only a press secretary can tell the public anything about the company)	Mostly unguarded, many participants, varied (e. g., no rules about telling outsiders about the company)
Goals	Efficient performance	Effective problem solving
Goals set	Single, clear-cut	Multiple, within organizational restraints

Characteristics of Open Systems

One problem with both the bureaucracy and human relations organizational models is their narrow, incomplete focus, which ignores all other influences on the organization. For example, in a bureaucratic system, if sales of a home entertainment product decreased because consumers had less money to spend as a result of changes in the economy, the decrease in sales would be viewed as an "error" in evaluating the effectiveness of the bureaucracy. Realistically, this decrease in sales had nothing to do with the effectiveness of the production of the item. In an open system the organization would respond to those changes in the economy and make changes in the organization. The changes could be minor, such as adding sales messages showing how to use the home entertainment product for other purposes, or major, such as changing the entire product line. For example, in the 1970s Motorola stopped making many of the products that had been the basis for its success in the electronics industry for over forty years. It stopped making consumer-oriented products such as televisions and car radios and switched to industrial products such as computer components and cellular communications equipment. This led to market success in those fields (Roth, 1998).

Open systems theory suggests that there is no single correct way to reach a goal. The same results can be achieved from different starting points and by performing different internal activities. The most basic parts of the organization as a system are the input, output, and functioning of the organization. Clearly, from the point of view of systems theory, the most desirable organizational structure is one based on an open system form of organization. Open systems have a number of variations; Katz and Kahn (1978) developed a comprehensive description that includes ten characteristics common to all open systems.

1. *Importation of energy.* Open systems need to bring in some form of energy from the world outside the organization. This could be new employees, raw materials for manufacturing, or other organizations. When Gateway began to be successful, it quickly added more employees to assemble and ship computers to its customers.

2. *Throughput.* An open system changes the energy that comes into the system. People can be trained to clean offices, students can be educated, and televisions can be made. Gateway trained some assemblers to do technical support when that area required more personnel.

3. *Output.* Open systems take some products outside the organization. An engineering firm can build a bridge across a river, students can become teachers in the community, and televisions can be sold at electronics stores. At first Gateway sold its products only by telephone or on the Internet. Since that time it has added retail stores where its computer products can be ordered for home or office delivery.

4. Systems as cycles of events. The pattern of activities in an organization goes through a specific cycle that produces a continuing circular process. For example, a business uses raw materials and human labor to produce television sets that are sold, and the profits are used to obtain more raw materials and pay for more human labor. Gateway's early success allowed it to expand its product lines and offer more computer-related products for sale.

5. *Negative entropy.* "Entropy" means moving toward disintegration or death. In other words, organizations tend to run down and go out of business unless they constantly renew their sources of energy. **Negative entropy** means moving in the opposite direction of death, that is, becoming even more successful. In the example of Motorola, when management saw that the company was unable to compete successfully with the producers of certain

> **Negative entropy** Refers to the need for an organization to renew its resources and continually move toward organizational success.

electronics products, it brought in new people and new product lines (new sources of energy) in order to survive and emerge in an even more successful position. More recently Motorola did not enter the digital telephone market quickly enough and was outpaced by competitors such as Nokia. Since market and economic factors are changing constantly, an effective open system structure must always look ahead to the next change in order to maintain homeostasis within the organization.

6. Information input, negative feedback, and the coding process. In addition to the raw materials and human labor that are brought into the organizational system, *information input* also influences the system. The simplest type of information is *negative feedback*, which indicates that something is going wrong. When Gateway became very successful, it increased its production lines to meet the increased demands for its products but failed to increase the number of technical support positions. The company began to get letters from customers saying that although it had a good product, they were unhappy with the organization and the products because of their inability to get timely technical help.

   The *coding process* refers to the way the organization selects which incoming materials it will pay attention to and how these will be interpreted inside the organization. For example, if you are unhappy with one of your college classes, you and your classmates can give very low marks to the instructor on the departmental evaluation forms. The department chairperson may look at the forms and decide that he will pay attention only to forms that have detailed written comments in addition to numerical scores. He also may decide that he will talk with the instructor only if the evaluations have been poor for two semesters in a row. Even after the chairperson talks to the instructor, he may decide not to pay any attention to the poor evaluations if the instructor tells him that they were caused by two or three students who turned the entire class against her and if he believes her.

7. Steady state and dynamic homeostasis. Another characteristic of open systems involves the cycles that make up systems in organizations and the way outputs generate more energy for inputs. These repeated cycles make it possible for the organization to keep functioning and maintain a steady state. The constant motion of this cycle is the reason that this steady state is called dynamic homeostasis. Dynamic homeostasis may require greater and greater levels of organization and growth.

   The changes that a college makes as it grows and as community needs change illustrates this constant change and adjustment. A small college may start with only three departments and four administrators. As enrollment grows, the college may add faculty members, administrators, and departments. It has the same name and still educates students, but it is no longer the original small organization.

The most successful systems are the ones that can adapt to or anticipate changes to maximize their organizational functioning. If the college added a radiology technician program in health services to offer students more options, this could be a positive change. If it failed to find out that there was an oversupply of these technicians in the area surrounding the college, the college would be moving toward entropy rather than growth.

8. *Differentiation.* Open systems move in the direction of greater specialization and complexity. A company may start out making cola drinks. As it responds to information and changes in the external environment, it may add diet sodas and noncola sodas. It may create another division to make sports drinks. Each of these changes can help maintain the dynamic homeostasis of the organization.

9. Coordination and integration. As more divisions are added, it becomes necessary to keep all the parts functioning in relationship to the other parts. If the sports drinks division is doing very well, perhaps the diet soda division can take greater risks in experimenting with new drinks.

10. **Equifinality.** This characteristic represents one of the major assumptions of systems theory: There are many ways to achieve the same goal. This is the opposite of human relations and bureaucratic structures, which look for the ideal system structure that will fit every situation. It also contradicts the scientific management principle that there is one best way to shovel coal or assemble a gun.

> **Equifinality** A systems theory concept that assumes that there are many ways to achieve the same goal.

If an organization has all ten of these characteristics, has it found the perfect structure? One of the problems with systems theory structures is that they must always be in a state of change to be successful. There is constant juggling to keep the social and technological aspects of the organization in balance and moving toward the organizational goals.

The attempt of open systems theory to incorporate all possible variables into the organizational structure model is both an advantage and a disadvantage. It is an extremely complete explanation of how organizations come to be structured the way they are. It also makes it almost impossible to predict the best organizational structure to a manager who is looking for a set of guidelines on ways to structure her department or company. In fact, the concept of equifinality says that there is no single best way to reach a certain goal or structure the organization to reach that goal.

In many ways a systems theory structure is like a high-wire walker in the circus, who must constantly respond and adjust to information both from the external world and from inside his body to complete his walk from one end of the wire to the other. Each action he takes affects all the other parts of the system. One approach to systems theory that emphasizes the coordination of people and the technological part of the system is the sociotechnical systems approach.

Sociotechnical systems
An approach to organizational structure that assumes that social and technological factors have equal weight in determining the organizational structure.

Sociotechnical Systems Structures

The basic assumption of the **sociotechnical systems** approach is that both the social and the technological aspects of an organization must be studied in order to understand an organization's productivity problems. The primary task of management is to make sure that these two systems and all their subsystems are in harmony. A change, even one that appears to be an improvement, such as the mechanization of coal mining, will change the balance.

The research that led to the development of the sociotechnical systems approach was done about fifty years ago in English coal mines (Trist & Bamforth, 1951). Before the introduction of mechanization, coal miners had worked in small teams, with each group being responsible for mining a specific area. As work went on, the teams also developed into social groups, with relationships that went beyond the boundaries of the workday. After World War II, to accelerate recovery from the war, a mechanized assembly-line-like system was introduced to the coal mining process. From a technical standpoint the mechanization should have increased production levels dramatically, but that did not occur. While greater production was possible, the social structure of the miners had been destroyed by the new technology. The work groups no longer had independent identities, and workers no longer could point to individual or group accomplishments. The level of group and individual responsibility and control was reduced, and production suffered.

Interest in sociotechnical systems structure has been renewed as the technology of computers and information systems has become a part of everyday work life. Hornsby, Clegg, Robson, and McLaren (1992) report on a project designed to investigate ways to improve information systems by looking at human and organizational issues at the time the systems are being developed, rather than trying to correct problems as they occur. Other researchers have investigated social factors in areas such as the use of e-mail (Golden, Beauclair, & Sussman, 1992). Keller (1994) found that the fit between technology and information-processing needs in a research and development group in a company predicted project quality for the group. Each of these examples shows that both technological and social factors must be considered and balanced in successful organizations—as they are at PeopleSoft, Inc., a company that develops software to automate business processes such as payroll, manufacturing, and order fulfillment. From 1994 to 1998 PeopleSoft increased its staff from 650 employees to over 7,500, making it difficult to maintain social connections and identity in the organization. Some of the methods PeopleSoft uses to balance the human relations side of the organization include giving each new employee a distinctive backpack with room for all the necessary hardware, such as a laptop computer, the job requires. Every employee can access all databases, for example, product development and marketing, promoting a sense of trust and equality among the workers (Roberts, 1998). The emphasis is on providing employees with the tools they need to be productive workers, while using the same tools to promote the people side of the organization. If the software developed by PeopleSoft is not good, the company will go out of business, but if the employees do not stay, the same thing will happen.

Autonomous work groups Groups in which employees are given responsibility for planning and accomplishing their work.

Autonomous Work Groups

For the coal miners, part of the solution to mechanization of the mines was to restore **autonomous work groups,** in which the employee groups were given the responsibility for planning and accomplishing their work. The purpose of autonomous work groups is not to ignore technology but to give equal weight to social factors to achieve the best balance. Wall, Jackson, and Davids (1992) describe an unintentional application of this principle in a robotics assembly line in a manufacturing plant. The line combined the work of four humans and six robots. Each time a machine problem occurred with the robots, the human workers were told to contact the engineering support staff to correct the problem. This resulted in the production line being out of service over 40 percent of the time. When the researchers recommended letting the human workers correct most of the problems themselves without calling the engineering support staff, their suggestion was turned down because the repairs were believed to be too difficult for the workers to do on their own.

Louise Gubb/The Image Works

■ An autonomous work group often can fix problems quickly because it is at the site of the problem.

The entire plant except for this line had been operating on a pay incentive system. When the robotics assembly line was added to the pay incentive system, the human workers began attempting to correct problems themselves to reduce the time the line was shut down. The distant location of the engineering support staff made it very difficult for the engineers to reach the assembly line in less than fifteen minutes. Since the rate of the robot work was constant, the only way the human workers could increase their pay was to reduce the amount of time the line was shut down. The researchers following the progress of the human workers found that as they became more familiar with the mechanics of the robots, they were able to anticipate problems and reduce the number of times the line was shut down as well as the amount of shutdown time.

This research also illustrates one of the other principles of sociotechnical theory: the assumption that the best place to handle problems is at the place where they occur, at the lowest level possible. This looks a great deal like participatory democracy, but the goal is finding the most effective way to combine human and technological elements, not just to increase participation. Zemke (1987) suggests that the people most removed from interacting with the technology, top management, make many of the poorest technology decisions. For example, in the early 1990s a number of government offices in a midwestern state were redesigned to incorporate the use of computers. After the governor received reports that many employees were playing the games that came installed on the computers they were using, he ordered that the games be removed. Learning time for the new computer operators increased but productivity did not increase as a result of less game playing. One of the system trainers told the governor's staff that the trainers had been encouraging new computer users to play the card games in order to develop the coordination necessary for using the computer mouse. The games were restored. While some employees may have spent some business time playing card games, the overall result was positive.

Research results on the application of sociotechnical structures generally have been favorable (Pasmore, Francis, Haldeman, & Shani, 1982), although the many variables involved have been held responsible for research showing less favorable results (Pasmore, Petee, & Bastain, 1986; Wall, Kemp, Jackson, & Clegg, 1986). There has been renewed interest in this type of structure as computers and other technologies become an increasingly important part of people's everyday lives.

Advantages and Disadvantages of Systems Theory and Sociotechnical Theory

The concept of contingency theories is very appealing to I/O psychology as researchers look to the changes in the world of work in the twenty-first century. One of the most common projections about the structure of work in the new century is that it will indeed be changing constantly. In discussing the organizations of the new century, Susan Mohrman, a Senior Research Scientist at the Center for Effective Organizations at UCLA, suggests that the ability to change constantly and be flexible will be among the most important organizational and individual survival skills. She predicts that the person who is doing a good job will not be the person who is pleasing the boss but the person who is "contributing accomplishments that result in products and services that please customers." Making real contributions and pleasing customers are central characteristics of open systems and sociotechnical structures. Mohrman further suggests that a job will no longer be a defined set of tasks and activities but as an opportunity to earn money by using one's skills on a particular project or assignment. If an individual does not respond to changes in the system and technology and develop new skills and abilities, that individual will be out of work. As organizations continue to downsize, the employees who are the most flexible, have the broadest range of skills, and are most able to learn new ones will have the greatest chance of remaining employed when the workforce is reduced (Church, 1996).

This kind of work situation is frightening and difficult to interpret for many people. Employees look for reliable guides to explain "the system" in order to understand it and be successful in it. Many workers look to organizational culture and climate to provide this information.

ORGANIZATIONAL CLIMATE AND CULTURE

Organizational culture and climate are discussed together in this section, but first it is necessary to examine the differences between these concepts. This is not an easy task because there is some controversy about whether there is in fact any difference. Wilpert (1995) states that after twenty-five years of trying to develop clear definitions of these terms, there is still not complete agreement. Some psychologists believe that the terms are synonymous, some believe that "climate" is a subconcept of "culture," and some believe that these are related but different concepts. This last position is the one taken in this text.

Organizational culture is the deep pattern of basic assumptions that is passed on as the correct way to perceive, think, and feel in an organization. A successful organizational culture results in the survival of the organization; a dysfunctional culture results in the decline or death of the organization. **Organizational climate** refers to the individual perceptions of cultural events in an organization: how individual employees or groups interpret what happens in the organization. Let us look at examples of each of these concepts to make the differences clear.

One of the components of organizational culture is the physical layout and use of space in the organization. If a company's culture is based on an underlying

Organizational culture
The deep pattern of basic assumptions about shared values and beliefs in an organization.

Organizational climate
Individual and group perceptions of cultural events in an organization.

assumption that each employee is unique and works best when he or she is allowed to express that uniqueness, this will be evident in the physical features of the company. Perhaps employees are allowed to choose the furniture in their work areas and personalize their space with things they bring from home. One group may perceive this as a competition to show how important work is to them and will see family pictures or children's drawings as evidence that employees are not serious about work. Another group may regard this as a way to look more like upper management and will make all their furnishings exactly like the ones used by people in the top organizational levels. A third group may perceive this as a way to express how careful they are with company money and will only put items in their offices that they have brought from home. These differing perceptions represent evidence of organizational climate because they show how individuals or groups interpret the culture of the organization as it relates to physical space.

This example illustrates a difficulty in describing the culture of an organization that results from the influence of subgroups. Some of the subgroups in an organization may have values or beliefs that are different from those of the organization as a whole. For example, Jermier, Slocum, Fry, and Gaines (1991) examined a police department that projected a rigid appearance within the community. When groups of officers were interviewed in depth, the researchers found that only one of five subculture groups of officers conformed to the official culture. The other four groups had rejected the official culture or modified it to make it much softer and more flexible. Some researchers have suggested that organizational culture is more like the underlying personality of an individual and that organizational climate is more like the moods individuals experience from day to day (Kilmann, Saxton, & Serpa, 1985).

Levels of Organizational Culture

Organizational culture, like organizational climate, is a fairly new topic in I/O psychology. There appears to be a great deal of interest in these two topics as well as a great deal of discussion on how to study them and what they mean for organizations. Schein (1990) suggests that the best way to study organizational culture is to look at the three different levels that identify the culture in an organization (Figure 3.3).

The first level consists of observable artifacts. Artifacts include all the physical aspects of the organization, such as the physical layout, the dress code, the emotional intensity of the organization, the unofficial company stories, and the artwork on the walls. It also includes all the permanent records of the company, such as the annual report, the statements of its philosophy, and the personnel records. At Procter & Gamble, for example, a set of printed guidelines known as "Current Best Approaches" shows approved ways of handling such organizational activities as market research.

Figure 3.3

Levels of organizational culture.

Artifacts and Creations	Examples
Physical arrangements of offices and company	Open office design
How employees communicate with each other	Almost all communication written
Use of technology	Computer assistance in every area of the company
Values	**Examples**
Beliefs that end up being successful for the organization	The customer is always right. Rules were meant to be broken.
Basic Underlying Assumptions	**Examples**
Values accepted by almost everyone in the organization with few to no exceptions.	Solving problems has the highest organizational priority. Never sell a product at a loss. Employees want to do a good job.

Adapted from E. H. Schein. (1990). Organizational culture. Special issue: Organizational Psychology. *American Psychologist,* 45(2), 109–119.

The next level of organizational culture consists of the values of the organization. This includes the organization's norms, beliefs, founding documents, and philosophy in practice. For years the norm of conformity was valued so highly at Procter & Gamble that employees who suggested different ways to do things felt like outsiders. "I don't think they ever said, 'Individuality's bad,' but it felt that way," one worker explained (Brooker, 1999, p. 150).

Open-ended interviews often are used to ask employees why actions that have been observed in the organization are the way the are. For example, a consultant may find that memos left in one department are rarely shared with other departments even though instructions for sharing are included in the memos. The reason for this behavior may be revealed through interviews that uncover the organizational value that independent thought and action lead to research and progress at the company. Another part of the interview may reveal the value that the only employees who voluntarily cooperate with others are the ones who are not good enough to make it on their own. The uncovered values reveal the actual reason for the memo behaviors.

Interviews on values often provide the direction and material for the third and deepest level of organizational culture: the taken-for-granted, underlying, and unconscious assumptions that determine organizational feelings and behaviors. The method for uncovering these assumptions usually involves more intensive observations and more focused questions that lead the employees being interviewed to an extensive self-analysis on the organizational level. It is often difficult to reach this level because the basic assumptions are an unstated part of everyday life. It often takes an outsider who is trying to change these underlying assumptions to bring them to the attention of the employees. At Procter & Gamble, for example, the new chief executive officer, Durk Jager, appointed in January 1999, challenged the underlying assumption that employees should follow the established rules. In a videotaped speech sent to all the groups in the company, Jager downplayed the "Current Best Approaches" guidebook. He told employees that they should think for themselves. He also asked for new ideas through the company's internal communications network and offered rewards for the best ones.

One set of basic assumptions about organizational culture, which was described earlier in this chapter, was the Theory X and Theory Y systems developed by McGregor (1960). Once these basic assumptions are understood, it is easier to go back and correctly interpret some of the artifacts, or physical aspects, of the organization. If Theory X is a basic assumption at an organization, the interpretation of the observation of an employee playing a card game on her computer is that the employee is trying to avoid doing her assigned work. The correct meaning of such observations often is not clear until the basic assumptions are clearly understood. Bierma (1996) indicated that learning outside of formal training programs is the most valuable to employees for learning the corporate culture. This may be true because informal learning uses all three levels of culture identification.

Measurement of Organizational Culture

It is tempting to define the culture of the organization on the basis of a single story or series of events, but that will provide a far from complete picture. You may remember the story of the Disney employee, dressed in a character costume, who became ill and removed the head part of the costume to avoid soiling the uniform. Although he fainted after removing the costume head, he was fired because he had done it while he was among the guests. The Disney organization has a very strict set of rules about what is "onstage"—where the guests are—and what is "offstage"—where only employees are permitted. Taking off any part of the costume is allowed only offstage. From the perspective of the employees, this story shows how heartless the Disney organization can be, but it shows the guests how important it is to the organization to make a visit enjoyable for the guests.

Getting a complete picture of organizational culture requires time and the exploration of many different situations. Thinking about the ways anthropologists try to understand the culture of an extinct civilization can give some clues about the ways researchers try to understand the culture of an organization. Looking at artifacts is often the easiest way to assess a culture, but it is also one of the most risky because it is easy to interpret their meaning incorrectly. The Disney story could be interpreted in a number of ways, but it is only when the entire picture of organizational culture is drawn that it can be seen in context.

One of the ways to get an incomplete or incorrect picture of organizational culture is to look only at certain employees. Researchers have found that the top level of management often perceives the culture of the organization to be much more innovative and supportive than do either middle-level management or lower-level employees (Koberg & Hood, 1991). Survey instruments such as the Organizational Culture Inventory and the Corporate Culture Survey have been developed to gather information from employees at many different levels in the organization (Xenikou & Furham, 1996).

Person–Organization Fit

The relationship between an employee and the organizational culture has been examined in research on person–organization fit. This research explores the agreement between individuals' beliefs and behavior and those of the organizations that employ them. Typically, employees are attracted to organizations with cultures that match their own values (Judge & Cable, 1997; Sims & Keon, 1997), and once they are employed by an organization, the effects of person–organization fit appear to continue. Meglino, Ravlin, and Adkins (1989) found that when employees have values similar to those of their supervisors, they have higher levels of job satisfaction and organizational commitment.

A good fit between the person and the organization also has economic consequences for the organization. Sheridan (1992) found that newly hired accountants quit much sooner in companies with a culture that emphasizes work tasks as opposed to a culture that emphasizes interpersonal relationships. The economic cost of the more rapid departure of accountants from companies with a culture that emphasizes work tasks was over $6 million. While most research on organizational culture focuses on the social effects, monetary effects provide additional reasons for paying attention to the influence of the culture.

Creation of Organizational Culture

One approach to understanding the culture of organizations is to look at the process that creates that culture. One component is a critical incident that arouses certain behaviors that come to be adopted by the group. For example, a university in my state had a policy that if a professor was absent for any reason other than personal illness, and a substitute taught her class, the professor would have to pay for the substitute. When a faculty member's daughter was seriously injured in a car crash, the other faculty members decided to substitute without pay. The underlying issue here—"We help each other in a time of need without expecting anything in return"—can become a belief or assumption if the same behavior recurs in similar situations.

The second component in the development of culture in an organization is the society in which the organization is located. This can include the level of technology, market forces, and competitors. If a very large computer software company developed a product for which no other company was able to develop a good competing product, that organization might develop a belief to the effect that "Customers are stupid. They are willing to settle for whatever we give them." This could lead to very arrogant behavior from employees in their relations with customers. When and if another company developed a competitive product, the first company would have to change its cultural assumptions or it would not survive.

The third component of organizational culture development relates to the founder or succeeding leaders. When an organization is formed, the founder or founders provide a visible and clearly expressed model of how the company should be organized and how it should function. For example, although he is no longer alive, the founding assumptions of Sam Walton of Wal-Mart continue to be a very strong and observable presence in that company. From the greeters at the store entrances to the charitable donations, the basic assumption that "employees and customers are the most important part of any organization" is clearly present.

As the founder's beliefs are put into practice, some of these work out and some do not. As companies grow, subgroups often develop belief systems that may be different from that of the founder but are more successful for the group. As the use of computers grows in the workplace, some organization founders have kept up and changed with the times and others have tried to ignore computer-based technology. If some of the subgroups in an organization are able to incorporate computer-based technology successfully and work around the founder's aversion to computers, those subgroups may be able to contribute to the modernization and success of the company. Those subgroups also may contribute to the success of the organizational culture. Kanungo (1998) found that organizational culture is strongly influenced by the use of and satisfaction with computer-mediated communication within organizations.

Since so much of organizational culture lies below the surface, changes in the cultural system should be managed carefully so that they benefit the organization rather than destroy it. Although cataclysmic changes sometimes result in a better organization, planned changes usually are seen as more desirable and less disruptive. A number of methods of planned organizational culture change can result in a better organization.

■ Founders or leaders continue to exert influence over organizations whether they stay with the organization or not.

Organizational Culture Change

When the top executives of organizations plan changes in the organizational culture, they need to realize that from a systems structural point of view, cultural change is going on all the time in an organization, whether planned or not. You will recall that systems theory states that organizations constantly adjust in order to maintain homeostasis. Systems theory states that anything that is changed in an organization affects its culture—even a change as simple as one member of a work group leaving and being replaced by another person. The advantage of planning for cultural change lies in the degree of control that can be maintained and the ability to make the succeeding changes more beneficial and less destructive. The case study "Organizational Culture Change" shows how planning for organizational culture change made the process more successful for Chrysler Corporation.

[Case Study] ORGANIZATIONAL CULTURE CHANGE

In the early 1990s the Chrysler Corporation had a reputation for poor customer service and public relations and an outdated product line. Its market share was falling, and its fixed costs and losses were high. Top management decided that the problems were not with the structure of the organization or the employees but with the social structure and culture. To turn the company around, they developed a program of cultural change, Customer One. The values of the Customer One program are summed up in the motto "Whatever you do, do it with the customer in mind first, and the ancillary benefits will follow."

The new emphasis was on building a high-quality product with high levels of involvement early in the design process from everyone, including suppliers and customers as well as assembly line workers, product teams, and management. Suppliers were solicited for cost-saving suggestions, which resulted in savings of over $235 million in four years. Customers were asked to suggest improvements in vehicles rather than just rating the changes developed by engineers. Assembly line workers and mechanics were involved in production setups months before vehicle assembly began. Top management made a commitment to greater accessibility for all employees. Dealer incentives were based on quality and support for the Chrysler line.

Not only did the culture at Chrysler change, so did the bottom line measures of success. Overhead was cut $4.2 million in less than four years, the stock price quadrupled, and the company is once again profitable. In the process of changing the corporate culture, Chrysler found a number of keys to ensuring the success of the cultural change process:

1. Change does not happen overnight. One should plan on three to six years.

2. Patience, effort, and vigilance are critical factors.

3. It is best to start by changing small parts of the organization and then expand to more areas.

4. Good communication is the basis for successful cultural change. Keeping in touch with everyone involved can prevent many serious problems and correct them quickly if they occur. Misunderstandings are common during the organizational change process.

5. The managers and supervisors who are promoting the change must consistently model the behavior they want to see in other employees.

6. Change can become even more difficult once the turnaround begins.

7. The services of an experienced consultant can provide guidance and unbiased feedback.

Through purposeful, continued commitment to organizational culture change, Chrysler was able to change from "an aging dinosaur to a state-of-the-art profit maker," according to David Zatz of Chrysler.

From D. A. Zatz. (1994). Harnessing the power of cultural change. *The OD tool pack*, http://www.toolpack.com/culture.html

According to Trice and Beyer (1993), cultural changes in organizations fall into one of three basic categories. The first category is the overthrow and comprehensive change of the cultures of the entire organization. An example of this type of change occurred after a court order required the original Bell Telephone Company to divide into a number of smaller, independent regional communications companies. Some of the new regional companies tried hard to maintain the culture of the original company; others quickly asserted their own organizational cultural identity.

The second type of change occurs when only specific subcultures or subunits within an organization are singled out for change. For example, the food service staff in a large organization has developed a basic assumption that the employees know nothing about nutrition and it is the job of the food service staff to make them eat healthier food. Management may decide, however, that this basic assumption needs to be replaced. It may decide that the food service staff should serve the most popular food choices regardless of nutrition.

The third type of change results in a change of the entire organizational culture but is done gradually and slowly. For example, as the competition for high school graduates has increased among educational organizations, a number of colleges and universities have gradually changed their basic assumptions; they now consider students as customers who must be attracted to the schools, rather than seeing themselves as gatekeepers preventing unworthy students from entering their schools.

Although needed organizational culture changes can be made, an informal survey of management consultants (Kiechel, 1979) found that over 90 percent of American companies have been unable to carry out changes in corporate strategies that would lead to changes in corporate culture. Beyer and Trice (1978) suggest that this problem occurs because organizations decide to make a change, start the change process, but then fail to make the changes part of the everyday life of the organization. If an organization announces that no more routine memos will be circulated through departments but e-mail will be used instead, even if it makes sure each employee has the hardware and software necessary to use e-mail, it still may have trouble getting the employees to use this method. Perhaps the employees have the hardware and software but do not know how to use them. Training could solve this problem and overcome the resistance to making the change to e-mail, but other organizational culture features might prevent success. Perhaps the employees use the circulation of memos as a way to visit other employees and are unwilling to give up this method of sharing with other employees. Such problems are typical when organizations have a systems structure point of view. Trice and Beyer (1993) suggest that this is the nature of culture in organizations. They say, "Cultures are dynamic entities; they naturally give rise to all kinds of incremental changes." (p. 393). Harrison and Pietri (1997) suggest that team building as a part of organizational culture change may increase the likelihood of change because of support from the team members.

Accepting this point of view makes it difficult, if not impossible, to identify the best corporate culture. Many authors and researchers suggest that the best organizational cultures focus on values such as achieving productivity by supporting their employees, the importance of people as individuals, tolerance of failure, and informality as a way of promoting communication; these values are similar to many of the qualities of open systems and sociotechnical structures. While they may be very worthwhile beliefs, they may not fit all organizations. The best corporate culture appears to vary with the nationality (Den-Hartog et al., 1997) or the life cycle of the organization (Schein, 1985), or other factors such as the type of employees or economic cycles.

Measurement of Organizational Climate

Systems theory is illustrated in the concept of organizational climate. Climate refers to individual and group interpretations of certain features or events, and it may be different for different people in the same group of for those in different groups in the same organization. Managers who plan to make changes in the organizational culture should consider the effects on climate. The differences in perceptions among groups and individuals is well illustrated in a study by Kossek and Zonia (1993), which examined a university that made a conscious effort to change its culture in order to promote diversity among the employees. The researchers found that when formal organizational groups, such as the printing services department and the sociology faculty, had a greater percentage of women, the efforts of the university to promote diversity were viewed more favorably. Regardless of the organizational group, however, personal characteristics relating to race, ethnicity, and gender had stronger correlations with views of the university's promotion of diversity. Compared with white men, white women and members of racial and ethnic minorities placed a greater value on the university's efforts to achieve diversity.

Another study looked at differences in perception between people in an organization who regularly interacted with one another and people who did not regularly interact. The author of the study found that the interpretations of organizational events—such as firing a particular person or the construction of a new office building—were most similar among those employees who had the most interactions with one another (Rentsch, 1990).

As you saw earlier in this chapter, some researchers have suggested that organizational climate and job satisfaction are the same. Research such as Kossek and Zonia's university study and studies such as those by Pope and Stremmel (1992) indicate that while these concepts are related, they still most likely differ. Pope and Stremmel's study, involving workers at child-care centers, showed that job satisfaction measured the attributes of individuals and that organizational climate measured individual perceptions of attributes of the place of work—in this case the child-care center.

The view of organizational climate as specific to individuals or groups increases one's understanding of behavior in organizations, but it also makes it necessary to assess climate from the point of view of as many individuals and groups as possible to get accurate evaluations of the climate. Fortunately, the assessment of climate usually does not involve the in-depth interview methods associated with research on organizational culture, and so it is possible to get a large number of responses. Most research on organizational climate involves the use of questionnaires.

Some of these questionnaires have been developed to assess specific aspects of climate, while others assess climate as a whole. Examples of specialized questionnaires are the Military Equal Opportunity Climate survey (Dansby & Landis, 1991) and the Ethical Climate Questionnaire (Cullen, Victor, & Bronson, 1993). Figure 3.4 shows the types of items in these surveys. An example of a survey that looks at the entire climate is the Business Organizational Climate Index developed by Payne and Phesey (1971).

If climate is a measure of individual perceptions, a more accurate measure of climate should focus on what each individual says rather than generating an organizational summary or average. This would also help differentiate between organizational culture and climate. Koys and Decotiis (1991) developed a measurement scale designed to provide this type of individual focus, and they hope that it will influence the direction of psychological climate research in the future.

Figure 3.4

Typical items from an organizational climate survey.

---

1. Information goes upward and downward easily in my organization.

    True   False   Can't say

2. Almost every exception to a rule must be put in writing.

    True   False   Can't say

3. People at this company frequently spread rumors they know are not true.

    True   False   Can't say

4. Working together as a team is very important.

    True   False   Can't say

5. Top management is really interested in each employee.

    True   False   Can't say

6. Sharing information with other groups and departments is encouraged.

    True   False   Can't say

7. Doing extra work on your own time is encouraged by management and other employees.

    True   False   Can't say

Use of Climate and Culture in Organizations

Some psychologists have suggested that trying to examine organizational culture or climate is much like trying to search for the Loch Ness monster or the Abominable Snowman: Climate is very elusive, and the effort is unlikely to be successful. Most psychologists would agree that examining organizational culture and climate is not easy, but as knowledge about these concepts increases, examination and understanding begin to seem possible and important. Since at least the time of the Hawthorne Studies it has been known that social factors influence the work environment and that any attempt to develop a complete picture of the world of work must include people factors.

In recent years there has been increased interest in the ethical climate of organizations. If employees perceive that ignoring unethical behavior means that it is accepted or encouraged, there could be systemwide consequences for the organization. Recently, Sears, Roebuck and Company faced a lawsuit asserting that from 1989 to 1994 the company collected as much as $400 million for tire-balancing services that were never performed and then tried to cover up the fraud (*Wall Street Journal,* 1999). The lawsuit claimed that when the fraud was uncovered, Sears directed workers to destroy the tire-balancing machines and the counters connected to them. Employees claimed that Sears knew that most of the balancing services were never performed but pressured employees to sell the services anyway. Sears has denied the employees' charges, but in past years the retailer paid over $100 million to settle lawsuits charging unethical and illegal behavior. Although Sears made a monetary settlement in those lawsuits, the company said the errors were caused by an incorrect interpretation of rules rather than an intent to be unethical.

In contrast, a study of hospital nurses found that nurses who perceived the hospital as having a caring climate were more satisfied with their jobs and supervisors (Joseph & Deshpande, 1997). Many companies have decided to make the ethical climate clear by distributing a written code of ethics. At BellSouth the written code states, "Trust comes from doing the RIGHT THINGS for the RIGHT REASONS." At Texas Instruments the corporate citizenship statement says, "Our reputation for integrity, honesty and fairness goes back to our founders." This company also supports educational excellence among its employees and their families with programs ranging from a preschool child development center to generous financial support for continuing education. When what a company says and what it actually does are the same, the result is a highly ethical climate for employees.

Organizational Citizenship

In addition to the concern with ethical climate, many organizations have begun to examine the related concept of organizational citizenship among employees. *Organizational citizenship* refers to "individual contributions in the workplace that go beyond role requirements and contractually rewarded job achievements" (Organ & Ryan, 1995, p. 775). This includes behaviors such as volunteering to get sandwiches for several coworkers when one employee goes to the cafeteria, helping another employee unjam a copy machine, volunteering to stay late to complete a project, and assisting with a charity drive at work. In the Organ and Ryan meta-analysis of the reasons for this kind of behavior, job satisfaction was identified as the strongest contributor. Employees who perceive that rewards are given out very fairly in the organization and who are the most committed to the organization are the most likely to engage in organizational citizenship behaviors (Netmeyer, Boles, & McKee, 1997; Schappe, 1998).

Although organizational citizenship behaviors are outside the requirements of the job, employees feel that it is important that they be recognized for these behaviors in performance evaluations (Schnake & Dumler, 1997). However, if the behaviors are formally recognized in performance evaluations, they often become job requirements. Organ (1997) suggests that it may be less confusing to consider organizational citizenship behaviors as part of the context of the work environment. Such behaviors do not directly affect the actual performance of the tasks an employee is hired to do, but they influence the organizational culture, climate, and overall effectiveness.

At Texas Instruments employees are encouraged to volunteer in the community in many ways, such as tutoring students, serving as advisers to teachers and principals, and serving on the boards of nonprofit organizations or as education policy makers. For its part, the company makes numerous contributions to schools, community organizations, and universities. While the volunteer work and organizational contributions do not directly affect the task performance of employees, they contribute to an organizational culture strongly based on these underlying assumptions: "We all can help each other learn," "We owe something to the community rather than just taking from it," and "Learning never stops." Management at Texas Instruments strongly believes that organizational citizenship contributes to the company's success and effectiveness as a leader in the semiconductor industry (Engibous, 1999)

ORGANIZATIONAL EFFECTIVENESS

It is obvious that organizations must be effective to stay in existence. The questions that often are associated with organizational effectiveness are, "In what way do you mean effective?" and "How do you measure effectiveness?" The answer to the first question is that there are a number of possible answers. Cameron (1980) suggests that there are four basic facets to organizational effectiveness.

1. Is the organization accomplishing its goals? This typically refers to production or output, depending on whether this is a manufacturing or a service company.

2. Is the organization getting the resources it needs to continue functioning in its environment? If only two of eight computer manufacturers were able to get the computer chips they needed, those two would be seen as the most effective.

3. Is there little or no confusion or conflict within the organization? In other words, are the structure and culture of the organization productive or destructive? This refers to relationships among groups and individuals.

4. Are the stakeholders in the organization satisfied? **Stakeholders** are people who have any kind of investment (not necessarily monetary) in the organization's success. Typically, this includes stockholders, employees, and customers.

Each of these facets adds information for judging the effectiveness of an organization, and a number of different studies have used a variety of techniques for measurement (English, 1994; Judge, 1994). Among the measurement criteria are self-audits of activities, environmental scarcities, organizational size, financial and social performance, cost, profitability, efficiency, and decision-making variables. The identification of a number of facets of effectiveness and a variety of measurement techniques most likely indicates that organizational effectiveness has a number of dimensions rather than only one. Sampling more dimensions with more techniques is likely to result in a more complete measure of organizational effectiveness. More recently, two psychologists developed a computer-based system, *Effectiveness Consultant,* to assess organizational effectiveness (van der Heever & Coetsee, 1998). This system is based on input from nine accredited experts in business and organizational research. Organizational effectiveness is an emerging area of interest in I/O psychology, and as organizations move to "leaner" structures, it is more likely to generate greater interest.

Part of the effectiveness of an organization comes from the understanding of organizational culture and climate. Some researchers have suggested that the recent trend toward downsizing in organizations is a result of measurements of organizational effectiveness. Personnel audits show places to trim the organization but still maintain its success. There is no question that downsizing movements have made it important, on a personal and organizational level, to demonstrate measurable contributions to the success of the organization. The Government Performance and Results Act of 1993 is requiring federal agencies to adopt formal measures of organizational effectiveness and act on the results (Kravchuk & Schack, 1996). Even as downsizing is used to develop leaner organizations, research shows that firms that are strongly committed to human resource management practices in the areas of employee training and selection (d'Arcimoles, 1997; Delaney & Huselid, 1996) are higher in organizational effectiveness.

From a systems theory point of view, maintaining organizational effectiveness requires constant adjustment within an organization. When the changes are planned and the organization is committed to development, the chances of maintaining organizational effectiveness are greatly increased. Chapter 4 examines the planned change of organizational development and the organizational response to this change within the United States in regard to increasing diversity in the workplace.

MAIN POINTS

- Both the employees and the organization help determine the structure of an organization.

- The main principles of the bureaucracy are division of labor, merit-based employment, formal rules and procedures, a chain of command, and a span of control.

- Flat organizations have few levels of hierarchy and a small number of people reporting to a supervisor. Tall organizations have many levels and a large number of people reporting to a supervisor.

- Problems with bureaucratic structures include the inability to find the "ideal" bureaucracy, dissatisfaction among lower-level employees, and difficulty in changing the organization.

- Theory Y is an example of a human relations structure that considers employees as interacting social individuals.

- Systems theory as it is applied to organizational structure looks at organizations as dynamic, integrated parts that work toward the same goal.

- Organizational systems have inputs, outputs, and functions. Organizations that are responsive to change are called open systems.

- Katz and Kahn (1978) defined the ten major characteristics of an open systems structure, including the belief that there are many ways to reach the same goal (equifinality).

- Sociotechnical systems structure is a systems approach that gives equal weight to the social and the technical aspects of an organization.

- Autonomous work groups provide workers with opportunities for more responsibility for both social and technological control, emphasizing decision making at the lowest level possible.

- Organizational culture refers to the basic underlying assumptions of an organization.

- Organizational climate refers to individual perceptions of organizational culture.

- Culture can be examined by looking at the artifacts, values, and basic assumptions of an organization.

- The best organizational culture for an individual employee is the one with the set of values closest to the personal values of that employee.

- Organizational culture can develop from critical incidents affecting the organization, from cues coming from the society in which the organization is located, and from the founders or leaders of the organization.

- Organizational culture change occurs through overthrow, subunit changes, and gradual overall changes.

- Organizational climate often is measured by questionnaires answered by all or many employees.

- Organizational citizenship refers to employees' behaviors that are exhibited outside their regular job requirements but that benefit the organization.

- Organizational effectiveness refers to the success of an organization in meeting its goals, getting needed resources, minimizing conflict, and satisfying stakeholders.

KEY TERMS

Autonomous work groups	Negative entropy
Bureaucracy	Open system
Chain of command	Organizational climate
Closed system	Organizational culture
Contingency model	Sociotechnical systems
Division of labor	Span of control
Equifinality	Stakeholder
Flat organization	Systems theory
Homeostasis	Tall organization
Human relations structures	Theory X
Merit-based employment	Theory Y

REVIEW QUESTIONS

Answers to these questions can be found at the end of the book.

1. The main reason for the development of the bureaucratic structure was to give more control to top management.

   a. True   b. False

2. Which bureaucratic concept is best illustrated by a company's organizational chart?

    a. Division of labor

    b. Merit-based employment

    c. Formal rules and procedures

    d. All of the above

3. If you want to get as many promotions as possible in your working career, you should work for a _____ organization.

    a. systems

    b. flat

    c. tall

    d. business

4. The type of employee who would prefer to work in a bureaucracy most likely would be described as _____, _____, and _____.

5. An example of a human relations structure would be a Theory Y type of organization.

    a. True   b. False

6. Theory X assumes that employees want

    a. decreased responsibility.

    b. increased responsibility.

    c. a less bureaucratic structure.

    d. a people-friendly environment to work in.

7. Bureaucratic structures are usually examples of

    a. natural systems.

    b. open systems.

    c. closed systems.

    d. input-oriented structures.

8. Which systems characteristic would describe a company that converted from making baby food to making geriatric food supplements when the birthrate started to decline?

    _____

9. Dynamic homeostasis refers to the problem common to most organizations of maintaining a stable workforce.

    a. True   b. False

10. One of the advantages of applying systems theory to organizational structures is the ability to define the ideal organizational structure.

    a. True   b. False

11. Sociotechnical systems assume that the best level for making decisions in organizations is

    a. the highest level because those people have the most knowledge.

    b. the engineering level because those people are most familiar with the environment.

    c. in the human resources department, where they know the most about personnel.

    d. at the level where most of the effects of the decision occur.

12. What is one of the likely future characteristics of work that could make systems structures the best type of organizational structure? _____

    _____

13. Organizational culture generally refers to the national origin of the organization, and climate refers to features such as temperature and humidity.

    a. True   b. False

14. What are the three levels that are used to identify culture in an organization?

    a. _____

    b. _____

    c. _____

15. A good fit between an employee and an organization can lead to

    a. a more open culture.

    b. a more closed culture.

    c. monetary savings for the organization.

    d. employees staying on the job for a shorter time.

16. If a company replaces the elderly white male top management with a younger, more diverse executive group, this represents which type of organizational culture change?

    a. Gradual entire organizational change

    b. Subgroup change

    c. Overthrow change

    d. Involuntary change

17. Organizational climate most often is measured by giving questionnaires to many employees.

    a. True   b. False

18. What is one reason why it is important to consider culture and climate in an organization?

    _____

19. Organizational citizenship is important only during times of change in organizations because it can make change less stressful.

    a. True   b. False

20. The most common measure of organizational effectiveness is the profit the company makes.

    a. True   b. False

Use your browser to go to http://www.cybrblu.ibm.com/culture.html and examine IBM's discussion of its corporate culture. List five examples, given at this site, of artifacts of organizational culture, the first level of description of organizational culture. Among the types of organizational structures described in this chapter, which structure is IBM trying to use? Explain your answer.

WEB EXERCISE

4

The Changing Structure of the Organization: Diversity and Development

LEARNING OBJECTIVES
THE CHANGING STRUCTURE OF THE WORKPLACE
DIVERSITY ISSUES IN THE WORKPLACE
Benefits of Workplace Diversity
Racial and Ethnic Issues
Language Issues
Age Issues
Disability Issues

ORGANIZATIONAL DEVELOPMENT
Components of Organizational Development
Resistance to Change
Organizational Change Process: Action Method
Organizational Development Techniques
Case Study Diversity at Work
Organizational Transformation
Evaluating Organizational Development

Chapter Outline

Learning Objectives

After reading this chapter, you should be able to answer the following questions:

- What are the characteristics of an organization that has achieved diversity?
- How may racial and ethnic groups be treated unfairly in the workplace?
- How and why are older workers sometimes treated unfairly in the workplace?
- What are the issues that may prevent the full inclusion of workers with disabilities in the workplace?
- What do employers sometimes fear as the consequences of the Americans with Disabilities Act?
- What are the benefits of full inclusion in the workplace for workers with disabilities?
- What are the main components of organizational development?
- How does the action method promote organizational change?
- What are the typical methods of organizational development, and what are the main components of each method?
- How does diversity training promote organizational change, and what problems do diversity trainers encounter?
- What is organizational transformation, and how does it work?
- How can organizational development be evaluated, and what problems may need to be addressed?

THE CHANGING STRUCTURE OF THE WORKPLACE

In Chapter 3 the bureaucracy was examined as one of the earliest organizational structures. One of the dominant features of the bureaucracy is stability of the workplace; the formal rules and procedures make changes difficult and infrequent. The systems theory discussed later in that chapter emphasizes the almost constantly changing nature of the current workplace. While stability is valuable, the structure of the workplace is changing in many ways as the composition of the workforce becomes increasingly diverse. Greater diversity among employees is caused by a number of factors, including changes in the laws, changes in the characteristics of job applicants, and the desire of employers for the benefits of a diverse workforce.

As the workforce becomes more diverse, there will be a grater need for planning to make the best use of labor resources. The U.S. Bureau of Labor Statistics projected in 1996 that in the next ten years the number of white men in the labor force would continue to decrease while the number of women and Hispanic, African-American, and Asian employees would increase (Fullerton, 1997). While there definitely will be greater *workforce diversity* (employees who represent varied groups and populations), there may not always be greater *workplace diversity* (organizational structures that include varied groups and populations). Organizational development can help companies plan for greater workplace diversity and other changes in the work environment. Organizations that do not anticipate changes in the work environment rarely remain successful in a quickly changing world.

DIVERSITY ISSUES IN THE WORKPLACE

In 1995 the **Glass Ceiling Commission** issued a report on making full use of the nation's human resources. This commission was a twenty-one-member bipartisan group that was created by the Civil Rights Act of 1991. The purpose of the group was to study and recommend ways to eliminate the barriers minority group members and women experience when they try to move to higher levels in private sector organizations. As part of the commission's report, the secretary of labor cited a study showing that businesses committed to promoting minority and women workers had an average annual return on investment of 18.3 percent over a five-year period, compared with a return of 7.9 percent for the companies with the worst record of promoting women and minority workers.

The commission identified three types of barriers that women and minority workers face in achieving equality in the workplace. The first barrier is society, which may restrict educational and promotion opportunities to certain groups because of beliefs about those groups. This includes an unconscious preference for hiring employees who look like the people doing the hiring. The second barrier is corporate leaders who may use methods other than merit to select, promote, and evaluate employees. The third barrier is governments, which have kept inadequate and inconsistent records of employment status for different employee groups. This makes it difficult or impossible to monitor the employment status of those groups. The commission's report cited governments also for inconsistent monitoring and enforcement of existing laws and policies that forbid discrimination.

The commission found that the companies that were most successful at establishing and maintaining a diverse workforce were marked by five characteristics:

1. There is a visible commitment to workplace diversity starting at the top level and including the culture of the organization.

2. The top management acknowledges the value to the company of hiring and promoting minority group members and women. This objective is included in strategic business plans and goals.

3. Managers are held accountable for the hiring, development, and advancement of qualified employees. Pay and reward systems are tied to successful job performance alone.

Glass Ceiling Commission
A U.S. Department of Labor fact-finding group that assesses the status of women and minority groups in the workplace.

4. When research in the organization identifies specific barriers to full utilization of women and minority group members, the entire organization and all the employees work at changes until the barriers are eliminated.

5. The human resources department identifies and monitors the progress of high-potential minority and women employees to ensure that they have experiences that will qualify them to compete for leadership positions.

While these behaviors are advantageous for women and minority workers, the commission made it very clear that these policies must not unnecessarily deprive any other groups of their rights. The original intention of affirmative action policies was to identify underrepresented groups, set goals, and make plans for increasing the representation of those groups, and to terminate the program when the goals had been reached. The correct use of affirmative action programs is to open the system to find qualified employees who would not be likely to be included through the use of traditional selection methods. This was the point of the Glass Ceiling Commission's final report in November 1995, "A Solid Investment, Making Full Use of the Nation's Human Capital."

Benefits of Workplace Diversity

For some organizations workplace diversity is seen as a way to avoid lawsuits filed by employees who believe they have been unfairly discriminated against, but there are many positive benefits as well. The companies listed by *Fortune* magazine as the fifty best for minority employees outperformed a very strong Standard & Poor's 500 Index over a five-year period (Johnson, 1998). These results contradict the belief among some managers that investing in workplace diversity represents a financial loss to the company.

Richard Notebaert, chairman of Ameritech, indicated that there are at least four ways in which a commitment to diversity can enhance the financial performance of organizations (Notebaert, 1998):

1. A diverse workplace widens the pool of employees available to a company. The currently low unemployment rates have created competition for the best employees. An organization that is not willing to consider all potential employees is restricting its chances for success.

2. A diverse workplace enables a company to identify with its customers. This is really the basis of financial success for an organization. According the U.S. Department of Commerce, the buying power of Americans of African, Asian, and Hispanic descent is already $1 trillion. What company can afford to ignore that much buying power?

3. A diverse workplace makes companies far better prepared to succeed in the global marketplace. In the past twenty years Ameritech has gone from

providing telephone service in five midwestern states to offering a wide variety of communications-related capabilities in forty countries. The ability of employees to work effectively and sensitively with people whose cultures and experiences are different from their own is a skill that can be learned in a diverse workplace.

4. A diverse workplace adds genuine value to the expenditures companies make as they encourage the growth and strength of the communities in which they are located. Ameritech has consistently recruited minority contractors to supply some of its needs. One small African-American company that was nurtured by Ameritech for ten years went from being a company with four employees supplying $5,000 worth of wire and cable to being a company that did $7 million of business with Ameritech in 1998. Supporting diversity in the community also develops new potential employees and adds to the tax base of the community.

While organizations such as Ameritech clearly value a diverse workplace, other organizations have ignored or shown little interest in developing workplace diversity. The next several sections of this chapter examine different groups that contribute to diversity in the workplace and the issues involved in the full inclusion of women and minority employees.

Racial and Ethnic Issues

Since the 1990s there has been a movement to eliminate affirmative action goals from the workplace. The reasoning is that affirmative action has reached its goals and is no longer necessary. For example, the Bureau of Labor Statistics projects that by 2006 the white non-Hispanic proportion of the labor force will decrease to 73 percent (down from 80 percent in 1986) because of increases in minority group participation (Fullerton, 1997).

These statistics are only part of the story, however. Many people point to the need for affirmative action to promote minority group members in the workplace and keep them there. Among executives, over 98 percent are white, and the rate for leaving the workplace is much higher for minorities than for white employees (DeWitt, 1995; Glass Ceiling Commission, 1995a; Grossman, 2000). The higher the organizational level, the more unequal the numbers become. In 1990, African-American and Hispanic employees filled about 30 percent of middle management positions at large corporations but held less than 1 percent of the chief executive positions (Brown, 1990).

Although African-American employees are most often the focus of racial and ethnic issues at work, the increasing number of Hispanic-American and Asian-American employees has added another focus to those issues. By 2005 the black non-Hispanic and Hispanic labor forces will be nearly equal in size (U.S. Bureau of Labor Statistics, 1996). In certain communities other racial and ethnic minorities have encountered similar workplace problems. Asian and Middle Eastern employees often report unfair discrimination similar to that of other minorities.

It is possible to document companies, occupations, and jobs in which minority group members are not equally represented, on the basis of population or applicant figures. The problem with using numbers is that numbers do not identify the attitudes and beliefs that are behind the unfair practices. Industrial/organizational (I/O) psychologists are concerned with changing attitudes and meeting legal requirements to develop the most effective organization.

I/O psychologists also are concerned with what happens in organizations when minority employees are hired, so that those employees will remain and be promoted in the same way as majority applicants. Nondiscrimination policies and affirmative action may require equal treatment, but attitudes, social relationships, and other psychological factors may still represent barriers to overcome or differences to acknowledge. For example, evaluations by supervisors are typically crucial to promotion. Research shows that when the supervisor and the subordinates are of different races, the trust of the subordinates in the supervisor is significantly less than it is when the supervisor and the subordinates are of the same race (Jeanquart-Barone, 1993). Less trust leads to less sharing, and less mentoring can lead to fewer promotions.

In a survey of groups of employees in the regional office of a federal agency, each group (all men, all women, and men and women of color) reported similarly that it did not experience a common organizational culture—even though all worked for the same organization. This similarity of the way employees reported on the culture was based more on gender and race than on occupational factors such as job or organizational level (Fine, Johnson, & Ryan, 1990). One study indicated that in 1995, 89 percent of African-American employees believed they had to be better than white employees to get ahead at work, while only 30 percent of white employees had a similar belief (Grossman, 2000). Regardless of whether all employees agree, this perception affects the experience and feelings of African-American employees in the workplace.

In a study of job stress and coping behavior, researchers found that black employees were more likely than white employees to identify an individual, such as a supervisor or coworker, as a source of job stress (Stroman & Seltzer, 1991). This might be part of the reason African-American employees perceive less support from their supervisors and less independent decision making than do white employees (Igbaria & Wormley, 1992). When the subordinate was African-American and the supervisor was white, a researcher found less supervisory support, fewer developmental opportunities, and more discrimination (Jeanquart-Barone, 1996).

From a psychologist's viewpoint, it is the perception of the work environment that is critical to understanding how a person acts in that environment. The fact that an employer can show that all employees have equal access to company training programs does not mean that all employees feel they can apply for them. If African-American employees perceive that they are less likely to be chosen or less likely to complete a training program, they may not apply. It may take extra effort on the part of the employer to overcome those perceptions and get a larger number of African-American employees to apply for the program.

Another fast-growing minority in the workplace is the Asian-American worker. Asian-American employees have many of the same workplace concerns that other minorities have. In a study, Asian-American citizens reported about the same amount of workplace discrimination as Hispanic workers but less discrimination than black employees (Bell, Harrison, & McLaughlin, 1997). In Houston, from 1980 to 1990, the Hispanic population grew 75 percent but the Asian population grew 139 percent. The total number of Asians passed the number of Hispanics in that city.

Cultural differences may represent significant barriers for Asian-American workers. For example, in the United States small business owners quickly learn the importance of networking, establishing contacts that provide social resources for customers, good employees, and financing. One researcher found that the success of Asian-American small business owners was determined far more by large investments of financial capital and outstanding educational achievements on the part of the business owners (Bates, 1994). Also, Asian top executives were found to spend more blocks of time on a single project than American CEOs (Doktor, 1990); this means that American top executives were more likely to start a project, switch to another one, have a meeting, and then return to the original project during the course of a morning at work. Asian executives, on the other hand, were more likely to have fewer but longer meetings and spend more work time on single projects.

Managers at Eastland Bank in Rhode Island found that when they started a language and banking skills program for Southeast Asian students in that area, they became aware of many cultural differences that related to workplace behavior; they later included those differences in the training program (DiMase & Boyle, 1991).

Language Issues

How a person interprets a job situation is shaped by that person's individual experiences and the experiences of his or her race, gender, or ethnic group. In the case of many Hispanic employees, another part of the job experience is the language difference. Most African-American and white non-Hispanic employees share a culture based on the English language, which is the primary language for most of those employees. For many Hispanic employees, English is the second language. For a number of years psychologists have debated the extent to which language shapes the way a person thinks. Each language has words and expressions that are unique to it and express concepts that are difficult to translate into or understand in other languages.

There has been a great deal of debate on the issue, and some states have passed laws confirming English as the official language for government and the workplace. The right to use a different language is not specifically protected by civil rights laws, and some organizations cite business necessity for requiring English fluency in their employees. In a recent case an Office Depot store in Florida required that employees in the customer sales area use only English on the sales floor unless the customer preferred another language. Other languages could be used in the warehouse and break room (Finney, 1996). The business necessity reasons for this rule were customers' hesitancy to break into conversations in a foreign language and safety in situations that require a quick understanding of emergency messages.

The section on racial and ethnic issues in the workplace earlier in this chapter showed that different groups perceive the organizational climate differently. In Chapter 5 you will read about research showing that groups with the strongest identity have higher productivity and lower turnover. It is not unexpected, then, that research on Hispanic employees of the U.S. Navy's civilian workforce has shown that the Hispanic employees who were the most adapted to American culture had lower turnover rates than did the Hispanic employees who were the least acculturated (Booth-Kewley, Rosenfeld, & Edwards, 1993). This would add to the reasons for Office Depot's language rule and might suggest using a common language in the workplace whenever possible since language similarity is one of the strongest links among groups.

Even when words are translated directly, the meaning attached to those words can be different among different cultural groups. In a study of the Job Descriptive Index (JDI), which is discussed in Chapter 6, a Spanish translation of the JDI was given to three different groups to assess job satisfaction: bilingual U.S. Hispanic workers, U.S. Hispanic workers who spoke English primarily but who knew Spanish, and Mexican workers who spoke only Spanish. There were few differences in job satisfaction scores between the first two groups, but there were a number of significant differences in scores between the group that spoke only Spanish and the other two groups, showing that the JDI was perceived differently by the workers who spoke only Spanish (Drasgow & Hulin, 1987). The researchers suggested that both language and culture contributed to the perception of the translated JDI not being equivalent to the original JDI.

For some employers the goal of a common language for employees means financially supporting employees who are becoming proficient in the language needed on the job. One clothing manufacturer spent money to teach its non-English-speaking alteration tailors to learn enough English to read work directions and talk to customers (Cutler, 1991). A manufacturing firm in Illinois started a class in English as a second language that met twice a week for two hours on company time. The employees were so eager to learn that they asked to extend the class for another hour of their own time (*Training*, 1994).

Age Discrimination in Employment Act A federal law that makes discrimination against employees over age forty illegal.

Although language issues often focus on Hispanic-American employees, it is misleading to stereotype all Hispanic-American employees as having language problems at work and not look at the language problems of other employees. For example, a Hispanic-American who grew up in an English-speaking home and spoke English at school applied for a job at a manufacturing firm. On his résumé he had listed that he was bilingual but had not listed the second language: He had learned German in school and the military. When he went for an interview, the person who interviewed him started to speak in Spanish to make him more comfortable. Instead, it made him very uncomfortable because he had to tell the interviewer he could not understand a word she was saying!

Age Issues

Age is another component of workplace diversity. Older workers are remaining in or entering the workforce in higher numbers. By 2006 the median age of the labor force is expected to be higher than it has been any time in the previous forty-five years (Fullerton, 1997).

Workers over age forty have been protected by law for a number of years. The **Age Discrimination in Employment Act** and amendments to it protect those workers from being treated unfairly on the basis of age in terms of em-

Gale Zucker/Stock Boston

■ Older workers often can continue to make organizational contributions into their seventies and eighties.

ployment decisions about hiring, advancement and training, compensation, demotions, layoffs, terminations, and benefits. Full inclusion for older workers means choosing the best employee for the job regardless of age. Stereotypes and myths about aging have been one of the greatest barriers to full inclusion for older workers.

Knowledge Stereotypes

As is the case with the other groups discussed in this chapter, older workers are often the victims of stereotypes and false beliefs that discriminate against them. In some cases psychologists have contributed to those false beliefs. For example, for a number of years it was commonly thought that intelligence decreases with age, leading to a belief that older workers should not be given as much responsibility as younger workers. When group intelligence tests were given, people from middle age on typically seemed to show a decline in intelligence. A closer look at this research showed that much of this apparent decline was actually a decline in the speed of motor skills in reading the questions and marking the answers on the score sheet (Bischof, 1976).

Later research did show that there is an age-related decline in intellectual functioning, but it occurs much later than previous studies showed (Turner & Helms, 1986). This decline does not occur equally for all older people, and many people show very little decline until shortly before they die. In fact, verbal ability and general intelligence have been found to increase at least up to the normal retirement age (Birren, Cunningham, & Yamamoto, 1983).

Older people are actually superior to younger people in certain types of intelligence and memory. Older people are usually better in **crystallized intelligence,** which includes skills acquired through education and cultural experiences, such as verbal comprehension, numerical skills, and inductive reasoning. This is the kind of memory that would help a person score well on a game show such as "Jeopardy" if the motor skill of pressing the buzzer quickly were not a factor.

Fluid intelligence, which requires a person to organize or reorganize information directed toward problem solving, is a type of intelligence on which younger people score better than older people do. Retrieving information on a computer instead of looking it up in books may be more difficult for older people to learn. This does not mean that older people cannot or will not learn this skill, but it may take them longer. The next time you go to a library where the card catalog and periodical indexes have been replaced by computers, you probably will see a number of older people successfully retrieving information or even helping a younger student who is still learning how to use the computer system.

It appears that the older workers' willingness to view new technology as challenging rather than threatening plays a large role in their success at learning new jobs or skills. When employees age forty-five to sixty were interviewed about their perceptions of computers in the workplace, workers who

Crystallized intelligence
Intelligence based on skills acquired through education and cultural experiences.

Fluid intelligence
Intelligence based on the ability to organize information directed toward problem solving.

perceived computers as threatening complained much more about time pressure and health-related problems. Employees who viewed computers as challenging actively pursued information-seeking activities on the computers (Stauffer, 1992).

Work and Performance Stereotypes

Federal legislation in 1986 eliminated the age at which mandatory retirement can be imposed, except in a few specific cases. The government also has removed the upper limit of age-related employment protection. In other words, someone who is eighty years old may look to the Equal Employment Opportunity Commission to correct age-related employment discrimination. This is supported by research showing that the only performance decline for older workers occurs in jobs that require physical strength or speed (Aviolio, Waldman, & McDaniel, 1990).

Since most jobs do not involve those physical factors, a true equal opportunity employer would have no retirement age requirement but use only job performance to make employment decisions. The problem with this solution is that very few performance appraisals are totally objective, as you will see in Chapter 10.

The use of subjective elements in performance appraisals creates the possibility of bias whether it is intentional or not. Miller, Kaspin, and Schuster (1990) reviewed the effect that the type of performance appraisal method has on age discrimination lawsuits. They noted that subjective evaluations and recommendations from immediate supervisors provide a "ready mechanism" for discrimination. In one age discrimination case that an employer lost, the performance evaluation used was a rank-ordering system that was based on the assumption that performance declines with age, which obviously resulted in the oldest employees receiving the lowest ranks.

Researchers found two types of performance appraisal errors used to discriminate against older employees (Miller, Kaspin, & Schuster, 1990). The first error occurs when top management directs that the performance appraisal system be used to discharge an older employee who is still performing well on the job. This is illustrated by the previously mentioned rank-ordering system.

The second error occurs when a supervisor discriminates against an older employee by manipulating an age-neutral performance appraisal system. An example of this type of error is the case of *Krodel v. Department of Health and Human Services* (1982). The supervisor had already chosen a younger employee for the available promotion and had written a letter of recommendation that greatly exaggerated the younger employee's qualifications. The result was that this employee was placed on the list of those qualified for the promotion. The older employee was also on the qualified list. The supervisor was legally required to choose a qualified employee for the promotion, but it was unlikely that the younger employee would have been listed as qualified if he had been evaluated appropriately.

The researchers found that males between the ages of fifty and fifty-nine brought most age discrimination cases. Managerial or professional employees, workers whose jobs are most likely to include some degree of subjective evaluation (Miller, Kaspin, & Schuster, 1990), brought the most suits. Other researchers found that older sales representatives performed better than younger employees did when objective measures were used (Liden, Stilwell, & Ferris, 1996).

Some organizations that were eager to replace older employees with younger, lower-salaried employees later rethought the actual cost of losing a number of experienced workers all at once. Eastman Kodak changed its generous early retirement package not because of the cost of the package but because of its desire to keep experienced workers (Cowans, 1994).

As the unemployment rate drops, more organizations are looking to older workers to supply some of their labor needs (Kennedy, 1997). Some organizations, such as McDonald's, are advertising on television and in print for older employees. A survey showed that employers rate older workers high on basic literacy, commitment to the organization, skills, and experience (Waldrum & Niemira, 1997). Actions such as these appear to be moving in the direction suggested by the Glass Ceiling Commission: Organizations should be making the best possible use of the human resources that are available.

Disability Issues

The greatest legal change for workers with disabilities in recent times came with the passage of the **Americans with Disabilities Act (ADA)** in 1990. By the middle of 1994 this act covered all employers with fifteen or more employees. It forbids employers to discriminate against a person with a disability if that person is otherwise qualified for the job. The person must be able to do the essential functions of the job with or without **reasonable accommodation,** or changes in the workplace, to meet those needs of an employee with a disability that do not cause undue hardship to the organization or to other employees.

The ADA also covers people who are not currently disabled but have a record of having been disabled; this includes employees who are recovering drug abusers and those who have had cancer that is now in remission. Further, the act covers those who are treated as if they had a disability although they really do not. This might include someone who has bad facial scars from a fire and whose employer feels that it would be uncomfortable to work with him or her, although the employee is qualified to do the job.

Both before and after the passage of the ADA, employers, employees, including those with disabilities, and job applicants were concerned about the positive and negative effects of that legislation. It appears, however, that most employees were ready to welcome increased numbers of disabled workers; a survey reported

Americans with Disabilities Act (ADA) A federal law that makes it illegal to discriminate against a person with a disability if that person is otherwise qualified to do the job with or without reasonable accommodation.

Reasonable accommodation Changes in the workplace to meet the needs of a disabled employee that do not cause undue hardship to the organization or to other employees.

Disability A physical or mental impairment that substantially limits a major life activity.

by *HR Focus* (1992) showed that 52 percent of American workers believed that it would be fair to have their own work duties or schedules changed to accommodate new coworkers with disabilities.

One problem uncovered by the survey was that employees interpreted the term "disability" differently than the ADA did. Over half the workers surveyed believed that severe vision and hearing problems, wheelchair confinement, mental illness, and illiteracy should be considered disabilities. More recent court decisions have not always agreed with that response. For example, courts have struggled to decide whether substance abuse and repetitive stress injuries should be considered as disabilities. The ADA defines **disability** as a physical or mental impairment that substantially limits a major life activity, a record of such an impairment, or being regarded as having such an impairment. Major life activities include hearing, seeing, speaking, walking, breathing, performing manual tasks, personal care, learning, reproduction, child rearing, and working. A disability typically is permanent.

This definition does not include illiteracy, but it does include recovering substance abusers, cancer patients, AIDS and human immunodeficiency virus (HIV)-positive patients, people with certain learning disabilities, and diabetics; and it leaves open the possibility of adding others. In the first two years after the ADA was adopted, almost half the discrimination claims filed were for ailments not on the list of thirty-five worker impairments protected by the ADA (Verespej, 1994). Specifically excluded are employees whose difficulties at work stem from active use of illegal drugs, a compulsion such as gambling, sexual disorders, and sexual preference (Parry, 1991).

Many organizations have employed workers with disabilities not because the law required it but because hiring them made good business sense. When Xerox Corporation employed Peter Torpey as a computer engineer to design ink-jet printers, the company knew that accommodations would be needed for the blind engineer. The workplace adjustments included a computer speech synthesizer and a Braille keyboard. Xerox found that the adjustments were a good investment when Torpey's design successes made him one of the most valuable members of the design team (Dobbin, 1998).

Employees with disabilities are typically as good as or better than workers without disabilities. A study that compared janitorial employees who were disabled physically, mentally, and/or emotionally with janitors without disabilities found that the employees with disabilities performed at the same levels as or at higher levels than the employees without disabilities. This study found that the employees with disabilities had lower turnover and absence rates and were seen by their employers as more likely to advance in their careers (Ondusko, 1991).

Other studies have shown similar results for a variety of disabilities and employees (Johnson, 1993; Lysaker, Bell, Milstein, & Bryson, 1993). A snack food company in North Carolina found that when it started actively recruiting employees from a local vocational rehabilitation center, it reduced the annual employee turnover rate from 160 percent to 5 percent. Productivity rose from 60 percent to 90 percent of capacity. The increase in profits made it possible for the employer to offer full health benefits, paid vacations, and higher salaries to its employees (*Inc.*, 1995).

Employers' Fears of ADA

One of the fears organizations have about the ADA is that the requirement to make reasonable accommodation will be very costly. Three years after the ADA became law, research showed that less than 3 percent of the required accommodations cost more than $1,000. The average cost per accommodation was $121, and over two-thirds of the accommodations cost nothing (Clark, 1995). Companies are allowed tax credits for accommodations. Sears, Roebuck and Company, in fact, came out ahead financially by making reasonable accommodation for workers with disabilities. That retailer found that the average accommodation cost only $45, while firing and replacing an employee cost between $1,800 and $2,400 (Kazel, 1996) (Figure 4.1).

Figure 4.1

Many workplace accommodations are inexpensive, but they open the workplace to disabled employees.

TYPES OF SIMPLE WORKPLACE ACCOMMODATIONS FOR DISABLED EMPLOYEES

Buy adjustable desks and workstations when replacing equipment
Install grab bars in rest room facilities.
Upgrade emergency alarms to be both visible and audible.
Widen doorways.
Rearrange work areas to allow easy access for workers with assistance equipment.

While it may be difficult to judge whether a specific accommodation causes undue hardship, sometimes it does not require an extensive cost-benefit analysis to determine that a particular accommodation is not reasonable. For example, a secretary had a mental and emotional disability, caused by medication she was taking for depression, which made her unable to remember assignments she had been given. She was the secretary to an executive in a fast-paced, high-pressure office environment. She told her supervisor that if she did not take her medication, she would be too depressed to work. The supervisor took away many of her tasks and assigned them to another worker but kept the first secretary at the same pay. She then claimed that the change in job assignments was discriminatory; it caused her to be more depressed, and that led to her missing more days at work. At that point she was fired for missing too many workdays. She then filed a lawsuit against the company. The second secretary cost the company almost $40,000, and the legal bills were over $20,000. The company won the lawsuit but lost a great deal in the process. About 25 percent of the complaints filed over ADA issues are from workers who were hired and then came to believe that their companies did not make reasonable accommodation.

Most questions about what accommodations an employee may need can be asked only after a job offer has been made, but in some situations questions about accommodations can be asked in the initial interview. If an applicant has an obvious disability that would require an accommodation such as a wheelchair ramp, if a job applicant reveals a hidden disability such as diabetes, or if an applicant asks for reasonable accommodation, that person can be questioned to clarify the issue (Nomani, 1995).

One of the other fears employers have about the ADA is that medical insurance costs will increase dramatically when employees with disabilities are hired. In fact, the ADA does not require any special coverage for employees with disabilities. If a company excludes coverage for preexisting conditions, that applies to an employee with a disability. The only requirement is that all employees be treated the same with regard to benefit coverage. The ADA does cover people who are HIV-positive or who have AIDS. Since medical records must be kept separate from personnel records, the HIV/AIDS status of a job applicant may not be known in the organization unless special accommodations are required. There have been several legal challenges regarding medical coverage for those with HIV/AIDS, but there also have been medical discoveries that have lengthened and improved the life span of those patients. Employers are required to treat HIV/AIDS employees the same as any other employee, although there must be reasonable accommodation such as preventing the exchange of body fluids.

Another fear of employers is that the ADA will require them to keep employees who are substance abusers. While the ADA does protect recovering substance abusers, it does not require employers to keep employees who are still using illegal drugs as long as the company has followed the correct procedures for drug testing in the workplace. If current drug or alcohol use impairs an employee's job performance, the employer can take action against that employee.

A related fear for employers is the belief that they may be required to hire mentally ill people whose illnesses could result in workplace violence for which the employer will be liable. The ADA protects mentally ill employees, but it uses the criterion of reasonable accommodation. This means that an employer would not be required to allow an employee with a paranoid disorder to bring a gun to work because that employee believed someone might be trying to kill him. Employees cannot make up a mental illness; they must be able to verify the illness according to the *Diagnostic and Statistical Manual of Mental Disorders* that is used by mental health professionals. Research on a group of employees with schizophrenia-type disorders showed that they performed at least as well as other groups of disabled employees on a number of work measures (Lysaker, Bell, Milstein, & Bryson, 1993). Almost 13 percent of all complaints filed with the Equal Employment Opportunity Commission from 1992 through 1996 concerned discrimination against employees with a mental disability (Cashin, 1997).

Benefits and Successes of the ADA

In spite of the fears, most managers appear to agree with the primary intention of the ADA. A survey of 408 managers showed that they believed that hiring people with disabilities might actually improve their companies' ability to compete (Callahan, 1994). Another benefit of the ADA is that it has required organizations to look carefully at the job descriptions they use and remove nonessential job activities from those descriptions. A careful job analysis also might show that a task that is listed as essential is done only 5 percent of the time in that job and not only could be done but might be done better in other ways. One author used the example of a counselor in a residence for juvenile offenders. It had been listed as a job requirement that each counselor have a valid driver's license to transport juvenile offenders to court or the hospital. If there were five counselors on each shift, all of them would never leave at once to drive the juveniles, and so it was really only necessary that one or two counselors have a license. They might even have found that it was less risky and more cost-effective to have police officers take several of the offenders to court at one time (Greenberg & Bello, 1992). An engineering group at Xerox discovered that finding new ways to custom-tailor work applications made work more interesting and challenging for them. They said they were not bound by the way things were done in the past but looked for solutions outside the usual rules and boundaries (*HR Focus*, 1992).

If the ADA has the potential for making employees with disabilities an integrated part of the mainstream workforce, the years since its passage should have recorded increasing numbers of disabled workers. Unfortunately, that has not been true. Only half the 29 million disabled Americans age twenty-one to sixty-four are currently employed; they account for 14 percent of the employed population (Mergenhagen, 1997). This same article reports that about 85 percent of the legal claims of unfairness arising from the ADA were brought by current employees, not by applicants trying to enter the workforce.

One reason for these low figures is that the ADA requires employers to offer the same insurance coverage to workers with disabilities that it offers to all employees. In practice, this often means not covering or postponing coverage for preexisting conditions. People with disabilities who would lose subsidized medical coverage because they are employed may not be able to afford that loss and thus cannot accept an employment offer. The second reason reflects the fact that merely passing laws does not change attitudes. Like other employees, workers with disabilities may not choose to work in a hostile environment.

Even among work environments that are not hostile, many may not be fully accepting of employees with disabilities. A number of employers are dealing with attitude issues as part of the larger task of changing the whole organization or large parts of it through organizational development.

ORGANIZATIONAL DEVELOPMENT

If an organization is not effective or could be more effective, how can it be changed to improve? This important issue is addressed by **organizational development (OD)**, a process of planned change for the entire organization or a large part of it that is based on social science research methods.

Sometimes the desire for change is reactive; that is, something happens that requires the organization to change. For example, if the literacy level of job applicants falls so low that almost none of the applicants are at the reading levels required to work in the organization, the company may decide to make changes. The company may choose to change the jobs to require less literacy or to provide literacy training programs for the applicants. If the company does not change something so that the production process can continue, it will not survive. Reactive changes are made in response to another change, such as a threat to production, new competitors and customers, or new political and legal requirements.

Sometimes the desire for change is proactive; that is, the organization is doing well but wants to keep doing well and perhaps even do better in the future, and so it decides to make organizational-level changes. A current example of this kind of change is the increase in OD programs designed to promote the acceptance of cultural diversity in organizations. Other reasons for planning proactive changes include taking advantage of a new business opportunity and introducing new technology into the workplace.

Components of Organizational Development

Organizational development (OD)
A process of planned change for the entire organization or a large part of it that is based on social science research methods.

According to Porras & Silvers (1991), there are four components to OD: "(a) change intervention that alters (b) key organizational target variables that then impact (c) individual organizational members and the on-the-job behaviors resulting in changes in (d) organizational outcomes." (p. 52). Each of these components is a critical part of the change process (Table 4.1).

Table 4.1

COMPONENTS OF ORGANIZATIONAL DEVELOPMENT

Component of Organizational Development	Example
Change intervention	Consultant teaches team-building techniques to all supervisory personnel. Information technology department conducts training program for moving to a paperless office.
Key organizational target variables	Successful change to commission sales system for all salespeople. Successful change to a new office building.
Individual organizational members and their on-the-job behaviors	Successful change in sales teams rather than individual salespeople. Successful change in system's organizational structure.
Organizational outcomes	Higher profits, lower turnover, greater job satisfaction.

Change intervention refers to changes in work settings. These can be small changes in response to small clashes with factors in the environment, which result in minor changes in the work setting such as a one-day seminar on e-mail etiquette. Larger changes often are caused by an organization's desire to be prepared for the future by developing new methods and systems, such as new product lines.

Organizational target variables include four major types of variables: (1) organizing arrangements, such as the formal reward systems of incentive-based pay and ownership of the organization; (2) social factors, such as organizational culture and management style; (3) technology, such as tools, equipment, and machinery; and (4) the physical setting, such as interior design and office arrangements.

Changes in the individual job behaviors of employees basically involve making a new response to a new or old stimulus. These may be small changes, such as an improvement in skill levels among production workers, or they may be major changes in the entire focus of the organization, such as a change from being "production-driven" to being "customer-responsive." Changes in organizational outcomes include changes in organizational performance, such as productivity and efficiency, and individual changes such as learning new skills and abilities.

Managing all these components and arriving at positive organizational changes sounds like an awesome task and often is. Many OD designs are based on the systems theory model discussed in Chapter 3. That model is based on the

Change agent The person who directs organizational development in an organization; this may be someone inside or outside the organization.

principle that anything done to one part of an organization influences all the other parts. Even a minor change, such as upgrading the word-processing system used by one division of the company, can produce a ripple effect through all the other levels.

In the past OD often was thought of as "bringing in someone to stir things up a bit." This naive view led to some disasters, but it also led to a change in the focus of such development. Beer and Walton (1987) assert that the role of the manager has to be more that of an architect than that of a director. They say that the best OD consultants recognize that their influence is only for a very short term and that real success relates to OD becoming a general management skill. The role of the consultant is similar to that of a tutor who teaches a student a specific skill and then moves on to another student. In OD people in the organization learn new skills, which they apply in the organization. The consultant does not remain in the organization. Like a tutor, she moves on to another organization and another OD intervention.

This view fits a systems theory model because management-centered interventions are more likely to be modified and further changed on the basis of feedback from parts of the organization. A friend once told me that his group at work was being "developed." I said to him that sounded like a process done to film, which from his perspective was probably accurate. As with film that has been exposed, the result would be something different from what his work group started as. For film, the printed photo is the end of the process. Unfortunately, my friend also saw development as a terminal change in the behavior of his group.

In organizations that use a systems theory model, the end of one process is really the beginning of another cycle and perhaps further changes. An organization that does not make changes is likely to be an organization that is stagnating or declining. A manager who is a part of a dynamic organization is in an ideal position to direct those continuing adjustments and monitor the need for further change. McLean, Sims, Managan, and Tuffield (1982) suggest that this is a more realistic view because opportunities for organizational change are often unexpected. The role of the OD consultant in such a system becomes more that of a teacher developing skills in the managers than that of a person who "stirs the system up a bit." Regardless of who directs the organizational changes, this person often is referred to as the **change agent.**

Resistance to Change

Once managers have participated in successful OD changes, It is usually easier to interject more interventions, but getting management and employees to the point where they want the changes to occur is often a major hurdle in the process. Most people are somewhat resistant to changing what they know and feel comfortable with even if they see the change as desirable. Even though you may be eager to start a new job, you may be reluctant to leave your old job and old friends.

One of the goals of a successful OD intervention is to diminish resistance to change before the organization reaches the change or die point. Much of that resistance comes from employees' fears of losing jobs, coworkers, control over work, or status. Some of these fears may not be realistic, but they seem real to the people who have them. It may be easier for a manager to remedy these fears than for an OD consultant to attempt to relieve them. The manager is more of a stakeholder in the organization than is the outside consultant and may be seen as having more to lose if the change is not an improvement. When employees are involved in all steps of the change process, resistance to change is often lower because there is less that is unknown. Because resistance to change may come in many different forms, organizations need to be aware of that resistance and deal with it as part of the OD program. This leads to the next step: the actual intervention.

Organizational Change Process: Action Method

Although organizational change often is thought of as an ongoing process, most organizational change interventions use a series of stages to focus the activities. The **action method** of planned organizational change includes four stages: diagnosis, planning for change, intervention, and evaluation.

Diagnosis involves gathering information to interpret behavior in the organization correctly. Among the most common sources of data and methods of data collection are the following (Tichy, 1962):

1. Questionnaires given to many or all of the organizational stakeholders
2. A number of direct observations of behavior in the workplace
3. Interviews with individuals in key positions
4. Workshops with different groups to discuss group and individual perceptions
5. Documents and records of the organization

Often a combination of these methods will produce more information than any single method will. The goal is to get the greatest amount of high-quality information possible to make an accurate diagnosis.

If diagnosis is done correctly, planning for change (the next step) will be easier as clear needs become apparent. Even if the needs are clear, however, it may not be wise or reasonable to change all the diagnosed problems. This part of the planning process looks at which changes are most likely to produce the most desirable results. The choice of what changes to make also will influence the choice of organizational change methods. Many of the more common change methods are listed in Figure 4.2.

Action method An organizational development process that uses the steps of diagnosis, planning for change, intervention, and evaluation.

Figure 4.2
Methods of organizational change.

METHODS DISCUSSED IN THIS CHAPTER

Survey feedback
Team building
Process consultation
Organizational transformation

METHODS DISCUSSED IN OTHER PARTS OF THE TEXT

Individual consultations, such as counseling or coaching
Management by objectives
Job redesign, such as changing tasks or the work environment
Changes in personnel systems, such as performance appraisal and selection
Organizational design
Combination methods

During the intervention stage, the actual work with the employees is done by the consultant or the manager, or both. Since a variety of techniques may be used in a single situation, different change agents may be used during a single intervention. Evaluation, the fourth step, most commonly is done soon after the intervention, but the true picture of the effects often is seen when evaluation is done a number of times after the intervention.

In a true action method model the information gained in the last stage will lead back to the first stage. This reinforces the concept of the systems organizational model discussed in Chapter 3. Some authors have suggested that the action method model is more in line with Eastern traditions, such as Taoism and Confucianism, which see change as cyclical. This model views the organization as moving from one state to another and considers change to be the usual state of the organization (Marshak, 1993). A number of OD techniques can be used to promote organizational change.

Organizational Development Techniques

Early research in OD followed a model proposed by Lewin (1951) that started with "unfreezing," where the organization saw the need and planned to change. The next step was the actual change. The last step was "refreezing," where the changes were formally recognized and accepted as a part of the organization. While Lewin never suggested that the last step could not serve as the starting point for a new change process, he did suggest that the change process was uncomfortable and not a natural state for individuals and organizations. The next sections in this chapter examine more closely some of the specific techniques used during the intervention stage. You will see that a number of techniques incorporate each of Lewin's steps as part of successful OD.

Survey feedback A method of organizational development that is based on using questionnaires filled out by employees to give them feedback for planning for change in the organization.

Survey Feedback Method

One of the earliest OD techniques was the **survey feedback** method. This technique was developed in the 1950s when a psychologist working with Detroit Edison observed that little change occurred when survey results were reported to a supervisor and the supervisor did not discuss any plans for change with the subordinates. However, when the supervisor discussed the results with subordinates and made plans with them for changes, significant favorable changes occurred (Mann, 1961). These observations led to a very common, standardized method of organizational development that consists of the steps shown in Figure 4.3.

The first step is a planning step in which top management discusses the questionnaire, how it will be administered, and how the results will be used. The questionnaire is designed to assess employees' attitudes about specific work-related issues, such as job satisfaction, work atmosphere, management, company communications, policies, procedures, and customer relations.

The second step requires the questionnaire to be administered to every member of the organization. Third, someone outside the organization, such as a consultant, analyzes the results of the questionnaire so that the evaluation can be done objectively. Fourth, the results are reported back to each manager or group of managers, starting at the top.

Finally, after everyone is familiar with the data, each supervisor discusses the results with his subordinates to plan ways to solve the problems that were identified in the survey. This step may use the outside consultant to help generate or direct problem-solving interventions.

The survey feedback method has been shown to be an effective method for changing organizational behaviors in a number of different settings. Part of the reason for its effectiveness may be the long history of its use. Another part may be its low cost compared with some other methods; and a third part may be the involvement of everyone in the organization, leading employees to believe that management really does want to hear what they have to say.

The involvement factor becomes even more important if the feedback meetings lead to actual changes that are based on input from the employees. Born and Mathieu (1996) found that supervisors with the highest initial ratings in areas such as management supervision and supervisory communication made the

Figure 4.3
Steps in the survey feedback method.

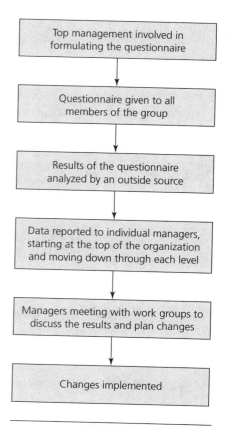

Top management involved in formulating the questionnaire

Questionnaire given to all members of the group

Results of the questionnaire analyzed by an outside source

Data reported to individual managers, starting at the top of the organization and moving down through each level

Managers meeting with work groups to discuss the results and plan changes

Changes implemented

greatest use of survey feedback results. When Bowers (1973) did a longitudinal study of the effects of different organizational change techniques in twenty-three organizations, he found that survey feedback systems were the most effective change strategy. Texaco's research and development department in New York used a survey feedback process that was repeated four times in five years. The results showed improvements in reducing sick time, resignations, and reworking. Patents and patent applications increased, as did the department's funding (Archer, Dorawala, & Huffmire, 1993). Another researcher developed a computer-based survey feedback program that he suggests can improve the facility of data collection and the accuracy of the results (Hirschfield, 1991).

As organizations become more multinational, a note of caution needs to be introduced. Putti (1989) suggests that in many Asian countries open discussion of organizational problems between subordinates and superiors is seen as undesirable. He cautions that national culture as well as organizational culture must be considered in making decisions about organizational change.

Team Building

One of the more popular OD techniques is **team building,** which focuses on improving the effectiveness of already established work groups. In a survey of *Fortune* 500 human resources executives, programs designed to improve organizational quality were used by 68 percent of those executives (*Training,* 1991). In another survey of 310 people who had participated in large-scale organizational change efforts, team building was the most frequently used change technique (Covin & Kilmann, 1991). The emphasis is usually not on teaching job-related technical skills but on teaching job-related interpersonal skills that allow members of the work team to accomplish their job functions more successfully.

The first step in team building is typically a diagnosis of where the group is going and how it is functioning, focusing on the identification of problems in the group. This can be done with the whole work team or with smaller subgroups. As a result of the diagnostic sessions, plans are made to produce changes in the group. Since it usually is not possible to make every change the group has identified, priorities often are established. Some common desires for change center on solving problems related to accomplishing work tasks, looking at and improving interpersonal relationships, and managing the group's culture (French & Bell, 1984). Sometimes more work-oriented projects for change are less threatening than are emotion-oriented changes. It may be a safer place to start the process (Bell & Rosensweig, 1978). Also, activities such as the outdoor educational experiences discussed in Chapter 10 may be part of the team-building process.

Team building
An organizational development method for improving the effectiveness of a work group through improved group interaction.

As part of the trend in employee empowerment, there has been a move toward using team building as a way to develop self-directed work groups (Cofsky, 1993; Wellins, 1992) in which all the team members share authority equally and function with supervision that is similar to coaching. Caution must be used to make sure the self-directed teams have been prepared to take on their responsibilities and trained in the skills that make self-direction work. Otherwise, a self-directed work team becomes a group in which no one is in charge and no one knows what to do. Weick (1993) discusses how this lack of preparation for self-direction could have contributed to the death of thirteen people in a fire, an emergency situation in which no one took charge. Self-directed work teams require team building, clarifying of goals and missions, agreeing on roles and responsibilities, improving relationships and interpersonal skills, and studying group dynamics, procedures, and processes for this to be a successful developmental activity (Arjas, 1991).

Although case studies do not provide a complete evaluation of the success of team building, they show that the process can work effectively. Apple Computer used team building to meet the changing requirements of global commerce. The team-building program led to the development of a worldwide commodity team network that would have to coordinate projects and supplies from every part of the world. After the team development process, Apple was able to increase revenues and volume of activity and reduce the cost of supplier management (Hamlin, 1994).

Several other studies have shown varying positive effects of team building on productivity (Bottger & Yetton, 1987; Buller & Bell, 1986; Harrison & Pietri, 1997; Mitchell, 1986). Bottom and Baloff (1994) suggest that the inconsistency of the results may be due to using team-building interventions when other methods would be more appropriate.

Process Consultation

The method of **process consultation** has a number of similarities to team building, but the emphasis is on the outside consultant teaching the team how to solve its own problems. Schein (1969) states that in process consultation the change agent teaches skills and values rather than just passing on knowledge about a task. In team building the focus is on getting the members of the work group to act cooperatively to accomplish the task. For example, Burke (1982) discusses the case of a corporate vice president whose subordinates responded incorrectly to his memos. He hired consultants to conduct a three-hour team-building intervention. During the intervention memos were shown on screens to the whole group, and then the group members prepared and discussed written responses. Only then did the vice president explain his intentions in writing the memo. Both the vice president and the subordinates cleared up some misunderstandings and were able to learn from the activity. Consequently, the number of the vice president's memos decreased 40 percent and the company saved almost $20,000 from the improved communications procedures.

Process consultation most often is used as a long-term intervention in an ongoing group. One psychologist compared process consultation to long-term psychotherapy (Landy, 1989), in that the consultant does not tell the client what to do but guides the client in learning and applying more successful techniques. Burke

Process consultation An organizational development method in which consultants work with people in the organization to help them learn to diagnose and solve their own problems.

(1982) indicates that process consultation may take a wide variety of forms but that the basic goal is to help the client "(1) to achieve a better understanding of the dynamics and characteristics of what is happening behaviorally within an interpersonal group, or intergroup setting, and (2) to act on that increased understanding in such a way that work will be improved and productivity increased." (p. 286).

In process consultations, while the consultant is working with one group, such as the sales, clerical, or production employees, the process may reveal other groups that have effects on it; at that point, the consultant may suggest involving the other groups. With several groups and issues to consider, the consultant will help the company decide how to make changes. At this point the consultant may remove herself from direct involvement and only check that the changes are proceeding smoothly. Longer time and greater involvement with the organization may lead the consultant to become a stakeholder in the organization and lose objectivity (Kahn, 1993). This may be a good reason to back away. The consultant usually returns to work on the evaluation, although a more objective third party also may work on it. If the evaluation indicates further need for development, the consultant may stay involved for some time.

More than any other OD method, this one requires a high degree of employee involvement, knowledge, skill, and commitment for the change to be successful. That commitment may help increase success in changing employees' attitudes and perceptions, as researchers found in a study of a medical center nursing staff (Weir et al., 1994). Rockwood (1993) lists four assumptions that must be met for process consultation to be a successful development method:

1. The problem in the organization that led to the need for change is the kind of problem that requires outside help to diagnose, but the diagnosis will be more accurate if the client participates in making it.

2. The client wants to make positive changes and has problem-solving abilities.

3. At the final decision point the client knows what intervention or solution will work best in the organization.

4. When the client participates to this degree, there will be an increase in the client's problem-solving abilities.

Process Consultation in Action

The following example of a process consultation shows how these four assumptions may lead to a successful change intervention. Joan Davis has been the president of a large university for slightly less than a year. Enrollment has continued to increase, and funding is at satisfactory levels. She feels that while the university seems to be progressing toward its goals, she is not really part of the picture. Her four direct subordinates, the vice presidents, seem to ignore her supervision. She meets with Ben Willis, a consultant, to plan a method to restructure the decision-making process. She tells Willis that she thinks the problem may center on her being a female; she is the first woman president of the university. She does not want to disrupt the successful functioning of the university, only to change the decision-making process.

Willis then schedules an introductory meeting with Davis and the four vice presidents to discuss contracting with the university to help diagnose and change the decision-making process. The four subordinates agree that they are unhappy with the current system because they feel overwhelmed with work. Willis begins by doing in-depth interviews with each vice president and Joan Davis. She and two of the vice presidents suggest interviewing the former president, who still lives near the university.

From the interviews and other observations, Willis concludes that the problem between Davis and her subordinates has resulted from the subordinates continuing to function as they had with the previous president. He was elderly and had remained on the job for several years more than he should have. When the vice presidents realized that the president was no longer able to fulfill his responsibilities, they decided to take charge until he could be persuaded to retire. This was planned as a temporary measure to protect him. When Davis was hired, they all were very pleased and supportive but did not change the way they had been functioning.

After discussing the results with Davis, Willis suggests several ways to intervene. Davis decides that since the vice presidents have been showing a high level of commitment to the university and a desire to change the way they function, the best intervention would be a daylong meeting with her and Willis. The purpose of the meeting will be to examine the results of Willis's interviews and observation and provide feedback to Davis and the vice presidents about their perceptions of her role and theirs. Davis feels it is important that she take charge of the meeting to emphasize her responsibility for decision making and supervision.

Davis and her subordinates agree on the problems but do not know how to make the necessary changes. Willis then makes a number of coaching and counseling suggestions, such as role reversal exercises and negotiation strategies. At the end of the daylong session Davis and the vice presidents agree that they have become aware of several ineffective patterns of behavior. They also have gained some insight into ways to change those patterns.

The group agrees to meet twice more, once with Willis and once by themselves, to work on the changes they have chosen to make. After the last meeting Willis sends evaluations to Davis and the vice presidents and meets with them one more time to assess their new level of effectiveness. The vice presidents say they are feeling much less pressure in their jobs because of their newly developed confidence in Davis's ability to lead the university. Davis says she is feeling much more successful in her role as university president because of the newly supportive and subordinate roles of her vice presidents. Willis agrees to meet with the group anytime it needs more help, but he is confident that they have learned a great deal. Learning how to apply the new skills on their own will help assure the success of the intervention after Willis's departure.

Diversity Training

Learning new attitudes and skills to apply in the workplace is also the focus of **diversity training**—educational programs that promote awareness and skill development to help employees function in a multifaceted workplace. This has become a popular training method in the last decade; in 1996, 74 percent of *Fortune* 500 companies reported that they had operational diversity training programs (Caudron, 1998). In Canada the Public Service Commission of the government has established a national Training Reference Centre to provide nationwide assistance in diversity training. In the United States private consultants do most diversity training. A recently released software program, *Dealing with Diversity*, uses computers to teach employees communication skills that focus on understanding and respecting individual differences.

The Workplace Diversity Network (*Network Newsletter*, 1995a) has identified two different types of diversity training. The first is awareness-based training designed to increase employees' diversity knowledge, awareness, and sensitivity. Many of these programs are similar to the sensitivity training and encounter groups discussed in Chapter 11. Awareness learning activities could include spending a day in a wheelchair to discover the kinds of feelings associated with a disability. A facilitator might ask a group of employees to think about a situation in which they felt different from everyone else, write down the feelings they associated with that experience, and then discuss what would have improved the situation.

The second type of diversity training is skill-based training, where the focus is on increasing information and assessing, building, and reinforcing interaction skills. Increased awareness and sensitivity may result, but they are by-products, not the main goal. At a time when many cultural groups are shown on television and in movies, it is difficult to realize that many people still have little actual contact with different groups. Lack of contact may produce incorrect information about people who differ from them. Diversity skill assessment might include discovering what information or misinformation employees have about workers from other cultures or backgrounds. For example, one of the most common forms of mistreatment of people in wheelchairs is speaking very loudly to them, as if they had a hearing impairment, or speaking to those who are with them rather than directly to the person in the wheelchair. Many organizations have started information programs about HIV and AIDS to counteract misinformation among employees because of misunderstandings and false beliefs people have about the illness.

Problems in Diversity Training. While diversity training seems to offer many positive ways to promote the acceptance of diversity in the workplace, a number of obstacles can prevent success. A 1992 survey of 1,405 companies found that only 5 percent of the respondents were doing "a very good job" of managing the diversity among their employees (Rice, 1994). One obstacle is the belief that a diverse workforce and organizational effectiveness are opposite goals. Some people believe that time allocated to workforce diversity training is time taken away from working toward organizational effectiveness. In reality, time allocated to workforce diversity training adds to organizational effectiveness.

The second obstacle is the false belief that laws such as civil rights acts and the ADA can change people's belief systems. Laws may be able to change behavior, which may ultimately, but not directly, lead to attitude change. The same is true of diversity training (Walters, 1995).

A third obstacle to the success of diversity training is the use of unqualified trainers. Many diversity trainers are indeed well-qualified professionals who can facilitate greater workplace diversity. There are currently no licensing standards or formal qualifications for this work. Managers need to ask consultants for references from other organizations where they have led diversity programs, rather than just asking a consultant if he can do diversity training. As with any other type of program or movement that becomes very popular very fast, organizations need to be cautious before contracting for diversity training.

A poor diversity training program may open a company to even greater liability. In 1993, R.R. Donnelly & Sons Co. in Chicago settled a class action racial discrimination lawsuit. Included in the settlement was an agreement to provide diversity training for all the employees, which the company did. In 1996 two other lawsuits were filed alleging discrimination and harassment related to participation in the training and the preparation of a diversity plan for the company. One indication of the failure of the diversity program was the decrease in minority hiring after the 1993 settlement. Some employees suggested that the training was window dressing rather than a real commitment by the organization (Markels, 1997). In 1995 a Federal Aviation Administration employee sued that organization for sponsoring a diversity training program that allowed women to grope him and encouraged participants to exchange racial insults (*New York Times*, 1995).

Successful Diversity Training. The *Network Newsletter* (1995b) included several commonsense suggestions for successful diversity training programs.

1. Avoid off-the-shelf, packaged programs in favor of programs that are tailored to the organization or group. If, for example, the packaged program has a lengthy section about learning to work with non-English speakers and all the workers at a company are already bilingual, this may not meet the organization's needs.

2. Avoid a program that is based on one or two large group lectures for the entire organization. It takes time, practice, and experience to change attitudes and behaviors. Large-group lectures may look good on year-end reports because they indicate that everyone in the organization has experienced diversity training, but they seldom lead to changed behaviors.

3. Have clear and simple goals. A reasonable goal for a diversity training program might be increased information for employees about their responsibilities for disabled coworkers, rather than the more general goal of feeling better about having coworkers with disabilities.

4. Make sure of the commitment and support of top management. If top management initiated the search for diversity trainers, this step may seem unnecessary. If the managers are not familiar with the program and the expected results, they may not approve of the program. A survey of human resources professionals indicated that the adoption and success of diversity training were linked to top management support (Rynes & Rosen, 1995).

5. Avoid programs that attack people for their beliefs. Many facilitators point out how difficult it is to make progress with a group when the leader starts by accusing everyone of being prejudiced. Attacking people and their beliefs makes them defensive rather than open and willing to learn.

6. Look for programs that focus on changing behaviors rather than opinions and belief systems. It is not possible to make everyone believe the same thing, but if all the employees have the same goal of success on the job, it is possible to find ways for them to work together cooperatively even with different beliefs.

7. Do not require diversity training. If employees know that diversity training is important to success in the organization, they will choose to attend the program if they want to succeed. Requiring attendance makes employees defensive and unwilling to learn. If attendance is required, employees sometimes try to prove that although their employer can make them go to the program, they cannot be forced to learn anything.

As the statistics at the beginning of this chapter indicated, the workforce is becoming increasingly diverse. Diversity training is smart strategic planning for a changing workforce. Organizational development emphasizes the need to look at new ways to solve old and new problems. Diversity training can help employees and employers learn some of those new methods and result in hiring new workers who may not have been considered before. See the case study "Diversity at Work."

[Case Study] DIVERSITY AT WORK

Sandia National Laboratories, the winner of the 1996 American Society for Training and Development (ASTD) Multicultural Network Award, has promoted diversity in the workplace for a number of years. Sandia is a government-owned, contractor-operated facility that provides scientific and engineering solutions for national defense, energy needs, technology, and the environment.

At Sandia diversity training starts at the organizational level, where it is one of the strategic goals. A specific corporate goal was changing Sandia's corporate culture from being strictly engineering- and science-oriented to being more business-oriented and people-sensitive. Within a five-year period the diversity planning department was to design and implement the diversity change process and transfer responsibility for the program to line management, with the human resources department remaining only in a supporting role.

The six diversity objectives established as part of strategic corporate plans were:

1. Determine areas for improvement in the workplace environment and implement processes and structures to address those issues.

2. Improve employees' experience of fairness and help Sandia attract future employees.

3. Develop a culture that fully utilizes all employees and recognizes diversity as a competitive advantage.

4. Project workforce diversity composition for the future. Compare the data with Sandia's workforce diversity and work to keep the company close to national statistics.

5. Establish and implement processes that support varied work styles and family needs.

6. Integrate diversity processes and structures with staffing, performance management, and leadership and management development.

Once the goals were in place at the organizational level, Sandia moved to diversity training at the individual, interpersonal, and managerial levels. Over three hundred employees became Diversity Champions, a group of volunteers who served as resources on diversity issues. Internal diversity trainers held education and awareness workshops and minimodules (short training sessions focused on a narrow topic). Division diversity councils, at the line organization level, identified diversity issues in their divisions and implemented division diversity action plans. Sandia also encouraged the development of affinity groups, driven and run by employees and organized around a particular topic or issue, such as the Disabilities Awareness Committee and the Black Leadership Committee. To gauge their success, diversity trainers at Sandia developed the Managing Diversity Progress Index (MDPI), which was designed for measurement and guidance.

Sandia has been pleased with the results of this companywide diversity training program, which met all its objectives. The program enhanced worker retention, empowerment, alignment, and productivity and brought different perspectives to problem solving. It also enhanced team dynamics and reduced harassment and discrimination complaints. Sandia now has a reputation as an employer of choice and therefore draws more qualified applicants.

From The organizational case for diversity: The 1997 fall forum visits Sandia National Labs. (1998). *The Network Newsletter,* 4(1), 1–6. *The Network Newsletter* is produced by The Workplace Diversity Network, a project of Cornell/L R and The National Conference; http://www.1lr.cornell.edu/depts/WDN/NetNews/

Organizational Transformation

One of the newest models of organizational change is **organizational transformation,** an OD method in which management directs change in the entire organizational vision for the future. This method has received growing attention as a

Organizational transformation An organizational development method in which management directs change in the entire organizational vision for the future.

promising way of meeting the challenges caused by the increasing number of consolidations, downsizings, and closures in the corporate world (Belasen, Benke, & DiPadova, 1996).

Porras and Silver (1991) compare this method of organizational change with other methods. They view OD as changing small pieces of the total system and organizational transformation as changing the entire organization's vision of its beliefs, purpose, and mission. The focus is on the future state of the organization that the large-scale change is meant to create. An example of an organizational transformation is the change in an organization from an organizational focus on quantity produced to a main focus on the quality of the product, where the entire organizational focus is modified.

Levy and Merry (1986) suggest that a change in corporate vision can happen in one of two ways:

1. Reframing, which changes the way members of the organization perceive reality. This could mean a change in interpreting the behaviors of employees, as discussed in the material in Chapter 3 on Theory Y and Theory X assumptions about workers' behavior. The change typically is accomplished by modifying attitudes and behaviors before the transformational change occurs. This can mean coping with changes in the world or government—for example, airlines changing to cope with deregulation.

2. Consciousness-raising, which makes employees aware of the transformational changes that are possible and leads to greater dissatisfaction with the way the organization is currently functioning. Techniques such as meditation and creativity exercises can lead to consciousness-raising (Porras & Silver, 1991).

Frame, Neilsen, and Pate (1989) examined the process of organizational transformation at the *Chicago Tribune,* which resulted from a 1985 strike involving more than a thousand workers at that newspaper's printing center. The center had been equipped with the most up-to-date machinery, but the organization had kept a long out-dated, strongly bureaucratic, competitive, low-trust environment. During the job action new workers were hired to replace the strikers, and top management saw an opportunity to transform the entire organization of the printing center. This included changing the mission statement of the printing center to a philosophy and orientation that was more of a partnership and customer-driven work environment.

A number of consultants worked with different groups in the organization to make those changes possible. Team building focused on measurement and results rather than group processes. Management introduced a new system of rewards based on results, not politics or seniority. The results were remarkable. Production costs decreased, and the employees received a 15 percent bonus over their base rate of pay within a year.

Not everyone agrees that the transformation was a success. Some researchers have criticized the change as representing a step backward in OD. Wardell (1989) suggests that what was called transformation was really a dictatorial senior management desire for change that did not involve the employees until the process was under way. Once top management set performance levels, the only input from employees was how they planned to reach those preset goals. Since union workers were replaced with nonunion employees, Wardell argues, employees lost the security of union protection and went along with the changes because they were afraid of losing their jobs.

Frame, Neilsen, and Pate suggest that the focus on results and the concern for excellence provide an example of the organizational transformations that must occur in many organizations if they are going to survive in the economic climate at the turn of the century. King, Nixon, and Pitts (1990) indicate that if managers learn to hold out a vision that inspires others, the managers are turned into leaders of leaders rather than leaders of followers. The vision of the leader is the trigger for the radical organizational change. The leader must identify and deal with obstacles that block that vision (Nutt & Backoff, 1997).

Organizational transformation represents a new direction in the field of OD. As more definition and evaluation are completed in this area, it will either be added as a component to the field, redefined, or discarded. The increasing need for major changes in the way people think about organizational structure will provide numerous tests of this method.

Evaluating Organizational Development

After examining a number of OD methods, the final question is still, "Does it work?" This is not a question that can be answered easily because so many factors contribute to the success or failure of OD programs.

At the most basic level an organization should be able to tell whether the intervention has made any difference, and if so, what difference. Some methods, such as survey feedback, appear to produce measurable results. Some changes take place over several years, as they did in the Texaco study discussed earlier in the chapter. The Texaco study, like most OD studies, examined only one organization in a field setting. The use of a control group may not be practical, but it can help determine the true effects of a development program. Without a control group there is always the possibility of a self-fulfilling prophecy. If a consultant goes to an organization and tells it that the program she is going to use will make things better, is it the program or belief in the program that has made things better? In most OD studies this is not an easy question to answer.

The question of a self-fulfilling prophecy bias enters when the measurement techniques used to evaluate the programs are examined. Most often the participants are asked about their reactions to the program, in contrast to the use of more quantitative measurement methods. It is easy to predict that knowing something has been done will produce positive reactions from the participants. If the consultant is the person who does the evaluation, his belief in the value of the program may influence the evaluation results. Another measurement problem involves the timing of the measurement. If the evaluation is done immediately after the intervention, will the results be different than they would be if they were done a year later? In general, positive effects tend to be greatest immediately after an intervention.

With so many potential pitfalls, is it possible to come to any conclusions about the effectiveness of OD? The answer is a qualified yes. One of the methods that appears promising in trying to answer this question is meta-analysis, which combines a number of studies in a statistical analysis. Several meta-analytic studies have shown generally positive results of OD (Beekun, 1989; Golembiewski, 1998; Guzzo, Jette, & Katzell, 1985; Neuman, Edwards, & Raju, 1989; Robertson, Roberts, & Porras, 1993) and have shown that the benefits outweigh the costs (Golembiewski & Sun, 1989). One study contrasted changes in employee behavior produced by OD with changes produced by employer-decreed policies. OD produced strong constructive changes in work, such as amount of time worked, and decreases in excused forms of nonwork, such as the number of sick days taken. When OD was abandoned in a cost-saving move and replaced by employer-decreed policies, most of the positive changes quickly vanished (Miners, Moore, & Campoux, 1994). The most successful OD interventions occur when the organizational culture and climate support sustained change (Schneider, Brief, & Guzzo, 1996). The best change agents appear to be those most knowledgeable about the organizational change process (Church, Waclawski, & Burke, 1996).

Most of the larger companies in the United States also appear to believe in the value of OD. A survey of *Fortune* 500 companies found that most of them had employees specifically assigned to OD (McMahan & Woodman, 1992). The next several years will add more information to the field as new methods are added and new types of organizations are used. The last several years have seen OD applied in church settings (Hair & Walsh-Bowers, 1992) and health and human service agencies (White, 1992), and one can expect many more applications in the future.

MAIN POINTS

■ I/O psychology is concerned with understanding how racial and ethnic minority employees perceive the workplace in a different way than majority group employees do.

■ African-American, Hispanic-American, and Asian-American employees are the largest groups of ethnic and racial minority employees.

■ Barriers to equality for racial and ethnic minority employees have to be eliminated, and organizations need to look for ways to promote equality at work.

■ Workers over age forty can compete equally with younger workers in most areas (physical strength and speed are exceptions).

■ Performance appraisals can be biased against older workers in several ways.

■ The Americans with Disabilities Act (ADA) requires that people with disabilities be treated fairly if they are qualified to do a job with or without reasonable accommodation.

■ Employers' fears about the ADA include high costs for accommodations and medical benefits and being required to keep substance abusers and dangerous mentally ill employees on the job. None of these fears are true.

■ The ADA has not increased the percentage of employees with disabilities in the workforce.

■ The four components of organizational development (OD), a planned change in an organization, are (1) change intervention that alters (2) key organizational target variables that then (3) affect individual employees and their job behaviors, resulting in (4) organizational outcomes.

■ Resistance to change must be faced for OD to be successful.

■ The action method of OD uses the four stages of diagnosis, planning for change, intervention, and evaluation.

■ Survey feedback is one of the earliest and most popular OD techniques.

■ Team building is an OD technique focused on teaching job-related interpersonal skills within a work team framework.

■ Process consultation is an OD technique that uses an outside consultant to teach work group members how to solve their own problems.

■ Diversity training in the workplace is directed toward increasing employees' awareness and skills in functioning in a diverse workplace.

■ Good diversity training programs are individualized for the organization, have clear goals, have support from top management, do not attack personal beliefs, work on changing behaviors, and are voluntary.

- Organizational transformation is a newer OD concept that is based on changing the entire organization's vision of its beliefs, purpose, and mission.

- A combination of factors, such as the timing of measurement and self-fulfilling prophecy, makes it difficult to evaluate the effects of OD, but in general, OD appears to be an effective method of changing organizations.

KEY TERMS

Action method
Age Discrimination in Employment Act
Americans with Disabilities Act (ADA)
Change agent
Crystallized intelligence
Disability
Diversity training

Fluid intelligence
Glass Ceiling Commission
Organizational development (OD)
Organizational transformation
Process consultation
Reasonable accommodation
Survey feedback
Team building

REVIEW QUESTIONS

Answers to these questions can be found at the end of the book.

1. The only purpose of affirmative action programs is to make sure companies reach minority hiring goals.

    a. True   b. False

2. One reason why minority workers leave organizations in greater numbers than other employees do may be that they

    a. do not value work as much as other employees do.

    b. perceive the work environment as hostile when other employees do not.

    c. do not like to work with people different from themselves.

    d. all of the above

3. Speaking a common language at work can be a way to help establish a common organizational culture as well as meet safety needs.

    a. True   b. False

4. When companies make a commitment to keeping women and minority employees in the workplace, they can expect

    a. less-qualified employees.

    b. greater training costs.

    c. better returns on investment.

    d. lower customer satisfaction.

5. Which of the following is typically better in older people than in younger people?

    a. Speed in assembly line tasks because older people have done the tasks for a longer time

    b. Fluid intelligence

    c. Motor control

    d. Crystallized intelligence

6. If a female job applicant was bald from a skin condition and was refused employment as a clerical worker because the manager thought the other employees would be uncomfortable, this person could be covered by the ADA.

    a. True   b. False

7. Most workplace accommodations cost

    a. over $500.

    b. about $125.

    c. over $1,000.

    d. nothing.

8. The first time questions about workplace accommodations can be legally raised is

    a. at the time of the interview (limited).

    b. after the interview.

    c. after a job offer has been made.

    d. after hiring.

9. Which of the following has been a problem for organizations as they try to meet the requirements of the ADA?

    a. Increased medical costs

    b. Inability to fire illegal drug users

    c. Inability to fire violent employees

    d. All of the above

    e. None of the above

10. Since the ADA has been in effect the proportion of employees with disabilities has increased to almost 40 percent.

    a. True   b. False

11. Organizational development (OD) refers only to *planned* organizational changes.

    a. True   b. False

12. The person who directs the changes of OD is called a(n)

    _____ _____.

13. Resistance to organizational change usually comes from a desire to

    a. sabotage OD efforts.

    b. leave the organization rather than change it.

    c. make management the change agent.

    d. keep things the same even if they are not so great.

14. The four steps in the action method of change are

    a. _____

    b. _____

    c. _____

    d. _____

15. The step that can follow evaluation in the action method of change is

    a. distancing employees from the change agent.

    b. the beginning of a new action method sequence.

    c. restoring order in the organization.

    d. restoring social relationships in the organization.

16. The survey feedback method requires only a sampling from the group or organization to fill out the survey data as long as the sampling is a representative one.

    a. True   b. False

17. List two of the measurable changes that have been found when the survey feedback method was used in organizations.

    a. _____

    b. _____

18. The focus of team building is

    a. learning interpersonal skills that will help the group function as a team.

    b. learning more efficient ways for work groups to do their assigned tasks.

    c. developing competitive team strategies.

    d. all of the above.

19. Which OD technique is most likely to end up with the consultant no longer working in the organization?

    a. Survey feedback

    b. Team building

    c. Process consultation

    d. Technical consultation

20. What are the two different types of diversity training?

    a. _____

    b. _____

21. The major difference between organizational transformation and other OD methods is that organizational transformation changes an organization by changing the overall vision for the future.

    a. True   b. False

22. List two of the problems that make evaluating OD difficult.

    a. _____

    b. _____

Use your browser to go to http://www.diversitydtg.com/tools/cool_quiz.htm to take the Interactive Diversity IQ Quiz. You should be able to answer many of the items correctly after having read this chapter, but you probably will acquire some new information. List the statements about workplace diversity that you learned as a result of taking this quiz. If you answered all the items correctly, list the three to five statements about workplace diversity that differ the most from your actual experiences.

WEB EXERCISE

5

Communication and Group Processes

LEARNING OBJECTIVES

COMMUNICATION

Conditions of Communication

Parts of the Communication Process

Problems in the Communication Process

Nonverbal Communication

Communication Networks

Formal Organizational Communication Patterns

Informal Organizational Communication Patterns

Computer-Based Communication

Case Study Communications at Work

GROUPS IN ORGANIZATIONS

Formal Groups

Informal Groups

Group Decision Making

Brainstorming

Groupthink

Social Loafing

Group Polarization

Group Cohesion

The Bottom Line

LABOR UNIONS

Reasons for Joining Unions

Changes in Union Membership

Comparisons with Nonunion Employees

Lack of Involvement with I/O Psychology

Ways to Use I/O Psychology to Rebuild Unions

Chapter Outline

This chapter continues the examination of organizations but looks at them in a different way. You will see how the communication process and group behaviors affect organizations. The last chapters touched on these issues when they looked at the kinds of communication most often associated with different types of organizational structures. Those chapters also examined the effects of the group in their discussions of topics such as team building in organizational development. This chapter examines these topics as major features in the study of organizational behavior.

COMMUNICATION

Some people have compared organizational communication systems to the human nervous system. This is a good comparison for a number of reasons. The nervous system is a vast integrated network that operates on a number of levels, much as organizational communication systems do. When something goes wrong in one part of the nervous system, it often has far-reaching effects on other parts of that system and the rest of the body. This is often true in organizational communication systems as well. A mislaid communication that never reaches the shipping department can affect a company's sales, its production rates for the next quarter, and layoffs of employees. From the average person's standpoint, it is often difficult to understand how each part of the nervous systems relates to all the other parts. From the standpoint of a professional industrial/organizational (I/O) psychologist studying organizational communication, it often seems that psychologists are only beginning to understand the communication process in organizations and the effects of the many variables in that process. As organizational topics such as those dealt with in the last few chapters receive increasing research attention, more information about the communication process should result. Better-quality research, such as experiments rather than case studies and natural observation, also should become more common.

Conditions of Communication

Communication is central to every aspect of organizational functioning. Many organizational situations require communication. Hunt (1980) suggests that at least one of the following conditions must be present in communication situations.

1. *Someone needs information.* People may give or ask for information in different situations.

2. *Someone needs social reinforcement.* Most people look to the work environment for at least some of their needs for recognition, self-esteem, and growth. Communication can help people meet those needs.

3. *Someone has directed someone else to communicate.* This can be a direct order, such as assigning a person to conduct an interview or prepare a presentation. It can be assumed that communicating is a required part of the job, such as that of a clerical supervisor.

4. *Someone communicates to achieve a goal.* This may be a simple, direct goal such as arranging vacation schedules for all the members of a department. It also may be a more complicated, below-the-surface goal such as the desire of one employee to show that she is a much better candidate for promotion than a competing employee (p. 31).

Parts of the Communication Process

There are number of elements common to any communication process. The model devised by Sanford, Hunt, and Bracey (1976) represents a middle ground between the most complicated and the most simple models of the communication process (Figure 5.1).

Figure 5.1

The Sanford, Hunt, and Bracey model of the communication process

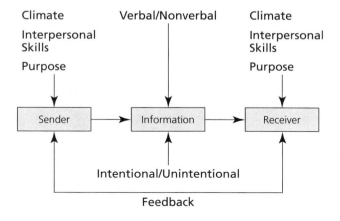

From A. Sanford, G. Hunt, and H. Bracey. (1976). *Communication behavior in the organization.* Columbus, OH: Charles E. Merril.

At the simplest level this model shows a **sender** transmitting a **message** (also called information) to a **receiver.** Each communication situation involves a climate (discussed in Chapter 3), a purpose, and the interpersonal skills of the sender and the receiver. The climate refers to how each person perceives the situation. The purpose is the reason for the communication as each person perceives it. Interpersonal skills refer to the social communication skills each person brings to the situation. Each person receives feedback from the other person. The message may be presented in a single medium, or channel, as in the case of a written memo, but often there are a number of other channels involved, such as nonverbal components and whether the communication was intentional or unintentional.

To make these concepts more understandable, let us use a simple example of a communication between a manager and an employee. Tina wants to tell Aaron about some new forms the human resources department is going to use to record interview data from job applicants. Tina is the head of the department, and Aaron is one of the hiring interviewers.

Sender

Tina is the sender of the information. She brings to this situation her perception of the climate in the department and the company, her purpose for communicating the information, and her skill in interpersonal communication. These three factors introduce a number of variables into the communication situation. If Tina has only recently been appointed head of the department,

Sender The person who originates a communication message.

Message Information that is sent during a communication.

Receiver The person for whom a communication message is intended.

Channel The medium that carries a message from the sender to the receiver, such as written memos or spoken words.

Media richness The intensity of the communication channel, with face-to-face communication being the most intense.

she may perceive the climate as one of resentment at her promotion. This can cause her to be more open and seek Aaron's support for the changes in the forms, or to establish more clearly her legitimate right to control the department by imposing those changes on Aaron. Her intended purpose is to get an interviewer to use the new interview forms, but she also may have a hidden agenda; for example, making the old form developed by Aaron appear to be damaging to the company. She can use her interpersonal skills to weigh each of these factors and choose the techniques that will build rather than harm the relationships in the department. Her choice of a medium to communicate her message is called the **channel.**

Channel

The medium used to communicate a message may include one or more of the following: face-to-face communication, telephone, meetings, written memos, formal reports, teleconferences, electronic mail, and mass media. The choice is determined by a number of factors. The theory called **media richness** suggests that the choice is determined by selecting the communication channel in which the level of communication value matches the uncertainty level of the task (Trevino, Daft, & Lengel, 1987). The richest channels of communication are, in descending order, face-to-face, telephone, electronic mail, and written. While some studies have supported this model (Trevino, Lengel, Bodensteiner, Gerloff, & Muir, 1990), others have pointed to different variables that can influence the choice of communication channel (Allen & Griffith, 1997).

In general, the more important the message is, the more important it is to use more than one channel. Multiple channels are especially important in communicating vital information such as upcoming layoffs and other major organizational changes. In one survey, employees indicated that during crisis events in the organization they strongly preferred receiving timely information from their direct supervisors. However, they reported that the initial information and ongoing information about a crisis often came from another source (Adams & Roebuck, 1997).

In our example, Tina could meet face to face with Aaron to explain the new interview form and provide written samples of the form and directions for its use. This is not a crisis situation, but it involves critical information. When more than one channel of communication is used, the most effective communication appears to occur when the message delivered from each channel is consistent with the messages from all the other channels (Grimes, 1990).

Receiver

Even with her careful planning, Tina cannot control how Aaron will receive her communication. Like Tina, he brings his perceptions of the climate, his purpose, and his interpersonal skills to the situation. If his perceptions of these three factors are similar to those of Tina, there is a greater chance that the communication will be transmitted and received correctly. One advantage of the Sanford, Hunt, and Bracey model shown in Figure 5.1 is that it shows the transmission of the message leading to feedback for both the sender and the receiver. This may occur more than once in the communication process. It provides a chance to check the correctness of the presentation and interpretation of the message and perhaps start another communication cycle. The communication cycle is not completed until the sender knows the information has been received correctly, on the basis of feedback from the receiver, not from the sender's personal assumptions.

Getting the receiver to interpret a message correctly is difficult even when the sender and receiver speak the same language and live in the same culture, but when language and culture are different, the problems can multiply. As a society becomes more multicultural, this becomes an increasingly important issue. Winters (1993) and Coward (1992) both suggest that companies should hire bilingual employees as a first step in cross-cultural communication. The second step is the correct transmission and reception of the message. Even when the language is correct, other parts of the communication process may present unintended messages. In different cultures gestures can be interpreted very differently. It is especially important to be aware of gestures and situations that are harmless or positive in one's own culture but negative in other cultures. These negative gestures may "speak" so loudly that the message does not get through.

Listening

Everyone understands that presenting or transmitting a message is an active process, but sometimes people forget that listening to a message as a receiver is also an active process. One study found that *active listening* was used only 2.3 percent of the time by managers. Involved listening, in which the listener processes the material into a personal frame of reference but does not give feedback to the sender, was used 23.3 percent of the time. The rest of the managers' listening experiences were passive, just letting the message be received 34.9 percent of the time, and detached, just being physically present while the message was presented but not attending to it (39.5 percent of the time) (Pearce, 1993).

Kelley and Ninan (1990) identified four components of active listening: understanding, nonverbal attentiveness, verbal responsiveness, and lack of distractions. In the example of Tina and Aaron, Aaron can demonstrate that he is actively listening to Tina's message by facing Tina, making eye contact, nodding his head, and telling her, "I'm glad to see this new interview form. I was becoming concerned about legal problems with the old form we've been using." He can ask about the starting date for using the new forms, what jobs they will be used

Michael Newman/PhotoEdit

■ Active listening is critical to good communication.

for, and whether all the questions need to be used in every interview. This can help Tina quickly assess Aaron's understanding of the message.

When the communication process works correctly, people are not as concerned about the details as they are when the process does not work. Understanding some of the pitfalls in advance may prevent them from interfering with communication. The next section examines some of the typical problems that can occur in the organizational communication process.

Problems in the Communication Process

Several problems that contribute to poor communication can result from using communication for more than one of the purposes described at the beginning of this chapter. In the example of Tina and Aaron, Tina may want to tell Aaron about the new forms and have him start to use them, but she also may want his approval of her new position as head of the department. Aaron may fail to tell Tina about problems he has encountered with similar interview forms because his performance review is scheduled soon and he is worried that she will not rate him well. Most errors in communication can be classified as errors of omission or errors of commission. **Errors of omission** are caused by deliberately leaving out information; **errors of commission** result from problems caused by something being added to the communication process.

Error of omission
A communication problem that is caused by leaving out parts of a message.

Error of commission
A communication distortion that results from adding information to the message.

Errors of Omission

Two of the most common problems in this category are filtering information and completely withholding information. In **filtering,** only parts of the message are held back. This is common with children, who quickly learn not to volunteer information that may lead to punishment. Employees may apply the same model and fail to send parts of messages or entire messages if they believe the result of full exposure would be harmful to them. Tesser and Rosen (1975) describe this as the **MUM effect:** minimize unpleasant messages. In the example of Tina and Aaron, his failure to tell her about problems he has had with similar forms would be an error of omission.

People who are in a position to regularly withhold information are referred to as **gatekeepers.** Sometimes withholding occurs because the gatekeeper believes that the receiver does not need to know the information. For example, a plant manager may not tell employees about a proposed layoff because he believes he can rearrange the budget to save most of their jobs. Whether the gatekeeper is part of top management, a secretary, or an administrative assistant, this role of deciding what information to hold back is one of considerable power (O'Reilly & Pondy, 1979). A study of managers and subordinates found that subordinates who reported to gatekeeping supervisors in the developmental area of a company were more likely to be promoted to managerial levels (Katz, Tushman, & Allen, 1995).

Errors of Commission

Errors of commission include exaggeration and information overload. Gaines (1980) referred to *exaggeraton* as "puffing", or accenting the favorable or unfavorable elements in a communication. Cohen (1958) found that as compared with employees who expected to be promoted, employees who did not realistically expect promotions sent more and longer messages unrelated to work. Their messages exaggerated the personal relationships between the employees, showing perceived social value rather than organizational value.

Information overload is often an organizational fact of life, occurring when employees receive more information than they can handle. Sometimes this is information that may not be helpful to them even if they could handle all of it. Some researchers blame information overload on the increased use of computers to communicate (Filipczak, 1994), but other researchers are developing computer software specifically to reduce information overload (*Canadian Banker*, 1994).

Nonverbal Communication

Nonverbal communication refers to everything that is part of the communication process other than the actual spoken or written words. Some researchers estimate that up to 90 percent of communication is made up of nonverbal elements (Buhler, 1991; Pearl, 1992). Costley and Todd (1987) divide nonverbal communication into five categories: body language, use of space, use of time, paralanguage, and artifacts (Table 5.1).

Filtering A communication distortion that results from withholding parts of a message.

MUM effect "Minimize unpleasant messages": A communication distortion resulting from not passing on information that would reflect unfavorably on the sender.

Gatekeeper A person whose role in the communication process allows him or her to withhold information.

Nonverbal communication All the components of a message except the spoken words. It includes features such as body language, paralanguage, and the use of space and time.

Table 5.1

TYPES OF NONVERBAL COMMUNICATION AND HOW THEY ARE USED AT WORK.

Type of Nonverbal Communication	Definition	Use at Work
Body language	Touching, posture, eye contact, facial expressions, and gestures	Burgoon (1982) found that high eye contact, close personal spaces, and leaning the body forward communicate intimacy. Fromme, Jaynes, Taylor, and Honold (1989) found that women were more comfortable using touch than men were.
Use of space	Distance or closeness between people as they communicate	Hall (1963) found that the personal distance zone (18 inches to 4 feet) and the social distance zone (4 feet to 12 feet) were used for most communication at work. Personal distance is used in friendship communications.
Use of time	How employees control time	The boss comes late to every meeting, making the subordinates wait.
Paralanguage	Nonverbal characteristics of the voice of the speaker, such as tone and volume	People who are being dishonest wait a longer time before they start speaking (Burgoon & Buller, 1994).
Artifacts	The way employees dress and the objects with which they surround themselves	O'Neal and Lapitsky (1991) found that people who dressed appropriately for a task were rated as more believable.

Considerable attention has been paid to the contribution of nonverbal factors to the communication process, but there is often conflicting information about its use and effectiveness (Lapakko, 1997). Research on the use of nonverbal communication elements to detect dishonesty has not reported detection rates better than the results of chance (DePaulo & DePaulo, 1989; Ekman, 1988; Vrij, 1993). Some individuals are better at interpreting nonverbal cues than others are, with women perceived as being better than men (Vrij & Semin, 1996).

With so much conflicting evidence, what conclusions can be drawn about the role of nonverbal communication? First, it is necessary to understand that nonverbal components are an influence on the communication process, not a separate language (Argyle, 1989). Second, the same gesture or intonation can be interpreted in a variety of ways. There are few hard and fast rules of interpretation unless the meaning is so clear that no interpretation is needed (the employee walks in, says he just won $40 million in a lottery, and leaves work an hour later). At the same time, it is necessary to understand that the most effective use of nonverbal communication is to convey additional information. Messages are more likely to be understood correctly when verbal and nonverbal messages are in agreement, just as they are when all the channels are delivering the same message.

Communication Networks

Up to this point you have been learning about communication between two people. Although a great deal of organizational communication follows this model, much communication goes from one person to a number of other people or goes through a number of people before reaching its final destination. A diagram of communication interaction among a number of people is called a **communication network.** As the communication process gets more complicated, it becomes more difficult to study the whole process in a laboratory situation. There has been some criticism that the simple network models studied in laboratory situations do not resemble actual organizational settings sufficiently; but looking at simple models often can provide a foundation for further research. Earlier laboratory research led to the development of more complicated network models, such as those investigated by Fulk and Boyd (1991).

Another researcher has suggested that the most realistic models of communication networks in organizations are those based on the systems theory structures discussed in Chapter 3 (Schwartz, 1986). Such a holistic view would include looking at formal and informal communication patterns as well as communication patterns that take place entirely within the organization and patterns that involve people outside the organization. Each communication network would be examined for the effect it had on the rest of the organization and how the organization affected the network.

The foundation for these newer models of communication networks still rests on basic network descriptions. Shaw (1978) identified the five major types of communication networks shown in Figure 5.2. The job titles used in each model show how these networks may be used in organizations. The chain, Y, and wheel patterns are described as **centralized networks** because information is channeled through single individuals. The circle and all-channel patterns are described as **decentralized networks** because messages can start anywhere and

Communication network
A model of message transmission in organizations in which more than one sender or receiver is involved.

Centralized networks
Communication systems that channel all information through a single person.

Decentralized networks
Message systems that use a number of starting points and directions for messages.

Figure 5.2
Network patterns of communication in organizations.

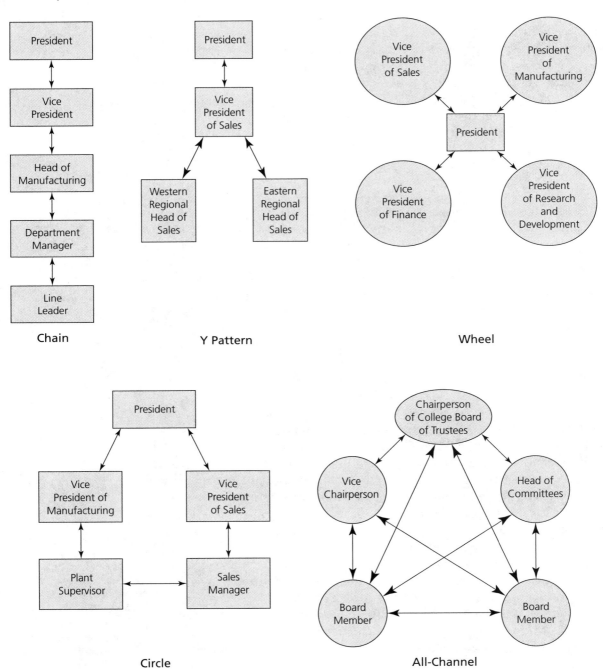

Chain

Y Pattern

Wheel

Circle

All-Channel

continue in a number of directions. The best use of each of these networks depends on work- and employee-related variables such as those listed below.

1. The employees with the highest level of job satisfaction are usually the ones in the most central positions in the networks, such as the person at the center of the wheel or the branching point of the Y. This person functions like a gatekeeper. The gatekeeper role becomes even more distinct in research about situations where members have reasons not to share information but try to gather more knowledge than the other group members do. In this situation the employees in the central positions do the least communicating (Bonacich, 1990).

2. Overall, employee satisfaction is greatest in the most decentralized networks, such as the circle and all-channel patterns. The more employees are involved in and feel empowered by the communication system, the greater their job satisfaction is (Marshall & Stohl, 1993).

3. Decentralized networks result in better performance when the tasks are more complicated, as in the case of a group charged with implementing acceptance of cultural diversity in an organization.

4. Centralized networks result in better performance when the tasks are uncomplicated and straightforward, as in the case of a university president informing employees about the schedule of staff activities the week before the semester starts.

Problems with using these basic network models in organizations include situations in which groups may be required to do both simple and complex tasks at the same time or in which quick, complicated decisions may be required. For example, it traditionally has been accepted that when quick, correct decisions are required in threatening conditions, centralized networks are the best network structure. Research has confirmed that decentralized structures result in slower decisions, although the quality is the same as it is in centralized structures (Turner, 1992). An additional problem in designating communication networks is that employees do not limit communication to formally designated networks. Many communication networks in organizations develop from informal friendship patterns. The next section looks at the differences between formal and informal communication structures.

Formal Organizational Communication Patterns

Formal organizational communication refers to the communication paths described on an organizational chart. The direction of formal communication can be downward, upward, or horizontal. Employees often use these communication paths as long as they find them effective. Organizations need to plan ways to ensure that effectiveness, as will be seen in the discussion of the directions of communication later in this chapter.

Formal organizational communication The communication paths shown on an organizational chart.

Downward communication
Messages that go from higher to lower organizational levels.

Upward communication
Messages that go from lower to high organizational levels.

Downward Communication

A great deal of formal communication in organizations goes from higher levels to lower levels. Higher-level employees need to direct and inform lower-level employees. Some of the most common methods of **downward communication** are memos, letters, telephone calls, fax messages, messages on bulletin boards, manuals, handbooks, and, more recently, voice mail and e-mail. Even with so many opportunities for communication, most employees report that they do not receive as much information from their superiors as they would like. Sometimes this may be caused by filtering, which occurs when supervisors perceive that subordinates do not need all the information from a report or document. Even if they do not need the information, subordinates are still distrustful when information is not given to them. Supervisors often do not like to pass on negative information, and so they censor downward messages. Research indicates that when electronic messaging is used most managers limit downward communication to objective information rather than emotionally charged or socially oriented information (Ku, 1996).

Misunderstandings in downward communication may occur when managers mistakenly believe they are doing a good job of communicating. Research shows that in general managers perceive themselves to be much better at communication than their subordinates perceive them to be (Schnake, 1990). One way to improve downward communication is for managers to explain the reasons behind their decisions and actions rather than just sending information downward (Brownell, 1991).

Upward Communication

Upward communication refers to planned, structured communications that go from a lower level to a higher level. As the issue of employee empowerment has received more attention in research on motivation and job satisfaction, methods of upward communication have become increasingly important. In an active upward communication system managers listen to and act on employees' suggestions and contributions. A survey of over a million employees found that only 34 percent felt that their companies listened to their problems and complaints; only 22 percent believed that their companies responded to those problems and complaints (*Personnel*, 1990). Part of the reason for such poor results may be misunderstanding about the upward communication process. The basic assumption in using upward communication is that employees and managers want to develop better ways of working and achieving together rather than simply giving employees a chance to list their complaints.

Some of the more common types of upward communication are the use of suggestion boxes, grievances, employee surveys, subordinate performance appraisals of superiors, and scheduled feedback meetings. For most of these methods to be effective, communication must go back to the subordinate to complete the cycle. One way to follow through on employees' suggestions is to give employees responsibility for following up and implementing their ideas (D'O'Brien, 1994). In this case, the company develops guidelines and oversees their administration and the employees gain more skills. Maritz, Inc., a St. Louis company, saved almost $12 million by approving over three hundred suggestions from employees (Walter, 1996). Often suggestion systems include a financial incentive for ideas that save money or make money for the company. An electronics company's president got some of his best cost-saving suggestions from employees after setting a goal of one suggestion per month from each of his 125 employees. He established a program for responding quickly to the suggestions, giving rewards for those that were used and giving reinforcement to the employees at daily meetings (*Inc.*, 1992).

Employee surveys promote feelings of trust and openness that are essential to successful upward communication programs. The surveys may cover current job practices or future improvements. A variation of the employee survey is the *reverse performance evaluation,* in which subordinates evaluate the supervisor on objective, job-related issues. Some supervisors feel defensive about this type of evaluation, but others look at it as additional information that will help them do their jobs better. The keys to success for upward communication systems are a corporate culture that encourages learning and change, employees who feel free to speak up without fear of retaliation, and managers who discuss feedback with their subordinates and use that feedback to make changes that lead to greater effectiveness. Upward feedback is a structured part of the communication process in an organization, and it must take place on a regularly scheduled basis, as Moravec, Gyr, and Freidman (1993) showed. Those researchers illustrated the practice of upward communication by using a survey at the Call Servicing division of AT&T. The formal upward feedback process uses a twenty-question survey instrument developed from the input of all levels of employees. Some of the questions are listed in Figure 5.3. Each manager uses this questionnaire with the people who report directly to him or her. Human resources personnel meet with the managers to discuss the results of the survey. Managers then meet with the subordinates, discuss the results, and develop action plans. AT&T is developing a computer-based version of this questionnaire that will allow data to be collected more frequently. Managers and subordinates have indicated that the process has been helpful and feel that it has increased personal and organizational effectiveness.

Horizontal Communication

Horizontal communication involves formal communication patterns from an employee to other coworkers. Increases in this type of communication usually are associated with greater organizational effectiveness because employees are encouraged to help each other with problems and share ideas (McClelland & Wilmot, 1990). When this is made a part of the formal communication structure, it indicates that the organization wants to encourage this type of communication and plans for it to occur rather than leaving it to occur by chance, informally.

Horizontal communication
Organizational messages that go from one employee to another employee at the same level in the organization.

Figure 5.3

Sample of items used in the upward communication survey at AT&T in 1993.

To what extent does the manager:	Almost always	Often	Sometimes	Seldom	Almost never	Do not know
AT&T CALL SERVICING SAMPLE UPWARD FEEDBACK INSTRUMENT						
Planning						
1. Develop plans that accurately anticipate future needs.	6	5	4	3	2	1
2. Communicate a consistent and clear direction for the team	6	5	4	3	2	1
3. Take actions that place the team above the individual.	6	5	4	3	2	1
Communication						
4. Communicate business issues in an understanding way.	6	5	4	3	2	1
5. Tell the truth about business issues and their effect on the team.	6 6	5 5	4 4	3 3	2 2	1 1
6. Help you and others understand your importance to overall business success.	6 6	5 5	4 4	3 3	2 2	1 1
Problem Solving						
7. Involve you and others in making decisions.	6	5	4	3	2	1
8. Address business problems in new and creative ways.	6	5	4	3	2	1
9. Use facts and measure as the basis for solving problems.	6	5	4	3	2	1
10. Identify problems completely before moving to solutions.	6	5	4	3	2	1

Developed by Karen Stoneman and Edward Bancroft, Wyatt Company, Chicago, and Carole Halling, AT&T Call Servicing, Chicago.

Informal methods of communication in organizations may be effective, but they have a number of drawbacks, as will be seen in the next section.

Informal Organizational Communication Patterns

While formal communication systems can be diagrammed or written in policy and procedure manuals, informal communication systems are often temporary and vague. Formal communication systems focus on company needs; informal communication systems focus on social needs.

The Grapevine

The most common **informal communication** systems in organizations are usually the grapevine, rumors, and gossip. In a survey of 22,000 shift workers, 55 percent said that most of their information came from the grapevine and only 11 percent cited upper management as their primary source of information (Boles & Sunoo, 1997). The **grapevine** is named for its similarity to the twisted, complex system of branches that are produced by a single grape plant. Using the grapevine communication system in an organization, a message may start out in one place and end up in a number of unplanned or unexpected places. In the corporate grapevine distortions occur, but most communications contain about 80 percent correction information (Mishra, 1990; Zaremba, 1988).

The best managers find ways to make the grapevine work for them instead of against them. Grapevines are most active during times of excitement and insecurity. When a corporate merger has been announced but no details about job changes have been given, the grapevine is very active as employees try to find out what will happen to them and their jobs. While the grapevine quickly spreads information that is not available from formal sources, the major reason for its growth and development is to satisfy social needs. Since the time of the Hawthorne Studies (Chapter 1), psychologists have recognized the importance of allowing and encouraging social relationships at work. These relationships require regular social contact, which often is provided by the grapevine. Alesse (1982) found that a strong grapevine communication system provides increased job satisfaction. Computer-based e-mail and groupware networks (see p. 169) have provided even more channels for the grapevine, but court rulings giving employers the right to examine employees' e-mail indicate that face-to-face contact will still be the preferred method for broadcasting grapevine information.

Instead of trying to destroy the grapevine, Zaremba (1988) suggests that managers cultivate it in three ways:

1. Use the informal network. Analyze it and find out what its branches are.

2. Be truthful and open about information that is sent on formal or informal networks.

3. Screen employees. If one talkative employee in an essential position is spending more time on the grapevine than with work-related matters, reassign or dismiss that employee. The grapevine exists along with work-related tasks, not in place of them.

Rumors

While the grapevine in general may promote better work among employees, one type of grapevine communication can disrupt or destroy the entire organization. **Rumors** are grapevine communications that are not based on factual evidence. In other words, they are not based on anything official from the organization.

Informal communication Ways of passing information in organizations other than those designated on the organizational chart.

Grapevine The informal communications system that exists in organizations.

Rumor Information communication that is not based on factual evidence.

Rumors have always been present in organizations, but the explosive growth of the Internet has provided a new source for rumors about people and organizations (Hutheesing, 1997). Davis (1967) discusses how rumors are spread and stopped in his story of a worker who cut two fingers on a machine one morning. By the afternoon the story was spreading throughout his company that an employee had lost his left hand at work that morning. The supervisors quickly made an announcement on the public address system that the most serious injury treated that day was two cut fingers and that the machine operator had returned to work. Note that they did not mention the rumor but quickly stopped its spread by introducing correct information. This seems to be one of the most effective methods to counteract the spread of rumors.

Whether a rumor starts seems to depend on a combination of personal anxiety, general uncertainty, belief in the possible truth of the rumor, and being a stakeholder in the outcome of the rumor (Rosnow, 1991). Rumors about unpleasant outcomes spread faster than do rumors about good outcomes (Walker & Blaine, 1991), and so those are the rumors to which management may need to pay the most attention. When a rumor does not have the potential to have harmful effects on the organization, the best choice may be to ignore it and let it die a natural death.

Gossip

Gossip consists of talk about real people in the organization, for the purpose of trading information, gaining influence and social control, or entertainment. Both men and women report very similar tendencies to gossip, although women gossip more about physical appearance (Nevo, Nevo, & Zehavi, 1993). Gossip can be one of the main methods for transmitting corporate culture. Although gossip can be hurtful and damaging, this is often not the intention.

Can gossip be stopped? If most gossiping is done for the purpose of entertainment, organizations may be able to find better, more work-related methods of providing involvement for employees. If gossiping is helpful in socializing new employees, developing better team spirit, or alerting managers to potentially harmful situations, it may be in the best interest of the organization to allow and even encourage some degree of gossiping. A department supervisor may count on the gossip her secretary collects to help run the department smoothly.

Computer-Based Communication

Computer-based communication
The transmission of messages in an organization that involves the use of computers for part or all of a transmission.

Whereas most informal communication takes place on a face-to-face level, the increasing use of computers in the workplace has led to several types of **computer-based communication**. It has been estimated that almost all white-collar workers have access to or use a computer at work. The computer is a different medium of communication from any others that have gone before it. Williams (1982) states, "The computer is the first communications technology to interact intellectually with its users. Most technologies only transform light, sound or data into electronic impulses for transmission, then reverse the process at the receiving end. Computers, by contrast, can accept or reject our messages, reduce or expand them, file them, index them, or answer back with their own messages" (p. 38).

Types of Computer-Based Communication

The most common uses of the computer for organizational communication are electronic mail (*e-mail*) and group exchanges such as networking and bulletin boards that allow the sharing of various kinds of information. Software designed to be used by group members to share information and connect their computers in a network is referred to as *groupware*.

Problems and Effective Use

Increased access to information through computers should lead to increased productivity. In reality, the average output of American information workers has not changed since the early 1960s, before large investments in technology began (*Economist*, 1990). Part of the problem may be caused by the wholesale adoption of computer-based communication without an assessment of needs or the best way to accomplish communication tasks.

One of the other dangers of computer-based communication systems is that the overwhelming amount of information available can lead to information overload. E-mail allows the quick distribution of memos to the entire organization rather than only to the appropriate people.

Another problem is the issue of e-mail privacy. The Electronic Communications Privacy Act of 1986 forbids unauthorized access to electronic communications. It does, however, permit employers to monitor e-mail that is sent or received in the course of doing business or if an employee gives permission for monitoring. Requests for permission to monitor employees' communications can be part of company policy. In a recent survey of human resource professionals, nearly 80 percent used e-mail but only 36 percent of their companies had formal, written e-mail policies (McCune, 1997). Recent court decisions about electronic communication generally have supported employers' rather than employees' interests (Cozzetto & Pedeliski, 1997).

One of the current trends in computer-based communication is connection to the Internet. Since the Internet has a number of excellent organizational applications, careful planning and training for Internet use should be beneficial to organizational communication. However, one of the most common results of adding computer-based communication systems is increased stress rather than better communication (Mantovani, 1994; Stone & Allen, 1990), although employees also report favorable evaluations of these systems (Compton, White, & DeWine, 1991). These results may indicate a need for better planning and training before Internet connections are installed rather than afterward.

The belief that computer-based communication prevents the development of impressions of the sender and receiver because of the lack of face-to-face contact also appears not to be true (Walther, 1993). Regular uses of computer-based communication systems have developed shorthand "emote icons" to restore some of the personalization missing from such communication. Some of those icons are illustrated in Figure 5.4.

F i g u r e 5.4

Some common "emote icons" (also called smileys) used in e-mail messages to convey emotion.

:-)	The basic smiley	:-(*)	That comment made me sick
;-)	The winking smiley	:-/	Skeptical smiley
:-(	The basic frowny	:-D	User is laughing
:-o	"Oh no!"	:-x	"My lips are sealed"
>:-/	Sick of smileys	>:-<	User is mad
:*	Kisses	B-)	User wears glasses
:-!	Foot in the mouth	:---------}	You lie like Pinnochio

When computer-based communication is used effectively, Fulk and Boyd (1991) suggest six specific organizational results:

1. More individuals participating as information sources in decision making but fewer persons making up the formal decision-making unit.

2. Fewer organizational levels involved in processing messages and giving permission for action.

3. Greater variation from organization to organization concerning the level at which particular types of decisions are made.

4. Less time devoted to decision-making meetings and quicker identification of problems and opportunities, leading to quicker decisions.

5. Higher-quality decisions.

6. Fewer human links in the information-processing network.

Communication Skills Training

As methods such as computer-based communication are added to organizations, the need for communication skills training becomes even more critical. Communication skills training involves at least four different kinds: writing skills, oral presentation skills, listening skills, and reading skills. Any program may involve one of these skills, a combination, or all of them. Communication skills training can involve the entire organization (Zamanou & Glaser, 1989) or only specific target sections within the organization. The communication skills training program at the Clyde Division of Whirlpool Corporation illustrates a typical training program; see the case study "Communications at Work."

[Case Study] COMMUNICATIONS AT WORK

The communication skills training program at the Clyde Division of Whirlpool Corporation is a typical training program. The company had reorganized into self-directed work teams; line supervisors—who previously had to communicate only with individuals—now had to coach individuals, make group presentations, and lead the work teams. The training program for them focused on reducing communication anxiety as well as teaching communication skills, which included computer literacy, engaging in interpersonal dialogues, making group presentations, and writing.

The training participants were volunteers. After nonparticipating line supervisors saw the positive changes in communication in those who completed the training, more of them volunteered for the program.

Three and again at six months after the training the participants were asked to describe what they had learned to do in the program and explain how they used those behaviors on the job. Before training, very few of the participants were able to apply any of the training objectives on the job; afterward they were able to use nearly all of them. The participants showed a 29 percent reduction in anxiety and an increase in their willingness to communicate. The supervisors saw line supervisors go from being team members to being team leaders.

From A. K. Watson and J. R. Bossley. (1995, April). Taking the sweat out of communication anxiety. *Personnel Journal, 74,* 111.

Communication skills become increasingly critical as more groups are used in organizational settings. The use of communication skills in group settings is examined in the next section.

GROUPS IN ORGANIZATIONS

The study of communication in organizations is closely linked to the study of groups in organizations. As you communication with others, you form bonds that result in groups being formed. Work groups generally consist of at least two employees who interact socially to meet a specific organizational goal. Some of these groups are formally defined by the organization, and others are informal groups that develop along with or in place of formal groups. This section looks at both types and the effects of groups on organizations. It also looks at the effects of a particular type of group, labor unions, in organizations.

Matrix structures A formal organizational group design that involves both the functional and the production divisions of an organization.

Project team A group assembled to work on a task from the earliest stages through completion. It disbands after the project is completed.

Work group A formal organizational collection of employees who have a common task but whose work does not depend on the other members of the group.

Work team A formal organizational collection of employees in which each person's work affects the other members' work in terms of completing the task.

Formal Groups

Formal groups tend to have more rigid patterns of status, authority, roles, and communication than do informal groups; those patterns are defined by membership, group rewards, and common goals. Some common types of formal groups in organizations are matrix structures, project teams, work groups, and work teams.

Matrix Structures and Project Teams

Matrix structures involve both the functional and the production divisions of an organization. Functional divisions relate to the way tasks are divided by their purpose within an organization—such as separate divisions for sales and for finance. Production divisions refer to the way tasks are divided for actual output—such as divisions that make a particular television set or car model. Matrix structures often are used in complex industries such as aerospace. In such groups employees may report to the functional division manager, for example, the head of engineering, and also to a production division manager, such as the person in charge of the *Challenger* spacecraft. Matrix organizations are characterized by a great deal of flexibility and adaptability so that they can change with rapidly changing conditions, such as those typical of the aerospace industry. Reporting to more than one supervisor can be a difficult situation, but the greater communication flexibility is an advantage in dealing with complex, creative work (Ford & Randolph, 1992).

A **project team** is similar to a matrix structure in that the group is assembled to develop a particular plan from its earliest stages through the completion of the project. This may be a group that is assigned to develop a new glucose-monitoring device for diabetic patients, test it, perfect it, and market it. Once the product is on the market, it may be assigned to another division that has been in charge of all diabetic products lines.

Work Groups and Work Teams

Work groups and work teams are similar in that both have a formal assignment from the organization. The work effort of a member of a **work group** does not depend on the other members; for example, the psychology department in a college is a work group, but each faculty member teaches his or her classes independently. If one professor is out, the others are able to teach their classes without interruption; they may even step in for the missing faculty member. **Work teams** require each member's cooperation to reach the end result. One of the simplest examples of a work team is an assembly line where the work of each person depends on the work of the previous person. If any person is absent from the work team and no one replaces that person, the group's work cannot be completed.

Informal Groups

Informal groups are groups that form naturally, for example car pools, people who eat lunch together, and parents with preschool children. The purpose of these groups is to meet personal goals. Those goals may help meet organizational goals, hinder them, or have little to do with them. One of the key factors determining membership is frequent interaction of the members, a critical factor in using groups to make decisions at work.

Group Decision Making

Types of Decisions

One of the most common uses for groups at work involves decision making; as the common saying goes, "Two heads are better than one." Group decision making can take several forms, depending on the task and the group.

- In **consultative decisions** the group leader makes the decision after receiving input from the group members. If the leader of a health and safety committee asked all the committee members for ideas about preventing workplace violence, looked at the suggestions, and then wrote a memo detailing the practices that would be used at the company, that would be a consultative decision.

- In a **democratic decision** the group members are given the authority to make the decision themselves. In the example of the health and safety committee, the group may discuss a number of methods and then jointly agree on which methods will be used at that company. The agreement usually is based on a majority vote, and so some members may not agree with the decision made by the group.

- In a **consensus decision,** all the members agree on the decision. Some members may believe that other choices would be better, but they all agree to support the decision of the group. One of the most common examples of consensus decision is in the jury system; all the members of a jury must agree on a verdict or punishment. In the health and safety committee example, the group may reach a consensus decision on installing physical safety barriers, although some members would prefer to hold safety seminars. Those members agree that it would be beneficial to install the barriers and perhaps hope that later the group may support the preventive seminars. Consensus decisions usually take longer to arrive at but tend to produce greater confidence in the decision and a better group climate (Neilsen & Miller, 1992). Consensus groups tend to reject more information input than do other types of groups, but this may be one of the ways that makes it possible for everyone to support the group decision (Propp, 1997).

Regardless of the method a group uses to arrive at a decision, the most basic question is whether there is an advantage to having a group rather than an individual make decisions. For a number of years it was accepted that groups produce

Informal group A naturally occurring collection of employees formed for the purpose of meeting personal goals.

Consultative decisions Judgments made by a group leader after receiving information from the group members.

Democratic decisions Judgments made by the entire group, typically by a majority vote.

Consensus decisions Group judgments that require all the members of a group to agree on the decision.

Group decision support systems (GDSS)
A computer-based system of network software that assists groups in generating and organizing ideas, editing shared work, and voting on alternatives.

higher-quality decisions than individuals do, but that groups take longer to make decisions (Kanekar, 1987; Michaelson, Watson, & Black, 1989). As more research was done and more work situations were examined, it became clear that the differences between group and individual decisions are not always clear-cut. It appears that when groups are formed to make a one-time decision, such as who to hire as office manager, individuals generally make better-quality decisions than groups do. When groups are formed to make a number of decisions over a longer time—such as the health and safety committee cited earlier—groups generally make better decisions (Gigone & Hastie, 1997). Other variables that may influence the quality of group decision making are task experience or group experience on similar tasks (Littlepage, Robison, & Reddington, 1997), how good decisions are defined (Gigone & Hastie, 1997), diversity of group members (Elass & Graves, 1997), status differences among members (Fiorelli, 1988), and other individual differences among members (LePine, Hollenbeck, Ilgen, & Hedlund, 1997). One goal of some computer-based group decision-making programs is to reduce the amount of *process loss,* the amount of time it takes to make decisions. This makes group decision making more advantageous.

Group Decision Support Systems

The use of computers in the group decision-making process is a fairly recent addition. This application is referred to as **group decision support systems (GDSS),** computer-based systems of network software that includes components for generating and organizing ideas, editing shared work, and anonymous voting on group alternatives from desktop computers (Aiken, Hawley, & Sloan, 1994–1995). Four different types of GDSS are commonly used (Table 5.2).

Since the group members' contributions are usually anonymous in GDSS, more comments are made, the comments are more critical and more likely to be added to

Table 5.2

TYPES OF GROUP DECISION SUPPORT SYSTEMS (GDSS)

GDSS	Example
Systems that support same-time and same-place interaction	Workstations at a conference table and terminals to access remote information
Systems that support same-place and different-time interaction	Project room where group members go to retrieve information
Systems that support same-time and different-place interaction	Videoconferencing systems
Systems that support different-place and different-time interaction	Electronic and voice mail systems

SOURCE: M. Alavi. (1991). Group decision support systems: A key to business team productivity. *Information Systems Management, 8,* 36–41.

by other group members, and status and expertise differences among group members are minimized (Dubrovsky, Kiesler, & Sethna, 1991; Sweeney, Soutar, Hausknecht, Dallin, & Johnson, 1997). The greater anonymity of GDSS may be an advantage in terms of incorporating multicultural employees into the organizational team. Daily and Steiner (1998) found that multicultural groups in the GDSS environment did more brainstorming than homogeneous GDSS groups or traditional decision-making groups. Other benefits of GDSS include improved decision quality and a greater degree of focus on the task (McLeod, 1992; Nunamaker, 1997).

The disadvantages of GDSS include taking a longer time to make decisions; more risky, unconventional, and extreme decisions; and lack of availability of the hardware and software needed (Benbassat & Lim, 1993; Keisler, 1992; Scott, 1992). More software companies are designing GDSS programs, and labor costs appear to be decreasing as these systems become more common (Aiken, Hasan, & Vanjani, 1996).

There is a less obvious problem related to the kinds of decision making used in GDSS. These systems are based on the assumption that decision making follows certain logical procedures and rules, which are incorporated into the software. At times the best decisions may be ones that are developed intuitively or more creatively. One study suggests that the continued use of GDSS may depend on the ability to incorporate other decision-making methods into the system (Pollock & Kanachowski, 1993). The kinds of decision making that appear to be most facilitated by GDSS involve complex projects, strategic planning, engagement planning, and review of client services (Campbell, 1990). These are the types of decisions that would appear to benefit most from a well-structured decision system. Compared to paper and pencil systems or no systems, GDSS show improved organization of the decision-making process (Poole, Holmes, Watson, & DeSanctis, 1993).

Part of the reason for the strong current interest in GDSS is the assumption that computer-based systems can eliminate some of the traditional problems of group decision making in face-to-face groups but retain the benefits. The following sections discuss brainstorming, groupthink, social loafing, and group polarization in face-to-face decision-making groups.

Brainstorming

A time-honored tradition in the group decision-making process is the use of **brainstorming** (Osborn, 1957). The basic structure of a brainstorming group requires a stated problem with members making contributions that can be stimulated by a contribution started by another member and added to by still other members. No one is allowed to criticize the ideas generated in this initial activity. At a later point the ideas are evaluated and modified and actions are planned. The ideal situation for brainstorming includes a group of seven to fifteen people, a balance between a casual meeting and the need to accomplish a task, and a method of recording the ideas that are generated.

Brainstorming A method of group decision making in which all the members meet, generate ideas without criticizing them, and evaluate the ideas as a group.

Social inhibition
The censoring effect that the presence of other people has on the behavior of group members.

Groupthink Poor group decision-making behavior resulting from a high degree of unity and desire for consensus among group members.

Problems

The basic assumption of brainstorming is that the group members will stimulate one another to generate more ideas than they would come up with on their own. Subjects in brainstorming experiments typically report that they believe groups generate more ideas than individuals do. This may result from individuals taking credit for more ideas than they actually produce when they are part of a group (Paulus, Dzindolet, Poletes, & Camacho, 1993). However, research comparing the number of quality of ideas generated by a brainstorming group with the number and quality of ideas generated by the same number of individuals acting alone showed that the output of the individuals was better (Diehl & Stroebe, 1987). Part of the reason for this is that even though members are told that no one should criticize any ideas, the members sometimes censor themselves as they think, "Oh, no, I can't say that. Everyone will think I'm so stupid." This is referred to as **social inhibition,** meaning that the presence of other people produces censoring. The brainstorming situations that result in the fewest and lowest-quality ideas include large groups, the presence of the experimenter or supervisor, and tape recording of the sessions as opposed to writing down ideas (Stroebe & Diehl, 1991).

Improving Brainstorming

A promising method to retain the good effects of brainstorming and counteract the effects of the presence of the group is the use of electronic brainstorming, with products such as IdeaFisher from Fisher Idea Systems. Participants use computers to enter ideas whenever they are ready and view all the ideas produced by other group members without any names attached. The main benefits are anonymity, which reduces social inhibition, and the spontaneous entry of ideas rather than participants having to wait for an opening (Cooper, Gallupe, Pollard, & Cadsby, 1998). Electronic brainstorming groups regularly outperform traditional brainstorming groups (Valacich, Dennis, & Connolly, 1994), and the participants indicate they are more satisfied with the electronic method (Gallupe, Dennis, & Cooper, 1992)

Although brainstorming can be a valuable group decision-making method, the best use of the method requires an awareness of the times when brainstorming is a poor choice. This includes times when the decision is entirely the supervisor's responsibility, when the topic could divide the participants even more, when the group is not used to generating ideas, and when the group is the wrong size (Thomas, 1991).

Groupthink

Groupthink is an unhealthy decision-making pattern that develops from a high degree of unity among group members and a desire for consensus (Janis, 1982). Among the factors that most often lead to groupthink are: a great deal of group cohesiveness ("us against them" feelings), a lack of outside sources of information, a leader who expresses strong feelings about particular solutions, a lack of decision-making procedures, group members who are very similar to one another, the perception of threats from outside sources, a belief that no better solutions are available, problems in the current decision-making process, and moral questions raised by the problem (Janis & Mann, 1977).

When groupthink controls the group decision-making process, there is a very low probability of a successful decision being made, as can be seen in the case of the *Challenger* spacecraft disaster of 1986. Kovach and Render (1987) examined the decision-making process that led up to approval for the takeoff and found that the management team at NASA exhibited many of these groupthink characteristics. All these conditions, taken together, would predict the no-cancellation decision that resulted in the explosion of the spacecraft. Most groupthink decisions do not risk a devastating loss of life, but many such decisions can lead to unfavorable outcomes.

■ Groupthink may have contributed to the *Challenger* spacecraft disaster of 1986.

To avoid groupthink in the decision-making process, Woodruff (1991) and Janis (1989) made a number of suggestions for stopping groupthink before it starts, including the following:

1. The kind of thinking that critically evaluates ideas and suggestions should be rewarded. Some groups even appoint a person to the role of *devil's advocate* to find flaws in proposed decisions. Part of this suggestion includes getting all the group members to provide input into the decision. If some group members say nothing, it is easy to assume that they agree with the rest of the group.

2. The larger group should be divided into smaller groups to evaluate the solutions, and group members should be encouraged to seek out more information individually from outside sources and experts to bring back to the group.

3. The leaders, who should be in control of the group and guide the procedures of the group in decision making, should at the same time remain impartial and not promote a particular decision.

4. If time permits, the group should hold a "second chance" meeting to reconsider the alternatives if rejected or try out the decision on a pilot basis, such as testing a new marketing approach in only one geographic area rather than the entire United States.

Social loafing The problem of members putting out less effort as a group than they would as individuals.

Free-rider theory An explanation for social loafing that is based on the belief that when group members see the work of the group progressing well, they believe their effort is not necessary.

Sucker-effect theory An explanation for social loafing that is based on the belief that if an individual member of a group believes that she or he is working harder than the rest of the group, that member will exert less effort to avoid being taken advantage of in the group.

Although groupthink has been studied for over twenty-five years, research support has been based mainly on case studies of decision disasters rather than on looking at the decision-making process as it results in good or bad decisions. Many laboratory studies have looked only at short-term decision quality and used only some of the components of groupthink (Aldag & Fuller, 1993). These criticisms do not mean that groupthink does not exist, only that it may be more complicated than was believed, as is typical of many real-life events as opposed to laboratory studies.

Social Loafing

Social loafing occurs when group members put out less effort as a group than they would as individuals. Social loafing has been studied for a number of years in I/O psychology and often is discussed in association with two other concepts: the free-rider theory (Kerr & Brunn, 1983) and the sucker-effect theory (Kerr, 1983; Robbins, 1995). Those concepts typically are used to explain why social loafing occurs. The **free-rider theory** suggests that if the group is doing a good job on the task it has been assigned, individual members can feel that their effort is not necessary and will reduce that effort. The **sucker-effect theory** suggests that when a group member perceives that she or he is working harder than the other members are and feels taken advantage of, that member will exert less effort to avoid being "suckered" into doing extra work.

An example of the sucker-effect is the occurrence of an absence culture. An absence culture suggests that employees deserve a certain number of group-defined days of absence, whether or not they are sick. If an employee does not take the group-defined number of absence days, he may feel that he is carrying an unfair share of the workload.

Another common explanation for social loafing is *diffusion of responsibility,* a situation in which the members feel that they can get lost in the group and no one will notice what they do as individuals (Latané & Nida, 1981). This assumption also has been used to explain group decisions that are more extreme than the decisions individual members would make.

The cure for social loafing would appear to be restoring individual responsibility; when group members know that their individual performance is being recorded, they are less likely to engage in social loafing (Everett, Smith, & Kipling, 1992; Robbins, 1995). Also, when the tasks assigned to the group are meaningful and achievable, social loafing is reduced (Atoum & Farah, 1993). Finally, threatening punishment for inadequate performance reduces social loafing (Miles & Greenberg, 1993). In a meta-analysis of seventy-eight studies, Karau & Williams (1993) found that the variables that had the greatest influence on whether group members would engage in social loafing were the chances of evaluation of individual performance, expectations about how other group members would perform, the meaningfulness of the assigned task, and the culture of the group. Using those variables, Shepard (1993) suggested three methods by means of which organizations might reduce social loafing: providing strong incentives for contributing, making each contributor and his or her contributions indispensable to the group, and decreasing the cost or effort of contributing to the group.

Group Polarization

Group polarization—the shift of a group to a more extreme position than the individual members' position—originally was studied as the risky shift phenomenon. The **risky shift phenomenon** suggests that groups will make a commitment to decisions involving greater risk rather than to the average of the decision risks that would be made individually. Although research confirmed this phenomenon, it also found evidence for a **cautious shift phenomenon,** in which group decisions were more conservative in terms of risk than were the decisions made by individuals. Both findings were incorporated in the concept of group polarization (Lamm & Myers, 1978).

The tendency toward caution or risk appears to be determined mainly by the majority viewpoint in the group. The movement toward the majority position fits an explanation of group polarization in which it is suggested that the minority members conform to the majority position. During group discussions the members of the majority convince themselves of the correctness of their decision and bring the minority members around to their viewpoint. The importance of group polarization lies not only in the risk levels of initial decisions but also in the effect it has on the future behaviors of group members. Once a group or an individual has made a decision, that group or person typically shows a strong commitment to the decision even when outside evidence shows that it was a poor choice. For example, in the 1980s and early 1990s, IBM suffered devastating losses because it decided to make its primary product large mainframe computer systems for organizations rather than desktop computers. Even when all indicators pointed to growth in desktop computers for the home and the office, the company stayed with its decision. One way to relieve such a problem is to have decisions following the initial one be made by a different group or person. Another reason for groups to move toward more extreme positions may be greater support from the group as it develops as "us-against-them" attitude and greater unity among the members. Attraction and unity among group members commonly are studied as aspects of group cohesion.

Group polarization
The tendency of a decision-making group to shift the group decision to a more extreme position than the average of the decisions of the individual members.

Risky shift phenomenon
The movement of groups toward decisions more dangerous than the decisions of the individual members.

Cautious shift phenomenon
The movement of groups toward decisions more careful than those of the individual members.

Group cohesion
The strength of the desire of
group members to remain part
of the group.

Group Cohesion

Group cohesion often is defined by the strength of the motivation of the group members to remain part of the group. Several different types of group cohesiveness can be found in work groups. In groups that are high in social cohesiveness the members want to extend discussions and engage in conversation. In highly task-cohesive groups the members want to complete the task quickly and efficiently. The general feeling in such highly cohesive groups is one of cooperation, with most behaviors directed toward group unity. There has been some disagreement on the contribution of group cohesiveness to productivity, but meta-analytic studies show a very significant relationship between group cohesiveness and good performance, with most of the effect caused by commitment to the task rather than by social attraction or group pride (Langfred, 1998; Mullen & Copper, 1994). One of the typical factors in group cohesion is high satisfaction among the members (Colarelli & Boos, 1992; Keller, 1986), which may translate into better performance and better attendance.

Group cohesiveness may result from the continued interaction required by either formal groups or informal groups. As long as a group's goals are the same as those of the organization, all the participants are satisfied. When the group's goal is different from the organization's (e.g., the work group sets standards for production far below those of the company), the company may try to diminish group cohesiveness, but if this attempt is successful, the company may lose some benefits. One of the quickest ways to reduce group cohesion appears to be to make the composition of the group more diverse as to gender, race, and organizational status (Jehn, Chadwick, & Thatcher, 1997).

The Bottom Line

With so many possible drawbacks, it may not seem worthwhile to use groups to make decisions. However, group decisions generally tend to be better than decisions made by individuals. To maximize the benefits and minimize the problems of group decision making, it is important to be aware of the problems before starting the group decision process and to incorporate safeguards to prevent those problems along the way.

A model of group decision making that incorporates many of the ways to prevent problems, yet demonstrates how many variables may be involved, is shown in Figure 5.5. This model may look complicated, but one could easily add even more variables. It is often difficult to determine which variables will be the most influential because that often depends on the specific situation. The next section looks at a specific example of groups in organizations, in this case, labor unions.

Figure 5.5

General group problem-solving model.

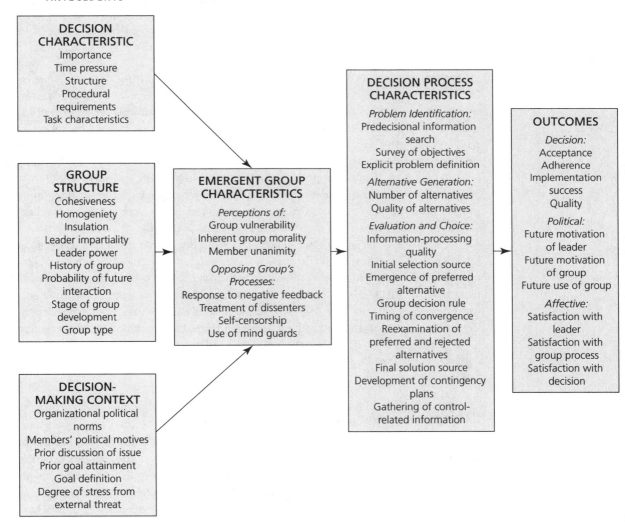

ANTECEDENTS

DECISION CHARACTERISTIC
Importance
Time pressure
Structure
Procedural requirements
Task characteristics

GROUP STRUCTURE
Cohesiveness
Homogeniety
Insulation
Leader impartiality
Leader power
History of group
Probability of future interaction
Stage of group development
Group type

DECISION-MAKING CONTEXT
Organizational political norms
Members' political motives
Prior discussion of issue
Prior goal attainment
Goal definition
Degree of stress from external threat

EMERGENT GROUP CHARACTERISTICS
Perceptions of:
Group vulnerability
Inherent group morality
Member unanimity

Opposing Group's Processes:
Response to negative feedback
Treatment of dissenters
Self-censorship
Use of mind guards

DECISION PROCESS CHARACTERISTICS
Problem Identification:
Predecisional information search
Survey of objectives
Explicit problem definition

Alternative Generation:
Number of alternatives
Quality of alternatives

Evaluation and Choice:
Information-processing quality
Initial selection source
Emergence of preferred alternative
Group decision rule
Timing of convergence
Reexamination of preferred and rejected alternatives
Final solution source
Development of contingency plans
Gathering of control-related information

OUTCOMES
Decision:
Acceptance
Adherence
Implementation success
Quality

Political:
Future motivation of leader
Future motivation of group
Future use of group

Affective:
Satisfaction with leader
Satisfaction with group process
Satisfaction with decision

Adapted from Ramon J. Aldag and Sally R. Fuller. (1993). Beyond fiasco: A reappraisal of the groupthink phenomenon and a new model of group decision processes. *Psychological Bulletin, 113*(3), 533–552.

LABOR UNIONS

Labor unions are a special type of group in the work environment. Typically, they do not show up on organizational charts, but they can have a strong influence on many aspects of organizations. In some organizations employees are required to be union members; on the other hand, some states forbid requiring union membership to get or keep a job.

Reasons for Joining Unions

In the past the relationship between unions and companies was characterized by opposition, but they needed each other to survive. Most unions were formed because of employees' dissatisfaction with management practices; they were intended to strengthen the bargaining position of employees on issues such as pay and safe working conditions. More recently, improving or maintaining benefits and gaining job security have become important reasons for joining a union. In the early years of union development in the nineteenth century bargaining was an all-or-none proposition: Workers got everything they asked for or got nothing. Give-and-take and compromise were not practiced until near the end of the nineteenth century.

This all-or-none strategy created strong feelings on both sides and might have led to even stronger positions for unions except for the effect of economic cycles on union membership. When the economy is doing well, unions that are oriented toward gaining economic benefits for their members tend to increase their membership. In economic recessions, unions that are oriented toward gaining job security for their members increase their membership. Currently some labor contracts are beginning to deal with quality of work life issues, but most contracts still focus on tangible, material factors in the work environment, such as pay and sick days.

Changes in Union Membership

The two different economic perspectives may have contributed to the decline of union membership in the United States. The American economy has continued to improve, but increasing numbers of workers have been displaced through downsizing and company reorganization. In 1997 only 14.1 percent of American workers had union contracts, whereas in the late 1950s about 35 percent of workers were union members. Greater employee participation and empowerment in the workplace may be another reason for the decline in unions. Union membership often is seen as a strong force for developing a cohesive group of employees, but management may not view this kind of group cohesion as favorable for the organization. However, researchers have found that satisfaction with the union and job satisfaction were the greatest predictors of employees' commitment to a company (Johnson & Jones-Johnson, 1992). Fullagar and Barling (1991) found that commitment to the union did not necessarily have a negative impact on commitment to the company, and vice versa.

Comparisons with Nonunion Employees

Although unions are perceived as being agents for obtaining better pay and benefits for employees, nonunionized employees often can improve their positions by comparing their positions to similar ones in unionized organizations. To stay competitive, companies may become more like the unionized companies. Nonunionized employees report higher levels of satisfaction with growth, pay, and supervision than unionized employees do (Gilmore, Fried, & Ferris, 1989). Although nonunionized employees typically have lower pay than unionized employees do, this difference may be offset by the cost of union dues. In the Gilmore, Fried, and Ferris study (1989) the researchers found that nonunion workers also had higher levels of internal work motivation. This may be a product of the collective bargaining process.

Lack of Involvement with I/O Psychology

Industrial/organizational psychologists have been far less involved in unions than they have been in other organizational groups. Part of the reason for this is the perception by unions that I/O psychologists are closely aligned with management. There has been a long tradition of I/O psychologists being hired to do surveys for management, some of which were used to prevent unions from being established or to break up a union (Huszczo, Wiggins, & Currie, 1984).

Some unions, however, are beginning to realize the benefits of paying for their own job satisfaction surveys before going into contract negotiations. When management suggests that there is no basis for a union saying that its members are unhappy with their work hours, the union can present documentation to support its position. If a large number of employees are dissatisfied, this can give the union added bargaining strength.

At best, most unions perceive I/O psychologists as neither helpful nor harmful but have no idea what use they could be to them. A survey in the 1980s showed that the most positive perception unions had of psychologists was that they could be trusted to keep employee information gathered in interviews confidential (Huszczo, Wiggins, & Currie, 1984).

Ways to Use I/O Psychology to Rebuild Unions

Labor unions in the United States are now going through major membership changes that may make them less resistant to obtaining the assistance of I/O psychologists. Although the percentage of workers who are members of unions

Decertificaton
The dismissal of a union at an organization as a result of union members voting to dismiss it.

is declining, the overall picture is one of great declines in membership and number of unions in the private sector and large gains in the public service sector. In 1992 the assistant to the secretary-treasurer of the AFL-CIO, Charles McDonald, predicted that by the year 2000 labor union membership in the private sector would include only about 5 percent of the workforce, which is close to the current 9.4 percent. This reduction would be caused not only by the failure of newly eligible employees to join unions; equally important, the number of employees lost through **decertification,** or the dismissal of a union, had quadrupled since the early 1960s.

What can unions do to change this pattern of decline, and how can I/O psychologists help them? If one looks at unions as actual organizations rather than just as opponents of companies, there are a number of issues on which I/O psychology is well suited to assist them. McDonald (1992) lists several ways in which unions must change for their survival.

1. Both labor unions and management must change their perceptions of each other. Instead of seeing each other as enemies working toward opposing ends, it would be more productive for unions and management to recognize their common goals. Cooke [1990] found that when employers collaborated with unions, the employers increased the monetary value of each employee to the organization.

■ Industrial/Organizational (IO) psychology can help unions and management avoid strikes in which each side loses more than it gains.

Jonathan Nourok/PhotoEdit

2. Unions must be willing to change and adapt in view of the fact that employees in many fields today do not look as automatically to unions to solve their problems as they did in the past. Some laws and government standards have replaced the need for union-negotiated hiring standards and work conditions. Better personnel selection methods for those in union leadership positions have become more important as well, as the field of labor relations has become more complex.

3. Unions should use more mass media advertising to attract membership and should promote legislation that would increase the financial advantage of union membership.

If McDonald's suggestions lead to a strengthening of unions, it would seem that they also would lead to a strengthening of the companies where the unions are located and greater involvement for I/O psychologists as well.

This chapter has come full circle: from looking at how individuals communicate and interact with one another to looking at how separate but closely related organizations—unions and companies—communicate and interact. As the next chapters look at other industrial and organizational topics, they will frequently use the information from the first five chapters.

MAIN POINTS

■ Communication in organizations occurs because someone needs information or social reinforcement, or because someone has been directed to communicate, or in order to achieve a goal.

■ Each communication involves a sender, a message, a channel, a receiver, and listening. The sender and the receiver each have a communication climate, a purpose, and interpersonal skills. The channel is the medium, such as the telephone or a letter, used to communicate a message. Listening involves active rather than passive participation.

■ Most errors in communication can be classified as errors of omission (something is left out) or errors of commission (something is added incorrectly).

■ Nonverbal communication is a problem when it sends information different from the verbal message. It is helpful when it adds useful information to the verbal message. Research on nonverbal communication shows how difficult it is to understand nonverbal messages correctly.

■ Communication networks are patterns that describe how groups of people communicate. The most common types of networks are centralized (chain, Y, and wheel) and decentralized (circle and all-channel).

■ Formal organizational communication refers to the communication paths seen on an organizational chart; those paths go upward, downward, or horizontally.

- Informal communication in organizations includes all communication outside the formal channels. The most common types of informal communication are the grapevine, rumors, and gossip.

- The computerization of many organizational functions has led to both improved communication and less efficient communication, depending on the work and communication situation.

- Training in communication skills usually involves teaching writing, oral presentation, listening, and reading.

- Some of the most common types of formal groups in organizations are matrix structures, project teams, work groups, and work teams. Informal groups are formed naturally to meet personal goals.

- Group decision making usually is done by consultative, democratic, or consensus methods. It also can be done using computers in group decision support systems (GDSS).

- Brainstorming, groupthink, social loafing, group polarization, and group cohesion are factors that influence group decision-making methods.

- The best decision-making groups are aware of potential problems and deal with them before they affect group decision making negatively.

- The main reason unions were formed was to improve the bargaining position of employees through the strength of a group.

- Union membership has gone through periods of increase and decrease; currently, it is decreasing in the private sector and increasing in the public sector. Most managers would prefer not to have unions in their organizations.

- I/O psychology was only minimally involved in unions in the past, mainly because of the belief of unions that I/O psychology is aligned with company management teams.

- Researchers predict that unions must change and adapt to new conditions in the workplace. One of the changes may be to use the expertise of I/O psychology to benefit unions in areas such as personnel selection and training.

KEY TERMS

Brainstorming	Consultative decisions
Cautious shift phenomenon	Decentralized networks
Centralized networks	Decertification
Channel	Democratic decisions
Communication network	Downward communication
Computer-based communication	Error of commission
Consensus decisions	Error of omission

Filtering
Formal organizational communication
Free-rider theory
Gatekeeper
Grapevine
Group cohesion
Group decision support systems (GDSS)
Group polarization
Groupthink
Horizontal communication
Informal communication
Informal groups
Matrix structures

Media richness
Message
MUM effect
Nonverbal communication
Project team
Receiver
Risky shift phenomenon
Rumor
Sender
Social inhibition
Social loafing
Sucker-effect theory
Upward communication
Work group
Work team

REVIEW QUESTIONS

Answers to these questions can be found at the end of the book.

1. Studies of communication in organizations are receiving less attention because they have been conducted for so long that almost everything is known.

   a. True   b. False

2. What are the four reasons for communicating in organizations?

   a. _____

   b. _____

   c. _____

   d. _____

3. The sender of a communication may become a receiver when he or she gets feedback about the message.

   a. True   b. False

4. The most media-rich communication channels are

   a. face-to-face and written channels.

   b. written and spoken channels.

   c. telephone and e-mail.

   d. face-to-face and telephone channels.

5. The problem in communicating in other languages involves both spoken and nonverbal messages.

   a. True   b. False

6. If you tell the department supervisor that there were eight returns today but fail to tell the supervisor they were all returns related to your incorrect statements about the use of the product, this is an example of

   a. the MUM effect.

   b. the MUTE effect.

   c. insufficient information.

   d. the erroneous information effect.

7. The temptation to get more information than one needs, just because the information is easily available, may lead to

   a. errors of omission.

   b. information overload.

   c. exaggeration.

   d. less use of computers in the communication process.

8. One of the most common problems involving nonverbal communication is the difference between verbal messages and nonverbal messages delivered by the same person at the same time.

   a. True   b. False

9. Noticing the extremely loud and harsh way in which the supervisor talks to a subordinate is an example of

   a. artifacts.

   b. body language.

   c. paralanguage.

   d. distancing.

10. One of the most common criticisms of communication network research is that too much of it is field-based and not done in a laboratory.

    a. True   b. False

11. If employee satisfaction is important in solving a complicated problem, the best communication network to use is probably

    a. chain.

    b. Y.

    c. wheel.

    d. all-channel.

12. Most formal communication goes downward because managers are usually the best communicators in an organization.

    a. True   b. False

13. List three of the five common upward communication methods.

    a. _____

    b. _____

    c. _____

14. If a company is planning a number of layoffs and a number of job changes for the remaining workers, the effect on the grapevine can be expected to be which of the following?

    a. Communication increases.

    b. Communication decreases.

    c. Communication stays the same.

    d. Communication centers on the lower levels of the organization.

15. The best way to stop rumors is to introduce rumors that present opposite statements.

    a. True   b. False

16. The greatest effect of computers on the communication process has been to increase the productivity of information workers.

    a. True   b. False

17. List one advantage and one disadvantage of computer-based communication.

    a. Advantage: _____

    b. Disadvantage: _____

18. List the four different types of communication training usually done by organizations.

    a. _____

    b. _____

    c. _____

    d. _____

19. The television actors in a long-running soap opera are most like a

    a. matrix organization.

    b. work group.

    c. work team.

    d. project team.

20. The group decision-making method that requires every group member to agree to and support the group's decision is called _____.

21. The advantages of group decision support systems include

    a. greater anonymity for members and their contributions.

    b. improved decision quality.

    c. greater use of computers at work.

    d. a greater degree of focus on the decision task.

    e. a, b, and c

    f. a, b, and d

22. Belief in the worth of brainstorming appears to be greater than the actual benefit from it.

    a. True   b. False

23. List two ways to avoid groupthink in decision-making situations.

    a. _____

    b. _____

24. The possible causes of social loafing include

    a. the sucker effect.

    b. diffusion of responsibility.

    c. the co-rider effect.

    d. a and b

    e. all of the above

25. The risky shift phenomenon and the cautious shift phenomenon are both forms of group polarization, but the risky shift refers only to situations that involve physical hazards for the group members.

    a. True   b. False

26. The best groups for getting work done are

    a. groups high in social cohesiveness, because the members like to be with one another.

    b. highly task-cohesive groups, because the members focus on the job.

    c. groups low in social cohesiveness, because social relationships will not interfere with getting the job done.

    d. none of the above

27. In the past, the relationship between unions and companies was usually co-operative because both knew they needed the other to survive.

    a. True   b. False

28. The proportion of workers covered by union contracts is currently

    a. over 50%.

    b. close to 100%.

    c. lower than 20%.

    d. almost zero.

29. Compared with unionized employees, nonunionized employees usually report

    a. lower pay.

    b. higher levels of pay satisfaction.

    c. greater work stress.

    d. a and b

    e. a and c

    f. all of the above

30. The two factors that are causing a decrease in union membership are new employees not joining unions and union employees decertifying their unions.

    a. True   b. False

31. List one of McDonald's (1992) three suggestions for increasing union membership.

    _____

Use your browser to go to http://www.webofculture.com/refs/gesture_mid_af.html. Choose three or more different countries. Find at least two examples from each country where a nonverbal communication is different than it is in our culture. Next to the description of what the nonverbal communication means in the foreign country, list what in means in our culture.

WEB EXERCISE

6

Motivation and Job Satisfaction

LEARNING OBJECTIVES
DEFINING MOTIVATION
THEORIES OF MOTIVATION
Need Theories
Job Design Theories
Cognitive Theories
Case Study Delivering Psychology at Work
Behavioral Theories
Emerging Theories

JOB SATISFACTION
Job Outcomes
Personal Factors in Job Satisfaction
Measurement of Job Satisfaction
Increasing Job Satisfaction

Chapter Outline

Learning Objectives

After reading this chapter, you should be able to answer the following questions:

- How is motivation defined in regard to work settings?
- What defines a need theory of motivation?
- What are the differences and similarities among Maslow's hierarchy of needs theory, Alderfer's ERG theory, and McClelland's need to achieve theory?
- What defines a job design theory of motivation?
- What are the differences and similarities between Herzberg's two-factor theory and Hackman and Oldham's job characteristics theory?
- What defines a cognitive theory of motivation?
- What are the differences and similarities among Adams's equity theory, Vroom's valence-expectancy-instrumentality theory, Locke and Latham's goal-setting theory, and Locke and Latham's high-performance cycle?
- What defines a behavioral theory of motivation?
- What are the differences and similarities between reinforcement theory and organizational behavior modification?
- How are motivation theories likely to be different in the future?
- How does job satisfaction relate to various job outcomes and personal factors?
- How is job satisfaction measured using the Job Descriptive Index, the Minnesota Satisfaction Questionnaire, and the Job in General Scale?
- What methods can be used to increase job satisfaction?

DEFINING MOTIVATION

If you have gone to work each day for the last several years, done all the tasks that were assigned to you, and received good evaluations, it is logical to conclude that you are motivated to do your job. Your behavior at work typically includes the three elements that are commonly used to define motivated behavior. According to Steers and Porter (1991), **motivation,** in regard to work behavior, energizes, directs, and sustains that behavior.

Although your behavior at work meets the definition of motivation, you might explain your motivation in a number of different ways. Perhaps you feel motivated because you see a great future with the organization. You also might say that although you are still doing what is required, you feel less motivated than you did when you started the job; you even may feel close to the point of burnout. Your supervisors and coworkers might describe your motivation in other ways.

Motivation The conditions that energize, direct, and sustain work behavior.

The concept of motivation is important in all aspects of the work environment. Employers want to hire the most motivated workers and maintain high motivational levels in their employees. This is the ideal situation, but a survey by the Public Agenda Foundation found that only about 16 percent of the workers interviewed put out the extra effort, care, and concern needed to do top-level work (Harari, 1994). With such low levels of highly motivated employees, it is no wonder that employers such as Columbo Frozen Yogurt, Digital Equipment, and Metropolitan Life Insurance have had salespeople walk over hot coals, literally, as a motivational exercise (Pereira, 1993) in an attempt to increase productivity, performance, and loyalty.

Although motivation has been an important concept since the beginnings of industrial/organizational (I/O) psychology, it has been a difficult concept to define and apply. A number of issues have been raised through the years as I/O psychologists have studied motivation in work settings.

The first problem is that the concept of motivation has been used in so many different ways that some psychologists argue that the term has lost its meaning. Being motivated seems desirable, but it can mean different things to different people. Limiting the definition of motivation to work behavior that is energized, directed, and sustained reduces some of the uncertainty associated with this concept.

The second problem is that motivation cannot be measured directly. It is inferred from the observable behaviors of workers, but it is not the same as their measured performance. If you and your spouse just had a baby, you still might be motivated to do well at work; however, your performance might suffer from the stress of caring for a baby. Motivation is not the same as desire because ability is necessary for motivated behavior. A person's desire to become a manager or head a company does not necessarily lead to success unless that person has the ability as well as the desire to perform.

A factor that is not the same as motivation but is closely related is job satisfaction, which is discussed in detail later in this chapter. The humanistic movement in I/O psychology suggested that the way to increase motivation is to increase happiness and job satisfaction. Researchers found that this was not always true. In fact, goal-setting theory, which also is examined in this chapter, suggests that highly motivated job behavior and performance lead to job satisfaction, not the other way around.

Despite these issues, motivation is such a basic concept in I/O psychology that it has attracted considerable attention. Researchers have suggested a variety of theories to explain how and why it works. The advantage of using a theory to explain motivation is that the theory provides an organizing framework rather than just hit-or-miss attempts to understand the concept.

THEORIES OF MOTIVATION

In the early years of I/O psychology Taylor's scientific management theory (Taylor, 1911) suggested that money is the key to motivating employees. The Hawthorne Studies, on the other hand, suggested that happiness, not money, is important in motivation.

As more was found out about people at work, both approaches were criticized for being simplistic and incomplete (Brayfield & Crockett, 1955; Roethlisberger & Dickson, 1939). These early theories were based on the assumption that employees are motivated by *needs,* deficiency conditions that lead to motivated behavior. Belief in these classic theories of motivation led to continued search for the need satisfaction that would lead to motivated behavior.

Need Theories

The common theme in need theories is that motivated behavior results from a desire to eliminate a deficiency, for example, eating food when one is hungry. Needs can be biological, such as hunger, or psychological, such as the need for social relationships. Three important need theories that have influenced I/O psychology are Maslow's hierarchy of needs, Alderfer's ERG theory, and McClelland's need to achieve theory.

Maslow's Hierarchy of Needs

Abraham Maslow spent a great deal of his professional life developing this theory of motivation, but it was only toward the end of his career that he turned his attention to ways to use the theory in organizational settings and other applications. In his *Eupsychian Management: A Journal* (1965) he applied his **hierarchy of needs theory** to a specific organizational setting he had observed.

Maslow believed that at any given time there is one category of needs on the hierarchy of needs (see Figure 6.1) that dominates people's behavior. The most basic needs are the physiological needs, including the need for air, water, and food, which people must satisfy to stay alive. Usually, people who are employed have already satisfied this level. The second level covers the need for personal safety and security. These needs include freedom from threats and dangers as well as having financial and other kinds of security. The third level deals with social needs, such as belonging, love, friendship, and affiliation. The fourth level focuses on needs for self-esteem, which include feelings of self-respect, self-confidence, recognition, and regard from one's peers. The fifth level is self-actualization, which Maslow described as "the desire to become everything that one is capable of becoming" (Maslow, 1943, p. 382). Although he did not define self-actualization in detail, Maslow offered examples of people he felt were self-actualized: Abraham Lincoln, Eleanor Roosevelt, Ghandi, Harry Truman, and Albert Einstein.

Hierarchy of needs theory A theory of motivation that holds that people progress up a pyramid of motivational steps from physiological needs to self-actualization.

Figure 6.1

Maslow's Hierarchy of Needs.

A. Physiological Needs

B. Safety and Security Needs

C. Social Needs

D. Esteem Needs

E. Self-Actualization Needs

This theory can be applied to the work environment in two ways. First, a supervisor may find employees who want to satisfy a particular need level through work, such as pay leading to financial security. Second, supervisors may find out what need level their employees want to satisfy (such as social needs) and then arrange the work environment to satisfy those needs (such as providing more opportunities for teamwork).

Although Maslow's theory has generated a great deal of popular interest, there has been little research support for it (Wahba & Bridwell, 1976). Some studies, such as the one by Sumerlin and Bundrick (1996) showing that male college students are closer to self-actualization than are homeless men with the save level of education, seem to be little more than common sense. Still Maslow's theory encouraged researchers to look beyond simple monetary or social explanations of motivation. It encouraged the development of more complicated models that view employees as whole persons, with lives outside work that influence their behavior at work.

Alderfer's ERG Theory

Clayton Alderfer developed a revision of Maslow's theory in an attempt to correct some of the problems research had revealed (Alderfer, 1969). One problem was the failure to confirm all five need levels. Alderfer suggested collapsing those five levels into three: existence (Maslow's physiological and safety needs), relatedness (Maslow's social needs), and growth (Maslow's esteem and self-actualization needs). Another problem was the failure to confirm the order for need satisfaction, from lowest to highest. Alderfer suggested that all three needs could operate at the same time. The result was his **ERG theory,** which states that existence, relatedness, and growth needs operate simultaneously to motivate behavior.

Although Alderfer's theory corrects some of the problems in Maslow's theory, it fails to use operational definitions for concepts such as growth needs. Also, even though Alderfer's up-and-down, all-at-once explanation of need levels may appear more realistic than Maslow's hierarchy, research support has been inconsistent. Some research is at least partially supportive (Fox, Scott, & Donohue, 1993; Wanous & Zwany, 1977). Overall, the theory's popular appeal and usefulness in guiding future research may be its main benefits.

McClelland's Need to Achieve Theory

David McClelland's **need to achieve theory** states that work motivation consists of three needs: the need to achieve, the need for power, and the need to affiliate (McClelland, 1961). People who score high on the need to achieve (NAch) find fulfillment through personal responsibility and the efforts they use to solve challenging problems. People who score high on the *need for power* have a strong drive to influence the behavior of other people. Scoring very high on the *need to affiliate* typically leads to placing a very high value on social relationships. Most of the research on these three needs in relation to work motivation has been focused on the need to achieve, because workers with a high level of this need are the most likely to do good work at any job.

Although McClelland's theory is a need theory, it is different from the two previously described theories in two important ways. First, NAch can be learned, unlike the desire for self-actualization, which Maslow says is innate. This means that employees who are low in NAch can be taught to increase their NAch levels (McClelland & Winter, 1969). Second, McClelland focuses on motivation in the work setting but Maslow and Alderfer see work behavior as only one part of motivation in life.

ERG theory A theory of motivation that states that existence, relatedness, and growth (ERG) needs operate at the same time to motivate behavior.

Need to achieve theory (NAch) A theory of motivation that suggests that the most satisfied workers are the ones who feel the greatest fulfillment through personal responsibility, leading to preset goals.

It would appear that if a company wanted to hire good workers, all it would have to do would be to find applicants high in NAch, but the solution is not that simple. First, workers high in NAch typically like to work alone so that they can have the greatest personal responsibility for their success. In a work situation that emphasizes teamwork, someone lower in NAch but higher in the need to affiliate may be a better choice.

Second, workers who are high in NAch prefer jobs in which they can get a great deal of concrete feedback on how they are doing at reaching their goals. Many jobs allow for only infrequent feedback, which is delivered long after the work has been done. One of the most frustrating jobs for a person high in NAch might be that of a social worker, where the clients control the outcomes and the employee often waits far into the future for feedback. McClelland stresses that people who are high in NAch get a great deal of joy and fulfillment from achievement. People high in NAch often choose to work long hours because they get personal satisfaction from reaching the goals they have set. Working as an independent computer consultant or programmer would be an ideal job for a person high in NAch.

The third problem in hiring people high in NAch relates to having to balance that need with people skills. Research shows that truly successful entrepreneurs are high in NAch but also have a strong commitment to others. This commitment is part of the need to affiliate because it involves social relationships (McClelland, 1987).

Although McClelland's theory is much more observable and testable than Maslow's or Alderfer's theories, it shares some of their weaknesses. The first problem is the lack of a clear definition of need. The second problem concerns the method of assessing NAch, which McClelland measured with the *Thematic Apperception Test (TAT)*. This test involves showing a person pictures like the one in Figure 6.2 and asking that person to tell a story about the pictures, in order to

Figure 6.2

A picture similar to the TAT pictures used to assess the need to achieve.

assess themes of achievement, affiliation, and power. For example, NAch is assessed by the number of times competition with a standard of excellence is mentioned. Even though McClelland developed a number of standard scoring systems, the scoring is still subjective, based mainly on the scorer's interpretations. This has made psychologists cautious about accepting the assessments, although more recent research using meta-analytic procedures has been more supportive (Spangler, 1992).

McClelland later examined the effect on the immune system of stress, the need for power, and the need to affiliate. He and his associates suggested that low stress and a strong need to affiliate have a positive effect on the immune system (Jemmott, Hellman, & McClelland, 1990).

Overall, the lack of clear research support for all the need theories has led to the development of other theories of motivation. Some of these theories relate motivation specifically to the work environment, the subject of the next section.

Job Design Theories

The common element in job design theories of motivation is arranging work in ways that will produce the best performance instead of satisfying deficiencies, as need theories suggest. Two important job design theories of motivation are Herzberg's two-factor theory and Hackman and Oldham's jobs characteristics theory.

Herzberg's Two-Factor Theory

Frederick Herzberg developed his **two-factor theory** as a result of a controversial study done by Herzberg, Mausner, Peterson, and Capwell (1957). Previous studies (Brayfield & Crockett, 1955) had shown no relationship between job satisfaction and work performance, but Herzberg's study found definite relationships between workers' attitudes and behaviors. His basic assumption was that satisfying employees' motivational needs causes high job satisfaction and performance. He believed that other studies had not found a relationship because of their assumption that job satisfaction (motivation) and job dissatisfaction are two ends of a continuum, when they are actually separate concepts.

Two-factor theory A theory of motivation that states that the working conditions leading to work dissatisfaction and work motivation are separate and different.

According to Herzberg, dissatisfaction is caused by the absence of what he called **hygiene factors,** which relate to the work environment and include supervision, interpersonal relations, physical working conditions, salary, company policy and administration, job benefits, and job security. If these factors are not satisfied, employees will report high levels of job dissatisfaction; if they are satisfied, employees will report no serious unhappiness at work.

Hygiene factors Elements in the work environment that cause job dissatisfaction if they are not present.

To reach high levels of job satisfaction, motivator factors also must be present. **Motivator factors,** which relate to the content of the work itself and the outcomes of that work, include achievement, recognition, the work itself, responsibility, and advancement. If you work as a transplant surgeon, you probably

Motivator factors Elements in the work environment that lead to job satisfaction if they are present.

Fundamental attribution error The belief that the behavior of others is caused mainly by personal factors and only slightly affected by situational factors.

Job characteristics theory A theory of motivation based on the assumption that certain core job elements in the work environment lead to job satisfaction.

Core job characteristics According to Hackman and Oldham, the job elements that are critical for job satisfaction to occur.

are a very motivated worker. Your work is challenging, you have a great deal of personal responsibility for the outcome of surgery, you are able to see dramatic changes for the better in patients, and you have been written about in magazines and professional journals.

Although the two-factor theory has a great deal of appeal on the surface, it has been suggested that it actually is an example of the **fundamental attribution error.** This concept states that people underestimate the importance of situational factors in explaining others' behavior and exaggerate the importance of personal factors in explaining the behavior of others (Ross, 1977). To develop his theory, Herzberg used interviews that asked workers to describe good and bad times at work and the events that caused those times (Herzberg, Mausner, & Snyderman, 1959). Several researchers have suggested that Herzberg's two factors only provide evidence of employees making fundamental attribution errors (Hinrichs & Mischkind, 1967; King, 1970) and do not demonstrate the existence of two distinct motivational factors. Other researchers have found that a number of motivator factors and hygiene factors seem to shift from one category to another, depending on the group of workers being studied (Dunnette, Campbell, & Hakel, 1967; Khojasteh, 1993). Despite criticisms of this theory, most I/O psychologists view Herzberg's major contribution as the development of job enrichment programs, which add motivator factors to the work environment by giving workers additional responsibilities. Job enrichment, which is discussed later in this chapter, is also part of the jobs characteristics theory.

Hackman and Oldham's Job Characteristics Theory

The **job characteristics theory,** developed by Richard Hackman and Gary Oldham, states that certain core job elements in the work environment lead to job motivation and satisfaction. Like Herzberg, these researchers agree that job enrichment usually leads to greater motivation and satisfaction (Hackman & Oldham, 1976).

Hackman and Oldham developed a questionnaire called the *Job Diagnostic Survey* (JDS) to assess which parts of a job influence satisfaction. Instead of Herzberg's two factors they identified five factors, each part of a continuum, that are critical to job satisfaction. These critical factors, called the **core job characteristics,** are

1. *Skill variety.* At the high end of the continuum skill variety means that workers are able to use a number of skills and abilities to perform their jobs. At the low end of the continuum, workers are able to use only a few of their skills in doing their jobs.

2. *Task identity.* At the high end of the continuum a worker is able to complete an entire product or a meaningful unit of work, such as bicycle. At

the low end a worker completes only a small part of the product, such as adding two screws to the dashboard on a car moving down the assembly line.

3. *Task significance.* At the high end of the continuum the worker's job has a critical impact on the lives of others, as in the case of a person who matches bone marrow donors with those who receive the bone marrow. At the low end the worker's job has little or no effect on other people, as in the case of a greeter who offers shopping carts to customers as they enter a store.

4. *Autonomy.* The high end of this characteristics is represented by an independent computer consultant who has total independence in planning, scheduling, and doing her work. The low end is represented by an assembly line worker who has no independence in terms of when, where, or how he does his work.

5. *Feedback.* At the highest end of the continuum employees get almost constant reports about how they are doing on the job, as in the case of an employee who works at a computer-monitored workstation where each hour a graph appears on the screen showing a comparison of each hour of performance levels for the last week. At the low end of the continuum employees get infrequent information about job performance, as in the case of a public aid caseworker who rarely sees the same clients twice and seldom hears about clients who have gotten off welfare.

In general, this theory suggests that workers like their jobs, are highly motivated, and have excellent job attendance and performance ratings when the work is interesting and meaningful and provides a great deal of responsibility for and information about how the work is going. This is diagrammed in Figure 6.3, which shows how the core job characteristics affect motivated behavior.

Hackman and Oldham (1976) used these core job characteristics to develop a formula to predict how motivating a particular job would be. The motivating potential score (MPS) uses the following formula:

$$MPS = \frac{(\text{skill variety} + \text{task identity} + \text{task significance}) \times \text{autonomy} \times \text{feedback}}{3}$$

Any high or low score in the skill variety, task identity, or task significance group can balance any other high or low score in this group. However, if the group score or the autonomy or feedback score is zero, there is no motivation in the job (because $0 \times 0 \times 0 = 0$). Hackman and Oldham suggested using this formula to motivate workers by finding ways to increase the value of the job characteristics. For example, a supervisor might delegate some decisions to subordinates, giving the subordinates greater responsibility and enhancing the meaningfulness of

Figure 6.3
Job characteristics model.

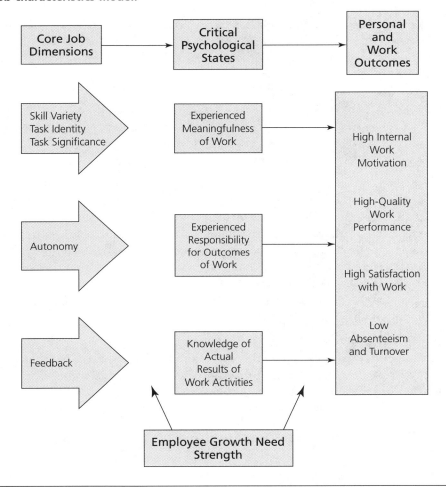

From J. R. Hackman & G. R. Oldham. (1976). Motivation through the design of work: Test of theory. *Organizational Behavior and Human Performance, 16,* 250–279.

their work. Cantanzaro (1997) suggested that this model could be used to change college psychology classes to find ways to increase each of the job characteristics to make students more motivated.

Research by Hackman and Oldham (1976) identified three additional factors that can moderate the motivated behavior predicted by their model:

growth-need strength, knowledge and skill, and satisfaction with the job context. **Growth-need strength** is the desire for personal growth and challenge on the job. Workers who want jobs with more growth opportunities are high in growth-need strength, while those who do not want growth opportunities are low in growth-need strength. Raising the values of all the core job characteristics will not raise the motivation of employees who are low in growth-need strength. Knowledge and skill factors refer to a worker's basic ability to do the job. A worker low in skill and knowledge will not feel more motivated by more responsibility or a greater number of tasks. This employee may have lower motivation because of frustration from the work.

Satisfaction with the job context factors is similar to Herzberg's hygiene factors. It includes satisfaction with pay, supervisors, peers, and the physical conditions of work. Hackman and Oldham agree with Herzberg's conclusion that a lack of satisfaction with these job context factors lowers motivation because workers focus their time and effort on these needs rather than on opportunities for growth and development.

Support for the job characteristics theory is mixed. The results of a meta-analysis of over two hundred studies (Fried & Ferris, 1987) supported some parts of the model but not others. Among the five core job characteristics, task identity showed the strongest relationship to work performance. Other studies have shown similarly mixed results (Johns, Xie, & Fang, 1992; Tiegs, Tetrick, & Fried, 1992).

Several researchers have suggested that moderator factors do not provide useful information because they restate the obvious. Saying that workers high in growth-need strength prefer jobs that provide opportunities for personal development and challenges is like saying that workers high in blue-color preference would rather work in blue-colored rooms. It is not surprising that research found that growth-need strength operates in the way Hackman and Oldham suggested (Fried & Ferris, 1987; Graen, Scandura, & Graen, 1986). Therefore, the most important finding of job characteristics theory may be that work motivation has more variables and components than early researchers believed. In addition, the theory has enhanced the understanding of job enrichment, which is discussed later in this chapter.

Cognitive Theories

Cognitive theories of motivation focus on the mental activities and perceptions by which people determine their motivation at work. These theories are based on a cognitive learning model that suggests that as people go through life, they process experiences into expectations about what will happen in certain types of situations. As people learn, they develop thoughts and feelings about the outcomes of certain behaviors. For example, most people develop

Growth-need strength
The desire for personal growth and challenge on the job.

Cognitive theories of motivation Motivational theories that focus on the thought processes and perceptions of employees.

Equity theory
A motivational theory based on the assumption that people want a fair return for the skills, experience, and other things they bring to the job when they compare themselves with others.

Inequity An unfair relationship between inputs and outcomes when an employee compares herself or himself to other employees.

beliefs about the fairness of the pay they receive. If people believe they are underpaid, they may quit or decrease their work output to match their beliefs about the pay scale. Three cognitively based theories of work motivation are: equity theory, valence-instrumentality-expectancy theory, and goal-setting theory.

Adams's Equity Theory

Equity theory, developed by Adams (1965), assumes that people want a fair return, in comparison with others, for the skills, experience, and other elements they bring to their jobs. When a person takes a job, she brings with her certain *inputs,* such as education, experience, and skills. People also expect certain *outcomes* from the job, such as pay, status, and benefits. According to Adams, workers want, in comparison with others, equity or fairness between the inputs and outcomes of their jobs.

The subjective perception of fairness by an employee, not objective reality, determines equity. For example, a highly paid surgeon may weigh his lengthy education and training against the earnings of top surgeons in the field. If he is paid about the same as the others, he may perceive that he has achieved equity between inputs and outcomes. Although nonsurgeons may feel that the surgeon's earnings are excessive, the balance of inputs and outcomes is perceived as fair by the surgeon. This is why equity theory is considered a cognitive theory of work motivation.

Workers who have achieved equity are unlikely to change anything about the work situation. When the work situation changes and is no longer considered fair, **inequity** is the term that describes a worker's perception. For example, if the surgeon developed a new procedure in his field that no one else could do, he might charge more for that surgery or ask for a larger office at the hospital to restore his feelings of equity.

Underpayment and overpayment are the two types of inequity, according to Adams. In the *underpayment* condition the worker perceives that her input is greater than the outcomes, compared with the outcomes others are receiving. In the *overpayment* condition the worker perceives that his input is less than the outcomes, compared with the outcomes others are receiving. In either condition Adams predicts that the discomfort caused by the inequity will cause the worker to restore equity by changing personal behavior in one of the following six ways:

1. *Change inputs.* Using this approach, the employee will work harder (overpayment) or do less work (underpayment) to make the inputs match the perceived outcomes others are receiving.

2. *Change outcomes.* Although an employee is unlikely to ask for less pay to restore equity, she may refuse a job title she feels she does not deserve.

3. *Leave the situation.* This is a more drastic resolution because it requires the employee to quit the job or transfer to a different area or type of work. This solution usually results from a very large inequity that has continued for some time.

4. *Change behavior toward comparable workers.* This means restoring equity by doing something with regard to the person with whom the worker compares herself. For example, the worker may encourage her colleagues to insist on more work being assigned to a team member who is not working very hard but is getting the same pay.

5. *Distort the situation.* In this approach the worker may, for example, make himself believe that his work is more valuable than the work of an employee who is receiving less money.

6. *Change the comparison.* This method involves changing the person to whom the worker is comparing herself. If a worker has been comparing herself to workers who have longer job tenure, she may decide to compare herself instead to workers who have been on the job as long as she has.

Other researchers have found that while many employees react in the ways Adams predicts, some employees react in other ways. Huseman, Hatfield, and Miles (1987) suggest that employees who behave in the ways Adams suggests are **equity sensitive.** Those workers try to maintain or restore equity in work situations. **Benevolents** are workers who prefer situations in which they get fewer outcomes from putting in greater effort than others do, in comparison. **Entitleds** are people who look for and want situations in which they get greater outcomes and give less effort than is the case among others with whom they can be compared.

Personality characteristics of employees determine which of these ways they will react. As might be expected, many more people feel entitled than feel benevolent. These people have a much higher threshold for overpayment inequity than for underpayment inequity (Sweeney, 1990). While entitleds and benevolents do not behave in ways that equity theory would predict, Huseman, Hatfiled, and Miles (1985) found that they do behave in the way a different motivation theory, expectancy theory (discussed in the next section) would predict. This research indicated that different motivation theories are effective with different groups and in different situations.

Early research on equity theory involving laboratory situations with pay as the outcome (Adams & Rosenbaum, 1962; Greenberg, 1982) was generally supportive. Later field studies also seemed to confirm most parts of this theory, although underpayment appeared to produce quicker and stronger changes than did overpayment. For example, Greenberg (1990) used equity theory to explain employee theft behavior after a company ordered a temporary pay cut at two manufacturing

Equity sensitive Refers to an employee who responds to inequity situations by trying to restore equity.

Benevolents Employees who believe they deserve unequally low returns from a job.

Entitleds Employees who believe they deserve unequally high returns from a job.

plants. The employees in one plant were given a complete and thorough explanation of the reasons for the pay cut, while those in the second plant were told only that the cut was necessary. The workers in the third plant received no pay cut and no explanation. During the period of the pay cut, the theft rate at the second plant was almost three times higher than that at the other plants. When pay was restored, the theft rate returned to the same level as at the other plants. Equity theory suggests that the employees were stealing as a way of increasing their outcomes in order to restore equity. The turnover rate in the plant that received the pay cut with no explanation also was much greater during the pay-cut period, demonstrating another of the possible reactions to pay inequity. Giving an explanation for the pay cuts appeared to prevent the theft and turnover increases.

Another study compared the performance of baseball players who completed salary arbitration in which player and team both gave final salary offers to an arbitrator (Bretz & Thomas, 1992). The arbitrator's choice between the two offers was significantly related to a player's performance before the arbitration period. If a player's performance had been very good, his offer was chosen more often. When a player's offer was not chosen in arbitration, he reacted to the perceived inequity with lower performance. He was also more likely to leave baseball or change teams, two other reactions to perceived inequity. This study demonstrates a clear comparison group—other baseball players—which is often not the case in other work settings.

■ The performance levels of professional baseball players have shown support for the equity theory of motivation.

Wendell Metzen/Index Stock

Overall, equity theory has contributed a number of improvements in the study of work motivation, such as recognizing that an employee's motivation exists as part of the social system of that employee as he compares himself with others (Summers & DeNisi, 1990). The influence of individual differences in personality in moderating equity theory has increased its predictive value (King, Miles, & Day, 1993). The most successful research involves predicting and explaining underpayment inequity. There generally has been less success in explaining and predicting behavior that results from overpayment inequity, although there seems to be support for the kinds of behavior changes resulting from overpayment that Adams would predict (Greenberg, 1988).

Equity theory also has been important in regard to the issue of equal pay for equal work in actual work settings. Greenberg (1988) and other researchers also have looked at status rather than pay as an outcome, taking the equal pay issue beyond the numbers on a paycheck.

Vroom's Valence-Instrumentality-Expectancy Theory

Valence-instrumentality-expectancy (VIE) theory explains that job behavior results from a combination of the factors of valence, expectancy, and instrumentality. For the last few decades this has been one of the most popular theories in I/O psychology. Originally described by Vroom (1964), it has been elaborated by several others, including Porter and Lawler (1968). Both equity theory and VIE theory are cognitive theories that assume that people can evaluate themselves and situations rationally and base their actions on those rational evaluations.

The formula used in VIE theory to predict employee work behavior has five major components. The first one is **job outcome,** the positive or negative results of job behaviors. Positive outcomes include getting paid and being promoted. Negative job outcomes include getting demoted and being fired. The second component is **valence,** an expression of the subjective value an employee attaches to a specific job outcome. Valence usually is rated on a scale of +10 to −10 based on the perceptions of the employee. This may be different for each employee in a department or team. It also differs for each possible job outcome.

The third component is **instrumentality,** the subjective value that indicates how much an employee believes that his job performance will influence a particular job outcome and how likely it is that he will obtain that outcome. Instrumentality uses a probability value (as discussed in Chapter 2 and the statistical appendix), but that value represents only the employee's perception; it is not an objective measure. An instrumentality value of 1.0 means that the employee believes the job outcome is 100 percent related to performance on the job and that the employee has the knowledge, skills, and abilities to do the job. A value of 0 indicates that the employee believes the job

Valence-instrumentality-expectancy (VIE) theory A motivational theory based on the relationship among valence, instrumentality, and expectancy, in regard to job behaviors.

Job outcome The results of job behaviors, such as pay or being fired.

Valence The subjective value an employee attaches to a particular job outcome.

Instrumentality The degree to which an employee believes that his or her performance on the job will influence a particular job outcome.

Expectancy The perception of an employee of how much his or her personal effort will influence his or her job performance and lead to certain outcomes.

performance has no relation to the job outcome and he is unable to do anything to obtain that outcome.

The fourth component is **expectancy,** the employee's perception of how much personal effort will influence her job performance and lead to a certain job outcome. This concept is unique to VIE theory. It is measured on a subjective probability scale of 0 to 1.0. A score of 0 means that the employee perceives no relationship between effort and job outcome. A score of 1.0 means that the employee is certain that the effort will result in the desired outcome.

The fifth component in VIE theory is *force,* the result of combining valence, instrumentality, and expectancy factors to predict the motivated behavior of an employee in performing a particular job behavior. Force is expressed as the result of a mathematical formula that combines values for valence, instrumentality, and expectancy.

The use of the VIE formula can be shown in predicting the work behavior of a grocery store stocker. The stocker may attach a valence of +9 to the job outcome of becoming the head of the produce department, but a valence of −3 to the job outcome of longer work hours associated with the promotion to department head. If the stocker found out that promotions are based only on performance evaluation scores, he probably would rate the instrumentality high because he consistently received high evaluation scores. If he knew that the grocery chain promoted to the department head job only employees who were graduates of a two-year college with good performance evaluation scores, he might perceive a high expectancy value if he had almost completed his degree in addition to having good evaluation scores. Using the VIE theory, it would be predicted that the grocery store stocker would be motivated to become the produce department head and would go after that job outcome actively.

Although there has been a great deal of research on various parts of this theory, few managers apply the theory to motivate employees. The formula that makes the theory measurable makes it less understandable to managers on the job. Although formulas suggest objective measurement, the VIE theory relies on subjective perceptions as the basis for many of the components in its formula. The problem of measurement of valence, instrumentality, and expectancy is mentioned by a number of researchers (Ilgen, Nebekr, & Pritchard, 1981; Schmidt, 1973; Wanous, Keon, & Latack, 1983).

Although ratings seem fairly stable for individuals, they are based on the subjective perception of each person. One study showed distinctive differences between men and women in job outcome preferences and the valence, instrumentality, and expectancy ratings related to those outcomes (Hollenbeck, Ilgen, Ostroff, & Vancouver, 1987). Expectancy theory typically is better at predicting the behavior of an individual making a choice between two courses of action than it is at predicting the behavior of groups or of individuals compared with the rest of the group (Kennedy, Fossum, & White, 1983; Muchinsky, 1977). While some psychologists have criticized this problem (Beach & Mitchell, 1990; Lord & Maher, 1990), other researchers (Porter & Lawler, 1968) have suggested that the theory needs to be even more complex to provide a complete motivational picture. The most consistent research results generally involve explaining and predicting the behavior of individuals rather than that of groups (Wanous, Keon, & Latack, 1983).

VIE theory works well only if people behave and make decisions in rational ways. When one researcher attempted to use expectancy theory to predict the effort college students would put into their courses, he found that the predictive value ranged from almost nothing to very high (Muchinsky, 1977). He believed that the extremely large variations in predictive value were caused by the extremely large variations in rationally based behavior among the students. What is rational in one theory is not always rational in another theory, however. Expectancy theory does a better job of explaining the behavior of the entitleds and benevolents of equity theory than equity theory does (Huseman, Hatfield, & Miles, 1985).

Expectancy theory continues to be one of the most popular theories of work motivation (Lee & Earley, 1992). It has been applied to a wide variety of settings, from predicting police productivity in enforcement of laws against driving under the influence of alcohol (DUI) (Mastrofski, Ritti, & Snipes, 1994), to predicting performance in complex computer projects (Watson & Behnke, 1991), to predicting the occupational choices of college students (Brooks & Betz, 1990). Although research tests may not provide complete support for expectancy theory, many provide at least partial support. In a meta-analysis of previous studies, Van Erde and Thierry (1996) found that different operational definitions and measurement techniques for each of the VIE components led to lower correlations than other researchers had found, although they found a positive correlation between the VIE model and a number of work-related criteria. Among the work applications suggested by this theory are making sure employees understand their work goals and how their performance will lead to certain rewards. Clarity of goals and the performance-reward relationship form the basis for the third cognitive theory of motivation, discussed in the following section.

Locke and Latham's Goal-Setting Theory
Goal-setting theory is based on the assumption that conscious, difficult, specific goals lead to increased job performance. One of the most popular work motivation theories among I/O psychologists (Lee & Earley, 1992), this theory is most directly attributed to the work of Locke (1968) and Locke and Latham (1984) over a thirty-year period. It is similar to expectancy and equity theory because it assumes that workers are rational and behave in logical ways.

Goal-setting theory
A theory of motivation based on the assumption that conscious, difficult, specific goals lead to increased job performance.

According to Locke and Latham (1990a), the goals that are best for increasing performance share five characteristics:

1. Difficult goals lead to the best performance (Wood, Mento, & Locke, 1987). Locke and Latham (1990b) reported that 91 percent of the studies they reviewed showed a positive relationship between goal difficulty and higher performance.

2. Specific difficult goals lead to better performance than do no goals or vague goals, such as "do your best." Meta-analyses by Wood, Mento, and Locke (1987) and Guzzo, Jette, and Katzell (1985) confirmed this in laboratory and field settings.

3. High levels of commitment to goals increase performance (Erez & Zidon, 1984; Wofford, Goodwin, & Premack, 1992; Wright, 1989) regardless of whether the goals are assigned or developed with worker participation (Locke & Latham, 1990a). Although a meta-analytic study by Donovan and Rodosevich (1998) confirmed the relationship between goal commitment and performance, this study also found that the relationship was weaker than originally believed.

4. To influence performance, workers must have specific feedback about the results of goal accomplishment (Locke & Latham, 1990a; Wilk & Redmon, 1998). The feedback can come from the supervisor, the worker, or the job.

5. Goal setting may be harmful if goals are set for the wrong reason or if there is goal conflict (Locke, 1996).

Goal setting has been used with speed skaters preparing for competition (Wanlin, Hrycaiko, Martin, & Mahon, 1997). For example, if a skater were aware of the world record in her event, she and her coach could decide to set her goal as coming within two seconds of that record at least four times before she competed in the Olympics. The skater's long hours of practice and training would show her commitment to the goal. She would receive feedback from the timing clock and the coach. The researchers in this study found a measurable increase in performance in both practice and competition.

When Locke and Latham (1990a) reviewed research on goal-setting theory, they concluded that people and situations are often more complicated than the original assumptions suggested. They found that a number of moderator variables can influence the success of this model in motivating worker behavior. The moderators they found to have the greatest influence on performance in goal-setting theory include the following:

- *Ability.* High- and low-ability workers improve their performance when difficult goals are set, but as the goals come closer to being impossibly high, high-ability workers continue to improve longer than do low-ability workers. Supervisors need an awareness of the ability levels of their employees to get the greatest motivational benefit from goal setting.

■ Swimmers preparing for Olympic competition illustrate Locke and Latham's goal-setting theory, like the skaters discussed in the text.

■ *Personality variables.* Employees with a high need to achieve perform best when they are assigned goals and receive feedback on their progress toward those goals. Employees with a low need to achieve do best when they participate in the goal-setting process. High self-esteem also appears to contribute to the successful attainment of goals (Von Bergen, Soper, & Rosenthal, 1996).

■ *Task complexity.* When tasks are simple, such as putting together items on an assembly line, goal-setting productivity gains are increased. When tasks are more complex, such as planning the human resource needs for an organization for the next five years, the goal-setting productivity gains are decreased.

■ *Situational factors.* When the job situation (such as a lack of information or materials) makes it more difficult for employees to complete a task, there is a decreased link between goal setting and performance.

■ *Internal versus external control.* Workers who believe their performance is determined by fate or the way others behave are **externally focused.** Workers who believe their performance is caused mainly by the choices they themselves make are **internally focused.** Internally focused workers typically perform better in goal-setting conditions because they believe more strongly in their ability to control the outcome of the situation. Commitment to the goal was also found to be higher in internally focused workers (Hollenbeck, Williams, & Klein, 1989).

Externally focused Refers to employees who believe that most work outcomes are caused by forces outside themselves.

Internally focused Refers to employees who believe that most work outcomes are caused by personal effort from inside themselves.

Self-efficacy An employee's perception of the chance that she or he is able to produce the behaviors that lead to certain job outcomes.

Most of these moderators can be combined in the concept of **self-efficacy,** a worker's evaluation of the likelihood of being able to perform the behaviors that will lead to a desired result (Bandura, 1986). The evaluation is based on past performance, adaptability, ability, use of resources, planning skills, and other personal factors. Research shows that high scores on self-efficacy measures typically are related to high levels of performance in goal-setting situations (Boyce & Bingham, 1997; Locke, Frederick, Lee, & Bobko, 1984; Wood & Locke, 1987).

Research evidence for goal-setting theory and its components is very strong. This theory has so much commonsense appeal that some critics have suggested it is not really a theory but a description of what employees, especially those in high-level positions, have always done. Two research studies contradict these critics. The first study showed that when scientists and engineers in a research and development center were assigned to either a control group or a group that had specific, difficult goals, the goal-setting group showed a significant increase in performance. That increase occurred even though the control group was aware of what was happening in the goal-setting group (Latham, Mitchell, & Dossett, 1978).

The second piece of research, one of the classic studies in goal-setting research (Latham & Baldes, 1975), showed that goal setting is not merely an obvious part of the work environment. This study looked at drivers of logging trucks who were only partially loading their trucks when they could have added almost 40 percent more to their loads and still have met the weight limits. Telling the workers to increase their loads without making the trucks overweight did not change their loading behaviors. Under the union contract the company could not introduce a pay incentive system to increase truckloads; instead, management approached the union with a goal-setting plan that would neither reward better performance nor punish poor performance. The goal for the truckers was set to make each load 90 percent of the maximum weight allowed. Performance improved within a week. Within a month the company increased its profits. One of the most common applications of goal setting, management by objectives (MBO) (see Chapter 10), has been used for years to increase employees' performance. The case study "Psychology at Work" shows how Federal Express applied goal setting to extend the benefits it had begun by using MBO.

[Case Study] DELIVERING PSYCHOLOGY AT WORK

The Federal Express Corporation wanted to expand the traditional management by objectives (MBO) goal-setting process that has supervisors write performance goals for subordinates after receiving input from the subordinates. The company developed what they called the 360-Degree Goal-Setting Program. Performance goals are written for each employee and the entire human resources department after input has been received from all internal customers (supervisors, top management, subordinates, coworkers, and representatives from other departments who interact with the employees) and external customers (clients, suppliers, community officials, and consultants). The benefit of using both internal and external customers is a more complete understanding of the expectations of employees and customers. Among the goals Federal Express developed for the human resources department were

- a twenty-four-hour response to e-mail and phone messages,
- a two-hour response time to emergency calls,
- a bimonthly meeting with employees at the workplace, and
- semiannual training sessions on topical subjects.

Federal Express found that the goal-setting program required more time to administer than did other programs it had used. This included training time for employees and managers. The advantages were precise measurement of and feedback on performance goals; greater accountability for employees' performance; and clear expectations for employees, managers, and supervisors.

Federal Express has been so pleased with the results of the pilot study of the human resources department that it has expanded the goal-setting program to other parts of the organization.

From J. F. Milliman, R. A. Zawacki, B. Schultz, S. Wiggins, & C. A. Norman. (1995). Customer service drives 360-degree goal setting. *Personnel Journal, 74,* 136–138.

One of the more recent applications of goal-setting theory is the **high performance cycle,** a circular description of how rewards for high levels of performance become an incentive for workers to maintain those levels. Locke and Latham (1990a, p. 201) stated that "all individuals learn at an early age that they perform better on a task if they pay attention to it, exert effort on it, and persist at it over time than if they do not." The process of the high performance cycle is shown in Figure 6.4. The relationship that the high performance cycle shows between motivation and job satisfaction is strong. This is very different from Herzberg's belief that job satisfiers and job motivators are separate factors.

Research evidence appears to support this hypothesis that rewards are the result of high performance levels and not the cause of those performance levels (Earley & Lituchy, 1991; Frayne & Latham, 1987; Latham & Frayne, 1989). It is likely that the high degree of interest in this concept and in goal-setting theory in general will generate many more studies. Part of the popularity of this theory comes from its wide applicability to different situations, from lacrosse teams, to university admissions offices, to sales representatives, to accident reduction programs.

High performance cycle
The application of a goal-setting theory that deals with continued high levels of motivated behavior and job satisfaction.

Figure 6.4

Locke and Latham's high-performance cycle.

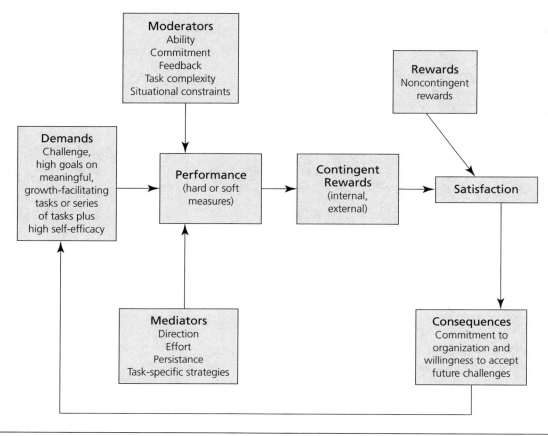

From E. A. Locke, & G. P. Latham. (1990a). *A theory of goal setting and task performance.* Englewood Cliffs, NJ: Prentice-Hall, p. 253.

Behavioral theories of motivation Explanations of motivated behavior that are based on the principles of operant conditioning.

Reinforcement theory A motivational theory that assumes that the occurrence of a behavior is strengthened or weakened by the reinforcers or punishments that follow it.

Behavioral Theories

Behavioral theories of motivation are based mainly on the principles of operant conditioning and assume that the positive or negative consequences of behaviors determine whether a behavior will be repeated or stopped (see Chapter 11). While cognitive theories focus on mental processes, behavioral theories focus only on directly observable and measurable behaviors.

Reinforcement Theory

One application of behavioral theories of motivation is **reinforcement theory,** which assumes that motivated behavior is caused by the consequences that follow a behavior. The most effective consequences are those that follow a behavior directly. *Reinforcers* are consequences that increase the occurrence of the behavior they follow. **Positive reinforcers** are consequences that increase a behavior when the employee gets something good, such as extra pay, a better office, or new tools. **Negative reinforcers** are consequences that increase a behavior when the employee avoids or escapes something bad, such as having to stay late to finish a project without extra pay. Negative and positive reinforcers strengthen behavior because the end result is something good or rewarding.

Any time a particular behavior increases, it is being reinforced even if the behavior is not desirable. One summer during college I worked at a large candy manufacturing company covering boxes of candy bars. It was boring work. One evening, when I got a small paper cut, I was removed from the assembly line to avoid getting blood on the candy bars and missed forty-five minutes of work. Other workers quickly realized that this was a way to get paid for doing nothing, which was very reinforcing. They began to get more and more paper cuts. The line leader stopped the paper cut frenzy by handing out bandages and rubber gloves rather than removing workers from the assembly line. She used *extinction*—the removal of reinforcement—to decrease our paper cut behavior. *Punishment*—the application of unpleasant consequences for certain behaviors—also can decrease the occurrence of a behavior. If the candy bar workers had been given a warning that led to disciplinary action for each paper cut, that punishment probably would have decreased their paper cut behavior.

In most cases it is better to use reinforcers rather than punishment, because punishment often leaves angry feelings even if used correctly. At best, punishment only gets an employee to stop doing a certain behavior. Stopping unsafe work behaviors is often an appropriate use of punishment, but it does not tell employees what to do in place of the unsafe behavior.

Schedules of reinforcement—the pattern of how often reinforcers are given after a desired behavior—are used to increase the occurrence of desired behaviors. If a behavior is reinforced every time it occurs, this is called *continuous reinforcement*. If reinforcement is given only some of the time after a behavior occurs, this is called *intermittent reinforcement*. The four types of intermittent reinforcement schedules are shown in Table 6.1, which indicates that many different reinforcers can be used to increase behavior. Money is a common reinforcer, but praise, attention, and feedback also can be effective if they are meaningful to the employee. The key to successful reinforcement of behavior is that the employee must value the reinforcer.

One group of researchers has supported the position that **extrinsic reinforcers** such as money and praise have less value than do **intrinsic reinforcers** such as self-satisfaction and accomplishment, which are personally satisfying and challenging for the employee. These researchers feel that extrinsic reinforcers may make intrinsic reinforcers less valuable because work is no longer done for the self-satisfaction

Positive reinforcer
A behavioral consequence that leads to the increased occurrence of a behavior because the person has received something good.

Negative reinforcer
A behavioral consequence that leads to the increased occurrence of a behavior because the person has avoided or escaped something bad.

Extrinsic reinforcers
External rewards, such as praise and money.

Intrinsic reinforcers
Rewards that are personally satisfying, such as self-satisfaction.

Table 6.1

SCHEDULES OF INTERMITTENT REINFORCEMENT

Schedule	Definition	Example
Fixed ratio reinforcement	Reinforcement given after a specific number of responses	Salesperson who receives a $100 commission for every ten television sets sold
Fixed interval reinforcement	Reinforcement given for the first correct response after a specific amount of time	Supervisor observes employee for two minutes and verbally praises employee for first correctly done behavior after the two-minute time period
Variable ratio reinforcement	Reinforcement based on a certain average number of responses	Slot machines programmed to pay off on an average of one time per one hundred lever pulls
Variable interval reinforcement	Reinforcement given after an average time interval	Supervisor averages four times a day verbally rewarding an employee for good work during a one-week period

it provides but only for an external reward, such as money. If the extrinsic reinforcer is then taken away, performance will decrease (Deci, 1975).

Research tests of the use of intrinsic reinforcers have provided information about the best use of both types of reinforcers. In boring, repetitive tasks, extrinsic reinforcers seemed to be more effective. When the tasks were challenging and gave workers opportunities to assess their competence through positive feedback, intrinsic reinforcers appeared to be very effective. Many situations have both intrinsic and extrinsic reinforcers (Campbell & Pritchard, 1976), and it may be difficult to know which reinforcer is operating. The effective use of reinforcers depends on both the person and the situation.

Organizational and Behavior Modification

When reinforcement theory and learning principles are used to change behavior throughout an organization, the result is organizational behavior modification. **Organizational behavior modification** is the systematic application of learning principles in order to change behavior in an entire organization or a large group within the organization. The focus here is on large-scale change rather than looking at a single individual. With its emphasis on directly measurable behavior, organizational behavior modification is preferred by many supervisors because of its clear, bottom line results.

Organizational behavior modification
The application of reinforcement theory on a companywide basis.

If a group of clerical workers typing form letters are not doing as many letters as management believes they could do, this system may be used to motivate them. After current levels of performance are recorded, the reinforcement behaviors and rewards are introduced. The employees may be given a bonus for letters beyond a certain required level per day. After they do a certain number of form letters, they may be allowed to work on a more creative typing project for a certain period. If the number of form letters completed increases only when the reinforcement program is used, it is likely that the behavior modification system has produced the improved behavior.

Most research confirms the effectiveness of organizational behavior modification (Hammer & Hammer, 1976). Unions and employees, however, often express concern that reinforcement systems are manipulative and treat employees like trained animals rather than human beings. Another concern is whether these systems result merely in a change in performance without a basic change in motivation.

Emerging Theories

None of the current theories of motivation seem to be totally comprehensive, but they provide important insights and lay the foundation for future theories. The common elements of existing theories indicate important areas for future research. For example, several theories consider the role of pay as a motivator, but from different perspectives. Herzberg's two-factor theory sees fair pay as eliminating dissatisfaction, similar to the emphasis in Adams's equity theory. Reinforcement theory views good pay as motivating performance. McClelland's need to achieve theory and Locke and Latham's goal-setting theory see pay as an extrinsic motivator that interferes with intrinsic motivation; these two theories also view setting and reaching goals as major components of motivation. Although Maslow's hierarchy of needs and McClellland's need to achieve theory are need-based, workers obviously apply some cognitive processing and rational thinking to meet their needs—indicating another area of overlap among theories. Although newer theories may be more complex, one psychologist (Kanfer, 1994) has suggested that in the coming years research on motivation will focus on three major topics: motivation and cognitive abilities, motivation in specific social situations, and typical versus maximum performance.

Emerging theories may be more complicated than the current theories, but they may clarify the connections between motivation and performance and motivation and job satisfaction. The motivation theories examined in this chapter show that job satisfaction leads to higher levels of motivation and performance (Herzberg, Mausner, Peterson, & Capwell, 1957) and that higher levels of motivation and performance lead to higher levels of job satisfaction (high performance cycle). The next section looks in more detail at the issue of job satisfaction in relation to motivation and performance.

JOB SATISFACTION

Most people relate job satisfaction to happiness on the job. This is close to the commonly accepted definition of **job satisfaction** as the level and direction of a worker's emotion and affect toward a job and a job situation (Korman, Greenhaus, & Baden, 1977). High levels of job satisfaction have been viewed as desirable from the time of the Hawthorne Studies, which led to the human relations movement in I/O psychology (see Chapter 1). From the human relations viewpoint, motivation is the result of increasing happiness on the job. Although later research showed that the relationship between motivation and job satisfaction is not that simple, the linkage between them has led to increased attention to job satisfaction as an important component in improving motivation.

While high levels of job satisfaction have been linked to positive outcomes, such as increased performance, low levels of job satisfaction have been linked to a variety of negative outcomes. Locke and Latham (1990a) identified six categories of employees' responses to job dissatisfaction: (1) job avoidance (quitting); (2) work avoidance; (3) psychological defenses, such as drug abuse; (4) constructive protest, such as complaining; (5) defiance, such as refusing to do what is asked; and (6) aggression, such as theft or assault. Among these categories, job avoidance, which is discussed later in this chapter, shows the strongest relationship to job satisfaction. The obvious relationship between these responses and lower organizational productivity and performance is one reason why employers are so interested in improving job satisfaction.

Job Outcomes

As is shown in Figure 6.5, job satisfaction is related to the job outcomes of performance, turnover, absenteeism, organizational commitment, and job involvement, which influence bottom line measures of organizational success. The personal factors related to job satisfaction, including gender, race, personality, and union membership, are discussed later in this chapter.

Job Performance

Although most I/O psychologists agree that job satisfaction is related to job performance, meta-analytic studies have shown only a weak relationship (Iaffaldano & Muchinsky, 1985). One of the most basic questions is whether increased job satisfaction causes increased job performance or vice versa.

For a number of years the popular belief was that increasing job satisfaction would lead to increased performance. Jacobs and Solomon (1977) found research support for the position that higher performance leads to increased job satisfaction when the higher performance is related directly to increased rewards. They

Figure 6.5

Correlates of job satisfaction, showing the two-way relationship
with job satisfaction.

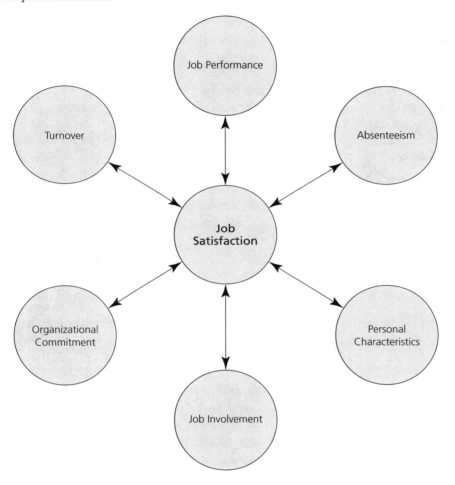

suggested that support for the opposite belief may have been caused by the finding of little or no linkage between performance and rewards. Goal-setting theory
provides further evidence to support Jacobs and Solomon, but the exact nature
of the relationship between job satisfaction and performance is not clear.

Turnover

Workers stay on the job or quit for a variety of reasons. Some of the reasons involve job satisfaction, and some do not. Indicating an intention to quit has been

Voluntary turnover Occurs when an employee leaves an organization by choice.

Involuntary turnover Occurs when an employee leaves an organization against her or his own desires.

Functional turnover A loss of an employee that benefits the organization.

Nonfunctional turnover The loss of an employee the organization wants to keep.

found to be a strong predictor of actually quitting. Studies that use job satisfaction scores to predict quitting at some point in the future (intent to leave) generally have been successful (Crampton & Wagner, 1994; Hellman, 1997; Krausz, Koslowsky, & Eiser, 1998).

Intent to leave may be a clearer link to job satisfaction because it relates to voluntary nonfunctional turnover. **Voluntary turnover** means that an employee chooses to leave an organization in contrast to being fired, which is called **involuntary turnover.** From the employer's point of view, turnover can be functional or nonfunctional. **Functional turnover** means that the organization benefits from the loss of an employee. This is the case when the employee is a poor worker. **Nonfunctional turnover** means that the organization did not want the employee to leave, because losing a desirable employee can be harmful to the organization.

A study by Hollenbeck and Williams (1986) found that slightly over half (53 percent) of job turnovers were actually functional turnovers. In a meta-analytic study relating job satisfaction, organizational commitment, and turnover and intent to leave, Tett and Meyer (1993) found that job satisfaction had the strongest linkage with turnover intent and turnover. Stedham and Mitchell (1996) found a significant relationship between voluntary turnover and job satisfaction in casino employees.

Although it seems logical to assume that the workers who keep talking about leaving are the ones who are the most dissatisfied on the job, that is not always true. One of the strongest factors in determining actual quitting behavior may be economic conditions. If there is not much chance of getting another job, a job without much satisfaction may be better than no job (Carsten & Spector, 1987). An employee who is dissatisfied but stays and a dissatisfied employee who has not quit yet affect other people. Nozar (1992) reports that at Omni Hotels one of the best solutions to unhappy guests was increasing the satisfaction level of the employees who had contact with guests. Gaertner and Nollen (1992) characterized these different types of employees as stayers (high job satisfaction), leavers (high job dissatisfaction), jilteds (lower job satisfaction and lower in-house career opportunities but greater career opportunities outside the company), and locked-ins (lower job satisfaction and few career opportunities inside or outside the company).

Absenteeism

Employees may be absent for a variety of reasons besides job dissatisfaction. This may be part of the reason meta-analytic studies relating job satisfaction and absenteeism have not found strong correlations (Farrell & Stamm, 1988; Hackett, 1989) or have found no correlations (Leigh, 1991). One possibility for these low correlations is that absence causes job dissatisfaction rather than job dissatisfaction causing absence (Tharenou, 1993). If an employee misses work often, he is more likely to receive poor performance appraisals, corrections from his supervisor, and pressure from peers. Those factors could increase his desire to leave the organization. Several researchers have found a relationship between higher absence levels and employees' intent to leave the organization (Krausz, Koslowsky, & Eiser, 1998; Van Yparen, Hagedoorn, & Gaurts, 1996).

At the opposite end, higher satisfaction levels have been found to contribute to decreased absenteeism. Two researchers cited a reduced absence rate among women in an organization after the introduction of casual dress days at work (Yates & Jones, 1998). Organizations often list improving job satisfaction and reducing absenteeism as reasons for adopting causal dress days.

When employees work in groups, the work groups often develop informal norms for the numbers of days of absence that are "deserved" in particular jobs. These norms make up the **absence culture.** If a company allows ten paid sick days a year, the group norm might be that one "deserves" six of those days whether or not one is sick. When Mathieu and Kohler (1990) looked at absence rates for individuals before and after they joined a work group, they found that the amount of time taken off from work after joining the group was closer to the group averages than it was to the previous individual averages.

Organizational Commitment

Organizational commitment is the degree of an individual's desire to remain with an organization. It is based on the strength of the employee's involvement and identification with the organization. Involvement may be based on loyalty to the company, fear of losing pension benefits, or feeling a moral obligation to stay, but the end result is a desire to stay. Organizational commitment is the opposite of intent to leave. It indicates how much effort an employee is willing to make to stay with the organization.

Generally, the relationship between job satisfaction and organizational commitment is positive (Stumpf & Hartman, 1984; Verma & Upadhyay, 1986). Like the issue of absenteeism, some researchers question whether organizational commitment causes job satisfaction or the other way around. Current research appears to indicate that a high level of organizational commitment probably produces a high level of job satisfaction (Ting, 1997; Vandeberg & Lance, 1992).

Job Involvement

While organizational commitment is commitment to the overall organization, **job involvement** is an employee's strength of identification with the job. A computer consultant could be strongly committed to the job of writing computer programs but have no involvement with the company for which he is working. This is typical of consultants, who frequently move from one organization to another. In general, research indicates that job satisfaction and job involvement are positively correlated with job satisfaction leading to job involvement (Mathieu & Farr, 1991; Mortimer & Lorence, 1989). This means if you have a high level of job

Absence culture
An informal group norm for the number of days of absence that are "deserved" in a particular job.

Organizational commitment The degree of an employee's desire to remain with an organization.

Job involvement The degree of an employee's identification with the job.

satisfaction in your current position, you most likely will intensify your interest in the job. This may include reading current job-related publications, talking with others in the field, or taking additional classes focused on the job.

Personal Factors in Job Satisfaction

A number of personal factors, such as age, race, and gender, have been found to correlate with job satisfaction. However, correlational research shows only that a relationship exists, not why it exists. For example, research generally has shown that job satisfaction increases with age (Brush, Moch, & Pooyan, 1987). This might lead to the conclusion that if a company wants workers to be high in job satisfaction, it should hire older employees, but there are other possible reasons for this correlation.

Perhaps as workers get older they move to higher-status positions in the organization; higher job status also correlates positively with higher job satisfaction (Guppy & Rick, 1996; Matkin & Bauer, 1993). One researcher found that when the age–job satisfaction relationship was looked at separately for three different status groups, different relationship patterns emerged for each group (Zeitz, 1990). Other researchers (Clark, Oswald, & Warr, 1996) have suggested that when other factors are controlled for, the relationship between age and job satisfaction actually has more of a U shape, with the lowest job satisfaction occurring among the youngest and oldest employees.

Like the complex relationship between age and job satisfaction, the relationship between gender and job satisfaction is modified by a number of variables. Some of the strongest relationships between gender and job satisfaction have been found in studies in which stress, harassment, and pay inequity were other variables (Black & Holden, 1998; Goldenhar, Swanson, Hurrell, Ruder, & Deddens, 1998; Piotrowski, 1998). As teamwork becomes more important in the workplace, both men and women have higher job satisfaction when they are part of gender-balanced work groups instead of single-sex work groups (Fields & Blum, 1997).

The relationship between race and job satisfaction follows a similar pattern. The relationship is stronger when other variables are added. When employees perceive racial discrimination in the workplace, job satisfaction decreases significantly (Sanchez & Brock, 1996).

Compared to the complex relationships between age, gender, and race, and job satisfaction, the relationship between more general personal characteristics and job satisfaction appears to be more stable and consistent. Researchers have found a positive correlation between overall satisfaction with life and job satisfaction regardless of gender, age, or race (Crohan, Antonucci, Adelmann, & Coleman, 1989; Judge & Watanabe, 1993). Staw, Bell, and Clausen (1986) found that people who expressed a positive attitude toward life in adolescence showed continuing higher levels of job satisfaction up to fifty years later. A relationship that lasts that long suggests that there may be genetic factors as well as environmental factors in job satisfaction. Some studies that looked at identical twins raised in separate environments showed a higher correlation between the adult twins' job satisfaction scores than would be predicted from looking at any two people in general (Arvey, Bouchard, Segal, & Abraham, 1989; Arvey, McCall, Bouchard, & Taubman, 1994; Keller, Bouchard, Arvey, Segal, & Dawis, 1992).

Although organizations may use research studies like these to find a reason not to provide an environment high in job satisfaction, this research is designed to show a possible genetic predisposition toward job satisfaction rather than a genetic cause for it. Environment is still a critical variable. In one study of twins broad genetic influence was found to account for 41 to 61 percent of the scores on the personality traits of neuroticism, extraversion, openness, agreeableness, and conscientiousness (Jang, Lively, & Vernon, 1996). Another researcher found that two of those traits—extraversion and a low degree of neuroticism—were significantly linked to job satisfaction (Tokar & Subich, 1997). This means that up to half the score on the personality traits is determined by environmental influences.

Even if research shows that job satisfaction starts with a genetic predisposition, environmental factors such as challenging work, an opportunity to participate at work, and fair pay are still important modifiers. Good managers want to find the best fit between the personality characteristics of the employee and the characteristics of the work environment. Several researchers have confirmed the importance of finding that fit (Holland, 1996; Oleski & Subich, 1996).

Measurement of Job Satisfaction

Measuring job satisfaction is important for tracking and assessing improvement. There are several commonly accepted measures of job satisfaction. The two most popular—the Job Descriptive Index (JDI) and the Minnesota Satisfaction Questionnaire (MSQ)—measure specific aspects of the job. These are called **facet measures of job satisfaction** because they examine separate components of job satisfaction, such as supervision and pay. Other measures, such as the newer Job in General Scale, which look at overall work satisfaction levels, are referred to as **global measures of job satisfaction.**

Most organizations prefer to use facet measures so that managers can determine which parts of a job should be changed. Some organizations create their own measures of job satisfaction, but it is often better to use a standardized scale. First, the standardized questionnaire has been tested and shown to be valid. Second, since the standardized measures, such as those now to be discussed, have

Facet measures of job satisfaction Measures that look at separate components of satisfaction, such as pay and supervision.

Global measures of job satisfaction Measures of overall work satisfaction levels.

been on the market for some time, there is a great deal of comparison data. This means that managers can easily determine whether dissatisfaction with certain facets is common to a particular job or if that dissatisfaction is unique within their organization. One group of researchers found over a hundred published research studies that used the Job Descriptive Index (Cook, Hepworth, Wall, & Warr, 1981).

Job Descriptive Index

The *Job Descriptive Index (JDI)* measures five facets of job satisfaction: pay, work, promotion opportunities, supervision, and coworkers. It was developed over twenty-five years ago (Smith, Kendall, & Hulin, 1969) and later was revised (Balzer et al., 1990). The JDI has been translated and given to over three thousand employees in at least six different countries (Hulin, 1987).

Figure 6.6 shows a sample of items from the JDI. The scale has a brief description of each facet and a number of adjectives or short phrases beside which employees write "yes," "no," or "can't decide" for each adjective or phrase. There are seventy-two descriptive adjectives or phrases in all. A score is determined for each facet.

The most common criticism of the JDI is that there may be more than five main facets (Yeager, 1981). Other researchers have suggested that the "can't decide" answer is more negative than positive and should be scored that way (Hanisch, 1992). While the ease of scoring and administering the paper and pencil version of the JDI has always been an advantage, a computerized version of the index has been developed that may make scoring and analyzing the results easier (Kantor, 1991).

Minnesota Satisfaction Questionnaire

The *Minnesota Satisfaction Questionnaire (MSQ)*, which measures twenty facets of job satisfaction (Weiss, Dawis, England, & Lofquist, 1967), has been researched and shown to have good levels of validity and reliability. The MSQ has short (twenty items) and long (one hundred items) forms. Each item is a short statement about a specific aspect of the job. Each item is marked "very dissatisfied," "dissatisfied," "neutral," "satisfied," or "very satisfied." Sample items are shown in Figure 6.6

In contrast to the JDI, the MSQ has been criticized for measuring too many facets, some of which overlap (Gillet & Schwab, 1975). Although the MSQ is not used as often as the JDI is, it is used frequently. A study previously mentioned in this chapter that related job satisfaction to genetics used the MSQ, which the researchers sorted into intrinsic, extrinsic, and general satisfaction scales (Arvey, Bouchard, Segal, & Abraham, 1989).

Figure 6.6

Sample items from the Job Descriptive Index and the Minnesota Satisfaction Questionnaire.

JOB DESCRIPTIVE INDEX

Think of your present work. What is it like most of the time? In the blank beside each word given below, write

____Y____ for "Yes" if it describes your work
____N____ for "No" if it does not describe it
____?____ if you cannot decide

Work on present job

_____ Routine
_____ Satisfying
_____ Good

Think of the pay you get now.How well does each of the following words describe your present pay? In the blank beside each word, put

____Y____ if it describes your pay
____N____ if it does not describe it
____?____ if you cannot decide

Present pay

_____ Income adequate for normal expenses
_____ Insecure
_____ Less than I deserve

Source: P. C. Smith, L. M. Kendall, & C. L. Hulin. (1985). Job Descriptive Index. In *The measurement of satisfaction in work and retirement* (rev. ed.). Bowling Green, OH: Bowling Green State University Press.

MINNESOTA SATISFACTION QUESTIONNAIRE

On my present job, this is how I feel about	Very Dissatisfied	Dissatisfied	Neutral	Satisfied	Very Satisfied
1. being able to keep busy all the time	_____	_____	_____	_____	_____
2. the chance to work alone on the job	_____	_____	_____	_____	_____
3. my pay and the amount of work I do	_____	_____	_____	_____	_____

Source: D. J. Weiss, R. V. Dawis, G. W. England, & L. H. Lofquist. (1967). *Manual for the Minnesota Satisfaction Questionnaire: Minnesota studies in vocational rehabilitation.* University of Minnesota, Vocational Psychology Research.

Job in General Scale

One of the more recent additions to measuring job satisfaction is a global measure of job satisfaction based on the JDI that is known as the *Job in General Scale* (Ironson, Smith, Brannick, Gibson, & Paul, 1989). It has shown fairly good reliability and may be useful in obtaining an overall measure of job satisfaction. The main disadvantage of this scale is that it does not give information about specific parts of the job, although it can provide a good basis for comparison between organizations and jobs.

Increasing Job Satisfaction

Although most managers would agree that increasing job satisfaction is desirable, there are limits on what organizations can do. Nobody can change personal factors

Job enrichment
A systematic program for increasing job satisfaction by giving additional responsibility to employees.

Job enlargement
Increasing the amount of tasks done or knowledge used by an employee on the job.

Job rotation Allowing employees to do different duties on a regularly scheduled basis.

such as age and race. Choosing employees on the basis of personal characteristics related to job satisfaction probably would lead to legal challenges because of the sometimes inconsistent relationship between job satisfaction and job performance.

In general, the work environment factors that are associated with higher job satisfaction are interesting work, job security, autonomy and self-management, low job stress, many participation and communication opportunities, fair pay, and objective performance appraisals. Job enrichment, which was mentioned earlier in this chapter in relation to Herzberg's two-factor theory, includes many of these factors. **Job enrichment** is a systematic program for increasing job satisfaction by giving additional responsibility to employees. Greater responsibility may be given in a number of ways. On the automobile assembly line, instead of just putting on windshield wipers, each worker could be part of a team that built an entire car. Quality control could become the responsibility of the work team or of each worker rather than the responsibility of a quality control inspector.

Job enrichment programs have been used in a number of organizations, with generally positive results. For example, Texas Instruments' defense systems and electronics groups established a job enrichment program that trained teams to have increased control over the production process. After six months the job-enriched teams had reduced the production cycle time 50 percent, decreased the scrap rate 60 percent, and increased productivity 30 percent (*Training and Development*, 1995).

Although the results of the job enrichment programs are generally positive, identifying the cause of those results remains a problem because factors other than enrichment may contribute to a program's success (Locke, 1975). Locke and Latham (1990a) suggest that the results are caused by the feedback and goal setting that often are incorporated into job enrichment programs. Umstot, Bell, and Mitchell (1976) found that when goal setting and job enrichment were combined, productivity and job satisfaction increased. In field settings it is particularly difficult to isolate one variable as being responsible for the changes that occur. Many programs are not just job enrichment programs but job enrichment programs combined with other programs.

Job enrichment is different from job enlargement and job rotation. **Job enlargement** means increasing the number of tasks done or amount of knowledge used by employees. It often leads to higher job satisfaction because the employees are using their abilities more fully, and if often includes higher pay. If employees were asked to do more work without an increase in pay, that could lead to job dissatisfaction. Job enlargement can be job enrichment if it also includes more responsibility, but it also can involve just doing more work.

Job rotation involves doing different tasks on a regular schedule. This is more than just doing the same job in different ways or places. For example, a maintenance employee who only scrubbed floors might be given a schedule that had him scrub floors one week, clean bathrooms the next week, paint the week after that, and do repair work the fourth week. If he only switched between floor scrubbing in different buildings or on different floors, that would not be job rotation. Job rotation has been most successful among employees who do boring, repetitive jobs.

In this chapter you have learned about the relationship between motivation and job satisfaction. In future chapters, such as Chapters 12 and 13, you will learn about other factors that have been related to motivation, job satisfaction, and performance.

MAIN POINTS

- Motivation at work refers to the conditions that activate, direct, and support continued work behavior. It is not the same as performance. Ability is necessary for motivation.

- Theories provide a framework for studying and applying motivation in order to raise the motivation levels of employees.

- Many of the early theories of work motivation were need theories based on eliminating deficiencies.

- Important need theories of motivation includes Maslow's hierarchy of needs theory, Alderfer's ERG theory, and McClelland's need to achieve theory.

- Job design theories of motivation stress ways to arrange the work environment to get the best job performance.

- Imporant job design theories of motivation include Herzberg's two-factor theory and Hackman and Oldham's job characteristics theory.

- Cognitive theories of motivation focus on how employees understand things as they relate to motivation at work. The emphasis is on individual perceptions.

- Important cognitive theories of motivation include Vroom's' VIE (valence-instrumentality-expectancy) theory, Locke and Latham's goal-setting theory, and Locke and Latham's high performance cycle.

- Behavioral theories of motivation are based on the principles of operant conditioning.

- Important behavioral theories of motivation include reinforcement theory and organizational behavior modification.

- In the future, motivation research may focus more on cognitive abilities, specific social situations, and typical versus maximum performance.

- Job satisfaction refers to the emotional content, or affect, people attach to a job or job situation.

- Job satisfaction typically correlates with job performance, but it is not certain which one causes the other.

- Job outcomes that are related to job satisfaction include turnover, absence, organizational commitment, and job involvement.

- Personal characteristics that are related to job satisfaction include age, race, gender, and genetics.

- Two of the most commonly used facet measures of job satisfaction are the Job Descriptive Index (JDI) and the Minnesota Satisfaction Questionnaire (MSQ). Both have been well researched.

- The Job in General Scale is a global measure of job satisfaction.

- Job enrichment (giving workers more responsibility) is a common technique for increasing job satisfaction, as are job enlargement and job rotation.

KEY TERMS

Absence culture
Behavioral theories of motivation
Benevolents
Cognitive theories of motivation
Core job characteristics
Entitleds
Equity sensitive
Equity theory
ERG theory
Expectancy
Externally focused
Extrinsic reinforcers
Facet measures of job satisfaction
Functional turnover
Fundamental attribution error
Global measures of job satisfaction
Goal-setting theory
Growth-need strength
Hierarchy of needs theory
High performance cycle
Hygiene factor
Inequity
Instrumentality
Internally focused

Intrinsic reinforcers
Involuntary turnover
Job characteristics theory
Job enlargement
Job enrichment
Job involvement
Job outcome
Job rotation
Job satisfaction
Motivation
Motivator factors
Need to achieve theory (NAch)
Negative reinforcer
Nonfunctional turnover
Organizational behavior modification
Organizational commitment
Positive reinforcer
Reinforcement theory
Self-efficacy
Two-factor theory
Valence
Valence-instrumentality-expectancy
  theory
Voluntary turnover

Answers to these questions can be found at the end of the book.

1. Motivation generally means that a person wants to work hard no matter what gets in the way of doing that.

   a. True

   b. False

2. Which of the following factors can modify motivated work behavior?

   a. Ability

   b. Other needs

   c. a and b

   d. None of the above

3. Need theories say that getting rid of a deficiency causes motivated behavior.

   a. True

   b. False

4. The five levels of Maslow's need hierarchy are

   a. _____.

   b. _____.

   c. _____.

   d. _____.

   e. _____.

5. The level of Alderfer's ERG theory most like Maslow's physiological needs is

   a. growth.

   b. relatedness.

   c. existence.

   d. goal needs.

6. The three types of needs McClelland believes influence people's behaviors are

   a. _____.

   b. _____.

   c. _____.

7. List two hygiene factors and two motivators according to Herzberg's two-factor theory.

   a. Hygiene Needs   b. Motivators

   _____   _____

   _____   _____

8. If you say your friend's good grades are due mainly to easy tests and his bad grades are caused mainly by his failing to study, you may be making a(n)

    a. cross-attribution error.

    b. inadequate sources error.

    c. functional fixedness error.

    d. fundamental attribution error.

9. List the five factors that Hackman and Oldham's job characteristics theory says are critical for job satisfaction.

    a. _____

    b. _____

    c. _____

    d. _____

    e. _____

10. Because the motivating potential score (MPS) formula is so precise, Hackman and Oldham's job characteristics theory has had the clearest research support among all the job design theories.

    a. True

    b. False

11. According to Adams's equity theory, if you went to college and graduate school but can only find a dead-end job that pays the minimum wage, you probably have feelings of

    a. cognitive inequality.

    b. inequity.

    c. disharmony.

    d. input/outcome adjustment.

12. People who do more work than others but get less pay are called _____; people who do less work than others but get more pay are called _____.

    a. equity-sensitive; equity-insensitive

    b. equity-entitled; equity-unentitled

    c. benevolents; entitleds

    d. input unequal; outcome unequal

13. One problem in trying to apply equity theory to an actual work situation is that there is no consistent way to predict those with whom employees will compare themselves.

    a. True
    b. False

14. If you believe that no matter how well you do your job, you never will be the head technician because the supervisor has three children she wants in that position, you probably have a low score in

    a. instrumentality.
    b. valence.
    c. expectancy.
    d. job outcomes.

15. The concept of _____ is unique to the VIE theory.

    a. force
    b. valence
    c. instrumentality
    d. expectancy

16. Popular support for the VIE theory is fairly strong.

    a. True
    b. False

17. As long as workers are committed to goals, it does not matter if the goals are assigned or developed through worker participation.

    a. True
    b. False

18. List two of the four moderators that influence behavior in goal-setting theory.

    a. _____
    b. _____

19. The concept of _____ is a combination of the effects of moderators on performance in goal-setting theory.

    a. force
    b. equitability
    c. social reference
    d. self-efficacy

20. The high performance cycle theory suggests that increasing job satisfaction leads to better performance.

    a. True

    b. False

21. Reinforcement theory applied to motivation focuses only on observable or measurable behaviors.

    a. True

    b. False

22. The most basic assumption of reinforcement theory is that _____ increase occurrence of behaviors and _____ decreases occurrence of behaviors.

23. If your supervisor says that if you send out one more incorrect part you will be fired, and therefore you carefully check each order to avoid sending out any wrong parts, this is an example of the use of which of the following?

    a. Positive reinforcement

    b. Negative reinforcement

    c. Punishment

    d. Neutral consequences, because you still have the job

24. If you are supposed to be paid every Friday but sometimes get paid on Thursday or Monday, this is a _____ schedule of reinforcement.

    a. continuous

    b. variable interval

    c. variable ratio

    d. fixed interval

    e. fixed ratio

25. If you work as a stay-at-home parent, you probably receive mostly _____ reinforcers.

    a. intrinsic

    b. extrinsic

    c. monetary

    d. meaningless

26. Even though reinforcement theory generally has been effective, unions and employees often oppose these types of programs.

    a. True

    b. False

27. Future theories of motivation are likely to be
    a. computer based.
    b. useful only on the international business level.
    c. less focused on social factors.
    d. based on additions to current theories.

28. Job satisfaction typically refers to
    a. emotional feelings toward work.
    b. emotional feelings and performance behaviors related to work.
    c. commitment to the job.
    d. all of the above.

29. Increasing job satisfaction usually causes an increase in job performance.
    a. True
    b. False

30. Turnover that benefits an organization is called _____.

31. The problem or problems in linking absenteeism to job satisfaction is (are) that
    a. people are absent for reasons other than low job satisfaction.
    b. work group norms may establish absence levels.
    c. absence may be the cause, not the result, of low job satisfaction.
    d. all of the above.

32. Organizational commitment and job involvement are basically the same concept because both relate to working.
    a. True
    b. False

33. According to recent research, if both your parents were high in job satisfaction, your level of job satisfaction probably
    a. relates to how they raised you.
    b. is similar to their level of job satisfaction.
    c. has nothing to do with their level of job satisfaction.
    d. relates more to the job you do.

34. List the two most common measures of job satisfaction.
    a. _____
    b. _____

35. Which of the following terms would describe a grocery store worker's job if she stocked the shelves one day, did checkout the next day, worked at the service desk the day after that, and handed out free samples another day?

    a. Job enrichment

    b. Job enlargement

    c. Job rotation

    d. Job involvement

WEB EXERCISE

Use your browser to go to:
http://www.ewgsa.org/Education/BusinessWise/Job_Satisfaction_Survey/job_satisfaction_survey.html
Take the job satisfaction survey and compare your results to the answers of the others who have taken this survey. What areas are better or worse in job satisfaction for you? What changes at work or in you would improve your job satisfaction score?

Leadership | 7

Chapter Outline

LEARNING OBJECTIVES

DEFINITIONS OF LEADERSHIP

THEORIES OF LEADERSHIP

Trait Theories

Behavioral Theory

Contingency Theories

Transformational and Charismatic Leadership

SUBSTITUTES FOR LEADERSHIP AND EMPLOYEE EMPOWERMENT THEORIES

Case Study Leadership at Work

POWER AND LEADERSHIP

Position and Personal Power

Bases of Power

Use of Influence

Power of Followers

PERSONAL VARIABLES IN LEADERSHIP

Gender Roles in Leadership

Racial Issues in Leadership

Cross-Cultural Management

BEING AN EFFECTIVE LEADER

> ## Learning Objectives
>
> After reading this chapter, you should be able to answer the following questions:
> - What is the difference between a leader and a manager?
> - What is the major assumption of trait theories of leadership? What is an example of a trait theory?
> - What is the major assumption of behavioral theories of leadership? What are the major components of each of the behavioral theories discussed in this chapter?
> - What is the basic assumption of contingency theories of leadership? What are the major components of each of the contingency theories discussed in this chapter?
> - What are transformational leaders and charismatic leaders? How are they different? How are they the same?
> - How can employee empowerment or other factors substitute for leadership?
> - What types and bases of power do leaders use?
> - What happens when the followers are the ones with power in a work situation?
> - How do personal variables such as age, race, and gender influence leadership?
> - What are the characteristics of an effective leader, according to Bennis (1993)?

What is the best way to lead a group of employees? Are the best leaders born or trained? Do work groups need leaders? These are some of the questions that industrial/organizational (I/O) psychologists studying the field of leadership have tried to answer for over a hundred years. As was discussed in Chapter 6, even if a good answer is found at one time, knowledge and situations change and the answers to these questions also may change.

Despite those changes, this long period of study should have provided some practical guidelines for choosing better leaders. In practice, however, the failure rate within management has been estimated to be at least 50 percent (DeVries, 1992; Milliken-Davies, 1992; Shipper & Wilson, 1991). There are at least two possible ways to deal with this problem. The first is to acknowledge that much is still not known about choosing and developing good leaders. As this chapter will show, researchers have learned a great deal about leadership over the years, and so lack of knowledge is not the issue.

The second possible approach is to realize that knowledge in this area is not being applied or is difficult to apply to actual work situations. This is the more likely cause of the problem. This chapter looks at some of the applications of effective leadership developed by I/O psychologists and at better ways to use knowledge about leadership. The chapter starts with some of the earliest views of leadership, developed by researchers using scientific management, and then deals with the newest interests in transformational and charismatic leaders. This examination of changes in leadership theory over the years shows the ways in which new knowledge and changing situations have shaped the study of leadership in I/O psychology.

Leadership The ability to persuade a follower to make a commitment to the goals of a group and work toward those goals.

DEFINITIONS OF LEADERSHIP

When people make lists of famous leaders, there is such diversity in their choices that it is difficult to imagine what those leaders have in common other than being in charge of something. One of the problems may be that each person has a different definition of leadership. A general definition of **leadership** focuses on the ability to persuade a follower to make a commitment to the goals of a group and work toward those goals.

With the focus on persuasion, Hogan, Curphy, and Hogan (1994) separate leadership from domination. From their point of view, leadership involves only persuasion, not force. It concerns persuading followers to put aside their individual desires and to work toward a goal that is good for the group. The benefits to individual members are a side effect, not the main focus. The leader, if she is effective, is a team builder. With the current emphasis on teams in the workplace, this is a critical skill.

The definition of leadership also leads to a further distinction between *leaders* and *managers* because of the way those terms are used in organizations; they often are used as if they referred to the same behaviors and positions. However, although the terms have much in common, they are not the same (Holloman, 1986; Kochan, Schmidt, & DeCotiis, 1975). A person or group at a higher level in the organization typically appoints managers to their positions. An example of a manager would be the head of a clerical group in a company who was appointed to that position by the head of business services. Leaders are typically chosen by the groups they lead. An example of a leader would be the head of a local union, elected by the union members.

There is a great deal of overlap between these two categories, and a wise manager will try to get the support of the group of which he in charge in order to be the most effective manager possible. At the same time, a good manager or leader will be aware of the differences between these categories. Bennis (1993) listed several major contrasts between managers and leaders (Table 7.1). According to Bennis, one of the major characteristics of leaders is their clear understanding of what they want to do both at the personal and professional levels. They have the strength to continue toward those goals in spite of setbacks or failures. Since most theories do not distinguish between managers and leaders, it may be useful to refer to Table 7.1 in looking at different leadership theories to see whether certain theories apply more to managers or to leaders, or equally well to both.

Table 7.1

DIFFERENCES BETWEEN LEADERS AND MANAGERS

Managers	Leaders
Administer	Innovate
A copy	An original
Maintain	Develop
Focus on systems and structures	Focus on people
Rely on control	Inspire trust
Short-range view	Long-range perspective
Ask how and when	Ask what and why
Eye on the bottom line	Eye on the horizon
Accept status quo	Challenge status quo
Classic "good soldier"	His or her own person
Do things right	Do the right thing

From W. Bennis. (1993). *An invented life: Reflections on leadership and change.* Reading, MA: Addison-Wesley, pp. 88–89.

THEORIES OF LEADERSHIP

In the same way that the different organizational structures discussed in Chapter 3 were linked to the research, knowledge, and culture of a particular time, leadership theories reflect the research, knowledge, and culture of particular periods in I/O psychology. At certain times either biological (nature) or behavioral (nurture) theories have been the more popular explanations of leadership. Biological explanations of behavior suggest that leaders are born, not made. Behavioral explanations suggest that leadership is learned through certain experiences. Most psychologists look to both explanations for a complete picture of human behavior. The leadership theories discussed in this chapter show a shift from biological explanations to behavioral ones, and a more recent shift back toward biological theories.

Trait Theories

Trait theory A leadership theory that is based on the assumption that effective leaders have certain characteristics, either learned or innate.

Trait theory often is seen as a direct outcome of the scientific management theory that was dominant in the early years of I/O psychology. Scientific management was based on the belief that workers operate the same way as the machinery they work on. If the owner of a company wanted a machine to do something at the company, he would list the tasks the machine was required to perform. He then would go out and find that machine or have one built and put it in place. The basic tenet of **trait theory** is that certain traits or characteristics are common to good leaders. If a company wants to hire good managers and leaders, it should make a list of the traits that are needed and then find someone with those traits and put her in the management position. The earliest trait theorists believed that good leaders are born with these traits and that these traits are a consistent part of a manager's personality. That position later was modified to indicate that the traits could be developed through experience; but the traits still were viewed as core personality characteristics of the leader.

Historical and Current Trait Theories

Trait theory often is referred to as the "great man" theory because this approach suggests that leaders are destined to lead and the early examples were exclusively men. When the first trait theorists started making lists of traits, there was not much opposition to this approach. One theorist might suggest that leaders should be ambitious, tolerant, and fair. Another psychologist might suggest that the trait of intelligence should be added to the list. As more psychologists found additional traits, it quickly became clear that trait theory was more complicated than it had seemed at first.

Part of the problem resulted from the method of identifying the traits of leaders. The typical method was to identify a group of outstanding leaders and then look for the traits they all had in common. Unless the same group of outstanding leaders was used each time, different traits would be identified. Even if the same group was used, different researchers could reach different conclusions about the traits that were critical. When researchers waited until people had become outstanding leaders before studying their traits, they left open the question of whether nonleaders had the same traits. If leaders and nonleaders had the same traits, this theory would not be helpful in predicting who would become leaders.

One explanation for the problems in early trait theories comes from later research on implicit theories of leadership. These theories suggest that as people go through life, they use their experiences with leaders to develop a model of what makes good ones. When people are asked to evaluate someone on his leadership abilities, they decide how good a leader he is on the basis of how well he fits their cognitive model of leadership (Lord, DeVader, & Alliger, 1986; Lord, Foti, & DeVader, 1984). For example, implicit leadership theories suggest that when presidents are seen as conforming to people's preconceived model of "presidential leadership," they are evaluated more favorably.

In much the same way that scientific management theory lost popularity after the Hawthorne Studies, trait theory also lost favor after these studies. Some researchers, however, continued to look for personality characteristics that were consistently associated with effective leadership. In recent years there has been renewed interest in this approach among I/O psychologists. Hogan, Curphy, and Hogan (1994) summarized the personality variables associated with effective

Surgency The leadership trait characterized by assertiveness, high energy and activity levels, and social involvement with others.

Intellectance The leadership trait characterized by imagination, cultural concern, and a broad range of interests.

Leadership motive pattern McClelland's theory that the most effective leaders combine high levels of the need for power and low levels of the need to affiliate.

leadership in work situations, drawing from a number of studies over the last several decades. The measures of effectiveness included compensation levels of the leaders, evaluations, and advancement over lengthy periods. They found that the traits associated most often with effective leadership were **surgency** (assertiveness, energy level, and social participation); emotional stability (adjustment and self-confidence); conscientiousness (working hard, being responsible, and being achievement oriented); agreeableness (friendliness and social support); and **intellectance** (being imaginative, being cultured, and having a broad range of interests).

Hogan, Curphy, and Hogan (1994) also examined ineffective leaders and found a high correlation with personality traits that made their subordinates reject their leadership attempts and prevented the leaders from building effective teams. These researchers suggested that the most effective leaders have the good personality characteristics and lack the "dark side" characteristics. They advised that as the workforce changes to more service jobs and bottom line measures become more critical for organizational survival, leadership selection and training based on personality traits will become even more essential.

McClelland's Leadership Motive Pattern

A specific trait theory that has received renewed interest in recent years focuses on a particular need: the need for power. Chapter 6 considered the need for power as one of the elements in McClelland's need to achieve theory. McClelland and Burnham (1976) and McClelland and Boyatzis (1982) found that the combination of a high need for power and a low need for affiliation was common to high-performing managers. The need for power was related to the desire to control other people, and the need to affiliate was related to the desire for social contacts. McClelland referred to this pattern of a high need for power and a low need to affiliate as the **leadership motive pattern.** He emphasized that the power exerted is power in the organization, not personal power.

A more recent study by Jacobs and McClelland (1994) showed high power levels among men and women who had received frequent promotions during a twelve-year period of employment in a large utility company. The researchers found a difference between the types of power used by men and women, however. Successful men were more likely to use reactive power (responding to a situation with a show of power), while successful women were more likely to use resource power (based on reserves of knowledge and skills). Spangler and House (1991) found that this leadership motive pattern, in combination with the achievement motive and an assessment of speech patterns, was strongly correlated to the effectiveness of U.S. presidents. When this approach is used for high-prestige and high-status jobs, it does a fairly good job of relating traits to job behavior. When it is applied to technical or engineering managers, it fails to relate well to job behaviors. This illustrates another problem with trait theory: It fails to account for behaviors in different types of situations that require different types of leader behavior, as is shown by the Hawthorne Studies.

Since the time of the Hawthorne Studies, research has shown that people are not machines and that they respond to social factors in the work environment at least as much as they respond to physical factors. A focus on the social behaviors at work led to the next type of leadership theory: the behavioral theory approach.

Behavioral Theory

The basic assumption of behavioral theories of leadership is that the important factor in determining leader effectiveness is what the leader does, that is, her behaviors rather than any of her personal characteristics. One of the earliest studies that promoted this point of view was conducted by Lewin, Lippitt, and White (1939). That study used boys' club groups, with leaders assigned to **authoritarian, democratic,** or **laissez-faire leadership styles.** The control of the leader ranged from complete (authoritarian) to shared (democratic) to none (laissez-faire). Although most of the boys liked democratic leaders the best, the group with an authoritarian leader got the most work done, which is an important consideration in most work settings.

Ohio State Studies

The desire to balance the need to get work done and to provide for social and other needs of employees led directly to the research done at Ohio State University starting in the late 1940s by Hemphill (1950), Shartle (1956), and others. Using the focus on behaviors of Lewin, Lippitt, and White (1939), those researchers developed a large list of behaviors of leaders. When they applied a factor analysis to their list of almost two thousand behaviors, they found that only two major factors represented all the behaviors: consideration and initiating structure.

Consideration behavior is focused on concern for the welfare of subordinates. This is a genuine concern that is reflected in mutual trust, warmth, and sharing between the supervisor and the subordinates. A leader who is highest in consideration might put an employee's need to be with his wife during a surgical procedure ahead of reaching a daily work goal. **Initiation of structure behavior** refers to the tasks required at work and getting them done. A leader who is highest in initiation of structure might try to persuade an employee with a bad case of the flu to stay on the job so that a particular work goal can be accomplished. While most leaders have a combination of consideration and initiation of structure behaviors, most of them, according to this theory, tend to be oriented more toward one or the other.

Authoritarian leadership style A leadership pattern in which the leader controls all the power in and decisions made by the group.

Democratic leadership style A leadership pattern in which the leader and each member share equally in the power and the decisions of the group.

Laissez-faire leadership style A leadership pattern in which the group members have all the power and decision-making authority in the group if they want it.

Consideration behavior Leadership behavior that is focused on the well-being of subordinates.

Initiation of structure behavior Leadership behavior that is focused on required tasks and their completion.

Measurement of Behavioral Theories

One of the major contributions of the Ohio State studies was the development of ways to measure the factors of consideration and initiation of structure. The *Leader Behavior Description Questionnaire (LBDQ)* (Hemphill, 1950) is filled out by subordinates; the *Leader Opinion Questionnaire (LOQ)* (Fleishman, 1960) is a description of ideal leader behavior completed by supervisors (Figure 7.1).

The items in each of these measurements are clearly descriptions of what leaders do rather than their personal characteristics. This is a much more concrete way of describing leaders and represents an improvement over many of the trait approaches. Another advantage is that behaviors can be taught in leadership training programs. It is much easier to teach a supervisor to "back up what the persons under you do" than to try to develop the personality characteristic of, for example, being socially supportive.

Research results generally have supported the Ohio State studies (Fleishman & Harris, 1962; Morse & Reimer, 1956), and this research has led to several managerial training programs, such as the Leadership Grid® program (Blake & McCanse, 1991). The basic assumption of such training programs is that the best leader is a person who is high in both consideration and initiation of structure.

Figure 7.1

Sample items from (a) the Leader Behavior Description questionnaire (LBDQ) and (b) the Leader Opinion questionnaire (LOQ).

(a)

Structure	Consideration
1. Schedules work to be done	1. Is friendly and approachable
2. Emphasizes the meeting of deadlines	2. Makes group members feel at ease when talking to them
3. Lets group members know what is expected of them	3. Does little things to make it pleasant to be a member of the group

(b)

Structure	Consideration
1. Put the welfare of your unit above the welfare of any person	1. Give in to your subordinates in your discussions with them
2. Encourage after-duty work by persons in your unit	2. Back up what persons under you do
3. Try out new ideas in the unit	3. Get approval of persons under you on important matters before going ahead

However, research on that pattern in the Leadership Grid (formerly known as the Managerial Grid®) failed to show that this is always the best leadership style (Larson, Hunt, & Osborn, 1976; Nystrom, 1978). Subordinates generally indicate greater satisfaction with high-consideration leaders (Greenspan, 1985), but those leaders show higher levels of job burnout (Dale & Weinberg, 1989).

Perhaps such findings are due to the conflict between initiation of structure demands by the organization and leadership consideration desires expressed by subordinates. It might be better for supervisors to give attention to both functions and balance them to achieve effectiveness. It is apparent that certain situations require consideration more than initiation of structure and that other situations require the opposite. In the most recent version of the Leadership Grid, more leadership styles were added to account for these variations in situations. Attention to the effects of different situations on leadership led to the development of contingency theories of leadership.

Contingency Theories

The basic assumption of **contingency theory** is that the effectiveness of a leader is determined by a combination of his or her characteristics and the environment of the leadership situation. Although it is not easy to change enduring personal characteristics, it may be easier to find situations that enhance the personality of the leader or change the situation to fit the personal characteristics of the leader. Fiedler's contingency theory has led to a leadership training program that is based on this assumption.

Fiedler's Contingency Theory

According to **Fiedler's contingency theory,** personality characteristics develop from experiences throughout people's lives and are difficult to change. Leaders are characterized as task oriented or person oriented—showing traits that are similar to initiation of structure and consideration in the Ohio State Studies.

The assessment of task or person orientation is done by using a measure called the **Least Preferred Co-Worker (LPC) scale.** The leader is asked to think of the employee she would least like to work with. Then she rates that employee on a scale that has a number of measures that consist of opposite pairs, such as friendly–unfriendly and tense–relaxed. The higher the number of positive choices, the higher the LPC score and the more person oriented the leader is. The higher the number of negative choices, the lower the LPC score and the more task oriented the leader is (Fiedler, 1978; Rice, 1978). Fiedler thought of this as determining the preferred style of a leader rather than determining the only style a leader could use. If a high-LPC leader had all his social needs met, he might give more attention to task accomplishment.

Contingency theory A leadership theory that is based on the assumption that the best leaders consider both their own characteristics and the leadership situation to determine the best way to lead.

Fiedler's contingency theory A leadership theory that states that the best leaders combine person orientation and task orientation in a variety of ways, depending on the work situation.

Least Preferred Co-Worker (LPC) scale A measurement scale developed by Fiedler to assess the person orientation or task orientation of a leader.

Leader–member relations
A situational variable that determines the degree of subordinates' liking of and support for a leader.

Task structure A situational variable that determines the clarity of job tasks and the behaviors needed to accomplish those tasks.

Leader Match Training
A leadership training program based on Fiedler's contingency theory.

The next step in this model requires evaluating the situation to identify features that are favorable or unfavorable to a leader's style, based on that leader's control over three situational variables: (1) **leader–member relations** (how much the subordinates like and support the leader); (2) **task structure** (how clearly the subordinates' job tasks are defined and how clear the path is to accomplishing those tasks); and (3) *leader position power* (the amount of legitimate authority the leader has to hand out rewards or punishment on the basis of her position in the organization).

According to this model, a low-control situation would occur if leader–member relations were poor and strained, the task structure was very unclear, and the leader had no legitimate authority in the organization. The opposite situation—high control—would occur if leader–member relations were strong and positive, the task structure and the ways to accomplish the task were very clear, and the leader clearly had a high degree of legitimate organizational authority. As can be seen in Figure 7.2, a low-LPC leader does best in either high or low situational control settings and a high-LPC leader does best in moderate situational control settings (Schriesheim, Tepper, & Tetrault, 1994). Fiedler's conclusion was that the setting determines the best leadership style. The combination of leadership style and situational control determines whether a person is in an effective or an ineffective leadership role.

Although each person may have intuitive feelings about her or his leadership style and situational control, Fiedler combined these elements into a leadership assessment and training program called **Leader Match Training** (Fiedler,

Figure 7.2

Relationship between Least Preferred Co-Worker (LPC) scores and the success of the leader in accomplishing the goals of the group.

Relationship-oriented leader High LPC score	Low performance	High performance	Low performance
Task- and relationship-oriented leader Middle LPC score	Average performance	Average performance	Average performance
Task-oriented leader Low LPC score	High performance	Low performance	High performance
	High degree of leader control over the situation	**Moderate degree of leader control over the situation.**	**Low degree of leader control over the situation**

Chemers, & Mahar, 1976). In this program leaders fill out assessments of the LPC scale, task structure, leader–member relations, and position power. Since Fiedler views task or relationship orientation as a trait of the leader, the training should be directed at finding the best situation for the leader or changing some elements of the situation to better fit the leader. For example, if a high-LPC leader found he was in a very low situational control setting, he might work to improve leader–member relations to raise the situational control score.

Leader Match Training has been a popular leadership training system because it provides a method to assess and change situations in a definite way. This is different from most leadership training programs, which focus on changing the leader in some way. The scales are easily administered and scored, and the information can be given back to the participants immediately for discussion. It is based on a theory that has received generally positive research support (Ayman & Chemers, 1991; Peters, Hartke, & Pohlmann, 1985; Strube & Garcia, 1981; Vecchio, 1983). The popularity of and research support for Leader Match Training have led to increased use of this system in organizations. There has been a fair amount of controversy, however, over how well Leader Match Training follows Fiedler's contingency theory (Chemers & Fiedler, 1986; Jago & Ragan, 1986a, 1986b).

Fiedler's Cognitive Resource Theory

One of the most positive aspects of Fiedler's leadership research has been his willingness to modify this theory as new information and research confirm or dispute it. His earliest contingency model (Fiedler, 1967) has been modified and has led to an additional theory: the cognitive resource model (Fiedler, 1986; Fiedler & Garcia, 1987). Despite the positive research on and success of the Leader Match Training program, Fiedler felt that there were missing pieces in people's understanding of leadership models and situations. This led to the development of **Fiedler's cognitive resource theory.** As the name suggests, this theory looks at how a leader's intelligence, technical competence, stress, and experience with the job influence leadership and group performance. On a commonsense basis, most people believe that the best leaders are the most intelligent and most experienced, and these characteristics are often among the criteria for selecting people for leadership positions. However, research shows virtually no relationship (Bass, 1981) between the intelligence and experience of a group's leader and the performance of the group. Cognitive resource theory attempts to explain these results by looking at how cognitive abilities relate to work situations. Among the relationships that Fiedler proposed are the following (Fiedler & House, 1994):

Fiedler's cognitive resource theory A leadership theory that is based on the assumption that the best leaders make use of their mental resources to determine the most effective ways to lead a group.

1. When leaders are in low-stress situations, they use their intelligence but not their experience to accomplish job tasks.

2. When leaders are in high-stress situations, they use their experience but not their intelligence to accomplish job tasks.

3. Directive leaders of supportive groups perform better if they use their intelligence in passing on orders and decisions to the group.

4. Nondirective leaders of nonsupportive groups do better if they are not as intelligent and are willing to be participative and listen to others.

5. The plans, decisions, and action strategies of the leader will be implemented only if the group is supportive of the leader.

Although cognitive resource theory often is seen as an extension of contingency theory, Fiedler suggests that they are complementary. The contingency model predicts when the leader will behave in a directive manner. It says (Fiedler & House, 1994):

1. Relationship-oriented leaders will be directive when they have high situational control.

2. Task-oriented leaders will be directive when they have moderate or low situational control.

Cognitive resource theory specifies the conditions under which the cognitive abilities of a leader can be used most effectively, as seen in the five situations listed just previously. As with contingency theory, research results generally have been supportive of cognitive resource theory in a number of different settings, but this theory also has generated criticism (Baril, Ayman, & Palmiter, 1994; Fiedler, McGuire, & Richardson, 1989; Gibson, Fiedler, & Barrett, 1993; Vecchio, 1990, 1992). Students often object that this theory involves so many variables that it is difficult to focus on what is critical in leadership. The next contingency theory provides a single focus for the leadership role.

Leader–Member Exchange Theory

The **leader–member exchange (LMX) model** (also known as vertical dyadic linkage theory) focuses on the relationship between the leader and each subordinate as the critical feature of leadership (Graen & Scandura, 1987). The basic assumption is that the leader does not behave exactly the same with each subordinate. Instead, the leader's behavior is based on which of two groups a subordinate belongs to. **In-group subordinates** are seen by the leader as competent, hardworking, and trustworthy. They get more support and understanding and have a more personal relationship with the leader. They are trusted to do important jobs. The leader sees **out-group subordinates** as incompetent, lazy, and untrustworthy. They receive directions through formal channels of authority and are given tasks that require little ability or responsibility. Clearly, most people would choose to be in-group subordinates. In-

Leader–member exchange (LMX) model A leadership theory based on the assumption that the quality of the relationship between the leader and each subordinate determines the effectiveness of the leader.

In-group subordinates Subordinates who are seen by the leader as competent, good workers.

Out-group subordinates Subordinates who are seen by the leader as undesirable workers.

group subordinates not only have much more freedom in their work activities, they also receive good performance evaluations even when they are not doing well (Duarte, Goodson, & Klich, 1993; Turban, Jones, & Rozelle, 1990) and therefore have more positive perceptions of the organizational climate (Kozlowski & Doherty, 1989).

How can one become an in-group subordinate and avoid being an out-group subordinate? Liden, Wayne, and Stilwell (1993) looked at 166 newly hired employees and their immediate supervisors during their first six months on the job. They examined expectations, perceived similarities, liking for each other, demographic similarity, and performance to determine the quality of leader–member exchange (LMX). They found that perceived similarity and liking for each other by both the leader and the subordinate had the greatest influence on the quality of LMX, while subordinates' performance ratings had much less influence. Ashkanasy and O'Connor (1997) confirmed the presence of higher LMX quality when the values of leaders and members are similar.

This research can provide only limited help to a subordinate who wants to be a member of the in-group. He might point out to a supervisor that they share a number of things in common, such as schools they attended and where they grew up. At the same time, there may be many dissimilarities that cannot be changed, such as age and gender. One resolution to this problem could be to train leaders to improve the quality of their LMX. Graen, Novak, and Sommerkamp (1982) found that training teaching supervisors to discuss work issues and work relationships with their subordinates significantly improved both productivity and job satisfaction. If leaders do not receive training in improving LMX quality, subordinates still can be successful in their careers if they are very good at their jobs. Graen and Wakabayashi (1984) found that young managers who ranked higher in quality of LMX, ability, or both received faster promotions and higher bonuses than did managers who were lower in both measures.

This research also demonstrates one of the problems with this theory. Although research generally has been supportive, some researchers feel that this is not a complete enough way to look at leadership unless other variables that could moderate the LMX effect are included (Dienesch & Liden, 1986). A more recent meta-analysis (Gerstner & Day, 1997) found significant relationships between LMX and a number of other variables, including job performance, satisfaction with supervision, overall satisfaction, commitment, role conflict, role clarity, and members' competence and turnover intent. A fairly common criticism of contingency theories in general is that so many variables influence effective leadership it is never possible to cover all the contingencies. The last contingency theory discussed in this section adds another factor that can influence the success of a leader.

Path-goal theory
A leadership theory based on the assumption that the most effective leaders make organizational goals and rewards clear to their subordinates and make it possible for the subordinates to reach those goals.

House's Path-Goal Theory

According to House (1971) and House and Mitchell (1974), three behaviors ensure a leader's success. Good leaders (1) help followers identify the paths that best lead to the goals of the subordinates, assuming that those goals are also beneficial to the organization; (2) acknowledge their followers' reaching those goals, with rewards that are meaningful to the followers; and (3) eliminate the barriers that might keep the followers from reaching their goals (Figure 7.3).

Using these behaviors, House's **path-goal theory** has a clear relationship to the valence-instrumentality-expectancy (VIE) and goal-setting theories that were discussed in Chapter 6. VIE theory states that employees will work hard if they value a goal and believe that they can attain it through their efforts. Goal-setting theory states that difficult specific goals motivate employees' behavior. The effort to combine motivation, job satisfaction, and leadership in one theory is seen as a definite advantage for this theory (Muchinsky, 1990). The complexity of combining so much in one theory has, however, led to limited research testing of different parts of the theory and conflicting results from one meta-analysis of it (Wofford & Liska, 1993), although an earlier meta-analysis (Indvik, 1986) was more positive. House (1996) revised some elements of this theory, but he may have made it even more complex and difficult to test.

Like LMX theory, House's theory emphasizes the relationship between the leader and each subordinate. The best leadership style for each lender–subordinate combination depends on the personal goals of the subordinates, the personal characteristics of the subordinates, and the attributes of the work situation. House and Mitchell (1974) defined four types of leadership behavior that should be used, depending on the particular combinations:

1. *Directive leadership.* A directive leader gives clear instructions to the subordinate about exactly what is to be done and how it is to be done. The subordinates have a very clear understanding of the job and how to obtain the rewards that are available.

2. *Supportive leadership.* A supportive leader's strongest commitment is to friendliness and the well-being of the subordinates. The subordinates are more likely to be interested in their work and to have higher self-confidence because of the leader's strong personal interest.

3. *Participative leadership.* A participative leader actively and genuinely involves the subordinates in every aspect of the work situation. The subordinates usually have a greater belief in their ability to accomplish the task and usually are very clear about the task and the methods used to accomplish it because they have contributed to both.

4. *Achievement-oriented leadership.* An achievement-oriented leader shows the characteristics of a good goal-setting leader. She sets challenging goals, expects

Figure 7.3
The role of the leader in House's path-goal theory.

Help subordinates
identify the best
paths to reach goals.

Remove barriers
to reaching goals.

Reward subordinates for reaching goals.

top-level performance from her subordinates, and expresses confidence that the subordinates will achieve the goals. The subordinates often feel a greater degree of challenge and move on to set goals that are even more difficult, as goal-setting theory would predict.

If a task is very complicated and the work group is composed of newly hired, inexperienced employees, a directive leader probably will be the most effective. By contrast, a supportive leader probably would be the most effective choice for a new project team planning the next new product for a company if the team was made up of employees whose group had experienced two previous failures. Although House's theory has generated a great deal of interest, lack of operational definitions of concepts such as *path* and *goal* has limited its usefulness. The interest generated by his theory has led to other leadership theories. House (1996) points to the substitutes for leadership and charismatic leader theories as developments of path-goal theory; this is discussed later in this chapter.

Vroom and Yetton's Decision-Making Model

The **Vroom and Yetton decision-making model** focuses on only one aspect of leadership behavior: decision making. Although making decisions may account for only a small part of leadership behavior, the decisions that are made by a leader often are regarded as critical in judging that leader's effectiveness. For example, think about how President Kennedy has been judged for his decisions to support an invasion of Cuba and to commit funds to land an astronaut on the moon. The Vroom and Yetton theory usually is classified as a prescriptive theory, meaning that it provides leaders with a way to choose the best decision-making method before going ahead. On the basis of a series of questions, the leader will arrive at a choice of one of five decision-making methods:

1. *Autocratic I.* The leader makes a decision without any assistance from or discussion with subordinates, using whatever information is available. A basic assumption is that the leader has the information needed to make the decision. It is not necessary for the subordinates to approve of the decision.

2. *Autocratic II.* The leader gets information from subordinates but makes the decision by herself. The leader may get information from the subordinates without sharing anything about the decision; decision acceptance by the subordinates is not required.

3. *Consultative I.* The leader talks to individual subordinates and shares the decision problem with some or all of them. The final decision is made by the leader, and it may not be the decision recommended by most or all of the subordinates.

4. *Consultative II.* The leader shares the decision problem with the entire group of subordinates but still makes the final decision, which may or may not be the decision recommended by the subordinates.

Vroom and Yetton decision-making model
A leadership theory that provides a decision pattern to help leaders find the most effective way to make decisions.

5. *Group.* The leader presents the decision problem to the entire group of subordinates, acts as a facilitator in helping the group reach a decision, but does not recommend a particular choice.

The final choice among these methods is determined by the answers to seven standard questions, as used in the following example of a department head who must choose which word-processing program to use in his department. This decision is diagrammed in Figure 7.4. The first question is, "Is the technical quality of this decision important?" Here the answer is yes because a poor technical choice could negatively affect the productivity of the department. The second question is, "Does the leader have enough information to make a high-quality decision?" The answer is no because the department head does not know which word-processing programs work best for the types of work done in the department.

The third question is, "Is the problem structured so that the leader knows what information is needed and how to obtain it?" Here the answer is yes because the department head knows that he needs a list of word-processing programs and knows that the head of information services maintains an up-to-date description and sample of those programs. The fourth question is, "Is it important for the subordinates to accept the decision for it to be an effective decision?" Here the answer is yes because the subordinates will be using the word-processing program every day. A program that does not fit their needs or preferences may lower their productivity.

The fifth question is, "If the leader makes the decision alone, is it likely that the decision will be accepted by the subordinates?" The answer here is no because the workers feel that the department head does not understand how they use a word-processing program on a daily basis. He is not close enough to make the best choice alone. The sixth question is, "Are the subordinates motivated to achieve the goals of the organization?" Here the answer is yes because everyone in the department has been there at least two years, and last year—when the company developed a program that gave each department a share of the profits it made—this group received one of the largest shares.

The seventh question is, "Is there likely to be conflict among the subordinates about the final choice for the entire group?" Here the answer is not used to help choose the decision method because of the answer to the sixth question. This answer indicates that the employees will work together cooperatively because they are all doing similar word-processing tasks and want to choose the program that will help all of them.

As you can see, this should lead to a group decision-making process. In this example only one good decision-making method results from the questions that are asked. In some situations, however, the answers to these questions may lead to several good methods.

Figure 7.4

The Vroom and Yetton decision model.

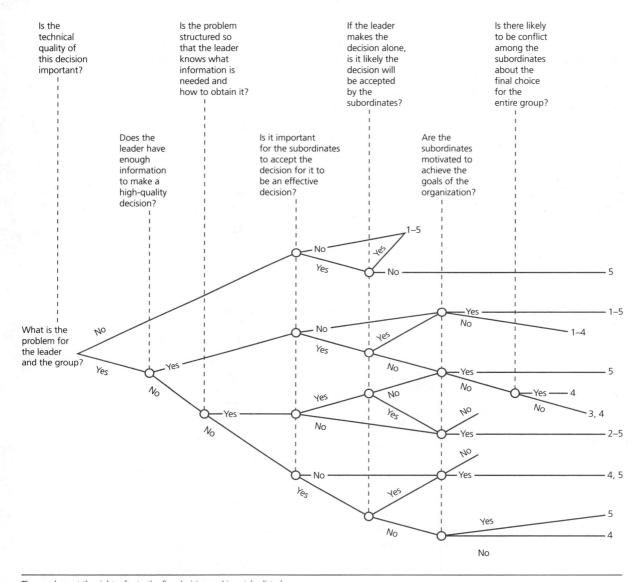

The numbers at the right refer to the five decision-making styles listed.
Adapted from V. H. Vroom & P. W. Yetton. (1993). *Leadership and decision-making.* Pittsburgh: University of Pittsburgh Press, p. 194.

To use this leadership model in actual work settings, managers are shown how to figure out what decision rules they actually use. They then are given feedback about how those rules differ from the ones suggested by the model. The last step is having the managers work through a number of case studies to practice making the correct choices according to the model. When the predictions of this model were used for actual decisions made by managers, researchers found that the decisions that fit the use of the model were more often successful, compared with decisions that did not fit the model (Vroom & Jago, 1988). Paul and Ebadi (1989) found that leaders who use the decision styles suggested by this model have subordinates who are more productive. Brown and Finstuen (1993) found that when this model was applied to decisions made by military officers in a graduate program, it was very successful at predicting the success or failure of those decisions on the basis of how closely the decisions conformed to the model.

Although research is generally supportive of Vroom and Yetton's theory, managers have indicated some discomfort with simply answering yes or no to the questions; in actual work settings many answers are partially yes and partially no. Vroom and Yago (1988) agreed that it would be better to substitute a five-point scale for the yes and no choices to grade each choice and they also added the following qualifiers to the decision process: information about the level of subordinates' development, how geographically spread out the participants are, and time requirements. This modified scale is referred to as the **Vroom and Yago theory.**

Although these factors add more realism to the model, they also make an already complex model even more so, which could discourage managers from using it. To increase the likelihood of managers using the model, a computer-based program was developed (Leadership Software, Inc., 1987) to guide managers through the decision steps. Although the Vroom and Yetton and Vroom and Yago models deal only with decision making, the ability to use them in actual job situations and leadership training programs is seen as a major advantage. The theories next to be considered are becoming increasingly popular, but they are often much less practical in actual job situations.

Transformational and Charismatic Leadership

Many leadership situations are based on an understanding between the leader and the followers. There is an implied social contract indicating that if the follower goes along with what the leader wants done, the follower will get certain benefits, such as pay, a promotion, or not getting fired. This is called **transactional leadership.** Constructive transactions result in positive consequences, such as getting a promotion. These transactions are viewed as more effective and satisfying than corrective transactions, which lead to negative consequences, such as a demotion (Bass, 1998).

Vroom and Yago theory
A leadership theory that adds more variables to the Vroom and Yetton decision-making model to make the leadership situation more realistic.

Transactional leadership
A leadership style that is based on a social contract between the subordinates and the leader, with the promise of rewards in return for certain behaviors.

Transformational leadership A leadership style in which the leader can change the interests and goals of individual subordinates into those of the group.

Charismatic leadership A leadership style that is based on the personal charm and emotional appeal of the leader.

Transformational Leaders

For some leaders, however, followers will do exceptional levels of work for what appears to be relatively little return. Steven Jobs, the founder of Apple Computer, persuaded several friends to commit large amounts of their time, energy, and effort to building the first Apple computers in his garage before he had even secured any orders for the machines. This situation typifies **transformational leadership.** A transformational leader gets followers to go beyond their self-interest and changes or transforms their goals into the greater goals of the group or organization. He gets the followers to do more than they have ever done before to meet the organization's goals (Barbuto, 1997; Bass, 1990b).

Bass (1985) found that the three major characteristics of a transformational leader are (1) charisma, (2) recognizing and encouraging each follower as an individual, and (3) providing the intellectual stimulation that gets followers to look at situations in new ways. The personality characteristics associated with transformational leadership are higher levels of pragmatism, nurturance, feminine attributes, and lower levels of criticism and aggression (Ross & Offerman, 1997). The use of transformational leadership has been associated with higher performance (Barling, Weber, & Kelloway, 1996; Howell & Avolio, 1993) and with greater perceived leader effectiveness and subordinate satisfaction with the leader (Deluga, 1991). A study of schoolteachers showed that the transformational leadership style is associated with lower burnout levels (Leithwood, Menzies, Jantzi, & Leithwood, 1996).

Bass (1990b) has suggested that transactional leadership styles are most appropriate in stable organizations. When the business climate becomes more turbulent, however, transformational leadership can meet the needs of a changing marketplace better because leadership behavior is based on a vision of the company, not just on moment-to-moment concerns. For Steven Jobs at Apple, his vision of a "computer on every desk" has been part of the company since its beginning in 1974. The introduction of the IMac computer, which could be up and running as soon as it was plugged in, provided further evidence of his vision of user-friendly computers for everyone. The IMac was introduced at a time of declining profits for Apple, when other types of computers were taking a greater market share.

Charismatic Leadership

The ability to inspire followers provides the link between transformational leadership and **charismatic leadership.** The followers of a charismatic leader do what the leader wants because of his or her personal charm, magnetism, and emotional appeal. Charismatic leaders inspire their followers to meet the personal goals of the leader, which may not be the goals of the organization.

Although the concept of charismatic leadership was proposed many decades ago by Weber (1947), it recently has received renewed interest. This renewal of interest has the advantage of many years of study that have led to a more complete definition of this system that is based on both the leader and the situation. House (1977) suggested that the conditions that promote charismatic leadership are unclear paths to goal achievement, the lack of a link between extrinsic rewards (such as pay) and the performance of individual workers, and instability in the organization and in social conditions. To test that suggestion House, Spangler, and Woycke (1991) rated the charisma of all U.S. presidents through Ronald Reagan. The charisma index for each president, assessed from historical documents, was influenced by both his personality and the conditions in the nation during his presidency. Threatening or crisis situations encourage the development of charismatic leadership. (McCann, 1997; Pillai, 1996).

Although each person may agree or disagree about whether a particular president is a charismatic leader, the characteristics and behaviors most commonly associated with this leadership style were summarized in the following list by Conger (1989) and DuBrin (1994).

1. Charismatic leaders have a vision they share with their followers. In his "I Have a Dream" speech, Martin Luther King, Jr., shared his vision of a country where people are not judged by the color of their skin.

2. Charismatic leaders excel at communications. Although many people disagreed with what Ronald Reagan was saying, he was given the nickname "the Great Communicator" for the way he presented his messages.

3. Charismatic leaders develop limitless feelings of trust among their followers. Every armed conflict produces examples of soldiers who are willing to follow their commanders even to death because of their faith in those leaders.

4. Charismatic leaders develop feelings of competence among group members by planning for their success. Herb Kelleher at Southwest Airlines convinced his turnaround crews that they could refuel and clean a plane and load baggage and refreshments in less than twenty minutes, half the industry average—and they did it.

5. Charismatic leaders have very high energy levels that contribute to an active leadership style. Herb Kelleher is described as "dynamic" by many employees and often seems to be everywhere, from working alongside plane crews on Thanksgiving to defending the right of Southwest to use a slogan by arm wrestling the president of another company. These characteristics contribute to the power and mystique of the charismatic leader.

Ethics of Charismatic Leadership

Among charismatic leaders, there have been a number of people who made the world a better place, but there also have been clearly destructive leaders, such as Hitler, heads of cults, and, more recently, financial criminals who caused large

| Ayatollah Khomeini of Iran | Adolf Hitler | President John F. Kennedy | General Colin L. Powell |

■ Charismatic leaders can be the best or the most destructive leaders.

financial losses for many people. What makes the difference between the two types? Howell and Avolio (1995) found a distinct difference in the ethical practices and behaviors of destructive versus beneficial charismatic leaders. Unethical charismatic leaders want power only for personal gain or to promote a personal vision. They do not tolerate opposition and require blind obedience from their followers. They do not consider the needs of their followers, and their only moral criterion is self-interest.

The exposure of unethical charismatic leaders should lead to a better understanding of the correct applications of charismatic leadership. At the same time, the current popularity of this theory is leading to an examination of organizations not traditionally studied in I/O psychology, such as volunteer organizations, social groups, and religious organizations, which often have charismatic leaders.

SUBSTITUTES FOR LEADERSHIP AND EMPLOYEE EMPOWERMENT THEORIES

The basic assumption of all the theories looked at so far is that leadership is necessary and important in all situations. Kerr and Jermier (1978), however, suggested that there are characteristics of workers, job tasks, and organizations that make the use of a leader unnecessary and may even make it impossible for a leader to contribute to a work group. This was not always accepted as true. Earlier, this chapter looked at a study of boys' club groups, conducted by Lewin,

Lippitt, and White (1939), which showed that with a laissez-faire leader, very little work was accomplished by the group and there was very low job satisfaction among the boys.

A laissez-faire leader often is called a nonleader because he has the title but exerts no leadership authority. Although most I/O psychologists regard this as a poor choice of leadership style, the findings of researchers such as Kerr and Jermier (1978) suggest that there are times when this style is the best choice. Howell, Bowen, Dorfman, and Kerr (1990) described the ideal situation for leadership substitution as being a closely knit group of highly trained workers in jobs with a high level of intrinsic satisfaction where computer technology is used for many managerial functions. Workers in such a setting have extensive professional education before they come to the organization or develop professional skills within the organization.

Although most work situations do not meet all these criteria, the indication is that in situations with some of these characteristics, it may be best for the leader to be less directive and give more authority and control to the workers. A study of secondary school teachers showed the substitutes for leadership dimension of professional orientation to be a significant predictor of organizational commitment. Several other substitutes for leadership dimensions were found to be significant predictors of teachers' job satisfaction (Burrows, Munday, Tunnell, & Seay, 1996). These criteria lead to a situation in which laissez-faire leadership is the best leadership style. However, although this theory may sound appealing, some critics have suggested that it is nothing more than an extension of path-goal theory (Schriesheim, 1997).

The **substitutes for leadership theory** gives some or all of the leadership functions to the workers if they are able to perform them well. In recent years the concept of **employee empowerment** has focused on giving employees greater control over the work environment, generally by giving them some of the functions previously controlled by their supervisors. The suggestion that employees may be able to do many of the functions assigned to managers sometimes has met with considerable resistance.

Organizations have had varying degrees of success with employee empowerment programs. Some of the failures occurred when empowerment was introduced in the workplace but not actually implemented. In one survey almost half the employees said they had opportunities to suggest ideas for improvements at work. The percentages ranged from 58 percent for middle managers to 38 percent for hourly workers. When those employees were asked whether any of their suggestions were used, the percentages remained high for middle managers (59 percent) but dropped to 18 percent for hourly workers (Durity, 1991).

Bennis (1993) says that when empowerment is real in organizations, four themes become evident in the everyday life of the organization:

Substitutes for leadership theory A theory that suggests leadership may not be necessary in all work situations.

Employee empowerment The practice of giving subordinates control of tasks and functions usually done by the supervisor.

1. People feel significant. They feel that their work behaviors make a difference to the success of the company.

2. Learning and competence matter. Mastery is important, but mistakes do not mean failure. Instead, they represent opportunities to get feedback about what to do differently the next time.

3. People are part of a community. Each person in the organization feels he or she is more than just an employee of an organization, in the same way that a family is more than a number of people who live in the same household.

4. The work is exciting.

While some employees may be unable or unwilling to be empowered, Tseo and Ramos (1995) view employee empowerment as a method for returning downsized or restructured organizations to a successful level, as is shown in the case study "Leadership at Work."

[Case Study] LEADERSHIP AT WORK

In the early 1980s Harley-Davidson, America's one remaining motorcycle company, was selling only 18 percent of the motorcycles purchased in the United States. Today the company proudly points to selling 49 percent of the motorcycles on the market. Its turnaround strategy included a strong emphasis on employee empowerment and quality. One of the goals was for employees and management to work toward a successful turnaround by developing a common passion for involvement in all parts of the organization.

One of the first changes management made was to get rid of the quality inspectors and train all the employees to keep track of their own quality. The workers created their own tolerance measurements. They were given instruments and computers to keep track of everything they produced.

The unions were included in the choice of which machinery was ordered and the design of new manufacturing processes. The unions also were involved in the choice of a new plant once the turnaround created a need for expansion.

To prepare employees to participate in decision making, all employees receive at least eighty hours of training per year. In addition, dealers receive three days of intensive training each year. The training topics are suggested by a dealer advisory council.

Employee participation extends to all parts of the business. Employees serve as models in the Harley-Davidson clothing catalog and volunteer at company rallies around the country that bring together customers, employees, and corporate brass. At the end of the rallies, Harley executives meet to answer the questions of the 250 to 300 Harley riders gathered at a town hall meeting. This is often like a meeting of old friends because the executives usually ride with the customers the day before the meeting. And if the company's engineers find ways for its suppliers to save Harley money, they get a share of the savings.

Clyde Fessler, vice president for business development, says, "Any type of business is cyclical. It's easy through the 'ups'; it's the relationships that get you through the 'downs.'"

From C. Fessler. (1998). How to be a loved company. *Best Practices,* http://www.csmus.com/article000005.htm.

POWER AND LEADERSHIP

Regardless of whether the employees, the leader, or both have the power in organizations, power is an important component of the leadership process. It is tempting to match the strong use of power with leadership effectiveness. A look at U.S. presidents shows that people admire presidents who were very powerful and discount the work of presidents who did not use power and influence in the same way. President Franklin D. Roosevelt was seen as a very powerful president for his aggressive programs to bring the country out of the Depression of the 1930s. President Jimmy Carter often was characterized as a "do-nothing" president because he used persuasion and influence far more than he directly exercised the power of the office.

Position and Personal Power

Leadership power typically comes from one of two sources. **Position power** comes from the job title and place on the organizational chart, such as vice president of sales. **Personal power** comes from the characteristics and skills of the leader, such as the charismatic leader discussed in the last section. French and Raven (1967) further divided these two types of power into three and two subtypes, respectively.

Bases of Power

The three subtypes of position power are legitimate power, reward power, and coercive power. **Legitimate power** is influence that is based on the formal organizational position of the leader. A salesperson may change the way she dresses because the head of the sales department has told her that he is imposing a new dress code. **Reward power** is influence that is based on the leader's ability to deliver rewards a worker values. If a supervisor can allocate desirable and undesirable work assignments each day, this is an example of reward power. A desirable job assignment can be given as a reward for high productivity, not as a bribe for future behavior.

Coercive power often is regarded by employees and managers as the least desirable type of power because it is based on the leader's ability to deliver punishments. If the supervisor makes a threat but the employee persists in the wrong behavior, punishment will follow. If no punishment follows the wrong behavior, the value of coercive power is lost (Raven, 1992). Even if a manager can get very

Position power Leadership control derived from the leader's legitimate status in the organization.

Personal power Leadership control derived from the characteristics and skills of the leader.

Legitimate power Influence that is based on the formal organizational position of the leader.

Reward power Influence that is based on the leader's ability to deliver things such as bonuses to subordinates.

Coercive power Influence that is based on the leader's ability to punish subordinates.

Expert power Influence that is based on the subordinate's belief that the leader knows more about the task than the subordinate does.

Referent power Influence that is based on the leader's personal attractiveness.

high production levels through the use of coercive power, the turnover and absence rates of subordinates can outweigh the production gains. The use of coercive power relates strongly to lower job satisfaction among employees (Hinkin & Schriesheim, 1989).

The two subtypes of personal power are expert power and referent power. **Expert power** is influence that is based on subordinates' belief in the superior task knowledge of the supervisor. The important factor here is the employees' belief in the leader's ability rather than the leader's actual ability. Expert power can be found even when an employee has very little positional power. In many organizations the employees in the information system department may be seen as having control over many people at many levels of the organization because they are believed to be the only people who can keep the computers operational.

Referent power is influence that is based on the personal attractiveness of the leader. This is most like the charismatic leadership discussed earlier. As with expert power, the main issue here is the followers' belief in the leader. With referent power, the belief is in the leader as a person rather than as a store of knowledge. A leader with referent power often is viewed as a role model for the subordinates. President Clinton said that his brief meeting with President Kennedy in the early 1960s was one of the events that inspired him to go into politics. Even if a leader with referent power makes poor decisions, the leadership often remains because this power is person-based rather than skill-based.

French and Raven's (1967) description of the bases of power has been in use for over three decades. A considerable amount of research has confirmed that leaders use these different types of power, and researchers have developed scales to assess which power bases are used by managers. One of the most recent measurement instruments of power bases was developed by Hinkin and Schriesheim (1989) (Figure 7.5). This measure has been shown to be valid and reliable. It is given to subordinates to assess the power bases of the people who supervise them. The use of this and similar scales has confirmed that the use of expert power and referent power generally leads to the best outcomes, including job satisfaction, high performance, and commitment (Podsakoff & Schriesheim, 1985; Rahim & Afza, 1993; Yukl, 1981).

One of the problems in applying the French and Raven model to actual work settings is the assumption that a leader's ability to influence subordinates is rooted in only one power base. If a younger employee is promoted to a supervisory position, he would be wise not only to use the legitimate power that the position gives him but also to try to develop expert power and referent power bases. He is much more likely to be successful by using this combination of power bases. While employees respond to legitimate requests made by supervisors, they respond more to referent power and expert power bases in leaders.

Figure 7.5

Measurement of French and Raven's power bases.

Instructions: Below is a list of statements which may be used in describing behaviors that supervisors in work organizations can direct toward their subordinates. First carefully read each descriptive statement, thinking in terms of your supervisor. Then decide to what extent you agree that your supervisor could do this to you. Mark the number which most closely represents how you feel. Use the following numbers for your answers.

5 = strongly agree	2 = disagree
4 = agree	1 = strongly disagree
3 = neither agree nor disagree	

My supervisor can

_____ 1. increase my pay level. (R)

_____ 2. make me feel valued. (RF)

_____ 3. give me undesirable job assignments. (C)

_____ 4. make me feel like he or she approves of me. (RF)

_____ 5. make me feel that I have commitments to meet. (L)

_____ 6. make me feel personally accepted. (RF)

_____ 7. make me feel important. (RF)

_____ 8. give me good technical suggestions. (E)

_____ 9. make my work difficult for me. (C)

_____ 10. share with me his or her considerable experiences and/or training. (E)

_____ 11. make things unpleasant here. (C)

_____ 12. make being at work distasteful. (C)

_____ 13. influence my getting a pay raise. (R)

_____ 14. make me feel like I should satisfy my job requirements. (L)

_____ 15. provide me with sound job-related advice. (E)

_____ 16. provide me with special benefits. (R)

_____ 17. influence my getting a promotion. (R)

_____ 18. give me a feeling I have responsibilities to fulfill. (L)

_____ 19. provide me with needed technical knowledge. (E)

_____ 20. make me recognize that I have tasks to accomplish. (L)

Letters after each statement have been added to indicate which power bases is being measured. (RF = referent).
Adapted from T. R. Hinkin & C. A. Schriesheim. (1989). Development and application of new scales to measure the French and Raven (1959) bases of social power. *Journal of Applied Psychology, 74*(4), 561–567.

Use of Influence

Although a supervisor may try to implement all of her subordinates' suggestions in order to encourage them to respond to her use of an expert power base, power bases rest on the ability to exert certain kinds of control, as is shown in the definitions of the power bases. The actual change in behavior or attitudes is referred to as **influence.** The methods used to produce these changes are called *influence*

Influence The exertion of control over others in a way that results in changes in behavior or attitude.

tactics. Yukl and Tracey (1992) identified nine different influence tactics from questionnaires filled out by subordinates, peers, and bosses of a group of managers (Table 7.2).

Although all these influence tactics have been used at some time, Yukl and Tracey (1992) found a great deal of variability in their effectiveness. The least effective tactics were pressure, coalition, and legitimating. If you consider the fact that law enforcement speed patrols are effective only when drivers can see the officers or know they are there, it is easy to understand why these tactics are the least effective. The most effective tactics were rational persuasion, inspirational appeal, and consultation. It is also easy to understand why these tactics work best. Most people like to think that they base decisions on facts rather than emotions. However, people can be convinced by the inspirational appeal to "go out there and win one" for an admired leader. The use of consultation makes followers feel that they and their ideas are important. Although these were the best and worst methods in general, Yukl and Tracey (1992) found that there were a num-

Table 7.2

YUKL AND TRACEY'S INFLUENCE TACTICS

Influence Tactic	How It Works
1. Rational persuasion	The leader uses logic and facts to persuade the followers that a request will lead to the desired outcomes.
2. Inspirational appeal	The leader uses an appeal to the followers' emotions and inspires confidence in their ability to do the job.
3. Consultation	The leader actively wants the followers to participate in work where their support is an important factor in getting the work done.
4. Ingratiation	The leader tries to get the followers in a positive frame of mind or to feel good about the leader before asking them to do something.
5. Exchange	The leader offers a trade of time, favors, or other benefits if followers do what he or she wants them to do.
6. Personal appeal	The leader asks for the followers' help based on the loyalty and friendship they feel toward her or him.
7. Coalition	The leader enlists other people to persuade the followers to do certain behaviors and tells them about the support of the others as the reason why they should agree to the request.
8. Legitimating	The leader bases his or her request on his or her position power authority in the organization.
9. Pressure	The leader uses demands, threats, or intimidation to get the followers to agree to his or her request.

ber of differences in effectiveness, depending on whether the influence appeal was directed at subordinates, peers, or superiors. If you want to persuade your boss to do something, you are most likely to use coalition or rational persuasion. From this research, it appears that the best choice would be to get all the facts and information together and then present them to the supervisor.

Although this discussion assumes that the use of influence or power leads to rightful outcomes, power and influence sometimes are used to achieve unjust outcomes. Kipnis (1976) found that supervisors with a great deal of position power, such as the ability to give raises or demotions and dismiss or transfer employees, relied on position power far more than personal power. In the last section, referent power and expert power bases (personal power) were said to lead to the best outcomes. Since high degrees of position power are associated with higher positions on the organizational chart, it is tempting for leaders with high position power to see themselves as far superior to their subordinates, and this can lead to conflict.

At the opposite end too little position power can lead to poor outcomes: Leaders with low position power often use threats of punishment (coercive power) even if they cannot enforce the punishment (Greene & Podsakoff, 1981). It appears that the best combination of personal power and position power is enough position power to get the job done along with the development of sources of personal power.

Power of Followers

If a great deal of attention has been focused on what the leader does or should do, very little attention has been focused on the role of the followers except as the leader influences them. The interaction between leaders and followers is a two-way relationship, with each one influencing the other whether in an informal social group or in the election of a president. At the national level, Winter (1987) found a history of greater electoral success for presidential candidates when the voters perceived the candidates as being more like themselves.

Although most research has examined how the leader influences the followers, followers can exert a great deal of influence over the leader as well. Lowin and Craig (1968) and Greene (1975) found that the performance of followers has a great deal of influence on the leader's behavior. When followers had poor performance records, leaders acted in more punishing ways (Sims & Manz, 1984). This could be an example of the fundamental attribution error (discussed in Chapter 6), which states that people tend to connect good performance in others with characteristics and causes outside of them and connect bad performance in others with factors within the person. If a group is performing well, the leader may point to her own skill in leadership, but if the group is performing poorly, she is more likely to see the cause as lack of effort by the group. At least one researcher

(Bar Tal, 1991) has confirmed the accuracy of this position. However, when he used an experiment based on Fiedler's contingency theory he found that the performance levels of the subordinates were determined more by the goals and motivations of the subordinates than by those of the leader. The area of follower research is new in the field of leadership, and research findings such as these suggest that more information about followers could lead to a more complete understanding of leaders.

PERSONAL VARIABLES IN LEADERSHIP

With the number of theories and situational variables involved in leadership, it is reasonable to expect that no two people lead in exactly the same way. When leaders have the same personal characteristics, such as gender or race, research has shown that those attributes add more variables to the leadership process. This section examines the effects of gender, race, and culture on leadership.

Gender Roles in Leadership

Research on the effects of gender on leadership has been mixed. Studies show that both women and men can be effective leaders (Dobbins & Platz, 1986; Drazin & Auster, 1987) and that men and women as leaders are perceived by themselves and others quite differently. Schein (1973) showed that when people were asked to describe "men in general," "women in general," and "successful middle managers in general," the descriptions of men and successful middle managers were very similar. By contrast, there was only a weak statistical relationship between the descriptions of women and the descriptions of successful middle managers. The traits that men and successful managers shared included leadership ability, self-confidence, objectivity, forcefulness, and ambition. Those characteristics typically are perceived as important for successful leadership. Schein suggested that these perceptions led to the less frequent choice of women for managerial positions because women did not fit the manager stereotype. This relates to the implicit theories of leadership discussed earlier in this chapter. In 1973 the United States was just beginning to apply the antidiscrimination laws of the 1960s, so it might seem that Schein's results may no longer be applicable.

In 1989, Heilman, Block, Martell, and Simon replicated and extended Schein's study and found that very little had changed in sixteen years. They asked people for descriptions of women in general, men in general, successful middle managers, men managers, women managers, successful men managers, and successful women managers. The descriptions of men in general still correlated far more with the descriptions of successful managers than did the descriptions of women in general. Only in the descriptions of successful managers and successful women managers was there a high degree of similarity. Even at that later time the people doing the ratings judged that "leadership ability" was more characteristic of successful male managers than of successful women managers, although they saw this trait as important for successful managers in general.

The adjectives applied to women managers and successful women managers compared with those of successful managers in general were the generally offensive characteristics "bitter," "quarrelsome," and "selfish." This seems to confirm the stereotype of the successful, high-powered career woman as a difficult person to work with. A further look at the qualities listed for successful managers in general shows some characteristics that are more similar to those of men in general than to those of women in general, however. Those characteristics include "curious," "helpful," "intuitive," "creative," "understanding," and "aware of others' feelings," which most people view as very positive.

This list of traits also seems to confirm the belief that successful male leaders are higher in task orientation and successful female leaders are higher in person orientation (Lauterbach & Weiner, 1996). Payne and Cangemi (1997) found that training could teach male and female leaders to incorporate both styles, but the backup styles still remained closer to the gender stereotypes. Eagly and Johnson (1990) did a meta-analysis of over 160 studies that compared the leadership styles of men and women and found that the stereotypes of task orientation and person orientation were true only in laboratory studies, not in field studies of real leaders.

One reason for the differences in these studies may be that field studies represent situations in which women must be perceived as effective leaders in order to be chosen for leadership positions. The laboratory studies offered the freedom to behave more as the subjects wanted to behave because their jobs did not depend on their behavior. Hackman, Hillis, Paterson, and Furniss (1993) found that masculinity was perceived as effective for both male and female leaders but that femininity was perceived as effective only when male leaders showed it.

Another meta-analysis showed that when women held autocratic or directive leadership positions, they were considered lower in effectiveness than men were (Eagly, Makhijani, & Klonsky, 1992). As the Heilman, Block, Martell, and Simon (1989) study shows, the perception of effective leadership is tied closely to descriptions of males. Thus, if women want to be promoted to leadership positions, they may believe that they must behave more like men than like women. In a laboratory study men and women both know that this is not a real-life situation and perhaps feel less need to conform to the stereotypes they find at work; research shows much greater gender differences in leadership styles in laboratory situations than in the field. This still does not mean that men and women lead in exactly the same way. Eagly and Johnson (1990) found that the leadership styles of men and women in both laboratory and field situations were more autocratic among the men and more democratic among the women.

Interactive leadership
A leadership style that is based on making the contact between subordinates and the supervisor positive for everyone involved.

As previous researchers had confirmed, each leadership style can be effective, depending on a number of situational variables, although subordinates generally indicate that they prefer democratic leaders. This may turn out to be an advantage for women as they find ways to profit from their leadership differences. Rosener (1990) described this new female leadership pattern as **interactive leadership,** because the emphasis is on the woman leader working to make her interactions with subordinates positive for everyone involved. The end result is a leader who is very similar to the transformational leader described earlier in this chapter. Transformational leaders have been shown to have a greater balance between masculine and feminine factors than do transactional leaders (Hackman, Furniss, Hillis, & Paterson, 1992).

Additionally, the women leaders in Rosener's (1990) sample were found to encourage participation in ways that were meaningful but did not give up control. One woman chief executive officer said that when she had a difficult decision to make, she asked employees what they would do in her position. She still made the final decision, but she had a much better basis for judgment. Interactive woman leaders also shared power and information. This can be dangerous if sharing power and information is seen as weakness or losing control, but the women managers all said that the positives of greater loyalty, trust, and openness made it worth the risk. Much like transformational leaders, these interactive female leaders worked to enhance the self-worth of the employees and energize them.

In another study female leaders engaged in more modeling and encouraging behaviors than did their male counterparts (Posner & Kouzes, 1993). As part of sharing power, those women freely gave credit to subordinates for good work and recognized them as people as well as employees. A study of the LMX theory found that women leaders showed more relationship concerns in their interactions than men leaders did (Fairhurst, 1993). Female interactive leaders typically indicated a very high degree of job satisfaction, and that enthusiasm was communicated to the employees. Those women indicated that this leadership style was a natural outcome of experiences that showed which behaviors got the best results.

In the past there were limited opportunities for women to learn leadership by being taken under the wing of a mentor in a higher position. More recent studies have shown that there are now more mentoring opportunities for professional women (Ragins & Cotton, 1991). The combination of greater mentoring opportunities and the development of a successful female leadership style (interactive leadership) may indicate that this society is moving toward greater leadership equity for men and women.

Racial Issues in Leadership

Thee is little doubt that certain racial and ethnic groups are more underrepresented in organizational leadership ranks than they are in the general population. In an *HRMagazine* survey (1991) the researchers found that African Americans,

Hispanic Americans, and Asian Americans held less than 1.5 percent of the senior executive positions in *Fortune* 1000 companies. In 1996, African Americans held fewer than 5 percent of executive, administrative, and managerial jobs (Hayes, 1998); whites held almost 97 percent of these executive positions. The remainder were held by nonresponders to the survey.

Although discrimination has been illegal for a number of years, gains in leadership positions for racial and ethnic minorities do not reflect as much progress as the overall employment picture does. *Hispanic Business* listed 287 Hispanic executives at 146 *Fortune* 1000 firms (*Hispanic Business*, 1998). In the previous *HRMagazine* survey, the new hires in the year of the survey showed 12.7 percent of the positions going to blacks, a figure similar to the percentage of African Americans in the general population. Only 5 percent of the managers hired in that year were black, and 5 percent of the officials and managers who lost jobs that year were black. This was not consistent across all the racial groups. Asian Americans accounted for only about 2.5 percent of the newly hired group but accounted for almost 5 percent of the new managerial positions.

Like women in management positions, members of racial and ethnic minorities often report feeling that a *glass ceiling* allows them to see what is possible in regard to leadership positions but does not give them access to those positions (Duleep &

Bob Daemmrich/Stock Boston

■ Although minoritiy group members are being hired in increasing numbers, they are not often found in leadership positions.

Sanders, 1992; Hylton, 1988; Zate, 1996). While most African-American managers agree that overt racism is rare, more subtle effects of prejudice seem to influence many corporate leadership decisions. In a survey of black executives and managers, over 95 percent felt that their corporate advancement had been hindered by racism (Braham, 1987). The more subtle occurrence of racism includes the perception of less encouragement to try new assignments and being sent to external development programs rather than to those inside the organization (Cianni & Romberger, 1995).

More overt occurrences of racism are shown in a study of the perception of managers in their ratings promotion potential for a group of managerial and professional employees who had received at least "above average" ratings. African Americans and Asian Americans were consistently rated lower than white employees were (Landau, 1995). In another study male and female managers were asked to describe "successful middle managers" and black and white stereotypes. The description of the successful middle managers was most similar to the white racial stereotypes (Tomkiewicz, Brenner, & Adeyemi, 1998).

In a similar study of Hispanic stereotypes and descriptions of managers, a group of business students in a master's program rated little difference between whites and Hispanics. Interestingly, this group rated "successful Hispanic managers" as being different from "Hispanics in general" (Tomkiewicz & Brenner, 1996). Even when members of ethnic and racial minorities are successful in managerial positions, that success is seen as different from the success of white managers. The success of black managers was perceived as more likely due to help from other people than to personal effort and ability—as in the case of white managers (Greenhaus & Parasuraman, 1993).

The overall corporate management experience appears to be much more negative for minority workers. When Greenhaus, Parasuraman, and Wormley (1990) asked several hundred black and white managers and their supervisors about their job experiences, blacks reported (1) feeling less accepted in their organizations, (2) having less discretion in their jobs, (3) receiving lower ratings from their supervisors, (4) being more likely to have reached a career plateau, and (5) experiencing lower levels of career satisfaction. Blacks with white supervisors reported less supervisory support and more discrimination than did black subordinates with black supervisors (Jeanquart-Barone, 1996).

Minority employees find a greater number of obstacles in reaching management ranks than do other employees. Braham (1987) found that a disproportionate share of minority group managers were in staff rather than line positions—for example, in human relations or employee assistance rather than in production or marketing. Line positions typically are perceived as the path to top executive positions. When cutbacks are made in organizations, the first layoffs usually occur among those in staff positions rather than line positions. Minority employees often report feeling that they had to work harder to reach management positions, and the farther they progressed up the corporate ladder, the greater the discrimination they encountered (Hylton, 1988).

Cross-Cultural Management

As managers find themselves supervising an increasingly diverse workforce, great numbers of managers and executives find themselves also having to manage in different cultural settings. As a result, the organizational relationship between leaders and subordinates often has numerous cultural factors. This may involve the manager being sent to another country or supervising groups of employees from other countries and other cultures in the United States. The likelihood of managers supervising in cross-cultural situations has increased greatly in the last several decades. The number of multinational companies in the fourteen largest countries went from 7,000 in 1969 to 24,000 in 1998 (Alden, 1998).

Management style is often closely related to the culture of the country in which a company is based. Studies have found significant differences in management style among American, European, and Asian countries (Hui & Graen, 1997; Rao, Hashimoto, & Rao, 1997; Suutari, 1996; Tayeb, 1994). The need for managerial effectiveness in cross-cultural settings has led to the development of formal cross-cultural management training programs in only about 30 percent of American organizations, but increases are expected. In a meta-analysis of twenty-one studies of the effectiveness of cross-cultural management training, Deshpanda and Viswesvaran (1992) concluded that such programs had a positive influence on the self-development, perception, adjustment, relationships, and performance of the managers.

Harrison (1992) found the best cross-cultural training included both cognitive and experiential programs. Cognitive training consisted of a programmed learning system, known as the cultural assimilator, that tests managers' knowledge of cultural differences and the effect of those differences in different cultures. Experiential training consisted of a behavior-modeling program in which the managers watched films of a person demonstrating and explaining correct behaviors in a problem situation, practiced the correct behaviors, and received feedback and reinforcement from the trainers.

BEING AN EFFECTIVE LEADER

After examining the different theories and variables of leadership, it may seem that the only realistic conclusion is that there is no consistently effective method of leadership because so many variables influence the process. Although there are many different leadership styles, situations, and variables, researchers have, however, found a number of common features among effective leaders in numerous situations. After holding a number of leadership positions, from provost to college president, and observing and interviewing numerous leaders, one author found that four competencies were always present to some degree in effective leaders (Bennis, 1993).

The first competency is the management of attention. A really effective leader has people wanting to join her. Followers are attracted by leaders' outstanding commitment to their goals, outcomes, and direction.

The second competency is the management of meaning. Followers may be attracted to a leader because of the leader's commitment and focus; but if the followers do not understand what the commitment is to or for, leadership cannot be effective. The most effective leaders use every part of themselves to convey meaning to their followers. A memo merely saying that an organization is going to be customer driven is not nearly as effective as having a manager who works in customer service one day each month and gives employees the authority to make on-the-spot refunds or adjustments for customers. A leader who says that all employees are equal and stops using an assigned parking space adds meaning to his words in a way that is understood by the employees.

The third competency is the management of trust. The issue here is constancy and predictability. Even if the followers do not agree with the leader, there is no doubt about where the leader stands and what she stands for. This relates to the first two competencies because the followers of a trusted leader know exactly what they are buying into over the long haul. One of the most common descriptions of ineffective leaders is that they cannot be trusted to be the same today as they were yesterday. Predictability sends the message that the leader is there for the long term and can be counted on.

The fourth competency is management of the self. The most effective leaders know what their strong and weak points are and know how to use their skills in the most effective ways. The management of self also means taking responsibility for one's actions. One leader Bennis (1993) cites said that he did not know what his most difficult decision was because he never worried about a decision after he had made it. He always accepted the possibility that it could be a wrong decision, but he would go on from there and not be overcome by doubt. The most effective leaders are willing to accept risk, knowing they can manage it.

Bennis's list of what it takes to be an effective leader agrees with a number of other studies of effective leadership. Studies by King (1990) and Conyne, Harvill, and Morganett (1990) stressed that effective leaders must be willing to take risks, be flexible, be willing to share power, be able to communicate the organization's goals and values, and be knowledgeable about themselves. Above all else, when effective leadership works, it is profitable for the organization, the leader, and the subordinates. One company president told me that he thought effective leadership is much like good art. Although he did not always know why the art was good or why the leadership was effective, he knew without a doubt when it was.

- Leadership involves getting followers to work on group rather than individual goals and is different from an appointed managerial position.

- Early theories of leadership focused on the traits needed by effective leaders. After a period of rejection, this theory is again finding favor. McClelland's leadership motive pattern is an example of a trait theory.

- Behavioral theories of leadership generally focus on the leadership behaviors of consideration and initiation of structure. The Ohio State University studies illustrate a behavioral leadership theory.

- Contingency theories of leadership focus on the combination of leadership characteristics and the environment. Fiedler's theories, LMX theory, House's path-goal theory, and Vroom and Yetton's decision-making model are examples of contingency theory.

- Fiedler's contingency theory led to the Leader Match Training program, which teaches leaders how to change situations to match their leadership preferences.

- Transformational and charismatic models of leadership are among the newest approaches to examining leadership.

- If subordinates are well trained and committed to a task, it may be possible to substitute those proficiencies for leadership positions, leading to employee empowerment.

- Power in leadership positions comes from either the position (job title) or the person (characteristics and skills). The three types of position power are legitimate power, reward power, and coercive power. The two types of personal power are expert power and referent power.

- Although power refers to actual control by the leader, changes in behavior result from the use of a number of different influence tactics by the leader. The use of referent power and expert power is most likely to lead to good outcomes for the group and the subordinates.

- In real work settings, power and influence are part of a two-way relationship between the leaders and the followers.

- Both men and women can be effective leaders, but research shows that men more often are seen as having the characteristics of good leaders.

- Recent research has suggested that women may be most effective as leaders when they develop a new leadership style referred to as interactive leadership.

- The low numbers of members of racial minorities in leadership positions appear to result from greater obstacles to reaching leadership positions rather than from lack of ability or skill.

- As organizations become more multinational, it will become important for leaders to be effective in many different cultural settings.
- Bennis (1993) says that the most effective leaders have competencies in the management of attention, meaning, trust, and self.

KEY TERMS

Authoritarian leadership style
Charismatic leadership
Coercive power
Consideration behavior
Contingency theory
Democratic leadership style
Employee empowerment
Expert power
Fiedler's cognitive resource theory
Fiedler's contingency theory
Influence
In-group subordinates
Initiation of structure behavior
Intellectance
Interactive leadership
Laissez-faire leadership style
Leader Match training
Leader–member exchange model (LMX)
Leader–member relations

Leadership
Leadership motive pattern
Least-Preferred Co-Worker (LPC) scale
Legitimate power
Out-group subordinates
Path-goal theory
Personal power
Position power
Referent power
Reward power
Substitutes for leadership theory
Surgency
Task structure
Trait theory
Transactional leadership
Transformational leadership
Vroom and Yago theory
Vroom and Yetton decision-making model

REVIEW QUESTIONS

Answers to these questions can be found at the end of the book.

1. The application of leadership theory research has led to very high success rates for managers in actual work situations.

    a. True   b. False

2. One of the major differences between managers and leaders is that

    a. managers are found only in lower levels of the organizations, and leaders are found at the top.

    b. managers are chosen by those above them, and leaders are chosen by their followers.

    c. managers have more power than leaders do.

    d. managers stay in their positions longer than leaders do.

3. Trait theory was a logical outcome of
   a. the Hawthorne Studies.
   b. bureaucracy research.
   c. scientific management.
   d. nurture explanations of behavior.

4. List two of the four traits that are believed to be found in effective leaders.
   a. _____
   b. _____

5. If a department head was very focused on meeting production quotas and reducing lost work time and was not concerned whether subordinates came to work when they were ill, that leader probably would score high on the dimension of
   a. initiation of structure.
   b. consideration.
   c. functionalism.
   d. need for power.

6. Contingency theories are based on the assumption that leadership effectiveness is determined by a combination of
   a. the situation and the top management of the organization.
   b. the situation and the sex of the leader.
   c. the characteristics of the leader and training of the subordinates.
   d. the characteristics of the leader and the environment of the leadership situation.

7. The leadership training system based on Fiedler's contingency theory is called
   _____

8. Which of the following is *not* a cognitive resource that Fiedler says is used by leaders?
   a. Stress of the leader
   b. Experience of the leader
   c. Personality of the leader
   d. Intelligence of the leader

9. Fiedler suggests that in high-stress situations, leaders should use

   a. their experience, not their intelligence.

   b. their intelligence, not their experience.

   c. intelligence and experience equally.

   d. the skills of the followers, not those of the leaders.

10. In the LMX model, subordinates who are trusted and have a more personal relationship with the leader are called the _____.

11. According to House's path-goal theory, a leader may have to use a different leadership style with each subordinate.

    a. True   b. False

12. The Vroom and Yetton decision-making model is limited because it can assess leadership effectiveness only after leadership decisions have been made.

    a. True   b. False

13. One criticism of the Vroom and Yetton decision-making model is that it

    a. can be used only at the highest levels of an organization.

    b. has never been tested with women leaders.

    c. is limited to yes or no answers when real situations may fall somewhere in between.

    d. is too simple to be useful.

14. The common element in transformational leaders and charismatic leaders is

    a. the situations that make those styles effective.

    b. the high level of intelligence of the followers.

    c. the low level of intelligence of the followers.

    d. loyalty to the leader, not to the organization.

15. List two of the characteristics of charismatic leaders.

    a. _____

    b. _____

16. If a group of research scientists who had been together for several years were close to a breakthrough on a new product, it might be possible for the group to function without a leader.

    a. True   b. False

17. Employee empowerment most often fails to work when
    a. followers try to get rid of most managers.
    b. managers do not actually give up control.
    c. the organization is too large.
    d. all of the above

18. If I do the things my department chairperson wants me to do because I have always been impressed by his ability to see both sides of an issue and his skill in getting faculty members to work together, the power base I am responding to is
    a. legitimate.
    b. expert.
    c. referent.
    d. coercive.
    e. reward.

19. The least effective influence tactics are
    a. personal appeal, coalition, and pressure.
    b. personal appeal, exchange, and pressure.
    c. personal appeal, ingratiation, and consolation.
    d. pressure, coalition, and legitimating.

20. The best combination of personal power and position power appears to be the least amount of position power possible and the development of more personal power.
    a. True   b. False

21. Although men and women both can be effective leaders, men more often are perceived as having the characteristics of successful leaders.
    a. True   b. False

22. The new female leadership pattern referred to as interactive leadership emphasizes
    a. women acting more like men to be successful leaders.
    b. leaders making the contacts they have with subordinates more positive for the leaders and the subordinates.
    c. women leaders spending more time with other women leaders as role models.
    d. women leaders interacting only with higher members in the organization to avoid being stuck in low-level positions.

23. One of the problems that members of racial minorities who want to become managers share with women who want to become managers is

    a. overt racism on the job.

    b. the promotion of many more men than women.

    c. lower managerial assessment test scores.

    d. lack of opportunities as a result of the glass ceiling effect.

24. Research has shown that the best cross-cultural management training programs involve

    a. language and culture training.

    b. cognitive and experiential training.

    c. language and social training.

    d. none of the above.

25. What are the four competencies Bennis (1993) believes are necessary for effective management?

    a. _____

    b. _____

    c. _____

    d. _____

WEB EXERCISE

Use your browser to go to http:/www.nwlink.com/~donclark/leader/bm_model.html, the home site for the developers of the Leadership GRID® developed by Blake and Mouton. Take the GRID quiz and indicate whether you do or do not agree with the assessment, and why.

Personnel
Psychology

Personnel Selection and Placement

8

LEARNING OBJECTIVES

THE IMPORTANCE OF PERSONNEL SELECTION

JOB ANALYSIS, DESCRIPTION, AND SPECIFICATION

RECRUITMENT
Recruitment Methods
Case Study Psychology in Personnel Selection
Factors That Influence Recruitment

METHODS OF PERSONNEL SELECTION
Application Blanks, Résumés, and Biodata
Interviews
Physical Examinations
Background and Reference Checks
Graphology and Miscellaneous Selection Methods
Assessment Centers

SELECTION DECISIONS
Diversity Issues and the Selection Ratio
Simple Regression Model
Multiple Regression Model
Multiple Cutoff Model
Multiple Hurdle Model
Utility Decisions

Chapter Outline

THE IMPORTANCE OF PERSONNEL SELECTION

Is finding the right job or the right person for a job a matter of luck or chance? Psychologists and other researchers have demonstrated that there are a number of reliable and valid methods for selecting people for jobs, but that does not prevent people from looking for a quicker, easier system. One organization went so far as to hire psychics to help it with personnel selection (Smith, 1995).

Personnel selection means choosing a person to fill an open job in an organization. The opening may occur for many different reasons, such as the departure of the current jobholder because of promotion, firing, or company growth. Technological improvements and changes can lead to retirements or new jobs. Whatever the reason for the job opening, the goal of personnel selection is always the same: choosing the best applicant for the job.

Good hiring practices make good financial sense for organizations. Hiring an incompetent employee can result in equipment damage, lost customers, more accidents, longer training times, and lower productivity among employees who depend on the work of a poor employee. Poor employees are absent and tardy more often than good employees are. And an organization that hires an inferior employee not only is losing the productivity of a better employee, it also may be allowing a competitor to get that benefit.

There are also less visible costs involved in hiring a poor worker. Not only does the hiring process have a cost, so does termination if the employee must be fired.

Personnel selection
The process of choosing the person who will be hired by using the results of screening measures.

Firing an employee who is past the probationary or trial period of employment can be even more difficult if the company does not operate in an **employment-at-will** state, where employees can be fired without good cause. Good workers may resent inferior employees who are getting the same pay but doing less work.

The higher or more technical the position is, the greater this cost is. The average cost of hiring the wrong employee is about $6,000 (Waddell, 1998). If a poor employee is hired, the organization may, in fact, find that it is less expensive to bring that employee up to an acceptable level than it is to fire and replace him.

The most cautious organizations concentrate on avoiding hiring a bad employee rather than on hiring the best employee (Cook, 1988). While most screening methods are designed to identify and reject undesirable applicants, the best methods also point to the best choice for the position (Yarborough, 1994). Some organizations divide the selection process into screening and selection segments. **Personnel screening** is done to eliminate unqualified applicants. The purpose of *personnel selection* is to combine all the screening elements so that the best employee is hired. **Personnel placement** involves putting the person selected into the actual job.

The selection process for higher-level positions generally takes longer than that for lower-level positions. At the college where I teach, the board of trustees takes at least a year to replace the president but the human resources department takes only four to six weeks to replace a clerical worker. Government regulations also can increase the time it takes to hire a new employee. At New York's transportation agency, government regulations have increased the hiring time for new employees to as long as five months; twenty years ago it took only two days. Organizations must be aware of the extra time that often is required to meet legal standards.

For any organization, the goal of the selection and placement process is to predict future behavior from past behavior, such as education and previous jobs, or from current behavior, such as scores on tests and interview records. This chapter looks at each selection element separately, but it is important to understand that the selection and placement of employees almost never are based on only one selection procedure. Usually the more important the job is, the more selection procedures are used. Selection and placement elements may be changed, dropped, or added depending on the job and the information from the evaluation of the selection process for that job.

JOB ANALYSIS, DESCRIPTION, AND SPECIFICATION

Before selection process decisions can be made, the organization must have up-to-date knowledge about the job that is being filled. This information is found in a **job analysis** that lists the tasks, duties, and responsibilities of a job and the skills, abilities, knowledge, and experience necessary to perform it. Sometimes a specialist

Employment at will
The principle that employers can hire and fire employees without a specific cause.

Personnel screening
The process of eliminating unqualified applicants as part of the selection process.

Personnel placement
After hiring an employee, choosing the job he or she will report to.

Job analysis A listing of the knowledge, skills, abilities, and experience needed to do a job correctly, as well as up-to-date information about the job itself.

Job description A list of the tasks performed in a job, the employee characteristics needed for the job, and the working conditions.

Job specification A list of the knowledge, skills, and abilities needed to perform a job.

from the human resources department prepares the job analysis, or a consultant may organize information received from various people in the organization. You will read about the job analysis process in detail in Chapter 10. A job analysis includes not only the behaviors that are needed on the job but also the background and experience an applicant must have to perform the job effectively. Job analysis also helps the organization meet the legal requirements of the hiring process. One requirement for demonstrating legal fairness is having a current job analysis that serves as the basis for the selection program (Clifford, 1994).

In the selection process, a job analysis is used to develop a job description and a job specification. A **job description** includes information about the tasks that must be performed as a part of the job, the equipment that must be used, the conditions of the work setting, the supervisory authority and hours and days of work, the salary, and the promotional structure. A **job specification** lists the knowledge, skills, abilities, and other qualifications required of the person who fills the job. The education and experience the jobholder must have also are included in the job specification.

Good research about each job is necessary for the development of a list of job requirements that can meet legal challenges. For example, a bank may include the requirement that all loan officers have a four-year college degree in finance. The bank must be able to demonstrate that loan officers with degrees perform significantly better than loan officers who do not have degrees if it wants to continue to use a four-year degree as a job requirement (see Figure 8.1).

Figure 8.1

A job description modified for use as a listing of a job opening.

POSITION: Senior Clerk

TYPE OF POSITION: Classified/clerical part-time

DESCRIPTION: Under the supervision of the Regional Coordinator, the clerk will act as receptionist, provide clerical support, assist in the registration of students, maintain records for military personnel, and act as student liaison.

REQUIRED QUALIFICATIONS: This position requires a high school diploma or equivalent (GED), a minimum of two (2) years of office experience, and knowledge of computer keyboard and computer software (WordPerfect 6.1 or Microsoft Word). Good organizational and communication skills are essential.

SALARY/HOURS: Minimum starting salary is $8.47 per hour. Hours are normally 12:00 P.M. to 5:00 P.M. Monday through Thursday and 9:00 A.M. to 2:00 P.M. on Friday but may vary according to the needs of the college.

Employers often include data from the job description and job specification in the information they provide to job applicants. This helps eliminate applicants who are unable to do the job, at the same time making applicants aware of all the job requirements. These goals are similar to the goals of the recruitment process.

RECRUITMENT

Recruitment is the process organizations use to attract qualified job applicants. The organization's goal is to attract the largest group of qualified applicants at the least expense, within legal limits. Employers often use a variety of recruitment methods. Past experience may guide a company to place advertisements in local newspapers for a lunchroom supervisor, for example, if that method has resulted in good applicants in the past. Sometimes an organization will try a cheaper method, not get enough good applicants, and then try a more expensive approach rather than settle for less qualified applicants.

Successful recruitment can more than pay for itself. Companies traditionally measured the success of their recruitment programs by using a ratio of the number of job offers to the number of job acceptances. Hanigan (1991) points out that the true indicator of a successful recruiting program is retention of the people who are hired. Starbucks Coffee has a turnover rate of 57 percent compared with an average of 250 percent for all retail stores and restaurants. The chairman of Starbucks, Howard Schultz, attributes much of that success to a program that empowers employees and encourages commitment to the organization, which attracts good employees to the company (Weiss, 1998).

Recruitment Methods

Organizations can recruit internally, externally, or both. **Internal recruitment** involves activities inside the company, such as posting vacancy notices on company bulletin boards and telling employees about job openings. **External recruitment** involves activities outside the company, such as advertisements in newspapers or listings with employment agencies and job fairs. Many of the common types of external recruitment sources are shown in Figure 8.2. Among both types of recruitment sources, a survey of human resources executives found that the top three sources were employee referrals, college recruiting, and executive search firms (Terpstra, 1996).

The best choice of recruitment methods depends on a variety of factors. For example, internal recruitment is usually cheaper than external recruitment, and

Recruitment The process of attracting qualified job applicants to an organization.

Internal recruitment Attracting applicants from within the hiring organization.

External recruitment Attracting applicants by using sources outside the organization.

Figure 8.2

External recruitment methods.

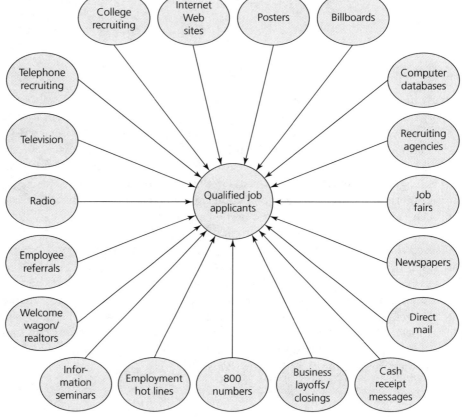

so organizations may try internal recruitment first. Then, if the job is not filled by this method, they will use external recruitment methods.

This pattern can create two distinct problems, however. A legal problem arises if potential job applicants outside the organization can show that this method unfairly excludes them from consideration for the job. There are not many jobs that are so specialized that only a person already working at the company will have the necessary skills. A new human resources director hired from outside the company will not know all the aspects of that position particular to that company but will have the general skills necessary to be a human resources director. Someone hired from within the organization may know that company better but may not have the best general human resources skills.

The second problem is that using only internal recruitment means that the organization always will hire the same type of employee. If the company is doing well and has hired outstanding people in the past, this may not be a problem. However, if less than excellent people have been hired in the past and the company is declining rather than growing, this may indicate a need for primarily external recruitment, in order to bring new people and ideas into the organization.

The greater expense of most external recruitment methods can be reasonable if better employees are chosen. High-turnover, unskilled-labor positions often can be filled successfully through unsolicited telephone calls, letters of application, and walk-ins—candidates who walk in off the street to apply for jobs (Fleishman, 1993). One researcher found that among bank tellers, the best performers after one year on the job were those who had been recruited through self-initiated walk-ins rather than through newspaper advertisements or employee referrals (Blau, 1990). These are all inexpensive methods.

Two external recruitment methods with which many students are familiar are college recruitment and job fairs. College recruiters often spend one or two days on a campus talking with students who are close to finishing their college work and students who want more information about their organizations. Since a campus recruiter is often the only representative of a company with whom a student has contact, the recruiter may have a great deal of influence on a student's attraction to and perception of the organization (Rynes, Bretz, & Gerhart, 1991; Turban & Dougherty, 1992). Companies often send out fairly young, successful employees as campus recruiters; this supports research showing that students rate much higher those recruiters who are more like them and who have an accurate perception of what the students are looking for in a job (Davis, Feild, & Giles, 1991; Royal & Austin, 1992). The most commonly asked questions in campus screening interviews involve college experience, work experience, strengths and weaknesses, and biographical background (DeBell & Dinger, 1997).

Job fairs often are sponsored by communities or community colleges. The purpose is to attract applicants, but job fairs (like campus recruitment) also increase awareness of and improve attitudes toward an organization. Companies represented at job fairs usually list job openings, collect résumés, and hand out a token from the company, such as a pad of paper or a key chain. Job fairs also may target a group that an organization would like to encourage to seek jobs. For example, two job fairs in Arkansas were targeted toward senior citizens and people with disabilities (Brown & Roessler, 1991), resulting in successful hiring and job retention for both groups. Others who have been targeted include blacks, Hispanics, and females, groups that companies want to attract in order to encourage diversity in the workforce.

Some companies have turned to the Internet and on-line services to create virtual job fairs (Frost, 1998; Greenblatt, 1998). The Westech Job Fair (www.vjf.com) advertises that is has over 25,000 high-technology career opportunities and a database of over 110,000 résumés. Several government agencies and not-for-profit groups also list job openings on the Internet.

Employers have been able to advertise job opportunities through on-line services such as Prodigy and America Online and on video shows offered by cable television services (*Personnel*, 1991). The Internet can be used for search engines, bulletin board systems, news groups, job banks, and company Web sites (Cook, 1997). Companies also can recruit from remote locations by videoconferencing (Ralston, 1997); and they are using computers to create databases of applicants that can be examined for current or future positions. Some examples of on-line and telephone-accessed résumé or job-listing databases are Job Bank USA, developed by the Society for Human Resource Management; JOBTRAK; and Military Outplacement (*HRMagazine*, 1992a) (see the case study "Psychology at Work").

[Case Study] PSYCHOLOGY IN PERSONNEL SELECTION

In the early 1990s Dime Savings Bank of New York found itself in the position of not having enough qualified applicants for jobs but lacking the money for more expensive external recruiting methods. The bank turned to telecommunications technology as a way to meet its recruitment needs. It was able to develop a voice mail system, the Dime JobLine, for about $1,500. The basic concept of JobLine is that applicants can call from any phone, anywhere, and find out what jobs are available at the bank.

The bank advertised the Dime JobLine in newspapers, in flyers, and by word of mouth. When applicants call the JobLine, the voice menu directs them to choose one of three geographic locations. After choosing full-time or part-time jobs, applicants hear a listing of all the jobs in that region. The listing for each job includes the job title, a brief summary of the qualifications required, and the hours of the job.

After listening to the job listing, an applicant is asked to leave a message with his or her name, the job of interest, and a phone number. Bank personnel retrieve the messages every day and then contact the applicants who seem qualified and invite them to interview for the open positions. Unqualified applicants are thanked for their interest and encouraged to call in the future. Job listings are changed each week.

Since starting JobLine, Dime Savings Bank has received an average of fifty calls a week. In the first year, fifty-five qualified applicants came for interviews and twenty-four were hired. Without JobLine, the average cost per hire was $1,529. With JobLine, the bank saved $36,969 in hiring costs the first year, making this an excellent investment in using technology for recruiting.

From A. M. Micolo. (1991). High-tech recruiting at low cost. *HRMagazine, 36,* 49–52.

If none of the cheaper methods draw enough qualified applicants, an organization may try the most expensive recruiting method per applicant, executive recruitment, sometimes referred to as headhunting. The job of an executive recruiting firm is to lure people away from competing organizations, often by offering increasingly well-paying positions. The placement firm usually receives about one-third of the first year's pay of a successfully placed employee (over $30,000 for an employee who is paid $100,000, for example).

Factors That Influence Recruitment

Regardless of the method used, research has shown that applicant factors, interviewer factors, and realistic job previews (discussed at the end of this section) all can influence the outcome of the recruitment process. From a recruiter's point of view, the most important characteristics for applicants are communication skills, enthusiasm, motivation, credentials, and a college degree. The least important characteristics are sense of humor, report-writing skills, summer or part-time job experience, ability to resolve conflict, and extracurricular activities (Atkins & Kent, 1988).

At the same time that recruiters are looking for certain characteristics and making decisions about applicants, applicants are making decisions about their interest in further contact with the company. This interest may be increased by a number of factors, such as satisfaction with the communication during the recruitment interview (Ralston & Brady, 1994), work flexibility (Verespej, 1993), the recruiter's competence, the sex composition of interview panels, and interview delays (Rynes, Bretz, & Gerhart, 1991). One researcher examined the factors that lead to decreased interest in an organization after recruiting efforts. Those factors included lack of preparation in the recruitment interview, poorly trained or uninterested recruiters, improperly focused presentations, and failure to understand how the recruiting firm is perceived on a college campus (Satterfield, 1991).

Part of the balancing act of being a recruiter involves meeting the expectations applicants bring to the selection process while not painting such an overly rosy picture of an organization that when applicants accept jobs, they leave, disappointed after a short time. One of the most common methods for avoiding this problem is a **realistic job preview,** an honest picture of the job that includes its good and bad aspects.

Researchers such as Gaugler and Thornton (1990) have found that realism in job previews generally lowers expectations about the organization and the likelihood of accepting a job offer. Although it may appear that lower job acceptance rates are not desirable, employees who have been exposed to realistic job previews typically stay in a job longer (Taylor, 1994) and are higher in job satisfaction (Suszko & Breaugh, 1986). Other researchers found that the most qualified applicants were the ones most likely to be influenced by negative information

Realistic job preview
A method for giving applicants an honest picture of the good and bad aspects of the job for which they are applying.

about a job. Applicants were found to give greater weight in general to negative information than to positive information about a job (Bretz & Judge, 1998). When a realistic job preview is combined with an attractive job and positive feelings toward the recruiter, the negative outcomes often associated with realistic job previews are reduced greatly (Saks, 1989).

Applicants are not always aware of the steps involved in job analysis and recruitment. As can be seen in Figure 8.3, the selection process is well under way by the time the prospective employee fills out an application blank or submits a résumé. The next sections of this chapter cover application blanks and other techniques that are part of personnel selection.

Figure 8.3
The personnel selection process.

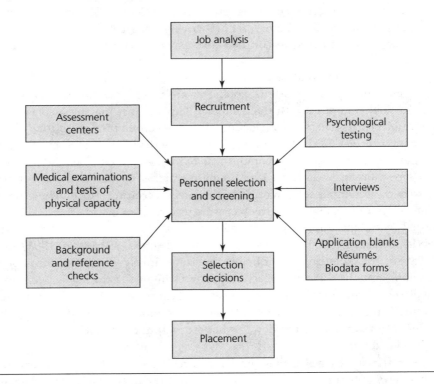

METHODS OF PERSONNEL SELECTION

Selection for a particular job may include some or all of the methods that are discussed here. Each method may be looked at as a way to reject an applicant, but each technique often is combined with others to produce a final acceptance or rejection decision. One of the parts of personnel selection—psychological testing—is so important that it is covered separately, in Chapter 9. Since the Equal Employment Opportunity Commission views all selection techniques as tests, the legal requirements of personnel selection also are covered in that chapter. Keep in mind that the standards of legal fairness that apply to tests also apply to all the selection methods discussed in the present chapter.

Application Blanks, Résumés, and Biodata

The basic assumption of each of these three methods is the same: Past behavior is a good predictor of future behavior. This is not a bad assumption as long as there is research that proves that the questions asked are related to performance on the job. Items about age, sex, race, arrest record, and religion must, by law, be left out of the screening and selection process. A study of eighty-eight organizations in the southeastern United States found that all the application blanks used by those organizations contained at least two "inadvisable" items that were legally questionable, such as items about age or race, with an average of 7.4 questionable items per form (Vodanovich & Lowe, 1992). Application blanks most commonly are used to screen out people who do not have the minimum qualifications listed in the job description and to develop a pool of qualified candidates for further screening or selection.

Some companies use computer-based programs to screen application blanks and résumés. Computer Sciences Corporation, a global technology consulting firm, stores all applicants' résumés in its internal database. When a position opens, human resources personnel search the database electronically for résumés that match the needed skills listed in the job specification (Ober, 1998).

The problem of faking answers on application blanks has received considerable attention recently because of the fear that an organization may be liable for an unqualified employee's behavior that results in harm to customers or other employees. Since application blanks are straightforward, the answers or qualifications that make an applicant look more desirable are usually obvious.

When applicants develop a pattern of inflating responses, they may give themselves away by rating themselves high on phony abilities as well as real ones. Anderson, Warner, and Spencer (1984) had clerical applicants rate themselves on a number of clerical tasks. Some were real abilities, such as the use of office equipment, but some were phony abilities such as "matrix solvency filing." The applicants who rated themselves highest on such "abilities" were found to be the worst typists. According to Fidelifacts, a New York company that investigates applications and résumés, about 30 percent of all applicants misrepresent themselves in some way (*Executive Female*, 1991). In general, the higher the position in an organization is, the more extensive is the amount of checking application blank information.

Weighted application blank An application form that assigns different values to each answer given by an applicant, on the basis of research on successful and unsuccessful workers in the job.

Résumé A summary of an applicant's job-relevant background and experience, drawn up by the applicant.

Biodata forms Application forms that ask for personal and social information to predict success on the job on the basis of information from past or current employees.

One way organizations try to increase the contribution made by application blanks to employee selection is to use a **weighted application blank.** This type of application blank gives points to each response the applicant makes. The highest number of points is given for answers that predict the greatest success on the job, on the basis of extensive research done at the organization. The factors that contribute the most to predicting job success are level of education and prior work experience (Lawrence, Salsburg, Dawson, & Fasman, 1982). For example, if research showed that applicants for a sales position had a 42 percent chance of being successful if they had not finished high school and a 65 percent chance if they had finished high school, four and six points would be given, respectively, for those answers. The application blank for this position would have enough scored items to establish a cutoff range for the entire application blank. Since the scores are based on research on actual job success, weighted application blanks usually are considered good predictors of performance on the job, and most applicants can see the relationship of the questions to the job.

The higher the position is, the more likely it is that the applicant will submit a **résumé** in place of or in addition to an application form. Since a résumé is similar to an application blank but is created entirely by the applicant, many organizations consider a résumé as more representative of the applicant than are answers to application blank questions. Dozens of books give résumé-writing hints, and there are a number of Internet resources that help applicants write a résumé, do a career search, and select a job listing. Two of these Internet sites are File Mine (www.filemine.com) and HotFiles (www.hotfiles.com). The most common suggestions are to make the résumé look attractive in terms of physical appearance, make sure there are no errors in typing or grammar, and, most of all, represent the applicant as favorably as possible without lying.

One type of application blank that may not have as obvious a relationship to the job is the **biodata form** (Owens, 1976). These forms often look quite similar to typical application blanks. The first differences applicants usually notice are the multiple-choice format and the use of questions that may not appear to be clearly related to the job or that involve data that seem to be discriminatory, such as age. The assumption behind this method is the same as that for the other methods in this section: Past behavior can predict future behavior. The difference is that biodata forms include more general behaviors, such as participation in sports activities in childhood, home ownership, and the number of years needed to complete college (Figure 8.4).

The development of a typical biodata inventory is illustrated by a study done by Russell, Mattson, Devlin, and Atwater (1990) that examined cadets at the U.S. Naval Academy. The cadets were asked to write autobiographical essays, which

---

Figure 8.4

Sample items from a biodata form.

Choose one answer for each question.

1. How many part-time jobs did you have during high school?
   a. 5 or more
   b. 3–4
   c. 1–2
   d. 0

2. How long have you been at your present address?
   a. more than 5 years
   b. 4–5 years
   c. 1–3 years
   d. less than 1 year

3. How many magazines do you usually read each month?
   a. more than 5
   b. 4–5
   c. 1–3
   d. 0

4. How much total time do you spend in vigorous exercise each week?
   a. more than 3 hours
   b. 2–3 hours
   c. 1–less than 2 hours
   d. 0

5. Where do you do most of your grocery shopping?
   a. discount warehouse
   b. food co-op
   c. grocery store chain
   d. independently owned grocery

6. How many department store charge cards do you own?
   a. more than 5
   b. 4–5
   c. 1–3
   d. 0

---

were used to generate biodata items. The items later were used with entering cadets to predict their success at the academy; the biodata inventory was found to be a good predictor of military and academic performance as well as leadership.

Despite research evidence of the value of biodata information in personnel selection, not many companies use this method. When personnel directors were asked why, they indicated that their companies did not have the time, money, and human resources to develop biodata inventories. However, they also said that they lacked knowledge about biodata inventories, and slightly more than one-quarter did not think this was a valid method of personnel selection (Hammer & Kleinman, 1988). Some of these concerns may be related to the fear of violating legal standards by asking prying questions that appear not to be job-related. A study by Mael, Connerly, and Morath (1996) indicates that people with more education and more positive attitudes toward biodata and the personnel selection measures used by organizations view fewer biodata items as invasive and not job-related. This study appears to point to the need for greater education and training for people involved in hiring new employees.

Interviews

The goal of a good employment interview is to obtain job-relevant information about the applicant and reduce bias factors as much as possible. Personnel selection interviews often are criticized in the same way that biodata inventories are: The questions asked may not all appear to be job-relevant. Actually, a greater concern is the issue of biased judgment by the interviewer. Interviews continue to be the most commonly used technique for personnel selection, but most research has reported their poor predictive value (Hunter & Hunter, 1984). More recently, however, research that looks at each kind of interview separately has indicated that interviews may have more value than was believed in the past (McDaniel, Whetzel, Schmidt, & Maurer, 1994).

Why isn't the goal to eliminate bias entirely from the interview process? When interaction between people is involved, it is not possible to be totally objective because some elements of the interview require judgment. Imagine that an applicant is asked to discuss what similar kinds of work she has done in the past. If she takes out a personal data sheet to refresh her memory, some interviewers may be impressed by her preparedness. Other interviewers may evaluate her more negatively because she used a written document instead of being able to recall the information.

Bob Daemmrich/Stock Boston

■ In a structured interview the interviewer often works from a set of prepared questions.

Although no single interview pattern fits all personnel selection situations, unstructured and structured interviews are the two types encountered most often in personnel selection.

Unstructured Interviews

In **unstructured interviews,** the interviewers ask whatever questions they want, whenever they want, and may change the questions for each applicant. There is no standard scoring system for the answers given in the interview. In addition to being legally questionable by not treating all applicants the same, this type of interview has been shown to contribute only slightly to good employee selection (Weisner & Cronshaw, 1988). Because there is no form to this type of interview and because the questions may change each time, organizations that give this type of interview may have trouble defending their use in terms of legal fairness, which requires all applicants to be treated the same.

Structured Interviews

Structured interviews consist of questions and acceptable responses that are determined before the interview. This type of interview is much more likely than an unstructured interview to meet the legal requirements for personnel selection by accurately predicting job performance (McDaniel, Whetzel, Schmidt, & Maurer, 1994). There are several types of structured interviews.

One type is the **situational interview,** which focuses on applicants' descriptions of how they would behave in a given situation, for example, what they would do with an employee who was performing a job very successfully but was not taking the required safety precautions. For such interviews the company uses job analysis to develop a list of situations based on behaviors that are critical to success or failure on the job. A sample of good, bad, and average responses is developed for each situation. Employees are usually very positive about situational interviews and try to respond accurately because they can see the relevance of the questions to the jobs for which they are applying (Weekley & Gier, 1987).

Another type is the **job-related interview,** generally conducted by someone in the human resources department or by the hiring supervisor. The questions that are asked are about past work experiences but are not specific to particular situations. For example, applicants may be asked to describe ways they have dealt with difficult subordinates in the past or about their previous experience with a particular kind of machinery.

Psychological interviews attempt to assess personal characteristics of applicants, such as dependability and the ability to handle stress. Such interviews usually are conducted only for higher-level positions and often are administered and interpreted by psychologists or management consultants. A type of psychological interview that combines other interview forms is the stress interview. It is assumed that if an applicant is asked whether he can handle stressful situations,

Unstructured interview
An interview in which different questions are asked of each applicant; the questions may have little relevance to the job.

Structured interview
An interview method in which the same questions are used in the same order for every applicant.

Situational interview
A structured interview technique that gives applicants specific job-related situations and asks how they would respond to each one.

Job-related interviews
Interviews that focus on past work experiences but are not specific to particular situations.

Psychological interview
An interview that focuses on assessing the personal characteristics of applicants.

the answer will be, "Of course I can. I'm really calm under pressure." A stress interview is used to get a behavioral sample rather than just a verbal response. It can become almost a situational interview when the applicant is placed in a stressful situation that has been arranged without his or her awareness of the purpose of the interview or activity. Some psychological interview techniques are used in assessment center evaluations, which are discussed later in this chapter. Regardless of the type of interview, doing the best interview possible will add to the success of the selection process.

Improving the Interview

Applicant Factors Although there seems to be little agreement about what actually is measured in an interview (Landy & Shankster, 1994), there does appear to be a fair amount of agreement about what should be assessed and shared during a selection interview. This is an opportunity to assess oral communication skills and appearance in both positive and negative ways. A *Wall Street Journal* article (1995) described an attractive, well-groomed recent college graduate who had gone to a great deal of effort to prepare for a job interview. She had excellent credentials and was very intelligent and articulate, but at her interview for a job working with health care administrators and physicians she wore sandals, a peasant blouse, and a large gold nose ring—and did not receive a job offer.

A selection interview is also a good time to clear up any information on the applicant's application blank or résumé that is inconsistent or incomplete and to amplify any job-related information that will contribute to the selection process. The interview is an excellent time for the interviewer to give applicants a realistic job preview.

Almost every organization uses interviews in the job selection process, and an applicant can influence the evaluation by her behavior during the interview. Research has shown that interviewers generally pay more attention to negative information than to positive information, and so applicants should be careful not to volunteer negative information (Rowe, 1989). If you are asked a direct question that could lead to a negative answer, such as "Why did you leave your job at the last company you worked for?" you should answer honestly but avoid blaming others, and give the reasons in as positive a way as possible.

Research indicates that the person who is offered the job is most often the one who makes the fewest mistakes in the interview and does well in the other selection steps. Many interviewers start with a mental image of the ideal jobholder and during the interview look for anything in the applicant that does not fit that stereotypical ideal (Arvey & Campion, 1982). The ideal jobholder should have a combination of job-related behaviors and characteristics, but with an interviewer who pictures a young, white male in the job, a woman may find herself rejected unless she dresses in a tailored business suit, for example (Forsythe, Drake, & Cox, 1985). The picture of the ideal applicant may be somewhat different from the actual appearance of an on-the-job employee. Even at a time when many organizations are allowing employees to wear less formal clothing, the traditional, conservative, dark-colored suit or dress is still the preferred interview clothing (Steinhauer, 1995).

Although many consultants offer a variety of suggestions about the best day of the week or the best time of the day that may improve the chances for an interviewee, research has not confirmed any of these suggestions (Willinghanz & Meyers, 1993). The one negative time factor to avoid is being late for the interview. Aamodt (1986) found that there was no difference in the hiring rate for applicants who arrived five to ten minutes early or on time, but no applicant who arrived late was hired.

As part of interview preparation, applicants need to find out as much about the company and the job as possible. A number of sources are usually available, such as company brochures, annual reports, Web sites, articles in periodicals, and current employees.

Even the most lengthy interviews represent a very short time for you as an applicant to present all your accomplishments and skills. Your application and résumé should have provided this kind of list, and so the interview becomes a time to supplement the list rather than redo it. One of the best ways to get interviewers to remember you is to use anecdotes or brief stories to emphasize your strengths: how you met challenges and how your actions benefited your employers or supervisors. It is easier to remember actual stories than lists of accomplishments. While you should think about what you say, you also should pay attention to how you say it. Nonverbal cues, such as making eye contact, can lead to higher interview scores (Aamodt, 1986; Amalfitano & Kalt, 1977). Even something as simple as wearing cologne or perfume can influence the interview score, depending on whether the interviewer is a woman or a man and the type of scent used (Fiore & Kim, 1997). Nonverbal information appears to have the greatest influence when the motivation or ability of the interviewer is low (Forrett & Turban, 1996). However, many interviewers believe they are much better at interpreting nonverbal cues than they actually are (*Sales and Marketing Management*, 1992).

Organizational Factors There are a number of actions the organization and interviewer can take to improve the quality of interviews and the personnel selection process. According to Campion, Palmer, and Campion (1997), the three most important factors in improving interviews are (1) the use of a job analysis to determine the questions, (2) the use of the same questions with each applicant, and (3) the use of better questions, such as questions about specific job situations.

One suggestion for reducing personal bias factors is to have the initial interviewing done by an interactive computer program rather than a person (Stamps, 1995; Thornburg, 1998). There are both advantages and disadvantages to this method. A bank that uses a computerized twenty-minute screening interview

First impression errors
A distortion of interview judgments caused by giving greater weight to information collected early in an interview.

Similarity errors
A distortion of interview judgments caused by the interviewer giving higher ratings to the applicants who are most like him or her.

Negative information errors A distortion of interview judgments caused by the interviewer paying more attention to bad information about the applicant than good information.

Contrast errors A distortion of interview judgments caused by the interviewer giving unfairly high or low scores on the basis of a comparison with previous applicants.

believes that this is more fair than traditional interviews because each applicant is treated exactly the same and that time is saved by weeding out underqualified people (Bulkeley, 1994). One of the initial beliefs about computer-based interviewing was that people would be more honest when they were not trying to impress an interviewer (Martin & Nagao, 1989). Other researchers found that the greatest amount of trying to create a favorable impression occurred during computer interviews (Lautenschlager & Flaherty, 1990), perhaps because applicants did not encounter the censoring gaze of an actual interviewer. Since one of the reasons for doing interviews is to assess the oral communication abilities of the applicant, computerized interviewing may be more of a screening than a final selection device.

Another way organizations can make interviews more accurate is to assure that the judgments made from interviews are largely based on job-relevant characteristics, rather than irrelevant personal features or errors. Structured interviews and knowledge about the job being filled help interviewers focus on job-relevant behaviors. Interviewer training can prevent some of the most common interview errors.

Among the most common errors are first impressions, contrast, similarity, and negative information. **First impression errors** result when the interviewer gives greater weight to information collected in the early part of the interview rather than giving equal weight to all the information gathered during the process. **Similarity errors** result from interviewers giving higher scores to applicants who are the most like themselves. **Negative information errors** result from the interviewer giving greater weight to negative information about the applicant than to positive information. **Contrast errors** occur when the interviewer rates the current applicant on the basis of how that person compares with previous applicants. The applicant does not have any control over this type of error. The best the interviewer can do is make herself as positively distinctive from the other applicants as possible so that comparisons are less likely to be made.

Most interviewer error training is directed toward making the interviewer aware of the presence of these errors and consciously trying to avoid them. This method appears to have had some degree of success (Arvey & Campion, 1982). Another method researchers have suggested for avoiding these errors is to have more than one interviewer. Although the cost is greater, the added value may offset the cost.

While there has been a great deal of research on various aspects of interviewing, studies show that very few organizations complete validation studies that prove the worth of the selection methods they use. Ryan and Sackett (1987) surveyed 163 psychologists who did personnel assessments and found that most said they did not validate any of the selection methods they were using. Arvey and Campion (1982) reported that many interviewers believe that they are good judges of people despite evidence to the contrary.

With so many qualifications to doing good interviews, should interviewing be a part of the selection process? Because interviewing is used in almost every selection process, the best answer would seem to be yes, as long as a trained interviewer is conducting a job-relevant, structured, situational interview. This is based on the work of McDaniel, Whetzel, Schmidt, and Maurer (1994), who conducted a meta-analysis of interview information from over 85,000 individuals that showed the usefulness of certain types of interviews in the selection process. The review of structured interviews by Campion, Palmer, and Campion (1997) also confirms the value of interviews in the personnel selection process.

Physical Examinations

Physical examinations are a selection technique that evaluates an applicant's physical skills, health, abilities, and disabilities. Organizations use several types of physical examinations, including medical examinations, physical ability tests, drug testing, and genetic and human immunodeficiency virus (HIV) screening.

Medical Examinations

Increasing concern about accidents and injuries and the accelerating costs of workers' disability and compensation claims has focused more attention on **medical examinations** and physical ability testing as part of the personnel selection process (Fleishman, 1988). The use of medical examinations has been redefined since the passage of the Americans with Disabilities Act (ADA) in 1990. This legislation, which was designed to protect disabled people at work as well as in other areas, has limited the usual preemployment medical examination in two ways. First, the examination may not be given until *after* a job offer has been made. Second, the medical examination can cover only job-relevant physical characteristics and must be required of all the employees entering that job (Fish, 1997). Since physicians often do not have specific information about job tasks and requirements, there may be little agreement between physicians assessing people applying for the same job unless there is a clear list of standards or limits (Hogan & Bernacki, 1981).

One way to provide greater standardization in medical examinations it to use the **Job Applicant Medical History Questionnaire** developed by Crump and Gebhart (1983). This is a form filled out by applicants for physically demanding jobs. The answers can allow the physician to target the applicant's past medical history. This is supposed to be used with a physician's manual developed by Fleishman (1975) that lists physical job requirements and distinguishes between allowable and disqualifying impairments. For example, mild hypertension might not disqualify a fire fighter, but severe hypertension might. One difficulty with this approach is that the ADA has made it illegal to eliminate an applicant because he has a medical condition that *could* be made worse by the demands of the job or

Physical examination
A personnel selection technique that focuses on physical skills, abilities, disabilities, and medical conditions that are relevant to the job.

Medical examination
A personnel screening technique that focuses on the job-relevant physical condition of an applicant.

Job Applicant Medical History Questionnaire
A personnel selection medical examination form featuring job-relevant items, which is filled out by the applicant before the physician's examination.

because he has a higher risk of injury on the job (Warner, 1991). The only legally acceptable criterion for disqualification is a medical condition that *would* make the person unable to do the job.

Being unable to do a particular physical task may not eliminate a person from the selection process if a reasonable accommodation can be made. For example, if a job requires being able to lift seventy pounds and an applicant can lift only sixty pounds, it appears that the person will not be able to do the job. However, if lifting seventy pounds is done only once a month and there are four other employees in the same job classification who can life that much, an applicant who can lift only sixty pounds may be an acceptable candidate if that person can take over the work of one of the other employees for thirty minutes once a month while the seventy-pound load is being lifted.

By combining medical screening with job analysis, the organization can focus on the physical demands of the job and not illegally base a decision on disabilities rather than abilities. Questions must be specifically related to the ability to perform physical functions that are critical to the job, not about physical or mental conditions in general (Warner, 1991).

Research has consistently shown that when information about disabilities is available during the selection process, such information influences the selection decision. For example, when college students rated hypothetical job applicants for a high-stress managerial trainee position or a low-stress bookkeeper position, the applicants were identified as having high blood pressure, allergies, or no adverse physical condition. The applicants with physical impairments were rated much lower for the manager trainee position (Wages, Manson, & Jordan, 1990). When actual managers and supervisors reviewed cover letters and résumés from applicants with a history of one of four forms of cancer or with pneumonia, together with a job description for the position, applicants with three of the four types of cancer were given hiring recommendations lower than those for the applicants with pneumonia (Bordieri, Drehmer, & Taricone, 1990).

Physical Ability Tests

One type of physical examination that traditionally has been used for physically demanding jobs such as police work and fire fighting is a **physical ability test.** These tests are designed to measure the physical skills required for a job. This is different from a medical examination in that it is given *before* a job offer has been made.

Physical ability tests
Personnel screening examinations that focus on the physical skills and capacities needed to perform a job.

Two issues have been raised about the use of physical ability tests. First, an increasing number of legal actions have challenged the validity of these tests in the selection and screening process. Second, there is a lack of published literature concerning the use and validation of physical ability tests in particular job settings (Arvey, Nutting, & Landon, 1992). This means that even though one might assume that being able to lift and carry a 175-pound dummy demonstrates a skill that is needed to be a firefighter, there is little proof that this ability is useful in predicting who will be a good fire fighter. Arvey, Nutting, and Landon (1992) suggest that the skills tested on physical ability examinations need to be related directly to the actual physical skills required on the job. Physical ability tests that are perceived as the most job-relevant have been found to be the most acceptable to employers and employees (Ryan, Gregouras, & Ployhart, 1996).

Organizations that worry about legal challenges may have problems with the use of physical ability tests because these tests, especially those involving upper body strength, historically have shown lower passing rates for women than for men (Fleishman, 1988). Fleishman suggested two ways of dealing with this issue. One way is to show that the physical ability or skill being tested is critical for correct job performance, so that the organization can legally hire more men than women if more men get passing scores. Some research has shown that tests of strength can be a good predictor of success in physically demanding jobs (Blakeley, Quinones, & Jago, 1992). Another researcher used a combination of laboratory and field tests to determine the minimum oxygen consumption demands for various fire-fighting tasks (Sothmann, Saupe, Jasenof, Blaney, & Furhman, 1990), showing that this may be a realistic approach.

■ Physical ability testing must evaluate the physical skills needed on the job.

Preemployment drug testing Urine and/or blood test screening for the presence of illegal drugs or drugs that could impair job performance.

Genetic testing Physical testing for the presence of inherited physical disabilities or predispositions.

The other method is to make physical ability testing part of a battery of physical examinations in which some of the tests do not result in unequal selection of men and women. For example, women often score as well as or better than men on tests of physical flexibility. If the total score of all the physical tests has been shown to be a good predictor of job success, this method can equalize the male–female selection ratio. Although physical ability tests appear to have the potential for misuse, they also appear to contribute positively to the selection process when they are used correctly.

Drug Testing

How likely are you to encounter **preemployment drug testing** the next time you apply for a job? A survey of large U.S. companies indicated that 80 percent of the responding companies use drug testing before or after hiring. In 1996 about one-third of all job applicants were tested for drug use (Greenberg, 1996). The proportion of companies with drug-testing programs has increased 277 percent since 1987 (*Managing Office Technology,* 1996). Lower unemployment rates appear to be bringing more drug-and alcohol-using applicants into the selection process (Knox, 1998). All the companies surveyed in one study said they have rejected applicants who tested positive for drugs (Gray & Brown, 1992). About 5 percent of preemployment drug tests done in 1998 came back positive for illegal substances.

The most common type of drug testing is done from a urine sample. The simplest type is a screening test that indicates the likely presence of a number of drugs. If that test is positive, a more specific confirmation test indicates which drugs are present. Because it is not considered a medical examination, preemployment drug testing can be done before general medical testing (Bresler & Sommer, 1992). Drug testing also can include testing for the presence of alcohol if it is job-relevant—as in the case of public transportation drivers. If applicants are aware that a company has a drug-testing program, this may be a strong deterrent to potential drug use (Borack,1998). Although there has been some concern that drug-testing programs may keep some applicants from applying for jobs, companies such as Red Lion Hotels and Motels believe that mandatory drug tests are a strong recruitment tool for attracting the most desirable job applicants (Jaquette, 1991; Mastrangelo, 1997).

Genetic Testing and HIV Testing

Two tests at the center of ethical and legal controversies are genetic screening and testing for the presence of HIV, the virus that causes acquired immune deficiency syndrome (AIDS). Some large organizations have looked at **genetic testing** as a way to screen applicants who may be susceptible to disabling (and costly) diseases. Only about 1 percent of employers use genetic testing for employees or applicants (*HRMagazine,* 1992b). Legally and morally, this is a difficult practice to justify, particularly in the selection process. It is not wrong for an employer to obtain this information, but it is illegal to use it to discriminate against applicants.

In 1995 the Equal Employment Opportunity Commission expanded the ADA to make genetic test–based discrimination illegal (Greengard, 1997). Previously in this chapter it was shown that information about disabilities influences hiring decisions, and genetic testing has been found to have a negative effect on the hiring of members of racial and ethnic minorities as well (Brady, 1993). Other problems with genetic testing include the accuracy of the results and whether the test determines the actual presence of a genetic disorder, such as sickle cell anemia, or only the potential for developing that disorder. Although many genetic disorders are costly in terms of insurance coverage, many of those disorders are not job-relevant in terms of the physical impairments they cause (Bumgart & DeJong, 1995; Cronin, 1993).

The cost of insurance coverage often is cited as a reason for testing for HIV. The problem with this reasoning is that it violates the law (Woolsey, 1993). Positive HIV status is a disability that is covered by the ADA. About 10 percent of ADA claims against employers are AIDS-related. The number of employees and applicants with HIV or AIDS is increasing as better treatment programs help reduce or eliminate the physical symptoms of the illness.

The only time **HIV testing** should be done as part of the selection process is when it is relevant to the job. For example, if someone with an unusual blood type was a paid blood donor, HIV testing would be job-relevant. It is not enough to think that an applicant's HIV status may be related to the job; there must be actual proof. One New York State health agency refused to hire an HIV-positive pharmacist, but the courts ruled against the department because fairly simple adjustments in the workplace could prevent any spreading of the infection (*Personnel Journal*, 1992). Most of those adjustments, in fact, should have been adopted as part of general safety practices regardless of HIV status.

> **HIV testing** A physical examination for the presence of the human immunodeficiency virus that causes AIDS.

Background and Reference Checks

Earlier in this chapter the usefulness of past performance in predicting future performance was discussed. Background and reference checks ask former employers and others who know an applicant to provide information about that applicant's past as part of an assessment of possible future performance. Legal challenges have influenced this area of personnel selection at least as much as they have influenced the use of physical examinations. Fear of being sued by former employees has limited a number of organizations to providing only neutral information, such as dates of employment and job title. In a survey in *Personnel Journal* (1993), 68 percent of executives from the 1,000 largest companies in the United States said that it was more difficult to check an applicant's references than it had been three years earlier. Seventy-five percent of those executives said

Negligent referral
The failure of a previous employer to warn a future employer about serious job-related problems in a job applicant.

Negligent hiring Careless hiring of an employee who causes harm to another employee, a customer, or a visitor to an organization.

that their own companies also are giving less information than they did in the past. Twenty-seven states have passed laws to protect employers when they release reference information about employees, as long as the employers are acting in good faith (Zachary, 1998).

The fear of lawsuits involving careless employee selection, brought by customers and current employees, may be more real than the fear of lawsuits from former employees. A search of lawsuits accusing employers of misrepresenting information about former employees showed that the employers usually win (Paetzold & Wilborn, 1992). Bias favorable to employers may, however, be changing as a result of a 1997 U.S. Supreme Court ruling (*Robinson v. Shell Oil*) that extended federal antidiscrimination laws to cover former employees suing over bad references written in retaliation for discrimination lawsuits filed by those employees (Bahls & Bahls, 1997). Companies often protect themselves by asking applicants to sign a release giving the organization permission to check references, former employers, and specific background items.

The fear of being sued has created another legal problem, however. Some employers are suing previous employers for **negligent referral.** This means that the previous employer failed to warn the future employer of a particularly serious job-related problem with a job applicant.

In light of such difficult legal questions, can it be worth using reference and background checks for personnel selection? The answer is yes for two reasons. First, National Referencing Corporation has found that using preemployment reference checks reduces job turnover 5 to 20 percent, depending on the job and industry (Dunn, 1995). The second reason for using reference and background checks is to avoid hiring someone who could put the company in a dangerous legal position. For example, if a company hires a repairperson with a long burglary record that it has not checked on, and the repairperson steals from a customer's home while making a service call, the company has damaged its reputation and exposed itself to being sued by the customer for failing to check the employee's burglary record. Many states do not allow employers to check arrest records, but most allow employers to check conviction records.

If a company carelessly hires an employee who causes harm to a customer, another employee, or a visitor, this forms the basis for a **negligent hiring** lawsuit against that company. The harm can be job-related, such as the employee not correctly repairing a furnace, leading to the death of a customer. Or it can be unrelated to actually doing the job, as in the example of an employee who steals from a customer. An organization protects itself against negligent hiring lawsuits by doing thorough background checks as well as using other selection procedures. The background check should include references, criminal record, drug tests, and general background information. The legal standard that the company must meet is the use of reasonable caution in finding a history of behavior that would make an employee unfit for the job. Most organizations check educational background (81 percent) and previous employment (79 percent), but only 37 percent check criminal records (Arthur, 1997).

Graphology and Miscellaneous Selection Methods

Each of the selection procedures discussed so far has been proved to contribute usefully to the selection process. **Graphology,** or handwriting analysis, has not, however—at least in the United States. The basic assumption in graphology is that examining handwriting characteristics such as size, slant, pressure, and rhythm can lead to conclusions about personality and mental traits: temperament, mental ability, sociableness, and work behaviors. This method has been used as part of personnel selection for over fifty years and is currently used by 9 percent of small U.S. companies, but only 5 percent of large businesses (Thatcher, 1997). Validity studies using subjects in the United States failed to show any value in using graphology for personnel selection (Rafaeli & Klimoski, 1983), but studies in Europe showed much better validity (Nevo, 1986). This method is much more popular in Europe than it is in the United States (Steiner & Gilliland, 1996). In the United States, applicants can refuse to have handwriting analysis included in the personnel selection process (Ocampa, 2000).

Two problems with the use of graphology in personnel selection are whether personality traits can predict job performance and whether more accurate tests can be used to assess personality traits if job-related. Both issues are examined in Chapter 9.

From time to time someone suggests that he or she has a quick, surefire method of finding a way through the job selection maze. Many of these methods are based on the personal belief systems of hiring managers or on very limited observations of behavior. The greatest danger of these tactics may be that they prevent the use of accurate and better selection methods. What can you do if you are asked to participate in any of these activities as part of personnel selection? You can always ask the person using these methods to explain their relationship to job performance, but you also might want to consider whether you want to work for an organization that does not use the best selection methods.

Assessment Centers

A number of organizations use a comprehensive personnel selection system known as an **assessment center,** which involves a series of tests, activities, and simulations that are scored by several trained raters. Although some large organizations set aside a specific physical location for these appraisals, the term *assessment center* refers to the evaluation process, not to where it takes place. The appraisals usually last several days and result in an overall rating that is based on

Graphology Assessment of personal characteristics from handwriting samples.

Assessment center A selection technique that uses multiple assessments of job-related knowledge, skills, and abilities by a number of evaluators who observe the applicants.

combining all the methods used and all the ratings given by each evaluator. Most companies use assessment centers for internal selection of candidates for promotion or for developmental purposes, but a growing number of larger organizations use them for external selection as well (Spychalski, Quinones, Gaugler, & Pohley, 1997).

Advantages and Disadvantages

One benefit of this process is that the applicant gets a realistic job preview, which can contribute to a better selection process both for applicant and organization. The expense of this method has limited its use mainly to large organizations and higher-level positions, although newer techniques that use computers and videotapes have brought application of the assessment center method to lower-level and entry-level positions as well.

The use of this method for selecting first-level supervisors had a positive effect on the performance of supervisors and generated a potential group of supervisors to be selected for further promotions (Campbell & Bray, 1993). However, only about 22 percent of *Fortune* 500 companies use this method. Over one-third of the organizations that do not use it list cost and time as their main reasons. The average cost per person assessed is between $750 and $1,000 (McDaniel, 1995). Although the apparent cost of an assessment center seems high, if the method results in better personnel selection, the cost may actually be lower than that of other, less effective methods. One study found that although assessment center selection cost almost ten times as much as an aptitude test, it produced much less discrimination against minority groups. The lower discrimination rate could make the assessment center more desirable than the cheaper aptitude test (Hoffman & Thornton, 1997).

This method is usually good at predicting organizational measures of job success such as salary level and number and frequency of promotions (Chan, 1996). This may result from the clear job relevance of the assessment activities. Applicants view assessment centers as being more job-related than are cognitive or mental ability tests (Macan, Avedon, & Paese, 1994).

Although assessment center scores are related to the number and frequency of promotions, there is still the question whether this is a result of the use of good selection methods or is due to other factors. Klimoski and Brickner (1987) suggest several other reasonable explanations for this strong relationship. One possibility is that employees are promoted because of their assessment center scores, not their performance. It is also possible that the same people who did the assessment center evaluations also do the promotional evaluations and make the same assessments each time, whether or not they are correct. There is also the possibility of a self-fulfilling prophecy bias (see Chapter 2); choosing a person to participate in an assessment center may give that person the belief that she can do the job well, and from that point on she behaves in ways that make that belief come true.

Assessment Center Development

The development of a good assessment center can be a time-consuming process, but correct design will have a positive effect on its success. Dulewicz (1991) outlined three steps to correctly designing an assessment center:

1. Program design involving the use of people with proven experience to conduct a job analysis and identify the key competencies, behaviors, and skill levels that are required for successful performance on the job

2. Training the assessors in the methods chosen and the correct use of evaluation techniques

3. Follow-up of assessment center participants and long-term monitoring of how the results are used

The specific evaluation exercises used in an assessment center depend on a number of factors, such as the purpose of the center, the personnel, and time limits. Some of the typical exercises that can be used are in-basket activities, leaderless discussion groups, simulations, individual interviews, paper and pencil exercises, oral presentations, and business games (discussed in Chapter 11).

The **in-basket exercise** consists of a series of memos, letters, and documents that might be part of the job the applicant is seeking (Fredericksen, 1962). A time limit is usually set, and so the applicant must prioritize the items and respond to the most important ones first. Applicants and organizations can see a clear relationship between this exercise and the actual behaviors required on the job, as is typical of most situational evaluation techniques.

A **leaderless discussion group** is an exercise that assesses leadership skills by assigning a problem to a group without a designated leader. The typical model involves giving the participants a problem to solve or discuss, such as how to reduce turnover among first-level supervisors without increasing organizational costs. No one is given the role of group leader, and sometimes the observer evaluators sit behind a smoked glass panel or videotape the activity remotely so that the discussion group does not look to them for leadership. The evaluators assess the emergent leadership skills of the group members, as well as cooperation, oral communication ability, and problem-solving techniques. This exercise has received more emphasis as organizations have increased the use of teams in the workplace.

Simulations are samples of job-related activities and behaviors. This can be very similar to situational interviews, which were looked at earlier in this chapter. For example, a candidate can be assigned to role-play a manager terminating a subordinate. To equalize the simulation for all applicants and reduce costs, videotapes may be used for part of the simulations (Fisher, 1992). Videotapes also can be used to re-create situations that might be difficult to bring into an assessment center setting, such as outdoor settings or those involving complex equipment. Simulations can be purchased from profession developers at a low cost, but this type of simulation may not be specific enough to obtain as much information as is needed.

In-basket exercise
A simulation activity that uses a sample of the documents a jobholder would find in her or his in-basket to which the job applicant is asked to respond.

Leaderless discussion group An assessment center exercise in which the applicants meet in a small group to solve job-related problems but no leader is assigned to direct the group.

Simulation An evaluation exercise used in assessment centers, which puts the applicant in a situation or activity similar to the actual job.

Bonnie Kamin/PhotoEdit

■ In a leaderless discussion group the group must solve a problem without an assigned leader. Each person contributes to the success of the task.

Paper and pencil exercises may include tests of problem-solving abilities, mental ability, and job knowledge, and are completed by each applicant individually. These tests are labeled paper and pencil exercises, but they also may be administered with computers. They may be objective tests or an assessment of writing abilities, such as writing a sales plan.

Some of these exercises may be related to oral presentations as well. The purpose of the oral presentation is to assess spoken communication ability. This can also be a simulation exercise if the applicant is a salesperson and is asked to do a sales presentation with material supplied in the assessment center or from a plan he previously developed.

Improving Assessment Centers

Although assessment centers often are pointed to as examples of good personnel selection, the cost and time they involve keep organizations looking for ways to improve their use. Among the suggestions for getting the greatest value out of the assessment center method are the following:

1. Make sure the purpose of the center is clear to both applicants and evaluators. For example, if no one is ever hired or promoted without high assessment center scores, that should be made known. If applicants are expected to

learn job skills as well as be evaluated, that also should be made clear (Spychalski, Quinones, Gaugler, & Pohley, 1997).

2. Use peer assessments and ratings by psychologists as well as the ratings of trained supervisors (Gaugler, Rosenthal, Thornton, & Bentson, 1987).

3. Look into other, cheaper methods before choosing to use an assessment center (Hunter & Hunter, 1984).

4. Use a behaviorally based evaluation system that does not overly rely on subjective managerial judgments (MacDonald, 1988).

5. Train the evaluators who work in the assessment center (Spychalski, Quinones, Gaugler, & Pohley, 1997).

SELECTION DECISIONS

In the most organizationally desirable situation, the selection process starts with a number of qualified applicants who are sifted down to highly qualified people who exactly match the number of job openings. However, this often cannot be achieved.

Diversity Issues and the Selection Ratio

One of the first considerations that influences the selection decision is the **selection ratio,** the comparison between the number of applicants and the number of job openings. The selection ratio has been shown to influence the final selection decision (Huber, Northcraft, & Neale, 1990).

The question of who is a qualified applicant has been the focus of charges of discrimination in the personnel selection process. Although statistics have shown an underrepresentation of certain racial, ethnic, religious, age, and gender groups in both applicants and final selection choices in the past, legal remedies have not always changed the numbers. A number of federal and state laws require organizations to show that they encourage diversity among applicants and value diversity in the final employee selection.

In spite of additional knowledge and a number of laws, many employers still select and place employees by trying to fit employees to the job rather than fitting the job to the employee. Some requirements are truly necessary for a particular job, but there is often more than one way to satisfy those requirements.

The focus of job analysis has changed from how a job is done to what the necessary job outcomes are. For example, if a receptionist position requires that someone be at the information desk during the nine hours a day the company is open, there is usually no reason why it has to be the same person for all those

Selection ratio
A comparison between the number of applicants and the number of people hired for a job.

hours. The company probably is already using a different employee during the receptionist's lunch break. It may be possible for two employees to share this one full-time job during a period when both have other responsibilities that prevent full-time employment. Compared with two part-time employees, the two job-sharing employees are less likely to leave the organization. Having experienced, consistent employees at the first contact point (the information desk) in an organization is an asset for a company.

As the number of nontraditional employees increases in the workforce and the number of traditional white male employees decreases, there will be greater need to look at jobs in nontraditional ways. It has been estimated that 75 percent of all new entrants to the labor force during the 1990s were women and minority group members. Nontraditional employees will need to be fully integrated into the workforce for organizations to continue to be successful.

Even when nontraditional applicants are encouraged to apply for positions, they may find that they are selected at lower rates than traditional employees are. The choice of which selection decision model to use can help correct this imbalance.

All the selection techniques discussed in this chapter and those that will be discussed in Chapter 9 have been shown to contribute to the accurate selection of employees. Some of the methods contribute more than others, but there is usually greater value in using more than one selection technique in the process. The choices that must be made typically involve which methods to use for a particular job selection process and how the scores should be put together to give the best value. Each of the following selection decision models can lead to good selection choices for different jobs in a variety of settings.

Simple Regression Model

The least complex method for judging the effectiveness of a selection technique is the **simple regression model** (see Chapter 2). Only two pieces of information are needed to construct this graph: the scores on the selection technique and the criteria for judging success on the job. The criteria of job success could include performance ratings, number of promotions in a stated period, length of time on the job, and number of disciplinary actions. Figure 8.5 shows a scatterplot of employees' scores on a weighted application blank and six-month performance ratings.

In this sample, the employees in square B are the people who got the highest scores on the weighted application blank and the highest performance ratings. The employees in square D are the people who got the lowest scores on the weighted application blank and the lowest performance ratings. If most of the dots are in these two squares, this test can be considered a good predictor of employees' performance because generally low scores are correlated with low performance and high scores are correlated with high performance. If a selection technique is not a good predictor of employee performance, the corre-

Simple regression model
A method for correlating job success with scores on a single selection measure.

Figure 8.5

A scatterplot chart for a simple regression selection model.

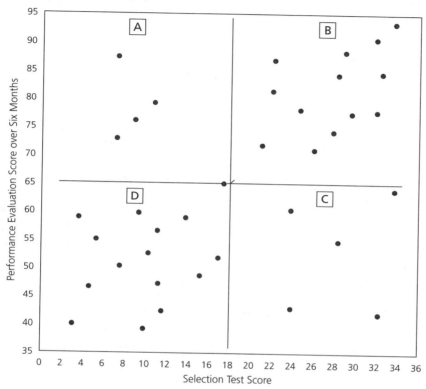

lation points will fall equally in all the squares. If most of the correlation points fall in the A and C squares, this means that the people who got the highest scores on the weighted application blank had the lowest performance ratings. This would not be desirable in this example, but if one looked at a scatterplot relating felony convictions and performance ratings, it would be better if most of the correlation points were in the A and C squares. This would mean that the people with the lowest number of felony convictions had the best performance ratings.

Although this is a very simple method, that simplicity leads to several problems. First, only one set of scores is related to the performance measure. Even when the score comes from a number of methods combined, as they are in an assessment center, it is still tempting, although incorrect, to believe that the good scores from the assessment center caused the good performance scores. A correlation only says that two things are related, and a third factor, say, job knowledge,

Multiple regression model
A selection method that shows the relationship between several combined scores and success on the job.

Multiple cutoff model
A selection model that uses a minimum score on each selection technique to determine the likelihood of success on the job.

may have caused both scores. There is also the question of whether one selection technique alone can account for job performance. Even if an applicant scores poorly on the interview, she may be an excellent employee because of her scores on the other selection methods.

Multiple Regression Model

The next method, the **multiple regression model,** can allow the applicant to make up for a poor score by using a number of selection methods to predict job performance. Since a high score in one selection device can compensate for a low score in another, this method also is referred to as a compensatory model. A graph of this model may look similar to a scatterplot used for the simple regression model, but the difference is the use of a number of selection methods that are combined and related to job performance rather than the use of only one selection method.

This method is a good choice when one low score may put an applicant below a minimum acceptable level but the applicant can compensate for that low score with very good scores on the other selection techniques. For example, an applicant for a sales position may score low on a test of personality factors related to success in sales positions but score very high on success in previous sales positions and the interview. His previous history of success in sales and his interview score would compensate for the low personality test score, and he might still receive a job offer.

There are situations in which multiple regression may be the best method for making selection decisions, but in other situations it may be a very poor choice. One problem with this approach is that it can hide serious difficulties that might prevent even minimum job performance. If a company were hiring someone to be an air traffic controller and that person did very well in the interview and the test of job knowledge but failed to meet the minimum score on the vision test, the two high scores could not make up for the vision score; vision is a critical requirement for air traffic controllers, who work with visual displays.

Multiple Cutoff Model

In a selection decision situation involving air traffic controllers, a better choice would be the **multiple cutoff model.** In this method, a minimum score is developed for each selection technique used. A score below the minimum on any of the selection techniques will eliminate the applicant. This is similar to a pass–fail test. For example, when you apply for a driver's license, in many states you are required to take a vision test, a written test, and a driving test. If you fail any one of these you cannot get a license, because each skill is critical to the ability to drive a car.

The problem of setting cutoff scores has raised a number of legal and professional issues. It seems logical to say that the cutoff score should be the minimum necessary to perform the job correctly. In the driver's license example, one could choose a number of different criteria for success at driving, such as the number of traffic law violations or the number of accidents, but it is difficult to assign an exact number of correct answers critical to being a good driver. Cascio, Alexander, and Barrett (1988) pointed to a cutoff score in the physical examination for the job of police officer in a city where 16 percent of the current police officers could not meet that score. The court decided that there was no proof that 16 percent of the city's police officers were unable to do the job, and the city was required to change the score.

Three requirements for a good cutoff score are that (1) the score be consistent with the results of a job analysis, so that only job-relevant behaviors are considered; (2) the score permit the selection of qualified candidates for the job; and (3) the score allow the organization to meet any legal requirements or hiring goals (Cascio, Alexander, and Barrett, 1988). In practice, this can be a very difficult task, and the researchers suggest that many organizations are trying to meet legal challenges by using more complex procedures to set cutoff scores.

One of the more complex procedures involves setting "bands" of passing scores and then selecting candidates from each succeeding band, from the highest to the lowest passing score (Cascio, Outz, Zedec, & Goldstein, 1991). The size of each band is determined by statistical methods. The hiring assumption is that all the applicants in each band are essentially the same in performance so that any person in that band can be selected with an equal chance of success, but that each higher band represents a greater chance for success at the job. It would be correct to choose people in the highest bands first if this were true. If an organization is trying to keep down the cost of the selection process, the multiple cutoff model may be a poor choice because this method requires administering all the selection methods to each applicant before making any selection decisions.

Multiple Hurdle Model

The **multiple hurdle model** reduces the cost by using a series of steps, or hurdles, that an applicant must pass before going on to the next step. The first hurdles usually involve the least expensive selection methods so that the more expensive methods are used with a smaller number of applicants. The method is more commonly used when there are a large number of applicants for a job and the job is critically important to the organization (Figure 8.6).

The selection of astronauts in the early years of space flight is a good example of the multiple hurdle approach. After the first satellites were launched, there was a great deal of interest in becoming an astronaut and many people requested applications. Whether an application was turned in was the first

Multiple hurdle model
A selection model that requires applicants to pass each step or test before going on the next step or test.

Figure 8.6

The multiple hurdle selection process.

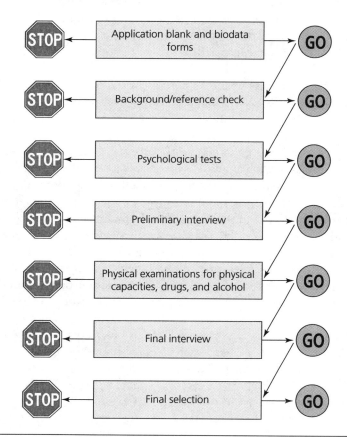

hurdle. Early astronauts were required to have experience as test pilots, and so applicants who did not have that experience were eliminated. The next hurdles consisted of reference and background checks and preliminary interviews. The final hurdles included mental and physical examinations and more extensive interviews.

One of the problems with this approach is the number of applicants who take themselves out of the selection process because of the time taken to pass each hurdle. It appears that applicants become more negative about an organization as the number of hurdles increases (Vecchio, 1996). This method has been challenged legally because different racial groups drop themselves out of the multiple hurdle process at unequal rates.

Utility Decisions

The final choice of a selection decision method and which selection techniques to use is often determined by a cost-benefit analysis. This commonly is referred to as establishing a **utility test** of the personnel selection process. On a common-sense level, it is obvious that even if an organization finds that an assessment center can predict success in the job of supermarket checker with a 95 percent accuracy rate, it probably will not use this method as part of the selection process for such a job because the cost would outweigh the benefit. This would be especially true if the organization found that a situational interview, which costs less than 5 percent of the price of the assessment center, could choose supermarket checkers with only a slightly lower accuracy rate.

A number of statistical methods can be used to compute the value to an organization of a particular set of selection methods (Hunter & Schmidt, 1982; Raju, Steinhaus, Edwards, & DeLessio, 1991), but even the most complicated methods do not consider all the factors that may contribute to the prediction of utility (Russell, Colella, & Bobko, 1993). No matter what utility analysis method is chosen, this is an important step in developing a personnel selection program. Not only does utility help determine the real value to the organization, research has shown that when evaluators are aware of the costs of personnel selection, they make different selection decisions (Huber, Neale, & Northcraft, 1987).

In the final analysis organizations must be sure that the selection methods they use are fair, useful, and cost-effective. Chapter 9 looks at the way personnel selection tests contribute to this equation.

Utility test An assessment of the cost-benefit ratio of using a particular selection test or method.

MAIN POINTS

- Screening, selection, and placement are separate parts of the selection process.
- A good job analysis and the resulting job description and job specification are the foundations of a good selection process.
- Recruitment, which can be internal or external, is necessary to make sure the organization has enough qualified applicants from which to choose.
- Application blanks, résumés, and biodata forms are personnel selection methods that rely on predicting future performance from records of past behavior.
- Weighted application blanks and biodata forms are methods that try to add value to the selection process by using something more than standard application blanks.
- Interviews are used in almost every selection process to assess oral communication skills and appearance.

- Interviews can be structured or unstructured. Situational, job-related, and psychological interviews are types of structured interviews.

- Applicants should be aware of interview factors they can control, such as dress and knowledge of the organization.

- Organizations can increase the value of interviews in personnel selection by training the interviewers and using job-relevant, structured situational interviews.

- The structure and use of physical examinations and tests as part of personnel selection have changed over the past thirty years as a result of legislation requiring proof of job relevance for including a specific physical skill or ability in the physical examination or test.

- Medical examinations must be job-relevant and can be given only after a job offer has been made.

- Physical ability tests, used for physically demanding jobs, assess the physical job skills that are required. These tests have faced numerous legal challenges for discrimination.

- Preemployment drug testing is being used by the great majority of organizations.

- Genetic and HIV testing present a number of ethical and legal issues for organizations and are not used often for personnel selection.

- Background and reference checks require a great deal of care in order to avoid legal challenges for negligent referral and hiring presented by former employees, other employers, and customers.

- Graphology and methods based on nonscientific beliefs have not been proved to be valid in the selection process.

- Assessment centers use a number of tests, activities, and simulations scored by several trained raters for personnel selection.

- Common exercises used in assessment centers include in-basket activities, leaderless discussion groups, simulations, individual interviews, paper and pencil tests, oral presentations, and business games.

- Selection decisions are determined by a number of factors, including the selection ratio, the value of each component to the selection process, and workplace diversity issues.

- Some of the common models for making selection decisions are simple regression, multiple regression, multiple cutoff, and multiple hurdle models.

- The final determinant of selection techniques is often the utility of a method, which involves the cost-benefit ratio.

Assessment center
Biodata forms
Contrast errors
Employment at will
External recruitment
First impression errors
Genetic testing
Graphology
HIV testing
In-basket exercise
Internal recruitment
Job analysis
Job Applicant Medical History
  Questionnaire
Job description
Job-related interviews
Job specification
Leaderless discussion group
Medical examination
Multiple cutoff model
Multiple hurdle model
Multiple regression model

Negative information errors
Negligent hiring
Negligent referral
Personnel placement
Personnel screening
Personnel selection
Physical ability tests
Physical examination
Preemployment drug testing
Psychological interview
Realistic job preview
Recruitment
Résumé
Selection ratio
Similarity errors
Simple regression model
Simulation
Situational interview
Structured interview
Unstructured interview
Utility test
Weighted application blank

Answers to these questions can be found at the end of the book.

1. Hiring poor employees can have both obvious and hidden costs to an organization.

   a. True

   b. False

2. The process of eliminating unqualified employees is known as _____.

3. A job description is

   a. the result of a job analysis.

   b. done before the job analysis.

   c. the same as a job analysis.

   d. b and c.

4. The recruitment process is considered successful when the person who is selected reports for the new job.

   a. True

   b. False

5. Which of the following recruitment methods may be legally challenged as unfairly discriminatory?

   a. Job fairs

   b. College recruiting

   c. Internal recruiting

   d. The use of cable television in recruiting

6. List three external recruitment methods.

   a. _____

   b. _____

   c. _____

7. According to recruiters, some of the most important characteristics for applicants to have are

   a. communication skills and motivation.

   b. enthusiasm and credentials.

   c. credentials and a degree.

   d. a and b

   e. all of the above

8. The first step in the personnel selection process occurs before the applicant fills out an application blank.

   a. True

   b. False

9. Biodata forms increasingly are replacing application blanks because of their greater validity.

   a. True

   b. False

10. A New York investigating company estimates that _____ of all applicants lie on application blanks and résumés.

    a. about one-third   c. about one-fourth

    b. about one-half   d. almost all

11. Which of the following methods do some personnel directors believe to be illegal?

    a. Weighted application blanks

    b. Biodata forms

    c. Interviews

    d. Résumés

    e. a and b

12. The two major types of interviews are _____ and _____.

13. Researchers have found the greatest validity for _____ _____ interviews.

14. What is most commonly assessed by the interview process?

    a. Previous work experience and vocational goals

    b. Response to job pressures and stress

    c. Group dynamics and sociability

    d. Oral communications skills and appearance

15. Research has shown that during an interview the interviewers generally pay more attention to finding out that you were fired from your last job than learning about the merit award you received.

    a. True

    b. False

16. What are the three interviewing errors over which an applicant can have some control?

    a. _____

    b. _____

    c. _____

17. Since interviews are used so much in the selection process, they are the most frequently validated selection method.

    a. True

    b. False

18. If a job requires you to be able to climb steps, your inability to do this will automatically disqualify you from that job.

    a. True

    b. False

19. The law requires that information about a person's disabilities be available from the beginning of the selection process to avoid discrimination.
    a. True
    b. False

20. What is one of the two problems in the use of physical ability tests in personnel selection?

    _____

21. What percentage of surveyed large U.S. companies use preemployment drug testing?
    a. 50 percent
    b. 80 percent
    c. 95 percent
    d. 75 percent

22. Which of the following jobs would legally permit HIV testing during personnel selection?
    a. Donor of clotting factor for the treatment of blood diseases
    b. Dentist
    c. Meat cutter
    d. Occupational therapist

23. The most common reason for employers *not* giving reference or background information is
    a. expense.
    b. lack of time.
    c. fear of lawsuits.
    d. unavailability of the information.

24. Which of the following methods has been shown to be a valid part of personnel selection?
    a. Interviews
    b. Graphology
    c. Phrenology
    d. Astrology
    e. all of the above

25. One of the requirements of an assessment center is
    a. a number of consecutive days of assessment.
    b. several assessors.
    c. a physical location set aside for the center.
    d. all of the above

26. Applicants view assessment centers as less job-related than other selection methods because they see them as playacting.
    a. True
    b. False

27. What are the three steps in setting up a good assessment center?
    a. _____
    b. _____
    c. _____

28. Which of the following is typically *not* an assessment center exercise?
    a. Physical ability tests
    b. Leaderless discussion groups
    c. Simulations
    d. Oral presentations

29. Which of the following selection decision models would be the best choice in applying for a position as a gymnast on the U.S. Olympic team if one was great in most areas but weak in floor exercises?
    a. Multiple regression
    b. Multiple cutoff
    c. Multiple hurdle
    d. any of the above

30. Which of the following selection decision models would be the best choice if there were over three hundred applicants for a single college teaching position?
    a. Multiple regression
    b. Multiple cutoff
    c. Multiple hurdle
    d. Expectancy chart

31. The utility of a selection decision process is determined by a comparison of the validity to the number of times the method is used.

   a. True

   b. False

WEB EXERCISE

Finding Your Dream Job Using the Internet

Using a search engine such as Excite, Yahoo, or Infoseek, type in the word "job." Choose one or two data bank sites, such as America's Job Bank (www.ajb.dni.us) or Monster Board (www.monster.com). Look for a specific job for which you would like to apply now or in the future. Print out the information about five different openings for this job, including the job description.

Employee and Organizational Testing

9

Chapter Outline

LEARNING OBJECTIVES
PURPOSE AND HISTORY OF EMPLOYMENT TESTING
LEGAL REQUIREMENTS OF TESTING
ETHICS AND TESTING
TYPES OF COMMONLY USED TESTS
   Mental Ability Tests
   Interest Inventories
   Personality Tests
   Aptitude and Achievement Tests
   Integrity (Honesty) Tests

WHAT MAKES A GOOD PSYCHOLOGICAL TEST?
   Reliability
   Validity
   Item Analysis
   Norms
   Standardization

CLASSIFICATON OF TESTS
   Power versus Speed
   Individual versus Group
   Paper and Pencil versus Performance
   Objective versus Subjective
   Language versus Nonlanguage
   Computerized Testing
   Case Study Selection Testing with Computers

CHOOSING THE RIGHT TEST
ADVANTAGES AND DISADVANTAGES OF USING TESTS
   Advantages
   Disadvantages

THE FUTURE OF TESTING

PURPOSE AND HISTORY OF EMPLOYMENT TESTING

"Time for your test." Your pulse begins to race, and you start to perspire. Most people do not like to take tests, even those who consider themselves good test takers or have done well on similar tests in the past. People are apprehensive about the results and what may be discovered about themselves. Test taking, however, is part of people's lives from the moment they are born (or even before birth).

Why is there so much testing if so few people like it? Is it really unavoidable? It is known that testing can improve the ability to make a medical diagnosis and predict outcomes. You certainly would prefer to have a doctor tell you that several very good tests have confirmed that you do not have a serious illness rather than have the doctor make a good guess that you are physically all right.

Most personnel selection and screening processes involve the use of psychological tests. The use of a good psychological test increases the likelihood that the most productive applicant will be chosen at the lowest cost to the organization. Like any good test, a useful psychological test is an accurate measure of behavior or knowledge. Not only does a bad test result in poor employee selection, the cost of making poor choices can be very high both for the organization and the employee.

What is the difference between effective and ineffective employee selection tests? Rudner (1992) states that the effectiveness of employment testing is determined by three factors. The first factor is the correlation between test scores and job productivity. This means that the persons who score highest on the test are the most productive employees on the job and the persons who score lowest are the least productive. The second factor is the percentage of applicants being hired. Suppose only 2 percent of the applicants who took the test were actually hired. In that case the testing program might be too expensive a method for selecting employees. The third factor is the proportion of applicants classified as successful by the test. If 98 percent of the applicants pass the test, it would be more cost effective to hire all applicants and then dismiss the 2 percent who failed on the job. The effective use of tests in personnel selection has improved greatly since their first use by industrial/organizational (I/O) psychologists early in the twentieth century.

The use of tests as part of personnel selection began long before the beginnings of I/O psychology. It is said that in China's Han Dynasty (206 B.C. to A.D. 220) written examinations were used to select candidates for government positions.

The U.S. government began to use employment tests after the Civil War to end corrupt practices in the civil service system. As an aspect of the selection process, testing has been part of I/O psychology since at least 1908, when Walter Dill Scott agreed to help the American Tobacco Company select salesmen (Landy, 1993). There was a surge in the use of employment tests after the introduction of this type of testing by the military in World War I. Many of those early tests, however, were poor predictors of job success. It has been estimated that about 40 percent of the companies that began to use tests after World War I found that they did not work (Lasden, 1985).

New testing successes during World War II in areas such as airplane pilot selection led to another peak in employment testing in private businesses during the 1950s. The civil rights movement of the 1960s and the legal requirement of proving that employee selection tests were fair led, however, to another decrease in the use of those tests. In the 1980s the government's rules were weakened by changes such as reduced funding for the Equal Employment Opportunity Commission, which resulted in lower investigation rates. Also, organizations found more objective ways to show that testing could enhance the selection and placement process. The use of employment testing increased during the 1980s, but tightening job markets during economic growth periods may decrease the use of employment testing. In recent years government on both the national and state levels has become increasingly involved in legislation to prevent discrimination against job applicants caused by the use of employment tests.

Each time the use of employment tests has increased, I/O psychology has added more knowledge to increase the usefulness of those tests in selecting employees. For example, in recent years researchers have found that giving a group of tests rather than a single test can be a more effective hiring technique (Ardelean, 1993). Personality testing for personnel selection has increased in usefulness as the groups of people against whom job applicants are compared have become more like actual employees (Butcher, 1994).

The use of psychological testing in employment selection has undergone tremendous changes since the passage of the Civil Rights Act of 1964. Before that time the only evaluation of the appropriateness of a test was done by the employer, who looked to the test to increase the chances of selecting skillful, competent employees. This is still a major concern for employers. However, employers now must show also that any test they use is not discriminatory against several protected groups of applicants.

LEGAL REQUIREMENTS OF TESTING

In general, the government's main concern in employment testing is whether a test is used unfairly against individuals or groups that are protected by legislation. The categories protected include group membership based on race, color, religion, sex, national origin, age, disabilities, pregnancy, or Vietnam-era military service.

The term *discrimination* needs to be considered in regard to treating people unfairly through the use of a test. The purpose of an employment test is to differentiate between applicants who will be successful future employees and those who will not. Discrimination that is based on characteristics unrelated to the job is illegal; differentiating between applicants on the basis of their ability to do the job is legal. In this text, **discrimination** refers to unfair rejection of job applicants and **differentiation** refers to finding the difference between good and bad employees.

The best way to prove that an employer does not discriminate is, of course, to show that a test differentiates between good and bad workers regardless of group membership. The assumption is that each organization is sufficiently concerned with this issue that if a test is not helping select the best employees, the organization will not use it. Although the tightening labor market of the late 1990s and the early 2000s has led to a drop in employment testing according to a recent American Management Association survey (Armour, 2000), about 46 percent of the companies surveyed said they do employment testing. After the passage of the 1964 Civil Rights Act, many employers decreased or abandoned employment testing as they became fearful of expensive legal challenges of those tests. As research and legal judgments have shown the usefulness of such tests, their use has resumed and increased. In general, this has resulted in the use of professionally developed tests rather than ones designed by a specific employer for its own use. Although it may seem cheaper or more relevant for a company to use a homemade test, the hidden cost of trying to defend its use in court may exceed the cost of purchasing a professionally developed test.

Discrimination Unfair rejection of job applicants.

Differentiation Distinguishing between good and bad employees.

The intent of Title VII of the Civil Rights Act of 1964 and other legislation (the Age Discrimination in Employment Act of 1967, Americans with Disabilities Act of

1990, and Civil Rights Act of 1991) has never been to require employers to hire unqualified people but to prevent them from unfairly rejecting qualified applicants. The federal government organization in charge of monitoring the fair selection and placement of employees is the **Equal Employment Opportunity Commission (EEOC).** Many state and local agencies also monitor the selection process.

In most cases of unfairness the EEOC or other agencies find the problem to be an error of omission; that is, the organization is not aware that it is doing something illegal. (Perhaps the argument that there are so many laws that no one can keep track of them is justified here.) When organizations are notified about the unfair practice, they usually change the selection and placement process so that it will be fair, especially if the changes will lead to better employee selection. The organizations may have to pay back wages to people who were unfairly rejected or give them another chance to be hired under the new selection procedures. If necessary, the EEOC may sponsor legal challenges to force organizations to prove that their practices are not unfair or require corrections if they are unfair.

How can the EEOC tell the difference between an applicant who was appropriately rejected and an applicant who was unfairly rejected? A protected group of applicants must provide evidence of **adverse impact.** After that evidence is provided, the burden of proof shifts to the employer. The legal assumption is that the test is unfair unless the organization proves otherwise. Under the **Uniform Guidelines for Employee Selection Procedures** (Equal Employment Opportunity Commission, 1978), a test is said to have an adverse impact when its selection rate for any protected group, such as Asian Americans, is less than four-fifths (80 percent) of the rate for the identifiable group, such as white males, with the highest selection rate. This is know as the **four-fifths rule.** The **selection rate** is the number of people who will be hired for a job divided by the number of people available to be hired.

This means that employers have to figure the selection rate for each group. For example, an organization has 120 applicants who take a test—80 white and 40 black—of whom 60 pass the test: 48 whites and 12 blacks. The test has a selection rate for white applicants of 48/80, or 60 percent, and a selection rate for black applicants of 12/40, or 30 percent. Next, the organization must determine which group has the highest selection rate. The last step is to calculate the impact ratios. This is done by comparing the selection rates for the other groups to that of the group with the highest selection rate (the selection rate for a group is divided by the selection rate for the highest group). In this example one divides 30 percent by 60 percent (the black applicant selection rate by the white applicant selection rate) to get an impact ratio of 50 percent. This test will be judged to have an adverse impact on blacks, since their selection rate from the test is equal to only 50 percent of the selection rate for whites.

Equal Employment Opportunity Commission (EEOC) The federal agency that enforces nondiscrimination laws in the workplace.

Adverse impact The unfair rejection of minority group applicants that occurs when the minority group's selection rate is less than 80 percent of the majority group's rate.

Uniform Guidelines for Employee Selection Procedures The set of procedures that explains how employers must prove that their employment selection systems are not discriminatory.

Four-fifths rule The requirement that the selection rate for minority applicants be at least 80 percent of the selection rate for majority applicants.

Selection rate The number of people who will be hired for a job divided by the number of people available to be hired.

Reverse discrimination
Unfair rejection of majority group applicants in favor of minority group applicants.

Race norming The practice of adjusting test scores on the basis of racial group membership.

It is in the best interests of an organization to keep accurate and meticulous records so that it can show that a test does not discriminate unfairly against applicants (*Griggs v. Duke Power Co.*, 1971) or that each test has been used correctly for each job in which it is used as a selection measure (*Moody v. Albemarle Paper Co.*, 1973). Some companies have chosen not to use certain tests, even though their usefulness has been proved, because of the poor public relations this could generate in parts of the community.

Can an organization go too far in trying to avoid unfair discrimination? The term **reverse discrimination** has been used to describe the unfair rejection of majority group applicants in favor of minority group applicants. In the landmark case of *Bakke v. University of California* (1978) the courts ruled that whites as well as blacks could be victims of discrimination. Bakke had sued the university to prove that he had been rejected unfairly for admission to medical school on the basis of his race (white) rather than because of a lack of legitimate qualifications. He had higher scores than did some of the people who were accepted, yet he was rejected. The courts ruled that since black applicants with lower qualifications and test scores were accepted, Bakke's rejection was due only to the fact that he was white. He won the case, and the university was required to admit him to medical school. Rather than emphasizing reverse discrimination, many view this case as illustrating the point that no one is exempt from unfair discrimination.

In the two decades after the passage of the civil rights laws of the 1960s the United States Employment Services attempted to reduce past discrimination practices by adjusting test score standards for different racial groups. This practice is called **race norming.** It was made illegal by the Civil Rights Act of 1991, which declares it illegal to adjust test scores on the basis of race, color, sex, religion, or national origin (Brown, 1994; Gottfreson, 1994).

Once race norming was forbidden, some employers turned to the practice of *score banding.* When score banding is used, all employees within a given range of scores are considered to have the same score. This is similar to the practice in college of assigning one letter grade to all students who score in the same range. Perhaps in your class anyone who scores between 90 and 100 on a test receives an A. If an employer wanted to hire an A student for a job, a person with a score of 92 would be considered equal to a person with a score of 98 since they are within the same score band. If the person with the score of 92 belonged to a protected class that had been discriminated against in the past, the employer might choose to hire that person instead of the person with the score of 98. This is still a controversial system and is being challenged in several court cases.

Even a good test can produce unfair discrimination, depending on the method used to interpret the results. If several interpretation methods are used, each can be unfair in different ways. McKinney and Collins (1991) used three different methods of evaluating the test results of applicants for a skilled trades position. A method that was the most useful in applicant selection also had the most unequal effect on minority group applicants. The methods that produced the highest selection of minority applicants adversely affected white applicants.

Recently there have been calls for the elimination of affirmative action practices. **Affirmative action** refers to hiring plans that give preferential treatment to certain groups. The most recent Supreme Court ruling (*Adarand Constructors, Inc., v. Pena,* 1995) requires that this preferential treatment be used only to correct a specific unfair practice, not bias in general. Some government officials see this as the beginning of the end for affirmative action, and others see it as adjusting affirmative action programs to fulfill more correctly the purpose for which they were designed. The call for elimination has the support of psychologists who believe that the changes in employment testing since the 1960s caused by legislation have led to the replacement of research-oriented selection methods with compliance-oriented methods (Ryanen, 1988). Some states have dropped affirmative action quotas or are proposing to scale back those programs. When California stopped using affirmative action standards for admission to state colleges, the number of admitted underrepresented minorities declined 36 percent (Stecklow, 1998). Psychologists have found that apart from the statistical realities of affirmative action, support for those programs is strongly influenced by individual beliefs and interests (Bobo, 1998). For many people affirmative action practices raise questions about the ethics of employment tests in general.

Affirmative action
The practice of using a hiring plan that gives preferential treatment to certain groups because of unfair hiring practices in the past.

ETHICS AND TESTING

For job applicants some of the greatest concerns about psychological testing, aside from the possibility of failing a test, are that (1) a test will reveal more information than they want to have known, that (2) they are not sure who has access to the test results, and that (3) they are not certain what the test is intended to measure. The American Psychological Association (APA) is aware of the importance of these concerns and has developed a code of professional ethics for those involved in psychological testing (American Psychological Association, 1992). Among the responsibilities of I/O psychologists who use tests in applied settings is the requirement of explaining to the test taker what the test is designed to find out and what the information gained from the test may be used for. This means, for example, that if you were given a mental ability test as part of the selection process to become an arc welder, the results from that test could not be used as part of the selection process for promoting you to a supervisory position without your knowledge and approval. Along with this responsibility comes the requirement that the test has been proved to be an effective test for the job for which it is used.

It is not ethical to disguise the purpose of a test to give a false impression of what that test is measuring. This is a difficult ethical problem because the examiner may have to be rather general about the test in order to avoid biasing an applicant's answers. Suppose applicants are given an integrity test. They may be told that this is a test of values rather than an honesty test. Many people would become very guarded in their answers if they thought their honesty was being questioned, because most people believe that their values are correct. The point is not that deception should be used but that there are many ways of saying the same thing and the correct procedure is to use the statement that is most descriptive yet produces the least biased answers. After applicants take the test, their scores should be given to them, along with an explanation of the results in language they can understand.

The psychologist or test examiner should be able to explain how the organization assures confidentiality and guards against invasion of privacy. In general, access to test results is restricted to people who have a legitimate reason to examine the results and who understand the meaning of the scores. This might include the person interpreting the results, the person making hiring recommendations and/or decisions, and the test taker. The Freedom of Information Act of 1974 gives people access to all personnel information about them, including test scores, unless they specifically give up that right.

Only qualified people should construct, administer, score, and evaluate tests. This often means someone who has had specialized training the field. If a test is administered or scored by a computerized program, someone with the appropriate training in psychological testing must develop the program. This specialized training allows the testing expert to specify to the test administrator the times when the results should perhaps be qualified in terms of accuracy. As an example, if you took a reading test but broke your glasses on the way to the test, the examiner might offer to let you return later with no penalty. However, individual test administrators should not be allowed to change standardized testing procedures for subjective reasons. The administrators of the test can ask an applicant to return later, but they should not decide on their own to give the applicant more time to finish the test.

If you find any unethical practices in the use of employee selection tests, you should make the psychologists in the organization aware of this, as one of their ethical responsibilities is to report unethical practices to the APA or to a state licensing board. If the result of the unethical practice is employment discrimination, this should be reported to government agencies such as the EEOC.

TYPES OF COMMONLY USED TESTS

Organizations use many different types of tests as part of the employment selection process. Some tests are used more frequently than others are, and some may be job specific. It is important to know which tests one may encounter in applying for jobs.

Mental ability tests Tests that assess cognitive skills and abilities.

Mental Ability Tests

Nobody would question the statement that it requires more mental ability to be a nuclear physicist than to be a swimming pool cleaner. Exactly how much mental ability is required by each job, however, is a more difficult question. **Mental ability tests** differentiate between applicants on the basis of their cognitive abilities. Most of the mental ability tests used in personnel selection are brief screening tests designed to sort applicants into qualified versus unqualified categories on the basis of their test scores. Choosing the person with the highest score in a group may not always lead to employing the best worker, however. Although people with a very high mental ability score certainly could do a job such as making French fries, they are likely to become bored quickly and either leave or find non-job-related activities such as filling out crossword puzzles or playing games during work to keep them performing.

It seems logical to say that mental ability is related to job performance, yet research results have not always been very supportive of this notion (Schmitt, Gooding, Noe, & Kirsch, 1984). Other research seems to show that these tests relate to both actual job performance and success in training programs (Guion & Gibson, 1988; Hunter & Hunter, 1984; Wagner, 1997). Research by Tenopyr (1981) concludes that no other employee selection method is as good as paper and pencil mental ability tests, in comparison to more subjective selection methods. The mental ability tests showed less adverse impact and better test validity compared with the other selection methods.

One of the most popular group mental ability screening tests is the Wonderlic Personnel Test. This takes only twelve minutes to complete and consists of fifty items that measure verbal, numerical, and spatial abilities (Figure 9.1). The most successful use of this test has been in predicting success in low-level jobs, especially clerical ones. It is very useful for quickly estimating general intelligence (McKelvie, 1989). The items require the applicant to write in an answer, and so this test must be adapted for some motor-skill-disabled applicants. Although tests like this one have been the target of legal action by those who believe they are unfair to certain minority groups, there is extensive information about standards for many of these groups in sources such as the *Mental Measurements Yearbook*.

Figure 9.1

Sample test items from the Wonderlic Personnel Test.

REAP is the opposite of

1. obtain   2. cheer   3. continue   4. exist   5. sow   _____

Paper sells for 23 cents per pad. What will 4 pads cost?   _____

MINER   MINOR   Do these words

1. have similar meanings   2. have contradictory meanings

3. mean neither the same nor the opposite   _____

Some psychologists believe that the mental ability test that would be most fair to minority group applicants would be one developed by that minority population itself. Researchers have found that issues involved in the fair testing of different racial and ethnic groups include more than the differential use of language (Martocchio & Whitener, 1992). The growth of the Hispanic minority in the United States has led to further research on the special testing requirements for that group (Camara, 1992). These special requirements might include adjusting test scores to account for educational achievement and assessing the language proficiency of a test taker before a test is given.

Individual mental ability tests are not used very frequently in personnel selection because of the time they take and the cost compared with their value as a screening tool, but some parts of these tests may be used to evaluate particular skills or abilities. The full test may take several hours to give and several more hours to score. Tests such as the Wechsler Adult Intelligence Scale-Revised (WAIS-R) provide more precise information on a number of components of mental ability. This test is divided into verbal and performance areas, and each area is divided into several subtests. The verbal section includes subsections on information, comprehension, arithmetic, similarities, digit span, and vocabulary. The performance section is divided into subsections on digit symbol, picture completion, block design, picture arrangement, and object assembly. Such mental ability tests are more likely to be used as part of an assessment for an individual who is being evaluated for overall job abilities and interests, usually for an upper-level position such as a manager or executive (Figure 9.2).

Figure 9.2

Sample of items from an individual intelligence test similar to the Wechsler Adult Intelligence Scale-Revised

1. "Evolution," what does "evolution" mean?
2. Who was Alexander the Great?
3. What does "A penny saved is a penny earned" mean?
4. Repeat the following numbers in backwards order: 3, 8, 6, 2, 9
5. What is missing in this picture?

Interest Inventories

Interest inventories can be very helpful in focusing a person's training or education or directing a person's career development. They are unlikely to be used for initial selection and placement because organizations assume that applicants already have an idea about the jobs they want to apply for. Organizations may use interest inventories as part of an assessment center or training program selection process to help focus vocational goals. Schools often use these inventories to help students choose a career path. The underlying basis of such tests is that the more answers the test taker gives that are like the answers given by someone who is successfully doing that job, the more likely it is that the applicant will do well at that job and enjoy doing it. The most popular examples of these tests are the Strong Vocational Interest Blank/Strong-Campbell Interest Inventory and the Kuder Personal Preference Record (Figure 9.3).

If you score very high on a job scale in an interest inventory but find that you do not like the overall job, you should think about what parts of that job you do like rather than rejecting the overall results. For example, if you score very high on the scale for a minister but are not involved in a religion, maybe what you have in common with ministers is a strong desire to help people. Culture, gender, and genetics also have been found to influence the results of interest tests (Karayanni, 1987; Moore & Ollenberger, 1986; Spokane & Jacob, 1996).

Figure 9.3
Sample items from the Strong Vocational Interest Blank.

L = like   I = indifferent   D = dislike

Show your interest in these activities by using the key above. Give the first answer that comes to mind.

L I D   Making a speech
L I D   Doing research work
L I D   Repairing a clock
L I D   Cooking
L I D   Operating machinery
L I D   Writing reports
L I D   Discussing politics
L I D   Taping a sprained ankle

Personality Tests

There is a long history of controversy about the use of **personality tests,** which measure the personal characteristics of applicants, in the application process. Among the problems are whether these scores are accurate, whether personality factors really relate to job performance, whether these tests measure normal or deviant personality features, and whether this kind of test represents an invasion of privacy. If personality test scores are used to reject otherwise qualified applicants, the hiring organization may be ignoring such factors as motivation and creativity in job performance. Overdependence on these types of tests may contribute to the loss of creativity in an organization by leading to the rejection of applicants with a personality profile different from the one the company has determined to be successful (Taylor & Zimmerer, 1988).

The tests initially used in personnel selection, such as the Minnesota Multiphasic Personality Inventory (MMPI), often were based on how similar the applicant's test score was to the scores of diagnosed mental patients. This would be an excellent tool for clinical or counseling psychologists (for whom the test originally was developed) but it is not often relevant to the employee selection process. Most seriously mentally ill people would not be applying for jobs, and their illnesses often would be obvious without a personality test. Research results have shown little relationship between these deviance test scores and job performance (Guion, 1965).

Personality tests Tests that assess the personal characteristics of the test taker.

The MMPI has been revised, and other tests have been developed, such as the California Psychological Inventory (CPI), which focuses on more normal behavior. The classes and components of behavior represented on the CPI are as follows:

Class I. Measures of poise, ascendancy, and self-assurance. Components: dominance, capacity for status, sociability, social presence, self-acceptance, independence, empathy, and sense of well-being.

Class II. Measures of socialization, maturity, and responsibility. Components: responsibility, socialization, self-control, tolerance, good impression, and communality.

Class III. Measures of achievement potential and intellectual efficiency. Components: achievement via conformance, achievement via independence, and intellectual efficiency.

Class IV. Measures of intellectual and interest modes. Components: psychological-mindedness, flexibility, and femininity/masculinity.

See Figure 9.4 for an example of this type of objective personality test.

The most severe criticism of the use of personality testing in the employee selection process typically has been reserved for subjective personality measures such as the Rorschach Inkblot Test and the Thematic Apperception Test. Not only do the previously discussed difficulties with personality tests apply, these last two tests raise the issue of the accuracy of their scores. These tests require that the test takers express their feelings, emotions, and other personality factors by responding to an ambiguous stimulus, such as an inkblot (Rorschach) or an ambiguous picture (Thematic Apperception Test). The test examiner then interprets

---

Figure 9.4

Sample personality test items.

Items are similar to those on the MMPI or CPI.

Y = typical of me   ? = can't say   N = not typical of me

Answer these statements by using the key above. Give the first answer that comes to mind.

Y ? N   I do not tire quickly.
Y ? N   Most people will use somewhat unfair means to gain profit or an advantage rather than lose it.
Y ? N   I am worried about sex matters.
Y ? N   When I get bored, I like to stir up some excitement.
Y ? N   I believe I am being plotted against.

---

the responses. Although there are standards for scoring these tests, there is also a great deal of room for personal interpretation by the examiner, raising the issue of interrater reliability, discussed later in this chapter.

Since the 1980s there has been an attempt to make personality tests more job-relevant by using working populations as the comparison groups and developing tests that are specific to certain jobs (Saville, 1984). Much of this research has focused on the identification of the Big Five personality traits that are considered the primary personality characteristics (Digman, 1990): openness, conscientiousness, extraversion, agreeableness, and neuroticism (OCEAN). When many personality measures were compared with many personality dimensions for a number of specific jobs, Barrick and Mount (1991) found several consistent and valid predictors by employing the five-factor model. Conscientiousness consistently was related to job proficiency and training proficiency, and extraversion was a valid predictor for success in sales and managerial jobs. Other researchers found that the Big Five personality characteristics were useful predictors of success in flight attendant training programs (Cellar, DeGrendel, & Klawsky, 1996).

Aptitude and Achievement Tests

The same tests may be used for either aptitude or achievement purposes, depending on the applicant's experiences before the test. If an organization takes the best applicants for a job, puts them through a training program, and then tests them for the ability to do the job, it is using an **achievement test,** because the applicants were given the test after they all had had a similar educational experience: the training program.

If the test was given at the beginning of the application process and people were chosen for the job on the basis of the results of the test, this would be classified as an **aptitude test**. This means that the applicants developed this aptitude in an unknown way. They may have had a similar job before, have had certain relevant training or experiences, or have a natural ability for the job. Many different tests fit into this category.

Multiple Aptitude Batteries

Achievement tests Tests that assess particular job skills of the test taker after a formal training program.

Aptitude tests Tests that assess particular job skills of the test taker before formal training has taken place.

Multiple aptitude batteries are somewhat similar in use to interest tests. They are used most typically in vocational counseling rather than as screening instruments. These batteries give scores in a number of different job-related areas. For example, the General Aptitude Test Battery used by the government gives scores in mental ability, verbal aptitude, numerical aptitude, spatial aptitude, form perception, clerical perception, motor coordination, finger dexterity, and manual dexterity. This test battery requires about two hours to take. The Differential Aptitude Battery can be used in similar ways with high school students and adults. Flanagan's Employee Aptitude Survey is designed to be used with actual job applicants.

Specific Aptitude Tests

Specific aptitude tests are more likely to be used at the time of application for a job. Their purpose is to determine whether the applicant already has the ability required to do the job successfully. Sometimes these may be vision or hearing tests, but more commonly they involve motor functions, mechanical aptitude, or clerical aptitude.

Motor function tests involve some aspect of movement responses. Most of these tests concern hand skills, as in the case of the O'Connor Finger Dexterity Test and Tweezer Dexterity Test, and the Purdue Pegboard. The Tweezer Dexterity Test requires the applicant to put small metal pins in a hole by using a tweezer. Such tests usually are timed.

Mechanical aptitude tests may involve some motor responses but also include perceptual and spatial aptitudes and mechanical reasoning and information. Examples of these tests are the MacQuarrie Test for Mechanical Ability and the Bennett Mechanical Comprehension Test. Figure 9.5 shows sample items from the Bennett Test to demonstrate how mechanical reasoning and information can be tested.

F i g u r e 9 . 5

Sample items from the Bennett Mechanical Comprehension Test.

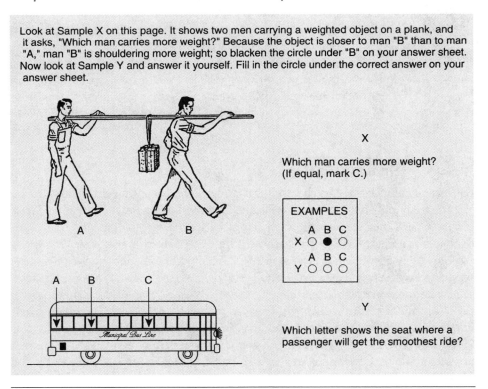

Look at Sample X on this page. It shows two men carrying a weighted object on a plank, and it asks, "Which man carries more weight?" Because the object is closer to man "B" than to man "A," man "B" is shouldering more weight; so blacken the circle under "B" on your answer sheet. Now look at Sample Y and answer it yourself. Fill in the circle under the correct answer on your answer sheet.

X

Which man carries more weight? (If equal, mark C.)

EXAMPLES

A B C
X ○ ● ○
A B C
Y ○ ○ ○

Y

Which letter shows the seat where a passenger will get the smoothest ride?

Source: *Bennett Mechanical Comprehension Test.* The Psychological Corporation.

Figure 9.6

A work sample test uses equipment and skills the same or similar to skills and equipment used on the job.

Spencer Grant/Stock Boston

In clerical aptitude tests the emphasis is usually on speed in perceptual skills. The General Clerical Abilities Test and the Word Processor Assessment Battery give the best scores to applicants who can do tasks such as filing and keyboarding most quickly and accurately. Tools such as the Computer Competence Test have been developed to assess computer skills and abilities.

Aptitude tests for specific vocations may be used as part of the initial screening process. The *Mental Measurements Yearbook* (Conoley & Kramer, 1992) which often is considered the authoritative reference book for testing, lists vocational aptitude tests for firefighters, cosmetologists, police officers, computer programmers, and salespersons, among others. This reference is updated every few years.

When organizations have difficulty finding qualified applicants, they may use application test scores to choose the best applicants and then give them further training for the job. After the training and before placement, some measure of achievement in the training program often is used to assess whether the trainees have completed the training well enough to be placed in the job. These tests may be as general as the National Test of Basic Skills, which measures reading and writing abilities, or they may be vocationally specific, such as the typing test illustrated in Figure 9.6. Sometimes these types of tests are referred to as work sample tests because actual job behaviors are measured.

Integrity (Honesty) Tests

For several decades there has been a great deal of controversy about the use of polygraphs (commonly but incorrectly called lie detectors) in employment testing. Some people believe they have contributed significantly to screening out potentially untrustworthy employees (Sackett & Harris, 1988); others believe that their limitations outweigh their usefulness (Murphy, 1987). The limitations include the ability of some people to fake answers, inaccurate measuring devices, the subjectivity of interpretations, and the rejection of honest applicants who have been assessed as dishonest.

Whether or not to use polygraphs was mainly a decision of the organization until the U.S. Supreme Court upheld the Employee Polygraph Protection Act of 1988, which outlawed the use of polygraph tests in employment testing by most private employers. Individual states also have passed laws on polygraph testing for employment purposes. Some states do not allow any polygraph use; in other states employers can ask an applicant to take the test but cannot require it.

Exemptions usually are given for security work and for jobs in drug manufacturing companies. Although it is not illegal to use a polygraph in all situations, many employers avoid its use because of the controversy surrounding it.

To replace the polygraph test, many organizations have switched to paper and pencil **integrity tests.** The purpose of these tests is to identify certain behaviors that correlate with being a dishonest employee by indirectly asking an applicant about his or her honesty. Integrity tests are composed of questions that typically are answered differently by honest versus dishonest employees. The tests contain items about attitudes as well as about actual theft. Figure 9.7 contains items similar to those used on many paper and pencil integrity tests.

Integrity tests Tests that assess the truthfulness or dishonesty of employees and applicants.

F i g u r e   9 . 7

Sample items from an integrity test.

---

1. Did you ever lie to a teacher or policeman?

2. Do you think people who steal do it because they always have?

3. If you saw another person stealing on the job, would you turn that person in to the boss?

4. When you are wrong, do you usually admit it?

5. Is it very important to you to be trusted?

6. Have you ever been disgusted with yourself because you did something dishonest?

7. Do you sometimes think that you are too honest?

8. Do you believe everyone is dishonest to a certain degree?

9. Do you agree with this: Once a thief, always a thief?

10. Is it worse if someone takes something from a small store rather than from a large chain store?

Scoring: Although the complete 88-question test is designed to provide a more accurate evaluation of your honesty, the following scoring scale offers an indication.

"Correct" answers: Questions 1–5, yes; 6–10, no. Your total number of "correct" responses: 1–3, high risk; 4–7, marginal risk; 8–10, low risk.

Source: Stanton Corp. Charlotte, NC.

As organizations have turned to paper and pencil integrity tests, more has been written about their value and use. The *Mental Measurements Yearbook* gives generally favorable information about the tests, but some psychologists have argued that they are not valid for assessing dishonesty in job applicants (Ones, Schmidt, &

Viswesvaran, 1996). Some of the drawbacks, besides those just mentioned, include applicants' right to privacy and the possible misuse of this information. In *Thompson v. Borg-Warner* (1994) the job applicant sued the company over the questions used in an employment integrity test. The court ruled that questions about attitudes toward illegal drug use and corporate authority could be interpreted as inquiring about political beliefs. It is illegal to ask questions about political beliefs or affiliation as part of employee selection. The company settled out of court.

Other people feel that the benefits of integrity tests outweigh their disadvantages (Zemke, 1986). The greatest advantage is the cost saving achieved by avoiding the hiring of dishonest employees—the saving of the cost of dismissal and of hiring and training a new employee after the dishonest employee is fired. Athlete's Foot Stores reported a decrease of 28 percent in theft losses after it started to use integrity tests for employee selection.

When an organization decides to do integrity testing, there are two distinct types of tests from which to choose (Sackett, Burris, & Callahan, 1989). Overt integrity tests are based on the assumption that unfavorable attitudes and perceptions on the employee's part, as well as a history of prior inappropriate job behaviors, can predict future undesirable behaviors on the job. Personality-based integrity tests assume that certain traits correlate with employee theft, including low impulse control and lack of conscientiousness (Murphy & Lee, 1994).

Using meta-analyses, Ones, Viswesvaran, and Schmidt (1993) found that both methods were valid even though questions about faking responses remained. Other studies (Alliger, Lilienfeld, & Mitchell, 1996; Cunningham, Wong, & Barbee, 1994) showed that even when people are given directions and motivation to fake responses on integrity tests, their scores are close to those of actual job applicants. Other researchers have found that integrity tests may predict organizationally disruptive behavior rather than employee theft (Ones, Viswesvaran, & Schmidt, 1993). Such findings may increase rather than decrease their value.

The ultimate decision on the use of paper and pencil integrity tests no doubt will depend on the outcome of legal challenges as well as changes in the tests. To reduce the number of challenges and increase the tests' value, the Association of Personnel Test Publishers (1990), the U.S. Congress's Office of Technology Assessment (U.S. Congress, 1990), and the American Psychological Association (Goldberg, Grenier, Guion, Sechrest, & Wing, 1991) developed a set of guidelines for the use of integrity tests in employee selection. The guidelines require that test publishers provide accurate information about the test and provide training and support for their clients. That support includes providing professional staff to help clients score and interpret a test. The test must not be biased against any protected groups, and all ethical standards must be maintained (Jones, Arnold, & Harris, 1990). Research comparing groups by age, race, and gender found that the only significant difference between the comparison groups was higher scores for women on overt integrity tests (Ones & Viswesvaran, 1998). The congressional and APA reports both identified several areas of concern in the use of integrity tests in employee selection, including the need for a more precise definition of integrity, less reliance on cutoff scores, and the need for independent research (Camara & Schneider, 1994). Some of the more common integrity tests are the Personnel Selection Inventory Test (PSI) and the Stanton Survey.

Reliability Consistency of test scores.

Test-retest method A way to prove the consistency of test scores by readministering a test after a period of time.

WHAT MAKES A GOOD PSYCHOLOGICAL TEST?

The easy answer to this question in regard to employee selection tests in general is that the psychological test should distinguish successful employees and unsuccessful employees in a specific job or field. However, underlying this question are others. For example, how do organizations know that a test is really indicating the difference between successful and unsuccessful employees, not just that between good and bad test takers? Can people improve their scores if they take the test at different times of the day or week? Would taking the test in a noisy room have an effect on test scores? Did the organization administer the test correctly? Is the group the applicant is being compared with the appropriate one? These kinds of questions are answered by looking at the characteristics that make a good test, including reliability, validity, norms, and standardization. These features will be discussed separately and then analyzed together in the discussion of test utility.

Reliability

Reliability in a test refers to the consistency of the score results over time. If you took an employment test at one company and received an almost perfect score and then took the same test at another company a week later and failed, you certainly would think there was something wrong with either you or the test. Once you ruled out things such as being sick during the second test or not being allowed the correct amount of time, you most likely would conclude that the test was not reliable and ignore the results. Reliability scores are reported as correlation coefficients. Reliability scores are the correlations between the scores obtained in each of the methods used to measure reliability. The best correlation between reliability measures would be very close to +1.00. However, in real life most psychologists consider correlation coefficients over +.80 quite good (Kaplan & Saccuzzo, 1993). There are several acceptable methods and formulas for measuring reliability.

Test-Retest

The **test-retest method** is the most basic reliability method. The same test is given to the same group of people at different times with a time interval between the administrations. The longer the time interval, the better (to minimize the possibility of subjects remembering the test questions). When the scores are

Parallel forms method
A way to prove the consistency of test scores by administering different forms of a test.

Split halves method
A way to prove the internal consistency of test scores by correlating the scores of two different halves of the same test.

compared, it can be determined whether a person's score has changed significantly from one testing to the other. The scores from the first test administration are correlated with those from the second to determine test-retest reliability. This is often a simple way to test for reliability, but it cannot be used if the test takers can improve their scores each time they take the test.

Companies usually do not use this method if they are developing their own selection tests, because the wait between the different times the test is given is not practical. Some tests do lend themselves to this type of reliability checking, however. A mental ability test or personality test often can be given to the same people at two different times, with the results compared for reliability. A test that measures a person's interests could be given more than once without the possibility that remembering questions from the first time the test was taken might change the scores the next time (Vansickle, Kimmel, & Kapea, 1989).

Parallel Forms

Often more than one version, or form, of a test is needed. For example, job applicants who go from one employer to another will not always take exactly the same test if parallel forms are used. Many group mental ability tests, such as the Wonderlic Personnel Test, come in several forms. In the **parallel forms method,** different versions of the same test are given to the same group of people. In addition to proving the reliability of the test, this method shows equivalence between forms. A high degree of correlation means that both tests are measuring the same behaviors. This was the method used by Pynes, Harrick, and Schaefer (1997) when they developed a selection test for a secretarial job at a state universities system. Two forms of the selection test were developed; the estimate of equivalence reliability between the two tests was .94, showing a high degree of agreement between the scores on the two forms.

Split Halves Method

Often it is not practical to give a test more than once. This is true in the case of college admission tests such as the American College Test (ACT) and Scholastic Aptitude Test (SAT). To determine whether these tests are reliable, the internal consistency of the individual test items is evaluated. The most commonly used method of establishing internal consistency is the **split halves method,** which compares the results from one half of the test with those from the other half. A more complicated method can also be used to correlate each test item with all other items on the test.

Interrater Reliability

With objective tests that have only one correct answer for each item, the same score should result regardless of how many different people score the test. When a test requires the scorer to evaluate each answer for correctness or when there may be more than one right answer or there are degrees of correctness—as in some individual mental ability tests and personality tests—each person grading the test may score it somewhat differently. The degree of agreement between test scorers is called **interrater reliability.** Ideally, if each person grading the test follows the same test manual, they all will arrive at the same score, but each examiner brings his or her own experiences, biases, and training to the test situation. The makers of published tests must prove that different examiners give similar scores on the same test. If they do not, the test lacks interrater reliability. Projective personality tests such as the Rorschach Inkblot Test often have the greatest disagreement between raters.

Validity

In addition to test scores being consistent, a good selection test accurately measures the behaviors and skills needed on the job. This raises the issue of **validity,** or whether a test measures what it is supposed to measure according to the people who made and use it. An organization that uses a test as part of the selection or placement process for computer programmers wants to know that the test really does differentiate between good and bad programmers. If the test seems to be unfairly biased against any protected group of applicants, the government requires proof that the test differentiates between good and bad programmers in a way that is not unfair to any protected group.

Some researchers believe that organizations must be willing to decrease the need for validity in order to reduce adverse impact. Maxwell and Arvey (1993) showed that organizations can decrease adverse impact by using the most valid selection tests.

There are a number of ways to prove that a test has validity when it is used for a specific purpose. **Criterion-related validity** shows that the test score is related to a measure of actual job performance, such as evaluations from superiors or the quantity and quality of production. **Descriptive validity** shows that the test measures an abstract trait, such as mental ability, that is necessary to do the job correctly or that the test directly measures skills or knowledge required on the job. Examples include mental ability screening tests given to managerial job applicants and a test of sterile procedures for a nursing assistant applicant in which the applicant has to perform the procedures as part of the screening test. Most people think of tests as paper and pencil exercises, but tests may be based on actual behavior as well.

Validity often is expressed numerically as a correlation coefficient between the test scores and an outside criterion, such as job performance. For example, the results of a welding test can be compared with the number of units welded and the number of errors made on the job. Although the ideal would be a correlation coefficient close to +1.00, in real life correlations in the range of .30 to .50 may be used. The correlation coefficient is a useful number, but it ignores

Interrater reliability The degree of agreement between test scoring by different examiners.

Validity The degree to which a test measures what it is supposed to measure.

Criterion-related validity A way to prove the effectiveness of a test by correlating the score with a subsequent measure of job performance.

Descriptive validity A way to prove the effectiveness of a test by correlating the score with measures of the nature or content of the job.

Predictive validity testing
A way to prove the effectiveness of a test by correlating scores with future measures of job performance.

Concurrent validity testing
A way to prove the effectiveness of a test by correlating test scores with current employees' performance measures.

important real-life considerations such as the selection ratio, the cost of administering or scoring the test, and the type of training program the company uses. Before an organization chooses a selection test, it should check validity studies in actual work settings.

Criterion-Related Validity

Criterion-related validity determines whether a test is related to a measure of actual job performance. There are two acceptable methods to show criterion-related validity. In **predictive validity testing** everyone who applies for a job is given the new test, hired, and later tested for on-the-job performance, which is compared to test scores. Ideally, everyone who applies is hired for the job, but realistically, an organization will continue to use its old methods to determine whom to hire while giving the new test. If the test has predictive validity, the employees with the highest test scores will have the highest performance evaluations and those with the lowest scores will have the lowest performance evaluations. Both of these results are necessary to tell the difference between good and bad employees. One of the obvious problems with this method is that an organization may end up hiring more people than it needs and some of those employees may, and probably will, create an unacceptable risk. What if the method were used to validate a test for nuclear power technicians? Could the employees at the low end of the test and the performance scale create dangerous situations on the job?

The other method of demonstrating criterion-related validity is called **concurrent validity testing,** which compares test scores and performance measures for employees already on the job. To validate a new selection test for computer programmers, the test is administered to people who are already employed as computer programmers. Next, the test scores are correlated with a measure of job performance, such as supervisors' evaluations. It is reasonable to assume that if the relationship between test scores and job performance looks something like the one in Figure 9.8, the test is differentiating between successful and unsuccessful programmers.

One of the problems here is that the scores and performance evaluations go down only to the 67 percent level. Is it possible that applicants who score 40 percent on the test could receive grade averages of 85 percent? It is possible but not likely. The problem is that it cannot be known for sure. Employees do not represent the range of test scores that would be found in job applicants. This is referred to as a range restriction. Employees who are not suited to the job often leave, voluntarily or involuntarily. Therefore, the range of people being tested is not as great as it would be if all applicants were tested. The other problem with this method results from using people who are doing the job the test measures. Even after a short time on the job, people change in terms of knowledge and skills. Are the current workers enough like the job applicants in the area being tested to respond as the applicants would? Again, the

Figure 9.8

Example of a test demonstrating concurrent validity.

Employee	Test Score	Job Performance
1	100%	100%
2	96%	95%
3	93%	94%
4	87%	85%
5	82%	82%
6	78%	74%
7	71%	70%
8	69%	71%
9	67%	67%

answer is usually yes. Giving the test a second time to people earlier in the employment process, after initially showing validity by using the method described above, can prove this.

Descriptive Validity

Although the government and organizations would prefer to use criterion-related validity, there are times when this is not possible or practical. The time and money required for predictive validity studies may make it impossible for some organizations to use them. It would not be reasonable to use a concurrent validity measure if there were only a few people in the job the test was being used for and there was only one minority worker among them. In these instances the government will accept the use of descriptive validity information. These methods depend largely on the judgments of psychologists or other professionals, and so employers must be very careful in their selection of experts in order to avoid legal problems. There are two commonly used methods of descriptive validity: content validity and construct validity.

Content validity is demonstrated by showing that a test measures a particular knowledge or skill required for the job. When job knowledge, skills, and abilities are extremely objective, it is easier to demonstrate content validity. This evaluation often starts by examining a well-done job analysis to determine the content of a job. Part of content validity concerns whether the test is a fair, unbiased sample of the area the test is measuring. If the test you take on this chapter contains a fair sample of all the material and excludes information not in this chapter, the test has content validity. If a selection test is closely related to the

Content validity A way to prove the effectiveness of a test by demonstrating that it representatively samples significant parts of the job.

Construct validity A way to prove the effectiveness of a test by demonstrating that a test score relates to an identified psychological trait that underlies successful job performance.

Face validity A way to indicate whether a test measures what it looks like it measures.

tasks required for the job, high validity and reliability correlation coefficients can be the result. Harrick, Schaefer, Pynes, and Daugherty (1993) used a selection test for a midlevel secretarial position that was based on twenty-five work tasks identified in the job analysis. The test contained eighty task statements, which were evaluated by over 1,500 secretaries and supervisors. The resulting selection test had high reliability and validity values.

Construct validity is used to show that a test is measuring an abstract trait such as mental ability, aptitude, leadership, or judgment that is necessary for a job. The general method of showing construct validity starts, like content validity, with a good job analysis and then an identification of the constructs, or traits, that are believed to be the basis for successfully performing the important work behaviors.

If an organization plans to hire someone to supervise computer salespeople who work independently in various cities, part of the job analysis might include "ability to supervise the salespeople in a way that promotes and encourages independent thought and action." This ability is the abstract construct the test is trying to measure. If a test is developed for this ability, construct validity may be used to prove that this is what the test really measures. One way to do this is to compare the results from this test with those of a test that most experts agree measures that trait.

Another way to show construct validity is by looking at other research. Company psychologists may find that independent leaders have been shown to get a large number of their subordinates promoted to supervisory positions. The psychologists then will look for a positive relationship between the applicants' test scores and the numbers of their subordinates promoted to become supervisors. They also will want to examine some negative correlations. They may find from research that independent leaders almost never use autocratic leadership techniques. Here they will look for a negative relationship between the applicants' tests scores and their use of autocratic leadership techniques. This means that people who get high scores on the organization's test use very few autocratic leadership techniques. Regardless of whether the behavior that is being correlated with the test comes from previous research or from the psychologists' own research, construct validity means that the test correlates with behavior. This is the process that was used by Frei and McDaniel (1998) when they found a connection between the personality traits of agreeableness, emotional stability, and conscientiousness and scores on a test for selecting customer service personnel.

Face Validity
Face validity evaluates whether a test measures what it looks like it is measuring. It is not a way of proving what a test actually measures and therefore cannot be used to satisfy government validity requirements. A test high in face validity measures just what it appears to measure.

Most employment and selection tests have fairly high face validity. The basic validation method used in tests with low face validity is the assumption that the more answers the applicant gives that are like the answers given by the members of a defined group—such as forest rangers or hostile people—the more likely the applicant is to be a member of that group. This is often the basis for including items on an interest test. The more answers the applicant gives that are like the answers given by people who are already dentists, for example, the more likely it is that the applicant will enjoy being a dentist. This is also the basis for including many items on personality tests. The more your answers are like those of aggressive people, the more likely it is that you yourself are aggressive.

Even though test items may be valid predictors, employees may be offended by questions that do not appear to apply directly to the job. In *Soroka v. Dayton Hudson* (1991), the case involved a test for the position of security guard that included questions about religious beliefs and sexual practices. The job applicant sued the company over the use of the test, claiming that those questions constituted an invasion of privacy because they did not appear to be relevant to the job of a security guard. Although this type of question had been used on other employment tests that were shown to have validity for the job, Soroka won the case and settled out of court.

Validity Generalization

How can one know whether the test an I/O instructor gives is valid for I/O students in another class or at another school? How can an organization know whether a test that is valid for computer technician selection at one company is valid for that purpose at its own company? This question is answered by **validity generalization,** which shows that a test that is valid in one job setting is valid in a similar job setting.

At one time psychologists thought that each company and job was unique in important ways. This meant that a test that was valid for clerical selection at one company would not be valid at another company until it was validated at that company. Studies such as that done by Hunter and Hunter (1984) have shown that this is not necessarily true. If there is a careful job analysis showing that the jobs at different companies are very much alike, the same test probably can be used at the second company if it has been shown to be valid at the first company. This saves a great deal of time and money and may contribute to more sharing among companies in developing selection tests. It also makes it possible for organizations with too few employees to do their own validity studies to use psychological tests. It also may contribute to a decline in the use of homemade tests and an increase in the use of published tests once an employer knows that a test that is good for similar jobs in other organizations most likely can be used in her organization as well. Local validity studies are an important way to confirm validity generalization work.

Validity generalization A way to prove validity that concludes that a test that is valid in one situation may be valid in another similar situation without independent proof of its validity.

There has been a great deal of discussion about the use of validity generalization since it was introduced in the 1980s. Some researchers (Schmidt, Law, Hunter, & Rothstein, 1993) found that certain statistical refinements can improve the value of the validity generalization work. Other researchers (Laosa, 1991) found that the usefulness of validity generalization is limited by issues such as the degree of support for a culturally diverse workplace. Culturally diverse groups may be different enough from one another to prevent the use of validity generalization. Despite criticisms of validity generalization, it is likely that the renewed interest in the use of tests in personnel selection will lead to increasing numbers of validity generalization studies.

Item Analysis

In addition to showing that an entire test is valid, each individual test item must be shown to be valid. An **item analysis** presents statistical evidence that each item discriminates between successful and unsuccessful employees. In an "ideal" test, the successful job performers select only the correct answers and the unsuccessful job performers divide themselves equally among all the other answer choices. Each item should be tested and revised until it meets all the criteria of job relevance and importance, clarity, and appropriate item statistics. Even if all these criteria are met, the items may be legally challenged, as was discussed above in the section on face validity with reference to *Soroka v. Dayton Hudson* (1991).

Norms

As the workforce has become more diverse, the issue of norms has become increasingly important. **Norms** are the average, or typical, performance of the group of people who were used to develop the test. That group of people is referred to as the **standardization sample**. The cutoff scores used by an organization may be above, below, or at the average score, depending on factors such as the selection ratio and the cost of training.

In the best situation, the group that was used to develop the test is exactly the same as the group among whom the test is being used. Many organizations use both the norms developed by the test publisher and those developed specifically within the organization. The most desirable tests are those that can be used with the greatest number of people. These tests usually have large numbers of people in the standardization sample that was used to develop the norms. As more nontraditional workers enter the workforce, we are finding a greater variety of test norms for specific groups. A single test may use different sets of normative scores for each of several groups. However, race may not be used as a basis for developing norms, as was made clear in the discussion of

Item analysis An evaluation of the validity of each individual item on a test.

Norms The average or typical performance of a large group of people on a test.

Standardization sample The group of people used to establish a test's norms.

race norming earlier in this chapter. It was made illegal by the Civil Rights Act of 1991. How the test is administered also may affect test norms. Silver and Bennett (1987) found that different norms were needed when the Minnesota Clerical Test was administered using a video display terminal like the one a secretary might use on the job.

Standardization Consistency or uniformity of the procedures for administering a test and the conditions under which it is given.

Standardization

Standardization means that a test is administered the same way each time. When you took achievement tests in school, each person was given the same number of sharpened pencils and the same time limit. Psychologists realize that factors other than pencils and time limits must be standardized as well. Many tests now come with instructions about room temperature, lighting, space, and time of day. These are all factors that should be standardized to provide the best testing situation. At best, standardization promotes the use of the same best test conditions, but by definition, it only means that the test always is administered in the same way. People often mistakenly believe that only printed tests given to large groups of people are standardized; other types of tests can be standardized as well.

CLASSIFICATION OF TESTS

The decision about which tests to use depends on a variety of factors. To help with such decisions, tests can be classified not only by subject matter but according to other characteristics. Some of these common types of characteristics are power versus speed, individual versus group, paper and pencil versus performance, objective versus subjective, and language versus nonlanguage.

Power versus Speed

Most tests depend on both speed and power to some extent, but one of the two may be the main focus. In a speed test, a person's score depends on how many items that person can complete in a given time. The items are usually fairly easy. An example might be a test requiring applicants to write a symbol in place of a number, as in the digit symbol test on the WAIS-R. On a power test all the test takers have enough time to complete all the items but usually do not because some of the items are so difficult that they cannot be completed. A mathematics test that starts with very easy problems and goes on to more difficult ones that require the use of answers from the earlier problems is an example of this kind of test. When test takers can no longer solve the problems, they must stop, since they do not have the ability required to go on to the next problem.

Individual versus Group

Group tests can be given to many people at the same time. An example is the Wonderlic Personnel Test. It is obviously cheaper to use this kind of test in terms of both administering and scoring, but it is difficult to allow for any modifications that may be necessary to ensure good test performance. For example, blind applicants may need to have the test read to them. As the name implies, an individual test is a test that is given to only one person at a time. The WAIS-R is an example of this kind of test. In an individual test the examiner not only makes modifications for certain test takers but also can get non-test information, such as emotional reactions, social skills, and cooperation. Individual tests are, of course, expensive to give since only one person at a time is tested and the examiner usually has to have extensive training in giving and scoring these tests.

Paper and Pencil versus Performance

In paper and pencil tests, all the items are printed on a form and the applicant answers the questions on the test form or on a separate sheet. A written test given to a class in Spanish is an example. The problem with such a test is that the students may know how to write Spanish but be unable to speak it correctly. This may be a poor test choice for assessing hands-on job skill. Performance tests require the applicant to do a task, often an actual job sample—as in the case of a nursing assistant having to demonstrate sterile procedures or the Federal Aviation Administration requiring pilot candidates to perform a specified set of maneuvers to receive their licenses. This type of test is realistic. However, it can be given to only one person at a time and may require expensive materials.

Objective versus Subjective

Objective tests have only one correct answer for each item and often can be scored by a machine. The multiple-choice tests given in many college classes are often objective tests. Many people can take these tests at the same time, and the simplicity of the scoring makes them quick and inexpensive to administer and get results. Subjective tests require a great deal of skill to interpret, and each person doing the scoring may score the test slightly differently. An essay examination would fall into this category. In either type of test the skills of the person taking the test can influence the scores. Some students are very good takers of multiple-choice tests and others do best on essay exams. To some extent, doing well on either type of test is a skill that can be learned. Many schools offer skills classes in test-taking procedures.

Language versus Nonlanguage

The great majority of tests that are used in employment selection involve language in administering the test, taking it, or both. However, if language use is not a relevant feature of the job someone is being selected for, a nonlanguage test may be used. Pictures or demonstrations can be used to give the directions. The Miniature Punch Press Test can be given in this way. Even portions of the WAIS-R, such as block design and object assembly, can be given in this way. This avoids bias against people who lack verbal skills when those skills are not important to the job. Certain disabled individuals also may benefit from a nonlanguage test.

Computerized Testing

As computers have become part of everyday life, they have become part of the testing process. Computers have been used to administer, score, and even interpret a number of selection tests. Computers often make the testing environment more accessible to disabled applicants. Although they were initially expensive, their growing use has helped reduce their cost. The expense of the hardware and software generally has limited the use of computerized testing to large organizations, such as the military, that do a large amount of testing.

Computerized tests can be either computer-based forms of paper and pencil tests or tests especially adapted for the computer (*computer adaptive testing* or *CAT*). When computers have been used to replace paper and pencils in testing, many researchers have found similar results on each type of test (Neuman & Baydoun, 1998; Potosky & Bobko, 1997). The advantages of computer-based testing include being able to give the test to a single individual at any time, the ability to give a different but equivalent test to each applicant, and quick scoring and feedback done by the computer program. The National Association of Securities Dealers uses this method to administer over 210,000 certification examinations a year at over a hundred centers nationwide and have the results available within twenty-four hours (Feuer, 1986). The U.S. Air Force has developed a computer-based test as part of its pilot candidate selection process (Carretta & Lee, 1993).

Computer-based tests can eliminate the problem of interrater reliability by reporting similar sets of scores in the same way each time. Computer-based tests are less biased and more objective than is the use of many different test administrators. Schmitt, Gilliland, Landis, & Devine (1993) developed a computer-based testing procedure for selecting secretaries. Some of the advantages were a reduction in the role of the test administrator, easy use at multiple test sites, quick feedback, fairness to applicants who already were familiar with computers, and easy entry of test scores into a centralized data bank.

Computer adaptive testing makes use of the ability to design computer programs that can choose questions based on the applicant's response to earlier questions on the test. A typical computer adaptive test starts with a question of average difficulty. If that question is answered correctly, the next question requires a higher ability level. If the first question is answered incorrectly, the next question is selected from a lower ability level. The computer adaptive test can give precise information by selecting questions from specific ability levels. Some of the advantages of using computer adaptive testing are a shorter administration time, increased and more useful information from the test results, and the ability to use different questions each time someone takes the test (O'Hare, 1997). An example of the development of a computer adaptive test in an organization is shown in the case study "Selection Testing with Computers."

[Case Study] SELECTION TESTING WITH COMPUTERS

When State Farm Insurance Company became concerned about security problems and a lack of parallel forms for its standard paper and pencil test for computer programmers, it turned to computerized adaptive testing (CAT) to meet its needs. The job applicants were college graduates with majors in computer science or with a strong background in that field.

State Farm had the test items developed by computer programmers who were knowledgeable about programming and test writing. The company tested concurrent validity by giving the test items to a group of computer programmers and comparing the results with the programmers' job performance evaluation scores. The programmers took the test at a desktop computer. The items differed with each presentation of the test in order to deal with the issue of test security. The test began with the presentation of an item of medium difficulty, and then the questions got easier or harder based on the applicants' responses. After sixteen items had been presented, a final assessment of the applicant's ability was made. The goal of this test was to screen out the lowest-scoring applicants from the selection process.

The researchers found that the CAT test scores were very similar to the scores from the regular paper and pencil tests. Many times CAT can reduce testing time, but these researchers found that the testing time was about the same for both types of tests. Using the computer could allow this test to be administered at a variety of sites and at times other than regular work hours. Even without reducing the test time, the greater test security made this an improved testing process for State Farm.

From R. C. Overton, H. J. Harms, L. R. Taylor, & M. J. Zickar (1997). Adapting to adaptive testing. *Personnel Psychology, 50*(1), 171–185.

Computer adaptive testing is most common in the areas of aptitude and achievement testing, where applicants come to the job situation with a wide variety of skill levels. This kind of testing can more easily isolate specific categories in which a person requires further training and can save money by avoiding unnecessary training. An organization may find that a data entry clerk is very good at categorizing information but very poor at summarizing groups of data. This means that this person needs training only in that area, not in all data entry operations. If a person answers questions poorly in one category, the computer can switch to another category without the applicant completing all the questions in the first category.

Another type of computer adaptive testing involves improving existing ability tests, such as the Minnesota Form Board Test. By using the computer, the applicant can manipulate the parts into the new required positions (Pellegrino & Kail, 1982) (Figure 9.9).

The last type of computer adaptive testing is truly unique to the computer, as it is used to assess human capabilities that cannot be measured by printed tests (Fleishman, 1988). Examples are the ability to concentrate, time sharing, and the ability to function under different time pressures. One of the earliest uses of this kind of test was done by electric power companies to screen candidates for positions in energy control centers (Marshall-Meis, Eisner, Schemmer, & Yarkin-Levin, 1983). The critical nature of such jobs requires a great deal of sensory alertness and the ability to pay attention to more than one source of information at a time. The computer can easily simulate paying attention to several tasks at a time by having the applicant strike a computer key when any one of several displays on the screen reaches a predetermined point. Computer-based tests also have been used to present complex dynamic scenarios that are comparable to other simulations used in employee selection (Funke, 1993).

If an applicant is unable to write answers by hand but can record answers on a computer, this allows the organization to test that person fairly. Some computers even respond to voice activation. These kinds of modifications of the test may result in a more job-relevant evaluation of the applicant. For example, someone who is paralyzed and is applying for a job as a proofreader may be able to show his ability to function on the job by using a voice-activated computer.

Computerized programs have been developed that provide not only test scores but a written interpretation of those scores. One of the earliest programs for doing this was used for the Minnesota Multiphasic Personality Inventory (Rome, Swenson, Mataya, McCarthy, Pearson, Keating, & Hathaway, 1962). Vale, Keller, and Bentz (1986) developed computer-generated written reports for a group of psychological tests used for management and executive selection by a large national retail merchandising organization. To test the computer-generated reports against reports written by experts, the researchers gave both kinds to psychologists, who were asked to evaluate them. The computer reports were rated as

Figure 9.9

Items on the Minnesota Form Board Test that have been adapted for computer testing.

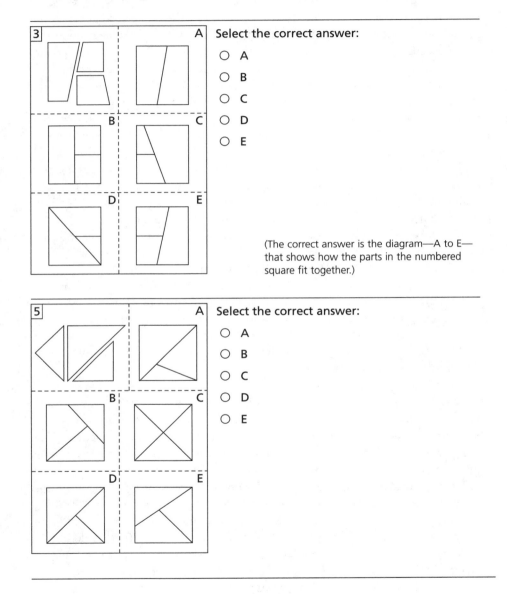

Select the correct answer:

○ A
○ B
○ C
○ D
○ E

(The correct answer is the diagram—A to E— that shows how the parts in the numbered square fit together.)

Select the correct answer:

○ A
○ B
○ C
○ D
○ E

more thorough and accurate, but the experts' reports were rated as better in picking out the important characteristics of the person being tested. Although it may be too soon to replace psychologists as interpreters of test results, it is easy to see

Figure 9.9 (continued)

Items on the Minnesota Form Board Test that have been adapted for computer testing.

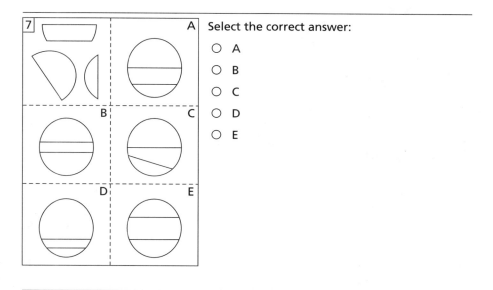

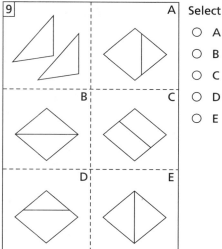

Source: R. Likert and W.H. Quasha (1995). *Revised Minnesota paper form board test.* San Antonio, TX: Psychological Corporation

the advantages of not having to train a new person to interpret tests each time there is a turnover in personnel and being able to draw on a number of expert interpreters through use of a computer program.

CHOOSING THE RIGHT TEST

How does an organization know which tests to use in employment selection and placement? The answer seems obvious: Use the best tests available for the job being filled or develop new tests. There are, however, many considerations that go into that decision. **Test utility,** or the usefulness of a test in a particular situation, must be measured to determine whether the test is helping the organization select and place successful employees.

The knowledge needed to make such decisions typically requires special expertise in the field of personnel testing, such as the skills of an I/O psychologist. The first step is to obtain a very specific job analysis or job description, as was discussed in Chapter 8. The job analysis for a clerical worker cannot just state that typing is required but must include information such as speed and knowledge of word processors or computers, job skills that can be measured objectively through testing.

After the job analysis has been completed, the next step involves locating all the tests that are available or constructing a new test to evaluate the abilities required for the job. It is usually less expensive and faster for the organization to use an existing test than to develop a new test. Reference books such as *Mental Measurements Yearbook* list many published tests. This book contains descriptive information about various tests and research information about how those tests have been used, their validity, and their reliability.

An overriding factor in many test decisions is cost—not just the cost of purchasing, developing, and administering the test but the overall organizational cost. Berger and Tucker (1987) developed a simple formula for determining the dollar value of testing, which involves the increase in accurate selections provided by the test (represented by a percentage), multiplied by the number of persons hired, then multiplied again by the salaries of the employees. For example, a company is recruiting twenty computer programmers and uses a test to select new employees. The test has improved the organization's selection accuracy by 25 percent, and the salary of each programmer is $40,000 per year. The cost of the testing program is $10,000. Gross saving in selection is 25 percent times twenty programmers times $40,000 per programmer, or $200,000. After subtracting the $10,000 cost of testing, the organization has a net saving of $190,000.

More complicated formulas can be used to determine the best cutoff test scores for an organization to use. These formulas can factor in important variables that affect employees' success, such as the expenses associated with accidents by truck drivers or the productivity of salespeople (Martin & Raju, 1992). The use of such statistical utility formulas has helped reduce the subjectivity of employment test selection. Harris, Dworkin, and Park (1990) found that many human resource practitioners based their test selection decisions on factors such as their personal beliefs about validity, their beliefs about the ease of passing the test rather than more objective measures mentioned above, and the perceived offensiveness of the tests to applicants. Other researchers found that even when utility analysis information is presented, managers may discount the information in favor of less reliable decision-making systems (Whyte & Latham, 1997). Still other researchers have suggested that managers' failure to use utility information is caused by the belief that such information is really a sales pitch (Cronshaw, 1997) or by their failure to understand the information (Carson, Becker, & Henderson, 1998).

Other ways of assessing the utility of a test include whether it results in improved performance evaluations and decreased turnover. If high turnover figures have been caused by the firing of poorly performing employees, an effective test may result in a significant cost saving. Turnover costs include not only the cost of replacing an employee but also the separation costs for that employee and the training costs for the new employee. Mercer (1988) showed how one organization calculated the turnover cost for one computer programmer to be over $20,000. Before changing the hiring process, that organization averaged a 28 percent turnover rate per year. After it changed its selection tests to make them more valid, turnover was reduced to 9 percent per year and the organization saved over $120,000 a year in reduced turnover costs.

There is also a cost in not using tests in the most optimal way. The government has used the General Aptitude Test Battery (GATB) for a number of years. The usual process had been to hire randomly from the pool of everyone who achieved a minimal test level. Hunter (1983) estimated that the federal government could save $15.61 billion per year if test use was optimized, for example, by choosing employees who scored highest on certain sections of this test. He calculated that the increase in workforce productivity resulting from the four million workers hired by using the GATB would come to $79.36 billion per year. This optimal use of the test would require about $8.75 million per year, but the increase in correct selection and productivity would far outweigh that cost.

Organizations need to be sure that each test they use complies with the legal requirements of the EEOC guidelines and that the test is suitable in terms of administering and scoring. If the test requires a licensed psychologist for administration and scoring and the organization does not already employ a psychologist, it may not be worth it to hire one. Test publishers generally provide information about administration and scoring with a description and samples of the test.

ADVANTAGES AND DISADVANTAGES OF USING TESTS

Advantages

In contrast to the other methods used in personnel selection and placement, psychological testing has some distinct advantages. In many cases, a large number of people can be tested in a short time, compared with the lengthy process of interviewing. Many tests can be scored quickly and thoroughly, especially with the assistance of computers. Compared to other methods, tests are often the most objective method of selection. Personal bias plays a much greater role when subjective evaluations are required, as in interviews or reviewing recommendations.

The most important advantage to many organizations is usually cost savings. Not only does a good psychological test help prevent selecting a poorly performing employee, the cost of testing is often lower than that of other selection methods, especially when an organization has determined how much the correct use of testing contributes to the overall selection process.

The best predictive tests for success on the job and in training tend to be mental ability tests. Over 78 percent of psychologists involved in the selection process say that they use this kind of test (Ryan & Sackett, 1987). However, aptitude and achievement tests may be the most distinctly job-relevant. Several aptitude tests combined into a test battery can at times improve the selection process even more than can the use of a single test (Riggio & Sotoodeh, 1987). For published tests, especially those that have been in existence for some time, such as the Wonderlic Personnel Test, there is a great amount of research information available. This is often not true for selection methods such as interviews and application blanks. Overall, psychological testing can be one of the most objective, cost-efficient parts of the selection and placement process.

Disadvantages

Does this mean that organizations should rely solely on psychological tests to select employees? No, because no single method of selection is perfect. In the current testing boom, special attention should be paid to the problems that are unique to psychological tests. Lasden (1985) suggests that even if a test is used extensively, organizations cannot accept the results blindly. IBM developed a Programmer Aptitude Test (PAT) in the 1950s that was used all over the United States for the next ten years until studies in the 1960s showed that half the top scorers turned out to be below-average programmers.

Much like the commercials on television, information from test publishers may fail to tell the whole truth or make exaggerated claims. Overreliance on test results relative to other selection methods may lead to a poor selection program in general. One of the advantages of testing—the quickness and ease of administering and scoring—may contribute to this overreliance.

Since the 1950s people such as William Whyte, in *The Organization Man* (1956), have been critical of the tendency of companies to develop sameness in behavior, personality, and style among successful employees. Personality tests in particular may contribute to this corporate profile by identifying one personality type as the most successful and rejecting all others. This narrow use of personality testing may reject a number of applicants who can do the job but do not fit the profile. A major source of innovation and change within an organization consists of employees who are able to think "outside of the box."

If applicants know in advance what an organization is looking for, is it possible to fake test results? Unfortunately, the answer is sometimes yes. One study (Furham, 1990) had people complete four tests of personality used in personnel selection. They were supposed to answer the questions on these tests as if they were the ideal candidates for the job of librarian, advertising executive, or banker. All these tests were susceptible to faking. That is, when the person taking the test tried to answer like an ideal banker candidate, that was what the test reflected. Personality tests seem especially subject to this problem, and many published tests, such as the MMPI, include a number of lie scales to detect fakers.

The ultimate responsibility for the correct use of a test lies with the organization that uses that test, which should make certain that the test is administered in the proper setting, scored correctly, administered and scored by someone with the appropriate level of training, and used correctly in the decision-making process. Too often, less than qualified people are allowed to be a part of the testing process.

THE FUTURE OF TESTING

Although there has been a resurgence in the use of testing, many organizations do not use testing for hiring or selection. The government and military lead the test use field, with 38 percent of those departments and groups doing some form of psychological testing. Only 21 percent of manufacturers use any tests. How likely you are to be tested also depends on the type of job for which you are applying. Companies surveyed by the American Management Association (2000) indicated that only 6.1 percent tested job skills for all applicants, but 56.3 percent tested applicants in selected job categories such as word processing. The conclusion of the study indicates that not only are you far more likely to encounter psychological tests as part of the job selection process than was the case in the past, but before you are allowed to show a particular job skill, you probably will have to demonstrate proficiency in basic mathematics and reading skills.

MAIN POINTS

- Psychological tests have been used in I/O psychology since the early part of the twentieth century.

- The Civil Rights Act of 1964 and other laws prohibit the use of tests that discriminate on the basis of race, color, religion, sex, national origin, age, disability, or Vietnam War veteran status.

- The Equal Employment Opportunity Commission is the federal government agency that monitors employment testing for bias.

- The American Psychological Association monitors and gives guidelines for the ethical use of psychological tests.

- Mental ability tests are used to measure the different components of cognitive abilities. These tests are usually good predictors of job performance and success in training programs.

- Interest inventories are used to assess job and career interests.

- Personality tests are used to assess personal characteristics and behaviors. They are controversial in terms of job relevance, although recent improvement may increase their validity.

- Aptitude tests and achievement tests are used to assess specific job skills and job knowledge. These are often job-relevant because they test specific job skills.

- Integrity tests have been used to replace polygraph tests, although their use is controversial.

- The characteristics of a good psychological test are validity, reliability, appropriate norms, and standardization.

- Reliability refers to the consistency of test scores. It can be assessed by the test-retest method, the parallel forms method, or the split halves method.

- Interrater reliability refers to similarity between examiners in scoring and interpreting test results.

- Validity concerns whether a test really measures what it is supposed to measure. The types of validity are criterion-related validity (measured by predictive or concurrent validity studies) and descriptive validity (measured by content or construct validity studies).

- Face validity assesses whether a test appears to measure what it is supposed to measure.

- Validity generalization allows a test to be used with similar groups in different organizations.

- Item analysis is used to judge the validity of each test item.

- Norms are the average or typical performance of a large group of people on a test.

- Standardization refers to how a test is administered (instructions given, level of lighting in the examination room, etc.) so that all conditions are the same for all test takers.

- Tests can be classified by characteristics such as power versus speed, paper and pencil versus performance, objective versus subjective, and language versus nonlanguage.

- Computers can be used to create a fairer testing environment for disabled applicants and to administer, score, and interpret tests. Computers also have been used to improve existing tests and measure abilities that cannot be measured by printed tests.

- Before choosing a selection test, an organization must complete an extensive and specific job analysis and job description.

- Sources such as the *Mental Measurements Yearbook* can be used to locate published tests.

- The choice of a particular test for personnel selection depends on factors such as validity, fairness, applicability, and cost.

- Compared with other selection methods, testing can have several advantages, such as lower cost and objectivity, and can lead to improved performance evaluations and decreased turnover.

- Testing may have disadvantages, such as faking and incorrect test usage.

- Organizations are increasing the use of testing in personnel selection, and one is more likely to encounter tests as part of the application process now and in the near future.

KEY TERMS

Achievement tests	Discrimination
Adverse impact	Equal Employment Opportunity Commission (EEOC)
Affirmative action	
Aptitude tests	Face validity
Concurrent validity testing	Four-fifths rule
Construct validity	Integrity tests
Content validity	Interrater reliability
Criterion-related validity	Item analysis
Descriptive validity	Mental ability tests
Differentiation	Norms

Parallel forms method
Personality tests
Predictive validity testing
Race norming
Reliability
Reverse discrimination
Selection rate
Split halves method

Standardizatoin
Standardization sample
Test-retest method
Test utility
Uniform Guidelines for Employee
 Selection Procedures
Validity
Validity generalization

LEGAL RULINGS AND LEGISLATION INFLUENCING PERSONNEL SELECTION DECISIONS

Adarand Construction Co. v. Pena (1995). The U.S. Supreme Court ruling that limited affirmative action programs to correcting specific evidence of past discrimination or a strong imbalance in the workforce or labor pool.

Age Discrimination in Employment Act of 1967. The federal law that prevents discrimination in the hiring process for people age forty or over.

Americans with Disabilities Act of 1990. The federal law that prevents discrimination against people with disabilities who are otherwise qualified for a job.

Bakke v. University of California (1978). The U.S. Supreme Court decision that established the unfairness of reverse discrimination.

Civil Rights Act of 1964. The federal law that prohibits discrimination based on race, age, or sex.

Civil Rights Act of 1991. The federal law that extended the protection provided by the 1964 Civil Rights Act and outlawed race norming.

Griggs v. Duke Power Co. (1971). The U.S. Supreme Court decision that required employment selection tests to be directly job-relevant.

Moody v. Albemarle Paper Co. (1973). The U.S. Supreme Court decision that required organizations to validate an employment test for each separate job in which it is used as a screening measure.

Soroka v. Dayton Hudson (1991). The court decision that eliminated some valid test items that may appear to be irrelevant.

Title VII of the Civil Rights Act of 1964. The part of the Civil Rights Act of 1964 that prohibits discrimination in the hiring process.

Thompson v. Borg-Warner (1994). The federal court ruling that limits the type of questions used on integrity tests.

Answers to these questions can be found at the end of the book.

1. The psychological tests used in personnel selection and placement measure
   a. knowledge of psychology.
   b. ability to interpret psychology test results.
   c. behavior.
   d. genetic characteristics.

2. Psychological testing as part of the selection process in the United States dates back to
   a. the Civil War.
   b. the early 1960s.
   c. the early 1900s.
   d. none of the above

3. Economic factors as well as legal factors may influence how much employment tests are used.
   a. True
   b. False

4. List four federal laws that prevent the use of discriminatory employment tests.
   a. _____
   b. _____
   c. _____
   d. _____

5. The federal agency that monitors the use of psychological tests in employment selection is the _____ _____ _____ _____.

6. The four-fifths rule requires organizations to hire four-fifths of the minority applicants who apply for jobs.
   a. True
   b. False

7. _____ _____ means unfairly rejecting majority group applicants in favor of less qualified minority group applicants.

8. One of the ethical requirements for using psychological tests is that in order to eliminate secrecy the results be shared freely with anyone who asks to see them.
   a. True
   b. False

9. Which of the following tests is least likely to be used in an organization's personnel selection process?

    a. Mental ability tests

    b. Interest inventories

    c. Aptitude tests

    d. Honesty tests

10. A recent change in personality tests for employment selection has been to use _____ populations for the norms.

11. If new workers were given a motor function test at the end of a training program, that test would be classified as a(n) _____ test.

12. In clerical aptitude tests the emphasis is usually on

    a. telephone skills.

    b. ability to follow orders.

    c. ability to make independent decisions.

    d. speed.

13. Match each item at the left with the term that best describes it.

    _____ Mental ability test   a. General Aptitude Test Battery

    _____ Personality test   b. Wonderlic Personnel Test

    _____ Interest test   c. an essay history test

    _____ Multiple aptitude battery   d. Miniature Punch Press Test

    _____ Motor function tests   e. Purdue Pegboard Test

    _____ Nonlanguage test   f. Kuder Personal Preference Record

    _____ Subjective test   g. California Psychological Inventory

14. The _____ outlawed the use of most polygraph tests in employment selection.

15. Integrity tests are being used as replacements for polygraph tests.

    a. True

    b. False

16. Which of the following is *not* a characteristic of a good psychological test?

    a. Normalization

    b. Standardization

    c. Reliability

    d. Validity

17. When people who are already employed by an organization are used to establish the validity of a test for the job they do, this method is called _____ _____.

18. When a personality test looks like a test of interior decorating skills, this test most likely lacks

    a. standardization.

    b. content validity.

    c. face validity.

    d. reliability.

19. For a test to be considered reliable, the correlation coefficient should be at least +.90.

    a. True

    b. False

20. The concept that explains a psychology instructor defending the validity of a midterm examination by explaining that it has been proved to be valid in the past with many similar groups of psychology students is _____ _____.

21. A test that can be given to people only once can never be shown to be reliable.

    a. True

    b. False

22. Which of the following validity methods will the Equal Employment Opportunity Commission accept to show the validity of a test?

    a. Content validity

    b. Face validity

    c. Concept validity

    d. Normative validity

    e. all of the above

23. If a test administrator makes certain that room temperature and lighting are the same every time a test is given, the administrator is concerned with the _____ of the test.

24. If you believed your instructor might purposely try to give you a failing grade, which type of test would make it most difficult to do this?

    a. nonlanguage test

    b. power test

    c. performance test

    d. objective test

25. Computer programs have been used to produce written interpretations of test scores.

    a. True

    b. False

26. Computer programs for testing may be used by only one person in one location at a time.

    a. True

    b. False

27. The first step in selecting a test for an organization is to get a list of all the available tests.

    a. True

    b. False

28. Mental ability tests are typically _____ in validity, _____ in fairness, _____ in applicability, and _____ in cost.

29. The turnover cost of replacing a single poorly selected computer programmer was found to exceed

    a. $5,000.

    b. $10,000.

    c. $20,000.

    d. $50,000.

30. The most directly job-relevant tests are _____ and _____ tests.

31. Test publishers have sometimes been found to exaggerate or slant claims for the tests they publish.

    a. True

    b. False

32. It is possible to fake answers on some selection tests.

    a. True

    b. False

33. When applicants fail basic skills tests, most organizations put them in remedial programs and then retest them.

    a. True

    b. False

34. The chances of your being required to take tests as part of the job selection process are likely to decrease in the near future.

    a. True

    b. False

Use your browser to go to http://outofservice.com/you and take the personality test based on the Big Five personality dimensions discussed in this chapter. To which of the five dimensions does each question refer? Submit your answers and print the results. Do you agree with your evaluation? Why or why not? What jobs do you think might fit your personality profile, and why?

WEB EXERCISE

10

Performance Appraisal

LEARNING OBJECTIVES

PURPOSE OF PERFORMANCE APPRAISALS
Individual Purposes
Organizational Purposes

WHAT MAKES A PERFORMANCE APPRAISAL FAIR?

JOB ANALYSIS
Methods of Job Analysis
Job Evaluation and Comparable Worth

METHODS OF PERFORMANCE APPRAISAL
Outcome-Based Methods
Absolute Standards Methods
Relative Comparisons Methods

ERRORS IN PERFORMANCE APPRAISAL
Halo Errors
Leniency and Severity Errors
Central Tendency Errors
Contrast and Similarity Errors
Recency Error
Frame of Reference Errors

WHO DOES THE PERFORMANCE APPRAISAL?
Immediate Supervisor
Subordinate Appraisal
Peer Evaluation
Self-Evaluation
Human Resources Department and Assessment Centers
Multiple Raters
Case Study Appraisals at Work

PERFORMANCE APPRAISAL INTERVIEWS

IMPROVING PERFORMANCE APPRAISALS

EVALUATING PERFORMANCE APPRAISAL PROGRAMS

Chapter Outline

If you are hired to pick all the apples in an orchard in three days and do it in two, should you receive an excellent performance evaluation and a monetary bonus as a reward? What if the owner found that you damaged 20 percent of the apples you picked or that you were such a good picker that the owner would lose money by promoting you to crew chief or you found out that one of last year's pickers was paid double what you were paid for the same work? This simple example raises some of the questions organizations face in evaluating employees in the best way for the organization and the employees. **Performance appraisal** seems to be a very straightforward concept: It means measuring the output of a worker that contributes to productivity. Either you do the job correctly or you do not.

In a perfect world, performance appraisals would involve only objectively measurable job-relevant features evaluated by totally objective raters. Accurate performance appraisals become even more important when one looks at how many other work functions are related to these scores. In Chapters 8 and 9, performance appraisal scores were discussed as criteria for evaluating the validity of personnel selection measures. In Chapter 11, performance appraisal scores will be analyzed as criteria for evaluating the success of training programs. If employee performance appraisal scores are valid and reliable, the validity of the training and selection programs can be confirmed. If those scores are not valid and reliable, they cannot be used to confirm the effectiveness of the other programs. A strong relationship between performance appraisal scores and other scores will be meaningless if the performance appraisal scores are not valid and reliable.

Performance appraisal
The process of measuring the output of an employee that contributes to the productivity of an organization.

Despite these difficulties, it is possible to do good performance appraisals, and finding good ways to evaluate the performance of employees is a worthwhile goal for organizations. This chapter looks at some of the problems in performance appraisal as well as many of the solutions.

PURPOSE OF PERFORMANCE APPRAISALS

Organizations often use performance evaluations for multiple purposes (Cleveland, Murphy, & Williams, 1989), although the major use usually determines the type of evaluation. For example, if a company wants to use performance appraisals as a method for selecting managerial candidates for promotion, it will be most interested in assessing which people have the strongest management skills. If the company is going to downsize and wants to identify the most expendable workers, it will be most interested in assessing those who have the weakest job skills. If the company wants to encourage growth among employees, input to workers will be an important aspect of performance appraisal.

Individual Purposes

For the individual employee, appraisal represents an opportunity for feedback. Frequent feedback is important for developing new behaviors and improving current behaviors. Everyone likes to know how he or she is doing. I liked writing this textbook on a computer because my word processor provides a current word count. I set a weekly goal and was able to evaluate my daily performance by looking at the word count. Employees are sometimes fearful of performance appraisals because they have received no feedback beforehand and enter the appraisal interview with a fear of the unknown. Have you ever taken a test, been unsure about how you did, and then waited weeks for the instructor to return the test scores? If you had not taken any quizzes or received any feedback from class assignments before the test, you might have been even less sure about your performance.

Several of the motivational theories discussed in Chapter 6 are based on the assumption that employees like to do a good job and are pleased when their performance improves. A well-done performance appraisal can help employees meet their growth needs and make realistic career plans. Performance appraisals also can show employees how they are advancing toward specific job and career goals. By pinpointing deficiencies that can be corrected through training, appraisals help individuals improve while helping the organization achieve its goals.

Most people would not mind performance appraisals if they were completely objective *and* were used only for improving performance. The problem comes when a performance appraisal is unfairly subjective and can be used for punishment, such as firing or demotions, or unfair distributions of merit pay. Should performance appraisals be used that way? Unfairly subjective appraisals are usually illegal as well. The legal standards that apply to job selection methods (Chapter 9) apply to performance appraisals.

What about the use of performance appraisals for punishments such as firing and demotions? If the appraisal is done correctly, this is an appropriate use for it. In the same way, if appraisals are done correctly, they can be used appropriately to award merit pay. Remember the general definition of performance appraisal? Using that definition, if an employee is not contributing to the productivity of an organization, transfer, training, firing, or demotion may be an appropriate response.

Organizational Purposes

Often organizations use performance appraisals for more than one purpose. A survey of over 100 organizations showed that the most common uses of performance appraisal information were for salary administration, performance feedback, and identification of employees' strengths and weaknesses. The least common uses were evaluation of personnel systems, such as selection and training, and the identification of organizational developmental needs (Cleveland, Murphy, & Williams, 1989) (Table 10.1).

There is nothing wrong with using performance appraisals for more than one purpose, if the uses do not conflict with each other. Research shows that the expected use has a strong influence on the ratings (Zedeck & Cascio, 1982), and so the different purposes must be complementary rather than contradictory.

Table 10.1

USES OF PERFORMANCE APPRAISAL INFORMATION

Most Common Uses	Least Common Uses
Salary administration	Evaluation of personnel systems
Performance feedback	Criteria for validation research
Identification of individual strengths and weaknesses	Identification of organizational development needs
Documentation of personnel decisions	Reinforcement of authority structure
Recognition of individual performance	Personnel planning
	Determination of organizational training needs

Adapted from J. N. Cleveland, K. R. Murphy, and R. E. Williams. (1989). Multiple uses of performance appraisal: Prevalence and correlates. *Journal of Applied Psychology, 74*(1), 130–135.

Jawahar and Williams (1997) did a meta-analytic study that showed that when performance appraisals are used for administrative purposes such as pay raises or promotions, ratings are more lenient than they are when used for developmental purposes. When there is more than one purpose, raters tend to complete the appraisal form using only what they believe to be the most important purpose and ignoring the other purposes (Cleveland, Murphy, & Williams, 1989).

Even when the appraisal purposes do not conflict directly, different uses may lead to different results. For example, when appraisals are used for decisions about merit pay, the evaluators must compare individuals with one another to allocate the merit pay. When appraisals are used to improve work performance, the evaluator has to focus only on the individual employee and areas where developmental activities such as training can be helpful.

WHAT MAKES A PERFORMANCE APPRAISAL FAIR?

While most people do not object to fair performance appraisals, many employees are fearful of being evaluated unfairly because they are often dependent on a person like their supervisor for the evaluation. Employers also are concerned about the fairness of performance appraisals. In a survey of *Fortune* 100 companies employees cited three important issues (Thomas & Bretz, 1994):

1. The acceptance of the appraisal system by those being rated
2. Whether employees believe the process is fair
3. Whether employees believe the results are fair

These issues concern both the legal fairness of the evaluation and the fairness of the skills and abilities being evaluated, as well as how the evaluation is done.

A few organizations have found an interesting method for dealing with the complicated issue of doing legally fair performance appraisals. Those organizations have taken the position that if they do not do any performance appraisals, they cannot get into legal trouble. This approach not only is legally wrong, it also is harmful to the organization since a number of valid organizational purposes can be served by performance appraisals.

Although the general applications of the law are fairly clear, specific judgments on topics such as methods of job analysis and standards for performance appraisals sometimes are in conflict (Cascio & Bernardin, 1981). The most important legal performance evaluation requirement is that it be based on job-related factors. When organizations encourage workplace diversity, this issue becomes even more critical. To decide on promotions, the organization needs to be able to show that the person who was promoted was more qualified than the person who was not. To dismiss an employee, the company must show that he or she has not been performing at an acceptable level. Each of these requirements can be met by correctly done and documented performance evaluations.

The most comprehensive law covering these practices is Title VII of the Civil Rights Act of 1964 (Chapter 9). The Equal Employment Opportunity Commission is charged with monitoring performance appraisals for discrimination. In an analysis of 295 U.S. circuit court decisions from 1980 to 1995, Werner and Bolino (1997) found that the most important performance appraisal elements in court decisions favorable to organizations were the use of job analysis, the provision of written instructions, agreement among the raters, and allowing employees to review the results. Although training the raters did not quite reach statistically significant levels, it remains an important factor in court decisions. Since legal requirements for fair performance appraisal are based on the use of only job-related information, the next section looks at ways to do job analyses that lead to the use of job-relevant behaviors.

JOB ANALYSIS

Job analysis is the process of gathering information about the job-oriented and worker-oriented elements of a job. The most common elements used are the activities necessary to do the job; the physical equipment and machinery needed for the job; standards of acceptable performance; the knowledge, skills, and abilities required for the job; the physical location of the job; and the outcome of doing the job.

Most job analyses combine job-oriented aspects and worker-oriented aspects. **Job-oriented evaluations** focus on organizational features, such as productivity, and the tasks, duties, and responsibilities needed to perform the job. **Worker-oriented evaluations** focus on the characteristics of the workers, such as the skills and abilities they must have to do the job correctly.

Although this chapter discusses job analysis in terms of its use in performance appraisals, job analyses are used for a number of purposes. A job analysis is important for selection procedures (Chapters 8 and 9), training (Chapter 11), organizational development (Chapter 4), and other organizational actions and decisions. If an appropriate job analysis has been completed before the selection process begins, the performance appraisal process may already have completed one of the steps.

Methods of Job Analysis

There are a variety of methods for gathering information during the job analysis process. The most common methods involve observation, interviews, critical incidents, or published structured assessment methods. Recently, some

Job analysis The process of gathering information about the job-oriented and worker-oriented elements of a job.

Job-oriented evaluation A job analysis that focuses on organizational features such as productivity, tasks, duties, and responsibilities.

Worker-oriented evaluation A job analysis that focuses on the characteristics of the worker—such as knowledge, skills, abilities, experience, and education—that are necessary to do a job correctly.

computerized methods have been used to aid the job analysis process as well. Let us look at these methods in terms of how to do them and the advantages and disadvantages of each one.

Observation

A supervisor, a human resources specialist, or a consultant can do observations of a worker on the job. The advantage of having human resources specialists or consultants observe workers is that those people usually have been trained in correct methods of observation. The observers can either watch for and record the elements that make up a job analysis or work from a checklist of items. The checklist also can be used to indicate how many times an element of a job is observed. The requirements for using the observation method include observing for a long enough period to do an accurate analysis and observing often enough to sample all possible items.

Doing a job analysis by observing workers raises the possibility of a Hawthorne effect, because the presence of an observer can change behaviors. If a clerical worker sometimes calls a friend in printing services for help to get her work done ahead of other projects, she is unlikely to make that kind of call while being observed. If those calls make it possible for her to complete her work on

Dick Blume/The Image Works

■ Observing an employee at work is a common method of obtaining job analysis information.

time, a job analysis based on observations that do not include the phone calls may not be accurate. The best use for observation techniques is in the case of routine jobs that involve obvious behaviors—such as making telemarketing calls. Observation will not work for jobs that mainly involve thought processing, such as planning and decision making.

Another type of observation is self-observation, in which the employee observes himself on the job and keeps a diary or log of the job analysis elements. The advantage of this method is that it can cover a longer period and may include behaviors that other observers would not notice. The disadvantages include taking time away from the employee's job and having the employee edit the diary to make it look more favorable. Pine (1995) found that among a group of corrections officers, 45 percent reported doing tasks that had been added to the job analysis checklist as fake items. The officers also exaggerated the time they spent on various tasks.

Interviews

Interviews can be done on the job or elsewhere by some of the same people who do observations for a job analysis. Employees can be interviewed separately, in groups, or with their supervisors. The advantages of interviews are the ability to get reports on infrequently occurring behavior, information about thought-processing skills, and input from more than one person. The disadvantages include having employees censor their answers to look better or make their jobs appear more complicated and failing to remember all the important components. Interviews can be unstructured or structured, like the employment interviews discussed in Chapter 8. Although unstructured interviews may seem less formal and more comfortable for the employee, structured interviews are more likely to produce information useful for the job analysis.

Critical Incidents

Critical incidents are a listing of the crucially good and crucially bad parts of a job. This method of gathering information was developed as a means of defining a job in terms of the concrete and specific behaviors that are necessary to perform that job successfully (Flanagan, 1954). Developing this kind of analysis is a two-step process. In the first step incidents that illustrate effective or ineffective job behaviors are collected from supervisors, employees, and anyone else who is knowledgeable about the job. In the second step someone who is trained in job analysis or performance evaluation classifies the incidents in groupings that are appropriate for the job being analyzed. For example, a hospital might use this method to do a job analysis of the nursing assistant job. After getting incident statements from nursing assistants, nurses, administrators, and other health care personnel, the evaluator would group the behaviors in categories such as "direct patient care" and "documentation of patient care."

Critical incidents A method of job analysis that defines a job in terms of the specific effective or ineffective job behaviors of an employee.

Structured assessment methods Professionally constructed and published organizational job analysis systems.

One of the advantages of this method is the focus on critical behaviors, not those behaviors that may occur on the job but are not critical to good or bad performance. However, this technique is based on the assumption that the people who submit incidents can tell the difference between critical and noncritical behaviors. It also depends on the ability of those people to recall the incidents from memory if they are not keeping a diary or a log.

Structured Assessment Methods

Structured assessment methods are professionally constructed and published organizatonal job analysis systems. Two of the most popular structured job assessment methods have been in use for a number of years: the *Position Analysis Questionnaire (PAQ)* and *Functional Job Analysis (FJA)*.

McCormick and others developed the Position Analysis Questionnaire (PAQ) as a worker-oriented form of job analysis. The questionnaire is designed to be used by a job analysis specialist who interviews workers and supervisors while the job is being performed. The reading level (appropriate for college graduates) could make it difficult for supervisors or employees to fill out the questionnaire on their own (Ash & Edgell, 1975).

This system breaks jobs down into 194 elements grouped in six categories: information input, mental processes, work output, relationships with other persons, job context, and other job characteristics (McCormick, Jeanneret, & Meacham, 1972). The job elements are rated on some or all of six scales: "extent of use," "importance to the job," "amount of time," "possibility of occurrence," and "applicability." Most of these scales are graded from very high to very low levels. The category "does not apply" is added to each scale.

The PAQ has been criticized for the difficulty of updating the information in the questionnaire to reflect changes in jobs and for the difficulty of understanding the computer analysis of the questionnaire (Bemis, Belenky, & Soder, 1983). The low cost and widespread use (Levine, Ash, & Bennett, 1980) may compensate for those problems, however. Another way to deal with the problem of its high (college graduate) reading level could be the use of the *Job Element Inventory* developed by Cornelius and Hakel (1978). This is a structured questionnaire that is modeled on the PAQ but has a much lower reading level. Because the PAQ is so popular, there is a great deal of comparative data about jobs that have been analyzed using it. Professional job analysts have indicated a preference for this method of job analysis (Levine, Ash, Hall, & Sistrunk, 1983), and research indicates that experts in job content get the most accurate results with this method (Harvey & Lozada-Larsen, 1988).

The second structured method of job analysis, Functional Job Analysis (FJA), was developed for the 1965 edition of the *Dictionary of Occupational Titles (DOT)*. The current edition of the *DOT* uses a more complex classification system than the earlier edition did. In this method of job analysis, workers' functions are classified according to three hierarchies—data, people, and things—on the basis of interviews or observations or both by a job analysis specialist (Fine & Wiley, 1971). The specialist first reviews any written material, such as previous classifications. Each hierarchy goes from very simple to very complex functions in the hierarchy. The complete range for each of these hierarchies is shown in Figure 10.1.

Figure 10.1
Functional job analysis (FJA) categories and job examples.

DATA HIERARCHY

Most complex   **Least complex**

Synthesizing

       Coordinating, innovating

         Analyzing

           Computing, compiling

            Copying

               Comparing

Chief Financial Officier   Intake worker

PEOPLE HIERARCHY

Most complex   **Least complex**

Mentoring

     Negotiating

       Supervising

         Consulting, instructing, treating

          Coaching, persuading, diverting

            Exchanging information

              Taking instruction, helping, serving

Mediator   Restaurant table cleaner

THINGS HIERARCHY

Most complex   **Least complex**

Precision working, setting up

       Manipulating, operating and controlling, driving and controlling

           Handing, feeding and offbearing, tending

Custom clock maker   Cafeteria tray worker

- *Data hierarchy.* Assesses an employee's involvement with information and ideas in the job.
- *People hierarchy.* Assesses an employee's involvement with people in the job.
- *Things hierarchy.* Assesses an employee's involvement with equipment, tools, and machinery in the job.

A complete FJA process also includes assessment on a Worker Instruction Scale and three General Education Development Scales of reasoning, mathematics, and language. The coding system of data, people, and things developed from this method is used by the U.S. Employment Service to classify jobs; this has led to widespread use of the FJA. This type of job analysis requires a fairly high investment of time and effort to complete, but it can be useful in showing exactly where a worker's time and effort are spent. A study in a nursing home showed that even when the nursing assistants were involved in direct caregiving (69 percent of total tasks), their orientation was not primarily toward the residents. In this study the tasks with the greatest psychosocial components were those that were performed least frequently (Brannon, Streit, & Smyer, 1992). Although doing things (bed making, for example) and dealing with data (writing down resident information, for example) are important, one would generally expect the people component to receive the greatest attention.

Each job analysis method has advantages and disadvantages, but which one is the best or most useful? That depends on a number of factors, including time, money, and the purpose of the job analysis (Landy & Shankster, 1994). If possible, the answer is often to use a combination of methods and to use these systems on a continuing basis. A good way to keep the job analyses up to date is to schedule periodic reviews of all the job analyses used in the organization. An important reason to keep job analyses up to date is that pay or compensation often is determined from a job evaluation, which is partially developed from the job analysis.

Job Evaluation and Comparable Worth

One of the other common uses for job analysis information is to help develop the job evaluation. **Job evaluation** refers to the process of establishing a job's worth, or value; this usually is done in monetary terms. Job evaluation has become more important because fair employment legislation requires greater proof that maintaining unequal pay levels for similar jobs is justified. The concept of equal pay for equal work is called the principle of **comparable worth**. In the past, organizations managed to keep pay rates lower for many women by using different job titles although the work was essentially the same. When correct job analyses are done, these artificial differences often become apparent and better job evaluations are done.

Job evaluation The process of using a job analysis and other information to establish the monetary worth of a job.

Comparable worth The principle of paying equally for the same work regardless of the job title or jobholder.

Starting with the **Equal Pay Act of 1963,** the intent of the federal government has been to require equal pay for jobs that require equal skill, effort, and responsibility and that are performed under similar conditions. In general this law was meant to correct the lower pay levels that many women were receiving for doing the same work as men. Organizations were allowed only to raise pay levels, not lower them, to make them equal. Legal challenges have required some corrections, but those corrections have not been as extensive or costly as many businesses feared. First, to sue an organization, the employees must be able to show that the company purposely discriminated in pay levels and that the motive for the unfair pay levels was to discriminate. Second, the costs have been much lower than predicted, in most cases about 1 to 2 percent of the organizational payroll for up to five years (Patten, 1988).

Some organizations shorten the job evaluation process by using a system called **direct market pricing,** in which they assign pay values to jobs on the basis of the current labor market, not an internal job evaluation. This means looking at what the job pays in other companies and looking at the available labor pool, and then setting the pay rate for the job. It is more difficult to defend job evaluation practices that are done this way, but it is certainly much quicker.

Another way to reduce the time required is to use a computerized job analysis program such as the S.M.A.R.T. system used at Liberty Mutual Insurance (Barry & McLaughlin, 1996). One government agency in London was able to decrease the size of the evaluation staff and reduce the number of records by half when it switched to a computerized job evaluation system (*Personnel Management*, 1992).

One of the most difficult steps in job evaluation is choosing the relevant **compensable factors**: job elements that determine the monetary worth of the job. Factors such as years of experience are objective and easy to measure, but what about the mental effort required by a job? It is easy to say that a doctor should be paid more than a nursing assistant because the doctor needs many more years of education, but is there a difference in the mental effort demanded by these positions? Should there be compensation for mental effort, and if so, how can that effort be measured?

Effort is one of the factors that must be considered under the Equal Pay Act, but including a factor that vague can present even more complications. The Americans with Disabilities Act has added further hurdles by requiring that only essential job functions be considered in the job analysis (Karsten, Schroeder, & Surrette, 1995). Organizations are left with the dilemma of deciding whether to include marginal job functions in determining the job evaluation. If workers with disabilities cannot perform nonessential job functions, should their job positions pay less? If those workers can perform the nonessential job functions, should their job positions pay more? There are no easy answers that can satisfy legal requirements, employees, *and* employers.

Equal Pay Act of 1963
A federal law requiring equal pay for jobs that require equal skill, effort, and responsibility and that are performed under similar working conditions.

Direct market pricing
A method of job evaluation based on what similar jobs pay in other companies and on the available labor pool.

Compensable factors
The job elements that, added together, determine the monetary worth of a job.

One way to overcome this problem is to use a job analysis method that will help determine the compensable factors. The PAQ has been shown to have a high reliability in job evaluations, and 9 of the 187 job elements assessed by the PAQ have been shown to be good predictors of a job's value (Belcher & Atchison, 1987; Burgess, 1984; Treiman, 1979). Most organizations use some form of job evaluation (Armstrong, 1995) to make the performance appraisal process more accurate. However, the job evaluation is still done in the context of this society, possibly bringing unfair biases to the job evaluation process. One study (Lewis & Stevens, 1990) found that changing the identification of a jobholder from male to female lowered the worth assigned to that job when all other factors were held constant.

No one has suggested abandoning job evaluation and the search for comparable worth, but it is important to realize that change is not always easy. Job evaluation remains the most open and flexible option available to reward employees in a fair, equitable way in a variety of work settings; this is the reason job analysis and job evaluation must be done before performance appraisals (Duftel, 1991).

Once the job analysis and job evaluation have been completed, the final step is to decide what method or methods of performance appraisal will be used. A number of factors go into this decision. The following section examines many of the common performance appraisal methods and their usefulness in different situations.

METHODS OF PERFORMANCE APPRAISAL

Performance appraisal can be done in many ways, and often a combination of methods is used to evaluate employees. Most employees feel that objective methods are the fairest, but some jobs and behaviors are difficult to measure in objective ways. Let us look at a system that classifies appraisal methods in three categories: outcome-based methods, absolute standards methods, and relative comparison methods (Bernardin & Beatty, 1984). **Outcome-based methods** are based on the results of work performance. They are concerned not with the ways the employee does his or her work but with what the employee produces. In **absolute standards methods** the evaluator indicates whether an employee's performance meets a standard that is described on the appraisal form. This is usually a yes or no judgment. **Relative comparisons methods** often are referred to as personnel comparison methods because the evaluator is required to weigh one employee's performance against another employee's performance.

Outcome-based methods Performance appraisal methods that use measurable or countable data on the results of work performance.

Absolute standards methods Performance appraisal methods based on comparing an employee's behavior with a model described in a performance statement.

Relative comparisons methods Performance appraisal methods that compare an employee's job performance with another employee's job performance.

Outcome-Based Methods

Outcome-based methods often are referred to as objective criteria because they involve using measurable or countable data, such as how many windshield wipers an employee attaches each hour or how many cellular phones made by a work group are rejected by the quality controller each day. In a survey of *Fortune* 100 companies, 80 percent of the companies reported using outcome-based approaches for executives and managers and 70 percent used them for professional employees. Outcome-based systems and less objective methods were used equally (31 percent and 32 percent, respectively) for hourly employees (Thomas & Bretz, 1994). In your work experience you probably have encountered at least one of the outcome-based measures listed in the following paragraphs.

Quantity and Quality of Work

Quantity and quality of work measures often are used to get a more meaningful picture of productivity. A worker can be very good on one of these measures without being good on the other, and so using them together provides better information. If you made more French fries than anyone else did at McDonalds but did it by undercooking every batch, you should not receive a good performance appraisal. Although this method is used most commonly to assess lower-level positions, it also can be used for a lawyer who is judged by how many hours of client work he generates for his firm and a surgeon who is judged by the success rate of her operations.

The underlying assumption in these measures is that the employee's job can be rated in terms of quantity and quality of work and that the employee has control over those factors. When 240 public sector and private sector employees were compared on quantity and quality of work, it was found that quantity was highest in the thirty to thirty-nine-year-old workers but quality was higher in the older groups (Rao & Rao, 1997).

Personnel Data Methods

Personnel data measures include the kinds of elements typically recorded by the human resources department, such as absenteeism, tardiness, and accident rate. Although these elements have the advantage of being objectively measurable, a number of judgment issues are involved. For example, it is a common assumption that when an employee is absent, she is not being productive, but creative personnel may get some of their best ideas when they are not interrupted by office routines. There is also the question of when absenteeism truly affects an organization's productivity. Tardiness measures and accident measures are numerically objective, but they, like absentee measures, are subject to questions about their actual effect on productivity. Another problem with personnel data concerns inadequate record keeping. Unless very exact standards are used in recording personnel data, the conclusions drawn from these data may be inaccurate and unfair.

Management by Objectives

Drucker (1954) first used management by objectives as a system for measuring the effectiveness of employees or groups as they contributed to the

Management by objectives (MBO)
A performance appraisal system that measures the effectiveness of an employee or group in terms of goals set by the supervisor and the employees or group.

achievement of goals that determined an organization's success. **Management by objectives (MBO)** measures only the results, not the employee's or group's behavior in reaching the goals. This method has a number of elements in common with goal setting (Chapter 6). Although this is a results-oriented system, one caution must be mentioned in terms of setting goals. The MBO system seems to imply that each new goal must be higher than the previous goal to indicate progress, but in some cases continuing to achieve at high levels may be an acceptable goal.

Another potential problem with MBO is the assumption that individual success always leads to organizational success. While organizational and individual goals often may move toward the same end, it is possible for them to move in opposite directions. Bernardin and Beatty (1984) give the example of a school system in bad financial condition for which the organizational goal was to restore fiscal health while the individual teachers' goals included spending more time on planning, organizing, and supplementing classroom materials—which required greater expenditures to be successful.

With these limitations, can MBO be an effective method of performance appraisal? A meta-analysis of research studies appears to say yes. Rodgers and Hunter (1991) found that sixty-eight of seventy studies involving MBO showed productivity gains. The most important factor in the success of the system was the support of top management. When top management support was high, the average productivity gain was 56 percent; when support was low, average productivity gain was only 6 percent. Another study showed that the level of use of MBO appraisals remained steady through the mid-1990s, demonstrating continuing interest in this system (Smith, Hornsby, & Shirmeyer, 1996).

Computerized Performance Appraisal

Computerized performance appraisal is one of the newest types of evaluation. The computer has been used in two different ways in the performance appraisal process. In the first type of use the organization employs a software program to develop a structured performance appraisal process. After the supervisor enters data, the program generates reports about individual employees and organizational comparisons (Rafferty, 1990). Providing a system that produces impartial, consistent documentation of employee evaluation helps organizations avoid lawsuits alleging unfair evaluation of performance (Belanger, 1991). Most of these programs include a legal checker to alert evaluators about the use of certain words or terms. These programs can be especially useful in smaller companies in which there are no human resources departments or specialists in performance evaluation. A survey showed that less than half of upper-level managers were aware of the existence of computerized performance appraisal systems (Flowers, Tudor, & Trumble, 1997).

The second type of use of computers in performance appraisal is to monitor and record employees' work behaviors. A telephone-based collection agency might use a computer to monitor the length of calls and the dollar amount collected by each employee. The IRS Automated Collection system used this type of monitoring for employees, who then were interviewed about the effects of the system. Some employees responded positively to the opportunity for greater feedback and objective performance measures, but others responded negatively to the invasion of privacy and felt that the monitoring made them focus only on the aspects of the job that could be objectively measured (Chalykoff & Kochan, 1989). By focusing only on such job features, the company may inadvertently reinforce behaviors such as handling a large volume of calls rather than paying the careful attention to detail that lengthier calls require. Some labor unions are beginning to include this topic in the negotiation process, and this may lead to modifications or more limited use of the method.

One problem that can result from the use of computer-generated reports is overacceptance of the appraisals. Employees may feel that a computer-generated appraisal is more accurate than an appraisal made by the supervisor because they see computers as being unbiased. Thus, for example, researchers found that students significantly changed their self-appraisals of purported psychic abilities on the basis of randomly assigned positive or negative feedback from a computer-based appraisal system (DeLaers, Lundgren, & Howe, 1998). If the computer appraisal is based on inaccurate information, it will not provide an accurate appraisal.

Absolute Standards Methods

In the absolute standards methods of performance appraisal, an employee's performance is compared with a statement on a rating scale and the evaluator decides whether the employee's performance meets the standard described in the statement. Each employee is compared with the statements on the appraisal form, not with the other employees. The final values of the appraisal may be compared across employees, but the goal of this system is evaluation of the individual. A number of systems use this format.

Graphic Rating Scales

Graphic rating scales are the most commonly used method of performance appraisal (Borman, White, Pulakos, & Oppler, 1991). The evaluator decides how much of a trait or behavior an employee displays on a scale that usually has a range of five to seven points. Samples of graphic scales are shown in Figure 10.2.

The underlying assumption in the use of graphic rating scales is that the traits being assessed are related to actual job performance. For example, it is easy to say

Graphic rating scales A performance appraisal method based on assessing how much of a trait or behavior an employee displays on a graduated measure.

Figure 10.2

Examples of graphic rating scales.

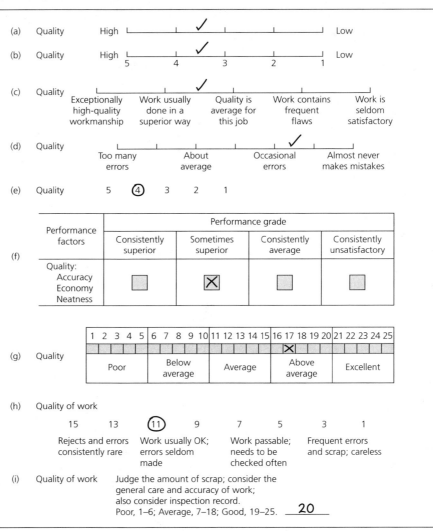

From *Personnel Testing* by R. M. Guion. Copyright 1965 by McGraw-Hill.

that traits such as decisiveness are related to managerial ability and performance, but research consistently has shown poor correlations (Brumback, 1972). If these traits are more operationally defined, as they are in Figure 10.2, it is possible to provide behavioral anchors for the traits being measured. This should lead to a more performance-oriented appraisal.

A recent suggestion for improving graphic scales is to make them less precise, that is, to allow the evaluator to indicate a range on the scale rather than an exact point. Researchers say that confining evaluators to a single point on the scale may give the impression of a degree of precision that is not really there (Hesketh, Pryor, & Gleitzman, 1989). The continued popularity of graphic rating scales despite their drawbacks most likely is due to the ease of development, use, and scoring.

Behavioral Rating Scales

Researchers have attempted to correct the problem of vague trait statements on graphic scales by using specific behavioral descriptions at a number of points along a rating scale. Some of the most commonly used behavioral rating scales are the **Behaviorally Anchored Rating Scale (BARS),** the **Behavioral Observation Scale (BOS),** and the **Behaviorally Anchored Discipline Scale (BADS).**

BARS (Smith & Kendall, 1963) and BOS (Latham & Wexley, 1981) both start with a list of critical incidents or job behaviors derived from a job analysis. Job dimensions or categories such as "organizational skills" then are identified. Statements that represent actual behaviors—exceptionally poor or good, and average—are developed for each dimension. For rating a college instructor in the job category of organizational skills, an example of the highest rating might be "Follows the course syllabus; presents lectures in a logical order, and ties each lecture into the previous one." An example of an average rating statement might be "Prepares course syllabus but follows it only occasionally; presents lectures in no particular order but does tie them together." An example of the lowest rating statement might be "Makes no use of a course syllabus; lectures on topics randomly with no logical order" (Bernardin, 1977).

Examples of specific behaviors are developed for each rating statement as well as the spaces between them, and a numerical scale (such as 1 to 10) is developed for the statements. The evaluator is asked to indicate which point on the scale best describes an employee on that job dimension. The point chosen can be based on documentation by the supervisor (the best method) or on an expectation of what the supervisor believes the employee's behavior on that dimension would be.

One of the advantages of this method is the use of concrete behavioral statements for the points on the scale. There should not be many different interpretations of "excellent" or "poor" behavior by the various raters. The time it takes to arrive at these concrete statements is one of the drawbacks to this method. Because it is based on actual job behaviors, it meets Equal Employment Opportunity Commission requirements. To meet those requirements on a continuing basis, however, an organization that uses BARS must be aware of any changes in the job that would require a change in the statements or anchor points. A beneficial side effect of the steps needed to develop this system is the involvement of

Behaviorally Anchored Rating Scale (BARS) A performance evaluation method based on comparing employees' job behaviors with specific performance statements on a scale of good to bad.

Behavioral Observation Scale (BOS) A performance assessment method that is based on the frequency of job behaviors.

Behaviorally Anchored Discipline Scale (BADS) A performance appraisal system that focuses on employees' misbehaviors, such as absenteeism and theft.

employees in the appraisal process, which can increase their positive feelings about performance appraisal and lead to more positive outcomes (Silverman & Wexley, 1984). Researchers found that employees were more satisfied and perceived evaluations as more fair when the evaluations were based on a BARS or BOS system rather than a trait scale (Latham & Seijta, 1997).

BOS is somewhat of a variation of BARS. The major difference is that BOS requires the supervisor doing the appraisal to indicate the frequency of the critical behavior. In the example of the college instructor, the statement "Instructor follows prepared syllabus in lectures" would be followed by a scale of 1 (never) to 5 (always). This method can be seen as giving more information to employees about the behaviors they should continue performing; but in practice, the ratings are based on the evaluator's memory of the employee's behavior rather than actual observation, and this may discredit the method (Mount & Thompson, 1987).

The BADS system uses a format similar to that of BARS, but the focus is on employee misbehaviors that relate to organizational citizenship, such as tardiness, absenteeism, insubordination, and theft. The exact degree of misconduct is tied to specific disciplinary reports. As in the BARS method, the use of objective data is designed to make judgments less subjective and give employees a clearer definition of what is expected (Kearney & Whitaker, 1988)

Checklists

Checklists can range from a simple list of statements, on which the evaluator checks those that apply to an employee and leaves blank those that do not, to weighted lists that carefully assign relative values to each statement. The problem with a simple checklist is the assumption, not always correct, that each statement has equal value in appraising performance. For example, few people would assign equal value to items on a checklist for a bank teller that say, "Dresses in a professional way" and "Has frequent account shortages."

In a weighted checklist each statement is assigned a value or weight that is based on the amount it contributes to good job performance. The critical incident method of job analysis often can be used as a starting point for this system. Supervisors could rate the job analysis statements for the relative amounts of effective and ineffective job performance that the behavior described in the statement contributes to the job being appraised. One of the problems with checklists and graphic scales is that it is relatively easy to fake a good or bad response set. If a supervisor wants to make a subordinate look like a poor performer in an evaluation, unless the employee is willing to challenge the evaluation legally, it is very easy to give a poor rating with a graphic scale or checklist. Fortunately, most supervisors want to do a fair and effective job in performance appraisals. If there is a realistic concern that faking is a problem, the method next discussed will reduce the likelihood of its occurring.

Checklists A performance evaluation method that relies on having the evaluator place a mark next to appraisal statements that describe the behaviors of the employee being evaluated.

Forced Choice System

The **forced choice system** of appraisal requires the evaluator to choose between three to five statements describing positive, negative, or neutral job-relevant statements. A sample of forced choice items is shown in Figure 10.3.

Forced choice system A performance appraisal method that requires the evaluator to choose between several behavioral descriptions, some of which are blind items and some of which are real items.

Figure 10.3

Sample of forced choice items used for evaluating a college instructor.

Choose the two statements in the following group that are most typical of your psychology instructor.

_____ 1. Is willing to explain concepts more than once.
_____ 2. Lectures with confidence.
_____ 3. Uses films, guest speakers, and group projects to supplement lectures.
_____ 4. Presents lesson objectives at the beginning of each class.

The statements that are used can be gathered from critical incidents job analysis, but the difficulty of developing a good forced choice instrument is a major drawback. After the statements are listed, evaluators are asked to indicate which ones are most typical of very poor employees only and which are most typical of very good employees only. This is called the discrimination value of a statement or item. A high-discrimination item would be a statement that was said only about very good or very bad employees. In Figure 10.3 only items 1 and 3 were found to discriminate between good and bad college instructors. A low-discrimination item would be said equally about all employees, such as items 2 and 4 in the figure.

After this step the evaluators are asked to rate the statements for preference values, that is, whether a statement appears to be something employees would like to have said about them during an evaluation or whether it appears to be something undesirable. All four items in the figure are regarded as equally favorable. To make a single appraisal item like this one, there would be four or five statements (one might be a discrimination-neutral statement), all of which were close to equal in preference value. However, two statements would be good discriminator statements and two would be poor discriminator statements. The person filling out the performance appraisal would check the two statements that best described the employee, choosing from the group of four or five statements. Only the two high-discriminator statements, if chosen, would contribute to the employee's appraisal score. The other two or three statements are blind statements that would not contribute to the appraisal. Statistically, the likelihood of being able to fake a good or poor employee appraisal is about at the level of chance.

Mixed standard scale
A performance appraisal system that randomly lists good, average, and bad behaviors for a job and requires the evaluator to compare the employee being evaluated to each statement.

The development of this kind of instrument is time-consuming and difficult. It therefore is rarely used, except when there are special needs, as in a company with supervisors who show a great deal of favoritism where faking good appraisals could be an issue. The supervisors who do the appraisal may have negative feelings about their own trustworthiness when they are told that the appraisal instrument includes blind items that will not be added to the employee's evaluation if they are selected. Since the employee receives a score for the total evaluation, this method cannot be used to give the employee feedback about particular strengths or weaknesses. The next method corrects some of these problems and looks at a range of good to bad behaviors in each category.

Mixed Standard Scale

As with the forced choice system, the development of the **mixed standard scale** starts with a list of critical incidents or job behaviors developed from a job analysis. In this method the next step is to classify those items into groups, such as job knowledge and judgment. The groups are divided further into job behaviors that represent each of the groups, and evaluators are asked to choose, from this list of job behaviors, examples of someone doing excellent, average, and unsatisfactory work in that area. In the job knowledge group, in rating a college instructor there may be statements such as the following:

Good: The instructor includes current developments in lectures and covers a range of viewpoints.

Average: The instructor presents accurate information on a variety of topics during lectures.

Poor: The instructor includes much out-of-date and incorrect information in lectures.

If there were twelve job groups, this would result in a total of thirty-six statements. The statements are arranged randomly on the appraisal form, and the person doing the evaluation is asked to put a plus sign next to a statement if the employee's performance is better than what is described in the statement, a minus sign if the employee's performance is worse, and a zero if a statement is a correct description of the employee's behavior.

The advantage of this system is that the evaluator must consider each statement separately rather than just noting that the employee is a good performer and should get a top numerical rating. Bernardin and Orban (1990) found that using a mixed standard scale instead of a graphic rating scale to evaluate police officers resulted in a lower likelihood of nonperformance variables (such as keeping one's desk area clean) being included in the performance appraisal. Prien, Jones, and Miller (1977) developed a computerized form for the mixed standard method that helps reduce the amount of time required to process these evaluations; that had been one of the obstacles to greater acceptance of this method.

Relative Comparisons Methods

Three of the most common comparison evaluation methods are ranking, paired comparisons, and forced distributions. As a student, you probably are familiar with the first and last methods, although paired comparisons have a long history in industrial/organizational (I/O) psychology because they were first used by Walter Dill Scott to evaluate military personnel during World War I (Chapter 1).

Ranking

Ranking simply lists all the employees being evaluated in order from best to worst. The raters usually start by filling in the employees at the top and bottom of the list and then move toward the middle. The middle area often represents the most difficult decisions because the employees' job behaviors are not that distinct from one another. When the numerical ratings for two or three employees are exactly equal, those employees sometimes are given the same rank. This may have happened when your high school senior class was ranked on the basis of grade averages. The problem with using this system in the appraisal process is that the rating tells employees that one is better than all the others ranked below him, and so ties in rank often are seen as representing some type of subgroup ranking in spite of the tie in rank. If there are several ties among employees, this is probably not an appropriate appraisal method. Researchers have suggested that ranking methods might be more useful if they were combined with another appraisal method (Chiu & Alliger, 1990) or if the ranking process was modified (Miner, 1988).

Paired Comparisons

In **paired comparisons** each employee is compared with every other employee on each job dimension being evaluated. Supervisors sometimes see this as a simpler system than ranking because only two employees have to be compared on one dimension at a time, but the number of individual evaluations can become overwhelming. If your instructor wanted to use this method to evaluate the students in your class, she would list the job dimensions to be used, such as test scores, class participation, reading assignments, extra-credit work, and group assignments. She then would rate each student in comparison with the others on those dimensions.

The formula to find out how many comparisons must be made on each job dimension is number of comparisons = $n(n - 1)/2$, where n is the number of students. If there were only five students in your class, the total number of comparisons would be only 10, but if there were 25, the total number would be 300. This is a workable system only when the number of employees being evaluated is rather low. When Scott developed this system, he suggested that the limit should be 10 soldiers. One use of this method that would make assessment easier

Ranking A performance appraisal method that requires the evaluator to list all the employees being appraised in order from best to worst.

Paired comparisons A performance appraisal system that requires the evaluator to compare each employee with every other employee on each characteristic or behavior being evaluated.

Forced distribution
A performance appraisal system that requires the evaluator to place a certain percentage of employees in each evaluation grade on the basis of a normal curve distribution.

Halo (devil) errors Unfair judgments made when knowledge of one trait or behavior biases the evaluation of other traits or behaviors.

would be with groups in which there is a great deal of competition, such as for merit pay (Pedrini & Pedrini, 1982). The end result of a paired comparison evaluation is a ranking by the number of preferred selections each employee receives, which makes the final ranking less subjective.

Forced Distribution

Forced distributions are the basis for the "grading curve" used by many instructors. This method is based on the assumption that a large number of people have characteristics or behaviors that fall into a pattern described as a normal or bell-shaped curve (see the Statistical Appendix). The distribution pattern for a normal curve is 10 percent in the highest category, 20 percent in the next category, 40 percent in the middle category, 20 percent in the next category, and 10 percent in the lowest category. This translates into A, B, C, D, and F grades in a class. The problem here is that all assignments to these categories are relative to the other employees rather than being based on an absolute level of performance. When Merck & Co. adopted a forced distribution appraisal system, that company included a correction for this problem in case the chosen distribution did not reflect the distribution of employee performance (Murphy, 1993).

This section has examined some of the common methods of evaluating performance and their advantages and disadvantages. At the beginning of this chapter it was noted that job performance can be influenced by a number of other factors. The next section looks at some of the errors commonly made during the evaluation process.

ERRORS IN PERFORMANCE APPRAISAL

It would be nice to assume that each person who does performance appraisals is totally objective and that the method used is very close to the perfect choice. Although most organizations try to achieve this goal, the combination of human raters and imperfect instruments can lead to several errors in performance appraisal. The more subjective the performance appraisal instrument is, the more open the appraisal is to these errors. The most common errors and problems are discussed next.

Halo Errors

Halo (devil) errors are errors that can result in incorrect evaluations (positive or negative) of employees; these errors occur when the knowledge of one trait or behavior influences the evaluation of other traits or behaviors. If an instructor gives a student a higher score on an essay examination than the student actually deserves, because the instructor saw the student doing a lot of writing in class, this can be a halo error. The student might have been writing an essay for another class rather than taking notes for the current class. This can be seen as contaminating the criteria used for the performance evaluation.

Leniency and Severity Errors

Have you ever had an instructor who had a reputation as one of the "really tough ones who flunk everybody"? This is the problem in **leniency and severity errors,** or errors caused by the evaluator being consistently too easy (leniency) or too hard (severity). The method of correcting this type of errors, a forced distribution, may involve trading one problem for another. Another common way to avoid this type of error is to require more than one evaluator to do the appraisal to see whether there is an error or a correct performance evaluation.

The issue of leniency errors in both appraisal inflation and grade inflation has received a great deal of attention in recent years. Over the past thirty years college grades have included increasing numbers of A and B grades, yet scores on college entrance tests have dropped over this period (Farley, 1995). Some managers and employers feel that the same type of inflation may be occurring in performance appraisals. It appears that the purpose of the appraisal contributes to the occurrence of leniency errors. It was noted earlier in this chapter that when performance appraisals are used for administrative purposes, such as pay raises and promotions, the appraisals are more lenient than they are when they are used for research, feedback, or employee development (Harris, Smith, & Champagne, 1995; Jawahar & Williams, 1997). Performance appraisals also become more lenient when the rater knows she will deliver the results in person to the employees (Waung & Highhouse, 1997).

Central Tendency Errors

Central tendency errors occur when all an evaluator's ratings are incorrectly clustered around the middle of the scale. Several typical situations may encourage such errors. If raters are told to write a justification only for very high or very low appraisal scores and can use check marks for middle scores, there is a temptation to make the easy choice and choose the middle scores.

Also, supervisors may incorrectly group scores around the middle if they previously made an extreme evaluation (positive or negative) that turned out to be wrong. If a supervisor recommended an employee for a promotion on the basis of his very high performance appraisal results and the employee was promoted but failed at the new job, his new supervisor might question the initial performance appraisal. Rather than taking that kind of risk again, the first supervisor might stick with middle ratings. Requiring the rater to use a forced distribution would correct this error, but this could be a matter of trading one problem for another.

Leniency and severity errors Unfair consistently high or low evaluations of employees and their performance.

Central tendency error An unfair grouping of performance evaluations at the middle of the scale.

Contrast and similarity errors Unfair evaluations of employees that are based on how their behavior is similar to or different from the behavior of the evaluator.

Recency error An unfair evaluation of an employee based only on that employee's latest performance, not his or her performance over the entire evaluation period.

Frame of reference error A performance appraisal unfairly influenced by factors outside the job, such as race, gender, age, and HIV status.

Contrast and Similarity Errors

Contrast and similarity errors can be characterized as follows. In *contrast errors* people are rated lower than they should be because they are behaving differently than the rater would in the job, independent of the correctness or efficiency of the method. Everyone develops systems and shortcuts, but objective evaluators have to be able to separate their personal preferences from their evaluations of the way work is done by others. This type of error also can occur when an evaluator who has done a job for a number of years unfairly gives a lower rating to a newer employee who cannot do the job as well as the evaluator can. A *similarity error* occurs when the evaluator rates an employee higher than he deserves because the employee does things the same way the rater does, regardless of how good or bad the result is.

Recency Error

Although a performance appraisal is supposed to cover the entire evaluation period, people's memory is usually much better for more recent events that it is for more remote events. An evaluator who gives much greater weight to recent performance than for performance over the entire period is making a **recency error** if an extraordinary situation has affected the most recent performance. An example would be an employee who had been a productive team member, willing to stay and work long hours on projects until two months ago, when she started a graduate training program that met in the evenings. If she were given a lower rating based only on the last two months of work instead of the entire year, that would be a recency error.

Frame of Reference Errors

Frame of reference errors include making factors outside the scope of the job, such as age, gender, race, and HIV status, part of the performance appraisal. This sometimes is referred to as the problem of criterion contamination. This type of error often is discussed in regard to diversity training (Chapter 4).

It often is difficult to separate a factor such as gender from factors that actually contribute to performance, but when studies look at only one or two factors at a time, the influence of that type of factor becomes clearer. The problem with using laboratory studies (Chapter 2) is that they may not reflect real-life situations.

In a fairly typical study of the effect of gender on performance evaluations in a laboratory setting, Dobbins, Cardy, and Truxillo (1986) had male and female undergraduates read and evaluate two descriptions of high-performing professors and two descriptions of low-performing professors. The professors were described only as either male or female. The true level of performance was known for each professor and was used to judge the fairness of students' evaluations.

Male professors were rated higher than their true level of performance, and female professors were rated lower.

Beliefs about the cause of males' and females' performance also can influence the ratings they receive. Greenhaus and Parasuraman (1993) found that even among very successful women managers, the cause of their success was less likely to be attributed to their ability than to help from others, and this was reflected in lower performance appraisals. This study also compared the factor of race in performance appraisals and found that the successful performance of black managers also was more likely to be attributed to help from others than to ability; this led to the perception of black managers as being poorer prospects for career advancement.

A number of studies have documented the negative effects of racial factors in performance evaluations when the raters' race was different from that of the employees' (Kraiger & Ford, 1990; Pulakos, White, Oppler, & Borman, 1989). Researchers such as Sackett and DuBois (1991) have suggested that the conclusion that raters give higher evaluations to members of their own race may be an illusion when the results of many studies are combined. One reason for this discrepancy may be that some research findings show only a small difference (Motowidlo & Tippins, 1993; Waldman & Avolio, 1991) or a difference only in one type of evaluation, such as when the evaluator and employee are of different races rather than the same race (Waldman & Avolio, 1991).

When Murphy, Barlow, and Hatch (1991) looked at legal challenges to performance evaluation that were based on racial discrimination, they found that the court rulings were basically the same as those required by any legal performance appraisal. Supervisors were required not to deviate from internal company policies and procedures and to give accurate performance evaluations uniformly and consistently to all subordinates. Following these standards produced unbiased, fair performance appraisals in most situations.

If an older person is not performing as well as a younger person is, is it fair to give the older person a lower performance rating? Yes, if the appraisal is an accurate assessment. Research suggests that performance appraisal discrimination against older workers may be a form of contrast error (Ferris & King, 1992). These studies indicate that the greater interpersonal distance between the older and younger workers, and the influence of subordinates, may be the cause of unfair evaluations. When a person significantly younger than the employee being appraised does the appraisal, he may have difficulty dealing with the differences between himself and the employees being evaluated. In a study designed to look at the effects of age on both objective data (comparison of sales to objective) and subjective data (the performance appraisal) for over two hundred salespeople, the objective data showed almost no age-related differences, while the subjective data reflected some age-related evaluations (Day, 1993).

Another factor that has been examined for its influence on the performance appraisal process is HIV status in cases where the person being evaluated has tested positive for HIV, the virus that causes AIDS. The question here is whether appraisals are discriminatory. A preliminary investigation matching HIV-positive sailors with HIV-negative sailors found lower overall evaluations for the HIV-positive sailors, suggesting that knowing an employee's HIV status before appraisal may unfairly influence the evaluation (Bohnker, 1992). As with any other disability, the legal requirement is that a person's disability cannot be used to bias the evaluation.

Although all these personal factors can be seen to influence the appraisal process, the effect of each one individually is relatively small, which may encourage some organizations to discount them. The problem here is that, although the effect of each factor is small, the total may be much more than research investigating one or two factors at a time may show. Ilgen, Barnes-Farrell, and McKellin (1993) concluded, after looking at the role of errors in performance appraisal, that although evidence shows that errors influence the actual performance appraisal, they may not reduce the overall rating accuracy. The most logical position on the effect of errors on the performance appraisal process is to make everyone aware of their presence, attempt to minimize their effects, and be vigilant in monitoring for unfair effects of errors during the appraisal.

An element that has been looked at only recently is a consideration of who is doing the performance appraisal. Do you think you would be easier on yourself in an evaluation than your supervisor would be? Would the appraisal be better if it included information from more than one rater? The next section looks at the different people who do performance appraisals.

WHO DOES THE PERFORMANCE APPRAISAL?

Most of the time an employee's immediate supervisor does the performance appraisal. In fact, the supervisor's opinion accounts for one-half to three-fourths of the final appraisal (Thomas & Bretz, 1994). For professional and hourly employees, the influence of the immediate supervisor on the final performance evaluation was greater than that of all the other evaluation sources combined. Those other sources included supervisors at a higher level than immediate supervisors; self-evaluation; peers; and miscellaneous categories, including subordinates. The least weight was given to ratings done by peers.

Immediate Supervisor

How well does the immediate supervisor do on performance appraisals? Research suggests that conclusions about *supervisor ratings,* compared with those from sources such as peers or self-evaluations, generally show some degree of agreement, although the level of agreement can change with a number of factors (Duarte, Goodson, & Klich, 1994; Farh, Werbel, & Bedeian, 1988; Malka, 1990). Some studies show a fairly high degree of agreement between evaluation sources; others show a greater leniency effect for peer raters. Part of this difference may result from different types of evaluators viewing different job elements as more or less crucial to the appraisal of performance. One researcher (Mount, 1983) found that managers base their appraisals primarily on the specific tasks that are part of the job, such as the ability of a teller to give correct change to a customer. Mount found that the workers themselves base their appraisals primarily on overall performance rather than a specific task or incident.

Subordinate Appraisal

One of the least frequently used sources of appraisal information is **subordinate appraisal.** In business this method most often is used in connection with the highest positions in an organization, where there are few peers or immediate supervisors to do evaluations. Recent changes in appraisal methods have included more subordinate appraisals, pointing to the need for better training for all employees who do appraisals. Training of appraisers, especially those, such as subordinates, who usually have little experience in this area, often is cited as a way to improve the performance appraisal process. When nurses were asked about their preferences in the appraisal process, they preferred ratings done by supervisors, peers, and themselves to ratings done by subordinates (Jordan & Nasis, 1992). Part of this preference may come from the belief of those being rated that they must solicit good feelings from their subordinates to get good ratings.

Peer Evaluation

Peer evaluation is an appraisal done by people who work at an equal level in the organization. The Thomas and Bretz *Fortune* 100 survey (1994) found that this method was used the most at the executive level and that no organization used it at the level of hourly employees. Twisleton (1992) cited some of the problems with peer review such as reciprocity ("If I don't support you with a good evaluation now, what will you do when I need your support in the future?"), collusion ("How about if we all agree to give each other great evaluations?"), and trust ("If I give you a good evaluation, you might give me the promotion I know I deserve.") Kennedy (1993) suggests that dealing with these issues and training in evaluation procedures can improve peer review as an appraisal system. The greatest acceptance of peer appraisal appears to result when the appraisal is used for developmental rather than evaluative purposes (McEvoy & Buller, 1987).

Subordinate appraisal
A performance evaluation done by those in a lower position than the person being evaluated.

Peer evaluation
A performance appraisal done by those at the same level as the person being evaluated.

Self-Evaluation

A survey of *Fortune* 500 companies indicated that over half those companies did not use *self-evaluation* as part of the performance appraisal process (Wells & Spinks, 1990). However, the more focused Thomas and Bretz *Fortune* 100 survey (1994) found that among companies that used self-evaluations, this form of appraisal accounted for 5 percent of total appraisal information weight at all levels, from executive to hourly employees. Some researchers (Budman & Rice, 1994; Meyer, 1991) suggest that the growing use of self-evaluations is consistent with a more participative management style that contributes to employee empowerment.

Although there may be concern that employees will be too easy on themselves in order to get a good performance evaluation, when correct performance appraisal procedures are followed there appears to be significant agreement between supervisory ratings and self-ratings (Somers & Birnbaum, 1991). Two factors that appear to influence self-evaluations are cultural context and self-esteem levels. One study found unusually low self-evaluation scores among Taiwanese workers (Farh, Dobbins, & Cheng, 1991), which the researchers attributed to a modesty bias among Asian workers. Further research by Yu and Murphy (1993) with Chinese workers did not confirm these modesty-based low self-evaluation scores, but this may still be a factor in certain cultural contexts. The role of self-esteem in self-evaluations appeared when Farh and Dobbins (1989) had a group of undergraduate students complete self-appraisals and self-esteem scales. Those researchers found that more lenient self-appraisals correlated with higher self-esteem levels. Another researcher found that employees are more likely to agree with and incorporate feedback from others if the feedback is consistent with their self-appraisals (Korsgaard, 1996). Although self-evaluations can be used at all levels in organizations, the greatest use is typically at upper-level positions that usually have the least objectively measurable performance appraisal elements.

Human Resources Department and Assessment Centers

Two other sources of performance appraisal information that are used less often than others are the human resources department and assessment centers. The advantages of using human resources department personnel for performance appraisal are the use of trained specialists, the use of people who can be more objective because they are less personally involved with the person being evaluated, and avoiding taking someone away from production duties to do performance appraisals. The involvement of the human resources department at this point also may help that department make personnel plans that meet the needs of the organization. An evaluator from the human resources department may be a good choice when there is a great deal of disagreement between a supervisor and an employee about the employee's performance appraisal. The disadvantages of using human resources department personnel are the limited amount of contact they have with the person and the job she or he is doing, which may be a major drawback in doing accurate performance appraisals.

Assessment centers, which were discussed in Chapter 8, usually are limited to fairly large organizations. Their role in performance appraisal generally lies in selecting the most promising candidates for promotions and managerial training programs. This is a costly method, and although performance on assessment center tasks has been shown to be a good predictor of later job effectiveness and success, smaller organizations usually can identify potential managers and executives in less expensive ways.

Multiple Raters

One way to improve performance appraisals is to use more than one source for an appraisal, a method discussed in detail later in this chapter. For many organizations this means the use of a multiple rater arrangement method called **360-degree feedback** (London & Beatty 1993). In this system performance appraisals come from everyone who has contact with the employee: supervisors, peers, subordinates, people from other companies, and populations such as customers and suppliers. This can been seen as an outcome of the organizational stakeholder concept discussed in Chapter 3. In a survey of *Fortune* 1000 firms, 22 percent of those companies were found to use some form of multiple rater performance appraisals (Bohl, 1996). Although groups such as customers and clients usually are not included in performance appraisals, 360-degree systems often are seen as providing more complete feedback to employees.

One of the problems in using a 360-degree system is getting all the participants to trust the process. Subordinates and clients may feel especially vulnerable if an employee finds out that they gave negative ratings, and so they may give more lenient ratings. Research on multiple rater systems shows the lowest degree of agreement between self-evaluations and other rater evaluations (Furnham & Stringfield, 1998). Employees may be tempted to inflate their self-evaluations when the performance appraisal system is used for administrative and personnel decisions such as pay raises. The *Fortune* 1000 survey mentioned previously found that over 90 percent of the companies that use 360-degree appraisal systems use them at least in part for personnel decisions, a factor that may decrease the accuracy of the appraisals, as discussed earlier in this chapter.

The general feedback from companies that have adopted 360-degree systems typically has been positive. Companies such as the basic industry division of Nalco, a chemical company in Illinois, have reported reduced turnover and better communication (Murphy, 1997). In the case study "Appraisals at Work" PhotoDisc enthusiastically endorses the 360-degree appraisal system.

360-degree feedback A system in which performance appraisals are done by everyone who has contact with the employee: supervisors, peers, subordinates, people from other companies, and populations such as customers and suppliers.

[Case Study] APPRAISALS AT WORK

How valuable are 360-degree performance reviews? Mark Torrance, president of PhotoDisc, claims that his company *cannot* afford not to do 360-degree reviews. This highly competitive digital-stock-photography company uses performance reviews mainly for employee development, and so the reviews are optional and are done six months before the performance evaluation that is used to set salary levels.

Employees and supervisors agree on six to ten reviewers for the employee. Immediate supervisors and people who report to the person under review are automatically included in the reviewer group. Each reviewer completes a three-page form that typically takes less than thirty minutes to finish. To keep the results confidential, PhotoDisc pays a consultant $50 per person to compile the results and share a summary of them with the employee and his or her supervisor. After the employee and supervisor discuss the feedback, the employee proposes a development plan to the supervisor. The development plans include specific strategies for addressing issues raised during the review. For example, after one technician found that many of his coworkers agreed that he needed to improve his desktop publishing skills, he signed up for a number of classes. The vice president of sales and marketing found out that her staff thought she was inaccessible, something that she felt none of them would have told her directly.

While PhotoDisc is sold on the value of 360-degree reviews, the consultant who helped develop their program cautions, "It's very hard to get people to change their behavior. You need specific goals, an action plan, and a mentor to remind people."

From S. Gruner. (1997, February). Feedback from everybody. *Inc.*, p. 102.

So far this chapter has dealt with making good choices in doing performance appraisals, but from the employees' perspective the most important part of this process is finding out the results and what the results mean to them personally. This is the role of the performance appraisal interview.

PERFORMANCE APPRAISAL INTERVIEWS

Performance appraisal interview A formal, regular, scheduled meeting of an employee and a supervisor to discuss the performance appraisal.

The **performance appraisal interview** is a time for the supervisor and the employee to share information, give feedback to each other, and make plans for future performance goals. It is not a once-a-year, fifteen-minute salary-setting meeting between a supervisor and an employee. If this is the only time subordinates and supervisors discuss performance issues, the goals and needs of the organization and the employee are suffering. Although formal performance appraisal interviews may take place only a few times a year, informal feedback to the employee should be frequent, specific, and directed more positively than neg-

J. Pickerell/The Image Works

■ The performance appraisal interview can be a positive experience for all participants.

atively. Most employees are performing more correctly than incorrectly, and feedback to them should reflect this.

Should these brief informal sessions replace the formal appraisal interview? The answer is no for several reasons. The first reason is to meet legal challenges. Feild and Holley (1982) found that organizations were much more likely to meet legal challenges to performance appraisals successfully when they were able to document regular formal performance appraisal interviews. The second reason is that many supervisors do not like to be judgmental and especially do not like to deliver negative information (Rapp, 1978), and so some supervisors would never do performance appraisal interviews if they were not required to. A survey of *Fortune* 100 companies found that the companies averaged less than four hours per year evaluating hourly employees. This included observing and documenting performance, completing the actual evaluation, and conducting the performance appraisal interview. This is much too close to the undesirable fifteen-minute salary-setting interview previously mentioned. The entire appraisal process for executives and managers was not much better, averaging only eight hours per employee per year (Thomas & Bretz, 1994). A survey of 140 midwestern firms found that 92 percent of those companies used performance and review sessions, but most of them did the reviews only at yearly intervals (Smith, Hornsby, & Shirmeyer, 1996).

Since performance appraisal interviews are necessary and can be beneficial to the employee, the supervisor, and the organization, how can organizations make these interviews more productive? The first step in planning for the performance appraisal interview should be to clarify the purpose of the interview for the supervisor and the employee. In a survey of research literature Wilson and Goodall (1985) found that appraisal interviews were used for various purposes. These included providing feedback on performance, counseling and providing help, discovering what an employee is thinking, teaching an employee to solve problems, helping an employee discover ways to improve, setting performance goals, and discussing compensation.

This is a great deal to accomplish in a single interview, and some of these goals may work against the others. It is difficult to discuss methods for improving performance and to accept feedback about negative behaviors if the same interview is used to set salary levels. A study of clerical employees and their managers in regard to setting rules for the performance appraisal interview found that the most potentially harmful disagreement was over the stated purpose of the appraisal session (Williams, 1989). Although a number of purposes can be served by the appraisal interview, the most common uses are giving feedback to the employee and organizational planning and development.

Once the purpose of the interview is clear, both the employee and the appraiser should prepare by reviewing all the material that will be part of the interview. Although appraisers have often participated in doing the evaluations, they still need to review the material and plan how it will be presented in the interview. Preparation by the employee also can lead to a better evaluation during the performance appraisal interview.

If employees understand the purpose of the interview and the materials to be used, they may feel less of a need to be on guard and defensive and may feel more secure about the fairness of the appraisal. Silverman and Wexley (1984) showed that when employees participated in developing the rating instrument used in the performance appraisal interview (BARS), they showed more favorable perceptions of the interview and had more positive outcomes afterward. Stano (1983) found that employees who were rated by their supervisors as outstanding contributors to a good performance appraisal interview were perceived as mature, positive, confident in their ability to do the job, and expressive of a genuine desire to learn and improve by actively seeing the experience and knowledge of the supervisor.

From the employee's perspective, the performance appraisal interviews that produce the greatest satisfaction and effectiveness ratings are those that combine judgmental and developmental components and include a high degree of participation by both the employee and the supervisor. Focusing on both past and future goals is also an important factor in the success of the interview (Keaveny, Inderrieden, & Allen, 1987). Greenberg (1986) surveyed over two hundred middle managers for factors that they believed to be critical to fair performance evaluations. He found several factors that directly concerned the performance appraisal interview, including two-way communication and the ability to challenge and/or rebut the evaluation. Greenburg also mentioned the following concerns: the importance of soliciting input from the employee before the interview, and using it; the evaluator's familiarity with the employee's work; ratings based on actual performance; and recommendations for salary or promotion based on the rating.

Overall, it appears that a number of rather distinct steps could remove much of the dread that sometimes is part of a performance appraisal interview for both the employee and the appraiser. These steps should contribute to the accuracy and effectiveness of the entire appraisal process, which is the focus of the next section.

IMPROVING PERFORMANCE APPRAISALS

Good performance appraisals should be reliable, valid, practical, and accepted by the users. These factors have been an accepted part of psychology for a number of years (Thorndike, 1949). Since the earliest studies of performance appraisals, information has accumulated on how to achieve this goal in practice as well as theory. Ilgen, Barnes-Farrell, and McKellin (1993) in their look at performance appraisal research in the 1980s and Thomas and Bretz in their *Fortune* 100 survey (1994) made a number of suggestions for improving the performance appraisal process. They concluded that several distinct changes demonstrated by research would help meet the criteria for a good performance appraisal. Among their suggestions were the following:

1. Ratings should be made immediately after observations. Ratings made after a delay of a day or more were less accurate than those done immediately after observation (Heneman & Wexley, 1983). What if evaluations are completed only twice a year? The formal instrument might be completed only twice a year, but keeping a diary and written comments throughout the period would produce better evaluations (DeNisi & Peters, 1996).

2. The stated purpose of the evaluation has to be the same as the use that is made of the performance appraisal information. Since performance appraisals commonly are used for more than one purpose, this may be difficult. It may involve using different evaluations for each purpose or at least more than one instrument when purposes such as pay setting and feedback are both involved (*Supervision,* 1998).

3. Rater training should be focused on his or her accuracy rather than the elimination of errors (Pulakos, 1984). Rater error training reduced the number of errors but did not improve the accuracy of the appraisals. Pulakos (1986) suggested that rater training should be specific to the requirements of the evaluation.

4. There should be a better understanding of the cognitive or thought processes raters use to arrive at their evaluations. For example, how long does it take an evaluator to decide whether an observed behavior is relevant to the appraisal, and does that affect what the evaluator records?

5. Employees should be more involved in the design, development, and administration of the appraisal system. This echoes Greenberg's (1986) suggestions for improving employees' perceptions of fairness in the appraisal process. This also should reduce defensiveness and resistance.

6. An environment should be created in which performance information is viewed as a resource that managers can use to develop subordinates. Employees also should recognize the career development potential in the performance appraisal process.

7. Multiple raters should be used. This not only reduces the possibilities of error that result from relying on a single source, it also increases the comfort level of an evaluator when she knows she is not solely responsible for what happens to the employee as a result of the evaluation.

If a company adopted all these suggestions, would it have an excellent performance appraisal system? Perhaps, as long as the company had done an evaluation of the performance appraisal system. This last step is often ignored but is critical to determining the worth of the appraisal system.

EVALUATING PERFORMANCE APPRAISAL PROGRAMS

It seems logical to say that performance appraisal systems are good if they do what they were designed to do. If the purpose of the appraisal system is to develop employees to their greatest potential in the organization, how can the company tell whether the appraisal system is accomplishing this? It is not a very measurable goal, and without being stated in more directly measurable terms, it would not be a very good criterion for evaluating a performance appraisal program. A second problem is that many companies use performance appraisals for more than one purpose. Is it possible for the appraisal program to accomplish some of these goals but not others? This may occur more often than companies would like.

One way to evaluate an appraisal program is to ask the people who are being rated for their assessment of the system. The factors mentioned by Greenberg (1986), cited in the section on performance appraisal interviews, included a number of elements that employees felt were critical to a fair performance appraisal. A number of other researchers have reported similar concerns among other groups of employees (Banner & Graber, 1985; Bretz, Milkovich, & Read, 1992; Inderrieden, Keaveny, & Allen, 1988; Jordan & Nasis, 1992; Morano & Deets, 1986).

According to Landy and Farr (1983), some sophisticated utility formulas can be applied to evaluate the monetary value of the use of a performance appraisal program. Although they predict that the use of such utility formulas (discussed in Chapter 9) will become commonplace, the complicated analysis required to use them may prevent their widespread adoption.

On a simpler level, Phillips (1987) suggests several red flags that can be raised to assess problems in the performance appraisal process. The same red flags can be used to assess the success of the program. The five elements he advises examining are as follows:

1. Examine the distribution of the ratings. This does not mean that a normal curve distribution must be shown for each organization. In a successful organization it can be assumed that lowest-performing people were never hired or left before performance evaluations were done. When a leniency bias appears to exist, organizations may not perceive it as a problem because they believe they have already dismissed the poorest performers (Thomas & Bretz, 1994).

2. Compare individual and group appraisals across time. There should be a degree of agreement with and improvement from previous performance appraisals.

3. Ask managers and employees when they last did or received an appraisal, looking for agreement between the two dates and an appropriate time interval between appraisals.

4. Ask the human resources department whether managers have had problems trying to discharge employees for unsatisfactory performance revealed during performance appraisals.

5. Ask supervisors whether they have ever acquired an unsatisfactory employee as a result of the recommendations and/or evaluations of other supervisors in the organization. This is a method of assessing supervisors on how well they do performance appraisals. Only 22 percent of the companies in a survey evaluated managers on this skill (Thomas & Bretz, 1994).

Although this list may not be technically sophisticated, it represents a good start. The beginning of this chapter looked at the many purposes and uses for performance appraisal information. A step toward making performance appraisals more equitable is for organizations to understand that how much they get out of a system is based on how much they are willing to put in. Performance appraisal success is an area that promises a great deal of return for the investment.

Many organizations have reported successes and positive experiences with the performance appraisal process. For example, Temple-Inland's forests division reported a great deal of satisfaction with a performance appraisal system developed by a company resource team. The team was asked to evaluate the system in the next year and suggest adjustments (Sorensen & Franklin, 1992). Pet

Incorporated and Nufield Hospitals System both reported success with their performance appraisal systems when they incorporated a number of the suggestions that have been covered here in the section on methods to improve performance appraisals (Haston & Pawlak, 1990; Wilson & Cole, 1990).

MAIN POINTS

- Organizations often use performance appraisal for a number of purposes. Some of the most common purposes are salary administration, performance feedback, and identification of employees' strengths and weaknesses.

- Fair employment law requires that performance appraisal be based only on job-related factors.

- Job analysis is a process of gathering information about the job-oriented and worker-oriented elements of a job before doing performance appraisals.

- Some common job analysis methods are observation, interviews, critical incidents, the Position Analysis Questionnaire (PAQ), and the Functional Job Analysis (FJA).

- Job evaluations are used to set the monetary value of a job and determine the comparable worth of different jobs on the basis of the compensable factors of each job.

- Performance evaluation instruments can be classified as using outcome-based methods, absolute standards methods, and relative comparison methods.

- Outcome-based methods involve objective measures, such as quantity and quality of work, personnel data, management by objectives (MBO) systems, and computerized performance appraisal.

- Absolute standards methods compare employees' behavior to a statement on a rating scale that represents a criterion for performance. Examples of these methods are graphic rating scales, BARS, BOS, BADS, checklists, forced choice systems, and mixed standard scales.

- Relative comparison methods contrast employees with each other. Examples of these methods are ranking systems, paired comparisons, and forced distributions.

- The best appraisal systems often use more than one of all these methods.

- Errors in performance appraisal usually result from imperfect raters and imperfect appraisal instruments rather than from purposeful bias.

- Some of the typical appraisal errors are halo (devil), leniency and severity, central tendency, contrast and similarity, recency, and frame of reference errors.

- Sources of performance appraisal information include the immediate supervisor (the most common source), subordinates, peers, the employee herself or himself, the human resources department, and assessment centers.

- Regularly scheduled performance appraisal interviews are important sources of information for employees and supervisors. They also help organizations successfully meet legal challenges to performance appraisals.

- Employees and supervisors need to be sure they are clear on the purpose of the appraisal interview and to prepare for it.

- The performance appraisal process could be improved by making ratings right after making observations, making the purpose and use of the evaluations the same, training raters and understanding the cognitive factors they use, involving employees more in the process, and using multiple raters.

- Performance appraisal programs should be evaluated on a regular basis to make sure they are accurate and fair.

KEY TERMS

Absolute standards methods
Behavioral Observation Scale (BOS)
Behavioral Anchored Rating Scale (BARS)
Behaviorally Anchored Discipline Scale (BADS)
Central tendency error
Checklists
Comparable worth
Compensable factors
Contrast and similarity errors
Critical incidents
Direct market pricing
Equal Pay Act of 1963
Forced choice system
Forced distribution
Frame of reference error
Graphic rating scales
Halo (devil) errors

Job analysis
Job evaluation
Job-oriented evaluation
Leniency and severity errors
Management by objectives (MBO)
Mixed standard scale
Outcome-based methods
Paired comparisons
Peer evaluation
Performance appraisal
Performance appraisal interview
Ranking
Recency error
Relative comparison methods
Structured assessment methods
Subordinate appraisal
360-degree feedback
Worker-oriented evaluation

REVIEW QUESTIONS

Answers to these questions can be found at the end of the book.

1. Doing accurate performance appraisals is an easily achievable goal for organizations.

   a. True   b. False

2. Individuals and organizations often have _____ reasons for wanting performance evaluations.

   a. different

   b. the same

   c. illegal

   d. unrealistic

3. What are the most common organizational reasons for doing performance appraisals?

   a. _____

   b. _____

   c. _____

4. Fair employment law does not apply to the performance appraisal process because it is concerned only with the hiring process.

   a. True   b. False

5. The first step in the performance appraisal process is to

   a. choose an evaluation form.

   b. determine the worth of the job.

   c. do a job analysis.

   d. decide which employees to evaluate.

6. One problem with using observation to do a job analysis is

   a. having too many people observe the employee at one time.

   b. the Hawthorne effect.

   c. the inability to observe workers on all shifts.

   d. all of the above

7. The critical incidents method is used only to analyze a job, such as nursing, where life-and-death decisions must be made.

   a. True   b. False

8. Two of the common structured job analysis methods are

   a. _____.

   b. _____.

9. Job evaluation must be done before job analysis because the value of a job determines how to do that job.

   a. True   b. False

10. Comparable worth issues have disappeared now that men and women almost always receive equal pay for equal work.

    a. True   b. False

11. The three categories of performance appraisal methods are

    a. _____.

    b. _____.

    c. _____.

12. Quantity and quality of work are the fairest ways to measure performance because they cannot be influenced by any outside factors.

    a. True   b. False

13. The goal statements in management by objectives systems

    a. must show improvement each time goals are set.

    b. usually are written by the supervisor only.

    c. must be written in behavioral terms.

    d. most often are completed when they are written in general terms.

14. Which of the following is a problem with the use of computers in performance appraisals?

    a. When the computer is off-line, performance cannot be measured accurately.

    b. Some employees feel this method represents an invasion of their privacy.

    c. This method focuses only on countable aspects of the job.

    d. The reports that are generated by this system can be interpreted only by trained specialists.

    e. e and d

    f. b and c

15. The most commonly used method for performance appraisal is _____ _____ _____.

16. BARS, BOS, and BADS are actually the same system, and the different titles represent the different companies that developed them.

    a. True   b. False

17. The basic assumption in the mixed standard scale is that if good, bad, and average performance statements are randomly listed in the evaluation, the evaluator must consider each statement carefully before responding.

    a. True   b. False

18. List two methods of appraisal that could be used to compare employees with each other.

    a. _____

    b. _____

19. Most errors in performance appraisal result from evaluators purposefully faking good evaluations for their friends and bad evaluations for employees they dislike.

    a. True   b. False

20–26. Matching. Match each error type with an example. Error types may be used more than once.

———— 20. Students who attend every class obviously should get a higher grade than students who rarely attend.

———— 21. Women naturally make better child care workers than men.

———— 22. My boss said she gave me a bigger raise than I really deserved because she knew I had college bills for all three children.

———— 23. Don't take Mr. Thomas for math. He flunks over half his students every semester.

———— 24. If you give everyone a rating between 3 and 7 (on a scale of 1 to 10), you can save a lot of time because you will not have to fill out all that paperwork.

———— 25. Susan is usually a good teller, but last week, right before performance evaluations, she made such a mess that her supervisor had to stay an extra four hours to straighten out her accounts.

———— 26. The supervisor says, "I don't know what is wrong with Steven. He has been at this job for two months now, and I can still do the job better than he can, and I'm not even a worker anymore."

a. Halo (devil)

b. Leniency and severity

c. Central tendency

d. Contrast and similarity

e. Recency

f. Frame of reference

27. One of the problems with using multiple sources of information for performance appraisals is that evaluators in different positions base their appraisals on different job factors.

    a. True   b. False

28. Which of the following sources of evaluation information is most consistent with a participative style of management?

    a. Self

    b. Immediate superior

    c. Subordinate

    d. Peers

29. What is one reason why it is important to schedule performance appraisal interviews regularly?

    _____

30. The most heavily weighted source of appraisal information is

    a. peers.

    b. peers and subordinates together.

    c. human resources departments and assessment centers.

    d. immediate supervisors.

31. Only immediate supervisors need to prepare for performance appraisal interviews because it is their job to do the appraisal.

    a. True   b. False

32. List two factors that are cited frequently as contributing to successful performance appraisal interviews.

    a. _____

    b. _____

33. The rater training that contributes most to improving performance appraisals focuses on

    a. reducing errors.

    b. making raters better at delivering negative appraisals.

    c. improving accuracy.

    d. all of the above.

34. Utility formulas are useful for telling an organization which is the best appraisal instrument to use in performance evaluations.

    a. True   b. False

35. Using more than one rater in the performance appraisal process

    a. can reduce error possibilities.

    b. can increase error possibilities.

    c. can increase the discomfort level of the evaluators because they think someone is checking up on them.

    d. should be done only at the highest levels in an organization.

WEB EXERCISE

Use your browser to go to
http://www.people.memphis.edu/~hresources/employ-pa/pahome.htm
to view a performance appraisal form from the University of Memphis. This form is used for staff employees such as office personnel. Using the information you learned in this chapter, list at least ten specific points in the evaluation where concepts in this chapter are applied correctly or incorrectly. Make sure to indicate the specific part of the appraisal form and explain why it represents a correct or incorrect application of a concept.

Employee Training and Development

11

Chapter Outline

LEARNING OBJECTIVES

INDIVIDUAL AND ORGANIZATIONAL TRAINING PURPOSES
Workplace Literacy
New-Employee Orientation
Continuing Education and Career Development
Retirement Planning

ASSESSMENT OF TRAINING NEEDS
Organizational Needs Analysis
Task Needs Analysis
Person Needs Analysis

TRAINING OBJECTIVES

PRINCIPLES OF LEARNING
Classical and Operant Conditioning
Schedules of Reinforcement
Transfer of Training
Other Principles of Learning
Cognitive Learning
Readiness and Motivation
Role of the Trainer

TRAINING METHODS AND TECHNIQUES
Training at the Job Site
Off-the-Job-Site Training

EVALUATION OF TRAINING PROGRAMS
Training Evaluation Criteria
Design of Training Evaluation Models
Cost of Training Evaluation
Case Study Training Works On-Line

Learning Objectives

After reading this chapter, you should be able to answer the following questions:

- What is training in the workplace and what are the individual and organizational purposes for which it is used?
- What are the following types of training and how are they used: workplace literacy, new employee orientation, continuing education and career development, and retirement planning?
- How is the need for training assessed by the three types of training needs?
- How should training objectives be written?
- What principles of learning apply to workplace training? How do they apply?
- What are the most common types of training done at the job site? What are the advantages and disadvantages of each?
- What are the most common types of off-the-job-site training that are not technology based? What are the advantages and disadvantages of each?
- What are the most common types of off-the-job-site training that are technology based? What are the advantages and disadvantages of each?
- How should training programs be evaluated according to Kirkpatrick and Kraiger and according to Ford and Salas?
- What design models are used to evaluate training programs? What are the advantages and disadvantages of each?
- What methods can be used to evaluate the cost of training programs?

What is the best way to learn to be a welder? To learn how to assemble a television set? To learn to be a psychologist? The training and development of employees has a long history as part of industrial/organizational (I/O) psychology. Other areas of psychology, such as learning, educational, and school psychology, also have contributed to the knowledge of the best way to train employees. Training receives a large allocation of resources in the field of human resources. In 1996, U.S. companies with more than 100 employees reported budgeting $55.3 billion for formal training programs that involved 69 percent of their employees (*Training and Development*, 1998). With such strong interest, large amounts of research in similar fields, and a great deal of funding, helping organizations find the best ways to do employee training should be one of the most thoroughly studied and evaluated areas in I/O psychology. However, much of the available information is based on weak research methods, such as case studies and observations. There have been relatively few experimental studies in the field of training and development. Many organizations do only a brief survey of the participants directly after training sessions.

Why are better research methods not used more? Part of the answer is that training and development exist in the context of the entire organization. If workers seem to be doing a good job after completing a training program or if top management is strongly committed to training and development, the organization will assign more resources to this area even without proof of its value.

Training Practical education in a skill, job, or profession.

Another part of the answer comes from looking at who does the training and why training is done. Often the people directly involved in training are chosen not because of their background in psychology but because of their skills in doing a particular task or job. These people may know intuitively how to teach a skill or may have picked up some training techniques informally. However, the best trainers are those who know the skills and have been trained to instruct others. Without a background in psychology, education, or research methods, many trainers may not realize the importance of assessment and evaluation, let alone know how to do them.

Training usually refers to practical education in mastering a skill or job. This definition separates training from education, which refers to more general development. Lawrie (1992) indicates that training, education, and development are linked by the concept of change, but he clarifies the different kinds of changes each one produces. Training produces a change in skills, education produces a change in knowledge, and developmental learning produces a change in attitudes or values.

These three concepts overlap greatly and often are used interchangeably. As organizations come to understand that educating and developing employees may be as beneficial as training them, more companies are using educational terminology and programs to supplement training. They also are supporting the educational efforts of their employees by paying part or all of the costs. Training costs typically have been paid by the organization because training often is considered to provide a more direct benefit to the organization. Education is thought to provide a direct benefit to the employee but a less direct benefit to the organization. The reason for the difference is that training helps employees perform their assigned tasks, while education may help them advance their careers or prepare for better jobs with other employers. As organizations broaden their concept of training, new and different purposes for training are evolving. The next section considers the uses of training in organizations.

INDIVIDUAL AND ORGANIZATIONAL TRAINING PURPOSES

Training can be used for a variety of individual and organizational purposes. Among those purposes are increasing employees' basic literacy skills, providing orientation for new employees, providing continuing and career education for current employees, and looking toward the future with retirement planning.

Workplace Literacy

In general, if organizations can shift the cost of training to the employee or to other organizations, they will be able to reap economic rewards from that shift. However, if the number of qualified applicants is not sufficient, organizations themselves have to bear the costs of training. In the United States teaching basic skills (including literacy) has been the role of elementary and high schools. Many organizations have begun to offer basic literacy training programs because their current applicants do not have the literacy needed for the job. Among 250 small firms, 29 percent indicated problems in finding employees with adequate reading skills (Szabo, 1992). Another study (Smith, 1995) found that 65 percent of the American workforce had reading skills below the ninth-grade level, which is defined as functional illiteracy. Some of these workers are literate in a language other than English, and so companies are teaching English literacy or English as a second language classes as well. In 1998, the National Institute for Literacy reported that American businesses had lost over $60 billion in productivity as a result of a lack of basic skills among employees. The same report noted that 75 percent of unemployed Americans have reading and writing problems (National Institute for Literacy, 1998).

Rebecca Cooney/NYT Pictures

■ Workplace literacy training has become an important training issue.

An example of basic skills and literacy training in the workplace is the partnership between Lone Star Steel and Northeast Texas Community College (Rosenberg, 1993–94). The program was initiated by the Job Training and Partnership Act program in Texas, which sponsors on-the-job training for skill-deficient job applicants. Lone Star and the community college determined the need for greater workplace literacy, built support for the training program, developed and presented the written project proposal, performed a job task analysis, and designed the curriculum.

Although companies are concerned with basic skills in order to obtain qualified employees, there are additional economic reasons for becoming involved in workplace literacy. The Business Council for Effective Literacy estimates that illiteracy costs at least $6 billion a year in welfare and unemployment programs (Rabin, 1992). When Magnavox evaluated its literacy program, it estimated that the training saved the company about $2,300 per month in reduced scrap and rework in 1991 (Ford, 1992). The monetary benefit of literacy and basic skills training is clear, but the benefit of other types of training is not always as obvious.

New-Employee Orientation

When employees join an organization, there is a period before they become productive for the organization. During that time they are becoming oriented to the company as well as to their specific jobs. The international executive search firm Battalia and Associates estimated that it takes six months to a year for a new executive to become acclimated and show real signs of performance (Cohen, 1990). Through its executive orientation program, that firm was able to reduce the adjustment time to three or four weeks for their placements.

The monetary benefit of new-employee orientation programs results not only from reducing the time it takes to become a productive employee but also from reducing turnover costs. If employees become frustrated because they never catch on to "the rules of the game" or are fired for not using methods that never were explained to them, the cost of replacing them can be much higher than the cost of a simple orientation program. In 1999, the United States Department of Labor estimated that it cost one-third of a new employee's annual salary to replace that employee (Reh, 1999).

Many different types of new-employee orientation programs can be developed to meet the needs of an organization. Programs in current use range from videotape presentations in complex structured organizations (Hale, 1992) to requiring the new employees of a small business to meet one on one with top managers within their first five days on the job (*Inc.*, 1992). Many programs include giving the new employees handbooks that provide information about the organization. A handbook may include a map of the company, an organizational chart, and the history and future of the company as well as its policies, procedures, work rules and safety requirements, and performance expectations. In recent years companies that focus on teamwork have expanded their orientation programs to include an introduction to team-based organizational systems and communications and problem-solving activities (Tyler, 1998). What most programs have in common is the goal of building a "loyal, committed group of employees who understand the organization's culture and resources and know how to help their own growth and development while working with others" (Leibowitz, Schlossberg, & Shore, 1991).

Continuing Education and Career Development

Continuing education and career development are part of the focus on employees as valuable organizational resources. Organizations that look beyond employees' current performance levels and job titles not only help their individual employees but assure the company's future success. Even if an employee is doing an excellent job now, planning for her or his continuing education and career development will promote higher performance in the future.

Continuing education can involve more than additional learning about the current job. It may involve learning a new job in the same organization. This is often referred to as **retraining** or **cross-training.** Statistics have shown that in the year 2000, 75 percent of all employees would need a significant amount of retraining (Waldron, 1993). Companies such as Intel, Chevron, and Sun Microsystems have found that it is cheaper to retrain employees than to fire them and hire new ones with the needed skills (Stuller, 1993). The Worker Adjustment and Retraining Notification Act (WARN) of 1996 makes it legally more desirable to retrain workers who may have been dismissed during a layoff.

Continuing education to upgrade skills in a job has proved to be profitable for organizations. Kenworth of Canada, a manufacturer of heavy trucks, started an intensive in-house training program for workers in their forties. The training included discussion groups as well as hands-on work on a mock-up truck. In the two years after the program began, production was up 19 percent and hours spent correcting manufacturing defects dropped to one-fifth of the previous total (Southerst, 1992). Organizations have also developed alliances with local colleges, universities, and schools to provide the highest-quality continuing education (Barnshaw, 1992). More recently, on-line courses and distance learning education have helped expand the resources for continuing education (Boyers, 1997; Brands, 1997). The advantage of these learning programs is that there are no limits in terms of time schedules or distance. Some universities have begun offering degree programs over the Internet.

Retraining Learning to do a current job in a new way or learning a new job in the same organization.

Cross-training Learning to do more than one job within an organization.

Continuing education that focuses on the entire career span of an employee often is referred to as **career development**. Career development or planning most often is seen as the individual's responsibility. Career development and planning obviously help each person as an individual, but why should organizations be involved in a process that may result in an employee finding a job with another organization? The answer is that although there may be a time when it is in the best interests of the organization for an employee to leave, there are benefits to the organization while that employee is still there. Nova Corporation of Canada has established a career development program for employees who are losing their jobs to downsizing as well as for employees who are remaining with the company (Wensky & Galer, 1997). Additional organizational benefits of such development programs include correcting performance deficiencies, maximizing performance, aligning employees' skills to promotional needs, cross-training for greater organizational flexibility, and developing a career path (Lipsett & Youst, 1994). Unfortunately, most managers do not perceive the company human resources department as a good source of career-planning advice (Welch, 1997). They feel that these departments are out of touch with the latest developments and act only as agents for the company.

One counselor-educator (McDaniels, 1989) says that in the new century the most successful organizations will be involved in planning for the entire life span of their employees. Super (1992) identified four distinct career stages through which employees pass in their work life (Table 11.1). Career development, like all

Career development
Planning for an employee's entire work life.

Table 11.1

SUPER'S STAGES OF CAREER DEVELOPMENT

Career Stage	Time Period	Organizational Behaviors
Exploration stage	Early work years	Developing future employees and new employees
Establishment stage	Early to middle work years	Encouraging the development of career anchors (employee knowledge of the most desirable work, values, and motives)
Maintenance stage	Late to middle work years	Maximizing employee productivity and organizational benefit
Disengagement stage	Last work years	Preparing for retirement and/or work continuation

training programs, may take a variety of forms to meet both employee and organizational needs. Russell (1991) lists self-assessment tools, individual counseling, information services, assessment programs, and developmental programs as aids to career development that have been used since the 1970s. Among more recent career development methods are computer- and Internet-based career-planning systems (Hanks, 1996; Koonce, 1997). Younger employees report greater satisfaction with computer-based systems, but the greatest success occurs when employees use those systems to establish a match between themselves and the career opportunities offered by the organization. As was noted in earlier chapters, good matches between organizations and employees lead to increased job satisfaction. Even though job satisfaction typically increases with age, older employees in the disengagement or decline stage of their careers still look to the company to provide continuing training and assistance; this is why more organizations are offering retirement planning.

Retirement Planning

One of the newest additions to employee training has been retirement or preretirement planning. As the number of aging workers increases, this area is expected to continue to grow. Formal planning has been shown to increase positive attitudes toward retirement (Multran, Reitzes, & Fernandez, 1997).

Financial planning is the most common type of assistance offered as companies attempt to shift the financial responsibility for retirement to employees. There are a number of computer-based and Internet programs, such as Quicken Financial Planner and RetireReady Deluxe, that companies have made available to their workers (Foust, 1997). A model of a comprehensive retirement planning program can be found at Adolph Coors Company, which offers a free seven-week program that covers financial planning, insurance, legal affairs, housing, personal safety, and health issues (Fuentes, 1992). Retirement planning makes it clear that training is a never-ending process. The next section looks at methods for assessing training needs so that a program will meet both the organization's and the employee's needs at the time the program is offered.

ASSESSMENT OF TRAINING NEEDS

The introduction of new computer software, such as the newest version of Windows, often generates a number of new training programs. Before purchasing or developing these training programs, companies should find out whether they are needed. A needs assessment may show that only two employees will be affected by the software change, in which case a companywide training program is not needed.

Even though it appears logical that training needs should be assessed before training programs are begun, a survey by Saari, Johnson, McLaughlin, and Zimmerle (1988) of 611 very large companies indicated that only 27 percent had a regular program for assessing management training needs. The most commonly used system for assessing training needs was developed by McGehee and Thayer (1961). It consists of three different types of training needs analysis: organizational, task, and person analyses.

Organizational Needs Analysis

Organizational needs analysis deals with finding out how training can assist the organization in achieving its goals. The question this raises is, "What are the goals of our organization?" If a company is downsizing, is it cheaper to fire all the people whose jobs are being eliminated or to provide retraining and assistance to find other jobs for those employees? The cost of unemployment compensation and hiring new workers may make retraining of current workers a better choice. An American Management Association survey (1999) shows over one-half of the organizations used training as a way to reduce turnover.

As organizations become multinational, an organizational analysis could show that diversity training, including an awareness of other cultures, will make a company more competitive in the global marketplace. A study by Black and Mendenhall (1990), which reviewed research on cross-cultural training, showed that such training can be effective in developing skills, facilitating adjustment to other cultures, and improving job performance. Additional issues at this level include the available labor pool, other diversity training issues, the resources available in the organization, and the values of the organization in regard to reaching its goals. Larger companies often routinely include strategic planning and goal setting as part of corporate development. Small organizations that struggle to survive from day to day may feel they are able to respond only to crisis needs, such as having enough workers present to run a production line that day. Longer-range planning for organizational needs could help them avoid "management by crisis" by preventing crisis situations.

Task Needs Analysis

Task needs analysis is the next type of needs assessment that must be done before training programs are developed. The information that is needed to do task

Organizational needs analysis An assessment of how training can assist an organization in achieving its goals.

Task needs analysis An assessment of the knowledge, skills, abilities, and other behaviors needed to do a job.

needs analysis is developed from a job analysis (Chapter 10). A job analysis should result in a list of the *knowledge, skills and abilities,* and *other behaviors* (KSAOs) necessary to perform the tasks that make up the job. Once the KSAOs have been identified, they can be examined to see which tasks employees can be expected to be able to do when they are hired. For example, newly hired bank tellers can be expected to have strong mathematics skills for handling transactions and good communications skills for dealing with customers. The bank can expect that it will need to train the tellers to operate its computerized system for recording transactions.

Even this straightforward area of task analysis is changing as the structure of work changes. As jobs have come to require more mental abilities and fewer physical abilities, researchers have suggested that there is a need to examine mental abilities as an important aspect of task analysis (Tannenbaum & Yukl, 1992). These researchers also advise that the rapid changes in technology will demand better planning for future training as well as greater flexibility. This means using methods such as cross-training to allow employees to learn more than one job. Also, the method of task analysis is changing as computer software is developed to assist in this process. *Training Needs Monitor* and *Needs Assessment Naturally* are computer-based programs that can support some task analysis activities as well as some organizational and person analysis activities (*Training*, 1994). As more software programs are developed, the cost should drop and the quality should improve.

Person Needs Analysis

The third type of needs analysis is **person needs analysis.** It centers on identifying which employees should be trained and how much training each employee should receive. To get the most from their training budgets, organizations must avoid wasting training dollars on employees who already have the needed skills or will not benefit from training. A typical person needs analysis is shown in Figure 11.1.

The most common sources of information for person analysis data are performance evaluation records, ability tests, critical incidents, information, and surveys of supervisors. Ford and Noe (1987) found that self-assessment adds information to the training needs analysis for lower-level and middle-level managers. Self-assessment requires employees to report the training they need. Lower-level managers reported higher needs for administrative skills than middle managers did.

Person needs analysis
An assessment of which employees should be trained and how much training each employee should receive.

In summary, before organizations implement training programs, they need to do a great deal of assessment to make sure that training is the best way to meet the organization's and employees' needs. Training needs assessment also should lead to clear objectives for training programs.

Figure 11.1

A portion of a person needs analysis for a sales position.

EMPLOYEE TRAINING NEEDS ASSESSMENT		
Employee		
Skill	Current need	Future need
1. Telephone skills		
2. Customer interaction skills		
3. Dress and grooming		
4. Independent development of sales plans		
5. Call back /follow-up skills		
6. New product knowledge		
7. Sales presentation skills		

TRAINING OBJECTIVES

Training programs that are satisfying for the employees and the organization begin with clear, specific, operationally defined objectives. This means that the training objectives must be expressed in precise terms and that there must be a way to measure the outcomes. For example, a company wants to train its shipping department personnel to be more cost-efficient. Instead of a general training objective such as "train employees to stop wasting money," the training objective must be written in behavioral terms and use operational definitions. (The use of operational definitions in hypothesis formation was discussed in Chapter 2.) A correctly written objective for this shipping department training program could be: "At the end of the two-day container placement training program employees will choose the smallest container that allows for at least one inch of packing material on all sides for at least 85 percent of the daily packaging tasks."

This is a well-written training objective because it makes clear the specific task employees are to learn. It also provides a way to measure the success of the training program after the employees are back on the job. Operational terms are usually objectively measurable. Students should be very clear about the task or skill they are to learn, and the trainer or supervisor should be able to judge whether the program has been successful. Clear and specific goals have been shown to enhance job performance (Latham, Steele, & Saari, 1982), which is an important goal for training programs. One further area must be considered before implementing a training program: the principles of learning that will be used in the program.

PRINCIPLES OF LEARNING

The basic principles of learning have been studied and researched for 100 years, and many of those principles apply to employee training. This section examines some of the major learning principles as they apply to employee training.

Classical and Operant Conditioning

Two of the major methods of conditioning or learning are classical conditioning and operant conditioning. **Classical conditioning** involves responses linked to reflexes or involuntary responses, such as Pavlov's dogs salivating at the sound of a bell. Classical conditioning has very limited applications in training in I/O psychology; an example would be learning the association between a warning light going on and a piece of machinery shooting a blast of air in the worker's face. After a time one can expect the employee to increase his blinking rate at the sight of the warning light, before the blast of air hits his eyes.

A large proportion of employee training is based on **operant conditioning** or variations of it. The central concept of operant conditioning is that rewarding a behavior will increase the occurrence of that behavior and punishing a behavior will decrease its occurrence. Training programs typically are designed to increase behavior, and so they should focus on rewarding correct behaviors. If the objective is to stop employees' unsafe behaviors through training, the focus may be on punishing incorrect or unsafe behaviors.

In thinking about rewards, or **reinforcers,** most people think about money or other tangible prizes. However, social reinforcers—such as telling someone she is

Classical conditioning
A training method that is based on linking behaviors to reflexive responses.

Operant conditioning
A training method based on the use of rewards and punishment for voluntary behavior.

Reinforcers Rewards that increase the incidence of desired behaviors.

doing a good job—and feedback—such as telling someone he is doing a job correctly—are valuable at work, especially in the training process. When one reinforces a behavior, one makes it stronger, which is usually the goal of training.

Schedules of Reinforcement

How often should one reinforce a behavior? To make training efficient, it is important to increase the incidence of the correct behavior as quickly as possible, and so it makes sense to reinforce the correct behavior every time it occurs. This is called **continuous reinforcement.** Many trainers argue that this is much too time-consuming, but continuous reinforcement saves time by quickly increasing the occurrence of desired behaviors and possibly avoiding the development of undesirable behaviors. Think about a new sales clerk who needs to learn how to process a sale. If the supervisor stays with him for an hour or two and reinforces every correct action, the clerk may quickly learn how to process sales correctly. In addition, the clerk will not have to unlearn incorrect behaviors. Continuous reinforcement strengthens a behavior quickly, but it is not a practical way to supervise after a training program is completed because this would be the only activity the supervisor would have time to do. Before the end of training the supervisor should change to one of the other methods or schedules of reinforcement. The other schedules of reinforcement that are used commonly are fixed ratio, fixed interval, variable ratio, and variable interval reinforcement, which were discussed in Chapter 6.

In skill training it sometimes is possible to master the entire skill correctly after a few attempts—such as putting a few wires in at the correct points in a car's steering system. In other cases the trainee does the task correctly, but not at the level required by the job. The training technique of shaping can bring an employee to the required level of performance. During a training program a trainer may reinforce an employee for coming closer and closer to the final performance level. The trainer needs to keep reinforcing for improvement, not for maintaining the lower level of performance. If you want clerical employees to be able to process sixty form letters a day, you might start out by reinforcing them for one correct letter, then five correct letters, then twenty correct letters, and so on, until they are doing sixty per day.

Transfer of Training

Getting people to perform correct behaviors during training programs is a good first step, but to complete the training program, they must learn to apply those behaviors correctly on the job. This is the process of **transfer of training.** Without transfer of training, training cannot be achieved unless it is done directly on the job. The best transfer of training occurs when the training situation is as much like the real situation as possible (Allen, Hays, & Buffardi, 1986), allowing employees to practice the new skills they learn (Binder, 1990). The new learning is built on a base of previous learning (Hollenbeck & Ingols, 1990). The work group and the supervisor are

Continuous reinforcement Rewards that follow every correct repetition of the desired behavior.

Transfer of training The application on the job of skills learned in a training situation.

supportive of the employees and the new behaviors, and the employees have the opportunity to perform the new behaviors on the job (Ford, Quinones, & Sego, 1992).

When new behaviors are applied correctly on the job, this is called positive transfer of training. Transfer of training also can be negative. This occurs when the skills and tasks learned in training not only are not helpful but actually interfere with the application of the correct skills. This can happen when positive transfer elements, such as critical job skills, are not present. Negative transfer of training can contribute to dangerous situations, as occurs when trainees believe that they have a skill because they have been practicing a new behavior for some time. However, instead of the correct new behavior, they have been practicing an incorrect one. For example, if a forklift driver trainee practices lifting pallets of empty boxes rather than the full boxes used by the company, she may not be able to lift full boxes on the job correctly.

Other Principles of Learning

In addition to transfer of training, several principles of learning guide the development of training programs. These principles include massed versus distributed practice, whole or part learning, and active practice of training materials. **Massed practice** refers to training that is done in one or a few long sessions. **Distributed practice** refers to learning that takes place over a number of short sessions. In general, distributed practice allows more time to process material. Bouzid and Cranshaw (1987) trained students and typists on twelve basic word-processing functions in either massed or distributed practice sessions. They found that the distributed practice students performed significantly better both at the end of training and one week later on a retention test. This research and other studies suggest that students should use distributed practice sessions to study for tests rather than "cramming."

Whole and part learning looks at whether the whole task should be presented at once or should be broken into smaller parts, with each part mastered in turn. One article (Swanson & Law, 1993) suggests that combining the two methods may produce the best results. The researchers recommend first presenting the whole task to be learned, then breaking the task into parts, and then again assembling it into the whole. For someone learning cardiopulmonary resuscitation (CPR) this would mean starting with a presentation of the entire process, then breaking it down into separate tasks, such as checking the neck pulse, and working on that task until it was mastered. The last step would be putting the separate tasks together to do a complete CPR.

The principle of **active practice** shows that having the learner participate dynamically in the learning process enhances learning. Charney, Reader, and Kusbit (1990) trained two groups in a computerized spreadsheet program. The group that learned the program by actually solving problems scored better on the performance tests at the end of the program. This type of approach also aids the transfer of training because it is easier to see how the training is going to be used on the job.

Massed practice Development of a skill during one or a few long sessions.

Distributed practice The development of a skill during many short practice sessions.

Whole and part learning Developing a new skill all at once (whole) or by putting together a number of separate pieces (part).

Active practice Learning in which the learner participates directly in the task to be learned.

Cognitive Learning

Each of these principles of learning focuses on observable behaviors. In recent years there has been an attempt to acknowledge parts of the learning process that are not directly observable, or cognitive learning. This is the third type of learning that applies to employee training as it is used in I/O psychology. The study of cognitive learning involves an examination of the thought processes that underlie learning. This approach states that people respond in a certain way because they have come to expect a reward for that response. The response is a result of a mental concept of what leads to a reward, not only of past reinforcement of behavior.

For example, a sales clerk decides to smile at customers more often after watching a successful clerk who smiles frequently. This is an example of cognitive learning by observation. One type of observational learning that has direct application in the training process is behavior modeling, which involves trying out new behaviors after they have been observed. Behavior modeling and other types of cognitive-based learning are discussed later in this chapter.

Readiness and Motivation

Readiness and motivation to learn can have a strong influence on the learning process. For many years psychologists assumed that if trainees were put in training programs, they would be ready and eager to learn. They started to rethink that assumption when they found that the results of training were not always positive. As they questioned why some results were neutral or negative, they found that a number of factors can contribute to the results. One factor was whether the trainees had the basic mathematics and literacy skills to profit from training. If trainees did not have those skills, correcting those deficiencies could enhance the likelihood of success in the training program (Carnevale, Gainer, & Meltzer, 1990).

Training in basic skills and literacy is not the entire answer, however. What if employees believe that if they are successful in a training program they will be given more responsibilities but without an increase in compensation or a promotion? Nordhaug (1989) conducted posttraining interviews with Norwegian employees and identified three different dimensions of payoffs from training: "motivation to learn" (increased interest in the subjects of the courses), "career development" (increased autonomy and production), and "psychosocial development" (increased self-confidence). Without these payoffs, trainees may believe that the training is not worth the effort.

When employees develop the belief that training is not worthwhile or do not believe they can be successful at it, this is called **resistance to training.** The result can be a loss of valuable employees and skills. For example, one of the biggest problems in training older employees in computer skills is not the learning itself but the employees' belief that they cannot learn the skills.

Resistance to training
The desire to avoid new learning situations.

Self-efficacy Belief in one's ability to perform a task.

Research has found that it is not enough to want to be successful in a training program; belief in one's ability to be successful is also important. A trainee's belief that he or she can be successful in performing a task is called **self-efficacy.** Gist, Schwoerer, and Rosen (1989) looked at managers who were being trained in the use of computer software and found that the managers with higher self-efficacy before and during training performed better on a timed computer task at the end of the training. Being successful at a training program can itself increase self-efficacy scores, which can contribute to success in later training programs. When researchers looked at the expectations and desires of over six hundred naval recruits, they found that the trainees who had their expectations and desires fulfilled in the training program developed greater organizational commitment, self-efficacy, and motivation than did the recruits whose expectations were not met (Tannenbaum, Mathieu, Salas, & Cannon-Bowers, 1991).

Is it possible to increase self-efficacy before training starts? Kaeter (1994) says that one of the best ways to prevent resistance to training is to create a "training culture" in which training is valued, put into practice, and shown to be effective in meeting goals. She also suggests emphasizing the personal benefits of training and keeping track of the day-to-day attitudes of employees who are entering training. The concept of a training culture should improve outcomes for trainees. Creating a climate that encourages and promotes success in training may benefit employees even if they believe that "everyone does okay in training here" rather than believing in their personal control of the training outcomes. The long-range goal, however, still should be to increase job and career involvement through feelings of greater personal control of the outcomes, because employees lowest in job and career involvement have been found to benefit the least from training programs (Noe & Schmitt, 1986).

Creating a training climate also can encourage greater voluntary participation in training. Voluntary participation in training programs has been shown to result in higher motivation to learn, greater learning, and more positive reactions to learning (Tannenbaum & Yukl, 1992). If participation is voluntary, an employee is more likely to feel that the company is interested not only in training that will benefit the organization but also in her or his development.

Role of the Trainer

The role of the trainer can have long-term consequences for both the trainee and the organization. Do you remember the best and worst teachers you ever had? What stands out in your mind as major differences? Some of the same criteria apply to trainers. In general, the best trainers are people who are knowledgeable about the subject or skills they are teaching and have learned about methods of teaching.

Too often trainers in organizations are chosen only because they are doing their current nontraining jobs very well. Laird (1978) calls this the "good worker" trap. He says that when trainers are chosen only because they are good at the jobs for which employees are being trained, the organization is losing a good worker and gaining a bad trainer. Laird also discusses the problem of the trainer who focuses only on the one characteristic of a great teacher that she remembers and then uses only that single characteristic to the exclusion of other important characteristics. For example, a trainer may remember how his math teacher's sense of humor helped make the class more interesting and then may build his entire training system around telling jokes.

Another problem, according to Laird (1978), is selecting a trainer because of personality traits rather than demonstrated skills. It is easy to list personality traits that may be helpful in training, but how a trainer uses those traits is the critical issue. Perhaps trainers should have warmth, but if they must be able to engage in two-way communication and respond appropriately to information from trainees, why not look for those skills? In most cases it is easier to measure skills than personality traits. Training the people who themselves do training in organizations is one of the major concerns of the American Society for Training and Development, which is the professional organization for training specialists. It provides information and resources both for professional trainers and for organizations.

The following guidelines, developed by Campbell (1988) and summarized in Tannenbaum and Yukl (1992), are a good outline of the critical features of an effective training program:

1. The instructional experiences that make up the training method should use the cognitive, physical, or motor processes that lead to mastery of the skill that is being taught. For example, if one is learning a motor behavior such as driving a truck, the training program should include doing the skills one will need to do, such as shifting gears.

2. The learner should be persuaded to practice the skill or task actively. For example, one should perform the steps in setting up a spreadsheet program instead of just hearing a lecture about those steps.

3. All available sources of relevant feedback should be used, and the feedback should be accurate, credible, timely, and constructive. In a computerized training program, the trainee may hear a beep after each wrong keystroke, and a chart may pop up on the screen every five minutes showing current progress. Twice a day the supervisor may go over the hourly records, chart the daily progress, and give the trainees feedback about their progress.

4. The instructional process should increase trainees' self-efficacy and expectations that the training will be successful and lead to valued outcomes. For example, the training should begin with simple behaviors that can be mastered easily and then progress to more complex behaviors as the trainees become more confident.

5. Training should be adapted to differences in trainees' aptitudes and prior knowledge. This means that someone who already can do the first level of a training program should not be required to relearn it just because all the trainees are required to complete each step in order.

Figure 11.2
Steps in the training process.

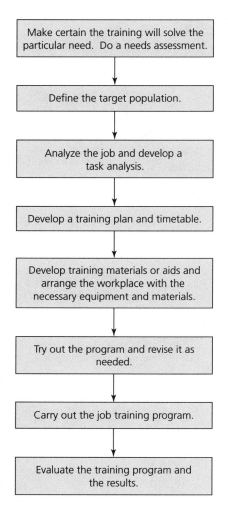

Make certain the training will solve the particular need. Do a needs assessment.

↓

Define the target population.

↓

Analyze the job and develop a task analysis.

↓

Develop a training plan and timetable.

↓

Develop training materials or aids and arrange the workplace with the necessary equipment and materials.

↓

Try out the program and revise it as needed.

↓

Carry out the job training program.

↓

Evaluate the training program and the results.

Adapted from A. B. McCord. (1987). Job training. In R. L. Craig (Ed.), *Training and development handbook: A guide to human resource development* (3rd ed., pp. 363–382). New York: McGraw-Hill.

On-the-job training
Learning that takes place while one is doing the job.

With so many different parts to the training process, it may be helpful to see how all the pieces of a program fit together in an overview of the process, such as the model shown in Figure 11.2, which is adapted from McCord (1987). As you can see in the first steps in the figure, previous sections of this chapter have focused on the preparation for training. The next step involves actually doing the training. To continue the training process, it is necessary to look at specific methods and types of training that are designed to meet a variety of needs.

TRAINING METHODS AND TECHNIQUES

Training can be done either on the job site or away from work. Either location has advantages and disadvantages. In looking at these locations, this section examines the advantages and disadvantages specific to each method.

Training at the Job Site

On-site training has a number of advantages, including realism, transfer of training, and less time lost from work. This section covers the on-site methods of on-the-job training, job instruction training, vestibule training, job rotation, apprenticeship training, and mentoring.

On-the-Job-Training

One of the most common types of training at the job site is **on-the-job training**. This method is used by over 93 percent of the companies Saari, Johnson, McLaughlin, and Zimmerle (1988) surveyed. Organizations often look to on-the-job training as an inexpensive way to get employees up to the needed production levels quickly.

The problems are often less obvious than the benefits. If training is done on the job, expensive equipment can be damaged or the trainees can interrupt other employees' work. The person assigned to be the trainer may be resentful of having to do one more job without receiving additional compensation. Although the trainer may be doing her own job well, she may not be good at teaching others to do that job. The best use of this type of training takes place when the training involves a simple skill that can be learned quickly without danger to the employee or the equipment, and the trainer has demonstrated good training skills.

Many of the best elements of on-the-job training can be illustrated in a study of bank tellers. In an experiment involving the training of bank employees, ten tellers received positive, immediate, graphic, and specific feedback as well as social reinforcers from their supervisors. The control group of tellers did not receive feedback or reinforcement. The tellers who received on-the-job training improved on four of six dimensions of high-quality service, and customers reported improved transaction quality (Luthans, 1991).

Job Instruction Training

Job instruction training, which was developed during World War II, uses four simple steps that often are referred to as "tell, show, do, and review." It involves a lecture by the trainer, a demonstration, a performance tryout by the trainee, and a critique of the trainee's performance. To illustrate this method, Camp, Blanchard, and Huszczo (1986) use the example of an employee learning to use a computer terminal (Figure 11.3).

Vestibule Training

If the possibility of damaging work equipment is too much of a hazard, a compromise that still allows training to be done at the work site is **vestibule training.** Vestibule training is done with the same equipment and tools used on the job, but it is done next to the actual work area so that it does not interrupt production. Transfer of training is very high, and the trainers often are people who have been trained in teaching methods as well as the required job tasks or skills. The main disadvantage of this method is the cost of the equipment and trainers. If the production area is very crowded, it may be difficult to find a place to duplicate the work setting.

Job Rotation

An on-site method that may enhance job satisfaction is **job rotation.** With this method employees are trained in a variety of jobs by doing each job for a period of time. The period may be as short as a week or as long as a year. An example that has long been in existence takes place in the last years of medical school for doctors in training. Each doctor can choose four specialty areas to work in for three months each.

This is a method that often is used for entry-level management positions to increase the scope of experience within the company and improve a trainee's understanding of how the different parts of the organization work together. The increase in job satisfaction results from increasing the variety of jobs and enriching the work environment.

Apprenticeship Training

A method of on-site training that also may include off-site training is the apprenticeship program. **Apprenticeship training** takes place over several years and

Job instruction training
A learning method that uses the four steps of tell, show, do, and review.

Vestibule training Training done adjacent to the actual work area with the same equipment and tools.

Job rotation Training done by cycling through a variety of jobs or positions.

Apprenticeship training Lengthy training in a skill or trade that involves a combination of supervised on-the-job work and classroom instruction.

Figure 11.3

Steps in the job instruction training process.

1. Tell. Explain to trainee the need to learn this task, ask what the trainee knows, and motivate trainee.

"All of our files are being computerized." "Have you ever used a computer terminal before?" "This should make it much easier to get personnel records."

2. Show. Trainer demonstrates the skill.

Trainer turns on terminal, accesses personnel records, prints them.

3. Do. Trainee does the task.

Trainee turns on the computer, accesses personnel records, and prints them.

4. Review. Feedback is given to employee.

Employee either did the skill correctly and goes back to work, or trainer goes back to step 2.

usually includes supervised work on the job as well as classroom instruction. Wages and responsibilities typically increase over the period of apprenticeship. The advantage usually lies in the combination of receiving training from highly skilled people in the field and getting structured classroom learning. This is often an excellent way to learn a skilled trade, such as carpentry or plumbing, that requires hands-on skills and independent thought and action. Chrysler Corporation and the United Auto Workers union resurrected an apprenticeship program for the skilled trades in 1996 after they estimated that half the skilled-trades employees at Chrysler would retire before 2005 (Jackson, 1996). Research has shown that graduates of apprenticeship programs earn more money, work more hours a year, and rise to supervisory positions in greater numbers than do other workers (Gitter, 1994). A disadvantage of this method of training results from restricted access to the training program. Minority groups have pressed for more equal access to apprenticeship programs, and government guidelines appear to be equalizing entry into those programs (Wexley & Yukl, 1984).

Mentoring A formal or informal relationship in which a more experienced worker helps a less experienced worker develop job- and career-related skills.

Mentoring

A form of apprenticeship training that has received a great deal of attention in recent years is mentoring. **Mentoring** involves an experienced worker who "adopts" an inexperienced worker in order to help that person along her or his career path. Formal and informal mentoring relationships have been in existence for many years. Professors and students and top athletes and beginning athletes have been a part of the tradition. In a formal mentoring relationship a senior employee is assigned to nurture the career and job development of a newer or younger employee. This may involve regularly scheduled meetings or discussions as well as informal interactions.

Mentoring also has been used as an informal method of management training for a number of years, and women's groups have promoted setting up formal mentoring programs for women to increase their numbers in these programs. The eagerness of women to be part of these programs makes sense when the benefits of such a relationship are examined. In a study of 404 graduates of undergraduate and graduate business programs, researchers found that even when they controlled for variables such as training, job experience, the organization, and several demographic factors, career mentoring was associated with a faster and higher promotion rate as well as with greater compensation, particularly when the mentor was a white male (Dreher & Cox, 1996; Whitely, Dougherty, & Dreher, 1991).

Companies also are using mentoring programs to increase diversity in the workplace and retain women and minority employees (Perez, 1997). Both the person who is being mentored and the organization gain valuable assets from mentoring, but the mentor also benefits from the process. Crandell (1994) lists several ways in which mentoring can further the career of the mentor: (1) the mentor can develop a reputation as a talent scout who can groom discoveries as well as pick them, (2) the protégé can keep the mentor informed about the culture and attitudes at a different level of the company, increasing organizational knowledge for the mentor, and (3) the protégé can act as a sounding board and help with the mentor's key projects.

Off-the-Job-Site Training

Off-the-job-site training includes any training that takes place at a location other than the place where the job is performed. Training away from the job site gives an organization access to many more methods and learning situations. There is also no disruption of operations. Organizations use a variety of off-site training methods, ranging from nonparticipatory methods such as lectures to participatory methods such as role playing. These methods can be classified according to their use of technology.

Nontechnology Methods

Nontechnology methods of training include lectures, role playing, behavior modeling, sensitivity training, case studies, conference training, the incident method, and outdoor experiential training.

Lectures Although they are used frequently, lectures often are dismissed as a poor way to accomplish training. Are lectures good for education but not for training? A great deal of the effectiveness of any training method depends on the correct use. If one wants to train a large group of employees on a new simplified safety procedure, lectures may be one of the best choices. Much of the effectiveness of the lecture method depends on the skill of the lecturer.

One way a lecturer can improve is through her willingness to ask for questions and facilitate group discussion. Although lectures often are considered as nonparticipatory, learners can do a great deal to increase their level of participation. Elfner (1980) found that students in a lecture course on management increased their knowledge of management principles much more than did a control group that received no training. The lecture method produced results similar to those from the discussion-focused sections of the course, with the lecture students doing slightly better on the test at the end of the course.

Role Playing Most people are familiar with **role playing** from childhood games. As a training exercise at work, students are assigned a specific organizational role and told to act as if they were in that position. Other trainees or the trainer may assume roles as well. The other trainees are assigned to observe the interaction and take notes on effective and ineffective actions. Very often there is a time limit, after which the trainer guides a discussion of what worked and what did not and why.

In role reversal the trainee does not play himself but instead plays the person receiving the communication. This is done to get the trainee to understand how it feels to be on the other side. A number of organizations have used role reversal and role playing to teach employees the emotional results of sexual harassment on the job (Brown & Codey, 1994; Thacker, 1992) and for cultural diversity training (Thompson, 1992).

Role playing A training method in which the learner practices new ways of interacting.

For role playing to be effective, the trainer needs to create an atmosphere in which the trainees feel safe experimenting and trying out behaviors. Both a benefit and a drawback to role playing is the fact that the training is not done on the job. The benefit is that there are no bad consequences at work if the trainee models the behavior ineffectively and if there is a chance to try the behavior before using it on the job. The drawback is that the trainees know the situation is not real and may use behaviors different from those they actually would on the job. In work settings role playing has been effective in producing changes in a number of on-the-job behaviors. For example, Wiswell and Lawrence (1994) used role playing to develop better feedback skills when managers gave feedback to the employee they had rated as the least effective in the work group.

Behavior Modeling   One application of cognitive learning to the training process is **behavior modeling,** which is learning that develops from watching another person (the model), then practicing the behavior and being reinforced for repeating it. It is based on observational learning according to Bandura's (1986) social learning theory. Bandura states that observational learning takes place in four steps: (1) paying attention to and sorting out the critical features of the model's behavior, (2) remembering the behavior by watching someone do it, (3) reproducing the behavior, and (4) being motivated to learn and use the behavior, which entails feedback and reinforcement. Behavior modeling has been used chiefly in management training, but there are numerous applications at all training levels. One study (Simon & Werner, 1996) compared behavior modeling, self-paced study, and lecturing for training in computer skills. The subjects were novice computer users at a U.S. Navy site. Cognitive learning and skill learning were highest in the behavior-modeling group.

Some researchers indicate that behavior modeling may be the most popular technique for teaching interpersonal and leadership skills (Baldwin, 1992). It is important that the model and the situation closely resemble what is required on the job because the success of this method depends on transferring the knowledge to the actual job situation. In a true behavior-modeling program, the skills practiced in training are the same as the skills used on the job. This is different from role playing, because the learner is trying to repeat the behavior of the model, not just try out various behaviors.

Sensitivity Training   Each of the techniques previously discussed includes emotional components, such as competitiveness and understanding another person's feelings. Emotional components in the training process are referred to as affective skills. **Sensitivity training** provides direct training in affective abilities in interpersonal interactions in a group setting. The goal of sensitivity training is greater awareness of the affective content of one's own behavior and how it influences others. This type of training also should provide a greater understanding of the way groups work and possibly help develop additional methods of learning for the

Behavior modeling
A training method in which the learner watches someone doing an action and then tries to repeat that action.

Sensitivity training
Experiential learning of emotional skills and behaviors.

participants. A number of organizations have begun using sensitivity training to develop multicultural awareness and diversity training (Gardner, Keller, & Piotrowski, 1996; Sachdev, 1997). The small size of the training group (usually eight to twelve members) encourages extensive interaction among the participants.

Although many group arrangements are possible, sensitivity training groups have certain basic characteristics in common.

1. *Here-and-now-focus.* The content of the training is the current discussion between the members. Often no agenda or discussion topic is assigned, but the content emerges as the participants interact with one another.

2. *Self-disclosure.* Learning can take place only if the participants reveal to the group their feelings about what is happening in the group.

3. *Feedback.* By getting and giving feedback about their self-disclosures, the participants learn how they are perceived by others and the importance of feedback that is specific and constructive.

4. *Climate of experimentation.* The premise of sensitivity training is that the group creates a "cultural island" of support and trust, in which the participants feel safe letting down their facades and can learn from their emotional reactions.

Research on the effectiveness of sensitivity training often lacks a good experimental design and has difficulty defining what should be measured. Overall, the most successful use of this training method appears to occur when the organization as a whole and individual supervisors are supportive of the trainees' attempts to change their behavior back on the job (Wexley & Latham, 1981).

Case Studies, Conference Training, and the Incident Method A method of training that has a number of similarities to sensitivity training is the use of case studies. **Case study training** starts by providing the trainees with a written description of a problem situation in an organization. Enough details are given that the trainees can feel they have the information needed to make judgments and decisions to resolve the problem. The trainees usually are instructed to develop a solution and come up with a plan to put that solution into action. They often are required to explain how they arrived at the solution and give reasons to support the solution and the action plan. These activities may be done individually or as part of a small group; discussion of the solutions and the advantages and disadvantages of each one is done as part of the group. The leader of the group guides the trainees in discovering the pieces that contribute to the solution but is careful not to direct them toward a single solution because an important goal of case study training is to make students aware that there may be number of successful solutions to a problem, not just the one dictated by the instructor.

Case study training
Learning based on an in-depth analysis of a particular person or situation.

The reasoning behind the case study is that when a concrete example is used, the trainees will be able to apply the theory and principles in a realistic way and their participation in the process will lead to better learning. This is a very popular method, which has been used by a number of law and graduate business schools for over seventy-five years. Harvard Business School each year generates 300 to 350 field-based case studies and about 300 more case-related pieces of teaching material that are distributed to over 25 nations and 200 business schools worldwide (Stern, 1995).

Problems with this method can result from its incorrect use. If the cases used are not realistic or are too simplistic, learning and transfer of training can be decreased. If the trainees do not have enough background knowledge about organizational theory and problem solving to apply to the cases, little learning will take place. The trainer must be skillful in facilitating rather than dominating discussions and promoting a particular solution. She should encourage the trainees to explore all possibilities (Argyris, 1980).

Two variations of the case study method are conference training and the incident method. **Conference training** is a group discussion about a specific topic, led by someone with knowledge of that topic; an example would be a conference for first-level supervisors on how to implement Americans with Disabilities Act guidelines in the work situation. In the incident method the trainees are given a bare-bones case study about an event, such as a supervisor returning to the assembly line after a break and finding only three of twenty employees on the line. When he searches for the others, he finds them in the break room, with two of the employees throwing punches at each other. The instructor knows all the background information about this incident, but she gives the details only in response to specific questions from the trainees. The most common use for the incident method is training in situations that require skills such as handling employee grievances and investigating accidents.

Outdoor Experiential Training Many people compare the growth in the popularity of outdoor experiential training to the rise of sensitivity training in the 1960s and 1970s; increased self-awareness is an expected outcome of both methods. Like sensitivity training, **outdoor experiential training (OET)** requires risk taking, and as in sensitivity training, the learning occurs in the experience. It is a method that usually involves management-level employees in a three- to seven-day wilderness activity led by trained personnel. The experiences may range from trekking through a desert to climbing a mountain or navigating a river.

The common element in these experiences is a series of planned physically and mentally challenging tasks. Since they require physical agility, these experiences may represent a significant challenge to disabled employees, but that also may represent a significant benefit. One study of OET that included disabled participants found an enduring change in attitudes toward the disabled (Anderson, Schleien, McAvoy, Laid, & Seligman, 1997). These programs are believed to improve managers' skills in teamwork, problem solving, risk taking, self-esteem, and interpersonal communication (Clements, Wagner, & Roland, 1995). OET groups

Conference training
A learning method that involves a group discussion about a specific topic, led by someone with knowledge of that topic.

Outdoor experiential training (OET) Learning done in rustic areas to increase individual and group self-understanding through various risk-taking experiences.

must experience real emotions rather than the make-believe emotions of role playing. They also develop group awareness and problem-solving skills because some of the tasks require the close cooperation of the group members.

Research on the effectiveness of OET is meager, but some early studies showed more self-sufficiency and less conflict among OET groups after the training. According to Ewert and Heywood (1991), the groups that had a white-water rafting experience improved in cohesiveness, interdependency, and problem solving more than did groups that participated in land-based training courses. Two other researchers (Wagner & Roland, 1992) found nonsigificant effects for individual participants but group changes similar to those in the first study. These results are very tentative and must be accepted cautiously until further research that is more experimental is completed.

Eric Newrath/Stock, Boston

■ **Outdoor experiential training provides a physical, mental, and emotional challenges.**

Technology-Based Methods

Technology-based methods include audiovisual training, simulation training, business games, programmed instruction, and computer-assisted instruction.

Audiovisual Training Training using audio or video media or both often has been misused. As in lectures, the correct use of audiovisual training techniques can be effective. The most common methods include slides, films, videotapes or audiotapes, and the newer multimedia CDs and videodiscs. Computers also are being used to create multimedia training presentations. One of the problems with methods such as multimedia presentations is that when they become so popular that they seem to be a requirement rather than a choice, their effectiveness can be compromised. Goldstein (1993) cites the program *Sesame Street* as one of the best illustrations of the effective use of audiovisual training.

The decreasing cost of equipment and materials and hence their overuse has caused multimedia presentations to lose some of their effectiveness. Before choosing an audiovisual method, the instructor needs to assess whether that method will promote better learning. Although the initial cost of the program may be high, it may be cheaper than sending a trainer to many different locations to train one or two people. One study estimated the cost of a production-quality video to be between $2,000 and $3,000 (Maynard, 1995). It also may be cheaper than having a trainer repeat a presentation many times. One interesting use of audiotapes came from a company that had a number of salespeople who spent considerable amounts of time driving between sales calls. The sales manager created monthly "windshield chats"—tapes salespeople could play in their cars—to provide them with company news, sales strategies, and current statistics, presented in humorous motivational and informational skits (Cohen, 1994).

The worst use of audiovisual presentations is to repeat a passive experience like a lecture; the best use appears to be in the form of dynamic presentations. One pharmaceutical company compared groups whose training presentations used lectures, lectures supplemented with slides, and dynamically presented videotaped visuals of the main points of the message. The group that viewed videotape presentations had the best retention rate over a one-week period. The key to the effectiveness of the videotape appeared to lie in the more frequent repetition of the verbal message and the emphasis on action in the presentation (Gehring & Toglia, 1988). In an interesting application, the American Hotel and Motel Association developed a series of language-free videos to train line-level employees whose preferred language was not English (Mally, 1997). Audiovisual programs also can be a good method for distributing up-to-date information on topics such as violence in the workplace and sexual harassment.

Simulation Training **Simulation training** replicates part or all of a job in an off-site location, in the belief that the trainees will transfer the skills to the actual job situation. Some of the typical uses of simulation training are for pilot training and in cardiopulmonary resuscitation. This type of training often is used when errors would be extremely expensive or cause harm to the trainee or the organization. A very complex job can be divided into smaller training segments, each of which can be simulated. Simulations also allow a trainee to make mistakes that would be embarrassing in front of fellow employees.

Simulation training
Learning based on practicing skills in a replica of the work situation.

Virtual reality Computer-based simulation training that re-creates a three-dimensional environment.

Simulations can provide a unique training situation for crisis events that are rare and unplanned but require well-trained responses. An example is the mock robbery training done for banks and credit unions by the police department in Spokane, Washington (Moore & Gehrig, 1991). The department stages a robbery, and the bank or credit union employees practice their roles as employees. The employees learn about describing the suspects, securing evidence, law enforcement requirements, and danger points in a robbery. The use of a simulation can give the trainees many chances to learn what to do in a situation that offers only one chance for correct behavior.

The latest extensions of simulations involve the use of computers in developing complex management games and virtual reality situations. The assumption in the use of **virtual reality** is that it will make transfers of training better by adding more three-dimensional realism to the training situation. Virtual reality programs have been used in a wide variety of training situations, from those involving special operations air crews to those demonstrating specialized surgical techniques or training firefighters on aircraft carriers. Some researchers have cautioned organizations to consider drawbacks such as expense and motion sickness before adopting virtual reality programs (Wilson, 1993). The increased sophistication of computer-based technology may encourage the use of virtual reality programs when other methods would be a better and cheaper choice.

Tannenbaum and Yukl (1992) discuss the use of simulations in a variety of settings ranging from the military to industry, with applications for insurance agents, supervisors, negotiators, and industrial engineers. The amount of research on simulations has increased greatly over the last several years, resulting in information about a number of factors that can improve simulation training. Researchers have summarized some of the important variables that make this type of training successful. These include (1) careful planning of the entire training development sequence; (2) presentation of an appropriate model of the correct behaviors; (3) a clear description of the relevant skills; (4) adequate debriefing; and (5) opportunities for coaching, feedback, reinforcement, and practice of skills on the job.

Although there is a lot of research on each of these factors, there is much less research about the effectiveness of simulations as a method of learning skills needed on the job. Two reasons for the lack of this research are that many job requirements are long-term rather than immediate and that many other training experiences may be used in combination with simulation training so that it is difficult to sort out how much each method contributes to the success of training. When other types of practice and coaching are separated out, the answer may be that simulation training is not as effective as it should be. One simulations expert recalled that experienced helicopter pilots often "crashed" the simulators he had helped develop, although they had been flying real helicopters correctly for a long time. He also found that after he himself spent considerable time on the simulator without other kinds of training, he was unable to control the real helicopter (Mathews & Anselmo, 1994).

Business Games A type of simulation that is used mainly with management involves business games. Business games are uniquely adapted for teaching cognitive skills, such as problem solving, and showing how the parts of an organization interact. Trainees can see the effects of their decisions within minutes or hours. Keys (1986) lists the three characteristics of a good business game as (1) a case history of the industry and company in which the management team is going to operate; (2) a set of realistic rules guiding business decisions, requiring the participants to propose certain decisions at certain times and refrain from using price fixing and other similar controls; and (3) a computerized mathematical model that simulates a dynamic market, which allows the decisions of each team to influence the decisions of every other competing team. In the actual job setting it might take years to get the same feedback on a decision.

Some of the advantages of games over other training methods are that games are reusable, participants are more positive about games than about lectures, and the competition among participants tends to result in a high degree of involvement (Camp, Blanchard, & Huszczo, 1986). One popular game, Looking Glass, is played with a small group of top managers or business owners who run an imaginary company for a few days while being supervised by professional trainers (McAteer, 1991).

Programmed Instruction **Programmed instruction** is an individualized method of instruction that is based on the principles of operant conditioning discussed earlier in the chapter. Active practice of the material helps trainees learn and appears to be critical to the success of this method (Miller & Malott, 1997). Each statement in the program represents a frame or step in learning. The correct answers to each step are revealed after the trainee writes in an answer.

Programmed instruction often is confused with computerized instruction methods, perhaps because programmed instruction often is done using a computer, although printed booklets can be used as well. Many student study guides used in high schools and colleges are based on programmed instruction. Typically, programmed instruction has not been found to increase training scores or job performance scores, but the time used for training usually is decreased, resulting in cost savings (Nash, Muczyk, & Vettare, 1971). Since this is an individualized method, it may be a good choice when the total number of learners is high but there are only a few students at a time in many different locations.

One way to overcome the problem of pacing for different trainees is to use branching rather than linear programs. **Linear programs** require everyone to go through the same small steps to the end of the program. **Branching programs** channel the trainee into different segments (branches) of the program on the basis of the correctness of each answer. If a correct answer is given, the program goes on to a new area. If an incorrect answer is given, the program goes to another

Programmed instruction
An individualized method of instruction that is based on the principles of operant conditioning.

Linear programs
Programmed instruction methods that require everyone to go through the same small steps to the end of the program.

Branching programs
Programmed instruction methods that channel the trainee into different segments (branches) of the program on the basis of the correctness of each answer.

Computer-assisted instruction (CAI) Learning methods that are computer-based.

branch that provides further practice in development of the same concept. Computer-based programmed instruction is useful for training that changes often because of developments in technology that must be learned by employees such as computer technicians.

Computer-Assisted Instruction **Computer-assisted instruction (CAI)** refers to a number of training methods that are computer-based. The programmed instruction discussed in the previous section is a common use of CAI. In addition to its ability to make changes in the programs easily, CAI offers more possibilities for combining video and animation and creating student interest in the process. Do you remember the typing or keyboarding classes you took that seemed to involve endless typing drills? Instead of doing repetitive drills, you now can learn to type with CAI programs such as *Mavis Beacon Teaches Typing,* which do the same drills but make them computer-based games. As in programmed instruction, the steps are small and you receive frequent feedback and reinforcement for improvement.

Many of the advantages of CAI are similar to those of programmed instruction: providing a learning structure, giving immediate performance feedback, and allowing permanent record keeping of students' learning progress (Yaber & Malott, 1993). CAI also can help students gain confidence in their abilities through untiring repetitions. As organizations become more globally diverse, CAI instruction may become the method of choice for training in a wide spread of locations. However, it is important to maintain some human elements in the training situation; most adults report that they do not like being taught exclusively by a machine (Goldstein, 1993). The problem of employees being intimidated by computers may decrease in the future as more people use computers on and off the job.

One of the biggest drawbacks to CAI is the cost. The Office of Technology Assessment of the U.S. Congress estimated the cost of developing a CAI program at $1,000 to $10,000 for hardware and $50 to $10,000 for software and other materials. The time needed to develop the program was 8 to 300 hours (Rae, 1994). The same study indicated that 44 percent of the companies surveyed were using some computer-based training. The cost may decrease if programs can be used by more than one organization.

Among the newest audiovisual concepts are interactive videodisc, CD-ROM, and Electronic Performance Support System (EPSS) instruction. EPSS is a sophisticated and computer-based training system that helps employees learn to perform a task quickly with minimal supervision; it is receiving increasing attention among organizational trainers. These systems are more expensive variations of a computer-based training program. The use of touch-based screens and other interactive hardware allows trainees to select one of several choices of actions to follow a videotape segment they have just watched. The next videotape segment they see is based on their choice. Trainees can choose to go back and try different actions in combination with new choices and then see the results of those choices.

Preliminary research indicates that interactive videodisc instruction is an effective educational medium that is received positively by students (Pollard, 1992). One researcher (Yoder, 1993) compared learning of sterile medical techniques in linear video and in interactive video situations. The group trained by interactive video showed the greatest transfer of cognitive learning to actual skill performance in a clinical setting.

One advantage of this method lies in the ease of use and the interaction between the trainee and the presentation. The interaction required depends on the type of material being presented. Another advantage appears to be the shorter time needed for training. Several studies have shown similar gains in accuracy scores between computer-based and traditional training methods (Lee, Rutecki, Whittier, Clarett, & Jarjoura, 1997; Williams & Zahed, 1996). If the time reduction is substantial and there are conditions such as the need to train many employees a few at a time, interactive video training may be worth the cost. Despite the high cost of development, up to half the companies in a survey of professional training programs said they were using some form of this training method (*Training and Development*, 1998).

EVALUATION OF TRAINING PROGRAMS

Earlier in this chapter it was noted that in 1996 companies with over 100 employees were spending over $55.3 billion a year for training. Were they getting their money's worth? The need for measurement of training success has become more important for organizations. A study by Bell and Kerr (1987) indicated that although 90 percent of the training directors they surveyed thought it was important to do training evaluations, they did not do them because their companies did not require any evaluation of training. In 1997 an American Society for Training and Development (ASTD) executive survey showed that 90 percent of organizations were evaluating at least some of their training courses (American Society for Training and Development, 1997). The most commonly evaluated were customer service training courses, and the least frequently evaluated were awareness training courses. In general, companies were much more likely to measure training inputs, such as expenditures, rather than outcomes.

Training Evaluation Criteria

For over twenty years the standard framework for categorizing training criteria has been the one developed by Kirkpatrick (1998), which includes four levels of training effectiveness: reactions, learning, behavior, and organizational results.

Reactions measure the feelings of trainees toward the training and the training program. This is the most common type of training evaluation. The 1997 ASTD survey indicated that over 90 percent of organizations evaluate their courses at this level. Reaction assessments may be worded as fairly as possible, but the basic question remains: "Do you feel you got anything for the time and money you spent?" Most people like to think that they are well-informed consumers, and so even if they did not learn much, they might still say that they did. One author referred to reaction criteria as "love letters," adding that unless the training was really horrendous, love letters are all that reaction evaluations are likely to produce.

Learning measures the knowledge and skills actually mastered and the attitudes that were changed in the training program. For behavioral skills such as how to drive a truck, the learning is observable and its measurement is straightforward. In contrast, when the learning consists of greater self-awareness from outdoor experiential training, measurement becomes more difficult because the learning is more cognitive, or unobservable. The 1997 ASTD survey indicated that about 50 percent of the organizations used the learning level of evaluation.

Behavior measures performance back on the job in terms of the changes that occur after training. If the goal is to reduce accidents and the accident rate is lower on the job after training, behavior has been measured. This level of measurement was reported by about 30 percent of the organizations in the 1997 ASTD study.

Organizational results measure whether the cost of the training is justified by the organizational financial benefit of the training compared to the cost savings or greater profit generated after the training. This highest level of evaluation was used by only about 25 percent of the companies in the 1997 ASTD survey. Many factors other than the cost of the trainer and materials influence both cost and profit. For example, there is the cost of time away from work during training. There is also the cost back on the job before the employees reach peak productivity. These measures are easy to figure compared with measuring the value of training that focuses on outcomes such as team cohesiveness and greater self-awareness.

Although these four levels have been the standard of evaluation for a number of years, newer research suggests that they may not be the best choice in all situations. Holton (1996) criticizes the Kirkpatrick four-level model for failing to include intervening variables such as motivation, trainability, job attitudes, personal characteristics, and transfer of training conditions. He also points out the relatively small amount of research done on the Kirkpatrick model. Part of the reason why evaluation is not done thoroughly may be that organizations are not clear about the specific changes that should be expected from trainee learning and the assessment methods that are appropriate for those expectations. The 1997 ASTD survey indicated that over 50 percent of executives at companies that used the Kirkpatrick model perceived a lack of information on the evaluation and measurement of training programs. Kraiger, Ford, and Salas (1993) looked at complex learning theories and suggested that it would be more appropriate to assess the learning produced by training by examining three different types of outcomes: cognitive, skill-based, and affective (Figure 11.4).

Cognitive learning outcomes A method of assessing training that looks at verbal knowledge, how that knowledge is organized, and how it can be applied.

Cognitive learning outcomes look at verbal knowledge, how that knowledge is organized, and how it can be applied. Verbal knowledge may involve giving a

Figure 11.4
Methods of evaluating training effectiveness.

KIRKPATRICK'S FOUR LEVELS OF TRAINING

| Reactions | Learning | Behavior results | Organizational results |

KRAIGER, FORD, AND SALAS'S OUTCOMES OF LEARNING

Cognitive Outcomes

- Verbal knowledge
- Knowledge organization
- Cognitive strategies

Skill-Based Outcomes

- Faster, more fluid behaviors
- Automatic processing of new behaviors

Affective Outcomes

- Attitudes
- Motivation
  Disposition
  Self-efficacy
  Goal setting

trainee a test to see if she can name all the parts of a computer's central processing unit. The organization of the knowledge of that trainee may be assessed by testing to find out if she knows the correct sequence for adding sound and video enhancements to the computer. Application may be assessed by finding out if the trainee can answer questions about other ways to add sound to a computer if all the sound card openings are filled or why the computer will not work correctly if the correct sequence for installation is not followed.

The second category, **skill-based learning outcomes,** concerns the development of technical or motor skills, such as driving a truck. The three steps of this outcome are skill acquisition, the development of faster and more flowing behavior, and reaching the stage at which the behavior becomes almost automatic. For truck driving, being able to demonstrate turning, shifting, and other driving abilities can indicate skill acquisition. In the second stage the trainee can shift gears smoothly without concentrating on shifting while pressing the clutch and releasing the gas pedal. In the last stage the trainee can drive the truck competently while listening to the radio or can change speeds on a slippery road.

The third category, **affectively based outcomes,** concerns the measurement of attitudes and motivation. Attitudinal learning can be used to measure changes in values involving safety practices after a training program. These are usually

Skill-based learning outcomes An assessment of the development of technical or motor skills during training.

Affectively based outcomes An assessment of the development of attitudes and motivation during training.

self-reports from the trainees. Changes in motivational learning can be assessed by comparing the goal-setting abilities of trainees before and after a management training program. In general, participation in work-required training programs appears to increase job satisfaction and organizational commitment (Birdi, Allan, & Warr, 1997).

The three-part outcome system has a number of elements in common with the Kirkpatrick model, but it also has a number of advantages. This model sees each of the parts as being related to the others. Changing one type of outcome can produce changes in another outcome. Learning about the parts of a safety system may increase positive attitudes toward promoting safety at work. Kraiger, Ford, and Salas (1993) also believe that their outcome-based system will lead to a more accurate statement of training objectives and better demonstrations of the validity of training programs—that is, whether the programs do what they are supposed to do.

The issue of validity of training programs raises the question of how to measure whether training programs have worked; a number of experimental designs have been used.

Design of Training Evaluation Models

Posttest-Only Design

The easiest way to assess the validity of training is to give the trainees a test after training and see if they can do something that is required. This is called a **posttest-only design.** For example, after receptionists are trained in telephone-answering skills, the percentage of calls handled correctly could be recorded. The addition of a control group that did not receive training would show how much of the recorded change resulted from the training program. The problem with this method is that no information is provided about the level of performance before training.

Pretest–Posttest Design

One way to correct this problem is to give a test before training as well as after training. This is called a **pretest–posttest design.** For the receptionists this would mean recording the percentage of correctly handled calls before and after training. The problem with this design is that one cannot be sure that the training, not a variable such as new equipment, caused the change. The use of a control group that was not trained but had its phone calls recorded during the same period would rule out many of the other variables. This is better than the other methods, but it still leaves some questions. What if the nontraining group were aware that it was being deprived of training? That might make those employees work less and record lower scores at the end of training. Goldstein (1993) raises the question of timing for the posttest measure. If it is done immediately after training,

Posttest-only design
Training assessment that measures behavior only after training.

Pretest–posttest design
Training assessment that measures behavior before and after training.

there is no measure of on-the-job performance. Goldstein suggests using a second posttest measure some time after the trainees are back on the job.

Solomon Four-Group Design

The most sophisticated and most complicated method of training deals with these problems as well as the previously mentioned ones. This method is called the **Solomon Four-Group Design** (Solomon, 1949). The name comes from the use of four separate, randomly assigned groups: two control groups and two training groups. One control group and one training group are given pretests before training, and then both are given posttests after the latter group has completed its training. The other training and control groups are given posttests only, after the training group has been trained. These last two groups will allow the researchers to find out if just being aware that training is being conducted causes any effects. A comparison of these methods is given in Table 11.2.

Although the general preference of researchers is to choose the strongest research method possible, some research has suggested that the best method is determined partially by what questions must be addressed by training. Sackett and Mullen (1993) indicated that when the purpose of training is to certify a particular level of performance, such as the ability to perform certain safety skills, a posttest-only design with no control group may be adequate.

Solomon Four-Group Design A rigorous training assessment that measures behavior in a variety of situations before and after training.

Table 11.2

METHODS OF TRAINING PROGRAM EVALUATION

Design	Groups	How Groups Are Assigned	Pretraining Measurement	Posttraining Measurement
Posttest only	Trainees	Random or representative sample	No	Yes
Pretest–Posttest	Trainees	Random or representative sample	Yes	Yes
Posttest only Control group	Trainees Controls	Random Random	No No	Yes Yes
Pretest–posttest Control group	Trainees Controls	Random Random	Yes Yes	Yes Yes
Solomon Four-Group	Trainees A Trainees B Controls A Controls B	Random Random Random Random	Yes No Yes No	Yes Yes Yes Yes

Adapted from R. R. Camp, P. N. Blanchard, & G. E. Huszczo. (1986). *Toward a more organizationally effective training strategy.* Englewood Cliffs, NJ: Prentice-Hall, p. 159.

Cost of Training Evaluation

As with many other programs, an important component of training success is the cost of the program. There are many costs to training other than the obvious ones of the materials and the trainer. Among the factors listed in one study (Arvey, Maxwell, & Salas, 1992) were subject costs, such as time away from work, administrative costs, and item development. If these costs lead to significant improvements in performance, this is money well spent. The 1997 ASTD study of training practices in the highest- and lowest-performing companies showed greater training expenditures and a higher percentage of employees trained among the top-performing companies.

More recently, Internet-based training resources such as newsletters and actual courses have been developed (Greenblatt, 1997) to increase access to training and decrease the costs. The case study "Training Works Online" discusses one company's investment in Internet-based learning. The Web exercise at the end of the chapter gives you a chance to try on-line training yourself. It is possible to train to become a certified technical trainer by using Internet-based resources.

[Case Study] TRAINING WORKS ON-LINE

What happens when a company decides to distribute its service representatives across the country and 1,200 new and reassigned employees need to be trained? This is the question Aetna U.S. Healthcare faced in late 1996. David Blair, the training director, calculated that face-to-face training would cost $5 million for travel. He quickly investigated on-line training as the solution to this problem. After testing three different on-line training suppliers for six months, Aetna chose Ilinc of Troy, New York. The educational costs and software upgrades cost $450,000.

The employees and trainers were initially nervous about the new system, and early training sessions were marked by software and hardware problems. The employees wanted to know how they would get their questions answered, and the trainers were fearful that the technology would eliminate the need for their interpersonal skills. Actually, the skill of the trainers became a critical factor in the success of the program. The trainers found that long training sessions on the Web did not hold the trainees' attention. They changed the lessons into fifteen-minute sessions, with a *Jeopardy* type of game used to review the session.

Was it worth the effort? For Aetna, the answer is a definite yes. Aetna figures that it has saved $3 million so far and is expanding the system throughout customer services. The employees taught on the Web-based system scored 4 percent higher on training achievement tests than did workers who were taught face to face. The employees liked the short sessions and interactive materials. One trainee said, "I feel freer to ask questions." Another pointed out, "The teacher won't catch you if you yawn."

From L. Kroll. (1999, March 8). Good morning, HAL. *Forbes.* http://www.forbes.com/forbes/99/0308/6305118a.htm.

Some research has suggested methods that make utility analysis possible (Cascio, 1989; Deitchman, 1990; Mathieu & Leonard, 1987). Although the formulas are rather complicated, the ability to evaluate bottom line effectiveness has added another dimension to the evaluation of training.

Even if bottom line measures look only at direct costs, such as the cost of training materials compared with profit or savings, they still give information about the worth of training. One example of an organization that completely turned around its financial situation through a commitment to training illustrates this kind of evaluation. In ten years the Houston-based Wallace Company went from the edge of failure to winning a national award for quality in the workplace. The main change consisted of a companywide training program that everyone from the chief executive officer to warehouse workers had a role in developing. In a three-year period the direct cost of the training program was over $700,000, but sales rose from $52 million to $90 million, making the training a very profitable investment (Galagan, 1991). As with any case study, it is difficult to say that the commitment to training was totally responsible for the turnaround, but case studies in combination with methods such as those discussed in this chapter can provide the information needed to make good decisions about training at work.

MAIN POINTS

- Training and development as done by I/O psychologists consolidate knowledge from many other psychological specialties.
- Training usually means education in a particular skill or job.
- Common training purposes include increasing basic skills and literacy, orienting new employees, and providing continuing education and retirement planning.
- Training needs are assessed through the use of organizational analysis, task analysis, and person analysis.
- Training objectives are behavioral statements of what should be accomplished by a particular training program.
- The major types of learning used in organizational training programs are operant conditioning, cognitive learning, and, much less frequently, classical conditioning.
- Some important variables in the learning process are shaping, transfer of training, massed versus distributed practice, whole versus part learning, and active practice of materials.
- Trainee variables include motivation, readiness to learn, resistance to training, and self-efficacy.
- The characteristics of the trainer influence the outcome of training.

- Training is done either on or off the job site.

- Methods of on-the-job-site training include on-the-job training, job instruction training, vestibule training, job rotation, apprenticeship, and mentoring.

- Off-site training uses either nontechnology methods (lectures, role playing, behavior modeling, sensitivity training, case studies, conference training, the incident method, and outdoor experiential training) or technology-based methods such as audiovisual training, simulation training, business games, programmed instruction, and computer-assisted instruction.

- Training programs must be evaluated to judge their effectiveness. Usually they are evaluated by using the criteria identified by Kirkpatrick, which include re-actions, learning, behavior, and organizational results.

- Since many organizations do not use all Kirkpatrick's criteria, other researchers have suggested that cognitive, skill-based, and affective outcomes or criteria are more relevant.

- The major experimental designs for evaluating training programs are posttest-only design, pretest–posttest design, and the Solomon Four-Group Design.

- The organizational cost of training is an important factor in evaluating the training process.

KEY TERMS

Active practice	Mentoring
Affectively based outcomes	On-the-job training
Apprenticeship training	Operant conditioning
Behavior modeling	Organizational needs analysis
Branching programs	Outdoor experiential training (OET)
Career development	Person needs analysis
Case study training	Posttest-only design
Classical conditioning	Pretest–posttest design
Cognitive learning outcomes	Programmed instruction
Computer-assisted instruction (CAI)	Reinforcers
Conference training	Resistance to training
Continuous reinforcement	Retraining
Cross-training	Role playing
Distributed practice	Self-efficacy
Job instruction training	Sensitivity training
Job rotation	Simulation training
Linear programs	Skill-based learning outcomes
Massed practice	Solomon Four-Group Design

Task needs analysis
Training
Transfer of training

Vestibule training
Virtual reality
Whole and part learning

Answers to these questions can be found at the end of the book.

1. Over 65 percent of the American workforce is involved in some type of training each year.

   a. True   b. False

2. Which of the following can explain why little research has been done on organizational training programs?

   a. Top management does not care if it is done.

   b. There is a large labor pool that requires very little training.

   c. No one in the organization is trained in research methods.

   d. All of the above

   e. None of the above

3. The amount of the resources allocated to workplace literacy training is decreasing because the workforce is becoming more educated.

   a. True   b. False

4. The four developmental stages in an employee's career are

   a. _____.

   b. _____.

   c. _____.

   d. _____.

5. The three types of training needs analysis are

   a. _____.

   b. _____.

   c. _____.

6. A list of the knowledge, skills, and abilities needed to be a lens grinder at an optical company would be developed from which of the following?

   a. Person analysis

   b. Organizational analysis

   c. Job analysis

   d. Career analysis

7. Training objectives
   a. must be formulated before a needs analysis so that the organization knows what needs to look for.
   b. should be very general to cover as many training situations as possible.
   c. must be written in operational terms.
   d. cover only job analysis needs.

8. Learning that is based on the use of punishment or reinforcement right after the performance of a behavior is called
   a. classical conditioning.
   b. operant conditioning.
   c. transfer of training.
   d. oppositional conditioning.

9. The newest type of learning applied to organizational training is _____ _____.

10. Unless training is done directly on the job, transfer of training must always be considered.
    a. True   b. False

11. One problem with negative transfer of training is
    a. extra training time required because training is not done on the job.
    b. irregular use of reinforcers.
    c. inability to train more than one person at a time.
    d. false belief by the trainees that they actually know the skill.

12. Operant conditioning focuses on _____ behaviors, and cognitive learning focuses on _____ processes.

13. Research has found that trainees are successful in training programs regardless of their personal beliefs about the likelihood of success.
    a. True   b. False

14. What is the name of the professional organization for training trainers?

    _____

15. One of the greatest advantages to training on the job site is the transfer of training.
    a. True   b. False

16. Which of the following training methods gives the trainee a chance to learn several jobs?

    a. Job rotation

    b. Vestibule training

    c. Mentoring

    d. Job instruction training

17. The four steps of job instruction training are

    a. _____,

    b. _____,

    c. _____,

    d. _____.

18. Which of the following is a disadvantage of role playing?

    a. There is little trainee participation.

    b. The trainee may play the role to impress the instructor and the other trainees.

    c. There may be bad emotional consequences.

    d. It is very expensive.

19. The main goal of sensitivity training is to expose emotional weaknesses among trainees to prevent them from being emotionally weak on the job.

    a. True   b. False

20. If you are in a training session where the trainer tells you about an actual organization and the problems it currently has and then asks you to develop a solution, you probably are being trained using an _____ _____.

21. In which training technique could you be bitten by a snake or squirrel? _____ _____ _____

22. Two training methods that have been criticized for lack of minority trainees are

    a. job rotation and job instruction training.

    b. mentoring and apprenticeship.

    c. case studies and conference training.

    d. mentoring and outdoor experiential training.

23. If you learn to handle dynamite by training with nonexplosive sticks that look and feel like real dynamite, this is an example of

    a. audiovisual training.

    b. business games.

    c. computer-assisted instruction.

    d. simulation training.

24. A method of training, similar to a case study, that has a group of trainees play roles in a fictional business for several hours or days is called a(n) _____ _____.

25. Programmed instruction can be done only on a computer.

    a. True   b. False

26. Almost half of all companies are using some form of computer-assisted training.

    a. True   b. False

27. A method of computer-assisted instruction that allows trainees to choose different actions and try out a number of different scenarios is

    a. interactive videodisc training.

    b. linear programs.

    c. on-the-job training.

    d. all of the above

28. According to Kirkpatrick, the four types of training evaluation criteria are

    a. _____,

    b. _____,

    c. _____,

    d. _____.

29. Which measure of training effectiveness is used most often?

    a. Reactions

    b. Skill-based measures

    c. Cognitive outcomes

    d. All of the above

30. Which training evaluation design model is the most expensive to use?

    a. Pretest–posttest

    b. Unequal random selection

    c. Pretest–posttest with a control group

    d. Solomon Four-Group

WEB EXERCISE

Is it possible to receive good training over the Internet? Use your browser to go to http://www.learnonnet.com/ and try any of the "demo" selections. How did you do? Report what you did and did not like about the training exercises. Do you think this is a good way to learn? Why? Compare this to the review questions at the end of each chapter in this book. Which do you prefer, and why?

The Work
Environment

Job and Work Design

Chapter Outline

LEARNING OBJECTIVES

INTRODUCTION TO HUMAN FACTORS PSYCHOLOGY

EQUIPMENT DESIGN
Role of the Human Factors Psychologist
Roles of People and Machines
Displays
Controls

WORKSPACE DESIGN
Psychological Factors in Workspace Design
Workplace Envelope

COMPUTERS AND HUMAN FACTORS
Erogonomic Computer Workspace Design
Problems in the Computer Workspace
Computer Hardware and Software
Attitudes toward Computer Use
Virtual Reality

ROBOTS AND HUMANS

NONTRADITIONAL WORK SCHEDULES
Shift Work
Compressed Workweek
Flextime
Job Sharing

WORKPLACE DESIGN
Open Offices
Telecommuting
Case Study Telecommuting Works

QUALITY OF WORK LIFE

Learning Objectives

After reading this chapter, you should be able to answer the following questions:

- What is human factors psychology (engineering psychology or ergonomics)?
- What is the role of human factors psychologists in equipment design?
- What are the advantages specific to machines and to people in person–machine systems?
- How can human factors psychologists make good displays (visual, auditory, tactile, and olfactory) and controls (affordance and compatibility issues)?
- What factors contribute to good workspace design?
- How do human factors psychologists improve the use of computers in the workplace? What are some of the typical problems?
- What nontraditional work schedules have become part of the workplace? How can they best be used?
- What can human factors psychologists do to improve office design and telecommuting?
- What are quality-of-work-life programs, and how are they used at work?

Job and work design is an interesting area in industrial/organizational (I/O) psychology because of the many changes that have taken place in this field since the early years of I/O psychology. As was discussed in earlier chapters of this book, job design received attention from Frederick Taylor, whose scientific management theory stated that people are extensions of the machines they operate. The focus in scientific management was on finding the most mechanically efficient way to do each work task, as in Taylor's study of coal shoveling. The goal was to make people more machinelike and reliable, not to adapt the machine to the human operator.

With the Hawthorne Studies and the realization that people are different from machines, the focus of job design changed to finding ways to get human operators to make the fewest errors. This became a critical element in World War II. The extensive use of highly sophisticated technology during the war made the consideration of the human operator critical to the success of person–machine systems.

I/O psychology is uniquely suited to study the ways in which people are likely to use a particular equipment feature, whether or not that use is what the designer intended. The consideration of both the person and the machine in current I/O psychology work also is seen as an application of systems theory (Chapter 3). Systems theory suggests that anything that is done to one part of a system or organization influences every other part of that system or organization. The systems theory approach has moved human factors considerations into a more organizational perspective. Rather than considering only how a single worker can do her job more efficiently, a researcher in the human factors field also would look at how that employee's work influences the work of others and the outcomes for the entire department or organization. The human factors field continues to be very much a part of applied I/O psychology. Most of the people who work in that field see themselves as practitioners rather than theorists. Among the over four thousand members of the Human Factors Society, only about 47 percent hold doctorates, indicating a strong emphasis on practical applications (Knowles, 1986).

This chapter looks at the large body of work that attempts to define the best way to design jobs and places of work. It is apparent that this issue has become increasingly complicated since Taylor's time. The chapter also examines the tremendous influence this area has had in recent years as computers, robots, and other technological innovations have become commonplace at work. Human factors specialists have also become increasingly involved in modifying the workplace to meet the requirements of the Americans with Disabilities Act. The increasing use of technology often has made it more difficult to determine which functions humans will do and which functions machines will do. It also has made the careful choice of functions even more critical. In 1992 the Federal Aviation Administration allocated $22.9 million for human factors research on the interaction between planes and pilots and other airline staff. Finally, the chapter looks at some of the alternative work arrangements that have been used increasingly in recent years, such as flextime scheduling and telecommuting.

INTRODUCTION TO HUMAN FACTORS PSYCHOLOGY

The area of job and equipment design for people is referred to as **human factors psychology** or **engineering psychology.** In Europe and Canada, the term **ergonomics** is used most often to refer to the human factors field. The concern of the field is the design of the job in person–machine systems. Howell describes the human factors concept as "an adoption of both human and physical perspectives when designing things for people to use, whether they be simple hand tools or computer hardware and software, sophisticated weapons systems or entire office complexes and space stations" (Howell, 1991, p. 210).

More recently, some psychologists have suggested expanding the scope of this field into the area of cognitive design (Dowell & Long, 1998). **Cognitive design engineering** refers to the part of work that involves thought processes and tools for thinking rather than directly measurable structures such as office furniture and video displays. An application of cognitive engineering might focus on the problem-solving strategies workers use in dealing with malfunctions in a manufacturing process.

Human factors psychology The study of person–machine systems in I/O psychology.

Engineering psychology The study of person–machine systems in I/O psychology.

Ergonomics A term used mostly in Europe and Canada to refer to the study of person–machine systems in I/O psychology.

Cognitive design engineering An extension of engineering psychology that concerns the part of work which involves thought processes and tools for thinking.

Sanders and McCormick (1993) list two major objectives for the human factors field:

1. To increase effectiveness and efficiency in work and work-related activities
2. To increase values that workers find desirable, such as increased safety, less fatigue and stress, more comfort in use, greater acceptance by the user, increased job satisfaction, and improved quality of life

This definition and the objectives just listed emphasize the design of equipment for people. However, this remains a problem, as the following section explains.

EQUIPMENT DESIGN

Psychologists know a great deal about good equipment design and tools for human use, but one may wonder whether anyone looks at this information. Have you ever accidentally pressed the wrong button on a video camera or VCR and erased or failed to record something important? You may feel that it was stupid to make such a mistake, but good equipment design would make an accident like that almost impossible. People expect tools and equipment to have been designed to operate correctly the first time, but as the book *The Psychology of Everyday Things* points out, it usually takes five or six attempts for designers to get the design of a new product right for human users (Norman, 1988).

Although people expect products to work correctly the first time, that does not always happen. When new versions of computer software are released, "fixes" for the software soon start appearing. These are corrections for design flaws that were not apparent or were ignored until users started complaining.

Role of the Human Factors Psychologist

Part of the design problem in person–machine systems involves the two separate and unlike components (the person and the machine) that must function together to produce a desired output. A car and a driver are a good example of this type of interaction (Figure 12.1). Any number of problems with the person or the machine can produce undesired results. If the driver pushes the gas pedal but the speedometer does not work correctly, the whole system may stop working correctly.

The use of human factors professionals in every step of the design of person–machine systems could improve the success rates of those systems. Meister (1987) suggests that human factors information should be used in each of the five steps of person–machine system development: (1) system planning, (2) preliminary design, (3) detail design, (4) testing and evaluation, and (5) production. In practice, most human factors involvement occurs during testing and evaluation or

Figure 12.1

The person-machine system.

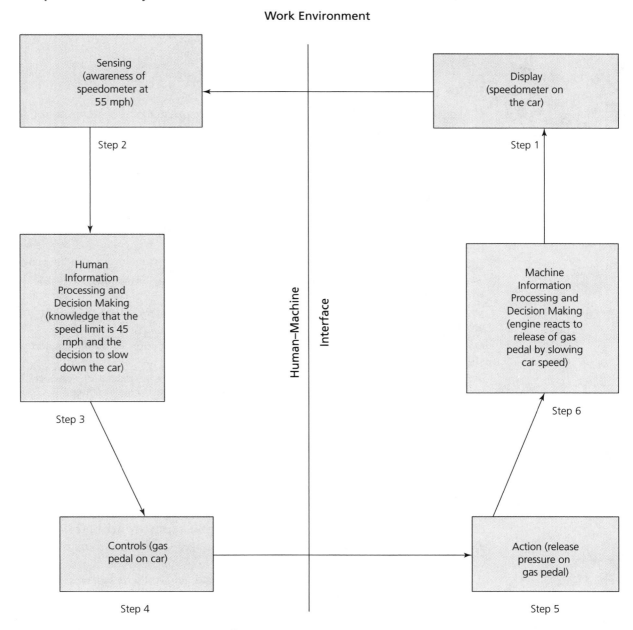

Adapted from W. C. Howell. (1991). Human factors in the workplace. In M. D. Dunnette & L. M. Hough (Eds.), *Handbook of industrial and organizational psychology* (p. 214). Palo Alto, CA: Consulting Psychologists Press.

after production, when the system is made operational. Howell (1991) believes that more organizations will decide to involve human factors professionals earlier in the design process as the number of lawsuits involving faulty design increases. Before the recent increase in such lawsuits, managers may have seen human factors specialists as spoilers of their elegant mechanical designs rather than partners in trying to develop the best system.

Roles of People and Machines

One of the first steps in the design process for person–machine systems is to decide which tasks the person will do and which ones the machine will do. Clearly, people have certain advantages over machines, just as machines have certain advantages over people (Table 12.1).

Table 12.1
ADVANTAGES OF HUMANS AND MACHINES IN PERSON–MACHINE SYSTEMS

Human Advantages	Machine Advantages
Better at dealing with events that occur very infrequently or are very unusual Better at interpreting meaning	Better at operating in a very hostile or dangerous setting, such as inside a nuclear reactor
More creative and unusual solutions to problems	Better at functioning for longer periods without fatigue
More flexible and better able to learn from errors and change	Fewer processing errors in calculations and other functions
Better at detecting a signal despite different noise factors, even at low levels	Stronger, react faster, and detect signals outside the range of human senses

The best person–machine systems combine the strengths of each part of the system and apply the best use of the system. For example, large radio telescopes systematically scan the heavens for unusual signals. When such a signal is detected, human operators decide whether it is a message from another world or random noise. However, that choice is not as straightforward as it sounds, and different interpretations have led to debates about extraterrestrial life. Back on earth, awareness of human and machine advantages can lead to more efficient and safer design of person–machine systems.

Drury and Sinclair (1983) predicted that machines would be better at detecting and measuring deformities in small steel cylinders because a machine can inspect parts more rapidly and identify flaws better than humans can. Those researchers found that the human inspectors outperformed the machines, however. The actual work task often required the humans to judge whether a particular combination of defects was serious enough to reject the cylinder, and those combined judgments were much better done by people.

For someone to process information correctly within a person–machine system, that person must be able to interpret the information from some type of display accurately and then use controls to operate the machine. The next section looks at the use of displays and controls to produce an effective person–machine system.

Displays

Display is the presentation of information to the human operator in a person–machine system. A human factors professional most often becomes involved when the information is presented indirectly. If a pilot watches a dial indicating the height of the plane rather than directly observing the plane scraping the top of a thirty-foot high tree, that is an indirect display.

Although presenting information to a person can involve any of the senses, the most common displays are visual or auditory or both, depending on the information that must be communicated. Visual displays should be chosen if the information is complex, if the message is long and can be dealt with later, and if it is too noisy for the person to hear a message. Auditory displays are better if the message is simple and short, if it must be taken care of immediately, and if the person receiving the message does not stay in one place (Sanders & McCormick, 1993). For example, a fire alarm would be better as an auditory display, but the directions for installing new computer hardware would be better as a visual display.

Visual Displays

Most people are familiar with a number of visual displays, such as the timer on a microwave oven and the speedometer in a car. One of the greatest success stories in human factors design was the change from the use of low-mounted brake lights on cars to the addition of one or more high center-mounted brake lights now required on all new cars sold in the United States. It has been estimated that when all cars are equipped with high center-mounted brake lights, 126,000 accidents, 80,000 fatal injuries, and almost $1 billion in property damage will be prevented each year, at the cost of just over $10 for each brake light (Sanders & McCormick, 1993).

The major issues in designing visual displays are (1) making sure the visual display really represents the information that needs to be presented, such as the direction in which a plane is turning, and (2) choosing the physical properties of the visual display, such as color. How well the display represents the information and the usefulness of the physical properties is based on the principle of mapping. **Mapping** is the relationship between the real world and the display. In one early airplane display, the visual information about the level of the wings was displayed as if the pilot were looking head on at another plane in a mirror image of what was

Display The presentation of information to the human operator in a person–machine system.

Mapping The relationship between a display and the real world.

Head-up display (HUD)
A display that gives visual information without requiring changing the level of one's eyes.

Annunciator A display that announces a change that requires immediate attention.

occurring in his plane. Until the display was changed to appear to be looking from the rear of the plane, numerous accidents resulted from pilots not mentally reversing the display image. Norman (1988) suggests that the best mapping is a natural arrangement of the display. Pilots look out from the cockpit of the plane, and so a good visual display should show that natural arrangement.

People typically recognize pictures more quickly than they recognize textual information, and so if time is a concern, pictures are a better choice for the display. It was found in one study that drivers could identify standard symbol signs about two times farther away than text signs (Kline & Fuchs, 1993). Keeping information in each visual display simple aids in correctly interpreting the display. In a complex structure such as a college classroom building, signs inside the building are more helpful than maps such as those given out during college orientation sessions (Butler, Acquino, Hissong, & Scott, 1993).

Another feature that can enhance the accurate interpretation of visual displays is the standard placement of the display, such as the display used for speedometers in cars. One problem with the speedometer is the necessity of taking one's eyes off the road and looking down to see the readings. Although drivers generally become good at glancing down for a second to look at the speedometer, driving performance could be improved if the display were at eye level. A **head-up display (HUD)** gives visual information without the necessity of changing eye level. In an experiment with HUD dashboard-mounted in-vehicle guidance system, drivers showed quicker reaction times than they did with a similar head-down display (Scrinivasan & Jovanis, 1997). Research on guidance systems in vehicles is important because those systems have not yet become standard in cars and it may be possible to find the best placement for the systems before they become standardized in less desirable locations.

The choice of color and the placement of the displays can add to the correct interpretation of a visual display. Chapanis (1994) found that red was perceived as indicating the greatest level of hazard, followed by orange, yellow, and white. Think about the visual displays on your car, such as the oil light. Do they use these colors correctly? A warning that does not appear unless the conditions change from normal to abnormal is called an **annunciator** because it announces a change that requires immediate attention. Most people would not look at an oil level gauge every minute or so to make sure that it was in the correct range but would pay quick attention to a flashing red signal.

Auditory Displays

Most car malfunctions are shown as visual displays, but it might be better to use auditory displays for the most critical malfunctions. As research cited earlier in this section showed, auditory displays are usually better than visual displays when immediate attention is required. Although very loud auditory signals are effective in getting people's attention, the nature of the sound used as a signal also influences how quickly a response is made. When Adams and Trucks (1976) tested a number of different warning noises ("wail," "beep," "whoop," "yeow," etc.), they found that the "yeow" and "beep" sounds produced the quickest reaction time. As towns and villages install new storm warning sirens, they are making use of this information.

The best auditory displays can be separated from background noise easily. One of the problems that contributed to the near disaster at the Three Mile Island nuclear plant in the late 1970s was having so many malfunctions indicated by similar auditory displays. At one point, over sixty separate auditory alarms were sounding, and the staff could not tell which ones were the most critical; this contributed to the failure to make the correct responses in time. Have you ever gone to answer the telephone and found that the ringing was on the television or radio? Like visual displays, auditory displays should be limited to the information needed for the person to make a response. The new fire alarm system at my college has a loud intermittent horn, a flashing white light, and speakers to broadcast messages. During one emergency evacuation the speakers were used to direct people to each of over forty building exits. The result was chaos as people tried to process too much auditory information. Now the alarm speakers are used to direct people to look at the evacuation map in each room to find the nearest exit. This is a much better use of an auditory signal. The reason for three systems (alarm, light, and speaker) was to make sure that everyone, including those with disabilities, would be warned. It turned out to be quicker to have other students assist the visually impaired students instead of having them listen to all the directions.

Tactile and Olfactory Displays

Although other senses are used far less than the visual and auditory senses for displays, at particular times tactile (touch) or olfactory (smell) displays may be the best choice. Tactile displays most often are used as substitutes for other kinds of displays, as in the vibrating pagers many people use.

Olfactory displays are limited in usefulness because of individual differences in the response to smells. A stuffy nose can limit olfactory sensitivity, and most people quickly adapt to new smells and stop attending to them. One of the most common olfactory signals is the addition of an odorant to natural gas so that if the stove or oven is on with no flame, a person can respond to the situation before any harm occurs. Many homes and apartments have auditory carbon monoxide detectors because that gas is odorless and has been responsible for many deaths.

Controls

Although the display gives information so that the person can make a decision, the person has to take action to make the machine respond. This is the purpose

Control The part of a person–machine system operated by the person to get the machine to do something.

Affordance The degree to which a control device allows only the intended use.

Compatibility The degree to which a control meets a person's expectations for its behavior.

Spatial compatibility The degree to which a control represents action in the real world.

Movement compatibility The degree to which moving a control represents movement in the real world.

of **controls,** which are used by the person to get the machine to do something. The gas pedal in a car is a type of control, as is the mouse on a computer. Most people do not think about good control design, because the control works and gets the job done well. When people do think about control design, it is usually because they are frustrated by bad design, such as a bathroom faucet that turns in the wrong direction. Some of the most important factors in good control design are affordance, compatibility, standardization, and the ability to choose the correct control.

Affordance

Affordance is the degree to which a control device's properties, such as shape and form, lead to the one intended use for the device. A doorbell with a single button is high in affordance because it is difficult to think of anything to do other than push the button. The best affordances give very strong clues about what the correct action should be. Door hardware often shows affordance problems. If a door has a handle, that suggests that the door can be opened by using the handle. The college where I work has a set of doors between two wings that have push bars on the inside and door handles on the outside. Only the inside push bars work for emergency exists, and this leads to students being caught in the courtyard between the wings when the outside handles do not work. The latest solution to this problem is the addition of a sign explaining that the door can be opened only from the inside. Norman (1992) says that a clear indication of an affordance problem is the addition of a sign to the device. The principle of affordance might suggest that all hardware be removed from the doors and the doors be designed to open electronically in an emergency.

Compatibility

Compatibility indicates how much the relationships between the person's actions and the machines' behavior are consistent with what people expect. High compatibility comes when a right turn on a car's steering wheel turns the car to the right. With low compatibility, the car would turn left when the wheel is turned right.

Sanders and McCormick (1993) list a number of important compatibility features, including spatial compatibility and movement compatibility. **Spatial compatibility** refers to the physical similarity between the controls and displays or the arrangement of the displays and controls. **Movement compatibility** refers to the degree to which moving a control represents movement in the real world.

Physical similarity relates to the mapping logic that was discussed earlier in this chapter. The example of the display that showed the plane in a mirror image of the view of the pilot out of the cockpit had poor physical similarity. A computer mouse that moves the cursor to the right when the mouse is moved to the right is an example of good physical similarity.

Arranging controls and displays to meet natural mapping requirements appears to be an easy task, but most machines are designed by mechanical designers, not human factors specialists. Although it might be mechanically efficient to put the controls for an electric stove in one line on the top of the stove, that is an arrangement that often leads to errors about which burner has been turned on. Avoiding arrangement problems is one of the reasons for the suggestion earlier in this chapter that human factors specialists be involved in the first steps in the design process. If you wanted to squirt fluid on the car windshield to clean the window, where is the first place you would look for the control? If your answer is that it should be close to the control for the windshield wiper, you are showing a good sense of human factors design.

An interesting example of purposefully violating these arrangement principles comes from word processor and computer keyboards. The most commonly used keyboards are called QWERTY keyboards from the arrangement of letters on one of the rows of keys. This keyboard makes some of the most frequently used keys the most difficult to reach (the "a" key, for example) and therefore slows down the typing action. This solved the problem with early typists who could type faster than the keys could return to their places, causing the typewriters to jam. Since jamming is no longer a problem, it would make sense to rearrange keyboards to resemble the Dvorak keyboard shown in Figure 12.2. While typists learned the new keyboard, performance would be lower. It is hard to change a hundred years of experience and equipment, but experienced typists could make a successful switch to the Dvorak arrangement. New typists would not have any behaviors to unlearn. The only keyboard design change that seems to be taking hold is switching to a split and tilted keyboard that allows a more natural wrist angle and causes less wrist and arm strain.

Although the QWERTY keyboard arrangement is not the most efficient, it illustrates the principle of standardization. When I switch from my computer at home to the one at the college and then to my laptop, I still have the same keyboard arrangement. Even if there is no logic, the standardization of a control can make it easier to operate. Many years ago my father taught me the jingle "Righty tighty, lefty loosey" to teach me the standardized way to turn screws and bolts.

Although it is good human factors design to have controls for similar actions grouped together, it is also important to be able to tell the difference between the controls and thus choose the correct one. My clock radio has four buttons in a single group, and too often I end up resetting the time rather than turning on the radio to play for an hour. Changing the first button to a bar would help prevent resetting the clock by accident.

Figure 12.2

QWERTY and Dvorak keyboard arrangements.

QWERTY KEYBOARD

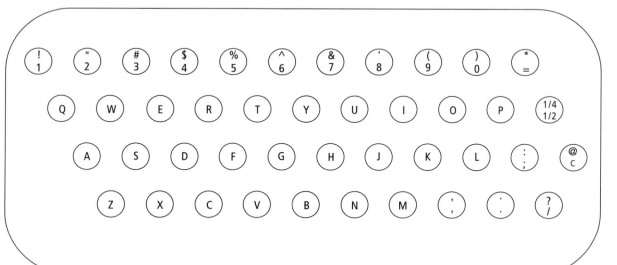

DVORAK SIMPLIFIED KEYBOARD

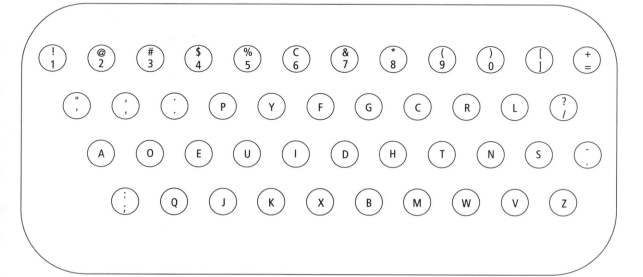

WORKSPACE DESIGN

Starting with Taylor, much of the work of human factors specialists focused only on correct equipment design. As the use of technology increased and became an integrated part of the workplace, it became apparent that the entire workspace had to be considered from a human factors perspective. Tom Wolfe in *The Right Stuff* discusses how the early capsules that were used to send humans into space had been designed to carry chimpanzees. The chimpanzees were strapped into the capsule to prevent them from moving around or changing any controls. When astronauts who were experienced test pilots replaced the chimpanzees, they wanted to be able to control some actions from inside the capsule, and so design changes were made to reduce frustration. The viewing window was placed in front of the astronauts rather than behind them. The astronauts were allowed to choose whether to leave the craft for a small rubber boat after the craft landed in the ocean or to stay in the capsule. These changes in workspace design changed feelings of frustration to feelings of satisfaction.

Psychological Factors in Workspace Design

It is relatively easy to base the physical design of the workspace on the physical features of average humans, but it is more difficult to include the psychological traits of people. Even when the technology works, psychological factors can prevent the best use of the equipment. A considerable amount of study has gone into designing office furniture to provide the physically best design for employees. Researchers found that when workers were allowed to adjust equipment to their own settings, even when those settings were less physically correct, workplace improvements occurred (Vink & Kompier, 1997).

Workplace Envelope

Workspace design focuses on two broad areas: the workplace envelope, which will be considered here, and the general office design, which will be looked at later in the chapter. The **workplace envelope** is the three-dimensional space in which a single individual works or, more generally, the space in which that person uses his or her hands. For the early astronauts, the interior of the small space capsule was the workplace envelope; for the American driver, it is the front left side of the car.

The goal of human factors design of the workplace envelope is to plan a physical space that is optimal for a person to perform a manual activity in a seated or standing position. Although it is fairly easy to measure a person physically and custom design a workplace envelope for that person, it is also very costly. The general practice is to use designs that fit about 95 percent of the population who will use the workplace envelope. That figure may be influenced by factors such as the

Workplace envelope The three-dimensional workspace in which a person uses her or his hands.

clothing a person is wearing, age, sex, ethnic group, and disabilities. For example, Rozier (1977) reported a 45 percent reduction in usable workspace for a person with a below-the-elbow amputation who uses a mechanical replacement arm. The Americans with Disabilities Act requires employers to make reasonable adjustments in the work environment for otherwise qualified individuals, making the question of design of the workplace envelope even more difficult. The city of Portland, Oregon, found that changing to adjustable furniture, which allows individualization of the workplace envelope, reduced the number of musculoskeletal disorder claims (Shihadeh-Gomaa, 1998).

To meet all the conflicting requirements of workplace envelope design, Sanders and McCormick (1993) offer a system of priorities for making choices about design elements. The purpose of this system is to make sure all the necessary requirements are included while recognizing that all the requirements are not equally important. The first priority concerns primary visual tasks; for example, placing a computer screen at the best distance from the user. The second priority concerns primary controls for interaction in the primary visual tasks. This could involve, for example, the placement of the keyboard and mouse for a computer user.

■ My home office meets most of the criteria for priorities in a good workplace envelope except for the papers on the floor.

The third priority concerns control–display relationships. This means putting the controls near the displays and providing compatible movement relationships. Both the mouse and the keyboard need to be close to the computer and the monitor. The words I see on the screen give immediate feedback about the correctness of my typing, and the mouse provides a mirror for its actions on the screen.

The fourth priority concerns the arrangement of elements that are used in a sequence. This is one area where my workplace envelope at home does not meet the standards. When I have to use several books or articles in sequence, I spread them in a partial circle on the floor around my chair. Ergonomically it would be much better to have them in a short file cabinet on the right side of my chair, between the chair and the wall.

The fifth priority is to locate conveniently those elements that are used frequently, such as a printer or scanner for a computer user. The sixth priority is to have consistency with other layouts within the system or in other systems, such as a computer user's setup at home and at work. Consistency with other layouts is important when a number of people use the same equipment or when there are frequent changes of workers. It is not too difficult to design a good workplace envelope for a computer user, but in places such as a nuclear control room with a huge number of controls and multiple priorities, satisfying each of these priorities is very difficult and nearly impossible in some instances.

The issue of priorities also becomes more critical when many different systems must be considered. The example of a workstation at a computer leads to the topic of computers and human factors, which has become a highly specialized area of human factors research in the last two decades.

COMPUTERS AND HUMAN FACTORS

In much the same way that knowing how to type was critical for secretarial success early in the twentieth century, knowing how to use a computer is now a requirement for almost every job from cashier at a Pizza Hut to chief executive officer (CEO) of a large insurance company. In a survey of 320 CEOs, chief operating officers, and strategic planners in large U.S. firms, 9 of 10 of those surveyed said that they believed computers had become vital to business in the United States (Turban, 1995).

In some cases the introduction of computers has changed the nature of the entire job dramatically. This is the case in the field of drafting, where hand drawing has been replaced in many situations by the use of computer-assisted design (CAD). The sales clerk and the supermarket checker rarely enter actual prices into a cash register anymore; instead, they pass merchandise and grocery items over a bar code scanner connected to a computer.

In other jobs the use of computers has assisted the employee but has not changed the actual work. This is typical of a manager who uses a computer-based program to schedule her workday, keep track of expenses, and send communications and other programs to help her make decisions at work. Craiger (1996) has suggested that many jobs would benefit from the use of a computer-based decision support system. The purpose of such a system is to provide a knowledge base that is far greater than that which a single person can bring to a problem-solving situation. This type of system also can use a large set of analytic rules to suggest which decisions have the greatest chances for success in a situation. The manager still evaluates and makes the final decision, but with much more information. Craiger also discusses a computer-based decision support system used in software development at IBM. At one step in the process, if the developer is taking too long at a particular task, the support system offers advice for completing the task. Earlier in this chapter it was stated that humans are better than machines when tasks are uncertain or not well defined. The computer-based decision support system shows a way in which a person and a machine can work together to enhance the ability of the person to make good decisions in uncertain situations.

Ergonomic Computer Workspace Design

Computers were heralded as a way of making jobs easier for employees, but the introduction of computers in the workplace has led to a number of problems involving physical stress and strain. A recent national study indicated that poorly set up computer workstations led to many problems such as neck, shoulder, and wrist stress and eyestrain (Sarkis, 2000).

Even when standards are set for physical factors in the computer-based workspace, research shows that there can be considerable disagreement between studies (Helander & Rupp, 1984). It is difficult to know which study to use for a particular group of employees. A second problem in using a fixed set of standards occurs when employees are observed establishing their own preferences for the physical arrangement of a computer workstation. When this is allowed, there is very little correlation between the workers' preferences and the settings expected from measuring human bodies (Cornell & Kokot, 1988; Grandjean, Hunting, & Piderman, 1983). Adjustable equipment appears to be one of the more successful solutions to these conflicts, and it also gives employees more of a sense of control over the work environment.

Problems in the Computer Workspace

Some of the problems of computer users are similar to those faced by anyone who spends long hours at a desk. Muscle stiffness and eyestrain can occur whether one is working at a computer terminal, using a sewing machine, or proofreading. Many of the eye problems reported by computer users are really problems with lighting in the workspace rather than problems caused by the video display terminal. These are problems that are not unique to computer usage, and methods to relieve them have been in use for years. Changes such as antiglare shields and the use of indirect rather than fluorescent lights reduce eyestrain in computer users (Anshel, 1997). Computers themselves have been used to help relieve these problems through the addition of a program that pops up on the screen after a specific amount of time and tells the employee to do certain muscle exercises at the desk to avoid strain. *Avoid Repetitive Motion Syndrome* from Micronite, Inc., is an example of this kind of program (Krasowska, 1996).

Another important problem that is not unique to computer use is **repetitive motion injury.** This is a painful condition that occurs when a small motor behavior is repeated many times during a shift. Repetitive motion injury was associated with work in meat- and poultry-processing plants in the past, but the claims of computer workers now make this injury the fastest-growing type of workers' compensation claim. In 1993 it was reported that repetitive motion injuries accounted for about 61 percent of all workplace illnesses (Mandelker,

Repetitive motion injury
An injury caused by many repetitions of a small motor behavior.

1993); four years later the injury rate appeared to be decreasing, however (Brostoff, 1997), but the Occupational Health and Safety Administration (OSHA) estimates that one in six heavy computer users will develop a repetitive motion injury (Levin, 1998).

Clerical workers and sales clerks and supermarket checkers, whose work is computer-based, contribute the most to the large increase in this type of injury. A clerical worker sits at a computer workstation, and a sales clerk or supermarket checker repeatedly passes items over a bar code scanner connected to a computer. The average cost of a repetitive motion injury claim is $14,726 but can go as high as $50,000 if surgery is needed, making it the costliest category per case of workers' compensation claims. This type of injury occurs more often when employers use computers to automate jobs rather than enhance jobs. Some clerical workers in this type of work setting have complained that it feels like they are working on an assembly line rather than in an office. Although the amount of physical force required is minimal, the pace does not allow for physical recovery of the muscles between repetitions. This is what leads to the injury.

One of the easiest solutions to this problem is to vary the work the employees do so that they do not repeat the same motions all day. Job enlargement (increasing job responsibilities) and job rotation (switching between a number of tasks), which were discussed in Chapter 6, could be used to increase job satisfaction and prevent repetitive motion injuries. In addition to increasing job satisfaction, these changes may reduce job stress, which has been found to contribute to repetitive motion injuries (Stephens & Smith, 1996).

Although repetitive motion injuries and eyestrain are real physical hazards of computer work, some of the work of human factors specialists may deal with employees' perceptions of computers rather than real physical problems. For example, early correlational research seemed to indicate a relationship between video display terminal (VDT) use and higher miscarriage rates among pregnant women. A National Institute for Occupational Safety and Health report (NIOSH, 1998) found no relationship between work at the video display terminals and either spontaneous abortions or premature birth. Another NIOSH (1997) study suggested that psychosocial factors common to VDT work, such as monotony, may contribute to other physical problems such as neck and head pain.

Computer Hardware and Software

Human factors specialists are also helpful in making equipment and design decisions about computer hardware that are based on the limitations of people in person–machine systems. In recent years computer hardware designers have found a number of ways other than the use of the keyboard to access the information on the video display. One of the most recent additions is a voice recognition system that converts speech directly into actions or text on the computer. Some common input devices are shown in Figure 12.3. If employers want employees to be able to position the cursor on the video display screen as fast as possible, the obvious choice is the touch screen. The problem with a touch screen is that it also has the lowest accuracy rate for cursor positioning. Although the trackball device is in the middle range for speed of input, it is the best for accuracy (Sanders & McCormick, 1993). If the time to correct errors is taken into account in the device decision, the fastest option is not the best choice for a computer user in an actual work situation.

Figure 12.3
Typical computer input devices.

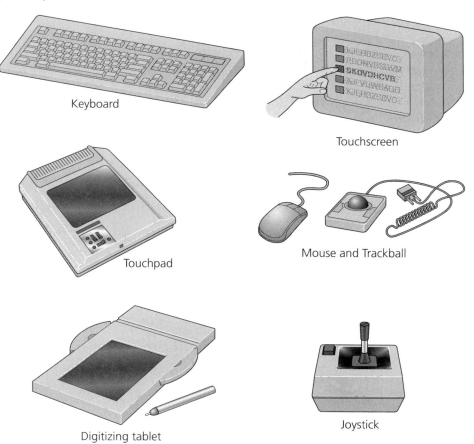

Keyboard

Touchscreen

Touchpad

Mouse and Trackball

Digitizing tablet

Joystick

Attitudes toward Computer Use

Another area of computer use at work that can benefit from the skills of a human factors specialist is the design of the software used by employees and the attitudes of employees toward computer use. These are closely related issues. If employees are fearful of using computers because they believe that the computer may replace them or are anxious about their ability with computers, even the best software programs will not be useful. One study found that previous coursework or computer literacy was the best predictor of computer use at work. The user-friendliness of the program was related only weakly to computer use, according to the study by Northrup, Kraemer, Dunkle, and King (1994).

This study illustrates an increasingly common problem in computer use. The people who make the hardware and the computer programs are experts in those areas, but the people who use them usually do not have expert knowledge and often have no knowledge at all. What appears simple or logical to an expert may be confusing to a novice. It is not enough to tell the experts to think like a novice. Howell (1991) points out that experts and novices in any field think in different ways about that field. There is no way to go back to an earlier level of understanding. For example, after almost thirty years in the field of psychology I find that sometimes when I write test questions that seem obvious and easy to me, that is not true for a beginning psychology student. I appreciate feedback from students about the questions I write because I use the students as my "experts" at being beginners in psychology.

Human factors specialists often can provide a link between the expert designer and the beginning user of computer hardware and software. Two interesting studies dealing with computer attitudes showed that when a computer task was labeled as "play" rather than "work" and the training situation was described as an "opportunity," employees, particularly younger ones, performed the task better and showed a higher motivation to learn (Martocchio, 1992; Webster & Martocchio, 1993). Negative attitudes toward computers have been linked to lower levels of job satisfaction and organizational commitment (Murrell & Sprinkle, 1993), and positive attitudes predicted increasing computer use at work (Winter, Chudoba, & Gutek, 1998). Other researchers found that people's trust in equipment is based mainly on their belief in its reliability. Any sign of failure, even in noncritical parts of the system, reduced trust in the entire system (Muir & Moray, 1996). In Chapter 11 of this book some of these issues were examined in greater detail. The role of the human factors specialist may be in designing training programs that not only provide knowledge but also deal with attitudes and fears.

Virtual Reality

Virtual reality programs are an area of human–computer interaction combining both hardware and software design issues. These programs are a type of simulation that re-creates all the elements of a real situation except for the worker actually

Virtual reality programs Computer-based programs that re-create all the elements of a real work situation, but without the consequences of making mistakes.

being there. The operator manipulates tools and controls that affect the program on the screen in the same way that action would work in real life. The advantage of virtual reality is that the operator can make mistakes and try out various possibilities without real-world consequences. A company called High Techsplanations has developed a number of virtual reality simulations for use in the medical field. Doctors can practice treating battlefield injuries or doing major surgical procedures without harming real patients if their actions are not done correctly (Zajtchuk & Satava, 1997). Other uses for virtual reality simulators include reducing test anxiety in college students and giving safety training at work (Blotzer, 1995; *R & D Magazine*, 1997).

As new technology develops, virtual reality devices are becoming increasingly realistic. They also are eliminating some of the problems of the early devices. Early helmets and goggles that were responsive to head movement often created nausea in the user because there was a brief time lag between the user moving her head and the helmet and goggles registering the change.

As virtual reality simulations improve and become more interactive, the uses for these devices will multiply. A recent research article found that students learned a complex motor skill better in a virtual reality setting than in an actual practice setting (Todorov, Shadmehr, & Bizzi, 1997). Many of these improvements have come from improvements in computer games for home use. The next section discusses another extension of human skills with machines, which has been used in the medical field and others areas.

ROBOTS AND HUMANS

Do you remember a few years ago when the *Pathfinder* robot traveled to and explored the Martian landscape? Scientists would have liked to go to Mars instead of sending a robot, but that was not possible at that time. In the videotapes of the *Pathfinder,* it appeared that the robot device was operating as a fully automated system. In common with all automated systems, however, this robotic device actually had humans involved in every step of the planning and execution of its mission.

Robots are mechanical devices that can be programmed to carry out a sequence of tasks. Most of those tasks involve movement or manipulation, as in the *Pathfinder's* exploration. Use in situations that would be very hazardous, as in space and under conditions of extreme cold, represent only a small proportion of industrial robot applications. It is much more common to find robots used to replace workers on routine but exacting jobs.

Car manufacturers use about one-quarter of the industrial robots in the United States. General Motors used the first industrial robot in the United States in a die-casting machine in 1961. Robots often are used in operations such as welding and painting. Their accuracy rate and productivity rate are higher than the rates of humans doing the same jobs, and the hourly cost is lower. One study found

Robot A mechanical device programmed by humans to carry out a sequence of tasks.

that the average cost of an assembly line employee was about $24 per hour, while the average cost of a robot was a little less than $6 per hour (Crocker & Guelker, 1988). The cost of the employee includes wages and fringe benefits, and the cost of the robot includes maintenance and depreciation. If the robot replaces more than one worker, the cost savings are multiplied. Part of the cost of the employee is the time—for coffee breaks and lunch, for example—when the employee is not productive. Robots are productive an average of 95 percent of the time on the job compared with 75 percent for the average blue-collar worker. Hidden costs of the employee include theft and sabotage and union negotiations and bargaining.

When robots are introduced into the work environment, sabotage is sometimes directed toward them because employees fear that they will be replaced by them. In the usual replacement formula each robot replaces two employees. Workers who are being replaced by robots may perceive sabotage as a way to keep their jobs. In some organizations special guard shields have been installed around robots to prevent sabotage.

Low-skill workers react more negatively than do high-skill workers to using robots at work (Chao & Koslowski, 1986). Low-skill workers see robots as more of a threat to their jobs, and high-skill workers perceive the use of robots as providing them opportunities to expand their skills. Although the use of robots is increasing in the United States, Japan has consistently led in the number of robots used in industry. Japan currently has over 350,000 robots in use, compared with about 100,000 in North America (Guidoni, 2000). Part of the reason for the higher numbers and greater acceptance of robots in Japan may be that a shortage of labor in that country has pushed the development of robots. In the United States robot development is related more to cost savings than to labor shortages. One of the few labor shortage–based robot programs in the United States involved the development of robots to clean rest rooms for the U.S. Postal Service (Bylinsky, 1992). This job is seen as undesirable, resulting in difficulty in filling the positions and high turnover rates. Some hotels are exploring the use of robots for jobs—such as food service—for which it is difficult to find and keep employees.

When robots are introduced into the work environment, one of the roles for I/O psychologists is to help create an atmosphere of acceptance. Crocker and Guelker (1988) list several ways in which employees can be prepared for the introduction of robots. First, employees need to feel that they will benefit from the robots. Workers are more accepting when they know they will not be laid off but will have more challenging jobs because a robot is doing the routine, repetitive actions.

Second, employees should feel that they, not the robots, are responsible for the company's achievement and success. This is an easy goal to lose sight of when robots are new and everyone pays attention to them. Workers sometimes feel that they are working for the robot, not the other way around. Companies need to keep the focus on the employees and reinforce their understanding of the robot as a tool to help them work better.

Third, companies should make sure that employees have many opportunities for growth and challenge at work. When the use of robots leads to greater automation, new methods to increase growth and challenge must be found. Methods for achieving this include providing more chances for socialization and instituting a job rotation system. Increased opportunities to socialize often are seen as a way to relieve the boredom of a routine, repetitive job. Job rotation is more valuable from the employer's point of view because the worker is learning more about the job and working rather than socializing.

Although it is not likely that employees soon will be working alongside robots like the ones in *Star Wars* (Figure 12.4), the future probably will see more use of industrial robots even in small organizations. It is better to prepare for the introduction of robots than to deal with problems after they are installed. One strategy for reducing person–machine problems is to automate everything that possibly can be automated. Howell (1991) cautions that this strategy can lead to increasingly inflexible systems that are not good for employees or the organization. Howell uses the example of the tragic person–machine system failure that occurred when a U.S. battleship shot down an Iranian civilian airliner that was mistakenly identified as an enemy aircraft. The crew was relying on information from the computers on the ship. When the computers gave incorrect information, the crew was not able to detect the mistake and interpreted the data to mean that the plane was descending for an attack when it actually was going higher in the sky. The crew lacked the ability to make the correct choices when the automated equipment made the wrong choices. Although robots and computers represent a tempting high-technology solution to person–machine problems, they may not always represent the best solution.

The use of robots represents a change in job design that is motivated by the introduction of technology. The next section looks at job design changes that are motivated by the human part of the system.

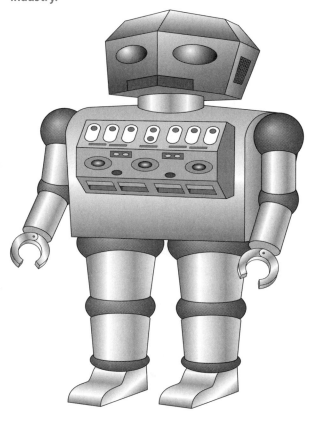

Figure 12.4

Many people's concept of industrial robots comes from robots in science fiction movies rather than the robots actually used in industry.

NONTRADITIONAL WORK SCHEDULES

Most people in the United States work hours other than the traditional "9 to 5." Although many people in full-time jobs work during the daytime from Monday through Friday, there are almost as many variations as there are places of work. If you live in or near a large city, you know that the rush hour is far longer than the hour before 9 A.M. and the hour after 5 P.M. Since the 1950s, the eight-hour (nine hours if lunchtime is unpaid) five-day workweek has been the standard. In the 1800s the hours of work often were limited by the number of daylight hours, but now the hours of work are limited only by the refusal to consider scheduling options.

One reason more companies have decided to use nontraditional work schedules is the increased numbers in the workforce of dual-income couples with children and of single parents. The stress associated with being a working parent will be discussed in Chapter 13.

The willingness of couples to adjust their work schedules to benefit their family schedules may involve their degree of commitment to the family and the job. Piotrkowski and Repetti (1984) suggest that two-income families may be either dual-career couples or dual-earner families. In dual-career couples both the husband and the wife have jobs that are very meaningful to them, involve a sequence of development—for example, from manager to vice president—and require a high degree of career commitment. In dual-earner families the husband and wife both work because of economic need and feel very little involvement in their jobs or careers. The economic value of the job is the focus of their commitment. They see their jobs as a means to earn a paycheck. Gilmore and Fanin (1982) added another type to this model: the couple in which both members work but the couple is concerned solely with developing the career of one of the partners because the other partner is working only to provide more family income. In this type of arrangement the second partner may take a job working a late afternoon or evening shift because it pays more money and the couple then does not have to pay for child care. The first partner has a job during daytime business hours that leads to greater development of his or her career.

Company involvement in care programs for children or other dependents can take many forms, including work scheduling arrangements. Alternative work arrangements such as flextime, telecommuting, and job sharing have been promoted as pro-family programs. Some of the most commonly used nontraditional schedules include those three systems and shift work.

Shift Work

Shift work is a way to meet staffing needs during times other than the typical daytime hours. Shift work is used when there is a need to have personnel on duty twenty-four hours every day, as in hospitals, international businesses, police

Shift work The use of afternoon and late-night work periods in addition to the usual day work.

Moonlighting Working a second or third job in addition to one's primary employment.

Circadian rhythms The twenty-four-hour functioning cycles of humans.

Compressed workweek Working the same weekly number of hours in fewer days per week.

departments, and fire departments. Shift work also is used when production demands cannot be met during a single daytime work period. With more retail stores, gas stations, and convenience stores staying open twenty-four hours a day, it is expected that the number of shift workers will increase. The increase in international operations also has led to an increase in shift work to match working hours in other countries.

Although most employees (61 percent) prefer to work a typical day shift, some employees prefer evening or late-night work hours (de la Mare & Walker, 1968). Among the people who choose to work evening or late-night hours, most of them would prefer to work a typical day shift but have other concerns that are more important than working during the day. Families with children may reduce child-care costs by having the mother and father work different shifts. Workers who are **moonlighting** may have only evening or late-night hours available for a second job. Shift workers in general, however, report more negative moods and chronic fatigue than nonshift workers do (Prizmic & Kaliterna, 1995).

Although there has not been agreement about the best rotation period when shifts are changed, many people agree that it is better to keep shifts fixed rather than rotating them at all (Frese & Okonek, 1984; Wilkinson, 1992). There are two possible reasons for these research findings. One reason is that rotating shifts disturbs the workers' **circadian rhythms**, the twenty-four-hour cycles of functioning by which most people live. Even if people have no time requirements involving family or job, they tend to structure each twenty-four-hour cycle into fairly constant periods of sleeping, waking, eating, and activity. Rotating shifts disrupt these circadian rhythms until a new rhythm is established. Workers with fixed shifts report many of these disturbances in their daily cycle during weekends or vacations. Rotating shifts also usually make it more difficult to coordinate child-care arrangements.

Fixed shifts allow more consistent opportunities for socialization away from work. Being able to go to the health club or golf course regularly with the same group of friends can prevent the lower satisfaction levels associated with evening or late-night shifts. Not surprisingly, workers with families report more dissatisfaction with evening or late-night shifts because they are out of step with members of the family who cannot change their hours of school or work (Smith & Folkard, 1993). One researcher suggests that it is better to change shifts quickly in a forward-rotating pattern (Knauth, 1996). This may give shift workers some access to typical family time patterns.

Compressed Workweek

Shift work, even during evening and late-night hours, maintains the standard of an eight-hour period of work per day. **Compressed workweek** schedules take the typical forty-hour workweek and contract it into three or four workdays per week. Are these longer hours exhausting or unsafe? Meta-analytic studies and other research have shown that fears about higher accident rates and lower productivity rates have not been confirmed (Moores, 1990; Vega & Gilbert, 1997). The greatest effect of the compressed workweek appears to be higher job satisfaction and lower absenteeism. Although employees working such schedules report an increase in fatigue, they do not appear to have lower productivity.

Organizations and employees find different advantages in compressed workweeks. Organizations may be able to decrease setup and cleanup time by doing it only four times rather than five times a week. If the company is closed on the fifth day, operating costs are reduced. Companies also may see the compressed workweek as a way of reducing the air pollution that results from employees' commuting. Bechtel Corporation in the San Francisco area started a schedule of nine-hour workdays on Monday through Thursday for all its employees. Each Friday half the employees work for eight hours in addition to the regular Monday through Thursday week.

For employees, the greatest advantages of the compressed workweek are the greater blocks of time off for personal and family activities, less weekly time spent in commuting, and lower child-care costs—if fees for such care are paid by the day or the other parent has different days off. In fact, absentee rates may go down because employees can schedule activities or appointments on the extra day off rather than taking time off from work (Moores, 1990).

Flextime

Flextime, which involves allowing some degree of personal choice in work scheduling, is one of the fastest-growing nontraditional methods of scheduling work. A survey by Hewitt Associates indicated that 68 percent of the surveyed employers offered some type of flexible scheduling option (Wells, 1997). Flextime is popular with both employees and employers. It leads to benefits for the organization, such as lower absentee rates, less overtime pay, higher productivity and job satisfaction, and less turnover (Estes, 1990). There is virtually no tardiness because the workday starts whenever the employee arrives. Employees report feeling that they have greater control over their jobs and lives. Flextime sometimes can be used in place of the employee absences allowed by the Family Medical and Leave Act of 1993 and the Pregnancy Sex-Discrimination Prohibition Act of 1978. Adjusting their work schedules may allow employees to remain on the job.

Some organizations use a totally flexible scheduling process known as **gliding time**, but most flextime schedules are set for a specific time period such as a month or more. When flextime is scheduled in this way, it is called a **flexitour**. Common to both types of flextime is the requirement of a particular set of hours during which all employees must be at work. For example, if an advertising company spent about a third of its time in group meetings that required the presence of all department members, the **core hours**, or required time, might be from 1 P.M. to 4 P.M. This would mean that employees could come in as early as 7 A.M. (with a

Flextime Allowing employees to choose their hours of work except for a certain number of core hours required for all employees.

Gliding time Flextime schedules in which employees are allowed to change their work hours with no prior notice.

Flexitour A flextime schedule in which employees are required to maintain a self-chosen schedule for a fixed period.

Core hours The central hours when all flextime employees are required to be present at work.

Bandwidth The total work hour span available to flextime employees for work scheduling.

one-hour lunch break) or work as late as 10 P.M. (with a one-hour dinner break) and still work for eight hours a day. The hours between 7 A.M. and 10 P.M. are called the **bandwidth** because they represent all the hours available for work.

Although flextime is very popular, it is not practical for all job situations. If a retail store is open from 8 A.M. to 9 P.M., flextime may meet staffing needs and give the employees greater control over their schedules. However, if no employee chooses to come in before 10 A.M., some employees will have to be assigned to the earlier hours. Some work, such as assembly line jobs, requires everyone to be there the entire time. In college classes, most instructors will allow some flexibility in scheduling but there are limited opportunities for a student to come in for the last half of one class and stay for the first half of the next class. One of the true flextime college schedules involves the use of video-based classes. Students watch a series of videotapes at the college library or in their own homes at any time they choose. The students also read a textbook on their own schedule. The instructor is available by telephone or in person if a student has questions. The student schedules tests in the learning center of the college during the hours the college is open. This is an excellent choice for students who have other responsibilities with erratic schedules, such as on-call paramedics and flight attendants. The use of Internet-based classes is also adding to college scheduling flexibility.

Job Sharing

Job sharing, in which a full-time job is divided between two employees, is a scheduling alternative that allows fewer hours at work but permits the employee to maintain professional involvement and have a regular work schedule. Some jobs are not adaptable to job sharing because they require a full-time commitment, but many others, such as a receptionist's or an accountant's position, can be divided into separate areas of responsibility that make job sharing possible. This may be an excellent scheduling choice during a period when two valuable employees are unable to work full-time because of child-care responsibilities or involvement in the care of an ill family member, although a 1999 study showed only 22 percent of surveyed organizations offered job sharing (Magruder, 2000). When employees maintain their involvement in the workplace, the return to full-time work does not require additional training time.

WORKPLACE DESIGN

As new work scheduling options lead to new ways of structuring work time, new designs for the workplace lead to new ways of structuring how a job is done. This section considers the physical design of office spaces and a new choice—

telecommuting—that eliminates the workspace at a company in most situations. Earlier in the chapter, the term *workspace* was used to refer to the organization of a workstation for an individual worker. When the workspaces of an entire group or organization are combined, this is the **workplace.**

Open Offices

When people complain about trying to get something done in a bureaucracy, they often mention the problem of going from one office to another and becoming lost in a maze of offices. When organizations make a conscious effort to move away from a bureaucratic structure, one of the changes they make is often to eliminate many of the little offices and locate groups of employees in large open work areas called open offices. **Open offices** can be groups of desks in one large area; or the larger area can be divided by temporary partitions that do not go all the way to the ceiling. Sanders and McCormick (1993) refer to the first type of design as a **bullpen office** and to the second design as a **landscaped office**.

Workplace The workspaces of an entire group or organization.

Open offices Office designs that eliminate individual offices or cubicles for each employee.

Bullpen offices Open offices that arrange the desks of employees in functional groups.

Landscaped offices Open offices that separate employee workspaces with partitions that do not go all the way to the ceiling.

Daemmrich/The Image Works

■ Landscaped open office designs often separate individual workplaces by using chest-high partitions.

Open office designs increase activity and interaction among employees (Ettorre, 1995) and decrease organizational costs, but they also have drawbacks. Employees, especially at the management level and above, report dissatisfaction with the lack of privacy and control (Davis, 1984; Sutton & Rafaeli, 1987). Private offices often are seen as status symbols as well. Moving to an open office plan may be regarded as a loss of status. Lower-level workers such as data entry operators and clerical workers may prefer an open office because of the increased opportunities to socialize. A combination system that may give back some of the employee control that is perceived as lost in the open office plan allows open office employees to schedule time in private work areas when they are working on a project that requires a lack of distractions. With open office designs, less money is spent on walls and doors but more money is spent on materials to reduce sounds and noise.

Telecommuting

Telecommuting sometimes is viewed as a return to the preindustrial days of working in the home. However, even though telecommuting employees may be alone in their homes, they are connected by telephone, fax, and computer as much as or even more than they would be if they were at the office. In preindustrial days work at home meant working independently of others, but this is not true for telecommuters because of all the ways they are connected to the office.

Telecommuting involves employees who typically would work at an office in a company. The employee still is doing the same office-based job, but in a more distant location, usually his home. He still has a private workspace that is assigned just to him.

As the popularity of flexible work arrangements has grown, a number of different terms have been used to describe these arrangements. Telecommuting can be confused with the work arrangement known as the **virtual office** because both arrangements involve an office away from the main company location. Virtual office arrangements involve taking away an employee's regularly assigned workspace and assigning workspaces on a temporary basis as needed or letting the employee set up a workspace anytime, anywhere, as needed. The virtual office arrangement most often is used with salespeople or field engineers who may use their assigned workspaces in the company only one day a week but work mainly away from the office. They are out on sales calls or in the field the rest of the time. It does not make economic sense to have space in the organization that is used less than 20 percent of the work time. If a salesperson knows he is going to be at the company all day Tuesday, he can call the scheduler on Monday and reserve a workspace for that day. The workspace will be equipped with everything the employee needs.

A variation of the virtual office is the **telecenter**, an office center that may be used by a number of employees from different organizations. It is located away from the main company site at a place closer to the employees' homes or sales lo-

Telecommuting Assigning employees to work from remote locations while still being connected to the main office location by computers, faxes, modems, and telephones.

Virtual office Eliminating assigned workspaces and giving employees mobile equipment, such as cellular phones and laptop computers, that allows them to use any place they work as an office.

Telecenter A remote office setting used as a temporary office location by virtual office employees.

cations. The employees can reserve an office or a conference room and can schedule administrative service support such as report duplication or telephone answering. When a virtual office employee is not in the office, she still is connected by portable equipment such as laptop computers and cellular telephones. The connections via the portable equipment are often the reason for confusion between telecommuting and virtual office arrangements. One of the common problems in both arrangements is that the ability to reach employees at any time of the day or night has blurred the concepts of "time at work" and "time away from work." There is still a need for boundaries to avoid the stress caused by never getting away from work.

Although both telecommuting and virtual office arrangements are recent alternatives, telecommuting has developed a larger base of organizations and employees. As many as 46 million employees are telecommuting for at least part of the workweek, and the number is expected to rise (Morrow, 1998). Telecommuting also has been in existence long enough for organizations and researchers to benefit from some early mistakes to make telecommuting programs more successful. This is shown in the case study "Telecommuting Works," which describes the use of telecommuting by the city of Portland, Oregon. Merrill Lynch & Company, Inc., has developed a two-week telecommuter training session for employees in which a laboratory setup simulates the home office environment (Girard, 1997). This allows employees to try out the setting and resolve problems before becoming telecommuters.

[Case Study] TELECOMMUTING WORKS

Can telecommuting be a successful work arrangement, or is it just the latest business fad? For the city of Portland, Oregon, the answer is an enthusiastic endorsement. After a six-month pilot project, the city has established a permanent telecommuting program for municipal staff.

The initial goal of the pilot project was reducing fuel consumption and air pollution by having fewer employees drive to and from work. Participants came from every sector of city employment, from hearings officers to office managers. They began working at home one day a week after a half-day training program.

Supervisors found that telecommuting improved employee morale, increased effectiveness, and boosted staff productivity. Employees found that the uninterrupted work time reduced stress and allowed for greater work continuity.

Among the employees who tried telecommuting during the pilot program is Nelda Skidmore, senior human resources analyst. While much of her work time is spent in meetings, Fridays in her home office are devoted to analysis, documentation, and report writing. She says that complex reports that might take several days to complete at the office often can be done in a single day at home. She stays in contact with the office through her computer and telephone and fax lines, including conference calls through speakerphones.

Another telecommuting success story is that of Jim Carlton, a computer-aided design and drafting specialist for the Bureau of Environmental Services. Carlton became a quadriplegic several years ago. If he had had to go to the office every day, he would have been able to work only part-time. Telecommuting has allowed him to continue doing full-time work. He works four- to ten-hour days at home. Carlton is connected to the city's computer network, which he uses for drawings, printing, and e-mail. A recently installed software program allows Carlton's supervisor to review his drawings, add comments, and return them.

The Portland Energy Office and the Oregon Office of Energy have combined to offer incentives and materials to help other organizations develop successful telecommuting programs. They offer tax credits and low-interest loans for equipment, publications, training, and ongoing assistance. Clearly, this has been a win-win situation for the city of Portland and its employees.

From Oregon Office of Energy. (1998). City of Portland gives telecommuting a thumbs up following a six-month test. http://www.cbs.state.or.us/external/ooe/cons/portl.htm.

A number of the earliest telecommuting arrangements resulted from the desire of organizations to keep employees who were extremely valuable but whose circumstances changed so that they no longer were able to come into the office every day. This could be a person who had moved with a spouse to a different community, a worker who recently had had an elderly parent come to live with him, or a person who had temporarily become immobile because of an accident. Two natural disasters—the Los Angeles earthquake of 1994 and the eastern seaboard blizzards of 1996—gave more desirability to telecommuting arrangements because of the ability of organizations to remain in business from telecommuting sites. A further impetus to the growth of telecommuting was provided by the Clean Air Act of 1990, which requires businesses that employ over 100 people in a single location to reduce employee commuting time 25 percent. Telecommuting from home reduces actual commuting time to zero on telecommuting days.

Although the reason for starting telecommuting was to maintain the work of employees, when this arrangement was used organizations found that it often led to increases in productivity. In a survey of telecommuters, three-fourths of the employees said they were more productive while telecommuting (Flynn, 1995) because they had fewer distractions. In a survey of *Fortune* 500 companies employers confirmed those gains (Greengard, 1994). Another benefit of telecommuting is the reduced need for office space. If two telecommuting employees use company office space only two days each week, those employees may be able to share one office instead of having separate offices. It has been estimated that employers can save $1,500 to $5,000 each year on office space costs for each employee who telecommutes. Telecommuting has opened employment possibilities to some employees who cannot come to a main office location. A disabled employee with a computer and a workstation adapted to his disabilities can be a positive addition to the human resources of an organization. If that worker already has the adapted equipment in his home, the additional cost to the employer may be much less than that of modifying office space at the company for her (Figure 12.5). Some states are allowing prison employees to do telecommuting work by working from the prison the same way other telecommuters would work from home (Metzger & Von Glinow, 1988).

Figure 12.5

Telecommuting can be a way for disabled employees to be active and productive by staying connected to the office from home.

Dennis Crews/Mercury Pictures

Although telecommuting sounds like a win-win situation for employers and workers, there are problems and limits to its usefulness. One of the most obvious issues is that certain jobs require a high degree of un-scheduled face-to-face contact or the use of equipment that cannot be moved. This means that at least some employees must be at the company location for the entire scheduled time each week. For example, hospital nurses and assembly line workers cannot make use of telecommuting. One of the early barriers to telecommuting was the inability of telecommuters to access visual information except for still pictures. Videoconferencing, which provides a real-time visual link between the telecommuter and the office, has helped eliminate this barrier.

For employers, some of the major concerns with telecommuting are loss of control over the employees and the workplace. This does not mean only the loss of direct face-to-face supervision but also the problem of the employer being required to maintain safety standards in the employee's home. Employers also are concerned with theft of company equipment from the employee's home and security for the work produced at home and sent electronically to the company. Training, prevention, and inspections can ease many of these concerns.

Employers also fear that if some employees are allowed to telecommute, the rest of the employees will feel that they should have that option as well and the organization will end up with no one at the office. While many employees still prefer to work at the company site, increasing numbers are indicating a preference for telecommuting work (Wilde, 2000). For employees, some of the major concerns are feeling out of touch with the office, lack of social contact, and loss of opportunities for promotion. The best telecommuting employees are often the best employees in general. They are self-disciplined, self-motivated, and resourceful about accomplishing their work. Most employees who telecommute divide their work time between home and the company. Most telecommuters work at home for one to three days per week on the average. Most telecommuting assignments last six to eighteen months before something occurs to bring the person back to the office. It may be a new project, a new job assignment, or a reorganization at the company.

The most successful way to think about telecommuting is to regard it as one of a variety of flexible work arrangements and to focus on remaining flexible while getting the work done. Telecommuting employees quickly learn that they cannot do full-time care of children or dependents and work full-time at a telecommuting station. However, if, for example, an elderly parent only needs someone to make lunch and assist her two or three times a day, telecommuting may be an excellent choice for the employee.

Flexible work arrangements designed to meet employees' and employers' needs is a central belief of the quality-of-work-life movement, which is the last topic in this chapter.

QUALITY OF WORK LIFE

The two major elements of **quality-of-work-life** programs are concern about the effect of work on employees as well as organizational goals, and using employee participation to solve organizational problems and make decisions (Nadler & Lawler, 1983). Sometimes quality of work life is considered part of organizational development or employee motivation and job satisfaction. The focus in these programs is on the individual employee, reinforcing the need for the flexible work arrangements discussed in the last section. Whether it is the physical design of the workspace or assigning work hours, it is becoming clearer that there is no "one size fits all" job and work design any more than there is "one size fits all" clothing design. Quality-of-work-life programs emphasize the fact that employees have responsibilities in addition to their jobs at the organization that can influence their behavior at work (Higgins, Duxbury, & Irving, 1992). Some organizations develop quality-of-work-life programs in association with the unions active in a company. If the programs are successful, both the union and the company benefit as employees give both equal credit for the success. If the programs are not successful, employees tend to blame management for the lack of success (Thacker & Fields, 1987).

As the cost of replacing workers increases, organizations are becoming more concerned about keeping good employees. Improving the quality of work

Quality of work life
The desire to improve organizational and employee goals and needs by increasing employees' participation in solving organizational problems and making decisions.

life is one method of reducing turnover rates as well as lowering the incidence of absenteeism, minor accidents, and grievances (Havlovic, 1991). It appears that employers could do much more to improve the quality of work life. Whereas 60 percent of Japanese office workers said their quality of work life had improved in the decade from 1981 to 1991, only 30 percent of American workers felt that way (*Training*, 1992). Even worse, the American figure represented a loss of 11 percentage points in the two years before the survey. The quality-of-work-life issues used in the survey included a number of topics discussed in this chapter and other topics, such as office space, safety, ergonomics, and general work attitudes.

Quality-of-work-life programs sometimes are regarded as meeting employees' needs at the expense of the organization's goals and needs. In a Canadian study (Duxbury & Haines, 1991) organizational decision makers said that they believed organizational goals and needs were more important than quality-of-work-life goals and needs. They also said that organizational goals and needs had priority in determining decisions about alternative work arrangements. Although it is not wrong to be concerned about organizational needs and goals, those decision makers saw employee and organizational needs as competing, not complementary. The definition of quality of work life given at the beginning of this section gives equal value to both sets of needs.

It is difficult to list the elements of a good quality-of-work-life program because each company, work setting, and group of employees has different needs and goals. These types of programs include consideration of many things: worker safety, shift scheduling, computer use, employee wellness and fitness, workplace ergonomics, employee evaluation, hiring of managers, building and office design, job reorganization, training programs, developing flextime and telecommuting programs, employee benefits, and conflict resolution. Wellness and fitness programs are discussed in Chapter 13 as part of the role of the employee assistance program. The essential elements in all these programs are employee participation and organizational commitment to employee participation. In most situations, quality-of-work-life programs have led to positive results. The explanation of the successes or the lack of success at times can be as complicated as the variety of programs. One possibility for program success other than improving the quality of work life may be the Hawthorne effect. Employees may respond positively to being noticed and included rather than to the actual work changes. Negative results could be caused by problems with the programs or by using employees who do not want to participate more at work. These alternative explanations indicate how complex these issues can become. Quality-of-work-life programs are driven by the desire of employees and organizations to improve the lives of employees in ways that will enhance their performance on the job, a major objective of I/O psychology.

MAIN POINTS

- Job and work design as an I/O specialty area is called human factors psychology, engineering psychology, or ergonomics, with a focus on person–machine interactions.
- People and machines each have distinct advantages in a person–machine system.
- The display part of the person–machine system gives information to the human operator. Good visual displays are based on good mapping, standard placement, and the correct use of color. Good auditory displays can be separated from other noises and contain only necessary information.
- Tactile (touch) and olfactory (smell) displays are less common but still are useful.
- Controls in a person–machine system are used by the operator to get the machine to do something.
- Some of the most important factors in good control design are affordance, compatibility, standardization, and ability to choose the correct control.
- Workspace design focuses on the workplace envelope and general office design.
- Some of the problems associated with computers in the workplace are difficulty in establishing standards, eyestrain, repetitive motion injury, and the attitudes of employees.
- Virtual reality computer programs simulate actual situations without the dangers that may be part of the actual situation.
- Robots are used in the workplace to carry out a programmed sequence of tasks, sometimes in situations too hazardous for humans, but more commonly to do repetitive, boring tasks.
- Nontraditional work schedules can be used to meet organizational and employee needs.
- Nontraditional work schedules include shift work, compressed workweeks, flextime, and job sharing.
- When companies eliminate individual offices, they create open office plans that feature groups of desks (bullpens) or use shoulder-high partitions between spaces (landscaped offices).
- Telecommuting employees continue to do the same work they did at the company site but do it at home, connected by computers, faxes, and other devices. They usually come into the office one or two days a week.
- Virtual office arrangements involve employees who most often work away from the office and use mobile equipment to stay connected to the company

but seldom come to the company site and have no regularly assigned office space.

■ Quality-of-work-life programs focus on the effects of work on employees while meeting organizational goals. Employee participation in problem solving and decision making is a necessary part of these programs.

KEY TERMS

Affordance
Annunciator
Bandwidth
Bullpen offices
Circadian rhythms
Cognitive design engineering
Compatibility
Compressed workweek
Control
Core hours
Display
Engineering psychology
Ergonomics
Flexitour
Flextime
Gliding time
Head-up display (HUD)

Human factors psychology
Landscaped offices
Mapping
Moonlighting
Movement compatibility
Open offices
Quality of work life
Repetitive motion injury
Robot
Shift work
Spatial compatibility
Telecenter
Telecommuting
Virtual office
Virtual reality programs
Workplace
Workplace envelope

REVIEW QUESTIONS

Answers to these questions can be found at the end of the book.

1. Current interest in job and work design focuses on ways to make people respond more as machines do.

   a. True

   b. False

2. The study of job and work design in I/O psychology is commonly known as

   a. ergonomics.

   b. human factors psychology.

   c. engineering psychology.

   d. all of the above

3. Which of the following is an example of a person–machine system?

   a. A person playing a movie on a VCR

   b. A person opening a can of cat food with a can opener

   c. A person reading a book

   d. a and b

   e. b and c

4. Which of the following is *not* an advantage of people over machines?

   a. Humans are better at dealing with the unexpected.

   b. Humans get fatigued less often than machines do.

   c. Humans are more adaptable.

   d. Humans are more creative.

5. What are the most common types of displays?

   a. _____

   b. _____

6. If the speedometer on your car were located on a transparent display on the windshield, this would be an example of

   a. a standardized display.

   b. a head-up display.

   c. good mapping.

   d. a pictorial display.

7. A clear glass door with no handles or any distinguishable handles would be described by designers as

   a. an incomplete design.

   b. high in affordance.

   c. low in affordance.

   d. high in compatibility.

8. A virtual reality game that uses a footpad to make it look like the operator is walking through the scene when he walks on the footpad would be described by a designer as

   a. high in compatibility.

   b. low in compatibility.

   c. high in standardization.

   d. high in differentiation.

9. The reason it is so difficult to get people to change from the QWERTY keyboard to the Dvorak keyboard is
    a. reduced typing speed for long periods.
    b. royalty cost to the person who patented the Dvorak keyboard.
    c. lack of affordance of the Dvorak keyboard.
    d. standardization of the QWERTY keyboard.

10. The role of a human factors specialist in workspace design is limited to the physical features of humans in person–machine systems.
    a. True
    b. False

11. What are the two most important priorities in the design of the workplace envelope for human beings?
    a. _____
    b. _____

12. The workplace injuries suffered by employees who work with computers are most like the injuries of
    a. supermarket checkers and poultry workers.
    b. electricians.
    c. electronic technicians.
    d. department store sales clerks.

13. A number of the problems associated with computer use in the workplace have been taken care of by research showing consistent standards for computer use.
    a. True
    b. False

14. Many of the fears people have about computers are fears of being replaced by computers or being unable to learn how to use computers.
    a. True
    b. False

15. Virtual reality programs have the advantage of
    a. being inexpensive to develop.
    b. allowing managers to supervise employees from a distance.
    c. not interfering with normal work operations.
    d. allowing learning mistakes without real-life consequences.

16. The workers who feel most threatened by the use of robots are
    a. high-skill workers who fear being replaced by robots.
    b. low-skill workers who fear being replaced by robots.
    c. clerical employees who fear being replaced by robots.
    d. managers who fear being replaced by robots.

17. Some of the problems in the use of robots in the workplace come from too much reliance on robots instead of not using them as much as they could be used.
    a. True
    b. False

18. The reason(s) fixed shifts should be preferred over rotating shifts is (are)
    a. disrupted circadian rhythms.
    b. difficulty in remembering work schedules.
    c. inability to use compressed workweek arrangements.
    d. loss of socialization opportunities.
    e. a and b
    f. a and d
    g. b and c

19. Research shows that the greatest problem with compressed workweeks is the increase in accidents from fatigue.
    a. True
    b. False

20. Flextime schedules that are totally flexible are called _____ _____, and flextime schedules that require commitment for a certain period of time are called _____.

21. When you go to work at a new job, you are shown a work area where all the desks for data entry operators are grouped in a single area. You are working in what kind of office arrangement?
    a. Landscaped
    b. Bullpen
    c. Product-driven
    d. Space-allocated

22. If you are an account artist in an advertising company and have a good graphics computer, modem, and fax machine at home, you may be able to persuade your supervisor that you could improve your productivity by

a. having a virtual office.

b. using flextime.

c. telecommuting.

d. working in an open office.

23. The best candidates for telecommuting work are employees who are doing poorly at the office because they are so easily distracted and will not have distractions at home.

a. True

b. False

24. One of the problems in developing successful quality-of-work-life programs is

a. the high cost.

b. the time away from work.

c. a management position that views employee and organizational needs as competing.

d. lack of interest among employees.

Use your browser to go to
http://www.pc.ibm.com/us/healthycomputing/we-wo.html
the IBM site for healthy computing. Compare the location where you usually use a computer with IBM's suggestions for workstation ergonomics (all parts) based on human factors (ergonomics) research. List the ways in which your workplace meets IBM's standards and the ways in which it does not. Indicate what changes you could make to meet IBM's standards for healthy computing.

WEB EXERCISE

13

Employee Stress, Safety, and Health

LEARNING OBJECTIVES
STRESS IN THE WORKPLACE
Stress and Productivity
Consequences of Stress
Contributors to Stress
Stress Management at Work

SAFETY IN THE WORKPLACE
Accidents, Injuries, and Illnesses at Work
Reducing and Preventing Accidents and Injuries at Work
Workplace Violence
Case Study Preventing Violence at Work

Chapter Outline

Learning Objectives

After reading this chapter, you should be able to answer the following questions:

- What is the relationship between stress and productivity?
- What are the organizational and personal outcomes of too much work stress?
- What are the typical organizational and personal contributors to stress? How do they influence stress at work?
- What individual and organizational methods of stress management are commonly used?
- What is the role of an employee assistance program in stress management?
- How safe or unsafe is the workplace for employees? What is the role of the Occupational Safety and Health Administration?
- What defines or should define an accident in the workplace?
- What are the organizational and personal contributors to accidents, injuries, and illnesses at work?
- How do design changes at work reduce the incidence of accidents and injuries?
- In what ways can human factors reduce accidents and injuries at work?
- How has violence affected the workplace?
- What actions should be taken to reduce violence in the workplace?

In the early years of the twentieth century stress and the health and safety of workers were not areas of concern in industrial/organizational (I/O) psychology. In the era of scientific management people were thought of as extensions of the machinery they operated. The Hawthorne Western Electric studies (Chapter 1) changed this basic assumption and looked at workers as complex human beings with emotional and social needs as well as physical needs. This chapter looks at the development of concern about the stress, health, and safety of employees and current applications of research in this field. This has become one of the most rapidly growing areas in I/O psychology, indicating increasing concern in organizations. The need for that concern is evidenced by surveys such as one that found that 89 percent of a sample of employees felt substantial or great pressure at work (*Journal of Accountancy*, 1997). The concern in organizations is evidenced by the growing number of workplace programs designed to promote safety, health, and stress reduction at work.

STRESS IN THE WORKPLACE

The stress-related effects of work are one of the most costly problems for many organizations. In Japan companies may be required to compensate the families of workers who die of stress from overwork. Current estimates in the United States

Stress The physical and/or psychological response to the demands made on a person.

of the cost of stress in the workplace range from $200 billion to $300 billion annually (Farren, 1999). Those costs include absenteeism; diminished productivity; employee turnover; accidents, direct medical, legal, and insurance fees; and workers' compensation awards. It makes good business sense to manage stress at work and reduce those costs as much as possible.

When stress management became a concern several years ago, many organizations decided that their goal would be to create a stress-free workplace. Not only is this unrealistic, it is undesirable. Without some stress, there can be no performance. **Stress** usually is perceived as something undesirable, but the general definition of the term pertains to the response of people to the demands placed on them. This includes many of the normal pressures most people experience at work. For example, a person's preparation for work could be measured as more stressful than resting in bed, but preparation for work usually is considered necessary and beneficial. However, if an employee raced frantically to get ready for work every morning, this usually would be considered too much stress.

One psychologist described the difference between stress levels that are too low, good, and too high by using the analogy of a violin string. If a violin string is pulled too tightly, only screeches and a broken string result. If the string is too loose, the tone of the music is not right. It is only when the string is tightened correctly that the best tone is produced. While getting ready for work in only fifteen minutes may be too much stress for many people, staying in bed all day represents too little stress or pressure to be productive.

Stress and Productivity

Many years ago Yerkes and Dodson (1908) graphed the relationship between stress and productivity (Figure 13.1). The middle area of the graph shows the stress levels that result in the greatest productivity. The goal of stress management programs in the workplace should be to find that area for each employee and maintain it within the organization. This is a very general and simple description of the relationship between stress and performance. The many different types of stress and organizational and performance variables may lead to other relationships between stress and productivity (Beehr, 1985).

Fortunately, most jobs do not involve the extreme emergency situations typical of the jobs of paramedics and police officers, but psychological and emotional stresses that build up slowly may lead to the same consequences. In some ways the jobs of paramedics and police officers may be better in terms of stress, because there is an awareness of the need to deal with the high stress levels that are produced. A day care worker whose job appears to amount only to playing with children all day may actually have stress levels as high as or higher than those of a police officer, as more and more stressors are added to her life.

When stress is viewed as the adaptation people make to changes in the environment, even positive events such as a vacation and winning a lottery become

Figure 13.1

The Yerkes–Dodson curve showing the relationship between stress and performance.

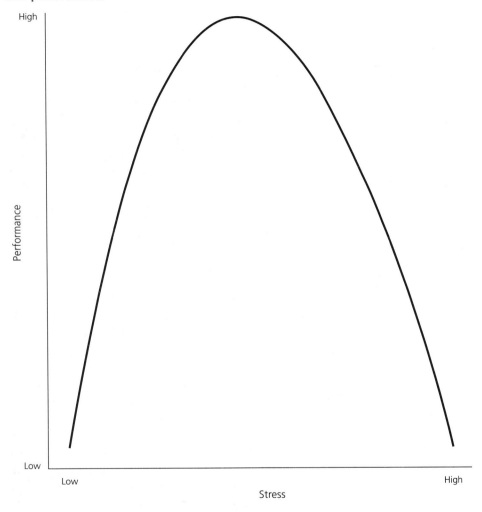

From R. M. Yerkes & J. D. Dodson. (1908). The relation of strength of stimulus to rapidity of habit-formation. *Journal of Comparative Neurology and Psychology, 18,* 459–482.

stressors. A person's reaction to winning a lottery—the increased heart rate, sweating, and a stomach tied in knots—sounds physically much like the reaction people have to rushing to work to avoid being late. The kind of stress that results from positive events is called **eustress** to distinguish it from negative stress, called **distress,** such as that caused by losing a job or being late for work (Golembiewski, Muzenrider, & Stevenson, 1986).

Stressors The characteristics or conditions that lead to stress.

Eustress Stress that arises from a positive experience.

Distress Stress that arises from a negative experience.

Too much stress, whether good or bad, can lead to undesirable consequences for the individual and the organization. The next sections of this chapter examine the consequences of stress, the sources of stress, and ways to manage stress levels.

Consequences of Stress

When stress is too high for too long, there are outcomes for the individual and the organization. The organizational outcomes may seem the most directly important to the company, but the hidden costs of the personal outcomes may exceed the direct organizational costs. Although the Bureau of Labor Statistics (1999) shows a decrease in occupational stress cases from 1992 to 1997, the absence rate for stress cases is more than four times the absence rate for all other nonfatal injuries and illnesses. Occupational stress cases decreased by 15 percent, but all other work-related injury and illness cases decreased by 21 percent.

Organizational Outcomes

The most common organizationally related outcomes of stress include absenteeism, tardiness, low performance, sabotage, and accidents. Several different types of absenteeism are related to stress. When an employee has a bad cold and stays home, this appears not to be stress-related because most people get several colds each year. But there is a link between stress and illnesses such as colds and flu: the greater vulnerability of the body to viral infections during periods of increased stress. Research confirms the relationship between high stress levels and higher rates of absenteeism (Jacobsen, Aldana, Goetzel, & Vardell, 1996; Vasse, Nijhuis, & Kok, 1998).

Prolonged high stress levels also may cause employees to call in sick when they are not physically ill. Those employees may feel that they are at the point where they need a mental health break, as one study documented in a group of nurses (Hackett & Bycio, 1996). Some organizations have begun to build such absences into their employee benefit plans, which allow an employee to say she is not coming in that day and not be required to give a reason. It could be argued that recovery from too much stress is just as important as recovery from the flu, but most employers allow sick days only for recovery from physical illnesses. Tardiness can be viewed as a small break from stress compared with the lengthier relief of being absent. Tardiness also may be a way to postpone the return to an unpleasantly stressful work situation. The employee who cannot seem to get to work on time and the employee who is always late returning from lunch or breaks may be avoiding the high stress levels in the work situation for as long as possible. These little breaks can add up to as much lost time as entire days of absence.

In terms of job avoidance, the ultimate response to stress is to quit the organization. High turnover levels can be a sign that stress at work has become too much for the employees to cope with (Dwyer & Ganster, 1991). When employees choose to stay in stressful organizations or professions, one of the factors that lessen the likelihood of quitting is commitment to the organization or profession. Jamal (1984) found that the most committed employees exhibit fewer negative effects of stress and show better coping skills in a stressful environment.

When a good employee leaves an organization, there is an obvious replacement cost. When employees stay on the job but respond to excessive stress with counterproductive behaviors, the costs may be less obvious but are just as high for the organization. High stress levels have been associated with employee sabotage, such as assembly line workers who might hang soda bottles in the door panels of cars in response to the pressures of their work. One study found that, among employees who were already predisposed to stealing from employers, high stress levels increased the likelihood of theft and the dollar amount of that theft (Jones & Boye, 1994). High stress levels also have been linked with a greater number of accidents (Matteson & Ivancevich, 1982).

Each of these organizational outcomes points back to the relationship between stress and performance. Numerous studies have shown a pattern in which increasing stress levels are related to lower performance levels (Jamal, 1984; Motowidlo, Packard, & Manning, 1986). Although most organizations are willing to accept temporarily lowered performance levels that result from a direct stressor, such as downsizing or relocating an office, the continued loss of performance from continuing high stress levels may be an avoidable cost. One of the problems here is that the stress-related problems may continue after the temporary stressor has been removed. One study reported continuing high stress levels among workers who originally had been designated as surplus employees during a downsizing operation, even though they were retained after the downsizing was completed (Armstrong-Stassen, 1997).

Personal Outcomes

The cost to the individual employee of work-related stress may be very high more often and in more cases than is believed. Most employees have heard of an executive driven by stress until he had a heart attack and died at his desk. The Japanese term *karoshi* is used to describe an employee who works himself to death. It is one of the leading causes of death among Japanese workers (*HR Focus*, 1992). In the United States there were 3,418 cases of occupational stress injuries and illness in 1997 (Bureau of Labor Statistics, 1999). The number of employees who say they experience too much stress on the job may be as high as 50 percent, and many of those employees may be exhibiting such negative effects of work-related stress as high blood pressure, heart problems, elevated serum cholesterol levels, and increased injury rates (Kenny, 1995).

The physical effects of stress often are not apparent unless the stress results from a crisis such as a car accident. Too much stress over long periods leads to negative results that can be both physical and psychological.

Karoshi A Japanese term used to describe an employee who works himself or herself to death.

General adaptation syndrome The three-stage model developed by Selye that describes how individuals react to stress, from alarm to resistance to exhaustion.

Fight-or-flight response The physiological arousal of a person in response to stress.

A number of years ago Hans Selye, a physician, developed a model of reactions to stress, dividing stress responses into three stages: alarm, resistance, and exhaustion (Selye, 1976). He called these three steps the **general adaptation syndrome.** In the alarm stage, a stressor is recognized and physiological change begins to occur. The initial response to a stressor is called the **fight-or-flight response.** Regardless of whether the person stays and confronts the stressor or runs away from it, the same initial pattern of physical responses begins. These responses include a surge of adrenaline and increases in heart rate and blood pressure, pupil dilation, and decreases in the digestive process, physiological changes that people would usually associate with increased stress. If the stressor is removed during this alarm stage, there are typically no long-term negative effects.

If the stressors are not removed, the person goes on to the stage of resistance. In this stage it appears that the person is meeting the demands of the increased stress levels because many of the symptoms of the alarm stage are no longer apparent. That surge of adrenaline that accompanied the initial fight-or-flight response occurs on a continuing basis. One therapist blames the increased pace of work for not giving employees time to bounce back from crises. Instead of a cycle of stress and recovery, there is only unending stress (Miller, 1988). Whereas the surge of adrenaline was helpful in dealing with the stressor at the beginning, the continuing elevation of the levels of that hormone can reduce the ability of the person's immune system to fight off disease.

In the last stage—exhaustion—the person's body is no longer able to produce enough adrenaline to cope with the stressor, and the early symptoms of the alarm stage reappear. The ultimate end of this stage is the death of the person from a stress-related illness such as a heart attack, or from the body's inability to fight off an illness such as pneumonia.

With such high stakes, it appears that the correct response is to remove the stressors long before the exhaustion stage is reached. Although that seems like a reasonable answer, research has shown considerable variation in employee and organizational responses to stress. People and organizations cause stress in a number of similar ways, but individual responses to the same stressor can be very different. The next section examines some personal and organizational variables that have been found to contribute to stress in employees.

Contributors to Stress

Researchers generally agree that neither the organization nor the individual alone is entirely responsible for high stress levels, but research also has shown that both can contribute to negative stress responses in different ways. The current increase in disability claims for work-related stress illness seems to indicate that greater weight is being given to organizational factors. Yet part of the apparent increase may actually be due to people's unwillingness to acknowledge their own contributions to a bad situation. Organizational and personal contributions to stress can produce lethal combinations, but personal choices and organizational factors also can lead to a reduction in stress. Although organizational and personal stress contributors are examined separately in the following sections, it is important to keep their combined effects in mind.

Organizational Contributors to Stress

Some of the most frequently cited organizational causes of stress are job and career uncertainty, technology, increased demand to learn new skills, increased demand for speed, lack of personal control, and poor workplace communications (Minter, 1991). Organizations that prevent stress from these sources are seen as desirable places to work, compared with organizations that deal with these factors only after the results of stress become apparent.

Demands of Work **Work overload** is the term used to indicate that speed and skill demands are too much for an employee. The overload may be quantitative or qualitative. If it is quantitative, there is too much work to do in the time available. Qualitative overload means that the work is too difficult for the employee to do. On a temporary basis work overload may be frustrating or exhausting; on a permanent basis it is a major source of stress, resulting in lower-quality work and lower job satisfaction (Kirmeyer & Dougherty, 1988).

The opposite of work overload is **work underload;** researchers have confirmed that it can result in stress (Johnson & Johnson, 1996). The most common form of work underload occurs when employees feel that they are not using their skills, training, and knowledge. Not having enough work activity also can be a source of stress. Hospital emergency room personnel often report that very slow times at work are as stressful as the busiest times.

Stress contributors that can result from mergers and downsizing include role ambiguity and role conflict. **Role ambiguity** results when employees are unclear about the responsibilities of their jobs. During a merger of companies there may be people from each company doing the same work, but they are unclear about how their jobs will be structured in the new organization. The three most common causes of role ambiguity are the complexity of organizations, the rate of change in organizations, and a managerial philosophy that believes in keeping information from employees (Kahn, Wolfe, Quinn, Snoek, & Rosenthal, 1964). In a meta-analysis, Jackson and Schuler (1985) found that role ambiguity and role conflict were related to lower organizational commitment and a stronger likelihood of leaving an organization, as well as lower employee participation and higher anxiety levels.

Role conflict results when an employee is caught between two competing sets of people who want different things. This often occurs when an employee reports to more than one supervisor. It is difficult to know which supervisor's demands are more important or urgent and who should be satisfied first. In recent years more attention has been given to the role conflicts created when employees are required

Work overload Stress caused by having too much work to do in the time available or not having the skills needed to perform the job.

Work underload Stress caused by not having enough work to do or not being able to use one's skills on the job.

Role ambiguity Stress caused when an employee is not clear about what she or he is required to do on a job.

Role conflict Stress caused by opposing demands that cannot both be met.

Technostress Stress caused by the never-ending demands of modern technology or by an employee's inability to use new technology, such as computers.

Sexual harassment Unwelcome sexual behaviors that are linked to conditions of employment, performance evaluation, or making a hostile work environment.

to behave in ways that conflict with their ethical beliefs, such as destroying material and saying that it never existed and lying for a supervisor who has gone off to play golf (Schwepker, Ferrell, & Ingram, 1997). Ethical role conflicts can overlap with personal contributors to stress in the workplace because each person may respond differently to questionable ethical situations just as each person may respond differently to the personal contributors to stress at work.

Technostress A more recently discovered organizational contributor to stress is **technostress.** This is stress resulting from fear of new technology or from the work overload caused by never getting away from work because of all the modern technology that creates constant contact with work. Laptop computers with modems, e-mail, and cellular telephones keep employees permanently in touch with their jobs. Employees who make use of this type of technology often report feeling that there is never any time that belongs to them. Other employees are anxious about their ability to keep up with the constantly changing technological requirements of the workplace. Fifty years ago, workers who learned drafting skills in school knew that they could use those skills throughout their careers. However, many drafting tasks have been replaced by computer-assisted design (CAD) programs that are upgraded continually, requiring new skills and learning and often leading to increased technostress for these workers.

Other organizational contributors to employee stress provide good examples of the concept of the person–environment fit. One employee may see as desirable what is stressful to another employee. Frequent work-related geographic moves typically are regarded as stressful, although not by all employees.

Sexual Harassment and the Hostile Work Environment Like the day care worker whose stress accumulates over time, the employee who experiences sexual harassment at work may show the cumulative effects of stress. While sexual harassment often is considered a women's issue, court cases have shown that men also can experience being sexually harassed.

Sexual harassment includes a wide variety of behaviors, such as unwelcome sexual advances, requests for sexual favors, and other verbal and physical conduct of a sexual nature. Harassment occurs when those behaviors are linked to conditions of employment, performance evaluation, or a hostile work environment. It requires a great deal of interpretation to determine when certain behaviors cross the line and become sexually harassing. A fire station bunkroom wall with pictures of naked women posted on it could be interpreted as creating a hostile work environment for women firefighters who must stay there while they are on duty. This is one of the five types of sexual harassment (Table 13.1) that are recognized as illegal behavior as well as producing a stressful work environment.

Although over 97 percent of companies have written policies about sexual harassment, the number of complaints has continued to increase. In 1999, the Equal Employment Opportunity Commission (EEOC) received 15,222 sexual harassment

Table 13.1

TYPES OF SEXUAL HARASSMENT

Type of Harassment	Example
Gender harassment	An engineering professor making fun of female engineering students by suggesting that women cannot concentrate with male students in the room
Seductive behavior	An employee leaving detailed fantasies about sexual behavior with another employee on that employee's desk each day
Sexual bribery	A supervisor who promises to inflate an employee's performance evaluation if she will have intercourse with him
Sexual coercion	A supervisor who threatens to put an employee on a bad work schedule if she does not go out with him
Sexual imposition	An employee who exposes himself to the worker next to him as they sit at adjoining desks

complaints, resulting in $50.3 million in benefits to the complainants (EEOC, 2000). Although this is a slight decrease from the previous year, it represents serious economic consequences for organizations. The costs involve reactions to stress such as absenteeism, lower productivity, and employee turnover, and sometimes legal costs as well (Petrocelli & Repa, 1992). Some of the costs are less obvious than others, as is true for many stressors. Piotrkowski (1998) found that increased sexual harassment was associated with decreased job satisfaction, greater distress, and greater alcohol use, factors that could have economic effects on organizations.

Organizations can take preventive action by making sure each employee knows the company policy on sexual harassment, by quickly and thoroughly investigating complaints, and by training employees about what situations are considered sexually harassing. In 1999 the EEOC issued a policy statement indicating the steps that organizations need to take to meet legal requirements (Table 13.2).

Table 13.2

EQUAL EMPLOYMENT OPPORTUNITY COMMISSION (EEOC) REQUIREMENTS FOR ORGANIZATIONS TO DEAL WITH SEXUAL HARASSMENT IN THE WORKPLACE

Distributing to all employees and enforcing a written antiharassment policy

Detailing in writing the procedure for employees to follow in making a formal complaint without fear of retaliation

Including the policy on sexual harassment in the company handbook and permanently posting it on bulletin boards

Training all employees on the types of conduct that violate sexual harassment policies

Complaints that will help the company take quick action should be specific and include documentation of the harassment, the names of witnesses, and a list of specific attempts to stop the harassment. In a study of sexual harassment court cases, Terpestra and Baker (1992) found that the victims were almost 100 percent successful in winning their lawsuits if there were witnesses and documentation and if the company had taken no action after being formally notified. Taking charge of the situation by complaining and seeing the behavior changed is an important step in reducing stress levels and restoring the emotional health of a harassed employee. Changing the behavior of the harassing employee is also an important step in restoring the emotional health of the organization because that action by the company clearly indicates that it will not accept sexual harassment in the workplace. Making employees aware of sexual harassment issues is often part of diversity training (Chapter 4).

Gender Attitudes Although gender attitudes have been changing throughout history, the stressful effects of the dramatic changes that have occurred in the last several decades have become apparent only recently. It may appear that working couples have jobs inside the home and outside the home, but Piotrkowski and Repetti (1984) suggest that this is actually a matter of three jobs divided between two people: two market jobs and one unpaid job in the household. Typically, the ways in which men and women relate to these paid and unpaid jobs has been unequal and very different (Zedeck & Mosier, 1990). For men, the perspective has most often been that work has been brought into the family environment. For women, the overlap has most often been in the other direction: Family concerns have been brought into the work environment.

In the late 1980s Felice Schwartz created a great deal of controversy by suggesting that some employed women do not want to focus on their careers to the degree required for continuing progress in the organization (Schwartz, 1989). This may be especially true when the woman has young children at home. A study of absenteeism rates for employees who cared for young children or parents found that caregiving for children had a great impact on absenteeism (Boise & Neal, 1996). When companies identified women they felt were not as job-committed as they believed men in the same position would be, the women were assigned to what has come to be called "the mommy track." The mommy track assigns these more family-oriented women to jobs that are less desirable and less likely to lead to advancement and career development but provide greater flexibility for attending to family needs. Some women felt this treated women as being less important than male employees, but others felt it was a way to give some women permission to pay more attention to their families than to work at a particular stage of life. While some women may find the mommy track desirable, women who want to resume a traditional career track may find little or no possibility for change. Jenkins (1997) reports on the problems female college professors encounter when they have children before completing the lengthy and time-consuming process of obtaining tenure.

Since most women still have the primary responsibility for home and family, it is logical that working couples identify issues such as child-care and care of older parents as mainly women's issues. The reason organizations have become involved in these issues is usually to reduce organizational costs, including the costs that are stress-related. In one year, Los Angeles Department of Water and Power workers indicated in an anonymous survey that they had missed 7,318 days of work because of child-care problems. The cost to the company was almost $1 million in salary and benefits. Company involvement in child and dependent care programs can take many forms. Some organizations offer paid child or dependent care as an option in a cafeteria-style benefit program that allows an employee to choose from several fringe benefits. Overall, Raber (1994) found that employees who made use of employee-sponsored child care programs had significantly higher job satisfaction and significantly lower levels of stress.

The reason organizations are willing to become involved in the child and dependent care issues of their employees can be traced to the numerous studies showing the organizational benefits of those programs. Zedeck and Mosier (1990) reported a number of studies showing that organizational support of these programs led to better productivity, stability, loyalty, and morale and to lower absenteeism, turnover, and tardiness.

J. Nourok/PhotoEdit

■ A woman brings a baby to a day care center.

Personal Contributors to Stress

There is little doubt that certain jobs are more stressful than others, but the responses of individuals to high- or low-stress jobs can be extremely different. A study by the National Institute on Workers Compensation and the American Institute of Stress cited inner-city high school teachers, police officers, miners, air-traffic controllers, customer service workers, and secretaries as having among the most stressful jobs in the United States. While some inner-city high school teachers and police officers show a number of negative stress outcomes, there are others who appear to thrive in their jobs. The difference may lie in personal factors that relate to stress. The sections following look at the personal factors of life changes, Type A and Type B personalities, hardiness, and burnout.

Life Changes At different times in their lives people are more or less resistant to job stress because of decreased or increased stress, respectively, outside work.

Holmes and Rahe (1971) developed a scale that assigned point values to changes in people's lives. The greater the change, the higher the number of points assigned to an event. Some of the events were positive (winning a lottery, taking a vacation), but many were unpleasant (getting a traffic citation, losing a job). This scale has been updated (Bhagat, 1983), but the basic assumption is the same. The greater the value of life change events is, the more likely it is that the person will experience health-related effects of stress. Table 13.3 shows some of the life change events and the values attached to those changes.

Table 13.3

STRESS EFFECTS OF LIFE EVENTS MEASURED IN LIFE CHANGE UNITS

Life Event	Number of Life Change Units
Death of spouse	100
Divorce	73
Marital separation	65
Imprisonment	63
Death of close family member	63
Marriage	50
Fired from job	47
Marital reconciliation	45
Pregnancy	45
Retirement	45
Sexual difficulties	39
Gain of new family member	39
Major business adjustment	39
Death of close friend	37
Change to a different career	36
Buying a house	31
Trouble with in-laws	29
Beginning or ending formal schooling	26
Trouble with boss	23
Change in residence	20
Change in eating habits	15
Vacation	13
Minor violation of the law	11

From R. S. Bhagat. (1983). Effects of stressful life events on individual performance and work adjustment processes within organizational settings: A research model. *Academy of Management Review, 8,* 660–671.

This approach has been criticized for assuming that everyone reacts to certain changes in the same way and for not accounting for different reactions at different stages of life (Kasl, 1981). There is still a positive correlation between increased life changes and increased health problems. Another criticism of this approach suggests that the events on the life change scale happen very infrequently but that everyday hassles, because they occur so frequently, can be as stressful as some life change events. Losing a job is generally more stressful than getting stuck in a traffic jam, but some researchers have suggested that situations that occur daily, such as traffic jams, can add as much stress as do some life change events (Savery & Wooden, 1994; Zohar, 1997). Life change events alone cannot predict exactly who will show health-related effects of stress and when those effects will occur, but change events are clearly contributors to overall stress.

Type A and Type B Personalities Another personal contributor to stress has been examined in research on the personality factors associated with coronary heart disease. While genetic factors, diet, and exercise all contribute, researchers found that a particular set of personality characteristics frequently was associated with heart disease even when the other factors were controlled (Freidman & Rosenman, 1974; Rosenman, 1978). The combined personality characteristics that are associated with coronary heart disease are aggressiveness, hostility, time urgency, and competitiveness. This combination is called the **Type A personality.** Personality characteristics that include being extremely easygoing are called the **Type B personality.** Freidman and Rosenman originally believed that Type A personality characteristics caused much more intense reactions to stressors: The more intense reactions led to the physical effects that caused the increase in heart disease.

Later researchers found that the link between Type A behavior and heart disease is not quite as direct as Freidman and Rosenman (1974) originally believed. Smith and Pope (1990) suggested that overall hostility and inappropriate reactions to hostility may be the underlying link between Type A personality and heart disease. Another possible link may be the generally higher arousal levels of Type A personalities even during rest times (Palmero, Codina, & Rosel, 1993; Smyth & Yardani, 1992). One researcher suggested that the most active ingredient in the Type A personality–heart disease link is the feeling of time urgency, which leads to chronic or continuous levels of arousal (Wright, 1991).

People with Type A personalities often are described as **polyphasic** because they frequently try to do more than one thing at the same time. They are impatient and often finish sentences for others in conversations. One of the consequences of modern technology is that it makes it possible for people with a Type A personality to have many separate tasks going on at the same time.

Another active ingredient in the Type A personality mix is a general unhappiness with, dislike of, and perceived threat from one's environment. A meta-analysis

Type A personality A set of personality characteristics, including aggressiveness, hostility, time urgency, and competitiveness, that may be linked to high rates of heart disease.

Type B personality A set of personality characteristics— described by the absence of Type A personality characteristics and by a generally easygoing lifestyle— that are linked to low rates of heart disease.

Polyphasic Having the ability and desire to do more than one activity at a time.

of studies relating Type A behaviors to heart disease showed a stronger relationship between the personality characteristic of negative affectivity and heart disease than between the global Type A personality and heart disease (Booth-Kewley & Freidman, 1987). **Negative affectivity** is characterized by the emotions of anger, hostility, and depression. A popular measure of the Type A personality is the Jenkins Activity Survey (JAS), samples of which are shown in Figure 13.2 (Jenkins, Zyzanski, & Rosenman, 1979). The JAS consists of fifty items that assess the Type A personality, but it is best at measuring the dimension of competitiveness (Matthews, 1982).

Figure 13.2

Sample of items from the Jenkins Activity Survey.

Directions: For each of the following items, please circle the one best answer.

1. Would people who know you well agree that you tend to get irritated easily?
   a. definitely yes
   b. probably yes
   c. probably no
   d. definitely no

2. Would people who know you well agree that you tend to do most things in a hurry?
   a. definitely yes
   b. probably yes
   c. probably no
   d. definitely no

From C. D. Jenkins, S. J. Zyzanski, & R. H. Rosenman. (1979). *The activity survey for health prediction, Form N*. New York: Psychological Corporation.

While the Type A personality often is viewed as undesirable, its higher arousal levels and greater feelings of time urgency can result in a better level of performance (Fekken & Jakubowski, 1990). Type A personalities usually also have higher levels of job satisfaction, which may be related to higher performance levels (Jamal, 1990). Type A personalities share a number of characteristics with the high need to achieve personality described in Chapter 6 and typically score high on need to achieve measures (Ganster, Schaubroeck, Sime, & Mays, 1991). This is the pattern of behavior that often is associated with the success of an entrepreneur or a self-employed consultant. One study showed that Type A personalities are less likely to cheat in academic settings, a factor that would confirm their need for individual accomplishment (Huss, Curnyn, Roberts, & Davis, 1993).

Research generally has been supportive of the correlation between the Type A personality and coronary heart disease, especially when a lengthy structured interview is used to assess the Type A personality (Schaubroeck, Ganster, & Kemmerer, 1994). Nevertheless, several researchers found that there are individuals in the Type A group who are very stress-resistant even in extended stressful situations.

Hardiness When researchers looked at chronically stressful situations, some individuals seemed to be relatively untouched by the negative consequences of long-term stress, regardless of the stressor. When the question was changed from "Who gets sick under stress?" to "Who stays healthy under stress?" researchers (Kobasa, Hilker, & Maddi, 1980; Kobasa, Maddi, & Kahn, 1982) found a personality characteristic that they called **hardiness.** People who are high in hardiness have a sense of commitment to family, work, and activities. They see themselves as being in control of their lives and look for and welcome challenges in all aspects of their lives. Hardiness allows a person to reject the negative effects of stress the way an inoculation allows a person to reject the polio virus. In a study of 112 cadets during a six-month training course, the number of illnesses and infections was significantly lower among cadets who were higher in hardiness (Solano, Battisti, & Stanisci, 1993). Another study found that students highest in hardiness showed the fewest blood pressure changes and the least arousal during a stressful task (Contrada, 1989).

People who are highest in hardiness appear to be able to look at stressful situations as representing a positive challenge that they will be able to overcome. Hardiness appears to result from certain background experiences and characteristics, including (1) diverse circumstances, with the opportunity to try many activities of moderate difficulty; (2) warmth and social support; and (3) a large number of rewarding experiences (Maddi & Kobasa, 1991). More recent research (Benishek, 1996; Bernard, Hutchison, Lavin, & Pennington, 1996) has suggested that the concept of hardiness may, however, be too simplistic to explain the stress resistance of these individuals. Other personality factors, such as ego strength, self-esteem, self-efficacy, optimism, and maladjustment levels, may be parts of the personality profile of stress-resistant persons. This recent research suggested that "health proneness" would be a better term for the stress-resistant personality. Factors that appear to contribute to health proneness include feelings of personal control and social support (Reich & Zautra, 1997).

Burnout At the opposite end of the continuum from people who are high in hardiness are employees who come to work but view each day with dread because they feel overwhelmed by stressors over which they have no control. These workers are described as suffering from **burnout.** Employees who are in "people" jobs—nurses, teachers, public aid caseworkers, and day care workers—are most likely to experience burnout. The process of becoming burned out usually is described as involving three separate but essential components (Jackson, Schwab, & Schuler, 1986), as is shown in Table 13.4.

Hardiness A personality trait that allows a person to be resistant to the negative effects of stress by viewing stress as a challenge rather than a negative event.

Burnout The state of physical, mental, and emotional exhaustion and cynicism caused by long-term job stress.

Depersonalization A stage
of burnout characterized by
viewing others as cases and
illnesses rather than as
people.

Table 13.4

COMPONENTS OF BURNOUT

Component	Characteristics	Example
Depersonalization	Employee develops a psychological distance between himself and clients, who are viewed negatively	A physician who refers to a patient as "the hot appendix in 203" rather than by name
Feeling of low personal accomplishment	Employee feels that no matter what she does, it will not make a difference	A social worker who feels that no matter what he does, no clients will get off welfare
Emotional exhaustion	Result of excessive psychological and emotional demands made on an employee	A teacher who continues to show up to work but grades no papers and sees no students during office hours

Unlike an employee who has a heart attack and stays home to recover, a burned-out employee continues to come to work each day, making it more difficult to detect the negative effects of stress. Burned-out employees are often rigid and inflexible because they are too exhausted and do not have the energy to be creative and find alternative solutions. A burned-out teacher may refuse to allow students to take a test any time other than the time it is scheduled, even if it would be reasonable to find some alternatives. Part of the exhaustion is a very real tiredness because a burned-out employee often starts as a committed employee who puts in many extra hours of work. One of the first signs of burnout is that although more hours are being spent on the job, less is accomplished.

Although it may seem that some degree of burnout is inevitable in many jobs, research has shown that a sense of personal control and social support from supervisors, peers, and family members can help protect employees from becoming burned out (Capner & Caltabiano, 1993; Huebner, 1994; Papadatou, Anagnostopoulos, & Monos, 1994). Diagnosing burnout in the early stages or preventing it is important to help organizations avoid the negative consequences of lower performance and quitting. One of the newest approaches to preventing burnout focuses on creating a better fit between the employee and the work situation and preventing poor decision making by the employee (Maslach & Goldberg, 1998). This approach emphasizes the interaction between the employee and the job situation.

There are several methods for measuring burnout, but the most common is probably the Maslach Burnout Scale (Maslach & Jackson, 1981). A sample of the items used to measure employee burnout is given in Figure 13.3.

Figure 13.3

Assessment of employee burnout with sample items from the Maslach Burnout Scale.

Each item is scored on a 6-point scale from 0 (never) to 6 (every day) for how often the employee taking the survey feels in the described ways about his or her job.

1. I feel emotionally drained by my work.
2. I feel frustrated by my job.
3. I feel used up at the end of the workday.
4. Working with people all day is really a strain for me.
5. I feel like I'm at the end of my rope.
6. I worry that this job is hardening me emotionally.
7. I've become more callous toward people since I took this job.

From C. Maslach & S. E. Jackson. (1981). The measurement of experienced burnout. *Journal of Occupational Behavior, 2,* 99–113.

Although it is possible to reduce burnout by developing a good social support system or not taking on more work than one can do, most jobs have some degree of stress associated with them. Whether that stress leads to greater or lower productivity depends on a combination of personal and organizational factors. The emphasis here is on a good person–environment fit. A rigid, inflexible person would find working in an unstructured computer software development company stressful but would find the high degree of structure in a very bureaucratic organization stress-reducing. This person–environment fit can be seen in the wide variety of stress management programs used in organizations. In an attempt to keep stress levels within productive ranges, many organizations have developed stress management programs to teach employees and supervisors ways to reduce stress organizationally and personally. The next section examines some of those programs and methods.

Stress Management at Work

Stress management programs at work may employ individual or organizational methods. Although organizations can reduce stress through better definitions of job roles, by preventing work overload, and by providing better training, the overwhelming focus of stress management programs has been on individual interventions (Ivancevich, Matteson, Freedman, & Phillips, 1990). When researchers looked for stress management programs that focused on organizational stressors as intervention targets, they found only four. Those programs were ones that included developing greater employee participation, establishing an employee stress reduction committee to provide suggestions to management, using flexible work schedules, and redesigning work.

Employee assistance program (EAP) The designated formal group in an organization that deals with individual employees' problems that affect job performance.

Employee Assistance Programs

Individually focused stress management programs are varied but are part of employee wellness programs administered by an employee assistance program (EAP) office. An **employee assistance program (EAP)** offers professional counseling to employees to prevent and treat problems at work. The programs are administered by employees within the organization (internal) or are contracted to outside consultants (external).

In general, EAPs do not try to change organizational contributors to stress in the workplace but attempt to make employees better able to cope with work stress. Over 82 percent of employees in the largest companies in the United States have access to EAPs that are part of the organization or are provided by an outside agency (Oss & Clary, 1998). Although EAPs first were used to treat existing problems such as alcohol and drug abuse, many companies have achieved better cost savings by preventing problems from the start. This has led to the development of wellness programs that focus on issues such as stopping smoking, weight loss, and heart disease prevention as well as stress management. Many EAPs are taking a larger view of contributors to stress and are developing programs in areas such as financial planning, caring for elderly parents, and sexual abuse as ways to prevent or deal with stress (Barrett, Scott, Gillespie, & Palmer, 1994; Gorey, Brice, & Rice, 1990).

Although stress management programs are a fast-growing EAP area, most programs have not been evaluated according to the research methods discussed in Chapter 2. Although the cost of EAPs is fairly low ($21 to $27 per covered employee), organizations need to be able to evaluate the return on that investment. Ivancevich, Matteson, Freedman, and Phillips (1990) report that more recent studies of stress management are using sound research methods that should lead to improvements in the quality of the programs. Studies such as those by Bellarosa and Chen (1997) looked at which stress management techniques had been found to be most effective. Relaxation was evaluated as the most practical intervention and physical fitness was rated as the most effective intervention. One of the beneficial outcomes of better evaluation of stress management programs is the ability to individualize programs for employees and organizations by referring to research findings—such as the different ways men and women experience stress (Jick & Mitz, 1985).

Methods of Stress Management

The best methods of stress management depend on both the individual and the organization. Some of the more common individual methods are exercise, meditation, relaxation techniques, cognitive approaches, time management, and goal setting. In a company in which the president encouraged employees to use meditation, the absence rate dropped 85 percent and the sick day rate dropped 30 percent among those who practiced meditation. The employees were followed for three years from the beginning of the program (Fritz, 1989). Relaxation techniques often include deep breathing methods and the relaxation response, a system similar to the deep physiological and mental rest provided by meditation (Benson, 1975).

Cognitive approaches to stress management emphasize changing the way an employee evaluates stress. A previous section of this chapter looked at individuals high in hardiness who view stressors as challenging rather than threatening. Lazarus (1991) discusses a method of using neutral or positive thoughts whenever stress is present to learn how to reevaluate the stressor.

Time management methods may focus on finding better ways to use the time that is available or taking control of time rather than letting it control the employee. Goal setting can be used to get an employee to set and achieve realistic goals and have a feeling of personal accomplishment.

Stress management is an important aspect of creating a healthy environment at work, but it is only one part. The next section looks at safety in the workplace as part of employee wellness and stress reduction.

SAFETY IN THE WORKPLACE

The concern for safety in the workplace is a rather recent development. In the early years of the twentieth century, if a worker was killed or disabled at work, the company might express regret to the worker's family, but the basic assumption was that the death or injury was the fault of the worker. In the 1930s social security legislation was passed that led to payments to the survivors of workers who died and disability payments for workers who were injured. The legislation provided payments no matter where the death or disability occurred, but it did encourage companies to look at safety in the workplace. A series of events in the 1960s, including the death of almost eighty West Virginia miners on the job, led to the passage of the Occupational Safety and Health Act of 1971. The **Occupational Safety and Health Administration (OSHA)** administers this legislation. It has developed safety standards for a number of work situations that represented workplace hazards people were already aware of (such as in mining and construction work) and hazards that people have become aware of only recently (such as secondhand smoke and workplace violence). Although there may be disagreement about acceptable levels of smoke and chemicals in the work environment, it is possible to set objective physical standards for a good workplace. Chapter 12 looked at several of these standards and the role of I/O psychologists in developing them. This section examines the role of the I/O psychologist in reducing and preventing accidents, illnesses, and violence at work.

Occupational Safety and Health Administration (OSHA) The federal government agency that oversees the health and safety of employees at work.

Accidents, Injuries, and Illnesses at Work

Even if OSHA did not inspect work sites and fine companies that violate written standards, most organizations still would try to reduce the number of accidents at work because of their cost. In 1998 the National Safety Council estimated the cost of work-related injuries to be over $25 million per year, mainly from time lost at work. Over six million workers were injured in work-related incidents in 1997.

Defining Accidents

An employee who is hit by a loose piece of machinery and has a broken arm is clearly an accident statistic, but he may not be counted as one. The most important criterion for determining an accident at work is time lost from work. This seems clear until one looks at the worker with the broken arm and finds out that he had the accident only minutes before he checked out for the day. He was able to return to work the next morning and be reassigned to a job that did not require the use of that arm.

Situations such as this often lead to substantial underreporting of accident rates by organizations. The reasons for wanting to report as few accidents as possible include avoiding having higher accident rates; maintaining a reputation as a safe place, in order to attract good workers; and avoiding penalties for unsafe work conditions. Instead of avoiding reporting accidents, organizations should be encouraged to report every accident, even if no time is lost, so that they can have the best information possible for avoiding future accidents.

OSHA can make sure that companies meet physical standards for safety, but there is not always much that it can do about the behavior of employees in preventing accidents. Regardless of the physical setting, the behavior of employees is the strongest contributing factor to accidents. Employees' behavior contributes even more to accidents when it is combined with unsafe equipment and procedures. While human error remains the major cause of accidents, the proportion of accidents it causes is declining. The number of accidents caused mainly by equipment and procedures has been increasing, however (Scherer, Brodzinski, & Crable, 1993). The strong relationship between people and equipment factors can be seen in the leading type of fatal accidents. Thirty percent of fatal work-related accidents in 1991 involved transportation (Castelli, 1993). Workers control the motor vehicles they operate, but poor procedures or operator errors in using the vehicles and poor equipment can operate in combination. The next section examines the human and workplace factors that contribute to accidents at work.

Organizational Contributors

As one might expect, the rate of accidents varies a great deal among different types of industries. Wholesale and retail trades account for a large portion of the work-related injury and illness total, but they employ many more people than

Jeffrey Blackman/Index Stock

■ The majority of on-the-job accidents involve workers and some type of vehicle.

mining does; at the same time, the associated injuries and illnesses tend to be less severe (Gloss & Wardell, 1984). The fatal injury rate is much higher in construction and mining. Across all types of industries, common contributors to accidents, injuries, and illnesses have been identified.

Physical Environment Many factors that are part of everyday work life can contribute to accidents. Noise is certainly part of people's lives both at work and outside work. When noise is so loud that it prevents hearing warning sounds, it becomes a factor in accidents. When noise is very loud for extended periods, it can lead to permanent hearing loss. The hearing loss usually occurs gradually and may not be considered a problem until it becomes severe (Ramsey, 1996). While hearing loss is the typical consequence, loud noise also has been associated with high blood pressure, heart disease, and psychiatric disorders (May, 1991; Theorell, 1990).

The term *illumination* refers to lighting levels in the work environment. Lighting levels that are too low to allow workers to see hazards or warnings can contribute to accidents and injuries, but lighting that is too high or produces glare also can lead to problems. Many companies use fluorescent fixtures to maintain even lighting levels. Safety organizations have investigated this type of lighting because of claims of a number of associated problems, such as skin problems. None of the studies have shown relationships between fluorescent lighting and skin conditions, however, and this type of lighting is no longer regarded as a problem at work. Although artificial lighting can maintain standard lighting levels, some organizations have found that the best lighting is the type that most closely replicates natural daylight; other companies use actual sunlight to supply a percentage of the light inside offices (Pierson, 1995).

In general it is better to have higher lighting levels than lower lighting levels, except in association with video display terminals. Too much lighting around those displays leads to glare and produces headaches and eyestrain. Brighter lighting for night shift workers increases alertness, possibly leading to a decrease in accidents (Campbell & Dawson, 1990).

Although most people prefer temperatures around 73 degrees and humidity levels about 45 percent, temperatures as low as 45 degrees or as high as 90 degrees can be tolerated without presenting a serious hazard to healthy people. The extremes of this range could be physically and psychologically uncomfortable and could be associated with lower work performance and increased accident rates when they are continuous over a number of hours or an entire work shift. The workers who are most likely to be exposed to excessive cold and its harmful effects are firefighters, outdoor workers, and refrigeration workers. Workers who are most likely to be exposed to excessive heat include cooks and bakers, cleaners, firefighters, and foundry workers. One study found significantly longer recovery times for firefighters who performed tasks in extremely high temperatures (Smith, Petruzzello, Kramer, & Misner, 1997).

Bad equipment design can be a contributing factor to accidents and injuries. Something as simple as the poor location of a stop button can lead to terrible injuries. In one example, a drill press operator who was wearing the heavy gloves required on the job caught a glove in a rotating drill bit. The on–off switch was too far away to reach, and in seconds the drill snapped off the worker's hand (Harrell, 1993). As computer use has increased, more attention has been focused on associated injuries. After much investigation, OSHA has rejected claims that the video display terminals (VDTs) used with computers give off excessive radiation. OSHA does continue to monitor the displays. More likely are problems such as eye fatigue and irritation, headaches, and dizziness. The change of physical features, such as the height of an employee's desk and chair and the lighting level, usually can eliminate these problems.

Another problem that often is associated with computer work is **repetitive motion injury** such as carpal tunnel syndrome, which leads to excessive pain in the wrist. Continuous and repeated motions cause such injury. Assembly line workers as well as employees who work with computers frequently report repetitive motion injuries. Changing equipment, such as providing wrist rests and different seating, and providing rest breaks often reduce or prevent these injuries.

Repetitive motion injury
An injury caused by many repetitions of a small motor behavior during the time at work.

Shift Work Although typically there are a smaller number of accidents during night shifts than during day shifts, night shift accidents tend to be more severe.

The smaller number may be a result of having fewer workers on the night shift or night employees being more aware of the need for alertness. Most accidents involving shift workers occur when they rotate work shifts. The change of sleeping and waking hours and the resulting fatigue may be responsible for many of these accidents. If workers must do shift work, they are better off staying on the same shift rather than switching. If workers must switch shifts, forward rotation and quickly rotating shifts are preferable (Knauth, 1996).

Sick Building Syndrome Open windows and doors are no longer found in many factories and offices as workplaces have become more energy-efficient. Such closed environments allow airborne pollution and illnesses to spread rapidly through the workplace. The result has been a dramatic increase in complaints of headaches, respiratory irritation, asthma, flulike symptoms, tightness of the chest, eye irritation, itchy skin, dizziness, and fatigue. When these symptoms occur in 10 to 20 percent of the workers in a building or area and the symptoms go away when the workers leave the building, this often is referred to as the **sick building syndrome (SBS)**. The causes of these symptoms can be poorly designed ventilation systems, a lack of fresh air drawn into the building, chemical compounds that evaporate in the air, tobacco smoke, and biological contaminants such as airborne viruses.

The U.S. Environmental Protection Agency (EPA) lists SBS as one of the five most important environmental issues in the United States. It estimates that 30 million to 75 million U.S. workers are at risk of becoming ill from indoor air pollution in the workplace. The EPA estimates that SBS costs organizations $66 billion per year. Although this seems to be a straightforward problem to correct, solutions have remained elusive. Many times an examination of a building shows no air quality readings in the unacceptable range for any of the common contaminants.

A possible answer to the continuing problems has come from researchers who found that a combination of contaminants, none of which alone was too high to be acceptable, could cause SBS problems. Another possible answer came when researchers found that some employees had developed a chemical sensitivity during the time they were exposed to a substance, such as carpet glue residue that remained in the environment even after the carpets were removed.

One difficulty in correcting SBS is that some architects and building managers believe that it is more of a psychological problem than a physical problem (Czander, 1994; Hughes & Holt, 1994). There is a precedent for that conclusion in the documentation of episodes in which many employees believe they are ill at the same time; this sometimes is referred to as **mass psychogenic illness**. This illness most often occurs among a group of workers who are friends. They believe they are ill, but there is nothing causing the symptoms. The workers most likely are doing simple, repetitive, boring jobs for low pay. This is most likely to occur among women who are dissatisfied with their work and have high levels of stress (Ryan & Morrow, 1992). These are not people who are faking an illness; they

---

Sick building syndrome (SBS) Symptoms of illness caused by the spread of airborne contaminants or pollution in tightly sealed buildings.

Mass psychogenic illness A stress-produced disability in which a number of employees at the same time believe they have developed a work-related illness.

suffer from a psychosomatic illness that is real to them even though the causes are psychological. Potera (1988) gives the example of a group of telephone operators who had to be evacuated twice in two days from their building because of symptoms of headaches, shortness of breath, dizziness, and nausea that the employees blamed on a strange odor. Investigation of all the physical possibilities showed that there was nothing wrong. When the workers agreed that the strange odor was gone, the symptoms disappeared.

If employees are really suffering as a result of SBS, the symptoms do not go away immediately after they leave the building but may improve over an extended period such as a weekend. Another difference is that SBS often shows up in particular physical locations within a building as a result of ventilation patterns. Mass psychogenic illness, on the other hand, spreads among members of social networks.

Ryan and Morrow (1992) suggest that the only way to make an accurate diagnosis of and distinction between SBS and mass psychogenic illness is to do a thorough physical assessment of the building, a good medical and neuropsychological evaluation of employees, a complete review of the symptoms when they occur, and a comprehensive examination of the stresses and strains of workers outside and inside the workplace. The researchers further suggest that the need for such a complex assessment method is one of the reasons that it is still difficult to diagnose these problems.

Personal Contributors

Looking at personal contributors to injuries and illnesses can isolate factors that may not be obvious in an organizational setting, including the accident-prone personality and other demographic characteristics associated with injury and illnesses.

Accident Proneness There is a belief that certain individuals are "accidents waiting to happen." Those individuals are believed to exhibit **accident proneness**; they have many more accidents than the average person does. Researchers have attempted to correlate certain personality characteristics with high accident frequencies to prove this belief. There have been numerous attempts to do this over the years, but none of them have led to the identification of the accident-prone personality (Sanders & McCormick, 1993).

Accident proneness
The belief that certain personality characteristics lead to a higher frequency of accidents in some individuals.

Accident liability
The theory that people are more or less prone to accidents in specific situations and that this liability can change over time.

What has been learned is that accident proneness refers more to the situation than to what the person does. For example, most people expect football players to have more job-related injuries than clerical workers who enter insurance claims at a computer. Very few people would think of a football player as being accident-prone. Sanders and McCormick (1993) suggest that it makes more sense to use the theory of **accident liability,** which states that people are more or less prone to accidents in specific situations and that this liability can change over time for each person. This theory fits well with other research findings that relate personal factors to accident rates.

Younger employees have the highest accident rate of any age group. As workers get older, they have increasingly fewer accidents (Shahani, 1987), but the accidents are four times more likely to be fatal (Moss, 1997). Younger workers are the least experienced and more often overestimate their abilities (Sanders & McCormick, 1993). Research has consistently shown a relationship between lack of job experience and a higher accident rate (Bryan, 1990).

Job Demands versus Capability This factor also fits with the theory that explains an increase in accident occurrence as an outcome of requiring workers to do more than they are capable of. Sanders and McCormick (1993) refer to this as the **job demand versus worker capability theory.** If a job requires more strength or more experience than a worker has, accidents can be expected to increase. Research shows that workers on ten-hour shifts have the most accidents during the last two hours of the shift, the time when fatigue makes them least able to meet the demands of the job.

Alcohol and Drug Abuse Some of the strongest correlations between personal factors and accident rates involve high accident rates among alcohol and drug abusers. One study showed that problem drinkers are 2.7 times more likely to have injury-related absences than are nonproblem drinkers (Webb, Redman, Henrikus, & Kelman, 1994). Data from the Health Interview Survey showed increasing rates of injury on the job associated with an increasing frequency of heavy drinking (Dawson, 1994). Another study found that employees who had used illegal drugs were five times more likely to have an on-the-job vehicle accident than were non-drug-using controls (Crouch, Webb, Peterson, & Buller, 1989). Delayed reaction time is often a factor in car accidents in which alcohol or drug use is involved.

Reducing and Preventing Accidents and Injuries at Work

Knowing the causes of accidents and injuries is only the first step; the real goal for an I/O psychologist is to reduce and prevent them. Lowering the accident and injury rate at work focuses on changing unsafe conditions, unsafe behaviors, or a combination of the two. The most successful programs usually look at both design and behaviors. Design changes are often more expensive but may be easier to accomplish in the long run because once they have been made, the goal of the program has been reached. With people factors, such as personnel selection and training, whenever new employees are added, the process must be repeated.

Design Factors

Design changes for safety focus on eliminating a particular injury or reducing the severity of the injury if an accident does occur. Sanders and McCormick (1993) discuss three design changes that meet these criteria. Since transportation injuries are the leading cause of work-related deaths, vehicle changes are used as examples (Figure 13.4).

Job demand versus worker capability theory A theory that explains higher accident rates as being caused by a job that demands more than an employee is capable of doing.

Figure 13.4

Safety design factors.

■ Exclusion designs make it impossible for a particular type of accident to occur. The side door on this van will not open until the car is in park, making it impossible to open the door while the car is being driven.

■ Prevention designs make it difficult, but not impossible, to do things that would lead to a particular accident. The fence around this pool makes it more difficult for the child to get to the pool, but if the gate is left unlocked or the child can climb over the fence, an accident can occur.

■ Fail-safe designs reduce the consequences or seriousness of an injury. The protective padding this hockey player wears may not prevent him from being injured, but it can reduce the seriousness of his injuries. He may receive a bad bruise instead of a broken leg.

Exclusion design A design change that makes it impossible for a particular type of accident to occur.

Prevention design A design that makes it difficult, but not impossible, to do things that would lead to a particular accident.

Fail-safe design A design that reduces the seriousness of an injury but does not always make the injury less likely to occur.

1. **Exclusion designs.** These designs make it impossible for a particular type of accident to occur. For example, newer heavy-equipment cranes have been designed so that it is impossible to put the crane bucket into operation unless the driver has the gearshift in the stop or parked setting. One of the problems with an exclusion design is that it can create a false sense of confidence. The design may cause workers to be more careless because they feel that the machine will not let an accident occur. Human alertness is necessary no matter how good an exclusion design is.

2. **Prevention designs.** These designs make it difficult, but not impossible, to do actions that would lead to a particular accident. Several years ago a number of car manufacturers promoted a design that did not allow a driver to shift into gear unless the driver's seat belt was fastened. Some drivers who felt that wearing a seat belt should be their own decision and not the car manufacturer's quickly found that the seat belt could be fastened behind the seat and still let them shift into gear. If an employee can override a safety shield on a saw by wedging a piece of wood over the latch, that worker still may incur serious eye injury from the saw.

3. **Fail-safe designs.** These designs reduce the seriousness of an injury but do not always make the injury less likely to occur. The use of air bags in cars does

not reduce the likelihood of car accidents but does reduce the severity of the injury in most cases. The death rate is much lower in car accidents involving cars equipped with air bags.

Human Factors

Each of the design factors listed above also shows the role of the person in preventing or reducing accidents and injuries. In the hands of an unsafe driver, even the best-designed car can be involved in an accident. The greatest emphasis in reducing accidents and injuries in the workplace has been placed on safety training for employees, but progress toward a safe workplace should begin before an employee is hired.

Selection The first step in accident and injury prevention occurs during the personnel selection process. This means choosing employees with the skills and abilities required for the job, as was previously suggested in the section on personal contributors to injury and illness. A correct match between job demands and employees' abilities should lead to a lower accident rate.

Another selection method that could reduce or prevent accidents would involve asking employees about unsafe behaviors during the employment screening process. Borofsky, Bielema, and Hoffman (1993) looked at rates of work-related accidents among employees of a resort hotel/conference center. The researchers compared the accident rate during a control time period with the rate during a two-year period when the Employee Reliability Inventory (Borofsky, 1992) was used as part of personnel selection. The accident rate on the job was significantly lower after this means of assessing unsafe behaviors was added to the selection process, and the cost of accidents on the job was reduced an average of over $32,000 per year.

The **Employment Reliability Inventory (ERI)** is designed to be used as a preinterview questionnaire. The answers lead to follow-up questions during the interview and reference checks. There are seven scales on the ERI assessing: freedom from disruptive alcohol and substance use, courteous job performance, emotional maturity, conscientiousness, trustworthiness, long-term job commitment, and safe job performance. Sample items from the scale are shown in Figure 13.5.

Training The most effective safety training programs emphasize learning to perform tasks safely, not just avoiding unsafe performance. Training to avoid accidents teaches an employee only what not to do, not what behaviors lead to safety at work. Racicot and Wogalter (1995) found that employees' use of safe behaviors increased when they watched a video of a role model actually working in a safe manner, rather than just hearing video or voice warnings about unsafe behaviors. When employees are given a chance to practice the procedures they have seen, this increases their ability to use those procedures on the job.

Interactive computer-based programs can allow the simulation of work events and enable employees to make choices about safer work behaviors. The consequences of their choices are shown, and the employees are allowed to repeat

Employment Reliability Inventory (ERI) A preinterview questionnaire designed to assess employee characteristics associated with unsafe job behaviors.

Figure 13.5

Sample of items from the Employee Reliability Inventory used to assess job applicants for unsafe behaviors that could lead to accidents on the job.

Directions: Job applicants are asked to respond yes or no to these statements about unreliable job behaviors.

1. Has your use of alcohol or drugs interfered with your performance on the job?
2. In your current job did you ever use drugs or alcohol on the job or at your workplace?
3. In the last year of your job did you either steal or take materials without proper authorization from the place where you work?
4. Were you ever fired, terminated or let go from a job for violence on the job?
5. In the last five years have you ever been convicted or had a finding of "sufficient facts" for a drug-related crime?

From G. L. Borofsky. (1992). Assessing the likelihood of reliable workplace behavior: Further contributions to the validation of the Employee Reliability Inventory. *Psychological Reports, 70,* 563–592.

a scenario or go on to another one. In a large organization with many employees starting jobs at different times this may be a very flexible, cost-effective alternative (Eisma, 1991). Unlike videotape presentations for new employees that show the traumatic consequences of unsafe behaviors, these interactive programs emphasize learning safe behaviors. Arousing high fear levels can lead to short-term changes in behavior, but rarely does this result in long-term changes after the shock wears off (Korman, 1991).

It is important for an organization to record unsafe behaviors accurately and document all the factors that contribute to accidents and injuries as a first step in designing a program to prevent those problems. Most accident report forms include the nature of the injury (sprain, cut, etc.), when and where the accident occurred (Tuesday, 10 A.M. at the entrance to the photocopy department, for example), the part of the body (head, back), the type of accident (fall, run over), the cause of the injury (equipment, body position), and other contributing factors (rain, poor visibility). Any additional information, including the near miss of an accident, which could lead to preventing a particular accident in the future, adds to the value of the report. A computer-aided incident data analysis program has been developed to help in the analysis and interpretation of accidents and injuries (Ness, 1994).

Safety Programs Once workers have been trained clearly and effectively in safe work practices, the next issue is getting them to use the safe procedures. A variety of safety programs have led to safer behaviors in the workplace; some of the more common are goal setting–feedback, behavior modification, problem solving, and safety awareness programs.

A standard goal setting–feedback program involves doing a job safety analysis, training in safe work practices, setting safety goals, providing feedback, and evaluating the results (Reber, Wallin, & Duhon, 1993). This type of program was used in one large industrial plant with 225 of the employees participating. First, safety procedures were defined and employees were assessed for their knowledge of them. Safety achievements were measured. Successively higher goals were used for each four- to five-week assessment period. In each period the goals were reached or exceeded. Employees were provided with feedback about their percentage of safety achievements during each assessment period. Safety scores of 90 percent, 99 percent, and 100 percent were accompanied by a significant decrease in accidents and time lost to injuries. The company estimated the safety savings to be at least $55,500 annually (Sulzer-Azaroff, Loafman, Merante, & Hlavacek, 1990).

Behavior modification programs emphasize the use of reinforcement for positive safety behaviors. The basic steps of a behavior modification program include targeting specific safety procedures, recording their occurrence, and then giving reinforcers for the correct behaviors. Many different types of rewards can be used as reinforcers, such as social praise, offering coffee and doughnuts, and giving bonuses or special privileges. Smith, Anger, and Uslan (1978) targeted reducing eye accident rates among twenty thousand workers in a shipyard. They chose eye injuries because they represented over 60 percent of the accidents there. The workers were praised for wearing protective eye equipment, but a control group was given no reinforcement for practicing eye safety procedures. At the end of the reinforcement period, the reinforced workers had reduced eye injuries 7.5 percent and the control group had reduced eye injuries 1.2 percent. The researchers cautioned that the success of behavior modification programs depends on the careful selection of the target behaviors and the correct choice and application of reinforcers.

Problem-solving safety programs emphasize the development of cognitive skills to allow workers to make better choices in potentially hazardous situations. These situations are often complex ones that involve a number of variables at once, as in the case of workers in nuclear power plants. Employees are taught how to identify emergencies, develop several action plans, and evaluate the choices. After the action, an evaluation of that choice is completed. This type of program often can be done with an interactive computer-based program similar to the one discussed previously in the section on the role of training in reducing accidents. Hytten, Jensen, and Skauli (1990) found a number of positive outcomes when this safety training method was used with offshore oil workers who were being trained for emergencies.

The goal of safety awareness programs is to increase attention to safe methods of work. Often this involves the use of posters showing safe procedures. In one program, used with a number of shipyard workers, posters were created showing the safe use of scaffolds. The posters were mounted in areas in which the employees were often found during the workday. The number of occupational accidents was reduced by calling attention to possible hazards (Saarela, 1989).

The ultimate goal of all safety programs is to promote a climate in which safe work behaviors are always valued. Organizations with a safety climate demonstrate a continuing commitment to a safe workplace. Employees perceive the company as fairly compensating them for on-the-job injuries and caring about their safety (Kunhomoidee & Karunes, 1991).

Another important component of a safety climate is the involvement of each employee in workplace safety (Dedobbeleer & Beland, 1991). When ServiceMaster Corporation made a significant shift to a safety climate by instituting a program that included preemployment screening, detecting and correcting hazards, actively involving employees in safety programs, and effectively managing injury claims, it was able to reduce workers' compensation claims by over $2 million and decrease the number of work-related accidents (Rogers, 1995). When safety is a priority for everyone in the workplace, it becomes a way of life and makes the workplace more healthy physically and mentally.

Workplace Violence

Accidents and injuries at work traditionally involved unsafe practices by employees or unsafe work conditions, such as equipment design, that led to problems. In recent years another cause of accidents and injuries has been added to the study of safety at work. This cause is workplace violence, which refers to deliberate assaults on workers by fellow employees, customers, former employees, or others. In 1996, 912 employees in the United States were killed at work by other people, and nearly 1 million workers were victims of violent crime in the workplace between 1987 and 1992 (Bureau of Labor Statistics, 1999). This makes murder the second highest cause of death on the job. Among female employees, workplace violence is the number one cause of death. Workplace violence has increased by over 30 percent from the annual average in the 1980s but has decreased each year since 1994.

The most common type of homicide on the job is murder during the commission of a crime such as a robbery. The most hazardous job in terms of homicide is that of driving a taxicab. Crime-related homicide also occurs among convenience store clerks, especially those who work late-night shifts. The second highest on-the-job homicide figures involve law enforcement and security officers. The nature of their jobs makes them more likely to come in contact with people who are more likely to commit acts of violence, but steps can be taken to reduce or avoid injury by using bulletproof windows and vests. An explosion of anger in another employee or a customer in the workplace, which results in an employee's death, is sudden and unexpected and typically is not planned for in designing the workplace. This type of assault accounts for 22 percent of the deaths at work. Four percent of these homicides represent the conclusion to domestic quarrels that started outside the workplace. Research has shown that a number of measures can protect the workplace against this type of violence, however.

Prevention

One of the first steps in preventing workplace violence is to screen employees for potential problems. Although coworkers commit only about 20 percent of workplace homicides, employers usually have more information available about their workers than about customers and clients. Data from previous workplace homicides have given a profile of the person who is mostly likely to commit workplace violence. In general this person is a man twenty-five to fifty years old. He has low self-esteem and is perceived as a loner. There is often a strong interest in the military and/or guns. The person who commits workplace violence that results in serious injury but not death is usually under thirty years of age and has a history of violence and drug and/or alcohol abuse. The workplace murderer is more likely to be over thirty years of age with no history of violence or substance abuse. This is the person who may be delusional, believing everyone is against him, and has few outlets for his frustration (Duncan, 1995; *Personnel Journal,* 1992). For example, in Fort Riley, Kansas, a soldier was involved in a number of counseling sessions with his squad leader. As his anger increased, he hid a shotgun in a wall locker before one of the sessions. When his anger and frustration reached an unmanageable level, he took the shotgun out of the locker and began firing randomly. The result was the death of one soldier, the injury of another soldier, and his own suicide.

Psychologists have had little success in predicting which employees are likely to become violent. Experts often disagree on the value of psychological tests in identifying potentially violent employees. These test scores are better at identifying employees who have already had problems with violent workplace behavior. Also, this psychological testing may involve an invasion of privacy and violate Americans with Disability Act standards for employees with psychological problems.

A less expensive and more acceptable method involves checking employment applications and references closely when people apply for work. During the preemployment interview an applicant should be asked about being disciplined or fired for fighting, assaults, or violations of safety rules, and about employment gaps.

A second step in preventing workplace violence involves making changes in the physical environment of the workplace to reduce or eliminate violence. OSHA requires employers to take all reasonable care to provide a safe workplace. Under the OSHA General Duty Clause, employers can be cited if there is a recognized risk of workplace violence and they do nothing to stop or prevent it. The Centers for Disease Control identified six factors that increase the risk of homicide in the workplace (CDC/NIOSH Alert, 1993):

1. Exchange of money with the public
2. Working alone or in small numbers
3. Working late-night or early-morning hours
4. Working in a high-crime area
5. Guarding valuable property or possessions
6. Working in a community setting

Many of these risk factors are present in late-night convenience stores. The National Association of Convenience Stores adopted a homicide reduction program that was first developed by 7-Eleven stores and that led to a 65 percent reduction in the robbery rate. The program included the following components:

1. Clearing windows for increased visibility, and improved lighting
2. Keeping little cash in the register
3. Posting signs about little cash in the register
4. Installing time-controlled safes that cannot be opened by cashiers
5. Altering escape routes
6. Training employees not to resist (Erickson, 1995)

Jerry Howard/Stock, Boston

■ One of the jobs in which an employee is most likely to get murdered is working late at night in a convenience store.

Another component was added when research showed that having more than one clerk on duty led to a decrease in the robbery rate and provided better eyewitness information if a robbery did occur. OSHA has targeted convenience stores because of their high incidence of workplace violence, but all employers need to look for ways to make the workplace secure from outsiders. This can include locking doors and limiting access, hiring security guards or other staff, improving lighting, using employee identification, and installing video cameras (Taylor, 1996).

The third step in prevention of workplace violence is safety awareness training for all employees. A survey found that fewer than 10 percent of companies provided formal training to all employees on dealing with workplace violence (Freidman, 1994). Employers must indicate a "zero tolerance" policy toward violence. Employees need to feel safe about reporting threats or problems that may lead to violence. Many employees are reluctant to report domestic problems because they are afraid they may be dismissed or not taken seriously. If threats are taken seriously by the organization, simple measures can prevent serious problems. A woman employee told her supervisor about threats being made by her ex-husband. The supervisor and the organization safety officer recommended that the employee be transferred from an easily accessible first floor office to a more secure office on the second floor. When the husband arrived intending to harm her, the relocation of the employee gave the company time to get help before violence occurred.

One aspect of safety awareness is increasing the level of employee awareness about the potential for violence in the workplace and teaching employees ways to defuse situations before they turn violent. Supervisors should know methods for introducing sensitive topics, such as layoffs and unsatisfactory performance ratings, that will usually produce less aggressive responses from employees. Supervisors should know how to defuse threats and anger before they turn into violence. The employee assistance program should be able to assist workers who show inappropriate responses at work. That program also can provide documentation for the human resources department. Some employee assistance programs offer classes in conflict resolution to help diffuse the threat of violence in the workplace. Conflict resolution programs may be one of the most effective prevention methods because many incidents of workplace violence involve people who already have had contact with one another. The success of violence prevention programs is shown in the case study "Preventing Violence at Work."

[Case Study] PREVENTING VIOLENCE AT WORK

After reading that forty-nine convenience store clerks had been killed on the job in 1990, the management at Dairy Mart Convenience Store decided that it wanted to protect its employees before violent episodes occurred. It also wanted employees to be able to feel safe at work. Following the National Institute for Occupational Safety and Health (NIOSH) guidelines, Dairy Mart implemented the following changes:

- More elaborate lighting and security systems were installed at stores.
- Trash is taken out only in the daytime.
- When the store managers make a bank deposit each day, they go at different times, are out of uniform, and keep the cash in a plain paper bag.
- Police officers are offered free coffee to encourage them to come into the stores.
- Windows are kept free of signs.
- Employees are trained in conflict resolution.
- Employees are told to greet each customer with a smile.
- The maximum amount of cash available in the store is $50.

While Dairy Mart did not release any numbers, it confirmed that these measures led to a large reduction in incidents of violence in its stores.

Other convenience store franchisers offered additional tips, such as checking job applicants for a criminal background. Research showed that over 50 percent of robberies were committed by current and former employees or with their cooperation. One franchise owner set up a video system so that employees could view mug shots and information on criminals who had committed similar crimes but had not been captured. The viewing was done during slow times at the store when employees did not have other duties.

Francis D'Addario, a security executive for Starbucks, emphasized the use of video cameras and alarm systems that work. Employees need to be held accountable for turning on alarm systems, changing videotapes, and keeping delivery doors locked.

Vermond Washington, an ex-convict who spent thirteen years in prison for armed robbery, suggests getting a trained guard dog and always having at least two employees on duty.

More than anything else, each of these experts stresses being prepared. It is much better to prevent violence at work than to deal with the consequences afterward.

From C. A. Gustke. (1997). Crimeproof your franchise. *Success, 44,* 75–77; R. Banham (1996, Fall). Defusing workplace violence. *Safe Workplace,* http://www.ncci.com/html/defusing.htm.

Crisis Teams

If violence occurs in the workplace, organizations should have plans for trained crisis teams to deal with the violence and its aftermath. Less than one-third of organizations report having a crisis management program, but more organizations report plans to develop such a program soon. The crisis management team should discuss possible scenarios and reactions. It should have plans and assignments for this type of situation, such as emergency phone numbers, designating a person to talk to the perpetrator until professional help arrives, sealing off unaffected areas of the workplace, and evacuating uninvolved employees (Ramsey, 1994).

After a crisis is resolved, employees often experience a number of negative emotions. Debriefing sessions conducted by the employee assistance program staff or other professionals can give the employees a chance to express those emotions in a safe and healthy way. They also can give the leaders a chance to assess employees who may need further help but are reluctant to ask for it (Thornburg, 1993). One problem with employees who appear to have recovered from the trauma of the violence is the occurrence of posttraumatic stress disorder. Flashbacks, nightmares, and anxiety attacks can be as incapacitating as the initial trauma itself. The likelihood of employees developing posttraumatic stress disorder appears to be related to the severity of the trauma and negative personal factors such as depression, anger, or drug abuse in the employees (Carlier, Lamberts, & Gersons, 1997).

The ultimate goal of workplace violence programs is to prevent problems before they occur. Statistics show that the amount of violence can be reduced and that prevention programs can be successful, but the most realistic position is to be prepared if violence does occur and to work actively to prevent problems. Organizations that make a strong commitment to the health and safety of their employees are viewed as far more desirable places to work and are able to hire and keep the best employees.

MAIN POINTS

- Stress-related problems at work cost $200 billion to $300 billion a year as a result of absenteeism, turnover, lower productivity, accidents, and medical and insurance costs.

- Some stress is necessary to produce motivated behavior, as was shown by Yerkes and Dodson (1908). Good stress is called eustress, and bad stress is called distress.

- Too much stress leads to consequences for the organization (absenteeism, tardiness, turnover, low performance, sabotage, and accidents) and for the individual.

- Personal outcomes of too much stress include the physical and mental effects described as the stages of Selye's general adaptation syndrome (alarm, resistance, and exhaustion).

- Organizational contributors to stress include the demands of work (work overload, work underload, role ambiguity and conflict), technostress, sexual harassment, and gender attitudes.

- Personal contributors to stress include life changes, a Type A personality, and burnout.

- Most stress management programs target individual employees' behavior and are administered through an employee assistance program.

- Some of the most common stress management methods are exercise, meditation, relaxation techniques, cognitive approaches, time management, and goal setting.
- The Occupational Safety and Health Administration monitors safety in the workplace.
- Accidents at work are defined mainly by lost work time.
- Human and workplace factors often combine to produce hazardous work situations.
- Organizational contributors to accidents and injury include the physical environment (noise, illumination, temperature, and equipment design), shift work, and the sick building syndrome.
- Personal contributors to accident and injury include greater accident liability rates among certain employees, excessive job demands, and substance abuse problems.
- Accident and injury prevention focuses on changing unsafe work conditions and behaviors.
- Workplace design changes to reduce accidents include exclusion designs, prevention designs, and fail-safe designs.
- Human factors in reducing accidents include selection, training, and safety programs.
- Some of the common types of safety programs involve goal setting–feedback, behavior modification, problem solving, and safety awareness.
- Violence in the workplace has become an increasing threat in recent years.
- Prevention of workplace violence includes screening employees for a history of violent acts, changing the physical environment to prevent violence, and helping employees learn violence-preventing behaviors and techniques.
- Organizations should have plans for crisis teams to deal with workplace violence when it occurs.

KEY TERMS

Accident liability
Accident proneness
Burnout
Depersonalization
Distress
Employee assistance program (EAP)

Employment Reliability Inventory (ERI)
Eustress
Exclusion design
Fail-safe design
Fight-or-flight response

General adaptation syndrome
Hardiness
Job demand versus worker capability
  theory
Karoshi
Mass psychogenic illness
Negative affectivity
Occupational Safety and Health
  Administration (OSHA)
Polyphasic
Prevention design
Repetitive motion injury

Role ambiguity
Role conflict
Sexual harassment
Sick building syndrome
Stress
Stressors
Technostress
Type A personality
Type B personality
Work overload
Work underload

Answers to these questions can be found at the end of the book.

REVIEW QUESTIONS

1. Eliminating all stress from one's life is the most productive way to deal with stress.

   a. True   b. False

2. Which of the following are stressors?

   a. Getting fired from a job

   b. Being trapped in a building on fire

   c. Going on vacation

   d. Having children

   e. a and b

   f. All of the above

3. Stress-related workers' compensation claims have been decreasing in recent years because of the increased use of stress management programs in organizations.

   a. True   b. False

4. Very high stress levels have been associated with which of the following?

   a. Increased illness rates

   b. Increased theft rates

   c. Death

   d. All of the above

5. The stage of the general adaptation syndrome that leads to the most negative outcomes is

   a. alarm because it is so strong.

   b. resistance because it takes so much effort to resist the stressor.

   c. exhaustion because the person has few physical reserves left.

   d. all the stages

6. Which of the following is *not* an organizational contributor to stress?

   a. Work overload

   b. Work underload

   c. Technostress

   d. None of the above

7. One of the most stressful times in an organization occurs during a merger because of the resulting role ambiguity.

   a. True   b. False

8. What type of sexual harassment is involved if the men in an office whistle at a woman in their department whenever she walks past them?

   a. Gender harassment

   b. Sexual seduction

   c. Sexual coercion

   d. Sexual bribery

   e. Gender illegality

9. The mommy track refers to

   a. the need for working mothers to exercise to reduce stress.

   b. a less desirable career path assigned to some working mothers.

   c. the career track of mothers who choose to leave the workforce when their children are born.

   d. males who take on the role of caregiver for their working wives.

10. Even if life changes are pleasant, they can result in increased stress levels.

    a. True   b. False

11. List two possible reasons for the correlation between the Type A personality and heart disease.

    a. _____

    b. _____

12. Which of the following characteristics is associated with high levels of hardiness?

    a. Overcoming personal conflicts

    b. Having an executive position in an organization

    c. The desire for challenges at work and outside work

    d. A nonstressful job

13. Burnout victims usually start as the least involved employees, and this lack of commitment causes the burnout.

    a. True   b. False

14. The role of the employee assistance program in stress management is *usually*

    a. managing programs to reduce individual stress levels.

    b. managing programs to reduce organizational stress levels.

    c. screening applicants to avoid hiring stressed employees.

    d. arranging hospitalization for the most stressed employees.

15. The most common definition of an accident at work involves how severe the injury is.

    a. True   b. False

16. Most researchers have come to regard the sick building syndrome as being real only in the minds of the employees.

    a. True   b. False

17. One of the differences between the sick building syndrome and mass psychogenic illness is

    a. the patterns of spread of the illness.

    b. the types of illnesses that result.

    c. the fact that only office workers suffer from sick building syndrome.

    d. all of the above.

18. Research on the theory of accident proneness shows that it probably would be more accurate to use the theory of

    a. accident repetition.

    b. psychosomatic prompting.

    c. accident availability.

    d. accident liability.

19. The personal factor most strongly related to accidents and injuries is
    a. the age of the worker.
    b. the sex of the worker.
    c. alcohol and drug abuse.
    d. the state of residence.

20. If the rails of a baby's crib are arranged so closely that the baby cannot put her head through them, this is an example of using _____ to prevent accidents.
    a. exclusion
    b. prevention
    c. a fail-safe method
    d. an extended method

21. The best safety training programs focus on showing unsafe behaviors so that employees do not do them.
    a. True   b. False

22. Which of the following is *not* a common type of safety program?
    a. Observational checklists
    b. Behavior modification
    c. Performance rating
    d. Problem solving
    e. None of the above

23. Increasing employees' awareness of safety can reduce the incidence of accidents.
    a. True   b. False

24. Murder is one of the top causes of death on the job.
    a. True
    b. False

25. List two workplace factors that increase the risk of homicide in the workplace.
    a. _____
    b. _____

26. The purpose of a crisis team at work is to subdue the perpetrator of the violent act.
    a. True   b. False

Use your browser to go to http://www.queendom.com/typea.html. Take the Type A personality test. What was your score? Do you think your score accurately reflects your personality? What changes could you make that would help you become more of a Type B personality? Which personality type do you find more desirable, and why?

Statistical Appendix

LEARNING OBJECTIVES
DESCRIPTIVE STATISTICS
  Measures of Central Tendency
  Normal and Skewed Distributions
  Measures of Variability

INFERENTIAL STATISTICS
  Point Estimation
  Hypothesis Testing
  Meta-Analysis

Appendix Outline

534

The purpose of this appendix is to introduce you to the statistical analysis of data. In an introduction such as this, students usually are not expected to do more than simple calculations. The main goal is to gain an understanding of how these analyses work, what they mean, and when to use them. Two major types of statistics are used in the analysis of data: descriptive statistics and inferential statistics.

DESCRIPTIVE STATISTICS

Descriptive statistics do just what the name implies: They describe data by organizing it. Descriptive statistics take a large amount of data, summarize it, and make it easier to understand.

Measures of Central Tendency

Measures of central tendency are concerned with the "typical" score in a distribution of scores. There are three measures of central tendency. The first measure is the **mode** (Figure A.1). The mode in the distribution in the figure is 73, since that is the most common score, which is the definition of the mode. If more people got a score of 15 than any other score on the first test in your class, the mode or typical score for your class would be 15.

The **median** is the score or measure where 50 percent of the scores are above that score and 50 percent of the scores are below it. It is the midpoint of the distribution of the scores. In Figure A.1, if the scores are put in numerical order, the midpoint is 63.5. When the midpoint falls between two numbers, the median is the midpoint between those two numbers.

Descriptive statistics Statistics that summarize and organize data.

Measures of central tendency Statistical procedures for finding the typical or average score in a distribution.

Mode The score in a distribution that appears the most frequently.

Median The score in a distribution where 50 percent of the scores are higher than that score and 50 percent are lower.

Figure A.1
Scores of students showing the mean, median, and mode.

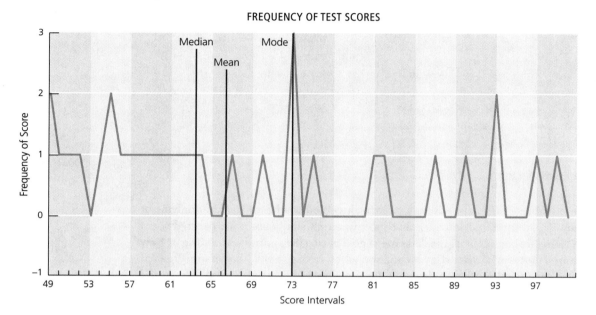

FREQUENCY OF TEST SCORES

The last measure of central tendency is the **mean**. A common name for the mean is the arithmetic average. The mean is computed as the total of the scores divided by the number of scores. In Figure A.1 the mean can be calculated by using the formula

$$\frac{\Sigma X}{N} = \overline{X} \qquad \text{or} \qquad \frac{1961}{30} = 65.4$$

where Σ (sigma) is the symbol for summation or addition, X is the symbol for the scores, and N is the symbol for the number of scores. The X with the line over it is the symbol for the mean. Although the mean, median, and mode provide valuable information, they cannot give a complete description of the data. There is no information about how the scores are distributed in the list of scores as part of the central tendency statistics. A number of common graphic patterns show the distributions of scores that occur when research data are looked at in graphs.

Mean The arithmetic average.

Normal curve A theoretical distribution used as the basis for certain statistical procedures. It often is referred to as a bell-shaped curve because of its characteristic shape, with the highest frequency in the middle and the lowest frequencies at the ends.

Normal and Skewed Distributions

The **normal curve** is the basis for many of the statistical analyses done in research. The normal curve represents the distribution of scores that will occur if a large number of observations are made and then graphed. For example, if a re-searcher measured the intelligence quotient (IQ) scores of 1,000 people, he most likely would get a distribution very close to the normal curve shown in Figure A.2. Looking at the graph, it is possible to see that most people have an IQ that is close to the average (100). The farther from the average an IQ score is, the less likely it is to occur. The defining feature of the normal curve is that it is symmetrical. The left side of the curve is the exact opposite, or a mirror image, of the right side, giv-ing the normal curve a distribution that is shaped like a bell. The greatest number of scores occur in the middle of the distribution, and the smallest number occur at either end.

Figure A.2

Example of the normal distribution of IQ scores.

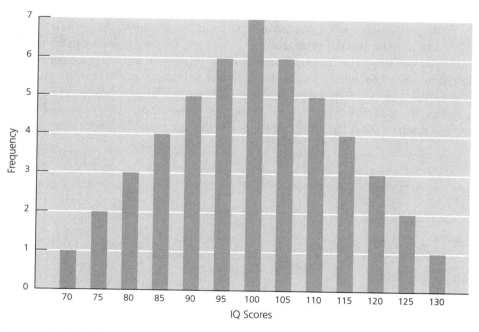

Not all data result in a normal distribution. If a student graphed the grades of a professor who gave very easy tests, the distribution would look like the graph shown in Figure A.3. Most of the students did very well, although a few did very poorly. This distribution is negatively skewed (skewed to the left) because the tail of the curve points in a negative direction (to the left). If the professor gave very hard tests and only a few students did well, the curve would be skewed to the right, or be positively skewed (Figure A.4).

Figure A.3
A negatively skewed distribution.

Figure A.4
A positively skewed distribution.

When a curve is normal, the mean, median, and mode are all the same. In Figure A.5 it can be seen that the mean, median, and mode are the same and all fall on the same place on the curve. Since the curve is symmetrical, the median must fall exactly in the middle of the curve. The mean also must fall exactly in the middle, since for every score a certain distance below the mean there has to be a corresponding score a certain distance above the mean. On the curve, the mode is the value under the highest point of the distribution, which is also the exact middle of the curve.

Figure A.5
The mean, median, and mode in a normal curve.

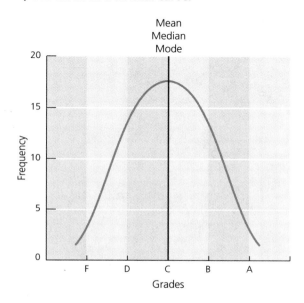

In a **skewed distribution,** the three measures of central tendency are not the same. Figure A.6 shows the mean, median, and mode in a graph of income in the U.S. The mode is the highest point in the distribution. The mean is toward the tail because of the extreme scores at the end of the distribution. Using income as an example, the extremely high income made by some people raises the mean income value. The median in a skewed distribution is always between the mode and the mean.

Skewed distribution
A distribution of scores in which the greatest number of scores occur near one end of the distribution.

Figure A.6

Location of the mean, median, and mode in skewed distributions.

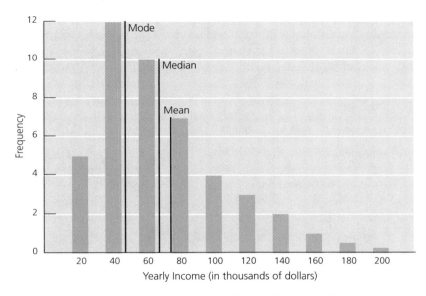

One of the problems with having three measures of central tendency is that it is sometimes possible to give a score that is mathematically correct while giving a misleading impression by using a particular measure of central tendency. Suppose a politician told voters that the average yearly income in the United States was $68,000 and that they should vote for her because she, as the incumbent, was responsible for that high yearly income. The opposing candidate tells the voters that the typical yearly income in the United States is only $40,000 and that voters should vote for him because he will make things better. Did one of the candidates lie? Probably not. The first candidate used the median as the measure of average, and the second candidate used the mode. Although both measures are numerically correct, they convey very different meanings. In a skewed distribution the median is the most representative measure of average because it is less affected by extreme scores than the mean is.

Measures of Variability

Although measures of central tendency say a great deal about the typical score in a distribution, they provide only half the information needed to get a complete description of a set of data. Assume that an employee has to train the workers in two departments, A and B. She finds that each department has a mean score of 50 on a measure of skill needed for the job. Can each department be trained the same way? The answer is not clear. The data in Figure A.7 show that even though the mean (and the median and mode as well) is the same in each department, the employees in the two departments are very different. The employees of department A are all very similar. In department B the employees range from very low to very high on the skill measured. Different teaching methods probably would have to be used in the two departments since the employees in each have such a different range of ability. Additional information is needed so that the correct training decisions can be made. Another statistical tool, measures of variability, supplies more information for this decision.

F i g u r e   A . 7

Distributions with the same mean but different variability.,

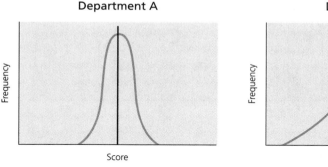

Measures of variability
Statistical procedures that measure how variable, or spread out, the scores in a distribution are.

Range In a distribution the highest score or measurement minus the lowest score or measurement.

Standard deviation (SD)
A measure of variability that is the basis for other statistical procedures because it divides the normal curve into equal intervals.

Measures of variability indicate how variable, or spread out, the scores in a distribution are. The **range** is the most basic measure of variability. The range is simply the highest score minus the lowest score. The most useful measure of variability is the standard deviation. The **standard deviation (SD)** indicates, more exactly than the range, how variable, or spread out, the scores in a distribution are. The larger the SD, the more variable the scores in the distribution. In Figure A.7 the distribution for department B is more variable. If the SD were calculated for both departments, the SD for department B would be larger. The formula for calculating the SD is shown in Figure A.8.

Figure A.8

Calculation of the standard deviation.

RAW DATA

Student Number	Grade
1	20
2	25
3	22
4	18
5	19
6	21
7	24
8	20
9	24
10	20

CALCULATION

Subject Number	X	$X - \bar{X}$	$(X - \bar{X})^2$
1	20	−1	1
2	25	+4	16
3	22	+1	1
4	18	−3	9
5	19	−2	4
6	21	0	0
7	24	+3	9
8	20	−1	1
9	24	+3	9
10	20	−1	1
	$\Sigma X = 213$	$\Sigma X - \bar{X} = 3$	$\Sigma(X - \bar{X})^2 = 51$

Standard deviation = SD = $\sqrt{\Sigma(X - \bar{X})^2/N}$ = $\sqrt{51/N}$ = $\sqrt{5.1}$ = 2.25

X = subject's raw score, $\bar{X}$ = mean, SD = standard deviation, Σ = sum

The SD is important because, together with the normal curve, it allows a researcher to calculate other measures that characterize a distribution of scores. Suppose two students took a test that had a mean of 100 and a standard deviation of 10. The first student received a score of 120, and the second student received a score of 90. How well did each student do? Is 120 well above average or only a little above average?

Figure A.9

Graph showing the percentage of population between two different standard deviations and the corresponding Z-scores (in parentheses).

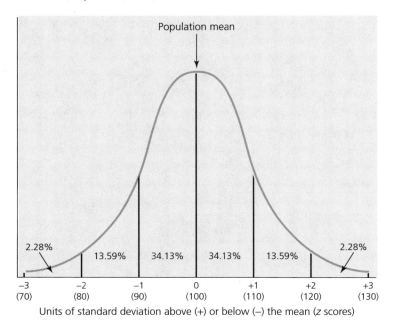

Population mean

2.28%
13.59%   34.13%   34.13%   13.59%
2.28%

| −3 (70) | −2 (80) | −1 (90) | 0 (100) | +1 (110) | +2 (120) | +3 (130) |

Units of standard deviation above (+) or below (−) the mean (z scores)

A score of 120 is 2 standard deviations above the mean [(120 − 100)/10 = 20/10 = 2] or +2 standard deviations. A score of 90 is −1SD. In a normal curve a certain percentage of the population always falls between plus and minus certain deviations. −1SD to +1SD contains 68.26 percent of the scores of the population, and −2SD to +2SD contains 95.44 percent of the scores of the population (Figure A.9). The same principle can be found on a normal curve table. Using the example above, it can be determined that 99.72 percent of the people taking the tests received scores between 70 and 130.

To determine how far above average a score of 120 is, start by looking at Figure A.9. The figure shows that a score of 120 is well above average, but that is not a precise statement. Using the numbers in Figure A.9, it is possible to determine that a score of 120 is better than the scores of 97.72 percent of the people who took the test. Fifty percent of the population have scores below the mean; 34.13 percent have scores between the mean and +1SD, and 13.59 percent have scores from +1SD to +2SD (50% + 34.13% + 13.59% = 97.72%). This means that a score of 120 is at the 97.72 percentile. **Percentiles** indicate how much of the population falls below a certain score. The student who received a score of 90 would be at the 15.87 percentile. Percentiles can be found for any score by using a normal curve table.

Another use for SD is to calculate **Z-scores.** Look at the data in Figure A.10 and assume that each person took a different test in a different subject. Each test has a different mean and standard deviation. Who did the best? Who did the worst? A Z-score is a number that tells how far from the mean a number is in SD units. The formula for Z-scores is

$$Z = \frac{X - \bar{X}}{SD}$$

Percentile The percentage of a population that falls below a given score.

Z-scores A statistical procedure that allows the comparison of different scores from distributions with different means and standard deviations.

Figure A.10

Example of four individuals' test scores on four different tests.

Subject 1	Subject 2	Subject 3	Subject 4
Test score: 50	Test score: 75	Test score: 100	Test score: 25
Class mean: 75	Class mean: 70	Class mean: 80	Class mean: 20
SD: 10	SD: 5	SD: 15	SD: 2

In this formula, X is the raw score, $\bar{X}$ is the mean, and SD is the standard deviation. Going through the calculations (Figure A.11), it can be seen that subject 4 did the best with a Z-score of $+2.5$ [$(25 - 20)/2 = +2.5$]; subject 1 did the worst with a Z-score of -2.5 [$(50 - 75)/10 = -2.5$]; and subjects 2 ($+1.0$) and 3 ($+1.33$) were in the middle. Graphing these results on a normal curve makes it easier to visualize these results. The larger the Z-score is, the farther from the mean a raw score is. A positive Z-score means that the raw score is above the mean; a negative Z-score means that the raw score is below the mean.

Figure A.11

Location of Z-scores of four subjects on the normal curve.

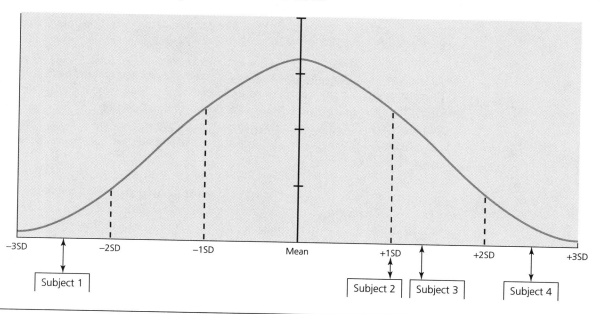

Inferential statistics
Statistical procedures that make it possible to arrive at judgments about a population by using a sample.

Point estimation
A statistical procedure that is used to estimate a population value by using a sample value.

INFERENTIAL STATISTICS

Although descriptive statistics make it possible to organize large amounts of data, even after they have been used, a researcher still does not know whether the results of her research have statistical meaning or significance. This is the purpose of **inferential statistics.** Inferential statistics are used to make conclusions about the total population that is being considered by using a sample. There are two types of inferential statistics: point estimation and hypothesis testing.

Point Estimation

The first type of inferential statistics is called **point estimation.** When a researcher uses point estimation, he tries to estimate the population value by measuring a sample. Political polls are a good example of point estimation. A pollster asks 1,000 people which of the candidates they are going to vote for. The pollster uses the results of the poll to estimate or infer how many people in the entire population are going to vote for each candidate.

If an employer asks twenty-five randomly chosen employees how many hours they work at home per week, the number given probably will be a good guess or estimate of how long the average employee works at home. This is an application of point estimation.

When the results of a political survey are printed, the report usually includes the margin of error as well as the point estimation. Whenever only a portion of the population is measured, there will always be some error. For example, if 44 percent of the people in the sample group say they are going to vote for candidate A and 41 percent say they are going to vote for candidate B, there may be a margin of error of 3 percent. This means that the actual vote for candidate A in the population could be anywhere between 41 percent and 47 percent and that the number of people in the population actually voting for candidate B could be anywhere from 38 percent of 44 percent. This is why a reporter may call a contest such as the one between candidate A and candidate B a dead heat. When the margin of error is considered, candidate B could be ahead in the contest.

The larger the sample is, compared to the total population, the smaller the margin of error is. Although the margin of error decreases as the sample size increases, the relationship is not a simple linear one. Figure A.12 shows a hypothetical example of how increasing the sample size has less and less of an effect on the margin of error.

Is it worth surveying an additional four hundred people to lower the margin of error from 4.5 percent to 4.0 percent? There is no right or wrong answer. It is a researcher's decision, based on the cost involved, the time it will take, and how precise the researcher needs to be.

Figure A.12

Example of how increasing survey size decreases the margin of error.

Sample size	Margin of error
100	6.0%
200	5.0%
400	4.5%
800	4.0%
1,600	3.9%

There is always a margin of error unless the entire population being considered has been measured. This is no longer a sample, since the whole population has been measured. The cost usually would prevent such a study. Most researchers try to use fewer subjects rather than more in order to save time and money. Depending on the type of research and analysis, a certain minimum number of subjects is required in each group to meet research requirements. Morse (1998) developed a computerized program to determine the minimum group size for good research.

Hypothesis Testing

The second type of inferential statistics is called **hypothesis testing.** Hypothesis testing judges whether one group—the experimental group—is different from another group—the control group—on the variable being measured. In correlational research, hypothesis testing judges whether the correlation is different from no relationship, or 0.

Since research is done with a limited number of subjects, there are two considerations: Will the results occur again? and Do the results apply to other situations or populations? **Statistical significance** answers these questions by determining the probability of the difference between groups on the variable being measured.

When an experiment or study is completed, the data have to be analyzed to find whether the independent variable had any effect or whether one group is different from another group. For example, did the subjects in the experimental group learn faster than did those in the control group, or are the workers at one plant more intelligent than the workers at a different plant? In both examples the question is whether the groups are different. In the first example the question is whether the experimental group is different from the control group. In the second example the question is whether the groups at the two plants are different.

Hypothesis testing
A statistical procedure that tests whether a group is different from another group in terms of a chosen variable.

Statistical significance
A statistical procedure that determines the probability that two groups are different on a chosen variable. In an experiment, it is the probability that the independent variable had an effect.

Significance or probability level The result of hypothesis testing procedures that determines the probability or odds that two groups are different on a chosen variable; in an experiment, it determines that the independent variable had an effect.

A variety of statistical procedures are used to determine statistical significance. A statistical analysis shows that the results of the experimental manipulations are not due to an accidental factor or chance; they are a result of the manipulations of the variables by the experimenter.

By convention, the lowest standard for statistical significance is the .05 **significance or probability level.** The .05 significance level means that the probability is 95 percent that the results of an experiment are caused by the experimental manipulations and are not due to chance. The other commonly used significance level is the .01 level. If an experiment is significant at the .01 significance level, it means that the probability is 99 percent that the results are caused by the experimental manipulations and are not due to chance. Statistical significance is typically reported as $p < .05$ or .01. The p stands for probability.

Replicating experiments is important to confirm the statistical significance of the results and to show the reliability of the research. Researchers can be more certain about the results if an experiment has been replicated. If an experiment reaches the .05 significance level, the researcher knows that the odds are 95 percent that the results were caused by the experimental manipulations and 5 percent that the results were due to chance. However, if the experiment is repeated and the same results occur, the odds are now .0025 (.05 $\times$ .05, or 25 out of 10,000) that the results of the experiment were due to chance.

Meta-Analysis

A more recent development in the statistical analysis of research findings is the meta-analysis (Glass, 1976; Rosnow & Rosenthal, 1989), which allows the results of many studies to be considered together. Since this analysis has influenced how research is done and how results are interpreted, it is discussed in Chapter 2.

MAIN POINTS

- Descriptive statistics summarize data. Inferential statistics are used to indicate that the results from a sample can be applied to a population.
- Descriptive statistics include measures of central tendency (mean, median, and mode) and measures of variability (range and standard deviation).
- Normal and skewed curves are used to represent the distribution of a set of scores graphically.
- Inferential statistics include point estimation and hypothesis testing.

- Statistical significance determines whether the independent variable had any effect in an experiment or if the results occurred by chance.
- A meta-analysis can be used to combine the results of a number of studies in one set of conclusions.

Descriptive statistics
Hypothesis testing
Inferential statistics
Mean
Measures of central tendency
Measures of variability
Median
Mode
Normal curve

Percentile
Point estimation
Range
Significance or probability level
Skewed distribution
Standard deviation (SD)
Statistical significance
Z-scores

REVIEW QUESTIONS

Answers to these questions can be found at the end of the book.

1. The three measures of central tendency are the _____, _____, and _____.

2. The _____ _____ is a measure of variability that is the basis for other statistical procedures.

3. Which of the following is *not* true about the normal curve?

   a. A certain percentage of the population always falls from minus a certain deviation to plus a certain deviation.

   b. The mean, median, and mode all have the same value.

   c. A curve can be skewed and still be normal.

   d. The standard deviation can be used to describe the results of an experiment in which the results resemble a normal curve.

4. You sample 100 people to see who they are going to vote for and then use the results to estimate how the rest of the population is going to vote. This is an example of

   a. hypothesis testing.

   b. inferential estimation.

   c. Z-scores.

   d. point estimation.

5. What would you use to compare your test score in this I/O psychology class to a friend's test score in English despite the fact that the tests have different means and different standard deviations?

   a. *Z*-scores

   b. Point estimation

   c. Hypothesis testing

   d. Modal estimation

6. If an experiment reaches the .05 significance level, it means that

   a. the odds are 5 percent that the independent variable had an effect.

   b. the odds are 95 percent that the independent variable had an effect.

   c. the odds are .05 percent that the dependent variable changed.

   d. the odds are 5 percent that the hypothesis was proved.

7. The commonly accepted probability or significance levels used in psychology are the _____ level and the _____ level.

Glossary

360-degree feedback A system in which performance appraisals are done by everyone who has contact with the employee: supervisors, peers, subordinates, people from other companies, and populations such as customers and suppliers.

Absence culture An informal group norm for the number of days of absence that are "deserved" in a particular job.

Absolute standards methods Performance appraisal methods based on comparing an employee's behavior with a model described in a performance statement.

Accident liability The theory that people are more or less prone to accidents in specific situations and that this liability can change over time.

Accident proneness The belief that certain personality characteristics lead to a higher frequency of accidents in some individuals.

Achievement tests Tests that assess particular job skills of the test taker after a formal training program.

Action method An organizational development process that uses the steps of diagnosis, planning for change, intervention, and evaluation.

Active listening Dynamic participation in the hearing of a message.

Active practice Learning in which the learner participates directly in the task to be learned.

Adverse impact The unfair rejection of minority group applicants that occurs when the minority group's selection rate is less than 80 percent of the majority group's rate.

Affectively based outcomes An assessment of the development of attitudes and motivation during training.

Affirmative action The practice of using a hiring plan that gives preferential treatment to certain groups because of unfair hiring practices in the past.

Affordance The degree to which a control device allows only the intended use.

Age Discrimination in Employment Act A federal law that makes discrimination against employees over age forty illegal.

Americans with Disabilities Act (ADA) A federal law that makes it illegal to discriminate against a person with a disability if that person is otherwise qualified to do the job with or without reasonable accommodation.

Annunciator A display that announces a change that requires immediate attention.

Applied research Research conducted to solve current, practical real-world problems.

Apprenticeship training Lengthy training in a skill or trade that involves a combination of supervised on-the-job work and classroom instruction.

Aptitude tests Tests that assess particular job skills of the test taker before formal training has taken place.

Artifacts Nonverbal communication messages based on the way the message sender is dressed or the objects around the sender.

Assessment center A selection technique that uses multiple assessments of job-related knowledge, skills, and abilities by a number of evaluators who observe the applicants.

Authoritarian leadership style A leadership pattern in which the leader controls all the power in and decisions made by the group.

Autonomous work groups Groups in which employees are given responsibility for planning and accomplishing their work.

Autonomy The core job characteristic that allows a great deal of independence and self-regulation on the job.

Bandwidth The total work hour span available to flextime employees for work scheduling.

Basic research Research conducted to find basic principles on which other research can build.

Behavior modeling A training method in which the learner watches someone doing an action and then tries to repeat that action.

Behavioral Observation Scale (BOS) A performance assessment method that is based on the frequency of job behaviors.

Behavioral theories of motivation Explanations of motivated behavior that are based on the principles of operant conditioning.

Behaviorally Anchored Discipline Scale (BADS) A performance appraisal system that focuses on employees' misbehaviors, such as absenteeism and theft.

Behaviorally Anchored Rating Scale (BARS) A performance evaluation method based on comparing employees' job behaviors with specific performance statements on a scale of good to bad.

Benevolents Employees who believe they deserve unequally low returns from a job.

Biodata forms Application forms that ask for personal and social information to predict success on the job on the basis of information from past or current employees.

Body language Nonverbal communication that includes touching, posture, eye contact, facial expressions, and gestures.

Brainstorming A method of group decision making in which all the members meet, generate ideas without criticizing them, and evaluate the ideas as a group.

Branching programs Programmed instruction methods that channel the trainee into different segments (branches) of the program on the basis of the correctness of each answer.

Bullpen offices Open offices that arrange the desks of employees in functional groups.

Bureaucracy Weber's rational, legal system of organizational structure with a hierarchical form.

Burnout The state of physical, mental, and emotional exhaustion and cynicism caused by long-term job stress.

Career development Planning for an employee's entire work life.

Case studies A research method in which one individual or thing is studied in detail.

Case study training Learning based on an in-depth analysis of a particular person or situation.

Cautious shift phenomenon The movement of groups toward decisions more careful than those of the individual members.

Central tendency error An unfair grouping of performance evaluations at the middle of the scale.

Centralized networks Communication systems that channel all information through a single person.

Chain of command Specification of the authority structure and responsibility in an organization.

Change agent The person who directs organizational development in an organization; this may be someone inside or outside the organization.

Channel The medium that carries a message from the sender to the receiver, such as written memos or spoken words.

Charismatic leadership A leadership style that is based on the personal charm and emotional appeal of the leader.

Checklists A performance evaluation method that relies on having the evaluator place a mark next to appraisal statements that describe the behaviors of the employee being evaluated.

Circadian rhythms The twenty-four-hour functioning cycles of humans.

Classical conditioning A training method that is based on linking behaviors to reflexive responses.

Closed system An organizational structure that is not responsive to internal and external changes in the environment.

Coding process The selection of which incoming information will be attended to.

Coercive power Influence that is based on the leader's ability to punish subordinates.

Cognitive design engineering An extension of engineering psychology that concerns the part of work which involves thought processes and tools for thinking.

Cognitive learning outcomes A method of assessing training that looks at verbal knowledge, how that knowledge is organized, and how it can be applied.

Cognitive theories of motivation   Motivational theories that focus on the thought processes and perceptions of employees.

Communication network   A model of message transmission in organizations in which more than one sender or receiver is involved.

Comparable worth   The principle of paying equally for the same work regardless of the job title or jobholder.

Compatibility   The degree to which a control meets a person's expectations for its behavior.

Compensable factors   The job elements that, added together, determine the monetary worth of a job.

Compressed workweek   Working the same weekly number of hours in fewer days per week.

Computer adaptive testing (CAT)   Testing done using a computer to replace other methods.

Computer-assisted instruction (CAI)   Learning methods that are computer-based.

Computer-based communication   The transmission of messages in an organization that involves the use of computers for part or all of a transmission.

Computerized performance appraisal   A method for performance evaluation that is assisted by the use of a computer or that uses a computer to monitor and count job behaviors.

Concurrent validity testing   A way to prove the effectiveness of a test by correlating test scores with current employees' performance measures.

Conference training   A learning method that involves a group discussion about a specific topic, led by someone with knowledge of that topic.

Consensus decisions   Group judgments that require all the members of a group to agree on the decision.

Consideration behavior   Leadership behavior that is focused on the well-being of subordinates.

Construct validity   A way to prove the effectiveness of a test by demonstrating that a test score relates to an identified psychological trait that underlies successful job performance.

Consultative decisions   Judgments made by a group leader after receiving information from the group members.

Content validity   A way to prove the effectiveness of a test by demonstrating that it representatively samples significant parts of the job.

Contingency model   An organizational structure system that suggests that the best organizational structure depends on being responsive to continuing changes in the environment.

Contingency theory   A leadership theory that is based on the assumption that the best leaders consider both their own characteristics and the leadership situation to determine the best way to lead.

Continuous reinforcement   Reinforcement that is given after every correct response.

Contrast and similarity errors   Unfair evaluations of employees that are based on how their behavior is similar to or different from the behavior of the evaluator.

Contrast errors   A distortion of interview judgments caused by the interviewer giving unfairly high or low scores on the basis of a comparison with previous applicants.

Control   The part of a person–machine system operated by the person to get the machine to do something.

Control group   In an experiment, the group that is not exposed to the independent variable. This group is compared to the experimental group to determine whether the independent variable had an effect.

Core hours   The central hours when all flextime employees are required to be present at work.

Core job characteristics   According to Hackman and Oldham, the job elements that are critical for job satisfaction to occur.

Correlation coefficient   A statistical procedure used to determine whether two variables are related to each other. If one changes, does the other one change?

Correlational study   Research done to determine whether changes in one variable are related to changes in another variable.

Criterion-related validity   A way to prove the effectiveness of a test by correlating the score with a subsequent measure of job performance.

Critical incidents   A method of job analysis that defines a job in terms of the specific effective or ineffective job behaviors of an employee.

Cross-training   Learning to do more than one job within an organization.

Crystallized intelligence   Intelligence based on skills acquired through education and cultural experiences.

Cumulative frequency graph   A graphic representation of data that shows incremental levels of a variable without returning to zero.

Curvilinear relationship   A relationship between two variables that can best be represented by a curved line. As one variable increases, so does the other, but only to a certain point. After that point, as one variable increases, the other decreases.

Data hierarchy   A category of the Functional Job Analysis that assesses an employee's involvement with information and ideas on the job.

Decentralized networks   Message systems that use a number of starting points and directions for messages.

Decertificaton   The dismissal of a union at an organization as a result of union members voting to dismiss it.

Democratic decisions   Judgments made by the entire group, typically by a majority vote.

Democratic leadership style   A leadership pattern in which the leader and each member share equally in the power and the decisions of the group.

Dependent variable   In an experiment, the variable that is measured. The change in the dependent variable should be due to the independent variable.

Depersonalization   A stage of burnout characterized by viewing others as cases and illnesses rather than as people.

Descriptive statistics   Statistics that summarize and organize data.

Descriptive validity   A way to prove the effectiveness of a test by correlating the score with measures of the nature or content of the job.

Devil's advocate   A person assigned to the role of finding fault with the decisions made by a group.

Differentiation   A systems theory concept that suggests that open systems move toward greater specialization and complexity.

Differentiation   Distinguishing between good and bad employees.

Diffusion of responsibility   An explanation for social loafing that is based on the belief that when individuals are members of a group, they feel they can get lost in the group and no one will notice what they do as individuals.

Direct market pricing   A method of job evaluation based on what similar jobs pay in other companies and on the available labor pool.

Disability   A physical or mental impairment that substantially limits a major life activity.

Discrimination   Unfair rejection of job applicants.

Disengagement stage   The career stage that focuses on leaving the work environment for retirement.

Display   The presentation of information to the human operator in a person–machine system.

Distress   Stress that arises from a negative experience.

Distributed practice   The development of a skill during many short practice sessions.

Diversity training   Educational programs that promote awareness and skill development to help employees function in a multifaceted workplace.

Division of Industrial and Organizational Psychology A division of the American Psychological Association group that later was incorporated as the Society for Industrial/Organizational Psychology.

Division of labor A clear definition of jobs in terms of their activities and responsibilities.

Double-blind control A research procedure in which the subjects and the researcher measuring the dependent variable do not know whether the subjects are in the experimental group or the control group.

Downward communication Messages that go from higher to lower organizational levels.

E-mail A letter written on a computer and transmitted through a computer network.

Employee assistance program (EAP) The designated formal group in an organization that deals with individual employees' problems that affect job performance.

Employee empowerment The practice of giving subordinates control of tasks and functions usually done by the supervisor.

Employment at will The principle that employers can hire and fire employees without a specific cause.

Employment Reliability Inventory (ERI) A preinterview questionnaire designed to assess employee characteristics associated with unsafe job behaviors.

Engineering psychology The study of person–machine systems in I/O psychology.

Entitleds Employees who believe they deserve unequally high returns from a job.

Equal Employment Opportunity Commission (EEOC) The federal agency that enforces nondiscrimination laws in the workplace.

Equal Pay Act of 1963 A federal law requiring equal pay for jobs that require equal skill, effort, and responsibility and that are performed under similar working conditions.

Equifinality A systems theory concept that assumes that there are many ways to achieve the same goal.

Equity sensitive Refers to an employee who responds to inequity situations by trying to restore equity.

Equity theory A motivational theory based on the assumption that people want a fair return for the skills, experience, and other things they bring to the job when they compare themselves with others.

ERG theory A theory of motivation that states that existence, relatedness, and growth (ERG) needs operate at the same time to motivate behavior.

Ergonomics A term used msostly in Europe and Canada to refer to the study of person–machine systems in I/O psychology.

Error of commission A communication distortion that results from adding information to the message.

Error of omission A communication problem that is caused by leaving out parts of a message.

Establishment stage The career stage that focuses on developing career anchors and accomplishment.

Eustress Stress that arises from a positive experience.

Exaggeration A communication distortion that results from giving extra emphasis to the favorable or unfavorable parts of a message.

Exclusion design A design change that makes it impossible for a particular type of accident to occur.

Expectancy The perception of an employee of how much his or her personal effort will influence his or her job performance and lead to certain outcomes.

Experiment A research study in which the researcher manipulates the independent variable and measures the dependent variable.

Experimental group In an experiment, the group that receives or is exposed to the independent variable.

Experimental realism Refers to how involved subjects become in an experiment. Do the subjects in the experiment act naturally and take the experiment seriously.

Expert power Influence that is based on the subordinate's belief that the leader knows more about the task than the subordinate does.

Exploration stage The career stage that involves planning for a first job or a new job.

External recruitment Attracting applicants by using sources outside the organization.

External validity A type of validity that allows the results of a study to be applied to other situations and other populations.

Externally focused Refers to employees who believe that most work outcomes are caused by forces outside themselves.

Extinction A behavioral consequence that leads to the decreased occurrence of a behavior by removing the reinforcer.

Extraneous variable Any variable that affects the outcome of an experiment but is not part of the experiment and therefore should be controlled.

Extrinsic reinforcers External rewards, such as praise and money.

Face validity A way to indicate whether a test measures what it looks like it measures.

Facet measures of job satisfaction Measures that look at separate components of satisfaction, such as pay and supervision.

Fail-safe design A design that reduces the seriousness of an injury but does not always make the injury less likely to occur.

Feedback The core job characteristic that provides frequent information about how an employee is doing on the job.

Fiedler's cognitive resource theory A leadership theory that is based on the assumption that the best leaders make use of their mental resources to determine the most effective ways to lead a group.

Fiedler's contingency theory A leadership theory that states that the best leaders combine person orientation and task orientation in a variety of ways, depending on the work situation.

Field experiment An experiment done in a real-life environment.

Field study A research method in which the researcher makes no manipulations but studies only what occurs in the environment naturally.

Fight-or-flight response The physiological arousal of a person in response to stress.

Filtering A communication distortion that results from withholding parts of a message.

First impression errors A distortion of interview judgments caused by giving greater weight to information collected early in an interview.

Fixed interval reinforcement Reinforcement given for correct responses after a specific period.

Fixed ratio reinforcement Reinforcement given after a specific number of correct responses.

Flat organization An organizational structure with few levels between the top and the bottom of the organization and many people reporting to a single supervisor.

Flexitour A flextime schedule in which employees are required to maintain a self-chosen schedule for a fixed period.

Flextime Allowing employees to choose their hours of work except for a certain number of core hours required for all employees.

Fluid intelligence Intelligence based on the ability to organize information directed toward problem solving.

Force The motivated behavior that results from a combination of valence, instrumentality, and expectancy.

Forced choice system A performance appraisal method that requires the evaluator to choose between several behavioral descriptions, some of which are blind items and some of which are real items.

Forced distribution A performance appraisal system that requires the evaluator to place a certain percentage of employees in each evaluation grade on the basis of a normal curve distribution.

Formal organizational communication The communication paths shown on an organizational chart.

Formal rules and procedures Written documents that specify and control organizational behavior in detail.

Four-fifths rule The requirement that the selection rate for minority applicants be at least 80 percent of the selection rate for majority applicants.

Frame of reference error A performance appraisal unfairly influenced by factors outside the job, such as race, gender, age, and HIV status.

Free-rider theory An explanation for social loafing that is based on the belief that when group members see the work of the group progressing well, they believe their effort is not necessary.

Frequency distribution A statistical method of arranging scores by categories.

Frequency polygon A line graph.

Functional Job Analysis (FJA) A structured method of job analysis that was the basis for an earlier edition of the *Dictionary of Occupational Titles*.

Functional turnover A loss of an employee that benefits the organization.

Fundamental attribution error The belief that the behavior of others is caused mainly by personal factors and only slightly affected by situational factors.

Gatekeeper A person whose role in the communication process allows him or her to withhold information.

General adaptation syndrome The three-stage model developed by Selye that describes how individuals react to stress, from alarm to resistance to exhaustion.

Generalization The use of research findings in situations that are similar, but not exactly the same.

Genetic testing Physical testing for the presence of inherited physical disabilities or predispositions.

Glass ceiling The place in the organizational structure above which employees who are discriminated against cannot be promoted.

Glass Ceiling Commission A U.S. Department of Labor fact-finding group that assesses the status of women and minority groups in the workplace.

Gliding time Flextime schedules in which employees are allowed to change their work hours with no prior notice.

Global measures of job satisfaction Measures of overall work satisfaction levels.

Goal-setting theory A theory of motivation based on the assumption that conscious, difficult, specific goals lead to increased job performance.

Gossip Information communication about people in an organization for reasons other than meeting organizational goals.

Grapevine The informal communications system that exists in organizations.

Graphic rating scales A performance appraisal method based on assessing how much of a trait or behavior an employee displays on a graduated measure.

Graphology Assessment of personal characteristics from handwriting samples.

Group cohesion The strength of the desire of group members to remain part of the group.

Group decision support systems (GDSS) A computer-based system of network software that assists groups in generating and organizing ideas, editing shared work, and voting on alternatives.

Group polarization The tendency of a decision-making group to shift the group decision to a more extreme position than the average of the decisions of the individual members.

Groupthink Poor group decision-making behavior resulting from a high degree of unity and desire for consensus among group members.

Groupware Computer software designed to be used by group members to share information and connect their computers.

Growth-need strength The desire for personal growth and challenge on the job.

Halo (devil) errors Unfair judgments made when knowledge of one trait or behavior biases the evaluation of other traits or behaviors.

Hardiness A personality trait that allows a person to be resistant to the negative effects of stress by viewing stress as a challenge rather than a negative event.

Hawthorne Studies A landmark series of research studies that changed the focus of early I/O psychology from scientific management to human relations.

Head-up display (HUD) A display that gives visual information without requiring changing the level of one's eyes.

Hierarchy of needs theory A theory of motivation that holds that people progress up a pyramid of motivational steps from physiological needs to self-actualization.

High performance cycle The application of a goal-setting theory that deals with continued high levels of motivated behavior and job satisfaction.

Hindsight bias The tendency of people to overestimate their knowledge or their ability to predict events once the answer is known or the results of a study occur.

Histogram A bar graph.

HIV testing A physical examination for the presence of the human immunodeficiency virus that causes AIDS.

Homeostasis A state of balance, or equilibrium, in the different parts of a system.

Horizontal communication Organizational messages that go from one employee to another employee at the same level in the organization.

Human factors or engineering psychology A specialty area in I/O psychology that focuses on the interaction between people and machines in the workplace.

Human factors psychology The study of person–machine systems in I/O psychology.

Human relations movement A movement that studies employees' attitudes, interpersonal relationships, and leadership styles to achieve better production.

Human relations structures An organizational design based on the assumption that interpersonal relations are the most important factor in an organization.

Hygiene factors Elements in the work environment that cause job dissatisfaction if they are not present.

Hypothesis A statement that predicts the results of an experiment.

Hypothesis testing A statistical procedure that tests whether a group is different from another group in terms of a chosen variable.

Importation of energy The process of bringing energy resources such as new employees and money into an organization.

In-basket exercise A simulation activity that uses a sample of the documents a jobholder would find in her or his in-basket to which the job applicant is asked to respond.

In-group subordinates Subordinates who are seen by the leader as competent, good workers.

Independent variable In an experiment, the variable that is manipulated or changed in order to study its effect.

Industrial/organizational psychology The application of psychological theory and methodology to the problems of organizations and the problems of groups and individuals in organizational settings.

Inequity An unfair relationship between inputs and outcomes when an employee compares herself or himself to other employees.

Inferential statistics Statistical procedures that make it possible to arrive at judgments about a population by using a sample.

Influence The exertion of control over others in a way that results in changes in behavior or attitude.

Influence tactics Methods of persuasion used to change followers' behavior.

Informal communication Ways of passing information in organizations other than those designated on the organizational chart.

Informal group A naturally occurring collection of employees formed for the purpose of meeting personal goals.

Information input Knowledge that comes into an organizational system and influences it, such as evidence of a decline in the sales rate.

Information overload A communication problem resulting from receiving more data than a person can process.

Initiation of structure behavior Leadership behavior that is focused on required tasks and their completion.

Inputs The skills, experience, knowledge, and other contributions an employee brings to a job.

Instrumentality The degree to which an employee believes that his or her performance on the job will influence a particular job outcome.

Integrity tests Tests that assess the truthfulness or dishonesty of employees and applicants.

Intellectance The leadership trait characterized by imagination, cultural concern, and a broad range of interests.

Interactive leadership A leadership style that is based on making the contact between subordinates and the supervisor positive for everyone involved.

Intermittent reinforcement Reinforcement that is given after an average of correct responses.

Internal recruitment Attracting applicants from within the hiring organization.

Internal validity Refers to a study in which the results can be due only to the experimental manipulations, not to outside variables or chance.

Internally focused Refers to employees who believe that most work outcomes are caused by personal effort from inside themselves.

Interrater reliability The degree of agreement between test scoring by different examiners.

Intrinsic reinforcers Rewards that are personally satisfying, such as self-satisfaction.

Involuntary turnover Occurs when an employee leaves an organization against her or his own desires.

Item analysis An evaluation of the validity of each individual item on a test.

Job analysis A listing of the knowledge, skills, abilities, and experience needed to do a job correctly, as well as up-to-date information about the job itself. Includes job-oriented and worker-oriented elements.

Job Applicant Medical History Questionnaire A personnel selection medical examination form featuring job-relevant items, which is filled out by the applicant before the physician's examination.

Job characteristics theory A theory of motivation based on the assumption that certain core job elements in the work environment lead to job satisfaction.

Job demand versus worker capability theory A theory that explains higher accident rates as being caused by a job that demands more than an employee is capable of doing.

Job description A list of the tasks performed in a job, the employee characteristics needed for the job, and the working conditions.

Job Descriptive Index (JDI) One of the common facet measures of job satisfaction.

Job Diagnostic Survey (JDS) A job satisfaction measure developed by Hackman and Oldham to assess which parts of jobs affect job satisfaction.

Job Element Inventory A structured job analysis method modeled after the Position Analysis Questionnaire, but with a lower reading level.

Job enlargement Increasing the amount of tasks done or knowledge used by an employee on the job.

Job enrichment A systematic program for increasing job satisfaction by giving additional responsibility to employees.

Job evaluation The process of using a job analysis and other information to establish the monetary worth of a job.

Job in General Scale A global measure of job satisfaction.

Job instruction training A learning method that uses the four steps of tell, show, do, and review.

Job involvement The degree of an employee's identification with the job.

Job outcome The results of job behaviors, such as pay or being fired.

Job rotation Allowing employees to do different duties on a regularly scheduled basis after training in each position.

Job satisfaction The level and direction of emotion, or affect, attached to a job and a job situation.

Job specification A list of the knowledge, skills, and abilities needed to perform a job.

Job-oriented evaluation A job analysis that focuses on organizational features such as productivity, tasks, duties, and responsibilities.

Job-related interviews Interviews that focus on past work experiences but are not specific to particular situations.

Karoshi A Japanese term used to describe an employee who works himself or herself to death.

Laboratory experiment An experiment done in a controlled environment.

Laissez-faire leadership style A leadership pattern in which the group members have all the power and decision-making authority in the group if they want it.

Landscaped offices Open offices that separate employee workspaces with partitions that do not go all the way to the ceiling.

Leader Behavior Description Questionnaire (LBDQ) A measure of the leadership behaviors of consideration and initiation of structure, which is completed by a leader's subordinates.

Leader Match Training A leadership training program based on Fiedler's contingency theory.

Leader Opinion Questionnaire (LOQ) A measure of ideal leadership behavior, completed by those in leadership positions.

Leader position power A situational variable that determines how much authority a leader has from his or her position in the organization.

Leaderless discussion group An assessment center exercise in which the applicants meet in a small group to solve job-related problems but no leader is assigned to direct the group.

Leadership The ability to persuade a follower to make a commitment to the goals of a group and work toward those goals.

Leadership motive pattern McClelland's theory that the most effective leaders combine high levels of the need for power and low levels of the need to affiliate.

Leader–member exchange (LMX) model A leadership theory based on the assumption that the quality of the relationship between the leader and each subordinate determines the effectiveness of the leader.

Leader–member relations A situational variable that determines the degree of subordinates' liking of and support for a leader.

Least Preferred Co-Worker (LPC) scale A measurement scale developed by Fiedler to assess the person orientation or task orientation of a leader.

Legitimate power Influence that is based on the formal organizational position of the leader.

Leniency and severity errors Unfair consistently high or low evaluations of employees and their performance.

Level of treatment   The varying amount or degree of the independent variable to which different groups in an experiment are exposed.

Linear programs   Programmed instruction methods that require everyone to go through the same small steps to the end of the program.

Linear relationship   A correlation in which the relationship between two variables can best be represented by a straight line.

Maintenance stage   Career stage that focuses on maximizing employee productivity and organizational benefit during the middle adult years.

Management by objectives (MBO)   A performance appraisal system that measures the effectiveness of an employee or group in terms of goals set by the supervisor and the employees or group.

Mapping   The relationship between a display and the real world.

Mass psychogenic illness   A stress-produced disability in which a number of employees at the same time believe they have developed a work-related illness.

Massed practice   Development of a skill during one or a few long sessions.

Matched groups   A method in which the subjects in an experiment are made equal or balanced on any variables or characteristics that may influence the outcome of the experiment.

Matrix structures   A formal organizational group design that involves both the functional and the production divisions of an organization.

Mean   The arithmetic average.

Measures of central tendency   Statistical procedures for finding the typical or average score in a distribution.

Measures of variability   Statistical procedures that measure how variable, or spread out, the scores in a distribution are.

Media richness   The intensity of the communication channel, with face-to-face communication being the most intense.

Median   The score in a distribution where 50 percent of the scores are higher than that score and 50 percent are lower.

Medical examination   A personnel screening technique that focuses on the job-relevant physical condition of an applicant.

Mental ability tests   Tests that assess cognitive skills and abilities.

Mentoring   A formal or informal relationship in which a more experienced worker helps a less experienced worker develop job- and career-related skills.

Merit-based employment   Job hiring based only on job-relevant factors.

Message   Information that is sent during a communication.

Meta-analysis   A statistical technique that allows the results of a number of studies to be combined and analyzed together to provide a single conclusion.

Minnesotat Satisfaction Questionnaire (MSQ)   A common facet measure of job satisfaction.

Mixed standard scale   A performance appraisal system that randomly lists good, average, and bad behaviors for a job and requires the evaluator to compare the employee being evaluated to each statement.

Mode   The score in a distribution that appears the most frequently.

Moonlighting   Working a second or third job in addition to one's primary employment.

Motivation   The conditions that energize, direct, and sustain work behavior.

Motivator factors   Elements in the work environment that lead to job satisfaction if they are present.

Movement compatibility   The degree to which moving a control represents movement in the real world.

Multiple cutoff model   A selection model that uses a minimum score on each selection technique to determine the likelihood of success on the job.

Multiple hurdle model   A selection model that requires applicants to pass each step or test before going on the next step or test.

Multiple regression model   A selection method that shows the relationship between several combined scores and success on the job.

MUM effect   "Minimize unpleasant messages": A communication distortion resulting from not passing on information that would reflect unfavorably on the sender.

Mundane realism   Refers to how closely the conditions of an experiment resemble a real-world environment and a real-world situation.

Need for power   The desire to influence the behavior of others and control them.

Need to achieve theory (NAch)   A theory of motivation that suggests that the most satisfied workers are the ones who feel the greatest fulfillment through personal responsibility, leading to preset goals.

Need to affiliate   The desire for social relationships.

Needs   Deficiency conditions that lead to motivated behavior.

Negative affectivity   A general personality trait described by the emotions of anger, hostility, and depression.

Negative entropy   Refers to the need for an organization to renew its resources and continually move toward organizational success.

Negative feedback   Information—such as evidence of a large increase in the turnover rate—that tells an organization or individual that it is doing something wrong.

Negative information errors   A distortion of interview judgments caused by the interviewer paying more attention to bad information about the applicant than good information.

Negative reinforcer   A behavioral consequence that leads to the increased occurrence of a behavior because the person has avoided or escaped something bad.

Negligent hiring   Careless hiring of an employee who causes harm to another employee, a customer, or a visitor to an organization.

Negligent referral   The failure of a previous employer to warn a future employer about serious job-related problems in a job applicant.

Nonfunctional turnover   The loss of an employee the organization wants to keep.

Nonverbal communication   All the components of a message except the spoken words. It includes features such as body language, paralanguage, and the use of space and time.

Normal curve   A theoretical distribution used as the basis for certain statistical procedures. It often is referred to as a bell-shaped curve because of its characteristic shape, with the highest frequency in the middle and the lowest frequencies at the ends.

Norms   The average or typical performance of a large group of people on a test.

Occupational Safety and Health Administration (OSHA)   The federal government agency that oversees the health and safety of employees at work.

On-the-job training   Learning that takes place while one is doing the job.

Open offices   Office designs that eliminate individual offices or cubicles for each employee.

Open system   An organizational structure that is responsive to internal and external changes in the environment.

Operant conditioning   A training method based on the use of rewards and punishment for voluntary behavior.

Operational definition   A precise, measurable explanation of the variables present in an experiment, including how the variables are manipulated and observed.

Organizational behavior modification The application of reinforcement theory on a companywide basis.

Organizational citizenship Individual contributions to the workplace that go beyond role requirements and contractually rewarded job achievements.

Organizational climate Individual and group perceptions of cultural events in an organization.

Organizational commitment The degree of an employee's desire to remain with an organization.

Organizational culture The deep pattern of basic assumptions about shared values and beliefs in an organization.

Organizational development (OD) A process of planned change for the entire organization or a large part of it that is based on social science research methods.

Organizational needs analysis An assessment of how training can assist an organization in achieving its goals.

Organizational psychology A specialty area in I/O psychology that looks at group influences on individual employees.

Organizational transformation An organizational development method in which management directs change in the entire organizational vision for the future.

Out-group subordinates Subordinates who are seen by the leader as undesirable workers.

Outcome-based methods Performance appraisal methods that use measurable or countable data on the results of work performance.

Outcomes The pay, status, and other returns an employee gets from a job.

Outdoor experiential training (OET) Learning done in rustic areas to increase individual and group self-understanding through various risk-taking experiences.

Output Products delivered to the outside world by an organization, such as televisions and teachers.

Overpayment An inequity relationship in which an employee gets a greater return from a job than he or she deserves, on the basis of inputs.

Paired comparisons A performance appraisal system that requires the evaluator to compare each employee with every other employee on each characteristic or behavior being evaluated.

Paralanguage Nonverbal characteristics of the voice of a message sender, such as tone, volume, speed, and pauses.

Parallel forms method A way to prove the consistency of test scores by administering different forms of a test.

Path-goal theory A leadership theory based on the assumption that the most effective leaders make organizational goals and rewards clear to their subordinates and make it possible for the subordinates to reach those goals.

Peer evaluation A performance appraisal done by those at the same level as the person being evaluated.

People hierarchy A category of the Functional Job Analysis that assesses an employee's involvement with people on the job.

Percentile The percentage of a population that falls below a given score.

Performance appraisal The process of measuring the output of an employee that contributes to the productivity of an organization.

Performance appraisal interview A formal, regular, scheduled meeting of an employee and a supervisor to discuss the performance appraisal.

Person needs analysis An assessment of which employees should be trained and how much training each employee should receive.

Personal power Leadership control derived from the characteristics and skills of the leader.

Personality tests Tests that assess the personal characteristics of the test taker.

Personnel data measures Performance appraisal based on human resources department information such as absenteeism, tardiness, and accident rate.

Personnel placement After hiring an employee, choosing the job he or she will report to.

Personnel psychology The area of I/O psychology that deals with employee recruitment and selection, training and development, performance appraisal, and job analysis.

Personnel screening The process of eliminating unqualified applicants as part of the selection process.

Personnel selection The process of choosing the person who will be hired by using the results of screening measures.

Physical ability tests Personnel screening examinations that focus on the physical skills and capacities needed to perform a job.

Physical examination A personnel selection technique that focuses on physical skills, abilities, disabilities, and medical conditions that are relevant to the job.

Pie chart A graphic representation of data that divides the data into segments like slices of a pie.

Placebo effect A change in the behavior of control group subjects resulting from their belief that they have been treated with the independent variable when they actually have been treated with something ineffective.

Pluralistic ignorance The belief that the results of scientific studies apply to other people but not to oneself, that one is somehow special or the exception.

Point estimation A statistical procedure that is used to estimate a population value by using a sample value.

Polyphasic Having the ability and desire to do more than one activity at a time.

Position Analysis Questionnaire (PAQ) A worker-oriented structured job analysis method.

Position power Leadership control derived from the leader's legitimate status in the organization.

Positive reinforcer A behavioral consequence that leads to the increased occurrence of a behavior because the person has received something good.

Posttest-only design Training assessment that measures behavior only after training.

Predictive validity testing A way to prove the effectiveness of a test by correlating scores with future measures of job performance.

Preemployment drug testing Urine and/or blood test screening for the presence of illegal drugs or drugs that could impair job performance.

Pretest–posttest design Training assessment that measures behavior before and after training.

Prevention design A design that makes it difficult, but not impossible, to do things that would lead to a particular accident.

Process consultation An organizational development method in which consultants work with people in the organization to help them learn to diagnose and solve their own problems.

Process loss The extra time it takes to make decisions when the decisions are made by a group rather than an individual.

Programmed instruction An individualized method of instruction that is based on the principles of operant conditioning.

Project team A group assembled to work on a task from the earliest stages through completion. It disbands after the project is completed.

Psychological interview An interview that focuses on assessing the personal characteristics of applicants.

Psychology The scientific study of behavior and mental processes.

Punishment An unpleasant consequence following certain behaviors, which leads to the decreased occurrence of these behaviors.

Quality of work life The desire to improve organizational and employee goals and needs by increasing employees' participation in solving organizational problems and making decisions.

Quantity and quality of work A performance appraisal based on the amount and grade of work performed.

Quasi experiment A research technique that is similar to but does not meet the strict requirements for a true experiment.

Race norming The practice of adjusting test scores on the basis of racial group membership.

Random assignment A method in which subjects are assigned by chance either to the experimental group or the control group in an experiment.

Range In a distribution the highest score or measurement minus the lowest score or measurement.

Ranking A performance appraisal method that requires the evaluator to list all the employees being appraised in order from best to worst.

Realistic job preview A method for giving applicants an honest picture of the good and bad aspects of the job for which they are applying.

Reasonable accommodation Changes in the workplace to meet the needs of a disabled employee that do not cause undue hardship to the organization or to other employees.

Receiver The person for whom a communication message is intended.

Recency error An unfair evaluation of an employee based only on that employee's latest performance, not his or her performance over the entire evaluation period.

Recruitment The process of attracting qualified job applicants to an organization.

Referent power Influence that is based on the leader's personal attractiveness.

Reinforcement theory A motivational theory that assumes that the occurrence of a behavior is strengthened or weakened by the reinforcers or punishments that follow it.

Reinforcer Any consequence that leads to an increase in the occurrence of a behavior.

Relative comparisons methods Performance appraisal methods that compare an employee's job performance with another employee's job performance.

Reliability Stability or constancy of results or test scores.

Repetitive motion injury An injury caused by many repetitions of a small motor behavior.

Replication Repetition of an experiment to see whether the same results will occur.

Resistance to training The desire to avoid new learning situations.

Résumé A summary of an applicant's job-relevant background and experience, drawn up by the applicant.

Retraining Learning to do a current job in a new way or learning a new job in the same organization.

Reverse discrimination Unfair rejection of majority group applicants in favor of minority group applicants.

Reverse performance evaluations An appraisal of a superior by subordinates.

Reward power Influence that is based on the leader's ability to deliver things such as bonuses to subordinates.

Risky shift phenomenon The movement of groups toward decisions more dangerous than the decisions of the individual members.

Robot A mechanical device programmed by humans to carry out a sequence of tasks.

Role ambiguity Stress caused when an employee is not clear about what she or he is required to do on a job.

Role conflict Stress caused by opposing demands that cannot both be met.

Role playing A training method in which the learner practices new ways of interacting.

Rumor Information communication that is not based on factual evidence.

Scatterplot   A graph of data from a correlational study.

Schedules of reinforcement   The pattern of how often reinforcers are given for a behavior.

Scientific management   The first widely accepted theory of management. Developed by Frederick W. Taylor, it was based on using the most efficient tools and motions to do a job.

Scientific method   The rules, procedures, and principles that guide scientific research.

Score banding   The practice of assigning the same test score to all test takers within a particular score range.

Selection rate   The number of people who will be hired for a job divided by the number of people available to be hired.

Selection ratio   A comparison between the number of applicants and the number of people hired for a job.

Self-efficacy   An employee's perception of the chance that she or he is able to produce the behaviors that lead to certain job outcomes.

Self-evaluation   A performance appraisal done by the employee being evaluated.

Sender   The person who originates a communication message.

Sensitivity training   Experiential learning of emotional skills and behaviors.

Sexual harassment   Unwelcome sexual behaviors that are linked to conditions of employment, performance evaluation or that contribute to making a hostile work environment.

Shift work   The use of afternoon and late-night work periods in addition to the usual day work.

Sick building syndrome (SBS)   Symptoms of illness caused by the spread of airborne contaminants or pollution in tightly sealed buildings.

Significance or probability level   The result of hypothesis testing procedures that determines the probability or odds that two groups are different on a chosen variable; in an experiment, it determines that the independent variable had an effect.

Similarity errors   A distortion of interview judgments caused by the interviewer giving higher ratings to the applicants who are most like him or her.

Simple regression model   A method for correlating job success with scores on a single selection measure.

Simulation   An evaluation exercise used in assessment centers, which puts the applicant in a situation or activity similar to the actual job.

Simulation study   A research method in which the study takes place in an artificial setting designed to look and respond like the real-world setting.

Simulation training   Learning based on practicing skills in a replica of the work situation.

Single-blind control   A research control in which the subjects in an experiment do not know whether they are in the control group or the experimental group.

Situational interview   A structured interview technique that gives applicants specific job-related situations and asks how they would respond to each one.

Skewed distribution   A distribution of scores in which the greatest number of scores occur near one end of the distribution.

Skill variety   The core job characteristic that centers on using a number of skills and abilities in a job.

Skill-based learning outcomes   An assessment of the development of technical or motor skills during training.

Social inhibition   The censoring effect that the presence of other people has on the behavior of group members.

Social loafing   The problem of members putting out less effort as a group than they would as individuals.

Sociotechnical systems   An approach to organizational structure that assumes that social and technological factors have equal weight in determining the organizational structure.

Solomon Four-Group Design A rigorous training assessment that measures behavior in a variety of situations before and after training.

Span of control The number of subordinates who report to a single supervisor.

Spatial compatibility The degree to which a control represents action in the real world.

Split halves method A way to prove the internal consistency of test scores by correlating the scores of two different halves of the same test.

Stakeholder Any person who has an investment, monetary or otherwise, in the success of an organization.

Standard deviation (SD) A measure of variability that is the basis for other statistical procedures because it divides the normal curve into equal intervals.

Standardization Consistency or uniformity of the procedures for administering a test and the conditions under which it is given.

Standardization sample The group of people used to establish a test's norms.

Statistical significance A statistical procedure that determines the probability that two groups are different on a chosen variable. In an experiment, it is the probability that the independent variable had an effect.

Stress The physical and/or psychological response to the demands made on a person.

Stressors The characteristics or conditions that lead to stress.

Structured assessment methods Professionally constructed and published organizational job analysis systems.

Structured interview An interview method in which the same questions are used in the same order for every applicant.

Subordinate appraisal A performance evaluation done by those in a lower position than the person being evaluated.

Substitutes for leadership theory A theory that suggests leadership may not be necessary in all work situations.

Sucker-effect theory An explanation for social loafing that is based on the belief that if an individual member of a group believes that she or he is working harder than the rest of the group, that member will exert less effort to avoid being taken advantage of in the group.

Supervisor ratings Performance appraisals done by an immediate-level or a higher-level manager.

Surgency The leadership trait characterized by assertiveness, high energy and activity levels, and social involvement with others.

Survey A research method that measures the verbal responses of subjects, usually in response to a series of questions.

Survey feedback A method of organizational development that is based on using questionnaires filled out by employees to give them feedback for planning for change in the organization.

Systems theory The belief that an organism or an organization must be regarded as an integrated whole, with any action in one part influencing all the other parts.

Tall organization An organizational structure with many levels between the top and the bottom of the organization and only a few people reporting to a single supervisor.

Task identity The core job characteristic that allows the completion of an entire product or job.

Task needs analysis An assessment of the knowledge, skills, abilities, and other behaviors needed to do a job.

Task significance The core job characteristic that centers on jobs that have a high degree of impact on the lives of others.

Task structure A situational variable that determines the clarity of job tasks and the behaviors needed to accomplish those tasks.

Team building An organizational development method for improving the effectiveness of a work group through improved group interaction.

Technostress Stress caused by the never-ending demands of modern technology or by an employee's inability to use new technology, such as computers.

Telecenter A remote office setting used as a temporary office location by virtual office employees.

Telecommuting Assigning employees to work from remote locations while still being connected to the main office location by computers, faxes, modems, and telephones.

Test utility How useful a test is in the situation for which it was designed.

Test-retest method A way to prove the consistency of test scores by readministering a test after a period of time.

Thematic Apperception Test (TAT) A series of ambiguous pictures used for storytelling to assess personality characteristics, including the need to achieve.

Theory A set of basic principles that explain and integrate a group of facts. Theories explain, interpret, and predict events.

Theory X McGregor's organizational structure based on the assumption that people dislike work and need close supervision to get work done.

Theory Y McGregor's organizational structure based on the assumption that people naturally look for satisfaction through work.

Things hierarchy A category of the Functional Job Analysis that assesses an employee's involvement with equipment, tools, and machinery of the job.

Throughput Changes in the resources brought into a system, such as training employees and manufacturing products.

Training Practical education in a skill, job, or profession.

Trait theory A leadership theory that is based on the assumption that effective leaders have certain characteristics, either learned or innate.

Transactional leadership A leadership style that is based on a social contract between the subordinates and the leader, with the promise of rewards in return for certain behaviors.

Transfer of training The application on the job of skills learned in a training situation.

Transformational leadership A leadership style in which the leader can change the interests and goals of individual subordinates into those of the group.

Two-factor theory A theory of motivation that states that the working conditions leading to work dissatisfaction and work motivation are separate and different.

Type A personality A set of personality characteristics, including aggressiveness, hostility, time urgency, and competitiveness, that may be linked to high rates of heart disease.

Type B personality A set of personality characteristics—described by the absence of Type A personality characteristics and by a generally easygoing lifestyle—that are linked to low rates of heart disease.

Underpayment An inequity relationship in which an employee puts more into a job than she or he gets from the job.

Uniform Guidelines for Employee Selection Procedures The set of procedures that explains how employers must prove that their employment selection systems are not discriminatory.

Unstructured interview An interview in which different questions are asked of each applicant; the questions may have little relevance to the job.

Upward communication. Messages that go from lower to high organizational levels.

Utility test An assessment of the cost-benefit ratio of using a particular selection test or method.

Valence The subjective value an employee attaches to a particular job outcome.

Valence-instrumentality-expectancy (VIE) theory A motivational theory based on the relationship among valence, instrumentality, and expectancy, in regard to job behaviors.

Validity Chapter 2: Evidence that the results of a research study were caused by the manipulations of the researcher, not by extraneous variables. Chapter 8: The degree to which a test measures what it is supposed to measure.

Validity generalization A way to prove validity that concludes that a test that is valid in one situation may be valid in another similar situation without independent proof of its validity.

Variable Anything that can be manipulated or measured.

Variable interval reinforcement Reinforcement given for correct responses after an average interval of time.

Variable ratio reinforcement Reinforcement given after a number of correct responses, based on an average number of responses.

Vestibule training Training done adjacent to the actual work area with the same equipment and tools.

Virtual office Eliminating assigned workspaces and giving employees mobile equipment, such as cellular phones and laptop computers, that allows them to use any place they work as an office.

Virtual reality Computer-based simulation training that re-creates a three-dimensional environment.

Virtual reality programs Computer-based programs that recreate all the elements of a real work situation, but without the consequences of making mistakes.

Voluntary turnover Occurs when an employee leaves an organization by choice.

Vroom and Yago theory A leadership theory that adds more variables to the Vroom and Yetton decision-making model to make the leadership situation more realistic.

Vroom and Yetton decision-making model A leadership theory that provides a decision pattern to help leaders find the most effective way to make decisions.

Weighted application blank An application form that assigns different values to each answer given by an applicant, on the basis of research on successful and unsuccessful workers in the job.

Whole and part learning Developing a new skill all at once (whole) or by putting together a number of separate pieces (part).

Work group A formal organizational collection of employees who have a common task but whose work does not depend on the other members of the group.

Work overload Stress caused by having too much work to do in the time available or not having the skills needed to perform the job.

Work team A formal organizational collection of employees in which each person's work affects the other members' work in terms of completing the task.

Work underload Stress caused by not having enough work to do or not being able to use one's skills on the job.

Worker-oriented evaluation A job analysis that focuses on the characteristics of the worker—such as knowledge, skills, abilities, experience, and education—that are necessary to do a job correctly.

Workplace envelope The three-dimensional workspace in which a person uses her or his hands.

Workplace The workspaces of an entire group or organization.

Z-scores A statistical procedure that allows the comparison of different scores from distributions with different means and standard deviations.

Chapter 1

1.d, 2.Hugo Münsterberg; Walter Dill Scott, 3.c, 4.e, 5.b, 6.d, 7.b, 8.d, 9.a, 10.c, 11.d, 12.b, 13.b, 14.b, 15.c

Chapter 2

1.applied; basic, 2.objective, 3.c, 4.replication, 5.d, 6.c, 7.independent; dependent, 8.control; experimental, 9.e, 10.random assignment; matched groups, 11.extraneous, 12.d, 13.operational definition, 14.c, 15.a, 16.pluralistic ignorance, 17.d, 18.hindsight bias, 19.c, 20.+1; −1, 21.related; strength; direction, 22.d, 23 b, 24.field study, 25.c, 26.d, 27.c, 28.a, 29.d

Chapter 3

1.b, 2.a, 3.c, 4.dependent; passive; docile, 5.a, 6.a, 7.c, 8.open, 9.b, 10.b, 11.d, 12.(one of) flexibility or increased change, 13.b, 14.a. observable artifacts; b. values; c. underlying assumptions, 15.c, 16.c, 17.a, 18.(one of) social factors influence the work environment or organizational culture and climate help an organization stay effective, 19.b, 20.b

Chapter 4

1.b, 2.b, 3.a, 4.c, 5.d, 6.a, 7.d, 8.a, 9.e, 10.b, 11.a, 12.change agent, 13.d, 14.a. diagnosis; b.planning for change; c.intervention; d.evaluation, 15.b, 16.b, 17.(two of) reduced sick time; fewer resignations; less redone work; increase in patents and patent application, 18.a, 19.c, 20.a. awareness; b.skill-based, 21.a, 22.(two of) length of time needed; lack of a control group; self-fulfilling prophecy bias; timing of measurement

Chapter 5

1.b, 2.a. someone needs information; b.someone needs social reinforcement; c.someone has directed someone else to communicate; d. someone communicates to achieve a goal, 3.a, 4.d, 5.a, 6.a, 7.b, 8.a, 9.c, 10.b, 11.d, 12.b, 13.(three of the following) suggestion boxes; grievances; employee surveys; reverse performance appraisals; scheduled feedback meetings, 14.a, 15.b, 16.b, 17.a (one of) greater participation; fewer organizational levels used to make decisions; greater organizational variety in the level where decisions are made; less time spent in meetings; higher-quality decisions; fewer human links; b.(one of) information overload; lack of planning; greater employment stress, 18.a.writing skills; b.oral presentation skills; c.listening skills; d.reading skills, 19.c, 20.consensus, 21.f, 22.a, 23.(two of) reward critical thinking; divide the larger group into smaller ones to evaluate the decision; leaders stay impartial; hold a "second chance" meeting to reconsider a rejected alternative, 24.d, 25.b, 26.b, 27.b, 28.c, 29.d, 30.a, 31.(one of) labor and management are changing their perceptions of each other; unions must be willing to change and adapt; increased value of union membership to employees

Chapter 6

1.b, 2.c, 3.a, 4.a.physiological needs; b.safety and security; c.social needs; d.self-esteem; e.self-actualization, 5.c, 6.a.need to achieve; b.need to affiliate; c.need for power, 7.a.(two of) supervision; interpersonal relations; physical work conditions; salary; company policy and administration; job security; b.(two of) achievement; recognition; work itself; responsibility; advancement, 8.d, 9.a.skill variety; b.task identity; c.task significance; d.autonomy; e.feedback, 10.b, 11.b, 12.c, 13.a, 14.a, 15.d, 16.a, 17.a, 18.(two of) ability; personality variables; situational factors; internal versus external controls, 19.d, 20.b, 21.a, 22.reinforcers (rewards); punishment, 23.b, 24.b, 25.a, 26.a, 27.d, 28.a, 29.b, 30.functional, 31.d, 32.b, 33.b, 34.a. Job Descriptive Index (JDI); b.Minnesota Satisfaction Questionnaire (MSQ), 35.c

Chapter 7

1.b, 2.b, 3.c, 4.(two of) surgency; emotional stability; conscientiousness; intellectance, 5.a, 6.d, 7.Leader Match Training, 8.c, 9.a, 10.in-group, 11.a, 12.b, 13.c, 14.d, 15.(two of) vision; good communications; inspiring trust; helping followers feel capable; having an action style of leadership, 16.a, 17.b, 18.b, 19.d, 20.a, 21.a, 22.b, 23.d, 24.b, 25.a.management of attention; b.meaning; c.trust; d.self

Chapter 8

1.a, 2.screening, 3.a, 4.b, 5.c, 6.(three of, see Figure 8.2): unsolicited telephone calls; walk-ins; college recruitment; job fairs; newspaper advertisements; television spots, 7.e, 8.a, 9.b, 10.a, 11.e, 12.unstructured; structured, 13.structured situational, 14.d, 15.a, 16.a.first impression; b.similarity; c.negative information, 17.b, 18.b, 19.b, 20.(one of): unfair discrimination; little proof that the abilities are needed on the job, 21.b, 22.a, 23.c, 24.a, 25.b, 26.b, 27.a.program design; b.training assessors; c.follow-up, 28.a, 29.a, 30.c, 31.b

Chapter 9

1.c, 2.c, 3.a, 4.Civil Rights Act of 1964; Title VII; Age Discrimination in Employment Act; Americans with Disabilities Act, 5.Equal Employment Opportunity Commission, 6.b, 7.Reverse discrimination, 8.b, 9.b, 10.working, or normal, 11.achievement, 12.d, 13.b; g; f; a; e; d; c, 14.Employee Polygraph Protection Act of 1988, 15.a, 16.a, 17.concurrent validity, 18.c, 19.b, 20.validity generalization, 21.b, 22.a, 23.standardization, 24.d, 25.a, 26.b, 27.b, 28.moderate; moderate; high; low, 29.c, 30.aptitude; achievement, 31.a, 32.a, 33.b, 34.b

Chapter 10

1.b, 2.a, 3.a.salary administration; b.performance feedback; c.identification of employees' strengths and weaknesses, 4.b, 5.c, 6.b, 7.b, 8.(two of) Position Analysis Questionnaire; Functional Job Analysis; Job Element Inventory, 9.b, 10.b, 11.a.outcome-based; b.absolute standards; c.relative comparison, 12.b, 13.c, 14.f, 15.graphic rating scales, 16.b, 17.a, 18.(two of) ranking; paired comparison; forced distribution, 19.b, 20.a, 21.a, 22.f, 23.b, 24.c, 25.e, 26.d, 27.a, 28.a, 29.(one of) meet legal challenges; make supervisors meet with subordinates, 30.d, 31.b, 32.(two of) agree on purpose; prepare; participate; combine judgment and developmental functions; base ratings on actual performance, 33.c, 34.b, 35.a

Chapter 11

1.a, 2.d, 3.b, 4.a. exploration; b.establishment; c.maintenance; d.disengagement, 5.a. organizational needs analysis; b.task needs analysis; c.person needs analysis, 6.c, 7.c, 8.b, 9.cognitive learning, 10.a, 11.d, 12.observable; unobservable, or thought, 13.b, 14.American Society for Training and Development, 15.a, 16.a, 17.a.tell; b.show; c.do; d.review, 18.b, 19.b, 20.case study, 21.outdoor experiential training, 22.b, 23.d, 24.business game, 25.b, 26.a, 27.a, 28.a.reactions; b.learning measures; c.behavior results; d.organizational results, 29.a, 30.d

Chapter 12

1.b, 2.d, 3.d, 4 b, 5.a. auditory; b. visual, 6.b, 7c, 8.a, 9.d, 10.b, 11.a. primary visual controls; b. primary controls that interact with the primary visual task, 12.a, 13.b, 14.a, 15.d, 16.b, 17.a, 18.f, 19.b, 20.gliding time; flexitour, 21.b, 22.c, 23.b, 24.c

Chapter 13

1.b, 2.f, 3.b, 4.d, 5.c, 6.d, 7.a, 8.a, 9.b, 10.a, 11.(two of) hostility; higher arousal levels; general unhappiness; negative affectivity, 12.c, 13.b, 14.a, 15.b, 16.b, 17.a, 18.d, 19.c, 20.a, 21.b, 22.e, 23.a, 24.a, 25.(two of) exchanging money with the public; working alone or in small numbers; working late-night or early-morning hours; working in high-crime areas; guarding valuable property; working in a community setting, 26.b

Appendix

1.mode; median; mean, 2.standard deviation, 3.c, 4.d, 5.a, 6.b, 7..05; .01

Aamodt, M. G. (1986, June). *Validity of expert advice regarding the employment interview.* Paper presented at the Tenth Annual Meeting of the International Personnel Management Association–Assessment Council, San Francisco.

Adams, J. S. (1965). Inequity in social exchange. In L. Berkowitz (Ed.), *Advances in experimental social psychology* (Vol. 2; pp. 267–296). New York: Academic Press.

Adams, J. S., & Roebuck, D. B. (1997). Exploring neglected terrain: Communication with employees during crises. *Organizational Development Journal, 15*(3), 63–74.

Adams, J. S., & Rosenbaum, W. B. (1962). The relationship of worker productivity to cognitive dissonance about wage inequities. *Journal of Applied Psychology, 46*(1) 161–164.

Adams, S., & Trucks, L. (1976). A procedure for evaluating auditory warning signals. In *Proceedings of the 6th Congress of the International Ergonomics Association and technical program for the 20th annual meeting of the Human Factors Society* (pp. 166–172). Santa Monica, CA: Human Factors Society.

Adler, P. S., & Borys, B. (1996). Two types of bureaucracy: Enabling and coercive. *Administrative Science Quarterly, 41*(1), 61–89.

Aiken, M., Hasan, B., & Vanjani, M. (1996, Winter). Total quality management: A GDSS approach *Information Systems Management, 13,* 73–75.

Aiken, M., Hawley, D. D., & Sloan, H. (1994–1995, Winter). How to improve bank meetings [group decision support systems]. *Journal of Retail Banking, 16,* 21–25.

Aldag, R. J., & Fuller, S. R. (1993). Beyond fiasco: A reappraisal of the groupthink phenomenon and a new model of group decision processes. *Psychological Bulletin, 113*(3), 533–552.

Alden, J. (1998, March–April). What in the world drives UPS? *International Business, 12*(2), 6–7+.

Alderfer, C. P. (1969). An empirical test of a new theory of human needs. *Organizational Behavior and Human Performance, 4,* 142–175.

Alesse, B. G. (1982, May 2–5). *Information discrepancy as a predictor of organizational satisfaction.* Paper presented at the Annual Meeting of the International Communication Association, Boston.

Allen, D. C., & Griffith, R. W. (1997, October). Vertical and lateral information processing: The effects of gender, employee class level and media richness on communication and work outcomes. *Human Relations, 50,* 1239–1260.

Allen, J. A., Hays, R. T., & Buffardi, L. C. (1986). Maintenance training simulator fidelity and individual differences in transfer of training. *Human Factors, 28*(5), 497–509.

Alliger, G. M., Lilienfeld, S. O., & Mitchell, K. E. (1996). The susceptibility of overt and covert integrity tests to coaching and faking. *Psychological Science, 7*(1), 32–39.

Amalfitano, J. G., & Kalt, N. C. (1977). Effects of eye contact on the evaluation of job applicants. *Journal of Employment Counseling, 14,* 46–48.

American Management Association. (1999). Retention: Challenges and solutions. 1999 AMA Human Resources Conference Onsite Survey. http://www.amanet.org/research/ specials/retent.htm

American Management Association. (2000). A 2000 AMA Survey: Workplace testing. *American Management Association Research Reports.*

American Psychological Association. (1981). *Specialty guidelines for the delivery of services by industrial/organizational psychologists.* Washington, DC.

American Psychological Association. (1992). Ethical principles of psychologists and code of conduct. *American Psychologist, 47,* 1597–1611.

American Society for Training and Development. (1997). National HRD (human resources development) executive Survey: Measurement and evaluation. http://www.astd.org/virtual_community/research/nhrd_executive_survey_97me.htm.

Anderson, C. D., Warner, J. L., & Spencer, C. C. (1984). Inflation bias in self-assessment examinations. *Journal of Applied Psychology, 69,* 574–580.

Anderson, L., Schleien, S. J., McAvoy, L., Laid, G., & Seligman, D. (1997). Creating positive change through an integrated outdoor adventure program. *Therapeutic Recreation Journal, 31*(4), 214–229.

Anshel, J. (1997, July 1). Computervision syndrome: causes and cures. *Managing Office Technology, 42,* 17–20.

Archer, E. D., Dorawala, T. G., & Huffmire, D. W. (1993, March–April). How Texaco R&D improved its organization. *Research Technology Management, 36,* 45–51.

Ardelean, E. (1993, July–December). Validation of a test battery for the selection and evaluation of foremen in the footwear industry. *Revue Roumaine de Psychologie, 37*(2), 153–164.

Argyle, M. (1989). Is nonverbal communication a kind of language? *Etc., 46*(2), 158–162.

Argyris, C. (1980). Some limitations of the case method: Experiences in a management development program. *Academy of Management Review, 5,* 291–298.

Arjas, B. K. (1991, June). Testing the teamwork theory. *Graphic Arts Monthly, 63,* 76.

Armour, S. (2000, August 8). Test? Forget the test—you're hired. *USA Today*, p. 1B.

Armstrong, M. (1995, September, 21). Measuring work: The vital statistics: IPD survey of job evaluation practices. *People Management, 1*, 43–35.

Armstrong-Stassen, M. (1997). The effect of repeated downsizing and surplus designation on remaining managers: An exploratory study. *Anxiety, Stress and Coping: An International Journal, 10*(4), 377–384.

Arthur, A. (1997, October). How much should employers know? *Black Enterprise, 28*, 56.

Arvey, R. D., Bouchard, T. J., Segal, N. L., & Abraham, L. M. (1989). Job satisfaction: Environmental and genetic components. *Journal of Applied Psychology, 74*(2), 187–192.

Arvey, R. D., & Campion, J. E. (1982). The employment interview: A summary and review of recent research. *Personnel Psychology, 35*, 281–327.

Arvey, R. D., Maxwell, S. E., & Salas, E. (1992). The relative power of training evaluation designs under different cost configurations. *Journal of Applied Psychology, 77*(2), 155–160.

Arvey, R. D., McCall, B. P., Bouchard, T. J., & Taubman, P. (1994). Genetic influences on job satisfaction and work value. *Personality and Individual Differences, 17*(1), 21–33.

Arvey, R. D., Nutting, S. M., & Landon, T. E. (1992). Validation strategies for physical ability testing in police and fire settings. *Public Personnel Management, 21*(3), 301–312.

Ash, R. A., & Edgell, S. A. (1975). A note on the readability of the Position Analysis Questionnaire (PAQ). *Journal of Applied Psychology, 60*(4), 765–766.

Ashkanasy, N. M., & O'Connor, C. (1997). Value congruence in leader–member exchange. *Journal of Social Psychology, 137*(5), 647–662.

Association of Personnel Test Publishes. (1990). *Model guidelines for pre-employment integrity testing programs.* Washington, DC: Association of Personnel Test Publishers.

Atkins, C. P., & Kent, R. L. (1988). What do recruiters consider important during the employment interview? *Journal of Employment Counseling, 25*(3), 88–103.

Atoum, A. O., & Farah, A. M. (1993). Social loafing and personal involvement among Jordanian college students. *Journal of Social Psychology, 133*(6), 785–789.

Austin, J. T., & Waung, M. P. (1994, April). Dr. Marion Bills: Allegan to Aetna. In L. Koppes (Chair), *The founding mothers: Female I/O psychology in the early years.* Symposium conducted at the Ninth Annual Conference of the Society for Industrial and Organizational Psychology, Inc., Nashville, TN.

Aviolio, B. J., Waldman, D. A., & McDaniel, M. A. (1990). Age and work performance in nonmanagerial jobs: The effects of experience and occupational type. *Academy of Management Journal, 33*(2), 407–422.

Ayman, R., & Chemers, M. M. (1991). The effect of leadership match on subordinate satisfaction in Mexican organizations: Some moderating influences on self-monitoring. *Applied Psychology: An International Review, 40*(3), 299–314.

Bahls, S. C., & Bahls, J. E. (1997, June). Point of reference: Providing references for former employees could put your business at risk. *Entrepreneur, 25*, 84–86.

Baldwin, T. T. (1992). Effects of alternative modeling strategies on outcomes of interpersonal-skills training. *Journal of Applied Psychology, 77*(1), 147–154.

Balzer, W. K., Smith, P. C., Kravitz, D. E., Lovell, S. E., Paul, K. B., Reilly, B. A., & Reilly, C. E. (1990). *User's manual for the Job Descriptive Index (JDI) and the Job in General (JIG) scales.* Bowling Green, OH: Bowling Green State University.

Bandura, A. (1985). *Social foundations of thought and actions: A social-cognitive view.* Englewood Cliffs, NJ: Prentice-Hall.

Banner, D. K., & Graber, J. M. (1985). Critical issues in performance appraisal. *Journal of Management Development, 4*(1), 26–35.

Barbuto, J. E., Jr. (1997). Taking the charisma out of transformational leadership. *Journal of Social Behavior and Personality, 12*(3), 689–697.

Baril, G. L., Ayman, R., & Palmiter, D. J. (1994). Measuring leader behavior: Moderators of discrepant self and subordinate descriptions. *Journal of Applied Social Psychology, 24*(1), 82–94.

Baritz, L. (1960). *The servants of power.* Westport, CT: Greenwood Press.

Barling, J., Weber, T., & Kelloway, E. K. (1996). Effects of transformational leadership training on attitudinal and financial outcomes: A field experiment. *Journal of Applied Psychology, 81*(6), 827–832.

Barnshaw, J. (1992). Educational resources in your own backyard. *Training and Development, 46*, 53–54.

Baron, R. A. (1995). *Psychology.* Needham Heights, MA: Allyn & Bacon.

Barrett, M. J., Scott, W., Gillespie, J., & Palmer, B. (1994). Women survivors of sexual abuse: EAP providers play a pivotal role. *Employee Assistance Quarterly, 9*(3–4), 149–159.

Barrick, M. R., & Mount, M. K. (1991). The big five personality dimensions and job performance: A meta-analysis. *Personnel Psychology, 44,* 1–26.

Barry, D., & McLaughlin, K. (1996, May). A S.M.A.R.T. method of compensation analysis. *HRMagazine, 41,* 80–83.

Bar Tal, Y. (1991). Followers' phenomenological field as an explanatory framework to Fiedler's situational favorability dimension. *Social Behavior and Personality 19*(3), 165–175.

Bass, B. M. (1965). *Organizational psychology.* Boston: Allyn & Bacon.

Bass, B. M. (1981). *Stodgill's handbook of leadership.* New York: Free Press.

Bass, B. M. (1985). *Leadership and performance beyond expectations.* New York: Free Press.

Bass, B. M. (1990a). *Bass & Stodgill's handbook of leadership* (3rd ed.). New York: Free Press.

Bass, B. M. (1990b). From transactional to transformational leadership: Learning to share the vision. *Organizational Dynamics, 18*(3), 19–31.

Bass, B. M. (1998). *Transformational leadership: Industrial, military and educational impact.* Mahwah, NJ: Lawrence Erlbaum.

Bass, B. M., & Barrett, G. V. (1981). *People, work and organizations.* Boston: Allyn & Bacon.

Bates, T. (1994). Social resources generated by group support networks may not be beneficial to Asian immigrant-owned small businesses. *Social Forces, 72*(3), 671–689.

Baumrind, D. (1985). Research using intentional deception: Ethical issues revised. *American Psychologist, 40,* 165–174.

Beach, L. R., & Mitchell, T. R. (1990). Image theory: A behavioral theory of decision making in organizations. In B. M. Staw & L. L. Cummings (Eds.), *Research in organizational behavior* (Vol. 12; pp. 1–41). Greenwich, CT: JAI Press.

Beehr, T. A. (1985). Organizational stress and employee effectiveness: A job characteristics approach. In T. A. Beehr & R. S. Bhagat (Eds.), *Human stress and cognition in organizations: An integrated perspective* (pp. 57–81). New York: Wiley.

Beekun, R. I. (1989). Assessing the effectiveness of sociotechnical interventions: Antidote or fad? *Human Relations, 42*(10), 877–897.

Beer, M., & Walton, A. E. (1987). Organization change and development. *Annual Review of Psychology, 38,* 339–367.

Belanger, K. (1991). Intelligent software for performance evaluations can be legal protection. *Employment Relations Today, 18,* 27–28.

Belasen, A. T., Benke, M., & DiPadova, L. N. (1996, Spring). Downsizing and the hyper-effective manager: The shifting importance of managerial roles during organizational transformation. *Human Resource Management, 35,* 87–117.

Belcher, D. W., & Atchison, T. J. (1987). *Compensation Administration* (2nd ed.). Englewood Cliffs, NJ: Prentice-Hall.

Bell, C., Jr., & Rosensweig, J. (1978). Highlights of an organizational improvement program in a city government. In W. L. French, C. H. Bell, Jr., & R. A. Zawacki (Eds.), *Organization development: Theory, practice and research* (pp. 380–392). Dallas, TX: Business Publications.

Bell, J. D., & Kerr, D. L. (1987). Measuring training results: Key to managerial commitment. *Training and Development Journal, 41,* 70–73.

Bell, M. P., Harrison, D. A., & McLaughlin, M. E. (1997). Asian-American attitudes towards affirmative action in employment: Implications for the Model Minority Myth. *Journal of Applied Behavioral Science, 33*(3), 356–377.

Bellarosa, C., & Chen, P. Y. (1997). The effectiveness and practicality of occupational stress management interventions: A survey of subject matter expert opinions. *Journal of Occupational Health Psychology, 2*(3), 247–262.

Bemis, S. E., Belenky, A. H., & Soder, D. A. (1983). *Job analysis: An effective management tool.* Washington, DC: Bureau of National Affairs.

Benbassat, I., & Lim, L. H. (1993). The effects of group, task, context, and technology variables on the usefulness of group support systems: A meta-analysis of experimental studies. Special issue: Group Support Systems. *Small Group Research, 24*(4), 430–462.

Benishek, L. A. (1996). Evaluation of the factor structure underlying hardiness. *Assessment, 3*(4), 423–435.

Benjamin, L. T. (1997). Organized industrial psychology before division 14: The ACP and the AAAP (1930–1945). *Journal of Applied Psychology, 82*(4), 459–466.

Bennis, W. G. (1993). *An invented life: Reflections on leadership and change.* Reading, MA: Addison-Wesley.

Bensen, H. R. (1975). *The relaxation response.* New York: Morrow.

Berger, R. M., & Tucker, D. (1987). How to evaluate a selection test. *Personnel Journal, 66,* 88 +.

Bernard, L. C., Hutchison, S., Lavin, A., & Pennington, P. (1996). Ego-strength, hardiness, self-esteem, self-efficacy, optimism and maladjustment: Health related personality constructs and the "Big Five" model of personality. *Assessment, 3*(2), 115–131.

Bernardin, H. J. (1977). Behavioral expectation scales versus summated scales: A fairer comparison. *Journal of Applied Psychology, 62*(3), 422–427.

Bernardin, H. J., & Beatty, W. (1984). *Performance appraisal: Assessing human behavior at work.* Boston: Kent.

Bernardin, H. J., & Orban, J. A. (1990). Leniency effect as a function of rating format, purpose for appraisal, and rater individual difference. *Journal of Business and Psychology, 5,* 197–211.

Beyer, J. M., & Trice, H. M. (1978). *Implementing change: Alcoholism programs in work organizations.* New York: Free Press.

Bhagat, R. S. (1983). Effects of stressful life events on individual performance and work adjustment processes within organizational settings: A research model. *Academy of Management Review, 8,* 660–671.

Bierma, L. L. (1996). How executive women learn corporate culture. *Human Resource Development Quarterly, 7*(2), 145–164.

Binder, C. (1990). Closing the confidence gap. *Training, 27,* 49–53.

Birdi, K., Allan, C., & Warr, P. (1997). Correlates and perceived outcomes of the psychological types of employee development activity. *Journal of Applied Psychology, 82*(6), 845–857.

Birren, J. E., Cunningham, W. R., & Yamamoto, K. (1983). Psychology of adult development and aging. *Annual Review of Psychology, 34,* 543–575.

Bischof, L. J. (1976). *Adult psychology.* New York: Harper & Row.

Black, J. S., & Mendenhall, M. (1990). Cross-cultural training effectiveness: A review and theoretical framework for future research. *Academy of Management Review, 15,* 113–136.

Black, M. M., & Holden, E. W. (1998). The impact of gender on productivity and satisfaction among medical school psychologists. *Journal of Clinical Psychology in Medical Settings, 5*(1), 117–131.

Blackburn, R. S. (1987). Experimental design in organizational settings. In J. W. Lorsch (Ed.), *Handbook of organizational behavior.* Englewood Cliffs, NJ: Prentice Hall.

Blake, R. R., & McCanse, A. A. (1991). *Leadership dilemmas—grid solutions.* Houston, TX: Gulf.

Blakeley, B. R., Quinones, M. A., & Jago, I. A. (1992). *The validity of isometric strength tests: The results of five studies.* Paper presented at the Seventh Annual Meeting of the Society of Industrial and Organizational Psychology, Montreal.

Blau, G. (1990). Exploring the mediating mechanisms affecting the relationship of recruitment sources to employee performance. *Journal of Vocational Behavior, 37*(3), 303–320.

Blotzer, M. (1995, January). Virtual reality: Real value for safety training. *Occupational Hazards, 57,* 121–122.

Bobo, L. (1998). Race, interests and beliefs about affirmative action: Unanswered questions and new directions. *American Behavioral Scientist, 41*(7), 985–1003.

Bohl, D. L. (1996, September/October). Minisurvey: 360-degree appraisals yield superior results, survey shows. *Compensation and Benefits Review, 28,* 16–19.

Bohnker, B. K. (1992). Performance evaluation impairment prior to HIV seropositive diagnosis: A preliminary Navy population-based study. *Aviation, Space and Environmental Medicine, 63*(3), 212–218.

Boise, L., & Neal, M. B. (1996). Family responsibilities and absenteeism: Employees caring for parents versus employees caring for children. *Journal of Managerial Issues, 8*(2), 218–238.

Boles, M., & Sunoo, B. P. (1997, November). Talk to your shiftworkers. *Workforce, 76,* 13.

Bonacich, P. (1990). Communication dilemmas in social networks: An experimental study. *American Sociological Review, 55*(3), 119–159.

Bond, M. H., & Smith, P. B. (1996). Cross-cultural social and organizational psychology. *Annual Review of Psychology, 47,* 205–235.

Booth-Kewley, S., & Freidman, H. S. (1987). Psychological predictors of heart disease: A quantitative review. *Psychological Bulletin, 101,* 343–362.

Booth-Kewley, S., Rosenfeld, P., & Edwards, J. E. (1993). Turnover among Hispanic and non-Hispanic blue-collar workers in the U.S. Navy's civilian work force. *Journal of Social Psychology, 133*(6), 761–768.

Borack, J. I. (1998). An estimate of the impact of drug testing on the deterrence of drug use. *Military Psychology, 10*(1), 19–25.

Bordieri, J. E., Drehmer, D. E., & Taricone, P. F. (1990). Personnel selection bias for job applicants with cancer. *Journal of Applied Social Psychology, 20*(3, Pt.2), 244–253.

Borman, W. C., & Cox, G. L. (1996, April). Who's doing what: Patterns in the practice of I/O psychology. www.siop.org/tip/backissues/tipapr96/borman/htm.

Borman, W. C., White, L. A., Pulakos, E. D., & Oppler, S. H. (1991). Models of supervisory job performance ratings. *Journal of Applied Psychology, 76*(4), 567–572.

Born, D. H., & Mathieu, J. E. (1996). Differential effects of survey-guided feedback: The rich get richer and the poor get poorer. *Group and Organizational Management, 21*(4), 388–403.

Borofsky, G. L. (1992). *Psychometric properties of the Employment Reliability Inventory (ERI)*. Boston: Bay State Psychological Services.

Borofsky, G. L., Bielema, M., & Hoffman, J. (1993). Accidents, turnover, and use of a preemployment screening inventory. *Psychological Reports, 73*(3, Pt. 2), 1067–1076.

Bottger, P. C., & Yetton, P. W. (1987). Improving group performance by training in individual problem solving. *Journal of Applied Psychology, 72,* 651–657.

Bottom, W. P., & Baloff, N. (1994). A diagnostic model for team building with an illustrative application. *Human Resource Department Quarterly, 5*(4), 317–336.

Bouzid, N., & Cranshaw, C. M. (1987). Massed versus distributed word processor training. *Applied Ergonomics, 18*(3), 220–222.

Bowers, D. G. (1973). OD techniques and their results in 23 organizations: The Michigan ICL study. *Journal of Applied Behavioral Research, 9,* 21–43.

Boyce, B. A., & Bingham, S. M. (1997). The effects of self-efficacy and goal setting on bowling performance. *Journal of Teaching in Physical Education, 16*(3), 312–323.

Boyers, K. (1997, November). Lessons from your desk. *Association Management, 49,* 50–53.

Brady, T. (1993, Autumn). Genetic testing: Medical and legal issues and DuPont's program. *Employment Relations Today, 20,* 257–266.

Braham, J. (1987). Top management: Is the door really open? *Industry Week, 236,* 64–66.

Bramel, D., & Friend, R. (1981). Hawthorne, the myth of the docile worker and class bias in psychology. *American Psychologist, 36,* 867–878.

Brands, K. M. (1997, October). Distance learning: Ernst and Young's satellite training network. *Management Accounting, 79,* 67.

Brannon, D., Streit, A., & Smyer, M. A. (1992). The psychosocial quality of nursing home work. *Journal of Aging and Health, 4*(3), 369–389.

Brayfield, A. H., & Crockett, W. H. (1955). Employee attitudes and employee performance. *Psychological Bulletin, 52,* 396–424.

Bresler, S. J., & Sommer, R. D. (1992, April). Take care in administering tests under ADA. *HRMagazine, 37,* 49–51.

Bretz, R. D., & Judge, T. A. (1998). Realistic job previews: A test of the adverse self-selection hypothesis. *Journal of Applied Psychology, 83*(2), 330–337.

Bretz, R. D., Milkovich, G. T., & Read, W. (1992). The current state of performance appraisal research and practice: Concerns, directions, and implications. *Journal of Management, 18,* 321–352.

Bretz, R. D., & Thomas, S. L. (1992). Perceived equity, motivation and final-offer arbitration in major league baseball. *Journal of Applied Psychology, 77*(3), 280–287.

Brooker, K. (1990, April 26). Can Procter & Gamble change its culture, protect its market share, and find the next Tide? *Fortune,* pp. 146–152.

Brooks, L., & Betz, N. E. (1990). Utility of expectancy theory in predicting occupational choices in college students. *Journal of Counseling Psychology, 37*(1), 57–64.

Brostoff, S. (1997, March 31). Repetitive stress injury dip found. *National Underwriter (Property and Casualty/Risk and Benefit Management), 101,* 23.

Brown, D. C. (1994). Subgroup norming: Legitimate testing practice or reverse discrimination. *American Psychologist, 49,* 927–928.

Brown, F. W., & Finstuen, K. (1993). The use of participation in decision making: A consideration of the Vroom-Yetton and Vroom-Jago normative models. *Journal of Behavioral Decision Making, 6*(3), 207–219.

Brown, L. (1990, November). Affirmative-action watch. *Black Enterprise, 21,* 24.

Brown, P. L., & Roessler, R. T. (1991). A job fair demonstration for senior citizens and people with disabilities. *Rehabilitation Counseling Bulletin, 35*(2), 82–90.

Brown, S. D., & Codey, H. C. (1994, November). Employee training may be the key to prevention of sexual harassment. *Labor Law Journal, 45,* 726–727.

Brownell, J. (1991, February). Middle managers: Facing the communication challenge. *The Cornell Hotel and Restaurant Administration Quarterly, 31,* 52–59.

Brumback, G. (1972). A reply to Kavanaugh. *Personnel Psychology, 25,* 567–572.

Brush, D. H., Moch, M. K., & Pooyan, A. (1987). Individual demographic differences in job satisfaction. *Journal of Occupational Behavior, 8,* 139–155.

Bryan, L. A., Jr. (1990, July). An ounce of prevention for workplace accidents. *Training and Development Journal, 44,* 100–102.

Bryan, W. L., & Harter, N. (1897). Studies in the physiology and psychology of the telegraphic language. *Psychological Review, 4,* 25–27.

Budman, M., & Rice, B. (1994). The rating game. *Across the Board, 31,* 34–38.

Buhler, P. (1991, September). Are you really saying what you mean? *Supervision, 52,* 18–20.

Bulkeley, W. M. (1994, August 22). Replaced by technology: Job interviews. *Wall Street Journal,* p. 81.

Buller, P. F., & Bell, C. H., Jr. (1986). Effects of team building and goal setting on productivity: A field experiment. *Academy of Management Journal, 29,* 305–328.

Bumgart, B. L., & DeJong, J. (1995, September). ADA: The bill of rights for AIDS patients. *Best's Review* (Life/Health Insurance Edition), *96,* 66–67.

Bureau of Labor Statistics, U.S. Department of Labor. (1999, Fall). Occupational stress: Counts and rates. *Compensation and Working Conditions Online, 4*(3): http://stats.bls.gov/opub/cwc/1999/fall/brief4.htm

Burgess, L. R. (1984). *Wage and salary administration: Pay and benefits.* Columbus, OH: Merrill.

Burgoon, J. K. (1982, May 2–5). *Relational messages associated with nonverbal behaviors.* Paper presented at the Annual Meeting of the International Communication Association, Boston.

Burgoon, J. K., & Buller, D. B. (1994). Interpersonal deception: III. Effects of deceit on perceived communication and nonverbal behavior dynamics. *Journal of Nonverbal Behavior, 18*(2), 155–184.

Burke, W. W. (1982). *Organization development: Principles and practices.* Boston: Little, Brown.

Burrows, L., Munday, R., Tunnell, J., & Seay, R. (1996). Leadership substitutes: Their effects on teacher organizational commitment and job satisfaction. *Journal of Instructional Psychology, 23*(1), 3–8.

Butcher, J. N. (1994, February). Psychological assessment of airline pilot applicants with the MMPI-2. *Journal of Personality Assessment, 62*(1), 31–44.

Butler, D. L., Acquino, A. L., Hissong, A. A., & Scott, P. A. (1993). Wayfinding by newcomers in a complex building. *Human Factors, 35*(1), 159–173.

Bylinsky, G. (1992, November 2). High-tech help for the housekeeper. *Fortune, 126,* 117.

Callahan, T. J. (1994). Managers' beliefs and attitudes about the Americans with Disabilities Act of 1990. *Applied H.R.M. Research, 5*(1), 28–43.

Camara, W. J. (1992). Fairness and fair use in employment testing: A matter of perspective. In K. F. Geisinger (Ed.), *Psychological testing of Hispanics* (pp. 215–231). Washington, DC: American Psychological Association.

Camara, W. J., & Schneider, D. L. (1994). Integrity tests: Facts and unresolved issues. *American Psychologist, 49*(5), 112–119.

Cameron, K. (1980). Critical questions in assessing organizational effectiveness. *Organizational Dynamics, 9,* 66–80.

Cameron, K. S., Freeman, S. J., & Mishra, A. K. (1991). Best practices in white-collar downsizing: Managing contradictions. *Academy of Management Executive, 5*(3), 57–58.

Camp, R. R., Blanchard, P. N., & Huszczo, G. E. (1986). *Toward a more organizationally effective training strategy.* Englewood Cliffs, NJ: Prentice-Hall.

Campbell, D. T., & Stanley J. C. (1963). *Experimental and quasi-experimental designs for research.* Chicago: Rand McNally.

Campbell, J. P. (1988). Training design for productivity improvement. In J. P. Campbell & R. J. Campbell (Eds.), *Productivity in organizations* (pp. 177–215). San Francisco: Jossey-Bass.

Campbell, J. P., & Pritchard, R. D. (1976). Motivation theory in industrial and organizational psychology. In M. D. Dunnette (Ed.), *Handbook of industrial and organizational psychology* (pp. 63–130). Chicago: Rand McNally.

Campbell, R. J., & Bray, D. W. (1993, Autumn). Use of an assessment center as an aid in management selection. *Personnel Psychology, 46,* 691–699.

Campbell, S. S., & Dawson, D. (1990). Enhancement of nighttime alertness and performance with bright ambient light. *Physiology and Behavior, 48*(2), 317–320.

Campbell, T. (1990, July). Technology update: Group decision support systems. *Journal of Accountancy, 70,* 47–48.

Campion, M. A., Palmer, D. K., & Campion, J. E. (1997). A review of structure in the selection interview. *Personnel Psychology, 50*(3), 655–702.

Canadian Banker. (1994). CBA plans to rescue bankers from information overload. *10,* 16–17.

Cantanzaro, D. (1997). Course enrichment and the job characteristics model. *Teaching of Psychology, 24*(2), 85–87.

Capner, M., & Caltabiano, M. L. (1993). Factors affecting the progression towards burnout: A comparison of professional and volunteer counseling. *Psychological Report, 73*(2), 555–561.

Carlier, I. V. E., Lamberts, R. D., & Gersons, B. P. R. (1997). Risk factors for posttraumatic stress disorder in police officers: A prospective analysis. *Journal of Nervous and Mental Diseases, 185*(8), 498–506.

Carnevale, A. P., Gainer, L. J., & Meltzer, A. S. (1990). *Workplace basics training manual*. San Francisco: Jossey-Bass.

Carretta, T. R., & Lee, M. J. (1993). Basic Attributes Test: Psychometric equating of a computer-based test. *International Journal of Aviation Psychology, 3*(3), 189–201.

Carson, K. P., Becker, J. S., & Henderson, J. A. (1998). Is utility really futile? A failure to replicate and an extension. *Journal of Applied Psychology, 83*(1), 84–96.

Carsten, J. M., & Spector, P. E. (1987). Unemployment, job satisfaction and employee turnover: A meta-analytic test of the Muchinsky model. *Journal of Applied Psychology, 72*(3), 374–381.

Cascio, W. F. (1989). Using utility analysis to assess training outcomes. In I. L. Goldstein (Ed.), *Training and development in organizations* (pp. 63–88). San Francisco: Jossey-Bass.

Cascio, W. F., Alexander, R. A., & Barrett, G. V. (1988). Setting cutoff scores: Legal, psychometric, and professional issues and guidelines. *Personnel Psychology, 41*(1), 1–24.

Cascio, W. F., & Bernardin, H. J. (1981). Implications of performance appraisal litigation for personnel decisions. *Personnel Psychology, 34*, 211–226.

Cascio, W. F., Outz, J., Zedeck, S., & Goldstein, J. L. (1991). Statistical implications of six methods of test score use in personnel selection. *Human Performance, 4*(4), 233–264.

Cashin, J. R. (1997, September). One flew over the workplace. *Best's Review, 98*, 80.

Castelli, J. (1993, January). Vehicles, falling objects, homicide kill most workers. *Safety & Health, 147*, 87.

Cattell, J. M. (1917). Our psychology association and research. *Science, 45*, 275–284.

Caudron, S. (1998, February). Diversity watch (Allstate Insurance and Pacific Gas & Electric). *Black Enterprise, 28*, 141–142.

CDC/NIOSH Alert. (1993). *Preventing homicide in the workplace*. Washington, DC: U.S. Department of Health and Human Services, Public Health Service, Centers for Disease Control and Prevention, National Institute for Occupational Safety and Health.

Cellar, D. F., DeGrendel, D. J. D., & Klawsky, J. D. (1996, Fall). The validity of personality, service orientation and reading comprehension measures as predictors of flight attendant training performance. *Journal of Business and Psychology, 11*, 43–54.

Chalykoff, J., & Kochan, T. A. (1989). Computer-aided monitoring: Its influence on employee job satisfaction and turnover. *Personnel Psychology, 42*, 807–834.

Chan, D. (1996). Criterion and construct validation of an assessment centre. *Journal of Occupational and Organizational Psychology, 69*(2), 167–181.

Chao, G. T., & Koslowski, S. W. J. (1986). Employee perceptions on the implementation of robotic manufacturing technology. *Journal of Applied Psychology, 71*(1), 70–76.

Chapanis, A. (1994). Hazards associated with three signal words and four colours on warning sings. *Ergonomics, 37*(2), 265–275.

Charney, D., Reader, L., & Kusbit, G. W. (1990). Goal setting and procedure selection in acquiring computer skills: A comparison of tutorials, problem solving and learner exploration. *Cognition and Instruction, 7*(4), 323–342.

Chebat, D., & Picard, J. (1991). Does prenotification increase response rates in mail surveys? *Journal of Social Psychology, 131*(4), 477–481.

Chemers, M. M., & Fiedler, F. E. (1986). The trouble with assumptions: A reply to Jago and Ragan. *Journal of Applied Psychology, 71*(4), 560–563.

Chiu, C. K., & Alliger, G. M. (1990). A proposed method to combine ranking and graphic rating in performance appraisal: The Quantitative Ranking Scale. *Educational and Psychological Measurement, 50*(3), 493–503.

Christensen, L. (1988). Deception in psychological research: When is its use justified? *Personality and Social Psychology Bulletin, 14*, 664–674.

Church, A. (1996, January). From both sides now: The changing of the job. *TIP* Newsletter, http://www.siop.org/backissues/tip95/church.html

Church, A. H., Waclawski, J., & Burke, W. W. (1996). OD practitioners as facilitators of change. *Group and Organizational Management, 21*(1), 22–66.

Cianni, M., & Romberger, B. (1995). Perceived racial, ethnic and gender differences in access to developmental experiences. *Group and Organizational Management, 20*(4), 440–459.

Clark, A., Oswald, A., & Warr P. (1996). Is job satisfaction U-shaped with age? *Journal of Occupational and Organizational Psychology, 89*(1), 57–81.

Clark, J. (1995, September). Does ADA work for disabled workers? *Kiplinger's Personal Finance Magazine, 49*, 140–141.

Clements, C., Wagner, R. J., & Roland, C. C. (1995). The ins and outs of experiential training. *Training and Development, 49*, 52–56.

Cleveland, J. N., Murphy, K. R., & Williams, R. E. (1989). Multiple uses of performance appraisal: Prevalence and correlates. *Journal of Applied Psychology, 74*(1), 130–135.

Clifford, J. P. (1994, Summer). Job analysis: Why do it, and how should it be done? *Public Personnel Management, 23,* 321–340.

Coates, J. F., Jarratt, J., & Mahaffie, J. B. (1990). *Future work.* San Francisco: Jossey-Bass.

Cofsky, B. (1993, April). Digital's self-managed accounting teams. *Management Accounting, 74,* 39–42.

Cohen, A. (1994). Staying in touch. *Sales and Marketing Management, 147,* 35.

Cohen, A. R. (1958). Upward communication in experimentally created hierarchies. *Human Relations, 11,* 41–53.

Cohen, J. (1990). Adjustment, executive style. *Personnel, 67,* 14.

Colarelli, S. M., & Boos, A. L. (1992). Sociometric and ability-based assignment work groups: Some implications for personnel selections. *Personnel Psychology, 13,* 187–196.

Compton, D., White, K., & DeWine, S. (1991, Winter). Techno-sense: Making sense of computer-mediated communications systems. *Journal of Business Communication, 28,* 23–43.

Conger, J. A. (1989). *The charismatic leader: Beyond the mystique of exceptional leadership.* San Francisco: Jossey-Bass.

Conoley, J. C., & Kramer, J. J. (Eds.). (1992). *The eleventh mental measurements yearbook.* Lincoln: Burros Institute of Mental Measurements, University of Nebraska.

Contrada, R. J. (1989). Type A behavior, personality hardiness, and cardiovascular responses to stress. *Journal of Personality and Social Psychology, 57*(5), 895–903.

Conyne, R. K., Harvill, R. L, & Morganett, R. S. (1990). Effective group leadership: Continuing the search for greater clarity and understanding. *Journal for Specialists in Group Work, 15*(1), 30–36.

Cook, J. D., Hepworth, S. J., Wall, T. D., & Warr, P. B. (1981). *The experience of work.* New York: Academic Press.

Cook, M. (1988). *Personnel selection and productivity.* New York: Wiley.

Cook, M. F. (1997, October). Choosing the right recruitment tool. *HRFocus, 74,* 57–58.

Cook, T. D., & Campbell, D. T. (1976). The design and conduct of quasi-experiments and true experiments in field settings. In M. D. Dunnette (Ed.), *Handbook of industrial and organizational psychology.* Chicago: Rand McNally.

Cooke, W. (1990). *Labor-management cooperation: New partnerships are going in circles?* Kalamazoo, MI: W. E. Upjohn Institute for Employment Research.

Cooper, W. H., Gallupe, R. B., Pollard, S., & Cadsby, J. (1998). Some liberating effects of anonymous electronic brainstorming. *Small Group Research, 29*(2), 147–178.

Cornelius, E. T., & Hakel, M. D. (1978). *A study to develop an improved enlisted performance evaluation system for the U.S. Coast Guard.* Washington, D.C.: Department of Transportation.

Cornell, P., & Kokot, D. (1988). Naturalistic observation of the adjustable VDT stand usage. *Proceedings of the Human Factors Society 32nd Annual Meeting* (pp. 496–500). Santa Monica, CA: Human Factors Society.

Costley, D. L., & Todd, R. (1987). *Human relations in organizations.* St. Paul, MN: West.

Covin, T. J., & Kilmann, R. H. (1991). Profiling large-scale change efforts. *Organizational Development Journal, 9*(2), 1–8.

Cowans, D. S. (1994, October 24). Kodak retouches benefits to slow retirements. *Business Insurance, 28,* 1.

Coward, N. C. (1992). Cross-cultural communication: Is it Greek to you? *Technical Communication, 39,* 264–266.

Cozzetto, D. A., & Pedeliski, T. B. (1997). Privacy and the workplace: Technology and public employment. *Public Personnel Management, 26*(4), 515–527.

Craiger, J. P. (1996, October). Traveling in cyberspace: An overview of computer-mediated work. *The Industrial-Organizational Psychologist (TIP)* http://www.siop.org/tip/backissues/tipoct96/craiger.htm.

Crampton, S. M., & Wagner, J. A., III. (1994). Percept-percept inflation in microorganizational research: An investigation of prevalence and effect. *Journal of Applied Psychology, 79*(1), 67–76.

Crandell, S. (1994). The joys (& payoffs) of mentoring. *Executive Female, 17,* 38–41.

Crocker, O. L., & Guelker, R. (1988, September). The effects of robotics on the workplace. *Personnel, 37,* 26–31.

Crohan, S. E., Antonucci, T. C., Adelmann, P. K., & Coleman, L. M. (1989). Job characteristics and well-being at mid-life: Ethnic and gender comparisons. *Psychology of Women Quarterly, 13*(2), 223–235.

Cronin, M. P. (1993). Hiring: This is a test. *Inc., 15,* 64–68.

Cronshaw, S. F. (1997). Lo! The stimulus speaks: The insider's view on Whyte & Latham's "The futility of utility analysis." *Personnel Psychology, 50,* 611–615.

Crouch, D. J., Webb, D. O., Peterson, L. V., & Buller, P. F. (1989). A critical evaluation of the Utah Power and Light Company's substance abuse management program: Absenteeism, accidents and cost. In S. Gust & J. Walsh (Eds), *Drugs in the workplace: Research and evaluation data.* (Monograph 91, pp. 169–93). Rockville, MD: National Institute on Drug Abuse.

Crump, C. E., & Gebhart, D. L. (1983). *Job Applicant Medical History Questionnaire*. Bethesda, MD: Advanced Research Resources Organization.

Cullen, J. B., Victor, B., & Bronson, J. W. (1993). The ethical climate questionnaire: An assessment of its development and validity. *Psychological Reports, 73*, 667–674.

Cunningham, M. R., Wong, D. T., & Barbee, A. P. (1994). Self-presentation dynamics on overt integrity tests: Experimental studies of the Reid Report. *Journal of Applied Psychology, 79*(5), 643–658.

Cutler, B. (1991, April). How many of your employees can read? *American Demographics, 13*, 16.

Czander, W. M. (1994). The sick building syndrome: A psychoanalytic perspective. *International Forum of Psychoanalysis, 3*(3), 139–149.

d'Arcimoles, C. H. (1997). Human resource policies and company performance: A quantitative approach using longitudinal data. *Organizational Studies, 18*(5), 857–874.

D'O'Brien, J. (1994, November). Throw out your suggestion box. *Supervisory Management, 39*, 1.

Daily, B. F., & Steiner, R. L. (1998). The influence of group decision support systems on contribution and commitment levels in multicultural and culturally homogeneous decision-making groups. *Computers in Human Behavior, 14*(1), 147–162.

Dale, J., & Weinberg, R. S. (1989). The relationship between coaches' leadership style and burnout. *Sport Psychologist, 3*(1), 1–13.

Dalziel, J. R. (1996). Students as research subjects: Ethical and educational issues. *Australian Psychology, 31*(2), 119–123.

Dansby, M. R., & Landis, D. (1991). Measuring equal opportunity climate in the military environment. Special issue: Racial, Ethnic and Gender Issues in the Military. *Internaltional Journal of Intercultural Relations, 15*(4), 389–405.

Davis, K. (1967). *Human relations at work: The dynamics of organizational behavior*. New York: McGraw-Hill.

Davis, K. R., Feild, H. S., & Giles, W. F. (1991). Recruiter-applicant differences in perception of extrinsic rewards. *Journal of Employment Counseling, 28*(3), 82–90.

Davis, T. R. (1984). The influence of the physical environment in offices. *Academy of Management Review, 9*, 271–283.

Dawson, D. A. (1994). Heavy drinking and risk of occupational injury. *Accident Analysis and Prevention, 26*(5), 655–665.

Day, N. E. (1993). Performance in salespeople: The effect of age. *Journal of Managerial Issues, 5*(2), 254–273.

de la Mare, G., & Walker, J. (1968). Factors influencing the choice of shift rotation. *Occupational Psychology, 42*, 1–21.

DeBell, C., & Dinger, T. J. (1997, November–December). Campus interviews: Some challenges to conventional wisdom. *Journal of College Student Development, 38*(6), 553–564.

Deci, E. L. (1975). *Intrinsic motivation*. New York: Plenum Press.

Dedobbeleer, N., & Beland, F. (1991). A safety climate measure for construction sites. *Journal of Safety Research, 22*(2), 97–103.

Deitchman, S. J. (1990). *Further explorations in estimating the military value of training*. IDA Paper P-2317. Alexandria, VA: Institute of Defense Analysis.

DeLaers, K. H., Lundgren, D. C., & Howe, S. R. (1998). The electronic mirror: Human–computer interaction and change in self-appraisals. *Computers in Human Behavior, 14*(1), 43–59.

Delaney, J. T., & Huselid, M. A. (1996). The impact of human resource management practices on perceptions of organizational performance. *Academy of Management Journal, 39*(4), 949–969.

Deluga, R. J. (1991). The relationship of leader and subordinate influencing activity in naval environments. *Military Psychology, 3*(1), 25–39.

Den-Hartog, D. N., Maczynski, J., Motowidlo, S. J., Jarmuz, S., Koopman, P., Thierry, H., & Wilderom, C. P. M. (1997). Cross cultural perceptions of leadership: A comparison of leadership and societal and organizational culture in the Netherlands and Poland. *Polish Psychological Bulletin, 28*(3), 255–267.

DeNisi, A. S., & Peters, L. H. (1996). Organization of information in memory and the performance appraisal process: Evidence from the field. *Journal of Applied Psychology, 81*(6), 717–737.

DePaulo, P. J., & DePaulo, B. M. (1989). Can deception by salespersons and customers be detected through nonverbal behavioral cues? *Journal of Applied Social Psychology, 19*(18, Pt. 2), 1552–1577.

Deshpanda, S. P., & Viswesvaran, C. (1992). Is cross-cultural training of expatriate managers effective: A meta-analysis. *International Journal of Intercultural Relations, 16*(3), 295–310.

DeVries, D. L. (1992). Executive selection: Advances but no progress. *Issues and Observations, 12*, 1–5.

DeWitt, K. (1995, April 20). Blacks prone to dismissal by the U.S. *New York Times*, p. A19.

Diehl, M., & Stroebe, W. (1987). Productivity in brainstorming groups: Toward the solution of a riddle. *Journal of Personality and Social Psychology, 53*, 497–509.

Dienesch, R. M., & Liden, R. C. (1986). Leader–member exchange model of leadership: A critique and further development. *Academy of Management Review, 11* 618–634.

Digman, J. M. (1990). Personality structure: Emergence of the five-factor model. *Annual Review of Psychology, 41,* 417–440.

DiMase, R. A., & Boyle, E. A. (1991, April). Eastland invests in untapped resources. *Personnel Journal, 70,* 53–54.

Dobbin, B. (1998, October 14). Eroding barriers. *Waukegan News Sun,* Sec. C, p. 1.

Dobbins, G. H., Cardy, R. L., & Truxillo, D. M. (1986). Effects of ratee sex and purpose of appraisal on the accuracy of performance evaluations. *Basic and Applied Social Psychology, 7*(3), 225–241.

Dobbins, G. H., & Platz, S. J. (1986). Sex differences in leadership: How real are they? *Academy of Management Review, 11,* 118–127.

Doktor, R. H. (1990). Asian and American CEOs: A comparative study. *Organizational Dynamics, 18*(3), 46–56.

Donovan, J. J., & Rodosevich, D. J. (1998). The moderating role of goal commitment on the goal difficulty-performance relationship: A meta-analytic review and critical analysis. *Journal of Applied Psychology, 83*(2), 308–315.

Dowell, J., & Long, J. (1998). Conception of the cognitive engineering problem. *Ergonomics, 41*(2), 126–139.

Drasgow, F., & Hulin, C. L. (1987). Cross-cultural measurement. *Revista Interamericana de Psicologia, 21*(1–2), 1–24.

Drazin, R., & Auster, E. R. (1987). Wage differences between men and women: Performance appraisal ratings versus salary allocation at the locus of bias. *Human Resource Management, 26,* 157–168.

Dreher, G. F., & Cox, T. H., Jr. (1996). Race, gender and opportunity: A study of compensation, attainment and the establishment of mentoring relationships. *Journal of Applied Psychology, 81*(3), 297–308.

Dreman, D. (1995, June 19). Outpsyching the market. *Forbes, 155*(13), 162–168.

Drew, C. J., & Hardman, M. L. (1985). *Designing and conducting behavioral research.* Elmsford, NY: Pergamon Press, Maxwell House.

Drucker, P. F. (1954). *The practice of management.* New York: Harper.

Drury, C. G., & Sinclair, M. A. (1983). Human and machine performance in an inspection task. *Human Factors, 25*(3), 391–399.

Duarte, N. T., Goodson, J. R., & Klich, N. R. (1993). How do I like thee? Let me appraise the ways. *Journal of Organizational Behavior, 14*(3), 239–249.

Duarte, N. T., Goodson, J. R., & Klich, N. R. (1994). Effects of dyadic quality and duration of performance appraisal. *Academy of Management Journal, 37*(3), 499–521.

DuBrin, A. J. (1994). *Applying psychology: Individual and organizational effectiveness.* Englewood Cliffs, NJ: Prentice-Hall.

Dubrovsky, V. J., Kiesler, S., & Sethna, B. N. (1991). The equalization phenomenon: Status effects in computer-mediated and face-to-face decision-making groups. *Human Computer Interaction, 6*(2), 119–146.

Duftel, L. (1991, July/August). Job evaluation: Still at the frontier. *Compensation and Benefits Review, 23,* 53–67.

Duleep, H. O., & Sanders, S. (1992). Discrimination at the top: American-born Asian and white men. *Industrial Relations, 31,* 416–432.

Dulewicz, V. (1991, June). Improving assessment centers. *Personnel Management, 23,* 50–53.

Duncan, T. S. (1995, April). Death in the office: Workplace homicides. *FBI Law Enforcement Bulletin, 64,* 20–25.

Dunn, P. A. (1995, February). Pre-employment referencing aids your bottom line. *Personnel Journal, 74,* 68–69.

Dunnette, M. D., & Borman, W. C. (1979). Personnel selection and classification systems. *Annual Review of Psychology, 30,* 477–525.

Dunnette, M. D., Campbell, J. P., & Hakel, M. D. (1967). Factors contributing to job satisfaction and dissatisfaction in six occupational groups. *Organizational Behavior and Human Performance, 2,* 143–174.

Durity, A. (1991). Empowered employees: Rhetoric or reality? *Personnel, 68,* 19.

Duxbury, L., & Haines, G., Jr. (1991, August). Predicting alternative work arrangements from salient attitudes: A study of decision makers in the public sector. *Journal of Business Research, 23,* 83–97.

Dwyer, D. J., & Ganster, D. C. (1991). The effects of job demands and control on employee attendance and satisfaction. *Journal of Organizational Behavior, 12,* 595–608.

Dyer, C. (1995). *Beginning research in psychology.* Cambridge, MA: Blackwell.

Eagly, A. H., & Johnson, B. T. (1990). Gender and leadership style: A meta-analysis. *Psychological Bulletin, 108*(2), 233–256.

Eagly, A. H., Makhijani, M. G., & Klonsky, B. G. (1992). Gender and the evaluation of leaders: A meta-analysis. *Psychological Bulletin, 111*(1), 3–22.

Earley, P. C., & Lituchy, T. R. (1991). Delineating goal and efficacy effects: A test of three models. *Journal of Applied Psychology, 76*(1), 81–98.

Eisma, T. L. (1991, May). User-friendly interactive software successfully trains workers in safety. *Occupational Health & Safety, 60,* 30.

Ekman, P. (1988). Lying and nonverbal behavior: Theoretical issues and new findings. Special issue: Deception. *Journal of Nonverbal Behavior, 12*(3, Pt.1), 163–175.

Elass, P. M., & Graves, L. M. (1997). Demographic diversity in decision-making groups: The experience of women and people of color. *Academy of Management Review, 22*(4), 946–973.

Elfner, E. S. (1980). Lecture versus discussion formats in teaching a basic management course. *Academy of Management Proceedings, 40,* 105–106.

Engibous, T. (1999, June 9). Reinventing TI. Sanford C. Bernstein & Company Strategic Decisions Conference, http://www.ti.com/corp/docs/investor/speeches/berns99/ index.htm.

English, G. (1994, May). The pursuit of efficiency: Untying the knot of bureaucracy. *Public Management, 76,* 16–19.

Equal Employment Opportunity Commission (1978). Adoption by four agencies of the "Uniform Guidelines on Employee Selection Procedures." *Federal Register, 43,* 38290–38315.

Equal Employment Opportunity Commission. (2000). Sexual harassment charges: EEOC & FEPAs combined: FY 1992–FY 1999: http://www.eeoc.gov/stats/harass.html

Erez, M., & Zidon, I. (1984). Effect of goal acceptance on the relationship of goal difficulty to performance. *Journal of Applied Psychology, 69*(1), 69–78.

Erffmeyer, E. S., & Mendel, R. M. (1990). Master's level training in industrial/organizational psychology: A case study of the perceived relevance of graduate training. *Professional Psychology Research and Practice, 21,* 405–408.

Erickson, R. J. (1995). Employer liability for workplace violence. *Tips on Employment Law, 5,* 1–7.

Estes, R. (1990). Effects of flexi-time: A meta-analytic review. *Applied H.R.M. Research, 1*(1), 15–18.

Ettorre, B. (1995, November). When the walls come tumbling down. *Management Review, 84,* 33–37.

Everett, J. J., Smith, R. E., & Kipling, K. D. (1992). Effects of team cohesion and identifiability on social loafing in relay swimming performance. *Internatinal Journal of Sport Psychology, 23*(4), 311–324.

Ewert, A., & Heywood, J. (1991). Group development in the natural environment: Expectations, outcomes and techniques. *Environment and Behavior, 23*(5), 592–615.

Executive Female. (1991, May–June). Root out tall tales. *14,* 12.

Fairhurst, G. T. (1993). The leader–member exchange patterns of women leaders in industry: A discourse analysis. *Communication Monographs, 50*(4), 321–351.

Farh, J. L., & Dobbins, G. (1989). Effects of comparative performance information on the accuracy of self-ratings and agreement between self- and supervisor ratings. *Journal of Applied Psychology, 74*(4), 606–610.

Farh, J. L., Dobbins, G. H., & Cheng, B. S. (1991). Cultural relativity in action: A comparison of self-ratings made by Chinese and U.S. workers. *Personnel Psychology, 44,* 129–147.

Farh, J. L., Werbel, J. D., & Bedeian, A. G. (1988). An empirical investigation of self-appraisal-based performance evaluation. *Personnel Psychology, 41*(11), 141–156.

Farley, B. L. (1995, June). "A" is for average: The grading crisis in today's colleges. In *Issues of education at community colleges: Essays by fellows of the mid-career fellowship program at Princeton University.* Princeton, NJ: Mid-Career Fellowship Program.

Farr, J. L. (1997, April 11). *Organized I/O psychology: Past, present and future.* Presidential address. Society for Industrial and Organizational Psychology, Inc., St. Louis, MO.

Farrell, D., & Stamm, C. L. (1988). Meta-analysis of the correlates of employee absence. *Human Relations, 41*(3), 211–227.

Farren, C. (1999, January/February). Stress and productivity: What tips the scale? *Strategy & Leadership, 27*(1), 36.

Feild, H. S., & Holley, W. H. (1982). The relationship of performance appraisal system characteristics to verdicts in selected employment discrimination cases. *Academy of Management Journal, 25,* 392–406.

Fekken, G. C., & Jakubowski, I. (1990). Effects of stress on the health of Type A students. *Journal of Social Behavior and Personality, 5*(5), 473–480.

Ferris, G. R., & King, T. R. (1992, May). The politics of age discrimination in organizations. *Journal of Business Ethics, 11,* 341–350.

Feuer, D. (1986). Computerized testing: A revolution in the making. *Training, 23,* 80–86.

Fiedler, F. E. (1967). *A theory of leadership effectiveness.* New York: McGraw-Hill.

Fiedler, F. E. (1978). Recent developments in research on the contingency model. In L. Berkowitz (Ed.), *Group processes* (pp. 209–226). New York: Academic Press.

Fiedler, F. E. (1986). The contribution of cognitive resources and behavior to organizational performance. *Journal of Applied Social Psychology, 16*(6), 532–548.

Fiedler, F. E., Chemers, M. M., & Mahar, L. (1976). *Improving leadership effectiveness: The leader match concept.* New York: Wiley.

Fiedler, F. E., & Garcia, J. E. (1987). *New approaches to effective leadership: Cognitive resources and organizational performance.* New York: Wiley.

Fiedler, F. E., & House, R. J. (1994). Leadership theory and research: A report of the progress. In C. L. Cooper & I. T. Robertson (Eds.), *Key reviews in managerial psychology: Concepts and research for practice* (pp. 97–116). New York: Wiley.

Fiedler, F. E., McGuire, M., & Richardson, M. (1989). The role of intelligence and experience in successful group performance. *Journal of Applied Sport Psychology, 1*(2), 132–149.

Fields, D. L., & Blum, T. C. (1997). Employee satisfaction in work groups with different gender composition. *Journal of Organizational Behavior, 18*(2), 181–196.

Filipczak, B. (1994, March). The ripple effect of computer networking. *Training, 31,* 40–47.

Fine, M. G., Johnson, F. L., & Ryan, M. S. (1990). Cultural diversity in the workplace. *Public Personnel Management, 19*(3), 305–319.

Fine, S. A., & Wiley, W. W. (1971). *An introduction to functional job analysis.* Kalamazoo, MI: W. E. Upjohn Institute for Employment Research.

Finney, M. (1996, January 24). Come se dice "diversity"? *HR Weekly Update,* 3–4.

Fiore, A. M., & Kim, S. (1997). Olfactory cues of appearance affecting impressions of professional image of women. *Journal of Career Development, 23*(4), 247–263.

Fiorelli, J. S. (1988). Power in work groups: Team members' perspectives. *Human Relations, 41,* 1–12.

Fish, M. M. (1997, April). Help wanted: The Americans with Disabilities Act and preemployment inquiries. *Risk Management, 44,* 63–64.

Fisher, R. (1992, May). Screen test [assessing job applicants using role-playing videos]. *Canadian Business, 65,* 62–64.

Flanagan, J. C. (1954). The critical incidents technique. *Psychological Bulletin, 51,* 327–358.

Fleishman, E. A. (1960). *The leader opinion questionnaire.* Chicago: Science Research Associates.

Fleishman, E. A. (1975). *Physical abilities analysis manual.* Bethesda, MD: Management Research Institute.

Fleishman, E. A. (1988). Some new frontiers in personnel selection research. *Personnel Psychology, 41,* 679–701.

Fleishman, E. A., & Harris, E. F. (1962). Patterns of leadership behavior related to employee grievances and turnover. *Personnel Psychology, 15,* 43–56.

Fleishman, S. T. (1993, Spring). A systematic approach to effective recruitment. *Employment Relations Today, 20,* 69–77.

Flowers, L. A., Tudor, T. R., & Trumble, R. R. (1997, May–June). Computer assisted performance appraisal systems. *Journal of Compensation and Benefits, 12,* 34–35.

Flynn, G. (1995, November). Telecommuters report higher productivity—and better home lives. *Personnel Journal, 74,* 23.

Ford, D. J. (1992). The Magnavox experience. *Training and Development, 46,* 55–57.

Ford, J. K., & Noe, R. A. (1987). Self-assessed training needs: The effect of attitudes towards training, managerial level, and function. *Personnel Psychology, 40,* 39–53.

Ford, J. K., Quinones, M. A., & Sego, D. J. (1992). Factors affecting the opportunity to perform trained tasks on the job. *Personnel Psychology, 45,* 511–527.

Ford, R. L., & Randolph, W. A. (1992). Cross-functional structure: A review and integration of matrix organizations and project management. *Journal of Management, 18,* 267–294.

Forrett, M. L., & Turban, D. B. (1996, Summer). Implications of the elaboration likelihood model for interviewer decision process. *Journal of Business Psychology, 10,* 415–428.

Forsythe, S., Drake, M. F., & Cox, C. E. (1985). Influence of applicant's dress on interviewer's selection decisions. *Journal of Applied Psychology, 70*(2), 374–378.

Foust, D. (1975, July 21). For the good life, hit "enter": Software and Web sites can help you plan for retirement. *Business Week,* p. 88.

Fox, J. B., Scott, K. D., & Donohue, J. M. (1993). An investigation into pay valence and performance in a pay-for-performance field setting. *Journal of Organizational Behavior, 14*(7), 687–693.

Frame, R. J., Neilsen, W. R., & Pate, L. E. (1989). Creating excellence out of crisis: Organizational transformation at the *Chicago Tribune. Journal of Applied Behavioral Science, 25*(2), 109–122.

Frayne, C. A., & Latham, G. P. (1987). The application of social learning theory to employee self-management of attendance. *Journal of Applied Psychology, 72*(3), 387–392.

Fredericksen, N. (1962). Factors in in-basket performance [Entire issue]. *Psychological Monographs, 76* (54).

Frei, R. L., & McDaniel, M. A. (1998). Validity of customer service measures in personnel selection: A review of criterion and construct evidence. *Human Performance, 11*(1), 1–27.

Freidman, M., & Rosenman, R. H. (1974). *Type A behavior and your heart.* New York: Knopf.

Freidman, S. (1994, September 6). Firms slow to manage security risk. *National Underwriter, 98*, 3.

French, J. R. P., & Raven, B. (1967). The bases of social power. In D. Cartwright & A. Zander (Eds.), *Group dynamics, research and theory* (3rd ed.; pp. 259–277). New York: Harper & Row.

French, W. L., & Bell, C. H. (1984). *Organization development* (3rd ed.). Englewood Cliffs, NJ: Prentice-Hall.

Frese, M., & Okonek, K. (1984). Reasons to leave shiftwork and psychological and psychosomatic complaints of former shiftworkers. *Journal of Applied Psychology, 69*(4), 509–514.

Fretz, B. R., & Mills, D. H. (1980). *Licensing and certification of psychologists and counselors.* San Francisco: Jossey-Bass.

Fried, Y., & Ferris, G. R. (1987). The validity of the Job Characteristics Model: A review and meta-analysis. *Personnel Psychology, 40*(2), 287–322.

Fritz, N. R. (1989). In focus. *Personnel, 66*(1), 5.

Fromme, D. K., Jaynes, W. E., Taylor, D. K., & Honold, E. G. (1989). Nonverbal behavior and attitudes toward touch. *Journal of Nonverbal Behavior, 13*(1), 3–14.

Frost, M. (1998, April). Old-fashioned career fairs gain favor online. *HRMagazine, 43*(5), 31–32.

Fuentes, J. J. (1992). How Adolph Coors helps employees with retirement planning. *Journal of Compensation & Benefits, 7*, 56–58.

Fulk, J., & Boyd, B. (1991). Emerging theories of communication in organizations. Special issue: Yearly Review of Management. *Journal of Management, 17*(2), 407–446.

Fullagar, C., & Barling, J. (1991). Predictors and outcomes of different patterns of organizational and union loyalty. *Journal of Occupational Psychology, 64*(2), 129–143.

Fullerton, H. N., Jr. (1997, November) Labor force 2006: Slowing down and changing composition. *Monthly Labor Review, 120*, 23–38.

Funke, U. (1993). Computer-based personnel selection with complex dynamic scenarios. *Zeitschrift für Arbeits und Organisationalpsychologie, 37*(3), 109–118.

Furham, A. (1990). Faking personality questionnaires: Fabricating different profiles for different purposes. *Current Psychology Research and Reviews, 8*(1), 46–55.

Furnham, A., & Stringfield, P. (1998, April). Congruence in job-performance ratings: A study of 360-degree feedback examining self, managers, peers and consultant ratings. *Human Relations, 51*, 517–530.

Gaertner, K. N., & Nollen, S. D. (1992). Turnover intentions and desire among executives. *Human Relations, 45*(5), 447–465.

Gaines, J. H. (1980). Upward communication in industry: An experiment. *Human Relations, 33*, 929–942.

Galagan, P. A. (1991). How Wallace changed its mind. *Training and Development, 45*, 22–28.

Gallupe, R. B., Dennis, A. R., & Cooper, W. H. (1992, June). Electronic brainstorming and group size. *Academy of Management Journal, 35*, 350–369.

Ganster, D. C., Schaubroeck, J., Sime, W. E., & Mayes, B. T. (1991). The nomological validity of the Type A personality among employed adults. *Journal of Applied Psychology, 76*, 143–168.

Gardner, O. S., Keller, J. W., & Piotrowski, C. (1996). Retention issues as perceived by African-American university students. *Psychology: A Journal of Human Behavior, 33*(1), 20–21.

Gaugler, B. B., Rosenthal, D. B., Thornton, G. C., & Bentson, C. (1987). Meta-analysis of assessment center validity. *Journal of Applied Psychology, 72*(3), 493–511.

Gaugler, B. B., & Thornton, G. C. (1990). Matching job previews to individual applicants' needs. *Psychological Reports, 66*(2), 643–652.

Gebhardt, D. L., & Crump, C. E. (1990). Employee fitness and wellness programs in the workplace. *American Psychologist, 45*, 262–272.

Gehring, R. E., & Toqlia, M. P. (1988). Relative retention of verbal and audiovisual information in a national training programme. *Applied Cognitive Psychology, 2*(3), 213–221.

Gerstner, C. R., & Day, D. V. (1997). Meta-analytic review of leader–member exchange theory: Correlates and construct issues. *Journal of Applied Psychology, 82*(6), 827–844.

Gibson, F. W., Fiedler, F. E., & Barrett, K. M. (1993). Stress, babble and the utilization of the leader's intellectual abilities. *Leadership Quarterly, 4*(2), 189–208.

Gigone, D., & Hastie, R. (1997). Proper analysis of the accuracy of group judgments. *Psychological Bulletin, 121*(1), 149–167.

Gilbreth, L. M. (1925). The present state of industrial psychology. *Mechanical Engineering, 47*(11a), 1039–1042.

Gillespie, R. (1991). *Manufacturing knowledge: A history of the Hawthorne experiments.* New York: Cambridge University Press.

Gillet, B., & Schwab, D. P. (1975). Convergent and discriminate validities of corresponding Job Descriptive Index and Minnesota Satisfaction Questionnaire scales. *Journal of Applied Psychology, 60*(3), 313–317.

Gilmore, C. B., & Fanin, W. R. (1982). The dual career couple: A challenge to personnel in the eighties. *Business Horizons, 25*(3), 36–41.

Gilmore, D. C., Fried, Y., & Ferris, G. R. (1989). The influence of unionization on job satisfaction and work perceptions. *Journal of Business and Psychology, 3*(3), 289–297.

Girard, K. (1997, October 27). Telecommuting lab eases the trip home. *Computer World, 31,* 69.

Gist, M. E., Schwoerer, C., & Rosen, B. (1989). Effects of alternative training methods on self-efficacy and performance in computer software training. *Journal of Applied Psychology, 74*(6), 884–891.

Gitter, R. J. (1994). Apprenticeship-trained workers: United States and Great Britain. *Monthly Labor Review, 117,* 38–43.

Glass Ceiling Commission (1995a, Spring). Good for business: Making full use of the nation's capital. Washington, DC: U.S. Department of Labor.

Glass Ceiling Commission (1995b, Fall). A solid investment: Making full use of the nation's human capital. Washington, DC: U.S. Department of Labor.

Glass, G. (1976). Primary, secondary, and meta-analysis of research. *Education Researcher, 5,* 3–8.

Gloss, D. S., & Wardell, M. G. (1984). *Introduction to safety engineering.* New York: Wiley.

Goldberg, L. R., Grenier, J. R., Guion, R. M., Sechrest, L. B., & Wing, H. (1991). *Questionnaires used in the prediction of trustworthiness in pre-employment selection decisions: An APA task force report.* Washington, DC: American Psychological Association.

Golden, P. A., Beauclair, R., & Sussman, L. (1992). Factors affecting electronic mail use. *Computers in Human Behavior, 6*(4), 297–311.

Goldenhar, L. M., Swanson, N. G., Hurrell, J. J., Jr., Ruder, A., & Deddens, J. (1998). Stressors and adverse outcomes for female construction workers. *Journal of Occupational Health Psychology, 3*(1), 19–32.

Goldstein, I. L. (1993). *Training in organizations* (3rd ed.). Pacific Grove, CA: Brooks/Cole.

Golembiewski, R. T. (1998). Dealing with doubt and cynicism about organizational change, the old-fashioned way: Empirical data about success rates in OD & QWL. In M. A. Rahim, R. T. Golembiewski, & C. C. Lundberg (Eds.), *Current topics in management* (Vol. 3, pp. 17–35). Stamford, CT: JAI Press.

Golembiewski, R. T., & Sun, B. C. (1989). Consulting is definitely worth the cost: Success rates in OD and QWL consultation. *Consultation: An International Journal, 8*(3), 203–208.

Golembiewski, R. T., Muzenrider, R. F., & Stevenson, J. G. (1986). *Stress in organizations: Toward a phase model of burnout.* New York: Praeger.

Gorey, K. M., Brice, G. C., & Rice, R. W. (1990). An elder care training needs assessment among employee assistance program staff employed by New York State government: Brief report of a systematic replication. *Employee Assistance Quarterly, 6*(2), 57–70.

Gottfreson, L. S. (1994). The science of politics of race norming. *American Psychologist, 49,* 955–963.

Graen, G., Novak, M., & Sommerkamp, P. (1982). The effects of leader–member exchange and job design on productivity and satisfaction: Testing a dual attachment model. *Organizational Behavior and Human Performance, 30,* 109–131.

Graen, G., & Scandura, T. A. (1987). Toward a psychology of dyadic organizing. *Research in Organizational Behavior, 9,* 175–208.

Graen, G. B., Scandura, T. A., & Graen, M. R. (1986). A field experimental test of the moderating effects of growth need strength on productivity. *Journal of Applied Psychology, 71*(3), 484–491.

Graen, G. B., & Wakabayashi, M. (1984). The Japanese career progress study: A 7-year follow-up. *Journal of Applied Psychology, 69*(4), 603–614.

Grandjean, E., Hunting, W., & Piderman, M. (1983). VDT workstation design: Preferred settings and their effect. *Human Factors, 25*(2), 161–175.

Gray, G. R., & Brown, D. R. (1992, November). Issues in drug testing for the private sector. *HR Focus, 69,* 15.

Greenberg, E. R. (1996, September). Drug testing now standard practice. *HRFocus, 73,* 24.

Greenberg, J. (1982). Approaching equity and avoiding inequity in groups and organizations. In J. Greenberg & R. L. Cohen (Eds.), *Equity and justice in social behavior* (pp. 389–436). New York: Academic Press.

Greenberg, J. (1986). Determinants of perceived fairness of performance evaluations. *Journal of Applied Psychology, 71*(2), 340–342.

Greenberg, J. (1988). Equity and workplace status: A field experiment. *Journal of Applied Psychology, 73*(4), 606–613.

Greenberg, J. (1990). Employee theft as a reaction to underpayment inequity: The hidden costs of pay cuts. *Journal of Applied Psychology, 73*(4), 606–613.

Greenberg, J., & Baron, R. A. (1993). *Behavior in organizations.* Needham Heights, MA: Allyn & Bacon.

Greenberg, S., & Bello, R. (1992). Rewrite job descriptions: Focus on functions. *HR Focus, 69*(7), 10.

Greenblatt, E. C. (1997, August). Web-based training. *Datamation, 43*, 4.

Greenblatt, E. C. (1998, January). Finding the right candidate online. *Datamation, 44*, 125.

Greene, C. N. (1975). The reciprocal nature of influence between leader and subordinate. *Journal of Applied Psychology, 60*(1), 187–193.

Greene, C. N., & Podsakoff, P. M. (1981). Effects of withdrawal of a performance-contingent reward on supervisory influence and power. *Academy of Management Journal, 24*, 527–542.

Greengard, S. (1994, September). Workers go virtual. *Personnel Journal, 73*, 71.

Greengard, S. (1997, July). Genetic testing: Should you be afraid? *Workforce, 76*, 38–44.

Greenhaus, J. H., & Parasuraman, S. (1993). Job performance attributions and career advancement prospects: An examination of gender and race effects. *Organizational Behavior and Human Decision Processes, 55*(2), 273–297.

Greenhaus, J. H., Parasuraman, S., & Wormley, W. M. (1990). Effects of race on organizational experiences, job performance evaluations and career outcomes. *Academy of Management Journal, 33*(1), 64–86.

Greenspan, M. (1985). Perceived leader behavior, individual dogmatism and job satisfaction. International Conference on Authoritarianism and Dogmatism (1984, Potsdam, NY). *High School Journal, 68*(4), 405–406.

Grimes, T. (1990). Audio-video correspondence and its role in attention and memory. *Educational Technology and Research and Development, 38*(3), 15–25.

Grossman, R. J. (2000, March). Race in the workplace. *HR Magazine, 45*(3), 41–45.

Guidoni, G. (2000, April 1). Automotive report—Robotic Renaissance. *Canadian Packaging, 53*, 17–18.

Guion, R. M. (1965). *Personnel testing.* New York: McGraw-Hill.

Guion, R. M., & Gibson, W. M. (1988). Personnel selection and placement. *Annual Review of Psychology, 39*, 349–374.

Guppy, A., & Rick, J. (1996). The influence of gender and grade on perceived worker stress and job satisfaction in white collar workers. *Work and Stress, 10*(2), 154–164.

Guzzo, R. A., Jette, R. D., & Katzell, R. A. (1985). The effects of psychologically based intervention programs on worker productivity: A meta-analysis. *Personnel Psychology, 38*, 275–291.

Hackett, R. D. (1989). Work attitudes and employee absenteeism: A synthesis of the literature. *Journal of Occupational Psychology, 62*(3), 235–248.

Hackett, R. D., & Bycio, P. (1996). An evaluation of absenteeism as a coping mechanism among hospital nurses. *Journal of Occupational and Organizational Psychology, 69*(4), 327–338.

Hackman, J. R., & Oldham, G. R. (1975). Development of the Job Diagnostic Survey. *Journal of Applied Psychology, 60*(1), 159–170.

Hackman, J. R. & Oldham, G. R. (1976). Motivation through the design of work: Test of a theory. *Organizational Behavior and Human Performance, 16*, 250–279.

Hackman, M. Z., Furniss, A. H., Hillis, M. J., & Paterson, T. J. (1992). Perceptions of gender role characteristics and transformational and transactional leadership behaviors. *Perceptual and Motor Skills, 75*(1), 311–319.

Hackman, M. Z., Hillis, M. J., Paterson, T. J., & Furniss, A. H. (1993). Leaders' gender role as a correlate of subordinates' perceptions of effectiveness and satisfaction. *Perceptual and Motor Skills, 77*(2), 671–674.

Hair, H., & Walsh-Bowers, R. (1992). Promoting the development of a religious congregation through a needs and resources assessment. *Journal of Community Psychology, 20*(4), 289–303.

Hale, B. J. (1992). Improve new-hire orientation. *Transportation & Distribution, 33*, 37.

Hale, M., Jr. (1982). History of employment tests. In A. K. Wigdor & W. R. Garner (Eds.), Ability testing: *Uses, consequences and controversies.* Washington, DC: National Academy Press.

Hall, E. T. A. (1963). A system for the notation of phonemic behavior. *American Anthropologist, 65*, 1003–1026.

Hamlin, C. (1994, Spring). Team building a global team at Apple Computer. *Employment Relations Today, 21,* 55–62.

Hammer, E. G., & Kleinman, L. S. (1988). Getting to know you. *Personnel Administrator, 33*(5), 86–92.

Hammer, W. C., & Hammer, E. P. (1976). Behavior modification on the bottom line. *Organizational Dynamics, 4,* 8–21.

Hanigan, M. (1991, July). Key campus strategies. *HRMagazine, 36,* 42–44.

Hanisch, K. A. (1992). The Job Descriptive Index revisited: Questions about the question mark. *Journal of Applied Psychology, 77*(3), 377–382.

Hanks, L. W. (1996, September). Career-planning software (Jump Start Your Job Skills and ResumeMaker Deluxe CD). *Macworld, 13,* 89.

Harari, O. (1994, September). Working smart. *Small Business Reports, 19,* 55–57.

Harrell, E. C. (1993). *Surviving in the workplace.* Milwaukee, WI: E.T. Publishing.

Harrick, E. J., Schaefer, D. O., Pynes, J. E., & Daugherty, R. A. (1993, Summer). Demystifying employment test validation: A process to get high validity coefficients. *Consulting Psychology Journal Practice and Research, 45*(3), 1–6.

Harris, M. M., Dworkin, J. B., & Park, J. (1990, Spring). Preemployment screening procedures: How human resource managers perceive them. *Journal of Business and Psychology, 4*(3), 279–292.

Harris, M. M., Smith, D. E., & Champagne, D. (1995, Spring). A field study of performance appraisal purpose: Research versus administrative based ratings. *Personnel, 48,* 151–160.

Harrison, E. L., & Pietri, P. H. (1997). Using team building to change organizational culture. *Organizational Development Journal, 15*(4), 71–76.

Harrison, J. K. (1992). Individual and combined effects of behavior modeling and the cultural assimilator in cross-cultural management training. *Journal of Applied Psychology, 77*(6), 952–962.

Harvey, R. J., & Lozada-Larsen, S. R. (1988). Influence of amount of job descriptive information on job analysis rating accuracy. *Journal of Applied Psychology, 73*(3), 457–461.

Haston, R. M., & Pawlak, T. M. (1990). Case study: Designing a performance management program. *Journal of Compensation and Benefits, 6,* 26–28.

Havlovic, S. J. (1991, Fall). Quality of work life and human resource outcomes. *Industrial Relations, 30,* 469–479.

Hayes, C. (1998, February). Life atop the crystal stair. *Black Enterprise, 28,* 107–108.

Heilman, M. E., Block, C. J., Martell, R. F., & Simon, M. C. (1989). Has anything changed? Current characterizations of men, women and managers. *Journal of Applied Psychology, 74*(6), 935–942.

Helander, M., & Rupp, B. (1984). An overview of standards and guidelines for visual display terminals. *Applied Ergonomics, 15*(3), 185–195.

Hellman, C. M. (1997). Job satisfaction and the intent to leave. *Journal of Social Psychology, 137*(6), 677–689.

Hemphill, J. K. (1950). *Leader behavior description.* Columbus: Ohio State University, Bureau of Educational Research.

Heneman, R. L., & Wexley, K. N. (1983). The effects of time delay in rating and amount of information observed on performance rating accuracy. *Academy of Management Journal, 26,* 677–686.

Herzberg, F., Mausner, B., Peterson, R. O., & Capwell, D. F. (1957). *Job attitudes: Review of research and opinion.* Pittsburgh, PA: Psychological Service of Pittsburgh.

Herzberg, F., Mausner, B., & Snyderman, B. B. (1959). *The motivation to work.* New York: Wiley.

Hesketh, B., Pryor, R., & Gleitzman, M. (1989). Fuzzy logic: Towards measuring Gottfredson's concept of occupational social space. *Journal of Counseling Psychology, 36*(1), 103–109.

Higgins, C. A., Duxbury, L. E., & Irving, R. H. (1992). Work–family conflict in the dual-career family. *Organizational Behavior and Human Decision Processes, 51*(1), 51–75.

Hinkin, T. R., & Schriesheim, C. A. (1989). Development and application of new scales to measure the French and Raven (1959) bases of social power. *Journal of Applied Psychology, 74*(4), 561–567.

Hinrichs, J. R., & Mischkind, L. A. (1967). Empirical and theoretical limitations of the two-factor hypothesis of job satisfaction. *Journal of Applied Psychology, 51*(2), 191–200.

Hirschfield, P. P. (1991, Spring). How employee feedback can boost organizational performance. *Employment Relations Today, 18,* 89–94.

Hispanic Business, (1998, January/February). 1998 corporate elite. p. 38.

Hoffman, C., & Thornton, G. C., III. (1997, Summer). Examining selection utility where competing predictors differ in adverse impact. *Personnel Psychology, 50*(2), 455–470.

Hoffman, K. (2000, April). Meeting of the minds—scientist and practitioner. *TIP.* www.siop.org/tip/tipApril00/11Hoffman.htm.

Hogan, J. C., & Bernacki, E. J. (1981). Developing job related pre-placement medical examinations. *Journal of Occupational Medicine, 23,* 469–475.

Hogan, R., Curphy, G. J., & Hogan, J. (1994). What we know about leadership: Effectiveness and personality. *American Psychologist, 49*(6), 493–504.

Holland, J. L. (1996). Exploring careers with a typology: What we have learned and some new directions. *American Psychologist, 51*(4), 397–406.

Hollenbeck, G. P., & Ingols, C. A. (1990). What's the takeaway? *Training and Development Journal, 44,* 83–84.

Hollenbeck, J. R., Ilgen, D. R., Ostroff, C., & Vancouver, J. B. (1987). Sex differences in occupational choice, pay and worth: A supply-side approach to understanding the male–female wage gap. *Personnel Psychology, 40*(4), 715–743.

Hollenbeck, J. R., & Williams, C. R. (1986). Turnover functionality versus turnover frequency: A note on work attitudes and organizational effectiveness. *Journal of Applied Psychology, 7*(4), 606–611.

Hollenbeck, J. R., Williams, C. R., & Klein, H. J. (1989). An empirical examination of the antecedents of commitment to difficult goals. *Journal of Applied Psychology, 74*(1), 18–23.

Holloman, C. R. (1986, January–March) "Headship" vs. leadership. *Business and Economic Review, 32*(2), 35–37.

Holmes, T. H., & Rahe, R. H. (1971). The social adjustment rating scale. *Journal of Psychosomatic Research, 15,* 210–223.

Holton, E. F., III. (1996). The flawed four-level evaluation model. *Human Resource Development Quarterly, 7*(1), 5–21.

Hornsby, P., Clegg, C. W., Robson, J. I., & McLarne, C. R. (1992). Human and organizational issues in information systems development. Special issue: Methods and Frameworks for System Design. *Behvior and Information Technology, 11*(3), 160–174.

House, R. J. (1971). Path-goal theory of leader effectiveness. *Administrative Science Quarterly, 16,* 321–338.

House, R. J. (1977). A 1976 theory of charismatic leadership. In J. G. Hunt & L. L. Larsen (Eds.), *Leadership: The cutting edge.* Carbondale: Southern Illinois University Press.

House, R. J. (1996). Path-goal theory of leadership: Lessons, legacy and a reformulated theory. *Leadership Quarterly, 7*(3), 323–352.

House, R. J., & Mitchell, T. R. (1974). Path-goal theory of leadership. *Journal of Contemporary Business, 3,* 81–97.

House, R. J., Spangler, W. D., & Woycke, J. (1991). Personality and charisma in the U.S. presidency: A psychological theory of leader effectiveness. *Adminstrative Science Quarterly, 36,* 364–396.

Howard, G. S. (1993). I think I can "I think I can": Reconsidering the place for practice methodologies in psychological research. *Professional Psychology Research and Practice, 24,* 237–244.

Howard, P. K., (1994). *The death of common sense: How law is suffocating Americans.* New York: Random House.

Howell, J. M., & Avolio, B. (1995, Autumn). Charismatic leadership: Submission or liberation? *Business Quarterly, 60,* 62–70.

Howell, J. M., & Avolio, B. J. (1993). Transformational leadership, transactional leadership, locus of control, and support for innovation: Key predictors of consolidated- business-unit performance. *Journal of Applied Psychology, 78*(6), 891–902.

Howell, J. P., Bowen, D. E., Dorfman, P. W., & Kerr, S. (1990). Substitutes for leadership: Effective alternatives to ineffective leadership. *Organizational Dynamics, 19*(1), 21–38.

Howell, W. C. (1991). Human factors in the workplace. In M. D. Dunnette & L. M. Hough (Eds.), *Handbook of industrial and organizational psychology* (pp. 209–269). Palo Alto, CA: Consulting Psychologists Press.

HR Focus. (1992, July). Workers are willing to accommodate coworkers with disabilities. *69*(7), 5.

HR Focus. (1992, October). Japan tries to take on a killer: Death from overwork. *69,* 18.

HRMagazine. (1991). The affirmative action pipeline. *36,* 59.

HRMagazine. (1992a). High-tech recruitment solutions. *37,* 54.

HRMagazine. (1992b). Genetic testing. *37,* 133–144.

Huber, V. L., Neale, M. A., & Northcraft, G. B. (1987). Decision bias and personnel selection strategies. *Organizational Behavior and Human Decision Processes, 40*(1), 136–147.

Huber, V. L., Northcraft, G. B., & Neale, M. A. (1990). Effects of decision strategy and number of openings on employment selection decisions. *Organizational Behavior and Human Decision Processes, 45*(2), 276–284.

Huebner, E. S. (1994). Relationships among demographics, social support, job satisfaction and burnout among school psychologists. *School Psychology International, 15*(2) 181–186.

Hughes, S. S., & Holt, B. A. (1994, July/August). Is sick building syndrome for real? *Journal of Property Management, 59,* 32–34.

Hui, C., & Graen, G. (1997). Guanxi and professional leadership in contemporary Sino-American joint ventures in mainland China. *Leadership Quarterly, 8*(4), 451–465.

Hulin, C. L. (1987). A psychometric theory of evaluations of item and scale translations: Fidelity across languages. *Journal of Cross Cultural Psychology, 18*(2), 115–142.

Hunt, G. T. (1980). *Communication skills in the organization.* Englewood Cliffs, NJ: Prentice-Hall.

Hunt, J., Carter, B., & Kelly, F. (1993, June). Clearly defined chain-of-command helps mobilize oil spill responders. *Occupational Health & Safety, 62,* 40.

Hunter, J. E. (1983). The economic benefits of personnel selection using ability tests: A state of the art review including a detailed analysis of the dollar benefit of the U.S. Employment Service placements and a critique of the low cutoff method of test use. *USES Test Research Report No. 47.* Washington, DC: Employment and Training Administration (DOL); Salt Lake City: Utah State Department of Employment Security, Western Test Development Field Center.

Hunter, J. E., & Hunter, R. F. (1984). Validity and utility of alternative predictors of job performance. *Psychological Bulletin, 96*(1), 72–98.

Hunter, J. E., & Schmidt, F. L. (1982). Fitting people to jobs: The impact of personnel selection on national productivity. In M. D. Dunnette & E. A. Fleishman (Eds.), *Human performance and productivity: Human capacity assessment* (pp. 232–284). Hillsdale: NJ: Erlbaum.

Huseman, R. C., Hatfield, J. D., & Miles, E. W. (1985). Test for individual perceptions of the job equity: Some preliminary findings. *Perceptual and Motor Skills, 61*(3, Pt. 2), 1055–1064.

Huseman, R. C., Hatfield, J. D., & Miles, E. W. (1987). A new perspective on equity theory: The equity sensitivity construct. *Academy of Management Review, 12*(2), 222–234.

Huss, M. T., Curnyn, J. P., Roberts, S. L., & Davis, S. F. (1993). Hard driven but not dishonest: Cheating and the Type A personality. *Bulletin of the Psychonomic Society, 31*(5), 429–430.

Huszczo, G. E., Wiggins, J. G., & Currie, J. S. (1984). The relationship between psychology and organized labor. *American Psychologist, 39*(4), 432–440.

Hutheesing, N. (1997, December, 15). Rumormongers. *Forbes, 160,* 54.

Hylton, R. D. (1988, August). Working in America. *Black Enterprise, 19,* 63–64.

Hytten, K., Jensen, A., & Skauli, G. (1990). Stress inoculation training for smoke divers and free fall life boat passengers. *Aviation, Space, and Environmental Medicine, 61*(11), 983–988.

Iaffaldano, M. T., & Muchinsky, P. M. (1985). Job satisfaction and job performance: A meta-analysis. *Psychological Bulletin, 97,* 251–273.

Igbaria, M., & Wormley, W. M. (1992, December). Organizational experiences and career success of MIS professionals and managers: An examination of race differences. *MIS Quarterly, 16,* 507–529.

Ilgen, D. R. (1990). Health issues at work: Opportunities for industrial/organizational psychology. *American Psychologist, 45,* 273–283.

Ilgen, D. R., Barnes-Farrell, J. L., & McKellin, D. B. (1993). Performance appraisal process in the 1980's: What has it contributed to appraisals in use? *Organizational Behavior and Human Decision Processes, 54,* 321–368.

Ilgen, D. R., Nebekr, D., & Pritchard, R. (1981). Expectancy theory measures: An empirical comparison in an experimental simulation. *Organizational Behavior and Human Performance, 28,* 189–223.

Inc. (1992). Getting new recruits on track. *14,* 114.

Inc. (1992, October). Productivity: Modernizing the suggestion box. *14,* 36.

Inc. (1995, December). Disabled workers: The unexpected advantage (Carolina Fine Foods). *17,* 119.

Inderrieden, E. J., Keaveny, T. J., & Allen, R. E. (1988). Predictors of employee satisfaction with the performance appraisal process. *Journal of Business and Psychology, 2*(4), 306–310.

Indvik, J. (1986). *Path-goal theory of leadership: A meta-analysis.* Presented at the meetings of the Academy of Management, Chicago.

Ironson, G. H., Smith, P. C., Brannick, M. T., Gibson, W. M., & Paul, K. B. (1989). Constitution of a Job in General scale: A comparison of global, composite, and specific measures. *Journal of Applied Psychology, 74*(2), 193–200.

Ivancevish, J. M., Matteson, M. T., Freedman, S. M., & Phillips, J. S. (1990). Worksite stress management interventions. *American Psychologist, 45*(2), 252–261.

Jackson, K. (1996, September 30). Program seeks to sell technical education. *Automotive News,* 23.

Jackson, S. E., & Schuler, R. S. (1985). A meta-analysis and conceptual critique of research on role ambiguity and role conflict in work settings. *Organizational Behavior and Human Decision Processes, 36,* 16–28.

Jackson, S. E., & Schuler, R. S. (1990). Human resource planning: Challenges for industrial/organizational psychologists.

Special issue: Organizational Psychology. *American Psychologist, 45*, 223–239.

Jackson, S. E., Schwab, R. L., & Schuler, R. S. (1986). Toward an understanding of the burnout phenomenon. *Journal of Applied Psychology, 71*(4), 630–640.

Jacobs, R. L, & McClelland, D. C. (1994). Moving up the corporate ladder: A longitudinal study of the leadership motive pattern and managerial success in women and men. *Consulting Psychology Journal of Practice and Research, 46*(1), 32–41.

Jacobs, R., & Solomon, T. (1977). Strategies for enhancing the prediction of job performance from job satisfaction. *Journal of Applied Psychology, 62*(3), 417–421.

Jacobsen, B. H., Aldana, S. G., Goetzel, R. Z., & Vardell, K. D. (1996). The relationship between perceived stress and self-reported illness-related absenteeism. *American Journal of Health Promotion, 11*(1), 54–61.

Jago, A. G., & Ragan, J. W. (1986a). The trouble with leader match is that it doesn't match Fiedler's contingency model. *Journal of Applied Psychology, 71*(4), 555–559.

Jago, A. G., & Ragan, J. W. (1986b). Some assumptions are more troubling than others: Rejoinder to Chemers and Fiedler. *Journal of Applied Psychology, 71*(4), 564–565.

Jamal, M. (1984). Job stress and job performance controversy: An empirical assessment. *Organizational Behavior and Human Performance, 33*, 1–21.

Jamal, M. (1990). Relationship of job stress and Type A behavior to employees' job satisfaction, organizational commitment, psychosomatic health problems and turnover motivation. *Human Relations, 43*(8), 727–738.

Jang, K. L., Livesly, W. J., & Vernon, P. A. (1996). Heritability of the big five personality dimensions and their facets: A twin study. *Journal of Personality, 64*(3), 577–591.

Janis, I. L. (1982). *Groupthink* (2nd ed.). Boston: Houghton Mifflin.

Janis, I. L. (1989). *Crucial decisions: Leadership in policymaking and crisis management.* New York: Free Press.

Janis, I. L., & Mann, L. (1977). *Decision making: A psychological analysis of conflict, choice, and commitment.* New York: Free Press.

Jaquette, L. (1991, February 25). Red Lion pleased with drug-testing program. *Hotel & Motel Management, 206*, 3+.

Jawahar, I. M., & Williams, C. R. (1997). Where all the children are above average: The performance appraisal purpose effect. *Personnel Psychology, 50*, 905–925.

Jeanquart-Barone, S. (1993). Trust differences between supervisors and subordinates: Examining the role of race and gender. *Sex Roles, 29*(1–2), 1–11.

Jeanquart-Barone, S. (1996). Implication of racial diversity in the supervisor–subordinate relationship. *Journal of Applied Social Psychology, 26*(11), 935–944.

Jehn, K. A., Chadwick, C., & Thatcher, S. M. B. (1997). To agree or not to agree: The effects of value congruence, individual demographic dissimilarity and conflict on work group outcomes. *International Journal of Conflict Management, 8*(4), 287–305.

Jemmott, J. B., Hellman, C., & McClelland, D. C. (1990). Motivational syndromes associated with natural killer cell activity. *Journal of Behavioral Medicine, 13*(1), 53–73.

Jenkins, C. D., Zyzanski, S. J., & Rosenman, R. H. (1979). *The activity survey for health prediction, Form N.* New York: Psychological Corporation.

Jenkins, D. (April 1, 1997). Mothering on the tenure track—Can we do it all? *Contemporary Women's Issues Database, 6*, 22–23.

Jermier, J. M., Slocum, J. W., Fry, L. W., & Gaines, J. (1991). Organizational subcultures in a soft bureaucracy: Resistance behind the myth and facade of an official culture. *Organization Science, 2*(2), 170–194.

Jha, S., Mishra, P. K., & Bhardwaj, G. (1994, Fall). Bureaucracy and role stress across three levels of technocrats. *Abhigyan*, pp. 17–22.

Jick, T. D., & Mitz, L. F. (1985). Sex differences in work stress. *Academy of Management Review, 10*, 408–420.

Johns, G., Xie, J. L., & Fang, Y. (1992). Mediating and moderating effects in job design. *Journal of Management, 18*(4), 557–676.

Johnson, G. J., & Johnson, W. R. (1996). Perceived over-qualification and well-being. *Journal of Social Psychology, 136*(4), 435–445.

Johnson, R. S. (1998, August 3). The 50 best companies for Asians, Blacks and Hispanics. *Fortune 138*(3), 94.

Johnson, V. A. (1993). Factors impacting the job retention and advancement of workers who are deaf. *Volta Review, 95*(4), 341–354.

Johnson, W. R., & Jones-Johnson, G. (1992). Differential predictors of union and company commitment: Parallel and divergent models. *Psychology: A Journal of Human Behavior, 29*(3–4), 1–12.

Jones, J. W., Arnold, D., & Harris, W. G. (1990). Model guidelines for preemployment integrity testing: An overview. In W. J. Jones (Ed.), *Preemployment honesty testing: Current research and future directions* (pp. 239–246). New York: Quorum Books.

Jones, J. W., & Boye, M. W. (1994). Job stress, predisposition to steal, and employee theft. *American Journal of Health Promotion, 8*(5), 331–333.

Jordan, J. L., & Nasis, D. B. (1992). Preferences for performance appraisal based on method used, type of rater, and purpose of evaluation. *Psychological Reports, 70*(3, Pt 1), 963–969.

Joseph, J., & Deshpande, S. P. (1997, Winter). The impact of ethical climate on job satisfaction of nurses. *Health Care Management Review, 22*, 76–81.

Journal of Accountancy. (1997, August). Pressure on the job. *184*, 18.

Judge, T. A., & Cable, D. M. (1997). Applicant personality, organizational culture, and organization attraction. *Personnel Psychology, 50*(2), 359–394.

Judge, T. A., & Watanabe, S. (1993). Another look at the job satisfaction-life satisfaction relationship. *Journal of Applied Psychology, 78*(6), 939–948.

Judge, W. Q. (1994, January). Correlates of organizational effectiveness: A multilevel analysis of a multidimensional outcome. *Journal of Business Ethics, 13*, 1–10.

Kaeter, M. (1994) Coping with resistant trainees. *Training, 31*, 110–114.

Kahn, R. L., Wolfe, D. M., Quinn, R. P., Snoek, J. D., & Rosenthal, R. A. (1964). *Organizational stress: Studies in role conflict and ambiguity.* New York: Wiley.

Kahn, W. A. (1993). Facilitating and undermining organizational change: A case study. *Journal of Applied Behavioral Science, 29*(1), 32–55.

Kanekar, S. (1987). Individual vs. group performance: A selective review of experimental studies. *Irish Journal of Psychology, 8*(1), 9–19.

Kanfer, R. (1994). Work motivation: New direction in theory and research. In C. L. Cooper & I. T. Robertson (Eds.), *Key reviews in managerial psychology: Concepts and research for practice* (pp. 1–53). New York: Wiley.

Kantor, J. (1991). The effects of computer administration and identification on the Job Descriptive Index (JDI). *Journal of Business and Psychology, 5*(3), 309–323.

Kanungo, S. (1998). An empirical study of organizational culture and network-based computer use. *Computers in Human Behavior, 14*(1), 79–91.

Kaplan, A. (1964). *The conduct of inquiry.* New York: Harper & Row.

Kaplan, R. M., & Saccuzzo, D. P. (1993). *Psychological testing: Principles, application, and issues* (3rd ed.) Pacific Grove, CA: Brooks/Cole.

Karau, S. J., & Williams, K. D. (1993). Social loafing: A meta-analytic review and theoretical integration. *Journal of Personality and Social Psychology, 65*(4), 681–706.

Karayanni, M. (1987, September). The impact of cultural background on vocational interest. *Career Development Quarterly, 36*(1), 83–90.

Karsten, M. F., Schroeder, M. K., & Surrette, M. A. (1995, July). Impact of the Americans with Disabilities Act on job evaluation. *Labor Law Journal, 46*, 436–439.

Kasl, S. V. (1981). The challenge of studying the disease effects of stressful work conditions. *American Journal of Public Health, 71*, 682–684.

Katz, D., & Kahn, R. L. (1978). *The social psychology of organizations* (2nd ed.). New York: Wiley.

Katz, R., Tushman, M., & Allen, T. J. (1995, May). The influence of supervisory promotion and network location on subordinate careers in a dual ladder RD & E setting. *Management Science, 41*, 848–863.

Katzell, R. A., & Austin, J. T. (1992). From then to now: The development of industrial/organizational psychology in the United States. *Journal of Applied Psychology, 77*(6), 803–835.

Kazel, R. (1996, March 11). ADA compliance without cost: Study catalogs Sears' cost-effective accommodations. *Business Insurance, 30*, 3.

Kearney, R. C., & Whitaker, F. (1988). Behaviorally anchored disciplinary scales (BADS): A new approach to discipline. *Public Personnel Management, 17*(3), 341–350.

Keaveny, T. J., Inderrieden, E. J., & Allen, R. E. (1987). An integrated perspective of performance appraisal interviews. *Psychological Reports, 61*(2), 639–646.

Keel, S. B., Cochran, D. S., Arnett, K., & Arnold, R. (1989, May). ACs are not just for the big guys. *Personnel Administrator, 34*, 98+.

Keisler, S. (1992, June). Group decision making and communication technology. *Organizational Behavior and Human Decision Processes, 52*, 96–123.

Keller, L. M., Bouchard, T. J., Arvey, R. D., Segal, N. L., & Dawis, R. V. (1992). Work values: Environmental and genetic issues. *Journal of Applied Psychology, 77*(1), 79–88.

Keller, R. T. (1986). Predictors of the performance of project groups in R&D organizations. *Academy of Management Journal, 29*, 715–726.

Keller, R. T. (1994, February). Technology-information fit and the performance of R & D project groups: A test of contingency theory. *Academy of Management Journal, 37*(1), 167–179.

Kelley, D. L., & Ninan, M. (1990, February 16–20). *Communication skills affecting listening satisfaction.* Paper presented at the Annual Meeting of the Western Speech Communication Association, Sacramento, CA.

Kennedy, C. W., Fossum, J. A., & White, B. J. (1983). An empirical comparison of within-subjects and between-subjects expectancy models. *Organizational Behavior and Human Performance, 32,* 124–143.

Kennedy, M. M. (1993). Where teams drop the ball. *Across the Board, 30,* 9–10.

Kennedy, M. M. (1997, September). Old dogs take heart. *Across the Board, 34,* 53–54.

Kenny, D. T. (1995). Stressed organizations and organizational stressors: A systemic analysis of workplace injury. *International Journal of Stress Management, 2*(4), 181–196.

Kerr, N. L. (1983). Motivation in small groups: A social dilemma analysis. *Journal of Personality and Social Psychology, 68,* 678–685.

Kerr, N. L, & Brunn, S. E. (1993). Dependability of member effort and group motivation loss: Free rider effects. *Journal of Personality and Social Psychology, 44,* 78–94.

Kerr, S., & Jermier, J. M. (1978). Substitutes for leadership: Their meaning and measurement. *Organizational Behavior and Human Performance, 22,* 375–403.

Keys, B. (1986). Improving management development through simulation gaming. Special Issue: Management Development for Productivity. *Journal of Management Development, 5*(2), 41–50.

Khojasteh, M. (1993). Motivating the private vs. public sector managers. *Public Personnel Management, 22*(3), 391–401.

Kiechel, W. (1979, September). Playing the rules of the corporate strategy game. *Fortune, 24,* 110–115.

Kilmann, R., Saxton, M. J., & Serpa, R. (Eds.). (1985). *Gaining control of the corporate culture.* San Francisco/London: Jossey-Bass.

King, A. S. (1990). Evolution of leadership theory. *Vikalpa, 15*(2), 43–54.

King, J., Nixon, B., & Pitts, G. (1990). Learning to lead. *Personnel Management, 22,* 65–67.

King, P. (1970). Clarification and evaluation of the two-factor theory of job satisfaction. *Psychological Bulletin, 74,* 18–31.

King, W, C., Miles, E. W., & Day, D. D. (1993). A test and refinement of the equity sensitivity construct. *Journal of Organizational Behavior, 14,* 301–317.

Kipnis, D. (1976). *The power holders.* Chicago: University of Chicago Press.

Kirkpatrick, D. L. (1998). *Evaluating training programs: The four levels* (2nd ed.). San Francisco: Berrett-Koehler.

Kirmeyer, S. L., & Dougherty, T. W. (1988). Work load, tension, and coping: Moderating effects of supervisor support. *Personnel Psychology, 41,* 125–139.

Klimoski, R., & Brickner, M. (1987). Why do assessment centers work? The puzzle of assessment center validity. *Personnel Psychology, 40,* 243–260.

Kline, D. W., & Fuchs, P. (1993). The visibility of symbolic highway signs can be increased among drivers of all ages. *Human Factors, 35*(1), 25–34.

Knauth, P. (1996). Designing better shift systems. *Applied Ergonomics, 27*(1), 39–44.

Knowles, M. (Ed.). (1986). *Human Factors Society 1986 directory and yearbook.* Santa Monica, CA: Human Factors Society.

Knox, N. (1998, February 22). Drug abuse problems are on the rise as the labor pool shrinks. *New York Times,* Section 3, p. 11.

Kobasa, S. C., Hilker, R. R., & Maddi, S. R. (1980). Remaining healthy in the encounter with stress. In *Work, stress, health* (pp. 10–15). Chicago: American Medical Association.

Kobasa, S. C., Maddi, S. R., & Kahn, S. (1982). Hardiness and health: A prospective study. *Journal of Personality and Social Psychology, 42,* 168–177.

Koberg, C. S., & Hood, J. N. (1991). Cultures and creativity within hierarchical organizations. *Journal of Business and Psychology, 6*(2), 265–271.

Kochan, T. A., Schmidt, S. M., & DeCotiis, T. A. (1975). Superior–subordinate relation: Leadership and headship. *Human Relations, 28,* 279–294.

Koonce, R. (1997, September). Using the Internet as a career planning tool. *Training and Development, 51,* 15.

Koppes, L. L. (1997). American female pioneers of industrial and organizational psychology during the early years. *Journal of Applied Psychology, 82*(4), 500–515.

Korman, A. K., Greenhaus, J. H., & Baden, I. J. (1977). Personnel attitudes and motivation. *Annual Review of Psychology, 28,* 175–196.

Korman, R. (1991, January 14). Training videos proliferate. *Engineering News-Record, 226,* 16.

Korsgaard, M. A. (1996). The impact of self-appraisal on reaction to feedback from others: The role of self-enhancement and self-consistency concerns. *Journal of Organizational Behavior, 17*(4), 301–311.

Kossek, E. E., & Zonia, S. C. (1993). Assessing diversity climate: A field study of reactions to employer efforts to promote diversity. *Journal of Organizational Behavior, 14*(1), 61–81.

Kovach, K. A., & Render, B. (1987, April). NASA managers and Challenger: A profile and possible explanation. *Personnel, 64*(4), 40–44.

Koys, D. J., & DeCotiis, T. A. (1991). Inductive measures of psychological climate. *Human Relations, 44*(3), 265–285.

Kozlowski, S. W. J., & Doherty, M. L. (1989). Integration of climate and leadership: Examination of a neglected issue. *Journal of Applied Psychology, 74*(4), 546–553.

Kraiger, K., & Ford, J. K. (1990). The relation of job knowledge, job performance, and supervisory ratings as a function of ratee race. *Human Performance, 3*(4), 269–279.

Kraiger, K., Ford, J. K., & Salas, E. (1993). Application of cognitive, skill-based, and affective theories of learning outcomes to new methods of training evaluation. *Journal of Applied Psychology, 78*(2), 311–328.

Krasowska, F. (1996, February). Software, sites can subdue strain. *Occupational Health and Safety, 65,* 20.

Krausz, M., Koslowsky, M., & Eiser, A. (1998). Distal and proximal influences on turnover intention and satisfaction: Support for a withdrawal progression theory. *Journal of Vocational Behavior, 52*(1), 59–71.

Kravchuk, R. S., & Schack, R. W. (1996, July/August). Designing effective performance-measurement systems under the Government Performance and Results Act of 1993. *Public Administration Review, 56,* 348–358.

Krodel v. Department of Health and Human Services, FEP 689 (D.D.C. 1982).

Ku, L. (1996, July). Social and nonsocial uses of electronic messaging systems in organizations. *Journal of Business Communications, 33,* 297–325.

Kunhomoidee, U. A., & Karunes, S. (1991). "Adequate compensation" and "care for employees' safety" as dimensions of organizational climate: Perceptions of management experts. *Journal of the Indian Academy of Applied Psychology, 17*(1–2), 13–19.

Laird, D. (1978). *Approaches to training and development.* Reading, MA: Addison-Wesley.

Lamm, H., & Myers, D. G. (1978). Group induced polarization of attitudes and behavior. In L. Berkowitz (Ed.), *Advances in Experimental and Social Psychology* (Vol. 11; pp. 145–195). New York: Academic Press.

Landau, J. (1995). The relationship of race and gender to managers' ratings of promotion potential. *Journal of Organizational Behavior, 18*(4), 391–400.

Landy, F. (1985). *Psychology of work behavior.* Homewood, IL: Dorsey Press.

Landy, F. H., & Farr, J. L. (1983). *The measurement of work performance: Methods, theory, and applications.* New York: Academic Press.

Landy, F. J. (1989). *Psychology of work behavior* (4th ed.). Homewood, IL: Dorsey Press.

Landy, F. J. (1993). Early influences on the development of industrial/organizational psychology. In T. K. Fagan & G. R. VandenBos (Eds.) *Exploring applied psychology: Origins and critical analyses.* (pp. 79–118). Washington, D.C.: American Psychological Association.

Landy, F. J., & Shankster, L. J. (1994). Personnel selection and placement. *Annual Review of Psychology, 45,* 261–296.

Langfred, C. W. (1998). Is cohesiveness a double-edged sword? An investigation of the effects of cohesiveness on performance. *Small Group Research, 29*(1), 124–143.

Laosa, L. M. (1991, September). The cultural context of construct validity and the ethics of generalizability. Special Issue: Educating Linguistically and Culturally Diverse Preschoolers. *Early Childhood Research Quarterly. 6*(3), 313–321.

Lapakko, D. (1997). Three cheers for language: A closer examination of a widely cited study of communication. *Communication Education, 46*(1), 63–67.

Larson, J. R., Hunt, J. G., & Osborn, R. N. (1976). The great hi-hi leader behavior myth: A lesson from Occam's razor. *Academy of Management Journal, 19,* 628–642.

Lasden, M. (1985, May). The trouble with testing. *Training, 22,* 78–81.

Latané, B., & Nida, S. (1981). Ten years of research on group size and helping. *Psychological Bulletin, 89,* 308–324.

Latham, G. P., & Baldes, J. J. (1975). The "practical significance" of Locke's theory of goal setting. *Journal of Applied Psychology, 60*(1), 122–124.

Latham, G. P., & Frayne, C. A. (1989). Self-management training for increasing job attendance: A follow-up and replication. *Journal of Applied Psychology, 74*(3), 411–416.

Latham, G. P., Mitchell, T. R., & Dossett, D. L. (1978). Importance of participative goal setting and anticipated rewards on goal difficulty and job performance. *Journal of Applied Psychology, 63*(1), 163–171.

Latham, G. P., & Seijta, G. H. (1997). The effect of appraisal instrument on managerial perceptions of fairness and satisfaction with the appraisal from their peers. *Canadian Journal of Behavioural Science, 29*(4), 275–282.

Latham, G. P., Steele, T. P., & Saari, L. M. (1982). The effects of participation and goal difficulty on performance. *Personnel Psychology, 35,* 255–268.

Latham, G. P., & Wexley, K. N. (1981). *Increasing productivity through performance appraisal.* Reading, MA: Addison-Wesley.

Lautenschlager, G. J., & Flaherty, V. L. (1990). Computer administration of questions: More desirable or more social desirability? *Journal of Applied Psychology, 75*(3), 310–314.

Lauterbach, K. E., & Weiner, B. J. (1996). Dynamics of upward influence: How male and female managers get their way. *Leadership Quarterly, 7*(1), 87–107.

Lawrence, D. G., Salsburg, B. L., Dawson, J. G., & Fasman, Z. D. (1982). Design and use of weighted application blanks. *Personnel Administrator, 27,* 47–53.

Lawrie, J. (1992). Differentiate between training, education and development. *Personnel Journal, 69,* 44.

Lazarus, R. S. (1991). Psychological stress in the workplace. *Journal of Social Behavior and Personality, 6,* 1–13.

Leadership Software, Inc. (1987). *Managing participation in organizations.*

Lee, C. S. C., Rutecki, G. W., Whittier, F. C., Clarett, M. R., & Jarjoura, D. (1997). A comparison of interactive computerized medical education software with a more traditional format. *Teaching and Learning Medicine, 9*(2), 111–115.

Lee, C., & Earley, P. C. (1992). Comparative peer evaluations of organizational behavior theories. *Organizational Development Journal, 10*(4), 37–42.

Leibowitz, Z. B., Schlossberg, N. K., & Shore, J. E. (1991). Stopping the revolving door. *Training and Development Journal, 45,* 43–50.

Leigh, J. P. (1991). Employee and job attributes as predictors of absenteeism in a national sample of workers: The importance of health and dangerous working conditions. *Social Science and Medicine, 33*(2), 127–137.

Leithwood, K., Menzies, T., Jantzi, D., & Leithwood, J. (1996). School restructuring, transformational leadership and the amelioration of teacher burnout. *Anxiety, Stress and Coping: An International Journal, 9*(3), 199–215.

LePine, J. A., Hollenbeck, J. R., Ilgen, D. R., & Hedlund, J. (1997). Effects of individual differences on the performance of hierarchical decision-making team: Much more than g. *Journal of Applied Psychology 82,*(5), 803–811.

Levin, A. (1998, October 5). Tech tools fight repetitive stress injuries. *National Underwriter, 102*(4), 44.

Levine, E. L., Ash, R. A., & Bennett, N. (1980). Exploratory comparison study of four job analysis methods. *Journal of Applied Psychology, 65*(3), 524–535.

Levine, E. L., Ash, R. A., Hall, H., & Sistrunk, F. (1983). Evaluation of job analysis methods by experienced job analysts, *Academy of Management Journal, 26,* 339–348.

Levy, A., & Merry, U. (1986). *Organizational transformation.* New York: Praeger.

Lewin, K. (1951). *Field theory and social science.* New York: Harper & Bros.

Lewin, K., Lippitt, R., & White, R. K. (1939). Patterns of aggressive behavior in experimentally created "social climates." *Journal of Social Psychology, 10,* 271–299.

Lewis, C. T., & Stevens, C. K. (1990). An analysis of job evaluation committee and job holder gender effects on job evaluation. *Public Personnel Management, 19,* 271–278.

Liden, R. C., Wayne, S. J., & Stilwell, D. (1993). A longitudinal study on the early development of leader–member exchanges. *Journal of Applied Psychology, 78*(4), 662–674.

Liden, R. D., Stilwell, D., & Ferris, G. R. (1996, March). The effects of supervisor and subordinate age on objective and subjective performance ratings. *Human Relations, 49,* 327–347.

Lindsley, D. B. (1988). *Fifty years of psychology: Essays in honor of Floyd Ruch* (E. R. Hilgard, Ed.). Glenview, IL: Scott Foresman.

Lipsett, L., & Youst, D. (1994). Develop your staffers with a plan. *Supervisory Management, 39,* 6.

Littlepage, G., Robison, W., & Reddington, K. (1997, February). Effects of task performance, member ability, and recognition of expertise. *Organizational Behavior and Human Decision Processes, 69,* 133–147.

Locke, E. A. (1968). Toward a theory of task motivation and incentives. *Organizational Behavior and Human Performance, 3,* 157–189.

Locke, E. A. (1975). Personnel attitudes and motivation. *Annual Review of Psychology, 26,* 457–480.

Locke, E. A. (1996). Motivation through conscious goal setting. *Applied and Preventive Psychology, 5*(2), 117–124.

Locke, E. A., Frederick, E., Lee, C., & Bobko, P. (1984). Effects of self-efficacy, goals, and task strategies on task performance. *Journal of Applied Psychology, 69,* 287–322.

Locke, E. A., & Latham, G. P. (1984). *Goal setting: A motivational technique that works.* Englewood Cliffs, NJ: Prentice-Hall.

Locke, E. A., & Latham, G. P. (1990a). *A theory of goal setting and task performance.* Englewood Cliffs, NJ: Prentice-Hall.

Locke, E. A., & Latham, G. P. (1990b). Work motivation and satisfaction: Light at the end of the tunnel. *Psychological Science, 1*(4), 240–246.

London, M., & Beatty, R. W. (1993). 360-degree feedback as a competitive advantage. *Human Resource Management, 32,* 353–372.

Lord, R. G., DeVader, C. L., & Alliger, G. M. (1986). A meta-analysis of the relationship between personality traits and leadership perceptions: An application of validity generalization procedures. *Journal of Applied Psychology, 71*(3), 402–410.

Lord, R. G., Foti, R. J., & DeVader, C. L. (1984). A test of leadership categorization theory: Internal structure, information processing and leadership perceptions. *Organizational Behavior and Human Performance, 34,* 343–378.

Lord, R. G., & Maher, K. J. (1990). Alternative information-processing models and their implications for theory, research and practice. *Academy of Management Review, 15,* 9–28.

Lowe, R. H. (1993). Master's programs in industrial/organizational psychology: Current status and a call for action. *Professional Psychology Research and Practice, 24,* 27–34.

Lowin, A., & Craig, J. R. (1968). The influence of level of performance on managerial style: An experimental object-lesson in the ambiguity of correlational data. *Organizational Behavior and Human Performance, 3,* 441–458.

Luthas, F. (1991). Improving the delivery of quality service: Behavioural management techniques. *Leadership and Organization Development Journal, 12*(2), 3–6.

Lysaker, P., Bell, M., Milstein, R., & Bryson, G. (1993). Work capacity in schizophrenia. *Hospital and Community Psychiatry, 44*(3), 278–280.

Macan, T. H., Avedon, M. J., & Paese, M. (1994, Winter). The effects of applicants' reactions to cognitive ability tests and an assessment center. *Personnel Psychology, 47,* 715–738.

MacDonald, D. R. (1988, February). Greater results from your assessment center. *Training and Development Journal, 42*(2), 50–57.

Maddi, S. R., & Kobasa, S. C. (1991). The development of hardiness. In A. Monat & R. S. Lazarus (Eds.), *Stress and coping: An anthology* (3rd ed., pp. 245–257). New York: Columbia University Press.

Mael, F. A., Connerly, M., & Morath, R. (1996). None of your business: Parameters of biodata invasiveness. *Personnel Psychology, 49*(3), 613–650.

Magruder, J. (2000, July 19). Working together/job sharing offers "best of both worlds." *Arizona Republic,* p. E1.

Malka, S. (1990). Application of multitrait-multirater approach to performance appraisal in a social service organization. *Evaluation and Program Planning, 13*(3), 243–250.

Mally, M. (1997, April 7). EI creates videos to solve language problems. *Hotel and Motel Management, 212,* 30–31.

Managing Office Technology. (1996, July). Drug testing grows, AMA study finds. *41,* 23.

Mandelker, J. (1993, April). Cumulative trauma increases workers' compensation claims. *Business & Health, 11,* 28–30.

Mann, F. C. (1961). Studying and creating change: A means to understanding social organization. In W. Bennis, K. Benne, & R. Chin (Eds.), *The planning of change* (pp. 605–613). New York: Holt, Rinehart & Winston.

Mann, S. E. (1996, November 25). Employee stress: An important cost in mergers. *Business Insurance, 30,* 24.

Mantovani, G. (1994, January). Is computer-mediated communication intrinsically apt to enhance democracy in organizations? *Human Relations, 47,* 45–62.

Markels, A. (1997, January 30). Workplace: A diversity program can prove divisive. *Wall Street Journal,* p. B1.

Marshak, R. J. (1993). Lewin meets Confucius: A review of the OD model of change. Special issue: Emerging Developments in Action Research. *Journal of Applied Behavioral Science, 29*(4), 393–415.

Marshall, A. A., & Stohl, C. (1993). Participating as participation: A network approach. *Communication Monographs, 60*(2), 137–157.

Marshall-Meis, J. C., Eisner, E. J., Schemmer, F. M., & Yarkin-Levin, K. (1983). Development of selection and evaluation methods in energy control centers, *ARRO Technical Report #3072/R83-14,* Bethesda, MD: Advanced Research Resources Organization.

Martin, C. L., & Nagao, D. H. (1989). Some effects of computerized interviewing on job applicant responses. *Journal of Applied Psychology, 74*(1), 72–80.

Martin, S. L., & Raju, N. S. (1992). Determining cutoff scores that optimize utility: A recognition of recruiting costs. *Journal of Applied Psychology, 77*(1), 15–23.

Martocchio, J. J. (1992). Microcomputer usage as an opportunity: The influence of context in employee training. *Personnel Psychology, 45*(3), 529–552.

Martocchio, J. J., & Whitener, E. M. (1992, May). Fairness in personnel selection: A meta-analysis and policy implications. *Human Relations, 45*(5), 489–506.

Maslach, C., & Goldberg, J. (1998). Prevention of burnout: New perspectives. *Applied and Preventive Psychology, 7*(1), 63–74.

Maslach, C., & Jackson, S. E. (1981). *The Maslach burnout inventory.* Palo Alto, CA: Consulting Psychologists Press.

Maslow, A. H. (1943). A theory of human motivation. *Psychological Review, 50,* 370–396.

Maslow, A. H. (1965). *Eupsychian management: A journal.* Homewood, IL: Richard D. Irwin.

Mastrangelo, P. M. (1997). Do college students still prefer companies without employment drug testing? *Journal of Business and Psychology, 11*(3), 325–337.

Mastrofski, S. D., Ritti, R. R., & Snipes, J. B. (1994). Expectancy theory and police productivity in DUI enforcement. *Law and Society Review, 28*(1), 113–148.

Mathieu, J. E., & Farr, J. L. (1991). Further evidence for the discriminant validity of measures of organizational commitment, job involvement and job satisfaction. *Journal of Applied Psychology, 76*(1), 127–133.

Mathieu, J. E., & Kohler, S. S. (1990). A cross-level examination of group absence influences on individual absence. *Journal of Applied Psychology, 75*(2), 217–220.

Mathieu, J. E., & Leonard, R. L. (1987). Applying utility concepts to a training program in supervisory skills: A time based approach. *Academy of Management Journal, 30*(2), 316–335.

Matkin, R. E., & Bauer, L. L. (1993). Assessing predeterminants of job satisfaction among certified rehabilitation counselors in various work settings. *Journal of Applied Rehabilitation Counseling, 24*(1), 26–33.

Matteson, M. T., & Ivancevich, J. M. (1982). *Managing job stress and health.* New York: Free Press.

Matthews, J., & Anselmo, J. (1994). Even good simulation has its limitations. *Aviation Week and Space Technology, 141,* 69.

Matthews, K. A. (1982). Psychological perspectives on the Type A behavior pattern. *Psychological Bulletin, 91,* 293–323.

Maxwell, S. E., & Arvey, R. D. (1993). The search for predictors with high validity and low adverse impact: Compatible or incompatible goals? *Journal of Applied Psychology, 78*(3), 433–437.

May, B. R. (1991, February). I can't hear you. *Supervision, 52,* 17–19.

May, D. (1999, April). Testing by necessity. *Occupational Health and Safety, 68*(4), 48–51.

Maynard, R. (1995, June). Making your message colorful and dynamic. *Nation's Business, 83,* 10.

Mayo, E. (1933). *The human problems of an industrial civilization.* New York: Macmillan.

McAteer, P. F. (1991). Simulations: Learning tool for the 1990's. *Training and Development, 45,* 19–22.

McCann, S. J. H. (1997). Threatening times and the election of charismatic U.S. presidents: With and without FDR. *Journal of Psychology, 131*(4), 393–400.

McClelland, D. C. (1961). *The achieving society.* Princeton, NJ: Van Nostrand.

McClelland, D. C. (1987). Characteristics of successful entrepreneurs. Third Creativity, Innovation and Entrepreneurship Symposium (1986, Framingham, MA). *Journal of Creative Behavior, 21*(3), 219–233.

McClelland, D., & Boyatzis, R. (1982). Leadership motive pattern and long-term success in management. *Journal of Applied Psychology, 67*(4), 737–743.

McClelland, D., & Burnham, D. H. (1976). Power is the great motivation. *Harvard Business Review, 54,* 100–110.

McClelland, D. C., & Winter, D. G. (1969). *Motivating economic achievement: Accelerating economic development through psychological training.* New York: Free Press.

McClelland, V. A., & Wilmot, R. E. (1990, August). Improve lateral communications. *Personnel Journal,* p. 32.

McCord, A. B. (1987). Job training. In R. L. Craig (Ed.), *Training and development handbook: A guide to human resource development* (3rd ed., pp. 363–382). New York: McGraw-Hill.

McCormick, E. J., Jeanneret, P. R., & Meacham, R. C. (1972). A study of job characteristics and job dimensions as based on the Position Analysis Questionnaire (PAQ). *Journal of Applied Psychology, 56*(2), 247–267.

McCormick, F., & Tiffin, J. (1974). *Industrial Psychology* (6th ed.). Englewood Cliffs, NJ: Prentice-Hall.

McCune, J. C. (1997, May/June). Get the message [company e-mail policy]. *Journal of Property Management, 62,* 42–44.

McDaniel, L. (1995, May). Group assessments produce better hires. *HRMagazine, 40*(5), 72–76.

McDaniel, M. A., Whetzel, D. L., Schmidt, F. L., & Maurer, S. D. (1994). The validity of employment interviews: A comprehensive review and meta-analysis. *Journal of Applied Psychology, 79*(4), 599–616.

McDaniels, C. (1989). *The changing workplace: Career counseling strategies for the 1990's and beyond.* San Francisco: Jossey-Bass.

McDonald, C. (1992). U.S. union membership in future decades: A trade unionist's perspective. *Industrial Relations, 31*(1), 13–30.

McEvoy, G. M., & Buller, P. F. (1987). User acceptance of peer appraisals in an industrial setting. *Personnel Psychology, 40,* 785–797.

McGehee, W., & Thayer, P. W. (1961). *Training in business and industry.* New York: Wiley.

McGregor, D. M. (1960). *The human side of enterprise.* New York: McGraw-Hill.

McKelvie, S. J. (1989, August). The Wonderlic Personnel Test: Reliability and validity in an academic setting. *Psychological Reports, 65*(1), 161–162.

McKinney, W. R., & Collins, J. R. (1991, Summer). The impact on utility, race and gender using three standard methods of scoring selection examinations. *Public Personnel Management, 20*(2), 145–169.

McLean, A. J., Sims, D. B. P., Managan, I. L., & Tuffield, D. (1982). *Organization development in transition: Evidence of an evolving profession.* New York: Wiley.

McLeod, P. L. (1992). An assessment of the experimental literature on electronic support of group work: Results of a meta-analysis. Special issue: Computer Supported Cooperative Work. *Human Computer Interaction, 7*(3), 257–280.

McMahan, G. C., & Woodman, R. W. (1992). The current practice of organizational development within the firm. *Group and Organizational Management, 17,* 117–134.

Meglino, B. M., Ravlin, E. C., & Adkins, C. L. (1989). A work values approach to corporate culture: A field test of the value congruence process and its relationship to individual outcomes. *Journal of Applied Psychology, 74,* 424–432.

Meister, D. (1987). System design, development and testing. In G. Salvendy (Ed.), *Handbook of human factors* (pp. 273–292). New York: Wiley.

Mercer. M. M. (1988). Reducing the costs. *Personnel, 65,* 36–42.

Mergenhagen, P. (1997, July). Enabling disabled workers. *American Demographics, 19,* 36–42.

Metzger, N. (1991). The changing health care workplace: A challenge for management development. *Journal of Management Development, 10,* 53–64.

Metzger, R. O., & Von Glinow, M. A. (1988). Off-site workers: At home and abroad. *California Management Review, 30,* 101–111.

Meyer, H. H. (1991, February). A solution to the performance appraisal feedback enigma. *Academy of Management Executive, 5,* 68–76.

Michaelson, L. K., Watson, W. E., & Black, R. H. (1989). A realistic test of individual versus group consensus decision making. *Journal of Applied Psychology, 74*(5), 834–839.

Miles, J. A., & Greenberg, J. (1993). Using punishment threats to attenuate social loafing effects among swimmers. *Organization Behavior and Human Decision Processes, 56*(2), 246–265.

Milgram, S. (1974). *Obedience to authority.* New York: Harper & Row.

Miller, A. (1988, April 25). Stress on the job. *Newsweek, 111,* 40–45.

Miller, C. S., Kaspin, J. A., & Schuster, M. H. (1990). The impact of performance appraisal methods on age discrimination in employment act cases. *Personnel Psychology, 43,* 555–578.

Miller, M. L., & Malott, R. W. (1997). The importance of overt responding in programmed instruction even with added incentives for learning. *Journal of Behavioral Education, 7*(4), 497–503.

Milliken-Davies, M. (1992). *An explanation of flawed first-line supervision.* Unpublished doctoral dissertation, University of Tulsa, Tulsa, OK.

Miner, J. B. (1988). Development and application of the rated ranking technique in performance appraisal. *Journal of Occupational Psychology, 61*(4), 291–305.

Miners, I. A., Moore, M. L., & Campoux, J. E (1994). Organizational development impacts interrupted: A multiyear time-serial study of absence and other time uses. *Group and Organization Management, 19*(3), 363–394.

Minter, S. G. (1991, April). Relieving workplace stress. *Occupational Hazards, 53,* 38–42.

Mishra, J. (1990, Summer). Managing the grapevine. *Public Personnel Management, 19,* 213–228.

Mitchell, R. (1986). Team building by disclosure of internal frame of reference. *Journal of Applied Behavioral Science, 22,* 15–28.

Moore, H. A., & Ollenberger, J. C. (1986, November). What sex is your parachute? Interest inventory/counseling models and the perpetuation of the sex/wage segregation of the labor market. *Work and Occupations, 13*(4), 511–531.

Moore, J. D., & Gehrig, R. L. (1991). Rehearsing for a robbery. *Security Management, 35,* 51–52.

Moores, J. (1990). A meta-analytic review of the effects of compressed work schedules. *Applied H.R.M. Research, 1*(1), 12–18.

Morano, R. A., & Deets, N. (1986). Keeping technologists on the road to the future. *Training and Development Journal, 40*(12), 38–41.

Moravec, M., Gyr, H., & Freidman, L. (1993, July). A 21st century communication tool. *HR Magazine, 38,* 77–79.

Morrow, J. (1998, February). House calls. *Success, 45,* 67–68.

Morse, D. T. (1998). MINSIZE: A computer program for obtaining minimum sample size as an indicator of effect size. *Educational and Psychological Measurement, 58*(1), 142–153.

Morse, N. C., & Reimer, E. (1956). The experimental change of a major organizational variable. *Journal of Abnormal Social Psychology, 51,* 120–129.

Mortimer, J. T., & Lorence, J. (1989). Satisfaction and involvement: Disentangling a deceptively simple relationship. *Social Psychology Quarterly, 52*(4), 249–265.

Moss, M. (1997, June 17). For older employees, on the job injuries are more often deadly. *Wall Street Journal,* p. A1.

Motowidlo, S. J., & Tippins, N. (1993). Further studies of the low-fidelity simulation in the form of a situational inventory. *Journal of Occupational and Organizational Psychology, 66*(4), 337–344.

Motowidlo, S. J., Packard, J. S., & Manning, M. R. (1986). Occupational stress: Its causes and consequences for job performance. *Journal of Applied Psychology, 71*(3), 618–629.

Mount, M. K. (1983). Comparisons of managerial and employee satisfaction with a performance appraisal system. *Personnel Psychology, 36,* 99–110.

Mount, M. K., & Thompson, D. E. (1987). Cognitive categorization and quality of performance ratings. *Journal of Applied Psychology, 72*(2), 240–246.

Muchinsky, P. M. (1977). A comparison of within- and across-subjects analyses of the expectancy-valence model for predicting effort. *Academy of Management Journal, 20,* 154–158.

Muchinsky, P. M. (1990). *Psychology applied to work: An introduction to industrial and organizational psychology* (3rd ed.). Pacific Grove, CA: Brooks/Cole.

Muir, B. M., & Moray, N. (1996). Trust in automation: II. Experimental studies of trust and human intervention in a process control simulation. *Ergonomics, 39*(3), 429–460.

Mullen, B., & Copper, C. (1994). The relation between group cohesiveness and performance: An integration. *Psychological Bulletin, 115*(2), 210–227.

Multran, E. J., Reitzes, D. C., & Fernandez, M. E. (1997, September). Factors that influence attitudes towards retirement. *Research on Aging, 19*(3), 251–273.

Münsterberg, H. (1913). *Psychology and industrial efficiency.* Boston: Houghton Mifflin.

Murphy, B. S., Barlow, W. E., & Hatch, D. D. (1991). Failure to evaluate accurately constitutes proof of discrimination. *Personnel Journal, 70,* 19–20.

Murphy, I. P. (1997, July 7). Firm uses feedback to cut turnover, save millions. *Marketing News, 31,* 15.

Murphy, K. J. (1993, Spring). Performance measurement and appraisal: Merck tries to motivate managers to do it right. *Employment Relations Today, 20,* 47–62.

Murphy, K. R. (1987). Detecting infrequent deception. *Journal of Applied Psychology, 72*(3), 611–614.

Murphy, K. R., & Lee, S. L. (1994, Summer). Personality variables related to integrity test scores: The role of conscientiousness. *Journal of Business and Psychology, 8,* 413–424.

Murphy, P. R., Daley, J. M., & Dalenberg, D. R. (1991). Exploring the effects of postcard prenotification on industrial firms' response to mail surveys. *Journal of the Market Research Society, 33*(4), 335–341.

Murrell, A. J., & Sprinkle, J. (1993). The impact of negative attitudes toward computers on employees' satisfaction and commitment within a small company. *Computers in Human Behavior, 9*(1), 57–63.

Murry, H. A., & Mackinnon, D. W. (1946). Assessment of OSS personnel. *Journal of Consulting Psychology, 10,* 76–80.

Myers, O. (1990, August). How come you do that? *Supervision, 51,* 6–8.

Nadler, D. A., & Lawler, E. E. (1983). Quality of work life: Perspectives and directions. *Organizational Dynamics, 11*(3), 20–30.

Napoli, D. S. (1981). *Architects of adjustment: The history of the psychological profession in the United States.* Port Washington, NY: Kennikat Press.

Nash, A. N., Muczyk, J. P., & Vettare, F. L. (1971). The relative practical effectiveness of programmed instruction. *Personnel Psychology, 24,* 397–418.

National Institute for Literacy. (1998). Fact sheet: Workforce literacy. http://www. nifl.gov.

National Institute of Safety and Health (NIOSH). (1997, July 31). *Musculoskeletal disorders (MSDs) and workplace factors.* http://www.cdc.gov/niosh/ergtxt7.html

National Institute of Safety and Health (NIOSH). (1998, January 7). Workplace VDT use not a risk factor for reduced birth weight, premature birth. http://www.cdc.gov/niosh/vdtrisk.html

Neilsen, M. E., & Miller, C. E. (1992). Expectations regarding the use of various group decision rules. *Journal of Social Behavior and Personality, 7*(1), 43–58.

Ness, Y. (1994, April). Number crunching software persuades management to expand the safety budget. *Occupational Health and Safety, 63,* 57–58.

Netmeyer, R. G., Boles, J. S., & McKee, D. O. (1997). An investigation into the antecedents of organizational citizenship behaviors in a personal selling context. *Journal of Marketing, 61*(3), 85–98.

Network Newsletter. (1995a, April). Basic models for managing diversity training. *1*(1). Retrieved April 9, 2000, from the World Wide Web: http://www.1lr.cornell.edu/depts/WDN/NetNews/1_1/Problemsolving.html.

Network Newsletter. (1995b, April). Tips for starting a diversity program. *1*(1.) Retrieved April 9, 2000, from the World Wide Web: http://www.1lr.cornell.edu/depts/WDN/ NetNews/1_1/problemsolving.html.

Neuliep, J. W. (1996). The influence of Theory X and Y management style on the perceptions of ethical behavior in organizations. *Journal of Social Behavior and Personality, 11*(2), 301–311.

Neuman, G. A., Edwards, J. E., & Raju, N. S. (1989). Organizational development interventions: A meta-analysis of their effects on satisfaction and other attitudes. *Personnel Psychology, 42*(3), 461–489.

Neuman, G., & Baydoun, R. (1998). Computerization of paper and pencil tests: When are they equivalent? *Applied Psychological Measurement, 22*(1), 71–83.

Nevo, B. (1986, July). *Graphology validation studies in Israel: Summary of 15 years of activity.* Paper presented at the International Association for Applied Psychology, Jerusalem.

Nevo, O., Nevo, B., & Zehavi, A. D. (1993). Gossip and counseling: The tendency to gossip and its relation to vocational interests. *Counseling Psychology Quarterly, 6*(3), 229–238.

New York Times. (1995, April 2). U.S. offered unusual class on "diversity training." Section 1, p. 34.

Newsweek. (1999, February 1). How the work force is changing, p. 58.

Noe, R. A., & Schmitt, N. (1986). The influence of trainee attitudes on training effectiveness: Test of a model. *Personnel Psychology, 39,* 497–423.

Nomani, A. Q. (1995, October 11). Limits are eased on job questions for the disabled. *Wall Street Journal,* Eastern edition, p. A5.

Nordhaug, O. (1989). Reward functions of personnel training. *Human Relations, 42,* 373–388.

Norman, D. A. (1988). *The psychology of everyday things.* New York: Basic Books.

Norman, D. A. (1992). *Turn signals are the facial expressions of automobiles.* New York: Addison-Wesley.

Northrup, A., Kraemer, K. L., Dunkle, D. E., & King, J. L. (1994). Management policy for greater computer benefits: Friendly software, computer literacy, or formal training. *Social Science Computer Review, 12*(3), 383–404.

Notebaert, R. C. (1998, November 1). Leveraging diversity: Adding value to the bottom line. *Vital Speeches of the Day, 65*(2), 47–49.

Nozar, R. (1992). Employee satisfaction gains importance [editorial]. *Hotel and Motel Management, 207,* 6.

Nunamaker, J. F. Jr. (1997). Future research in group support systems: Needs, some questions and possible directions. *International Journal of Human Computer Studies, 47*(3), 357–385.

Nutt, P. C., & Backoff, J. G. (1997). Facilitating transformational change. *Journal of Applied Behavioral Science, 33*(4), 490–508.

Nystrom, P. C. (1978). Managers and the hi-hi leader myth. *Academy of Management Journal, 21,* 325–331.

O'Hare, D. (1997). Cognitive ability determinants and elite pilot performance. *Human Factors, 39*(4), 540–552.

O'Neal, G. S., & Lapitsky, M. (1991). Effects of clothing as non-verbal communication on credibility of the message source. *Clothing and Textiles Research Journal, 9*(3), 28–34.

O'Reilly, C. A., & Pondy, L. R. (1979). Organizational communication. In S. Kerr (Ed.), *Organizational behavior.* Columbus, OH: Grid.

Ober, S. (1998). *Contemporary business communication* (3rd ed.). Boston: Houghton-Mifflin.

Ocampa. (2000). Handwriting analysis employers' guide. http://www.ocampa.com/analysis

Offerman, L. R., & Gowing, M. K. (1990). Organizational psychology. *American Psychologist, 45*(2), 427–458.

Olen, H. (1996, February). Getting a handle on flextime. *Working Woman, 21,* 55–56.

Oleski, D., & Subich, L. M. (1996). Congruence and career change in employed adults. *Journal of Vocational Behavior, 49*(3), 221–229.

Oliansky A. (1991). A confederate's perspective on deception. *Ethics and Behavior,* 1, 253–258.

Ondusko, D. (1991). Comparison of employees with disabilities and able-bodied workers in janitorial maintenance. *Journal of Applied Rehabilitation Counseling, 22*(2), 19–24.

Ones, D. S., Schmidt, F. L., & Viswesvaran, C. (1996, Summer). Controversies over integrity testing: Two viewpoints. *Journal of Business and Psychology,* 10, 487–501.

Ones, D. S., & Viswesvaran, C. (1998). Gender, age, and race differences on overt integrity tests: Results across four large-scale applicant data sets. *Journal of Applied Psychology, 83*(1), 35–42.

Ones, D. S., Viswesvaran, C., & Schmidt, F. L. (1993, August). Comprehensive meta-analysis of integrity test validities: Findings and implications for personnel selection and theories of job performance. *Journal of Applied Psychology, 78*(4), 679–703.

Organ, D. W. (1997). Organizational citizenship behavior: It's construct clean-up time. *Human Performance, 10*(2), 85–97.

Organ, D. W., & Ryan, K. (1995, Winter). A meta-analytic review of attitudinal and dispositional predictors of organizational citizenship behavior. *Personnel Psychology,* 48, 775–802.

Osborn, A. F. (1957). *Applied imagination* (rev. ed.). New York: Scribner.

Osipow, S. H. (1991). Observations about career psychology. *Journal of Vocational Behavior,* 39, 291–296.

Oss, M. E., & Clary, J. (1998, July 17). The evolving world of employee assistance. *Behavioral Health Management,* 18, 20–25.

Owens, W. A. (1976). Background data. In M. D. Dunnette (Ed.), *Handbook of industrial and organizational psychology* (pp. 609–644). Chicago: Rand McNally.

Paetzold, R. L., & Wilborn. (1992, May). Employer (ir)rationality and the demise of employment references. *American Business Law Journal,* 30, 123–142.

Palmero, F., Codina, V., & Rosel, J. (1993). Psychophysiological activation, reactivity, and recovery in Type A and Type B scorers when in a stressful laboratory situation. *Psychological Reports, 73*(3, Pt. 1), 803–811.

Papadatou, D., Anagnostopoulos, F., & Monos, D. (1994). Factors contributing to the development of burnout in oncology nursing. *British Journal of Medical Psychology, 67*(2), 187–199.

Parry, J. W. (1991). Employment under the ADA: A national perspective. *Mental and Physical Disability Law Reporter, 15*(5), 525–536.

Pasmore, W., Francis, C., Haldeman, J., & Shani, A. (1982). Sociotechnical systems: A North American reflection on empirical studies of the seventies. *Human Relations,* 12, 1179–1204.

Pasmore, W., Petee, J., & Bastain, R. (1986). Sociotechnical systems in health care: A field experiment. *Journal of Applied Behavioral Science,* 22, 329–339.

Patten, T. H. (1988). *Fair pay.* San Francisco: Jossey-Bass.

Paul, R. J., & Ebadi, Y. M. (1989). Leadership decision making in a service organization: A field test of the Vroom-Yetton model. *Journal of Occupational Psychology, 62*(3), 201–211.

Paulus, P. B., Dzindolet, M. T., Poletes, G., & Camacho, L. M. (1993). Perception of performance in group brainstorming: The illusion of group productivity. *Personality and Social Psychology Bulletin, 19*(1), 78–89.

Payne, K. E., & Cangemi, J. (1997). Gender differences in leadership. *IFE Psychologia: An International Journal, 5*(1), 22–43.

Payne, R. L., & Phesey, D. L. (1971). Stern's Organizational Climate Index: A reconceptualization and application to business organizations. *Organizational Behavior and Human Performance,* 6, 77–98.

Pearce, C. G. (1993, April). How effective are we as listeners? *Training and Development,* 47, 78–80.

Pearl, L. (1992, October). You are the message. *Agri Marketing,* 30, 44.

Pedrini, D. T., & Pedrini, B. C. (1982). Faculty or staff evaluations with paired comparisons. *Education, 103*(1), 105–106.

Pellegrino, J. W., & Kail, R. (1982). Process analysis and spatial aptitude. In R. J. Sternberg (Ed.), *Advances in the psychology of human mental ability* (pp. 118–132). Hillsdale, NJ: Lawrence Erlbaum.

Pereira, J. (1993, April 27). Bosses will do almost anything to light fires under salespeople [fire walking]. *Wall Street Journal,* p. 81.

Perez, J. (1997, September). Cracking the glass ceiling. *Hispanic Business, 19,* 31.

Personnel Journal. (1992, February). The potential workplace murderer. 71, 74.

Personnel Journal. (1992, July). Refusal to hire HIV-positive pharmacists violates Rehabilitation Act (of 1973) 71, 12.

Personnel Journal. (1993, May). Employers find it more difficult to check references. *72,* 20.

Personnel Management. (1992). New software for job evaluation cuts staff costs at local council. *24,* 11.

Personnel. (1990, May). Listening up—and down. *67,* Supplement to *HR Focus,* pp. 6–7.

Personnel. (1991, September). Beyond classified ads: Recruitment goes high tech. *68,* 5.

Peters, L. H., Hartke, D. D., & Pohlmann, J. T. (1985). Fiedler's contingency theory of leadership: An application of meta-analysis procedures of Schmidt and Hunter. *Psychological Bulletin, 97,* 274–285.

Petrocelli, W., & Repa, B. K. (1992). *Sexual harassment on the job.* Berkeley: Nolo Press.

Phillips, K. R. (1987). Red flags in performance appraisal. *Training and Development Journal, 41*(3), 80–82.

Pierson, J. (1995, November 20). If the sun shines in workers work better, buyers buy more. *Wall Street Journal,* p. B1.

Pillai, R. (1996). Crisis and the emergence of charismatic leadership in groups: An experimental investigation. *Journal of Applied Social Psychology, 26*(6), 543–562.

Pine, D. E. (1995). Assessing the validity of job ratings: An empirical study of false reporting on task inventories. *Public Personnel Management, 24,* 451–460.

Piotrkowski, C. S. (1998). Gender harassment, job satisfaction, and distress among employed white and minority women. *Journal of Occupational and Health Psychology, 3*(1), 33–43.

Piotrkowski, C. S., & Repetti, R. L. (1984). *Work and the family system: A naturalistic study of working-class and lower-middle-class families.* New York: Free Press.

Podsakoff, P. M., & Schriesheim, C. A. (1985). Field studies of French and Raven's bases of power: Critique, reanalysis, and suggestions for future research. *Psychological Bulletin, 97,* 387–411.

Pollard, C. (1992). Effects of interactive videodisc instruction on learner performance, learner attitude and learning time. *Journal of Instructional Psychology, 19*(3), 189–196.

Pollock, C., & Kanachowski, A. (1993). Application of theories of decision making to group decision support systems (GDSS). *International Journal of Human Computer Interaction, 5*(1), 711–794.

Poole, M. S., Holmes, M., Watson, R., & DeSanctis, G. (1993). Group decision support systems and group communication: A comparison of decision making in computer supported and nonsupported groups. *Communication Research, 20*(2), 176–213.

Pope, S., & Stremmel, A. J. (1992). Organizational climate and job satisfaction among child care teachers. *Child and Youth Care Forum, 21*(1), 39–52.

Porras, J. I., & Silver, R. C. (1991). Organizational development and transformation. *Annual Review of Psychology, 42,* 51–78.

Porter, L. W., & Lawler, E. E. (1968). *Managerial attitudes and performance.* Homewood, IL: Richard D. Irwin.

Posner, B. Z., & Kouzes, J. M. (1993). Psychometric properties of the Leadership Practices Inventory—Updated. *Educational and Psychological Measurement, 53*(1), 191–199.

Potera, C. (1988, November). Stress epidemics. *Psychology Today, 22,* 16.

Potosky, D., & Bobko, P. (1997). Computer versus paper and pencil administration mode and response distortion in noncognitive selection test. *Journal of Applied Psychology, 82*(2), 293–299.

Prien, E. P., Jones, M. A., & Miller, L. M. (1977). A job-related performance rating system. *Personnel Administrator, 22,* 1–6.

Prizmic, Z., & Kaliterna, L. (1995). Relationship between positive and negative affect and measures of tolerance to shiftwork. *Psychologia Croatica, 1*(3–4), 155–164.

Prochaske, J. O. (1993). I think we can. *Professional Psychology Research and Practice, 24,* 250–251.

Propp, K. M. (1997). Information utilization in small group decision making: A study of the evaluative interaction model. *Small Group Research, 28*(3), 424–453.

Pulakos, E. D. (1984). A comparison of rater training programs: Error training and accuracy training. *Journal of Applied Psychology, 69*(3), 581–588.

Pulakos, E. D. (1986). The development of training programs to increase accuracy with different rating tasks. *Organizational Behavior and Human Decision Processes, 38,* 76–91.

Pulakos, E. D., White, L., Oppler, S., & Borman, W. C. (1989). Examination of race and sex effects on performance ratings. *Journal of Applied Psychology, 74*(5), 770–780.

Putti, J. M. (1989). Organization development scene in Asia: The case of Singapore. *Group and Organization Studies, 14*(3), 262–270.

Pynes, J. E., Harrick, E. J., & Schaefer, D. (1997). A concurrent validity study applied to a secretarial position in a state universities civil service system. *Journal of Business and Psychology, 12*(1), 3–18.

R & D Magazine. (1997, February). Virtual labs speed product designs. 39, 24–26.

Raber, M. J. (1994). Women in the workplace: Implications for childcare. *Employee Assistance Quarterly, 9*(3–4), 21–36.

Rabin, A. T. (1992). Consequences of adult illiteracy reach far into the marketplace. *Occupational Health & Safety, 61*, 36.

Racicot, B. M., & Wogalter, M. S. (1995). Effects of a video warning and social modeling on behavioral compliance. *Accident Analysis and Prevention, 27*(1), 57–64.

Rae, L. (1994, April). Training 101: Choose your method. *Training and Development, 48*, 19–25.

Rafaeli, A., & Klimoski, R. J. (1983). Predicting sales success through handwriting analysis: An evaluation of the effects of training and handwriting sample content. *Journal of Applied Psychology, 68*(2), 212–217.

Rafferty, A. (1990, August). Tailor-made profiles ease performance reviews. *HRMagazine, 35*, 31–34.

Ragins, B. R., & Cotton, J. L. (1991). Easier said than done: Gender differences in perceived barriers to gaining a mentor. *Academy of Management Journal, 34*, 939–951.

Rahim, M. A., & Afza, M. (1993). Leader power, commitment, satisfaction, compliance, and propensity to leave a job among U.S. accountants. *Journal of Social Psychology, 133*(5), 611–625.

Raju, N. S., Steinhaus, S. D., Edwards, J. E., & DeLessio, J. (1991). A logistic regression model for personnel selection. *Applied Psychological Measurement, 15*(2), 139–152.

Ralston, G. (1997, April). Using videoconferencing for recruiting and training. *Telemarketing & Call Center Solutions, 15*, 68–69.

Ralston, S. M., & Brady, R. (1994). The relative influence of interview communication satisfaction on applicants' recruitment interview decisions. *Journal of Business Communications, 31*, 61–77.

Ramsey, R. D. (1994, August). Violence on the job: How safe is your workplace? *Supervision, 55*, 6–9.

Ramsey, R. D. (1996, September). Managing noise in the workplace. *Supervision, 57*, 3–5.

Rao, A., Hashimoto, K., & Rao, A. (1997). Universal and culturally specific aspects of managerial influence: A study of Japanese managers. *Leadership Quarterly, 8*(3), 295–312.

Rao, G. B., & Rao, S. S. (1997). Sector and age differences in productivity. *Social Science International, 13*(1–2), 51–56.

Rapp, B. (1978, May). You asked for it — but did you get it? *Public Management*, pp. 8–11.

Raven, B. H. (1992). A power/interaction model of interpersonal influence: French and Raven thirty years later. *Journal of Social Behavior and Personality, 7*, 217–244.

Reber, R. A., Wallin, J. A., & Duhon, D. L. (1993). Preventing occupational injuries through performance management. *Public Personnel Management, 22*(2), 301–311.

Reh, F. J. (1999, May 10) What good people really cost. http://management.about.com

Reich, J. W., & Zautra, A. J. (1997). Locus of control influences diathesis-stress effects in rheumatoid arthritis patients. *Journal of Research in Personality, 31*(3), 423–438.

Rentsch, J. R. (1990). Climate and culture: Interaction and qualitative differences in organizational meanings. *Journal of Applied Psychology, 75*(6), 668–681.

Rice, F. (1994, August 8). How to make diversity pay. *Fortune, 130*, 27–32.

Rice, R. W. (1978). Psychometric properties of the esteem for least preferred co-worker (LPC) scale. *Academy of Management Review, 3*, 106–118.

Riggio, R. E., & Sotoodeh, Y. (1987, August). Screening tests for use in hiring microassemblers. *Perceptual and Motor Skills, 65*(1), 167–172.

Robbins, T. L. (1995). Social loafing on cognitive tasks: An examination of the "sucker effect." *Journal of Business Psychology, 9*(3), 337–345.

Roberts, P. (1998, April). Humane technology—PeopleSoft. *Fast Company, 14*, 122.

Robertson, P. J., Roberts, D. R., & Porras, J. I. (1993). Dynamics of planned organizational change: Assessing empirical support for a theoretical model. *Academy of Management Journal, 36*(3), 619–634.

Rockwood, G. F. (1993). Edgar Schein's process versus content consultation models. *Journal of Counseling and Development, 71*, 636–638.

Rodgers, R., & Hunter, J. E. (1991). Impact of management by objectives on organizational productivity. *Journal of Applied Psychology, 76*(2), 322–336.

Roethlisberger, F. J., & Dickson, W. J. (1939). *Management and the worker.* Cambridge, MA: Harvard University Press.

Rogers, B. (1995, February). Creating a culture of safety. *HR Magazine, 40*, 85–88.

Rome, H. P., Swenson, W. M., Mataya, P., McCarthy, C. E., Pearson, J. S., Keating, F. R., & Hathway, S. R. (1962). Symposium on automation techniques in personality assessment. *Proceedings of Staff Meetings of the Mayor Clinic, 37*, 61–82.

Rosenberg, S. O. (1993–1994). A job training partnership with Lone Star Steel and Northeast Texas Community College. *Employment Relations Today, 20*, 391–397.

Rosener, J. B. (November–December 1990). Ways women lead. *Harvard Business Review, 68*, 119–125.

Rosenfeld, P., Edwards, J. E., & Thomas, M. D. (Eds.). (1993). *Improving organizational surveys: New directions, methods, and applications.* Newbury Park, CA: Sage.

Rosenman, R. H. (1978). The interview method of assessment of the coronary-prone behavior pattern. In T. M. Dembroski, S. M. Weiss, J. L. Shields, S. G. Haynes, & M. Feinlib (Eds.), *Coronary-prone behavior* (pp. 55–69). New York: Springer-Verlag.

Rosenthal, R. (1990). How are we doing in soft psychology? *American Psychologist, 45*, 775–777.

Rosnow, R. L. (1991). Inside rumor: A personal journey. Meeting of the Eastern Psychological Association (Philadelphia, PA). *American Psychologist, 46*(5), 484–496.

Rosnow, R. L., & Rosenthal, R. (1989). Statistical procedures and the justification of knowledge in psychological science. *American Psychologist, 44*, 1276–1284.

Ross, L. (1977). The intuitive psychologist and his shortcomings: Distortions in the attribution process. In L. Berkowitz (Ed.), *Advances in experimental social psychology* (Vol. 10; pp. 174–221). New York: Academic Press.

Ross, S. M., & Offerman, L. R. (1997). Transformational leaders: Measurement of personality attributes and work group performance. *Personality and Social Psychology Bulletin, 23*(10), 1078–1086.

Roth, D. (1998, July 6). First: From poster boy to whipping boy. *Fortune*, pp. 28–29.

Rowe, P. M. (1989). Unfavorable information and interview decisions. In R. W. Eder & G. R. Ferris (Eds.), *The employment interview* (pp. 77–89). Newbury Park, CA: Sage.

Royal, K. E., & Austin, J. (1992). Evaluation of hypothetical company recruiter by management students. *Psychological Reports, 70*(1), 89–90.

Rozier, C. K. (1977). Three dimensional work space for the amputee. *Human Factors, 19*(6), 525–533.

Rudner, L. M. (1992, Summer). Pre-employment testing and employee productivity. *Public Personnel Management. 2*(2), 133–150.

Russell, C. J., Colella, A., & Bobko, P. (1993). Expanding the context of utility: The strategic impact of personnel selection. *Personnel Psychology, 46*(4), 781–801.

Russell, C. J., Mattson, J., Devlin, S. E., & Atwater, D. (1990). Predictive validity of biodata items generated from retrospective life-experience essays. *Journal of Applied Psychology, 75*(5), 569–580.

Russell, J. E. (1991). Career development interventions in organizations. *Journal of Vocational Behavior, 38*(3), 237–287.

Ryan, A. M. & Sackett, P. R. (1987). Pre-employment honesty testing: Fakeability, reactions of test takers, and company image, *Journal of Business and Psychology, 1*, 248–256.

Ryan, A. M., & Sackett, P. R. (1987). A survey of individual assessment practices by I/O psychologists. *Personnel Psychology, 40*(3), 455–488.

Ryan, A. M., Gregouras, G. J., & Ployhart, R. E. (1996). Perceived job relatedness of physical ability testing for firefighters: Exploring variations in reactions. *Human Performance, 9*(3), 219–240.

Ryan, C. M., & Morrow, L. A. (1992). Dysfunctional buildings or dysfunctional people: An examination of the sick building syndrome and allied disorders. *Journal of Consulting and Clinical Psychology, 60*(2), 220–224.

Ryanen, I. A. (1988, December). Commentary of a minor bureaucrat. Special Issue: Fairness in Employment Testing. *Journal of Vocational Behavior, 33*(3), 379–387.

Rynes, S. L., Bretz, R. D., & Gerhart, B. (1991). The importance of recruitment in job choice: A different way of looking. *Personnel Psychology, 44*(3), 487–521.

Rynes, S., & Rosen, B. (1995, Summer). A field survey of factors affecting the adoption and perceived success of diversity training. *Personnel Psychology, 48*, 247–270.

Saarela, K. L. (1989). A poster campaign for improving safety on shipyard scaffolds. *Journal of Safety Research, 20*(4), 177–185.

Saari, L. M., Johnson, T. R., McLaughlin, S., & Zimmerle, D. M. (1988). A survey of management training and education practices in U.S. companies. *Personnel Psychology, 41*, 731–743.

Sachdev, P. (1997). Cultural sensitivity training through experiential learning: A participatory demonstration field education project. *International Social Work, 40*(1), 7–25.

Sackett, P. R., Burris, L. R., & Callahan, C. (1989). Integrity testing for personnel selection: An update. *Personnel Psychology, 42*, 491–529.

Sackett, P. R., & DuBois, C. L. (1991). Rater-ratee race effects on performance evaluation: Challenging meta-analytic conclusions. *Journal of Applied Psychology, 76*(6), 873–877.

Sackett, P. R., & Harris, M. M. (1988). Honesty testing for personnel selection: A review and critique. *Personnel Psychology, 37*, 221–245.

Sackett, P. R., & Mullen, E. J. (1993). Beyond formal experimental design: Towards an expanded view of the training evaluation process. *Personnel Psychology, 46*, 613–627.

Saks, A. M. (1989). An examination of the combined effects of realistic job previews, job attractiveness, and recruiter affect on job acceptance decisions. *Applied Psychology: An International Review, 38*(2), 145–163.

Sales and Marketing Management. (1992, April). What does body language really say? *144*, 40.

Sanchez, J. I., & Brock, P. (1996). Outcomes of perceived discrimination among Hispanic employees: Is diversity management a luxury or a necessity? *Academy of Management Journal, 39*(3), 704–719.

Sanchez, M. E., & Morchio, G. (1992). Probing "don't know" answers: Effects on survey estimates and variable relationships. *Public Opinion Quarterly, 56*, 454–474.

Sanders, M. S., & McCormick, E. J. (1993). *Human factors in engineering and design* (7th ed.). New York: McGraw-Hill.

Sanders, R. L. (1997, January). The future of the bureaucracy. *Records Management Quarterly, 31*, 44–46.

Sanford, A., Hunt, G., & Bracey, H. (1976). *Communication behavior in the organization.* Columbus, OH: Charles E. Merril.

Sarkis, K. (2000, May). Computer workers at risk for stress injuries. *Occupational Hazards, 62*(5), 33.

Satterfield, M. (1991, February). The six most common recruiting mistakes. *Journal of Accountancy, 171*, 97–100.

Savery, L. K., & Wooden, M. (1994). The relative influence of life events and hassles on work-related injuries: Some Australian evidence. *Human Relations, 47*(3), 283–305.

Saville, P. (1984). Purpose-made personality questionnaires. *Personnel Management, 16*, 47.

Schappe, S. P. (1998). The influence of job satisfaction, organizational commitment, and fairness perceptions on organizational citizenship behavior. *Journal of Psychology, 132*(3), 227–290.

Schaubroeck, J., Ganster, D. C., & Kemmerer, B. E. (1994). Job complexity, Type A behavior, and cardiovascular disorder: A prospective study. *Academy of Management Journal, 37*, 426–439.

Schein, E. (1985). *Organizational culture and leadership.* San Francisco: Jossey-Bass.

Schein, E. H. (1969). *Process consultation: Its role in organizational development.* Reading, MA: Addison-Wesley.

Schein, E. H. (1990). Organizational culture. Special issue: Organizational Psychology. *American Psychologist, 45*(2), 109–119.

Schein, V. E. (1973). The relationship between sex role stereotypes and requisite management characteristics. *Journal of Applied Psychology, 57*(1), 95–100.

Scherer, R. F., Brodzinski, J. D., & Crable, E. A. (1993, April). The human factor. *HRMagazine, 38*, 92–93.

Schmidt, F. L. (1973). Implications of a measurement problem for expectancy theory research. *Organizational Behavior and Human Performance, 10*, 243–251.

Schmidt, F. L. (1992). What do data really mean? Research findings, meta-analysis and cumulative knowledge in psychology. *American Psychologist, 47*, 1173–1181.

Schmidt, F. L., Law, K., Hunter, J. E., & Rothstein, H. R. (1993). Refinements in validity generalization methods: Implications for the situational specificity hypothesis. *Journal of Applied Psychology. 78*(1), 3–12.

Schmidt, F. L., Ones, D. S., & Hunter, J. E. (1992). Personnel selection. *Annual Review of Psychology, 43*, 627–670.

Schmidt, F. L., & Robertson, I. (1990). Personnel selection. *Annual Review of Psychology, 41*, 289–319.

Schmidt, W. C. (1997). World Wide Web survey research: Benefits, potential problems and solutions. *Behavioral Research Methods, Instruments, and Computers, 29*(2), 274–279.

Schmitt, N., Gilliland, S. W., Landis, R. S., & Devine, D. (1993). Computer-based testing applied to selection of secretarial applicants. *Personnel Psychology, 46*(1), 149–165.

Schmitt, N., Gooding, R. Z., Noe, R. D., & Kirsch, M. (1984). Meta-analyses of validity studies published between 1964 and 1982 and the investigation of study characteristics. *Personnel Psychology, 37*, 407–422.

Schnake, M., & Dumler, M. P. (1997). Organizational citizenship behavior: The impact of rewards and reward practices. *Journal of Managerial Issues, 9*(2), 216–229.

Schnake, M. E. (1990). Effects of differences in superior and subordinate perceptions of superiors' communication practices. *Journal of Business Communications, 27*(1), 37–50.

Schneider, B., Brief, A. P., & Guzzo, R. A. (1996). Creating a climate and culture for sustained organizational change. *Organizatonal Dynamics 24*(4), 7–19.

Schriesheim, C. A. (1997). Substitutes for leadership theory: Development and basic concepts. *Leadership Quarterly, 8*(2), 103–108.

Schriesheim, C. A., Tepper, B. J., & Tetrault, L. A. (1994). Least preferred coworker score, situational control and leadership effectiveness: A meta-analysis of contingency model performance predictions. *Journal of Applied Psychology, 79*(4), 561–573.

Schwartz, D. F. (1986, May 22–26). *A systems theory view of organizations as communications networks.* Paper presented at the Annual Meeting of the International Communication Association, Chicago, IL.

Schwartz, F. N. (1989, January–February). Management women and the new facts of life. *Harvard Business Review, 67*(1), 65–76.

Schwepker, C. H., Jr., Ferrell, O. C., & Ingram, T. N. (1997). The influence of ethical climate and ethical conflict on role stress in the salesforce. *Journal of the Academy of Marketing Science, 25*(2), 99–108.

Scott, C. (1992, February 21–25). *Using group decision support systems in teaching the small group communication course.* Paper presented at the 63rd Annual Meeting of the Western States Communication Association, Boise, ID.

Scott, W. D. (1903). *The theory of advertising.* Boston: Small, Maynard.

Scrinivasan, R., & Jovanis, P. P. (1997). Effect of selected in-vehicle route guidance systems on driver reaction times. *Human Factors, 39*(2), 200–215.

Selye, H. (1976). *The stress of life* (rev. ed.). New York: McGraw-Hill.

Shahani, C. (1987). Industrial accidents: Does age matter? In *Proceedings of the Human Factors Society 31st annual meeting* (pp. 553–557). Santa Monica, CA: Human Factors Society.

Shangraw, R. F. (1986). Telephone surveying with computers: Administrative, methodological and research issues. *Evaluation and Program Planning, 9,* 107–111.

Sharpe, D., Adair, J. G., & Roese, N. J. (1992). Twenty years of deception research: A decline in subjects' trust. *Personality and Social Psychology Bulletin, 18,* 585–590.

Shartle, C. L. (1956). *Executive performance and leadership.* Englewood Cliffs, NJ: Prentice-Hall.

Shaw, M. E. (1978). Communication networks fourteen years later. In L. Berkowitz (Ed.), *Group processes* (pp. 351–360). New York: Academic Press.

Shepard, J. A. (1993). Productivity loss in performance groups: A motivation analysis. *Psychological Bulletin, 113*(1), 67–81.

Sheridan, J. E. (1992). Organizational culture and employee retention. *Academy of Management Journal, 35*(5), 1036–1056.

Shihadeh-Gomaa, A. (1998, January). The right fit: Matching employees and workstations. *Risk Management, 45,* 37–38.

Shimberg, B. (1981). Testing for licensure and certification. *American Psychologist, 36,* 1138–1146.

Shipper, F., & Wilson, C. L. (1991, July). *The impact of managerial behaviors on group performance, stress and commitment.* Paper presented at the Impact of Leadership Conference, Center for Creative Leadership, Colorado Springs, CO.

Siding, T., Larsen, H. H., Gironda, L. A., & Sorenson, P. F. (1994). Back to the future: A pendulum in organization development. *Organization Development Journal, 12*(2), 71–83.

Silver, E. M., & Bennett, C. (1987). Modification of the Minnesota Clerical Test to predict performance on video display terminals. *Journal of Applied Psychology. 72*(1), 153–155.

Silverman, S. B., & Wexley, K. N. (1984). Reaction of employees to performance appraisal interviews as a function of their participation in rating scale development. *Personnel Psychology, 37,* 703–710.

Simon, S. J., & Werner, J. M. (1996). Computer training through behavior modeling, self-paced and instructional approaches: A field experiment. *Journal of Applied Psychology, 81*(6), 648–659.

Sims, H. P., & Manz, C. C. (1984). Observing leader behavior: Toward a reciprocal determinism in leadership theory. *Journal of Applied Psychology, 69*(2), 222–232.

Sims, R. L., & Keon, T. L. (1997, August). Ethical work climate as a factor in the development of person–organization fit. *Journal of Business Ethics, 16*(11), 1095–1105.

Smith, B. (1995, January). Psychics add new dimension in recruitment. *HRFocus, 72,* 3.

Smith, B. N., Hornsby, J. S., & Shirmeyer, R. (1996, Summer). Current trends in performance appraisal: An examination of management practice. *Advanced Management Journal, 61,* 10–15.

Smith, D. L., Petruzzello, S. J., Kramer, J. M., & Misner, J. E. (1997). The effects of different thermal environments on the physiological responses of firefighters to a training drill. *Ergonomics, 40*(4), 500–510.

Smith, L., & Folkard, S. (1993). The perceptions and feelings of shiftworkers' partners. *Ergonomics, 36*(1), 299–305.

Smith, M. J., Anger, W. K., & Uslan, S. S. (1978). Behavioral modification applied to occupational safety. *Journal of Safety Research, 10*, 87–88.

Smith, P. C., & Kendall, L. M. (1963). Retranslation of expectations: An approach to the construction of unambiguous anchors for rating scales. *Journal of Applied Psychology, 47*(1), 149–155.

Smith, P. C., Kendall, L. M., & Hulin, C. L. (1969). *Measurement of satisfaction in work and retirement.* Chicago: Rand McNally.

Smith, S. S., & Richardson, D. (1985). On deceiving ourselves about deception: Reply to Rubin. *Journal of Personality and Social Psychology, 48*, 254–255.

Smith, T. L. (1995). The resource center: Finding solutions for illiteracy. *HR Focus, 72*, 7.

Smith, T. W., & Pope, M. K. (1990). Cynical hostility as a health risk: Current status and future directions. *Journal of Social Behavior and Personality, 5*, 77–88.

Smyth, K. A., & Yardani, H. N. (1992). A path model of Type A and Type B responses to coping and stress in employed black women. *Nursing Research, 41*(5), 260–265.

Sohn, D. (1996). Meta-analysis and science. *Theory and Psychology, 6*(2), 229–246.

Sokal, M. M. (1987). *Psychological testing and American society: 1890–1930.* New Brunswick, NJ: Rutgers University Press.

Solano, L., Battisti, M., & Stanisci, S. (1993). Effects of some psychological variables on different disease manifestations in 112 cadets: A longitudinal study. *Journal of Psychosomatic Research, 37*(6), 621–636.

Solomon, R. L. (1949). An extension of control group design. *Psychological Bulletin, 46*, 137–150.

Somers, M. J., & Birnbaum, D. (1991). Assessing self-appraisal of job performance as an evaluation device: Are the poor results a function of methods or methodology? *Human Relations, 44*(10), 1018–1091.

Sonnenfeld, J. (1982). Clarifying critical confusion in the Hawthorne hysteria. *American Psychologist, 37*, 1397–1399.

Sorensen, R., & Franklin, G. M. (1992, August). Teamwork developed a successful appraisal system. *HRFocus, 69*, 3–4.

Sothmann, M., Saupe, K., Jasenof, D., Blaney, J., & Furhman, S. (1990). Advancing age and the cardiorespiratory stress of fire suppression: Determining a minimum standard for aerobic fitness. *Human Performance, 3*, 217–236.

Southerst, J. (1992). Kenworth's gray revolution. *Canadian Business, 65*, 74–76.

Spangler, W. D. (1992). Validity of questionnaire and TAT measures of need for achievement: Two meta-analyses. *Psychological Bulletin, 112*(1), 140–154.

Spangler, W. D., & House, R. J. (1991). Presidential effectiveness and the leadership motive profile. *Journal of Personality and Social Psychology, 60*(3), 439–455.

Spokane, A. R., & Jacob, E. J. (1996). Career and vocational assessment 1993–1994: A biennial review. *Journal of Career Assessment, 4*(1), 1–32.

Spychalski, A. C., Quinones, M. A., Gaugler, B. B., & Pohley, K. (1997). A survey of assessment center practices in organizations in the United States. *Personnel Psychology, 50*(1), 71–90.

Stamps, D. (1995, April). Cyberinterviews combat turnover. *Training, 32*, 43–47.

Stano, M. (1983, May). *Guidelines for the interviewee in the performance appraisal interview.* Paper presented at the annual meeting of the International Communication Association, Dallas, TX.

Stauffer, M. (1992). Technological change and the older employee: Implications for introduction and training. *Behaviour and Information Technology, 11*(1), 46–52.

Staw, B. M., Bell, N. E., & Clausen, J. A. (1986). The dispositional approach to job attitudes: A lifetime longitudinal test. *Administrative Science Quarterly, 31*, 56–77.

Stecklow, S. (1998, April 1). Minorities fall at universities in California. *Wall Street Journal*, p. A3.

Stedham, Y., & Mitchell, M. C. (1996). Voluntary turnover among non-supervisory casino employees. *Journal of Gambling Studies, 12*(3), 269–290.

Steers, R. M., & Porter, L. W. (Eds.). (1991). *Motivation and work behavior.* New York: McGraw-Hill.

Steiner, D. D., & Gilliland, S. W. (1996). Fairness reactions to personnel selection techniques in France and the United States. *Journal of Applied Psychology, 81*(2), 134–141.

Steinhauer, J. (1995, April 2). It's "The Gap" once you're hired, but job hunters must spiff it up: Interview suits are still navy after all these years. *New York Times*, Section 3, p. 13.

Stephens, C., & Smith, M. (1996). Occupational overuse syndrome: The effects of psychosocial stressors on keyboard users in the newspaper industry. *Work and Stress, 10*(2), 141–153.

Stern, A. L. (1995). A study in diplomacy. *Across the Board, 32*, 20–24.

Stone, W. S., & Allen, M. W. (1990). Assessing the impact of new communication technologies on organizational dynamics. *Consultation: An International Journal, 9*(3), 229–240.

Stroebe,W., & Diehl, M. (1991). You can't beat good experiments with correlational evidence: Mullen, Johnson and Salas' meta-analytic misinterpretations. *Basic and Applied Social Psychology, 12*(1), 25–32.

Stroman, C. A., & Seltzer, R. (1991). Racial differences in coping with job stress; A research note. *Journal of Social Behavior and Personality, 6*(7), 309–318.

Strube, M. J., & Garcia, J. E. (1981). A meta-analytic investigation of Fiedler's contingency model of leadership effectiveness. *Psychological Bulletin, 90*, 307–321.

Stuller, J. (1993). Why not inplacement? *Training, 30*, 37–41.

Stumpf, S. A., & Hartman, K. (1984). Individual exploration to organizational commitment or withdrawal. *Academy of Management Journal, 27*, 308–329.

Sulzer-Azaroff, B., Loafman, B., Merante, R. J., & Hlavacek, A. C. (1990). Improving occupational safety in a large industrial plant: A systematic replication. *Journal of Organizational Behavior Management, 11*(1), 99–120.

Sumerlin, J. A., & Bundrick, C. M. (1996). Brief Index of Self-Actualization: A measure of Maslow's model. *Journal of Social Behavior and Personality, 11*(2), 253–271.

Summers, T. P., & DeNisi, A. S. (1990). In search of Adam's other: Reexamination of referents used in the evaluation of pay. *Human Relations, 43*(6), 497–511.

Super, D. E. (1992). Career development and planning in organizations. In B. B. Bass, P. J. D. Drenth, & P. Weisenberg (Eds.), *Advances in organizational psychology: A review* (pp. 83–98). Newbury Park, CA: Sage.

Supervision. (1998, March). Multirater feedback and performance evaluations do not mix. *59*, 25.

Suszko, M. K., & Breaugh, J. A. (1986, Winter). The effects of realistic job previews on applicant self-selection and employee turnover, satisfaction and copy ability. *Journal of Management, 12*, 513–523.

Sutton, R. I., & Rafaeli, A. (1987). Characteristics of work stations as potential occupational stressors. *Academy of Management Journal, 30*, 260–276.

Suutari, V. (1996). Leadership ideologies among European managers: A comparative survey in a multinational company. *Scandinavian Journal of Management, 12*(4), 389–409.

Swanson, R. A., & Law, B. D. (1993). Whole-part-whole-learning model. European Conference on Educational Research (1992, Enschede, Netherlands). *Performance Improvement Quarterly, 6*(1), 43–53.

Sweeney, J. C., Soutar, G. N., Hausknecht, D. R., Dallin, R. F., & Johnson, L. W. (1997). Collecting information from groups: A comparison of two methods. *Journal of the Market Research Society, 39*(2), 397–411.

Sweeney, P. D. (1990). Distributive justice and pay satisfaction: A field test of an equity theory prediction. *Journal of Business and Psychology, 4*(3), 329–341.

Szabo, J. C. (1992). Boosting workers' basic skills. *Nation's Business, 80*, 38–40.

Tannenbaum, S. I., Mathieu, J. E., Salas, E., & Cannon-Bowers, J. A. (1991). Meeting trainees' expectations: The influence of training fulfillment on the development of commitment, self-efficacy and motivation. *Journal of Applied Psychology, 76*(6), 759–769.

Tannenbaum, S. I., & Yukl, G. (1992). Training and development in work organizations. *Annual Review of Psychology, 43*, 399–441.

Tayeb, M. (1994). Organizations and national culture: Methodology considered. *Organizational Studies, 15*(3), 429–446.

Taylor, F. W. (1911). *The principles of scientific management.* New York: Harper.

Taylor, F. W. (1947). *Principles of scientific management.* New York: Harper. (Original work published 1911)

Taylor, G. S. (1994). The relationship between sources of new employees and attitudes toward the job. *Journal of Social Psychology, 134*(1), 99–110.

Taylor, G. S., & Zimmerer, T. W. (1988). Personality tests for potential employees: More harm than good. *Personnel Journal, 67*, 60–61.

Taylor, H. (1997). The very different methods to conduct telephone surveys of the public. *Journal of the Market Research Society, 39*(3), 421–432.

Taylor, R. W. (1996). The rockem-sockem workplace. *Labor Newsletter, 26*, 6–9.

Tenopyr, M. L. (1981). The realities of employment testing. *American Psychologist, 36*, 1120–1127.

Terpestra, D. E. (1996, May). The search for effective methods. *HR Focus, 73*, 16–17.

Terpestra, D. E., & Baker, D. D. (1992). Outcomes of federal court decisions on sexual harassment. *Academy of Management Review, 35*, 185–194.

Tesser, A., & Rosen, S. (1975). The reluctance to transmit bad news. *Advances in Experimental Social Psychology, 8*, 192–232.

Tett, R. P., & Meyer, J. P. (1993). Job satisfaction, organizational commitment, turnover intention, and turnover: Path analyses based on meta-analytic findings. *Personnel Psychology, 46*, 259–293.

Thacker, J. W., & Fields, M. W. (1987). Union involvement in quality of worklife efforts: A longitudinal investigation. *Personnel Psychology, 40*(1), 97–111.

Thacker, R. A. (1992). Preventing sexual harassment in the workplace. *Training and Development, 46*, 50–53.

Tharenou, P. (1993). A test of reciprocal causality for absenteeism. *Journal of Organizational Behavior, 14*(3), 269–287.

Thatcher, M. (1997, May 15). A test of character. *People Management, 3*, 34–35+.

The Economist. (1990, June 16). Information technology: The ubiquitous machine. *315*(7659), 1–20. (Special Survey Section).

The Wall Street Journal (1999, June 17). Sears faces another suit on auto work, p. A3.

Theorell, T. (1990). Family history of hypertension: An individual trait interacting with spontaneously occurring job stressors. *Scandinavian Journal of Work, Environment and Health, 116*(Suppl 1), 74–79.

Thomas, S. L., & Bretz, R. D. (1994, Spring). Research and practice in performance appraisal: Evaluating employee performance in America's largest companies. *SAM Advanced Management Journal, 59*, 28–34.

Thomas, T. (1991, October). Knowing when to brainstorm solo. *Supervisory Management, 36*, 5.

Thompson, K. D. (1992). Back to school. *Black Enterprise, 21*, 56–57.

Thornburg, L. (1993, July). When violence hits business. *HRMagazine, 38*, 40–45.

Thornburg, L. (1998, February). Computer assisted interviewing shortens hiring cycle. *HRMagazine, 43*, 73.

Thorndike, R. L. (1949). *Personnel selection: Test and measurement technique.* New York: Wiley.

Tichy, N. M. (1962). *Managing strategic change.* New York: Wiley.

Tiegs, R. B., Tetrick, L. E., & Fried, Y. (1992). Growth need strength and context satisfactions as moderators of the rela-

tions of the job characteristics model. *Journal of Management, 18*(3), 575–593.

Ting, Y. (1997). Determinants of job satisfaction in federal government employees. *Public Personnel Management, 26*(3), 313–334.

TIP. (1998, June). What is an I/O psychologist? www.siop.org/tip/backissues/tipjune98.

Todorov, E., Shadmehr, R., & Bizzi, E. (1997). Augmented feedback presented in a virtual environment accelerates learning of a difficult motor task. *Journal of Motor Behavior, 29*(2), 147–158.

Tokar, D. M., & Subich, L. M. (1997). Relative contributions of congruence and personality dimensions to job satisfaction. *Journal of Vocational Behavior, 50*(3), 482–491.

Tomkiewicz, J., & Brenner, O. C. (1996). The relationship between race [Hispanic] stereotypes and requisite management characteristics. *Journal of Social Behavior and Personality, 11*(3), 511–520.

Tomkiewicz, J., Brenner, O. C., & Adeyemi, B. T. (1998). The impact of perceptions and stereotypes on the managerial mobility of African-Americans. *Journal of Social Behavior, 138*(1), 88–92.

Training and Development. (1995, June). Texas instruments gets from here to there. *49*, 40–41.

Training and Development. (1998, January). The 1998 ASTD state of the industry report. *52*, 1–8.

Training. (1991). Is quality priority one? *28*, 88.

Training. (1992, November). Workplace weather report: Partly cloudy. *29*, 68.

Training. (1994). Needs assessment software. *31*, 69.

Training. (1994, February). Learning English on company time. *31*, 64.

Treiman, D. J. (1979). *Job evaluation: An analytic review.* Washington, DC: National Academy of Sciences.

Trevino, L. K., Daft, R. L., & Lengel, R. H. (1987). Media symbolism, media richness and median choice in organizations: A symbolic interactionist perspective. *Communications Research, 14*, 553–574.

Trevino, L. K., Lengel, R. H., Bodensteiner, W., Gerloff, E., & Muir, N. K. (1990). The richness imperative and cognitive style: The role of individual differences in media choice behavior. *Management Communication Quarterly, 4*, 176–197.

Trice, H. M., & Beyer, J. M. (1993) *The cultures of work organizations.* Englewood Cliffs, NJ: Prentice-Hall.

Trist, E. L., & Bamforth, K. W. (1951). Some social and psychological consequences of the longwall method of coal-getting. *Human Relations, 4*, 3–38.

Tseo, G. K., & Ramos, E. L. (1995). Employee empowerment: Solution to a burgeoning crisis. *Challenge, 38*, 25–31.

Turban, D. B., & Dougherty, T. W. (1992). Influences of campus recruiting on applicant attraction to firms. *Academy of Management Journal, 35*(4), 739–765.

Turban, D. B., Jones, A. P., & Rozelle, R. M. (1990). Influences of supervisor liking of a subordinate and the reward context on the treatment and evaluation of that subordinate. *Motivation and Emotion, 14*(3), 215–233.

Turban, E. (1995). *Decision support and expert systems*. Englewood Cliffs, NJ: Prentice-Hall.

Turnage, J. J. (1990). The challenge of workplace technology for psychology. Special Issue: Organizational Psychology. *American Psychologist, 45*, 171–178.

Turner, J. S., & Helms, D. B. (1986). *Contemporary adulthood* (3rd ed.). New York: Holt, Rinehart & Winston.

Turner, M. E. (1992). Group effectiveness under threat: The impact of structural centrality and performance set. *Journal of Social Behavior and Personality, 7*(4), 511–528.

Twisleton, M. (1992). Implementing an appraisal system: A cautionary but honest tale. *Educational Psychology in Practice, 8*(3), 172–177.

Tyler, K. (1998). Take new employee orientation off the back burner. *HRMagazine, 43*(6), 49–57.

U.S. Bureau of Labor Statistics (1996, September 11). Labor force statistics from the current population survey: http://www.bls.census.gov/cps/pub/empsit_feb2000.htm.

U.S. Congress, Office of Technology Assessment. (1990). *The use of integrity tests for pre-employment screening* (OTA-SET-442). Washington, DC: U.S. Government Printing Office.

Umstot, D. D., Bell, C. H., & Mitchell, T. R. (1976). Effects of job enrichment and task goals on satisfaction and productivity: Implications for job design. *Journal of Applied Psychology, 61*(4), 379–394.

Valacich, J. S., Dennis, A. R., & Connolly, T. (1994). Idea generation in computer-based groups: A new ending to an old story. *Organizational Behavior and Human Decision Processes, 57*, 448–467.

Vale, C. D., Keller, L. S., & Bentz, V. J. (1986). Development and validation of a computerized interpretation system for personnel tests. *Personnel Psychology, 39*, 525–542.

Van De Water, T. J. (1997). Psychology's entrepreneurs and the marketing of industrial psychology. *Journal of Applied Psychology, 82*(4), 486–499.

Van Erde, W., & Thierry, H. (1996). Vroom's expectancy models and work-related criteria: A meta-analysis. *Journal of Applied Psychology, 81*(5), 575–586.

Van Yparen, N. W., Hagedoorn, M., & Gaurts, S. A. E. (1996). Intent to leave and absenteeism as reactions to perceived inequity: The role of social constraints. *Journal of Occupational and Organizational Psychology, 69*(4), 367–372.

van der Heever, P. K., & Coetsee, L. D. (1998). An expert system-based audit instrument to assess organizational effectiveness. *Organizational Development Journal, 16*(1), 29–44.

Vandeberg, R. J., & Lance, C. E. (1992). Examining the causal order of job satisfaction and organizational commitment. *Journal of Management, 18*, 153–167.

Vansickle, T. R., Kimmel, C., & Kapea, J. T. (1989, July). Test-retest equivalency of the computer based and paper-pencil versions of the Strong-Campbell Interest Inventory. *Measurement and Evaluation in Counseling and Development, 22*(2), 88–93.

Vasse, R. M., Nijhuis, F. J., & Kok, G. (1998). Association between work stress, alcohol consumption and sickness absence. *Addiction, 93*(2), 231–241.

Vecchio, R. P. (1983). Assessing the validity of Fiedler's contingency model of leadership effectiveness: A closer look at Strube and Garcia. *Psychological Bulletin, 93*, 404–408.

Vecchio, R. P. (1990). Theoretical and empirical examination of cognitive resource theory. *Journal of Applied Psychology, 75*(1), 141–147.

Vecchio, R. P. (1992). Cognitive resource theory: Issues for specifying a test of the theory. *Journal of Applied Psychology, 77*(3), 375–376.

Vecchio, R. P. (1996). The influence of employee screening on employee attachment. *Employee Responsibilities and Rights Journal, 9*(2), 119–129.

Vega, A., & Gilbert, M. J. (1997, Fall). Longer days, shorter weeks: Compressed work weeks in policing. *Public Personnel Management, 26*, 391–402.

Verespej, M. A. (1993, June 21). People-first policies: Work flexibility has become a recruiting tool. *Industry Week, 242*, 20.

Verespej, M. A. (1994, April 18). A Pandora's box of ailments: ADA is working—but not in the way it was intended. *Industry Week, 243*, 61–62.

Verma, O. P., & Upadhyay, S. N. (1986). Organizational commitment, job involvement and job satisfaction. *Indian Journal of Current Psychological Research, 1*(1), 24–31.

Vink, P., & Kompier, M. A. J. (1997). Improving office work: A participatory ergonomics experiment in a naturalistic setting. *Ergonomics, 40*(4), 435–449.

Viswesvaran, C, Varrick, M. R., & Ones, D. S. (1993). How definitive are conclusions based on survey data? Estimating robustness to nonreponse. Special issue: Innovations in Research Methods for Field Settings. *Personnel Psychology, 46,* 551–657.

Vodanovich, S. J., & Lowe, R. H. (1992, Fall). They ought to know better: The incidence and correlates of inappropriate application blank inquiries. *Public Personnel Management, 21,* 363–370.

Von Bergen, C. W., Soper, B., & Rosenthal, G. T. (1996). The moderating effects of self-esteem and goal difficulty on performance. *College Student Journal, 30*(2), 262–267.

Vrij, A. (1993). Credibility judgments of detectives: The impact of nonverbal behavior, social skills, and physical characteristics on impression formation. *Journal of Social Psychology, 133*(5), 601–610.

Vrij, A., & Semin, G. R. (1996). Lie experts' beliefs about nonverbal indicators of deception. *Journal of Nonverbal Behavior, 20*(1), 65–80.

Vroom, V. H. (1964). *Work and motivation.* New York: Wiley.

Vroom, V. H., & Jago, A. G. (1988). *The new leadership: Managing participation in organizations.* Englewood Cliffs, NJ: Prentice-Hall.

Waddell, J. R. (1998, February). Looking for Mr./Ms. Right. *Supervision, 59,* 16–18.

Wages, C., Manson, T., & Jordan, J. J. (1990). Effects of applicant's adverse medical history on college students' ratings of job applications. *Journal of Applied Social Psychology, 20*(16, Pt. 2), 1322–1332.

Wagner, R. J., & Roland, C. C. (1992). How effective is outdoor training? *Training and Development, 46,* 61–62.

Wagner, R. K. (1997). Intelligence, training and employment. *American Psychologist, 52*(10), 1059–1069.

Wahba, M. A., & Bridwell, L. T. (1976). Maslow reconsidered: A review of research on the need of hierarchy theory. *Organizational Behavior and Human Performance, 15,* 212–240.

Waldman, D. A., & Avolio, B. J. (1991). Race effects in performance evaluations: Controlling for ability, education and experience. *Journal of Applied Psychology, 76*(6), 897–901.

Waldron, H. L. (1993). Continuing education—an investment for your future. *Journal of Systems Management, 44,* 41–42.

Waldrum, S. B., & Niemira, H. G. (1997, Winter). Age diversity in the workplace. *Employment Relations Today, 23,* 67–73.

Walker, C. J., & Blaine, B. (1991). The virulence of dread rumors: A field experiment. *Language and Communication, 11*(4), 291–297.

Walker, R. (1997, February). Back to the farm. *Fast Company, 7,* 110.

Wall Street Journal (1995, February 27). Doomed days: The worst mistakes recruiters have ever seen. p. R4.

Wall, T. D., Jackson, P. R., & Davids, K. (1992). Operator work design and robotics system performance: A serendipitous field study. *Journal of Applied Psychology, 77*(3), 353–362.

Wall, T. D., Kemp, N. J., Jackson, P. R., & Clegg, C. W. (1986). Outcomes of autonomous work groups. *Academy of Management Journal, 29*(2), 280–304.

Walter, K. (1996, April). Employee ideas make money. *HR Magazine, 41,* 36–39.

Walters, F. M. (1995, June 1). Successfully managing diversity [address, March 8, 1995] *Vital Speeches of the Day, 61,* 480–500.

Walther, J. B. (1993). Impression development in computer-based interaction. *Western Journal of Communication, 57*(4), 381–398.

Wanlin, C. M., Hrycaiko, D. W., Martin, G. L., & Mahon, M. (1997). The effects of a goal-setting package on the performance of speed skaters. *Journal of Applied Sport Psychology, 9*(2), 212–228.

Wanous, J. P., & Zwany, A. (1977). A cross-sectional test of need hierarchy theory. *Organizational Behavior and Human Performance, 18,* 78–97.

Wanous, J. P., Keon, T. L., & Latack, J. C. (1983). Expectancy theory and occupational/ organizational choices: A review and test. *Organizational Behavior and Human Performance, 32,* 66–86.

Wardell, M. (1989). Tayloristic paternalism: A critique of the OD management style. *Journal of Applied Behavioral Science, 25*(2), 123–125.

Warner, D. (1991). Rules on medical tests for new hires. *Nation's Business, 79,* 29–31.

Watson, W. E., & Behnke, R. R. (1991). Application of expectancy theory and user observations in identifying factors which affect human performance on computer projects. *Journal of Educational Computing Research, 7*(3), 363–376.

Waung, M., & Highhouse, S. (1997, July). Fear of conflict and empathetic buffering: Two explanations for the inflation of performance feedback. *Organizational Behavior and Human Decision Processes, 71*, 37–54.

Webb, G. R., Redman, S., Henrikus, D. J., & Kelman, G. R. (1994). The relationships between high-risk and problem drinking and the occurrence of work injuries and related absences. *Journal of Studies on Alcohol, 55*(4), 434–446.

Weber, M. (1947). *The theory of social and economic organization* (A. M. Henderson & T. Parsons, Trans.; T. Parsons, Ed.). New York: Free press. (Original work published 1924)

Webster, J., & Martocchio, J. J. (1993). Turning work into play: Implications for microcomputer software training. *Journal of Management, 19*(1), 127–146.

Weekley, J. A., & Gier, J. A. (1987). Reliability and validity of the situational interview for a sales position. *Journal of Applied Psychology, 72*(3), 484–487.

Weick, K. E. (1993). The collapse of sensemaking in organizations: The Mann Gulch disaster. *Administrative Science Quarterly, 38*(4), 628–652.

Weir, R., Stewart, L., Browne, G., Robert, J., Gafni, A., Easton, S., & Seymour, L. (1994). The efficacy and effectiveness of process consultation in improving staff morale and absenteeism. *Medical Care, 35*(4), 334–353.

Weisner, W. H., & Cronshaw, S. F. (1988). A meta-analytic investigation of the impact of interview format and degree of structure on the validity of the employment interview. *Journal of Occupational Psychology, 61*, 275–290.

Weiss, D. J., Dawis, R. V., England, G. W., & Lofquist, L. H. (1967). *Manual for the Minnesota Satisfaction Questionnaire* (Minnesota Studies on Vocational Rehabilitation, Vol. 22). Minneapolis: University of Minnesota Industrial Relations Center.

Weiss, N. (1998, August). How Starbucks impassions workers to drive growth. *Workforce, 28*, 60–64.

Welch, J. (1997, November). Few managers trust HR for career advice. *People Management, 3*, 12.

Wellins, R. S. (1992, December). Building a self-directed work team. *Training and Development, 46*, 24–28.

Wells, B., & Spinks, N. (1990). How companies are using employee self-evaluation forms. *Journal of Compensation & Benefits, 6*, 42–47.

Wells, S. J. (1997, June 15). Honey, they've shrunk the workweek. *New York Times*, Section 3, p. 9.

Wensky, A. H., & Galer, S. M. (1997, August). Helping employees help themselves. *HRMagazine, 42*, 96–98.

Werner, J. M., & Bolino, M. C. (1997). Explaining U.S. courts of appeals decisions involving performance appraisals: Accuracy, fairness and validation. *Personnel Psychology, 50*, 1–24.

Wexley, K. N., & Latham, G. P. (1981). *Developing and training human resources in organizations*. Glenview, IL: Scott, Foresman.

Wexley, K. N., & Yukl, G. A. (1984). *Organizational behavior and personnel psychology* (rev. ed.). Homewood, IL: Richard D. Irwin.

White, D. B. (1992). New realities in the health and human service sector in the 1990's translate into new opportunities and challenges for O.D. *Organizational Development Journal, 10*(3), 1–10.

Whitely, W., Dougherty, T. W., & Dreher, G. F. (1991). Relationship of career mentoring and socioeconomic origin to managers' and professionals' early career progress. *Academy of Management Journal, 34*, 331–351.

Whyte, G., & Latham, G. (1997). The futility of utility analysis revisited: Why even an expert fails. *Personnel Psychology, 50*(3), 601–610.

Whyte, W. (1956). *The organization man*. New York: Simon and Schuster.

Wilde, C. (2000, April 10). The new workplace: Telework programs are on the rise. *Information Week, 781*, 189.

Wilk, L. A., & Redmon, W. K. (1998). The effects of feedback and goal setting on the productivity and satisfaction of university admissions staff. *Journal of Organizational Behavior Management, 18*(1), 45–68.

Wilkinson, R. T. (1992). How fast should the night shift rotate? *Ergonomics, 35*(12), 1425–1446.

Williams, F. (1982). *The communications revolution*. Beverly Hills, CA: Sage.

Williams. S. L. (1989, November). *The characteristics of an effective performance appraisal interview: A rules approach*. Paper presented at the 75th annual meeting of the Speech Communication Association, San Francisco.

Williams, T. C., & Zahed, H. (1996, Winter). Computer-based training versus traditional lecture: Effect on learning and retention. *Journal of Business Psychology, 11*(2), 297–310.

Willinghanz, M. A., & Meyers, L. S. (1993, Winter). Effects of time of day on interview performance. *Public Personnel Management, 22*, 545–550.

Wilpert, B. (1995). Organizational behavior. *Annual Review of Psychology, 46*, 59–90.

Wilson, G. L., & Goodall, H. L. (1985, April). *The performance appraisal interview: A review of the literature with implications for communication research.* Paper presented at the annual meeting of the Southern Speech Communication Association, Winston-Salem, NC.

Wilson, J., & Cole, G. (1990, June). A healthy approach to performance appraisal. *Personnel Management, 22,* 46–49.

Wilson, J. R. (1993). Virtual reality benefits may prove illusory. *Interavia/Aerospace World, 48,* 34–35.

Winter, D. G. (1987). Leader appeal, leader performance, and the motive profiles of leaders and followers: A study of American presidents and elections. *Journal of Personality and Social Psychology, 52*(1), 196–202.

Winter, S. J., Chudoba, K. M., & Gutek, B. A. (1998, November 30). Attitudes toward computer use: When do they predict computer use? *Information & Management, 34*(5), 275–284.

Winters, E. (1993). Preparing materials for use by the entire world or let 'em eat cake, speak English, and think as I do. *Technical Communications, 40,* 502–503.

Wiswell, A. K., & Lawrence, H. V. (1994). Intercepting managers' attributional bias through feedback-skills training. *Human Resources Development Quarterly, 5*(1), 41–53.

Wofford, J. C., Goodwin, V. L., & Premack, S. (1992). Meta-analysis of the antecedents of personal goal level and of the antecedents and consequences of goal commitment. *Journal of Management, 18*(3), 595–615.

Wofford, J. C., & Liska, L. Z. (1993). Path-goal theories of leadership: A meta-analysis. *Journal of Management, 19,* 857–876.

Wolf, S. G. (1986). *Meta-analysis: Quantitative methods for research synthesis.* Beverly Hills, CA: Sage.

Wood, R. E., & Locke, E. A. (1987). The relation of self-efficacy and grade goals to aca-demic performance. *Educational and Psychological Measurement, 47,* 1013–1024.

Wood, R. E., Mento, A. J., & Locke, E. A. (1987). Task complexity as a moderator of goal effects: A meta-analysis. *Journal of Applied Psychology, 72*(3), 416–425.

Woodruff, M. J. (1991, October). Understanding—and combating—groupthink. *Supervisory Management, 36,* 8.

Woolsey, C. (1993, February 15). AIDS limits violate ADA, official rules. *Business Insurance, 27,* 2.

Wright, L. (1991). Type A behavior pattern and coronary artery disease: A quest for the active ingredients and the elusive mechanism. In A. Monat & R. S. Lazarus (Eds.), *Stress and coping: An anthology* (3rd ed., pp. 275–300). New York: Columbia University Press.

Wright, P. M. (1989). Test of the mediating role of goals in the incentive–performance relationship. *Journal of Applied Psychology, 74*(5), 699–705.

Xenikou, A., & Furham, A. (1996). A correlational and factor analytic study of four questionnaire measures of organizational culture. *Human Relations, 49*(3), 349–371.

Yaber, G. E., & Malott, R. W. (1993). Computer-based fluency training: A resource for higher education. *Education and Treatment of Children, 16*(3), 306–315,

Yarborough, M. H. (1994, October). New variations on recruitment prescreening. *HR Focus, 71*(10), 1.

Yates, D. A., & Jones G. (1998). Casual dress days: Are there bottom-line impacts? *Organizational Development Journal, 16*(1), 107–111.

Yeager, S. J. (1981). Dimensionality of the Job Descriptive Index. *Academy of Management Journal, 24,* 205–212.

Yerkes, R. M., & Dodson, J. D. (1908). The relation of strength of stimulus to rapidity of habit-formation. *Journal of Comparative Neurology and Psychology, 18,* 459–482.

Yoder, M. E. (1993). Transfer of cognitive learning to a clinical skill: Linear versus interactive video. *Western Journal of Nursing Research, 15*(1), 115–117.

York, L., & Whitsett, D. A. (1985). Hawthorne, Topeka, and the issue of science versus advocacy in organizational behavior. *Academy of Management Review, 10,* 21–30.

Yu, J., & Murphy, K. R. (1993). Modesty bias in self-ratings of performance: A test of the cultural relativity hypothesis. *Personnel Psychology, 46,* 357–363.

Yukl, G. A. (1981). *Leadership in organizations.* Englewood Cliffs, NJ: Prentice-Hall.

Yukl, G., & Tracey, J. B. (1992). Consequences of influence tactics used with subordinates, peers, and the boss. *Journal of Applied Psychology, 77*(4), 525–535.

Zachary, M. K. (1998, January). References—between a rock and a hard place. *Supervision, 59,* 20–21.

Zajtchuk, R., & Satava, R. M. (1997, September). Medical applications of virtual reality. *Communications of the ACM, 40,* 63–64.

Zamanou, S., & Glaser, S. R. (1989, November 18–21). *Communication intervention in an organization: Measuring the results through a triangulation approach.* Paper presented at the Annual Meeting of the Speech Communication Association, San Francisco.

Zaremba, A. (1988, July). Working with the organizational grapevine. *Personnel Journal, 67,* 38.

Zate, M. (1996, January/February). Breaking through the glass ceiling [Hispanic executives]. *Hispanic Business, 18,* 30–32.

Zedeck, S., & Cascio. W. (1982). Performance appraisal decisions as a function of rater training and purpose of the appraisal. *Journal of Applied Psychology, 67*(4), 752–758.

Zedeck, S., & Mosier, K. L. (1990). Work in the family and employing organization. *American Psychologist, 45,* 240–251.

Zeitz, G. (1990). Age and work satisfaction in a government agency: A situational perspective. *Human Relations, 43*(5), 419–438.

Zemke, R. (1986, May). Employee theft: How to cut your losses. *Training, 23,* 74–78.

Zemke, R. (1987, February). Sociotechnical systems: Bringing people and technology together. *Training, 24,* 47–57.

Zohar, D. (1997). Predicting burnout with a hassle-based measure of role demands. *Journal of Organizational Behavior, 18*(2), 101–115.

Aamodt, M. G., 295
Abraham, L. M., 223, 224
Acquino, A. L., 460
Adair, J. G., 68
Adams, J. S., 156, 204, 205, 217
Adams, S., 461
Adelmann, P. K., 222
Adeyemi, B. T., 268
Adkins, C. L., 99
Adler, P. S., 83
Afza, M., 260
Aiken, M., 174, 175
Alavi, M., 174
Aldag, R. J., 181
Aldana, S. G., 496
Alden, J., 269
Alderfer, C. P., 197
Alesse, B. G., 167
Alexander, R. A., 311
Allan, C., 442
Allen, D. C., 156
Allen, J. A., 421
Allen, M. W., 169
Allen, R. E., 398, 400
Allen, T. J., 159
Alliger, G. M., 239, 338, 387
Amalfitano, J. G., 295
Anagnostopoulos, F., 508
Anderson, C. D., 289
Anderson, L., 433
Anger, W. K., 521
Anselmo, J., 437
Anshel, J., 468
Antonucci, T. C., 222
Archer, E. D., 136
Ardelean, E., 323
Argyle, M., 161
Argyris, C., 433
Arjas, B. K., 137
Armour, S., 324
Armstrong-Stassen, M., 497
Arnold, D., 338
Arthur, A., 303
Arvey, R. D., 223, 224, 294, 296, 298,
    299, 341, 444
Ash, R. A., 374
Ashkanasy, N. M., 247
Atchison, T. J., 378
Atkins, C. P., 287
Atoum, A. O., 178
Atwater, D., 290
Auster, E. R., 264
Austin, J., 285
Austin, J. T., 6, 11, 12, 17, 18, 19

Avedon, M. J., 304
Aviolio, B. J., 124, 254, 256, 391
Ayman, R., 245, 246

Backoff, J. G., 145
Baden, I. J., 218
Bahls, J. E., 302
Bahls, S. C., 302
Baker, D. D., 502
Baldes, J. J., 212
Baldwin, T. T., 431
Baloff, N., 137
Balzer, W. K., 224
Bamforth, K. W., 92
Bancroft, E., 166
Bandura, A., 212, 431
Banner, D. K., 400
Barbee, A. P., 338
Barbuto, J. E., Jr., 254
Baril, G. L., 246
Baritz, L., 6, 11
Barling, J., 183, 254
Barlow, W. E., 391
Barnardin, H. J., 370
Barnes-Farrell, J. L., 392, 399
Barnshaw, J., 414
Baron, R. A., 7, 67
Barrett, G. V., 15, 311
Barrett, K. M., 246
Barrett, M. J., 510
Barrick, M. R., 334
Barry, D., 377
Bar Tal, Y., 263
Bass, B. M., 15, 18, 245, 253, 254
Bastain, R., 94
Bates, T., 120
Battisti, M., 507
Bauer, L. L., 222
Baumrind, D., 67
Baydoun, R., 349
Beach, L. R., 209
Beatty, R. W., 395
Beatty, W., 378, 380
Beauclair, R., 92
Becker, J. S., 355
Bedeian, A. G., 393
Beehr, T. A., 494
Beekun, R. I., 146
Beer, M., 132
Behnke, R. R., 209
Beland, F., 522
Belanger, K., 380
Belasen, A. T., 144

Belcher, D. W., 378
Belenky, A. H., 374
Bell, C. H., Jr., 136, 137, 226
Bell, J. D., 439
Bell, M. P., 120, 126, 129
Bell, N. E., 222
Bellarosa, C., 510
Bello, R., 129
Bemis, S. E., 374
Benbassat, I., 175
Benishek, L. A., 507
Benjamin, L. T., 29
Benke, M., 144
Bennett, C., 347
Bennett, N., 374
Bennis, W. G., 237, 238, 257, 270
Bensen, H. R., 511
Bentson, C., 307
Bentz, V. J., 351
Berger, R. M., 354
Bernacki, E. J., 297
Bernard, L. C., 507
Bernardin, H. J., 378, 380, 383, 386
Beyer, J. M., 103
Bhagat, R. S., 504
Bhardwaj, G., 84
Bielema, M., 519
Bierma, L. L., 98
Binder, C., 421
Bingham, S. M., 212
Birdi, K., 442
Birnbaum, D., 394
Birren, J. E., 123
Bischof, L. J., 123
Bizzi, E., 472
Black, J. S., 417
Black, M. M., 222
Black, R. H., 174
Blackburn, R. S., 40
Blaine, B., 168
Blake, R. R., 242
Blakeley, B. R., 299
Blanchard, P. N., 427, 437, 443
Blaney, J., 299
Blau, G., 285
Block, C. J., 264, 265
Blotzer, M., 472
Blum, T. C., 222
Bobko, P., 212, 313, 349
Bobo, L., 327
Bodensteiner, W., 156
Bohl, D. L., 395
Bohnker, B. K., 392
Boise, L., 502

Boles, J. S., 107
Boles, M., 167
Bolino, M. C., 371
Bonacich, P., 163
Bond, M. H., 24
Boos, A. L., 180
Booth-Kewley, S., 121, 506
Borack, J. I., 300
Bordieri, J. E., 298
Borman, W. C., 9, 20, 381, 391
Born, D. H., 135
Borofsky, G. L., 519
Borys, B., 83
Bottger, P. C., 137
Bottom, W. P., 137
Bouchard, T. J., 223, 224
Bouzid, N., 422
Bowers, D. G., 136
Bowne, D. E., 257
Boyatzis, R., 240
Boyce, B. A., 212
Boyd, B., 161, 170
Boye, M. W., 497
Boyers, K., 414
Boyle, E. A., 120
Bracey, H., 154–155, 157
Brady, R., 287
Brady, T., 301
Braham, J., 268
Bramel, D., 16
Brands, K. M., 414
Brannick, M. T., 225
Brannon, D., 376
Bray, D. W., 304
Brayfield, A. H., 195, 199
Breaugh, J. A., 287
Brenner, O. C., 268
Bresler, S. J., 300
Bretz, N. E., 209
Bretz, R. D., 206, 285, 287, 288, 370,
    392, 393, 394, 397, 399, 400, 401
Brice, G. C., 510
Brickner, M., 304
Bridwell, L. T., 196
Brief, A. P., 146
Brock, P., 222
Brodzinski, J. D., 512
Bronson, J. W., 105
Brooker, K., 97
Brooks, L., 209
Brostoff, S., 469
Brown, D. C., 326
Brown, D. R., 300
Brown, F. W., 253

Brown, L., 118
Brown, P. L., 285
Brown, S. D., 430
Browne, G., 138
Brownell, J., 164
Brumback, G., 382
Brunn, S. E., 178
Brush, D. H., 222
Bryan, L. A., Jr., 517
Bryan, W. L., 5
Bryson, G., 126, 129
Budman, M., 394
Buffardi, L. C., 421
Buhler, P., 159
Bulkeley, W. M., 296
Buller, D. B., 160
Buller, P. F., 137, 393, 517
Bumgart, B. L., 301
Bundrick, C. M., 197
Burgess, L. R., 378
Burgoon, J. K., 160
Burke, W. W., 137, 146
Burnham, D. H., 240
Burris, L. R., 338
Burrows, L., 257
Butcher, J. N., 323
Butler, D. L., 460
Bycio, P., 496
Bylinsky, G., 473

Cable, D. M., 99
Cadsby, J., 176
Callahan, C., 338
Callahan, T. J., 129
Caltabiano, M. L., 508
Camacho, L. M., 176
Camara, W. J., 330, 339
Cameron, K. S., 21, 107
Camp, R. R., 427, 437, 443
Campbell, D. T., 47, 48
Campbell, J. P., 200, 216, 425
Campbell, R. J., 304
Campbell, S. S., 514
Campbell, T., 175
Campion, J. E., 294, 295, 296, 297
Campion, M. A., 295, 297
Campoux, J. E., 146
Cangemi, J., 265
Cannon-Bowers, J. A., 424
Cantanzaro, D., 202
Capner, M., 508
Capwell, D. F., 199, 217
Cardy, R L., 390

Carlier, I. V. E., 527
Carnevale, A. P., 423
Carretta, T. R., 349
Carson, K. P ., 355
Carsten, J. M., 220
Carter, B., 83
Cascio, W. F., 311, 369, 370, 445
Cashin, J. R., 129
Castelli, J., 512
Cattell, J. M., 11
Caudron, S., 140
Cellar, D. F., 334
Chadwick, C., 180
Chalykoff, J., 381
Champagne, D., 389
Chan, D., 304
Chao, G. T., 473
Chapanis, A., 460
Charney, D., 422
Chebat, D., 59
Chemers, M. M., 244–245
Chen, P. Y., 510
Cheng, B. S., 394
Chiu, C. K., 387
Christensen, L., 68
Chudoba, K. M., 471
Church, A. H., 95, 146
Cianni, M., 268
Clarett, M. R., 439
Clark, A., 222
Clark, J., 127
Clary, J., 510
Clausen, J. A., 222
Clegg, C. W., 92, 94
Clements, C., 433
Cleveland, J. N., 368, 369, 370
Clifford, J. P., 282
Coates, J. F., 23–26
Codey, H. C., 430
Codina, V., 505
Coetsee, L. D., 108
Cofsky, B., 136
Cohen, A., 435
Cohen, A. R., 159
Cohen, J., 413
Colarelli, S. M., 180
Cole, G., 402
Colella, A., 313
Coleman, L. M., 222
Colihan, J., 48
Collins, J. R., 326
Compton, D., 169
Conger, J. A., 255
Connerly, M., 292

Connolly, T., 176
Conoley, J. C., 336
Contrada, R. J., 507
Conyne, R. K., 270
Cook, J. D., 224
Cook, M. F., 281, 286
Cook, T. D., 48
Cooke, W., 184
Cooper, W. H., 176
Copper, C., 180
Cornelius, E. T., 374
Cornell, P., 468
Costley, D. L., 159
Cotton, J. L., 266
Covin, T. J., 136
Cowans, D. S., 125
Coward, N. C., 157
Cox, G. L., 20
Cox, T. H., Jr., 429
Cozzetto, D. A., 169
Crable, E. A., 512
Craig, J. R., 263
Craiger, J. P., 467
Crampton, S. M., 220
Crandell, S., 429
Cranshaw, C. M., 422
Crocker, O. L., 473
Crockett, W. H., 195, 199
Crohan, S. E., 222
Cronin, M. P., 301
Cronshaw, S. F., 293, 355
Crouch, D. J., 517
Crump, C. E., 4, 297
Cullen, J. B., 105
Cunningham, M. R., 338
Cunningham, W. R., 123
Curnyn, J. P., 506
Curphy, G. J., 237, 239, 240
Currie, J. S., 183
Cutler, B., 121
Czander, W. M., 515

Daft, R. L., 156
Daily, B. F., 175
Dale, J., 243
Dalenberg, D. R., 59
Daley, J. M., 59
Dallin, R. F., 175
Dalziel, J. R., 69
Dansby, M. R., 105
d'Arcimoles, C. H., 109
Daugerty, R. A., 344
Davids, K., 93

Davis, K., 168
Davis, K. R., 285
Davis, S. F., 506
Davis, T. R., 480
Dawis, R. V., 223, 224, 225
Dawson, D., 514
Dawson, D. A., 517
Dawson, J. G., 290
Day, D. D., 207
Day, D. V., 247
Day, N. E., 374
DeBell, C., 285
Deci, E. L., 216
DeCotiis, T. A., 105, 237
Deddens, J., 222
Dedobbeleer, N., 522
Deets, N., 400
DeGrendel, D. J. D., 334
Deitchman, S. J., 445
DeJong, J., 301
DeLaers, K. H., 381
de la Mare, G., 476
Delaney, J. T., 109
DeLessio, J., 313
Deluga, R. J., 254
Den-Hartog, D. N., 104
DeNisi, A. S., 207, 399
Dennis, A. R., 176
DePaulo, B. M., 160
DePaulo, P. J., 160
DeSanctis, G., 175
Deshpanda, S. P., 106, 269
DeVader, C. L., 239
Devine, D., 349
Devlin, S. E., 290
DeVries, D. L., 236
DeWine, S., 169
DeWitt, K., 118
Dickson, W. J., 12, 195
Diehl, M., 176
Dienesch, R. M., 247
Digman, J. M., 334
DiMase, R. A., 120
Dinger, T. J., 285
DiPadova, L. N., 144
Dobbin, B., 126
Dobbins, G. H., 264, 390, 394
D'O'Brien, J., 165
Dodson, J. D., 494
Doherty, M. L., 247
Doktor, R. H., 120
Donohue, J. M., 197
Donovan, J. J., 210
Dorawala, T. G., 136

Dorfman, P. W., 257
Dossett, D. L., 212
Dougherty, T. W., 285, 429, 499
Dowell, J., 455
Drasgow, F., 121
Drazin, R., 264
Dreher, G. F., 429
Drehmer, D. E., 298
Dreman, D., 4
Drew, C. J., 61
Drucker, P. F., 379
Drury, C. G., 458
Duarte, N. T., 247, 393
DuBois, C. L., 391
DuBrin, A. J., 255
Dubrovsky, V. J., 175
Duftel, L., 378
Duhon, D. L., 521
Duleep, H. O., 267–268
Dulewicz, V., 305
Dumler, M. P., 107
Duncan, T. S., 523
Dunkle, D. E., 471
Dunn, P. A., 302
Dunnette, M. D., 9, 200
Durity, A., 257
Duxbury, L., 485
Duxbury, L. E., 484
Dworkin, J. B., 354
Dwyer, D. J., 496
Dyer, C., 42, 45
Dzindolet, M. T., 176

Eagly, A. H., 265
Earley, P. C., 209, 213
Easton, S., 138
Ebadi, Y. M., 253
Edgell, S. A., 374
Edwards, J. E., 58, 121, 146, 313
Eiser, A., 220–221
Eisma, T. L., 520
Eisner, J. C., 351
Ekman, P., 160
Elass, P. M., 174
Elfner, E. S., 430
Engibous, T., 107
England, G. W., 224, 225
English, G., 108
Erez, M., 210
Erffmeyer, E. S., 28
Erickson, R. J., 524
Estes, R., 477

Ettorre, B., 480
Everett, J. J., 178
Ewert, A., 434

Fairhurst, G. T., 266
Fang, Y., 203
Fanin, W. R., 475
Farah, A. M., 178
Farh, J. L., 393, 394
Farley, B. L., 389
Farr, J. L., 6, 26, 29, 221, 401
Farrell, D., 220
Farren, C., 494
Fasman, Z. D., 290
Feild, H. S., 285, 397
Fekken, G. C., 506
Fernandez, M. E., 416
Ferrell, O. C., 500
Ferris, G. R., 125, 183, 203, 391
Feuer, D., 349
Fiedler, F. E., 243, 244–245, 246
Fields, D. L., 222
Fields, M. W., 484
Filipczak, B., 159
Fine, M. G., 119
Finney, M., 121
Finstuen, K., 253
Fiore, A. M., 295
Fiorelli, J. S., 174
Fish, M. M., 297
Fisher, R., 305
Flaherty, V. L., 296
Flanagan, J. C., 373
Fleishman, E. A., 242, 297, 299, 351
Fleishman, S. T., 285
Flowers, L. A., 380
Flynn, G., 482
Folkard, S., 476
Ford, D. J., 413
Ford, J. K., 391, 418, 422, 440, 442
Forrett, M. L., 295
Fossum, J. A., 209
Foti, R. J., 239
Foust, D., 416
Fox, J. B., 197
Frame, R. J., 144, 145
Francis, C., 94
Franklin, G. M., 401
Frayne, C. A., 213
Frederick, E., 212
Fredericksen, N., 305
Freedman, S. M., 509, 510
Freeman, S. J., 21

Frei, R. L., 344
Freidman, H. S., 506
Freidman, L., 165
Freidman, M., 505
Freidman, S., 525
French, J. R. P., 259, 260, 261
French, W. L., 136
Frese, M., 476
Fretz, B. R., 28
Fried, Y., 183, 203
Friend, R., 16
Fritz, N. R., 511
Fromme, D. K., 160
Frost, M., 286
Fry, L. W., 96
Fuchs, P., 460
Fuentes, J. J., 416
Fulk, J., 161, 170
Fullagar, C., 183
Fuller, S. R., 181
Fullerton, H. N., Jr., 115, 118, 122
Funke, U., 351
Furham, A., 99, 357
Furhman, S., 299
Furnham, A., 395
Furniss, A. H., 265, 266

Gaertner, K. N., 220
Gafni, A., 138
Gainer, L. J., 423
Gaines, J., 96
Gaines, J. H., 159
Galagan, P. A., 445
Galer, S. M., 415
Gallupe, R. B., 176
Ganster, D. C., 496, 506, 507
Garcia, J. E., 244–245
Gardner, O. S., 432
Gaugler, B. B., 287, 304, 307
Gaurts, S. A. E., 221
Gebhardt, D. L., 4, 297
Gehrig, R. L., 436
Gehring, R. E., 435
Gerhart, B., 285, 287
Gerloff, E., 156
Gersons, B. P. R., 527
Gerstner, C. R., 247
Gibson, F. W., 246
Gibson, W. M., 225, 329
Gier, J. A., 293
Gigone, D., 174
Gilbert, M. J., 477
Gilbreth, L. M., 12

Giles, W. F., 285
Gillespie, J., 510
Gillespie, R., 12, 13
Gillet, B., 224
Gilliland, S. W., 303, 349
Gilmore, C. B., 475
Gilmore, D. C., 183
Girard, K., 481
Gironda, L. A., 85
Gist, M. E., 424
Gitter, R. J., 429
Glaser, S. R., 170
Glass, G., 66
Gleitzman, M., 383
Gloss, D. S., 513
Goetzel, R. Z., 496
Goldberg, J., 508
Goldberg, L. R., 338
Golden, P. A., 92
Goldenhar, L. M., 222
Goldstein, I. L., 435, 438, 442
Goldstein, J. L., 311
Golembiewski, R. T., 146, 495
Goodall, H. L., 398
Gooding, R. Z., 329
Goodson, J. R., 247, 393
Goodwin, V. L., 210
Gorey, K. M., 510
Gottfreson, L. S., 326
Gowing, M. K., 20
Graber, J. M., 400
Graen, G., 246, 247, 269
Graen, G. B., 203, 247
Graen, M. R., 203
Grandjean, E., 468
Graves, L. M., 174
Gray, G. R., 300
Greenberg, E. R., 300
Greenberg, J., 7, 178, 205, 207, 398, 400
Greenberg, S., 129
Greenblatt, E. C., 286, 444
Greene, C. N., 263
Greengard, S., 301, 482
Greenhaus, J. H., 218, 268, 391
Greenspan, M., 243
Gregouras, G. J., 299
Grenier, J. R., 338
Griffith, R. W., 156
Grimes, T., 156
Grossman, R. J., 118, 119
Guelker, R., 473
Guidoni, G., 473
Guion, R. M., 329, 332, 338, 382
Guppy, A., 222

Gutek, B. A., 471
Guzzo, R. A., 146, 210
Gyr, H., 165

Hackett, R. D., 220, 496
Hackman, J. R., 200
Hackman, M. Z., 265, 266
Hagedoorn, M., 221
Haines, G., Jr., 485
Hair, H., 146
Hakel, M. D., 200, 374
Haldeman, J., 94
Hale, B. J., 413
Hale, M., Jr., 10
Hall, E. T. A., 160
Hamlin, C., 137
Hammer, E. G., 292
Hammer, E. P., 217
Hammer, W. C., 217
Hanigan, M., 283
Hanisch, K. A., 224
Hanks, L. W., 416
Harari, O., 194
Hardman, M. L., 61
Harms, H. J., 350
Harrell, E. C., 514
Harrick, E. J., 340, 344
Harris, E. F., 242
Harris, M. M., 336, 354, 389
Harris, W. G., 338
Harrison, D. A., 120
Harrison, E. L., 103, 137
Harrison, J. K, 269
Harter, N., 5
Hartke, D. D., 245
Hartman, K., 221
Harvey, R. J., 374
Harvill, R. L., 270
Hasan, B., 175
Hashimoto, K., 269
Hastie, R., 174
Haston, R. M., 402
Hatch, D. D., 391
Hatfield, J. D., 205, 209
Hathway, S. R., 351
Hausknecht, D. R., 175
Havlovic, S. J., 485
Hawley, D. D., 174
Hayes, C., 267
Hays, R. T., 421
Hedlund, J., 174
Heilman, M. E., 264, 265
Helander, M., 468

Hellman, C., 199
Hellman, C. M., 220
Helms, D. B., 123
Hemphill, J. K., 241, 242
Henderson, J. A., 355
Heneman, R. L., 399
Henrikus, D. J., 517
Hepworth, S. J., 224
Herzberg, F., 199, 200, 217
Hesketh, B., 383
Heywood, J., 434
Higgins, C. A., 484
Highhouse, S., 389
Hilker, R. R., 507
Hill, J. E., 48
Hillis, M. J., 265, 266
Hinkin, T. R., 260, 261
Hinrichs, J. R., 200
Hirschfield, P. P., 136
Hissong, A. A., 460
Hlavacek, A. C., 521
Hoffman, C., 304
Hoffman, J., 519
Hoffman, K., 30
Hogan, J. C., 237, 239, 240, 297
Hogan, R., 237, 239, 240
Holden, E. W., 222
Holland, J. L., 223
Hollenbeck, G. P., 421
Hollenbeck, J. R., 174, 208, 211, 220
Holley, W. H., 397
Holloman, C. R., 237
Holmes, M., 175
Holmes, T. H., 504
Holt, B. A., 515
Holton, E. F., III, 440
Honold, E. G., 160
Hood, J. N., 84, 99
Hornsby, J. S., 380, 397
Hornsby, P., 92
House, R. J., 240, 245, 246, 248, 250, 255
Howard, G. S., 60
Howard, P. K., 23
Howe, S. R., 381
Howell, J. M., 254, 256
Howell, J. P., 257
Howell, W. C., 455, 457, 458, 471, 474
Hrycaiko, D. W., 210
Huber, V. L., 307, 312
Huebner, E. S., 508
Huffmire, D. W., 136
Hughes, S. S., 515
Hui, C., 269
Hulin, C. L., 121, 224

Hunt, G., 154–155, 157
Hunt, G. T., 154
Hunt, J., 83
Hunt, J. G., 243
Hunter, J. E., 20, 292, 307, 313, 329, 345, 346, 355, 380
Hunter, R. F., 292, 307, 329, 345
Hunting, W., 468
Hurrell, J. J., Jr., 222
Huselid, M. A., 109
Huseman, R. C., 205, 209
Huss, M. T., 506
Huszczo, G. E., 183, 427, 437, 443
Hutchison, S., 507
Hylton, R. D., 268
Hytten, K., 521

Iaffaldano, M. T., 218
Igbaria, M., 119
Ilgen, D. R., 20, 174, 208, 392, 399
Inderrieden, E. J., 398, 400
Ingols, C. A., 421
Ingram, T. N., 500
Ironson, G. H., 225
Irving, R. H., 484
Ivancevich, J. M., 497, 509, 510

Jackson, K., 429
Jackson, P. R., 93, 94
Jackson, S. E., 21, 499, 507, 508
Jacob, E. J., 331
Jacobs, R., 218
Jacobs, R. L., 240
Jacobsen, B. H., 496
Jago, A. G., 253
Jago, I. A., 299
Jakubowski, I., 506
Jamal, M., 497, 506
Jang, K. L., 223
Janis, I. L., 176, 177
Jantzi, D., 254
Jaquette, L., 300
Jarjoura, D., 439
Jarmuz, S., 104
Jarratt, J., 23–26
Jasenof, D., 299
Jawahar, I. M., 370, 389
Jaynes, W. E., 160
Jeanneret, P. R., 374
Jeanquart-Barone, S., 119
Jehn, K. A., 180
Jemmott, J. B., 199

Jenkins, C. D., 506
Jenkins, D., 502
Jensen, A., 521
Jermier, J. M., 96, 256, 257
Jette, R. D., 146, 210
Jha, S., 84
Jick, T. D., 510
Johns, G., 203
Johnson, B. T., 265
Johnson, F. L., 119
Johnson, G. J., 499
Johnson, L. W., 175
Johnson, R. S., 117
Johnson, T. R., 417, 426
Johnson, V. A., 126
Johnson, W. R., 183, 499
Jones, A. P., 247
Jones, G., 221
Jones, J. W., 338, 497
Jones, M. A., 386
Jones-Johnson, G., 183
Jordan, J. J., 298
Jordan, J. L., 393, 400
Joseph, J., 106
Jovanis, P. P., 460
Judge, T. A., 99, 222, 288
Judge, W. Q., 108

Kaeter, M., 424
Kahn, R. L., 89, 499
Kahn, S., 507
Kahn, W. A., 138
Kail, R., 351
Kaliterna, L., 476
Kalt, N. C., 295
Kanachowski, A., 175
Kanekar, S., 174
Kanfer, R., 217
Kantor, J., 224
Kanungo, S., 101
Kapea, J. T., 340
Kaplan, A., 41
Kaplan, R. M., 339
Karau, S. J., 178
Karayanni, M., 331
Karsten, M. F., 377
Karunes, S., 522
Kasl, S. V., 505
Kaspin, J. A., 124, 125
Katz, D., 89
Katz, R., 159
Katzell, R. A., 6, 11, 17, 18, 19, 146, 210
Kazel, R., 127

Kearney, R. C., 384
Keating, F. R., 351
Keaveny, T. J., 398, 400
Keisler, S., 175
Keller, J. W., 432
Keller, L. M., 223
Keller, L. S., 351
Keller, R. T., 92, 180
Kelley, D. L., 157
Kelloway, E. K., 254
Kelly, F., 83
Kelman, G. R., 517
Kemmerer, B. E., 507
Kemp, N. J., 94
Kendall, L. M., 224, 383
Kennedy, C. W., 209
Kennedy, M. M., 125, 393
Kenny, D. T., 497
Kent, R. L., 287
Keon, T. L., 208, 209
Kerr, D. L., 439
Kerr, N. L., 178
Kerr, S., 256, 257
Keys, B., 437
Khojasteh, M., 200
Kiechel, W., 103
Kiesler, S., 175
Kilmann, R., 96
Kilmann, R. H., 136
Kim, S., 295
Kimmel, C., 340
King, A. S., 270
King, J., 145
King, J. L., 471
King, P., 200
King, T. R., 391
King, W. C., 207
Kipling, K. D., 178
Kipnis, D., 263
Kirkpatrick, D. L., 439–440
Kirmeyer, S. L., 499
Kirsch, M., 329
Klawsky, J. D., 334
Klein, H. J., 211, 220
Kleinman, L. S., 292
Klich, N. R., 247, 393
Klimoski, R. J., 303, 304
Kline, D. W., 460
Klonsky, B. G., 265
Knauth, P., 476, 515
Knowles, M., 455
Knox, N., 300
Kobasa, S. C., 507
Koberg, C. S., 84, 99

Kochan, T. A., 237, 381
Kohler, S. S., 221
Kok, G., 496
Kokot, D., 468
Kompier, M. A. J., 465
Koonce, R., 416
Koopman, P., 104
Koppes, L. L., 11, 12
Korman, A. K., 218
Korman, R., 520
Korsgaard, M. A., 394
Koslowski, S. W. J., 473
Koslowsky, M., 220–221
Kossek, E. E., 104
Kouzes, J. M., 266
Kovach, K. A., 177
Koys, D. J., 105
Kozlowski, S. W. J., 247
Kraemer, K. L., 471
Kraiger, K., 391, 440, 442
Kramer, J. J., 336
Kramer, J. M., 514
Krasowska, F., 468
Krausz, M., 220–221
Kravchuk, R. S., 108
Kravitz, D. E., 224
Ku, L., 164
Kunhomoidee, U. A., 522
Kusbit, G. W., 422

Laid, G., 433
Laird, D., 424–425
Lamberts, R. D., 527
Lamm, H., 179
Lance, C. E., 221
Landau, J., 268
Landis, D., 105
Landis, R. S., 349
Landon, T. E., 298, 299
Landy, F. J., 5, 6, 11, 15, 58, 137, 294, 323, 376, 401
Langfred, C. W., 180
Laosa, L. M., 346
Lapakko, D., 160
Larsen, H. H., 85
Larson, J. R., 243
Lasden, M., 323, 356
Latane, B., 178
Latck, J. C., 208, 209
Latham, G. P., 209–214, 212, 213, 217, 218, 226, 355, 383, 384, 420, 432
Lautenschlager, G. J., 296
Lauterbach, K. E., 265

Lavin, A., 507
Law, B. D., 422
Law, K., 346
Lawler, E. E., 207, 209, 484
Lawrence, D. G., 290
Lawrence, H. V., 431
Lawrie, J., 411
Lazarus, R. S., 511
Lee, C., 209, 212
Lee, C. S. C., 439
Lee, M. J., 349
Lee, S. L., 338
Leibowitz, Z. B., 414
Leigh, J. P., 220
Leithwood, J., 254
Leithwood, K., 254
Lengel, R. H., 156
Leonard, R. L., 445
LePine, J. A., 174
Levine, G. P., 374
Levy, A., 144
Lewin, K., 134, 241, 256–257
Lewis, C. T., 378
Liden, R. C., 247
Liden, R. D., 125
Lilienfeld, S. O., 338
Lim, L. H., 175
Lindsley, D. B., 5
Lippitt, R., 241, 256–257
Lipsett, L., 415
Liska, L. Z., 248
Littlepage, G., 174
Lituchy, T. R., 213
Lively, W. J., 223
Loafman, B., 521
Locke, E. A., 209–214, 210, 212, 217, 218, 226
Lofquist, L. H., 224, 225
Lovell, S. E., 224
Lowe, R. H., 28, 289
Lowin, A., 263
Lozada-Larsen, S. R., 374
Lundgren, D. C., 381
Luthas, F., 427
Lysaker, P., 126, 129

Macan, T. H., 304
MacDonald, D. R., 307
Mackinnon, D. W., 16

Maczynski, J., 104
Maddi, S. R., 507
Mael, F. A., 292
Magruder, J., 478
Mahaffie, J. B., 23–26
Mahar, L., 244–245
Maher, K. J., 209
Mahon, M., 210
Makhijani, M. G., 265
Malka, S., 393
Mally, M., 435
Malott, R. W., 437, 438
Managan, I. L., 132
Mandelker, J., 468
Mann, F. C., 135
Mann, L., 177
Manning, M. R., 497
Manson, T., 298
Mantovani, G., 169
Manz, C. C., 263
Markels, A., 141
Marshak, R. J., 134
Marshall, A. A., 163
Marshall-Meis, J. C., 351
Martell, R. F., 264, 265
Martin, C. L., 296
Martin, G. L., 210
Martin, S. L., 354
Martocchio, J. J., 330, 471
Maslach, C., 508
Maslow, A. H., 195–197, 217
Mastrangelo, P. M., 300
Mastrofski, S. D., 209
Mataya, P., 351
Mathieu, J. E., 135, 221, 424, 445
Matkin, R. E., 222
Matteson, M. T., 497, 509, 510
Matthews, J., 437
Matthews, K. A., 506
Mattson, J., 290
Maurer, S. D., 292, 293, 297
Mausner, B., 199, 200, 217
Maxwell, S. E., 341, 444
May, B. R., 513
Mayes, B. T., 506
Maynard, R., 435
McAteer, P. F., 435
McAvoy, L., 433
McCall, B. P., 223
McCann, S. J. H., 255
McCanse, A. A., 242
McCarthy, C. E., 351
McClelland, D. C., 197, 198, 199, 217, 240

McClelland, V. A., 165
McCord, A. B., 426
McCormick, E. J., 374, 456, 459, 462, 466, 470, 516, 517
McCormick, F., 41
McCune, J. C., 169
McDaniel, M. A., 124, 292, 293, 297, 344
McDaniels, C., 415
McDonald, C., 184–185
McEvoy, G. M., 393
McGehee, W., 417
McGregor, D. M., 85–86, 98
McGuire, M., 246
McKee, D. O., 107
McKellin, D. B., 392, 399
McKelvie, S. J., 329
McKinney, W. R., 326
McLarne, C. R., 92
McLaughlin, K., 377
McLaughlin, M. E., 120
McLaughlin, S., 417, 426
McLean, A. J., 132
McLeod, P. L., 175
McMahan, G. C., 146
Meacham, R. C., 374
Meglino, B. M., 99
Meister, D., 456
Meltzer, A. S., 423
Mendel, R. M., 28
Mendenhall, M., 417
Mento, A. J., 210
Menzies, T., 254
Merante, R. J., 521
Mercer, M. M., 355
Mergenhagen, P., 129
Merry, U., 144
Metzger, N., 21
Metzger, R. O., 483
Meyer, H. H., 394
Meyer, J. P., 220
Meyers, L. S., 295
Michaelson, L. K., 174
Micolo, A. M., 286
Mile, E. W., 207
Miles, E. W., 205, 209
Miles, J. A., 178
Milgram, S., 50
Milkovich, G. T., 400
Miller, A., 498
Miller, B. C., 48
Miller, C. E., 173
Miller, C. S., 124, 125
Miller, L. M., 386
Miller, M. L., 437

Milliken-Davies, M., 236
Milliman, J. F., 213
Mills, D. H., 28
Milstein, R., 126, 129
Miner, J. B., 387
Miners, I. A., 146
Minter, S. G., 499
Mischkind, L. A., 200
Mishra, A. K., 21
Mishra, J., 167
Mishra, P. K., 84
Misner, J. E., 514
Mitchell, K. E., 338
Mitchell, M. C., 220
Mitchell, R., 137
Mitchell, T. R., 209, 212, 226, 248
Mitz, L. F., 510
Moch, M. K., 222
Monos, D., 508
Moore, H. A., 331
Moore, J. D., 436
Moore, M. L., 146
Moores, J., 477
Morano, R. A., 400
Morath, R., 292
Moravec, M., 165
Moray, N., 471
Morchio, G., 59
Morganett, R. S., 270
Morrow, J., 481
Morrow, L. A., 515, 516
Morse, D. T., 46
Morse, N. C., 242
Mortimer, J. T., 221
Mosier, K. L., 4, 20, 502, 503
Moss, M., 517
Motowidlo, S. J., 104, 391, 497
Mount, M. K., 334, 384, 393
Muchinsky, P. M., 209, 218, 248
Muczyk, J. P., 437
Muir, B. M, 471
Muir, N. K., 156
Mullen, B., 180
Mullen, E. J., 443
Multran, E. J., 416
Munday, R., 257
Murphy, B. S., 391
Murphy, I. P., 395
Murphy, K. J., 388
Murphy, K. R., 336, 338, 368, 369, 370, 394
Murphy, P. R., 59
Murrell, A. J., 471
Murry, H. A., 16
Muzenrider, R. F., 495

Myers, D. G., 179
Myers, O., 84

Nadler, D. A., 484
Nagao, D. H., 296
Napoli, D. S., 29
Nash, A. N., 437
Nasis, D. B., 393, 400
Neal, M. B., 502
Neale, M. A., 307, 312
Nebekr, D., 208
Neilsen, M. E., 173
Neilsen, W. R., 144, 145
Ness, Y., 520
Netmeyer, R. G., 107
Neuliep, J. W., 86
Neuman, G., 349
Neuman, G. A., 146
Nevo, B., 168, 303
Nevo, O., 168
Nida, S., 178
Niemira, H. G., 125
Nijhuis, F. J., 496
Nikon, B., 145
Ninan, M., 157
Noe, R. A., 418, 424
Noe, R. D., 329
Nollen, S. D., 220
Nomani, A. Q., 128
Nordhaug, O., 423
Norman, C. A., 213
Norman, D. A., 456, 460, 462
Northcraft, G. B., 307, 312
Northrup, A., 471
Notebaert, R. C., 117
Novak, M., 247
Nozar, R., 220
Nunamaker, J. F., Jr., 175
Nutt, P. C., 145
Nutting, S. M., 298, 299
Nystrom, P. C., 243

Ober, S., 289
O'Connor, C., 247
Offerman, L. R., 20, 254
O'Hare, D., 350
Okonek, K., 476
Oldham, G. R., 200
Oleski, D., 223
Oliansky, A., 67, 68
Ollenberger, J. C., 331
Ondusko, D., 126

Ones, D. S., 20, 59, 337–338
Oppler, S., 391
Oppler, S. H., 381
Orban, J. A., 386
O'Reilly, C. A., 159
Organ, D. W., 107
Osborn, A. F., 175
Osborn, R. N., 243
Osipow, S. H., 22
Oss, M. E., 510
Ostroff, C., 208
Oswald, A., 222
Outz, J., 311
Overton, R. C., 350
Owens, W. A., 290

Packard, J. S., 497
Paese, M., 304
Paetzold, R. L., 302
Palmer, B., 510
Palmer, D. K., 295, 297
Palmero, F., 505
Palmiter, D. J., 246
Papadatou, D., 508
Parasuraman, S., 268, 391
Park, J., 354
Parry, J. W., 126
Pasmore, W., 94
Pate, L. E., 144, 145
Paterson, T. J., 265, 266
Patten, T. H., 377
Paul, K. B., 224, 225
Paul, R. J., 253
Paulus, P. B., 176
Pawlak, T. M., 402
Payne, K. E., 265
Payne, R. L., 105
Pearce, C. G., 157
Pearl, L., 159
Pearson, J. S., 351
Pedeliski, T. B., 169
Pedrini, B. C., 388
Pedrini, D. T., 388
Pellegrino, J. W., 351
Pennington, P., 507
Pereira, J., 194
Perez, J., 429
Petee, J., 94
Peters, L. H., 245, 399
Peterson, L. V., 517
Peterson, R. O., 199, 217
Petrocelli, W., 501
Petruzzello, S. J., 514

Phesey, D. L., 105
Phillips, J. S., 509, 510
Phillips, K. R., 401
Picard, J., 59
Piderman, M., 468
Pierson, J., 514
Pietri, P. H., 103, 137
Pillai, R., 255
Pine, D. E., 373
Piotrkowski, C. S., 222, 432, 475, 502
Pitts, G., 145
Platz, S. J., 264
Ployhart, R. E., 299
Podsakoff, P. M., 260, 263
Pohley, K., 304, 307
Pohlmann, J. T., 245
Poletes, G., 176
Pollard, C., 439
Pollard, S., 176
Pollock, C., 175
Pondy, L. R., 159
Poole, M. S., 175
Pooyan, A., 222
Pope, M. K., 505
Pope, S., 104
Porras, J. I., 130, 144, 146
Porter, L. W., 193, 207, 209
Posner, B. Z., 266
Potera, C., 516
Potosky, D., 349
Premack, S., 210
Prien, E. P., 386
Pritchard, R. D., 208, 216
Prizmic, Z., 476
Prochaske, J. O., 60
Propp, K. M., 173
Pryor, R., 383
Pulakos, E. D., 381, 391, 399
Putti, J. M., 136
Pynes, J. E., 340, 344

Quinn, R. P., 499
Quinones, M. A., 299, 304, 307, 422

Raber, M. J., 503
Rabin, A. T., 413
Racicot, B. M., 519
Rae, L., 438
Rafaeli, A., 303, 480
Rafferty, A., 380
Ragins, B. R., 266
Rahe, R. H., 504

Rahim, M. A., 260
Raju, N. S., 146, 313, 354
Ralston, G., 286
Ralston, S. M., 287
Ramos, E. L., 258
Ramsey, R. D., 513, 526
Rao, A., 269
Rao, G. B., 379
Rao, S. S., 379
Rapp, B., 377
Raven, B. H., 259, 260, 261
Ravlin, E. C., 99
Read, W., 400
Reader, L., 422
Reber, R. A., 521
Reddington, K., 174
Redman, S., 517
Redmon, W. K., 210
Reh, F. J., 413
Reich, J. W., 507
Reilly, B. A., 224
Reilly, C. E., 224
Reimer, E., 242
Reitzes, D. C., 416
Render, B., 177
Rentsch, J. R., 104
Repa, B. K., 501
Repetti, R. L., 475, 502
Rice, B., 394
Rice, F., 140
Rice, R. W., 243, 510
Richardson, D., 68
Richardson, M., 246
Rick, J., 222
Riggio, R. E., 356
Ritti, R. R., 209
Robbins, T. L., 178
Robert, J., 138
Roberts, D. R., 146
Roberts, P., 92
Roberts, S. L., 506
Robertson, I., 20
Robertson, P. J., 146
Robison, W., 174
Robson, J. I., 92
Rockwood, G. F., 138
Rodgers, R., 380
Rodosevich, D. J., 210
Roebuck, D. B., 156
Roese, N. J., 68
Roessler, R. T., 285
Roethlisberger, F. J., 12, 195
Rogers, B., 522
Roland, C. C., 433, 434

Romberger, B., 268
Rome, H. P., 351
Rosel, J., 505
Rosen, B., 142, 424
Rosen, S., 159
Rosenbaum, W. B., 205
Rosenberg, S. O., 413
Rosener, J. B., 266
Rosenfeld, P., 58, 121
Rosenman, R. H., 505, 506
Rosenthal, D. B., 307
Rosenthal, G. T., 211
Rosenthal, R., 55, 66
Rosenthal, R. A., 499
Rosenweig, J., 136
Rosnow, R. L., 55, 66, 168
Ross, S. M., 254
Roth, D., 89
Rothstein, H. R., 346
Rowe, P. M., 294
Royal, K. E., 285
Rozelle, R. M., 247
Rozier, C. K., 466
Ruder, A., 222
Rudner, L. M., 322
Rupp, B., 468
Russell, C. J., 290, 313
Russell, J. E., 416
Rutecki, G. W., 439
Ryan, A. M., 296, 299, 356
Ryan, C. M., 515, 516
Ryan, K., 107
Ryan, M. S., 119
Ryanen, I. A., 327
Rynes, S., 142
Rynes, S. L., 285, 287

Saarela, K. L., 522
Saari, L. M., 417, 420, 426
Saccuzzo, D. P., 339
Sachdev, P., 432
Sackett, P. R., 296, 336, 338, 356, 391, 443
Saks, A. M., 288
Salas, E., 424, 440, 442, 444
Salsburg, B. L., 290
Sanchez, J. I., 222
Sanchez, M. E., 59
Sanders, M. S., 456, 459, 462, 466, 470, 516, 517
Sanders, R. L., 85
Sanders, S., 267–268
Sanford, A., 154–155, 157

Sanson, N. G., 222
Sarkis, K., 468
Satava, R. M., 472
Satterfield, M., 287
Saupe, K., 299
Savery, L. K., 505
Saville, P., 334
Saxton, M. J., 96
Scandura, T. A., 203, 246
Schack, R. W., 108
Schaefer, D. O., 340, 344
Schapppe, S. P., 107
Schaubroeck, J., 506, 507
Schein, E. H., 96, 104, 137
Schein, V. E., 264
Schemmer, F. M., 351
Scherer, R. F., 512
Schleien, S. J., 433
Schlossberg, N. K., 414
Schmidt, F. L., 20, 67, 208, 292, 293, 297,
    313, 337–338, 346
Schmidt, S. M., 237
Schmidt, W. C., 58
Schmitt, N., 329, 349, 424
Schnake, M. E., 107, 164
Schneider, B., 146
Schneider, D. L., 339
Schriesheim, C. A., 244, 257, 260, 261
Schroeder, M. K., 377
Schuler, R. S., 21, 499, 507
Schultz, B., 213
Schuster, M. H., 124, 125
Schwab, D. P., 224
Schwab, R. L., 507
Schwartz, D. F., 161
Schwartz, F. N., 502
Schwepker, C. H., Jr., 500
Schwoerer, C., 424
Scott, C., 175
Scott, K. D., 197
Scott, P. A., 460
Scott, W., 510
Scott, W. D., 5, 323
Scrinivasan, R., 460
Seay, R., 257
Sechrest, L. B., 338
Segal, N. L., 223, 224
Sego, D. J., 422
Seijta, G. H., 384
Seligman, D., 433
Seltzer, R., 119
Selye, H., 498
Semin, G. R., 160
Serpa, R., 96

Sethna, B. N., 175
Seymour, L., 138
Shadmehr, R., 472
Shahani, C., 517
Shangraw, R. F., 59
Shani, A., 94
Shankster, L. J., 294, 376
Sharpe, D., 68
Shartle, C. L., 241
Shaw, M. E., 161
Shepard, J. A., 179
Sheridan, J. E., 99
Shihadeh-Gomaa, A., 466
Shimberg, B., 29
Shipper, F., 236
Shirmeyer, R., 380, 397
Shore, J. E., 414
Siding, T., 85
Silver, E. M., 347
Silver, R. C., 130, 144
Silverman, S. B., 384, 398
Sime, W. E., 506
Simon, M. C., 264, 265
Simon, S. J., 431
Sims, D. B. P., 132
Sims, H. P., 263
Sinclair, M. A., 458
Sistrunk, F., 374
Skauli, G., 521
Sloan, H., 174
Slocum, J. W., 96
Smith, B., 280
Smith, D. E., 389
Smith, D. L., 514
Smith, L., 476
Smith, M. J., 521
Smith, P. B., 24
Smith, P. C., 224, 225, 383
Smith, R. E., 178
Smith, S. S., 68
Smith, T. L., 412
Smith, T. W., 505
Smith B. N., 380, 397
Smyer, M. A., 376
Smyth, K. A., 505
Snipes, J. B., 209
Snoek, J. D., 499
Snyderman, B. B., 200
Soder, D. A., 374
Sohn, D., 67
Sokal, M. M., 10
Solano, L., 507
Solomon, R. L., 443
Solomon, T., 218

Somers, M. H., 394
Sommer, R. D., 300
Sommerkamp, P., 247
Sonnenfeld, J., 16
Soper, B., 211
Sorensen, R., 401
Sorenson, P. F., 85
Sothmann, M., 299
Sotoodeh, Y., 356
Soutar, G. N., 175
Southerst, J., 414
Spangler, W. D., 199, 240, 255
Spector, P. E., 220
Spencer, C. C., 289
Spinks, N., 394
Spokane, A. R., 331
Sprinkle, J., 471
Spychalski, A. C., 304, 307
Stamm, C. L., 220
Stamps, D., 295
Stanisci, S., 507
Stanley, J. C., 47
Stano, M., 398
Staw, B. M., 222
Stecklow, S., 327
Stedham, Y., 220
Steele, T. P., 420
Steers, R. M., 193
Steiner, D. D., 303
Steiner, R. L., 175
Steinhauer, J., 295
Steinhaus, S. D., 313
Stern, A. L., 433
Stevens, C. K., 378
Stevenson, J. G., 495
Stewart, L., 138
Stilwell, D., 125, 247
Stohl, C., 163
Stone, W. S., 169
Stoneman, K., 166
Streit, A., 376
Stremmel, A. J., 104
Stringfield, P., 395
Stroebe, W., 176
Stroman, C. A., 119
Strube, M. J., 245
Stuller, J., 414
Stumpf, S. A., 221
Subich, L. M., 223
Sulzer-Azaroff, B., 521
Sumerlin, J. A., 197
Summers, T. P., 207
Sun, B. C., 146
Sunoo, B. P., 167

Super, D. E., 415
Surrette, M. A., 377
Sussman, L., 92
Suszko, M. K., 287
Sutton, R. I., 480
Suutari, V., 269
Swanson, R. A., 422
Sweeney, J. C., 175
Sweeney, P. D., 205
Swenson, W. M., 351
Szabo, J. C., 412

Tannenbaum, S. I., 20, 418, 424, 425, 436
Taricone, P. F., 298
Taubman, P., 223
Tayeb, M., 269
Taylor, D. K., 160
Taylor, F. W., 195, 454
Taylor, G. S., 287, 332
Taylor, H., 59
Taylor, L. R., 350
Taylor, R. W., 525
Tenopyr, M. L., 329
Tepper, B. J., 244
Terpestra, D. E., 283, 502
Tesser, A., 159
Tetrault, L. A., 244
Tetrick, L. E., 203
Tett, R. P., 220
Thacker, J. W., 484
Thacker, R. A., 430
Tharenou, P., 220
Thatcher, M., 303
Thatcher, S. M. B., 180
Thayer, P. W., 417
Theorell, T., 513
Thierry, H., 104, 209
Thomas, M. D., 58
Thomas, S. L., 206, 370, 392, 393, 394, 397, 399, 401
Thomas, T., 176
Thompson, D. E., 384
Thompson, K. D., 430
Thornburg, L., 295, 527
Thorndike, R. L., 399
Thornton, G. C., III, 287, 304, 307
Tichy, N. M., 133
Tiegs, R. B., 203
Tiffin, J., 41
Ting, Y., 221
Tippins, N., 391
Todd, R., 159
Todorov, E., 472

Tokar, D. M., 223
Tomkiewicz, J., 268
Toqlia, M. P., 435
Tracey, J. B., 262
Trevino, L. K., 156
Trice, H. M., 103
Trist, E. L., 92
Trucks, L., 461
Trumble, R. R., 380
Truxillo, D. M., 390
Tseo, G. K., 258
Tucker, D., 354
Tudor, T. R., 380
Tuffield, D., 132
Tunnell, J., 257
Turban, D. B., 247, 285, 295
Turban, E., 467
Turnage, J. J., 21
Turner, J. S., 123
Turner, M. E., 163
Tushman, M., 159
Twisleton, M., 393
Tyler, K., 414

Umstot, D. D., 226
Upadhyay, S. N., 221
Uslan, S. S., 521

Valacich, J. S., 176
Vale, C. D., 351
Vancouver, J. B., 208
Vandeberg, R. J., 221
van der Heever, P. K., 108
Van De Water, T. J., 6, 8
Van Erde, W., 209
Vanjani, M., 175
Vansickle, T. R., 340
Van Yparen, N. W., 221
Vardell, K. D., 496
Varrick, M. R., 59
Vasse, R. M., 496
Vecchio, R. P., 246, 312
Vega, A., 477
Verespej, M. A., 126, 287
Verma, O., P., 221
Vernon, P. A., 223
Vettare, F. L., 437
Victor, B., 105
Vink, P., 465
Viswesvaran, C., 59, 269, 337–338
Vodanovich, S. J., 289
Von Bergen, C. W., 211

Von Glinow, M. A., 483
Vrij, A., 160
Vroom, V. H., 207, 253

Waclawski, J., 146
Waddell, J. R., 281
Wages, C., 298
Wagner, J. A., III, 220
Wagner, R. J., 433, 434
Wagner, R. K., 329
Wahba, M. A., 196
Wakabayashi, M., 247
Waldman, D. A., 124, 391
Waldron, H. L., 414
Waldrum, S. B., 125
Walker, C. J., 168
Walker, J., 476
Walker, R., 86
Wall, T. D., 93, 94, 224
Wallin, J. A., 521
Walsh-Bowers, R., 146
Walter, K., 165
Walters, F. M., 141
Walther, J. B., 170
Walton, A. E., 132
Wanlin, C. M., 210
Wanous, J. P., 197, 208, 209
Wardell, M. G., 145, 513
Warner, D., 298
Warner, J. L., 289
Warr, P. B., 222, 224, 442
Watanabe, S., 222
Watson, R., 175
Watson, W. E., 174, 209
Waung, M. P., 12, 389
Wayne, S. J., 247
Webb, D. O., 517
Webb, G. R., 517
Weber, M., 81, 83, 254
Weber, T., 254
Webster, J., 471
Weekley, J. A., 293
Weick, K. E., 137
Weinberg, R. S., 243
Weiner, B. J., 265
Weiner, S. P., 48
Weir, R., 138
Weisner, W. H., 293
Weiss, D. J., 224, 225
Weiss, N., 283
Welch, J., 415
Wellins, R. S., 136
Wells, B., 394

Wells, S. J., 477
Wensky, A. H., 415
Werbel, J. D., 393
Werner, J. M., 371, 431
Wexley, K. N., 383, 384, 398, 399, 429, 432
Whetzel, D. L., 292, 293, 297
Whitaker, F., 384
White, B. J., 209
White, D. B., 146
White, K., 169
White, L. A., 381, 391
White, R. K., 241, 256–257
Whitely, W., 429
Whitener, E. M., 330
Whitsett, D. A., 16
Whittier, F. C., 439
Whyte, G., 355
Whyte, W., 356
Wiggins, J. G., 183
Wiggins, S., 213
Wilborn, 302
Wilde, C., 483
Wilderom, C. P. M., 104
Wilk, L. A., 210
Wilkinson, R. T., 476
Williams, C. R., 211, 220, 370, 389
Williams, F., 168–169
Williams, K. D., 178
Williams, R. E., 368, 369, 370
Williams, S. L., 398
Williams, T. C., 439
Willinghanz, M. a., 295
Wilmot, R. E., 165

Wilpert, B., 95
Wilson, C. L., 236
Wilson, G. L., 398
Wilson, J., 402
Wilson, J. R., 436
Wing, H., 338
Winter, D. G., 197, 263
Winter, S. J., 471
Winters, E., 157
Wiswell, A. K., 431
Wofford, J. C., 210, 248
Wogalter, M. S., 519
Wolf, S. G., 67
Wolfe, D. M., 499
Wolfe, T., 465
Wong, D. T., 338
Wood, R. E., 210, 212
Wooden, M., 505
Woodman, R. W., 146
Woodruff, M. J., 177
Woolsey, C., 301
Wormley, W. M., 119, 268
Woycke, J., 255
Wright, L., 505

Xenikou, A., 99
Xie, J. L., 203

Yaber, G. E., 438
Yamamoto, K., 123
Yarborough, M. H., 281
Yardani, H. N., 505

Yarkin-Levin, K., 351
Yates, D. A., 221
Yeager, S. J., 224
Yerkes, R. M., 494
Yetton, P. W., 137
Yoder, M. E., 439
York, L., 16
Youst, D., 415
Yu, J., 394
Yukl, G., 20, 260, 418, 424, 425, 436
Yukl, G. A., 260, 429

Zachary, M. K., 302
Zahed, H., 439
Zajtchuk, R., 472
Zamanou, S., 170
Zaremba, A., 167
Zate, M., 268
Zatz, D. A., 102
Zautra, A. J., 507
Zawacki, R. A., 213
Zedeck, S., 4, 20, 311, 369, 502, 503
Zehavi, A. D., 168
Zeitz, G., 222
Zemke, R., 94, 338
Zickar, M. J., 350
Zidon, I., 210
Zimmerer, T. W., 332
Zimmerle, D. M., 417, 426
Zohar, D., 505
Zonia, S. C., 104
Zwany, A., 197
Zyzanski, S. J., 506

Absence culture, 178, 221
Absenteeism, 379
    child care, 502–503
    compressed workweek, 477
    job satisfaction, 219, 220–221
    stress, 496
Absolute standard methods of performance appraisal, 381–386
    behavioral rating scales, 383–384
    checklists, 384
    forced choice system, 385–386
    graphic rating scales of performance appraisal, 381–383
    mixed standard scale, 386
Accident liability, 516
Accident proneness, 516
Accidents
    age, 517
    alcohol/drug abuse, 517
    defining accidents, 512
    design factors to reduce, 517–518
    human factors to reduce, 519–522
    job demand vs. worker capability theory, 517
    organizational contributors to, 512–516
    physical environment and, 513–514
    rate, 379
    safety programs, 520–522
    shift work, 514–515
Achieve, need to, 197–199
Achievement-oriented leadership, 248–249
Achievement test, 334
Action method of planned organizational change, 133–134
Active listening, 157
Active practice, 422
Adolph Coors Company, 416
Adverse impact, 325
Advertising, psychological principles applied to, 5–6
Aetna U.S. Healthcare, 444
Affectively based outcomes, 441–442
Affiliate, need to, 197–199
Affirmative action programs, 327
    movement to eliminate, 118–119
    use and goal of, 117
Affordance in controls, 462
African Americans
    job stress, 119
    leadership and, 266–269

    racial and ethnic issues in workplace diversity, 120
    testing of, and legal issues of, 325
    in top management positions, 118–119
    in workforce, 115
Age Discrimination in Employment Act, 19, 122
    testing and, 324
Age issues, 122–125
    accidents, 517
    job satisfaction and, 222
    knowledge stereotypes, 123–124
    performance appraisal and frame of reference errors, 391
    performance evaluations, 124
    retirement age requirements, 124
AIDS. *See* HIV/AIDS
Airplane design, 17
Alcohol abuse, 517
Alderfer, Clayton, 197
American College Test, 340
American Hotel and Motel Association, 435
American Psychological Association, 18, 67–68
    ethics of testing, 327–328
    founding of, 5
Americans with Disabilities Act (ADA), 19, 26, 125–130, 377
    accommodations made for, 127–128
    benefits and successes of, 129–130
    defined, 125
    defining disability, 126
    employers' fears of, 127–129
    genetic test-based discrimination, 301
    HIV testing, 301
    medical examination, 297
    medical insurance coverage, 128, 129–130
    mentally ill employees, 128–129
    substance abusers, 128
    testing and, 324
    workspace design, 466
Ameritech, 117–118
Annunciator, 460
Apple Computer, 137, 254
Application blanks, 289–290
Applied research, 40
Apprentice training, 427–429
Aptitude tests, 334–336, 356
    multiple aptitude batteries, 334

    specific, 335–336
Army Alpha, 10
Army Beta, 10
Army General Classification Test, 16
Artifacts
    organizational culture and, 96–97
    use of, as nonverbal communication, 160
Asian Americans
    leadership and, 267–269
    racial and ethnic issues in workplace diversity, 120
    testing of, and legal issues of, 325
    in top management positions, 118–119
    in workforce, 115
Assessment centers, 303–307
    advantages/disadvantages, 304
    defined, 303
    improving, 306–307
    performance appraisal, 394–395
    steps for designing, 305–306
AT&T, 165, 166
Attribution bias, leadership and, 263–264
Audiovisual training, 434–435
Auditory displays, 460–461
Authoritarian leadership, 241
Autonomous work groups, 93–94
Autonomy, in core job characteristic, 202

Background checks, 301–302
Bandwidth, 478
Bar graph, 64
Basic research, 40
Behaviorally Anchored Discipline Scale, 383–384
Behaviorally Anchored Rating Scale, 383–384
Behavioral Observation Scale, 383–384
Behavioral theories of motivation, 214–217
    organizational behavior modification, 216
    reinforcement theory, 214–216
Behavioral theory of leadership, 241–243
Behavior criteria, 440
Behavior modeling as training, 431
Behavior modification programs, accident reduction and, 521
BellSouth, 106
Bell Telephone Company, 103
Benevolents, 205, 209
Bennett Mechanical Comprehension Test, 335

Bias
  hindsight bias, 51
  preventing in experiments, 46–47
Bills, Marion, 12
Bingham, Walter, 10
Bingham, Walter V., 6
Biodata form, 290–292
Body language, as nonverbal communication, 160
Brainstorming, 175–176
  improving, 176
  problems in, 176
Branching programs, 437
Bullpen offices, 479
Bureaucracy, defined, 81
Bureaucratic structures, 81–85
  advantages/disadvantages of, 83–85
  chain of command, 83
  division of labor, 81–82
  flat organizations, 83
  merit-based employment, 82
  principles of bureaucracy, 81–83
  rules in, 82, 84
  span of control, 83
  tall organizations, 83
Burnout, 507
Business games, 437
Business Organizational Climate Index, 105

California Psychological Inventory (CPI), 333
Career development, 415–416
  stages of, 415
Case studies
  communication skills training, 171
  computerized testing, 350
  defined, 60
  disadvantages of, 60
  diversity training, 142–143
  employee empowerment, 258–259
  goal-setting theory, 212–213
  leadership, 258–259
  motivation, 212–213
  as off-the-job-site training, 432–433
  organizational culture change, 102
  performance appraisal, 396
  personnel selection, 286
  scientific management, 8–9
  telecommuting, 48, 481–482

360-degree feedback, 396
  training, 444
  types of, 60
  uses of, 60
  violence in workplace, 525–526
Casual dress days, 221
Cautious shift phenomenon, 179
Centers for Disease Control, 523
Centralized networks, 161–163
  advantages of, 163
Central tendency errors, 389
Chain of command, 83
Challenger spacecraft disaster, 177
Change. See Organizational development
Change agent, 132
Change intervention, 131
Channel, in communication process, 156
Charismatic leaders, 254–256
  ethical issues, 255–256
  presidents as, 255
Checklists, in performance appraisal, 384
Chevron, 414
Child care
  absenteeism, 502–503
  nontraditional work schedules, 475, 476, 478
Chrysler Corporation, 102, 429
Circadian rhythms, 476
Civil Rights Act, 19, 116, 324, 347, 371
  testing, 325
Classical conditioning, 420–421
Classification, military, 9–10, 16
Clean Air Act, 482
Climate, in communication process, 156
Clinton, Bill, 260
Closed system, 88
Clothing, for interview, 294–295
Coding process, 90
Coercive power, 259
Cognitive design engineering, 455
Cognitive learning in training, 423
Cognitive learning outcomes, 440–441
Cognitive Resource theory, 245–246
Cognitive theories of motivation, 203–214
  equity theory, 204–207
  goal-setting theory, 209–214
  valence-instrumentality-expectancy theory, 207–209
College recruiters, 285, 287
Columbo Frozen Yogurt, 194
Communication, organizational, 153–171
  case study of communication skills training, 171

computer-based communication, 168–171
  conditions for, 154
  cross-cultural issues in, 157
  downward communication, 164
  filtering, 159
  formal organizational communication patterns, 163–166
  gatekeeper, 159
  gossip, 168
  grapevine, 167
  horizontal communication, 165–166
  informal organizational communication patterns, 166–168
  information overload, 159
  MUM effect, 159
  nervous system analogy for, 153–154
  nonverbal communication, 159–161
  parts of communication process, 154–158
  problems in communication process, 158–159
  rumors, 167–168
  upward communication, 164–165
Communication networks
  centralized networks, 161–163
  decentralized networks, 161–163
  patterns of, 162
Communication process, 154–158
  channel, 156
  climate, 155
  errors of commission, 158–159
  errors of omission, 158–159
  feedback, 157
  interpersonal skills, 155
  listening in, 157–158
  message, 155
  problems in, 158–159
  receiver, 156–157
  sender, 155–156
Comparable worth, 376–378
Compatibility in controls, 462–463
Compensable factors, 377
Compensation
  comparable worth, 376–378
  in equity theory, 204–207
  overpayment, 204–205
  underpayment, 204–205
Compressed workweek, 476–477
Computer-assisted instruction, 438–439
Computer-based communication

communication skills training, 170–171
   effective use of, 170
   problems of, 169
   types of, 169
Computerized adaptive testing, 350
Computerized performance appraisal, 380–381
Computer Sciences Corporation, 289
Computers/computer use, 92
   attitudes toward computer use, 471
   brainstorming, 176
   computer-assisted instruction, 438–439
   computer-based communication, 168–171
   ergonomic computer workspace design, 468
   group decision support system, 174–175
   hardware, 469–471
   for initial job interview, 295–296
   input devices, 469–471
   Internet-based learning, 444
   for job evaluation, 377
   older workers and, 123–124
   for performance appraisal, 380–381
   programmed instruction, 437–438
   repetitive motion injury, 468–469, 514
   software, 471
   task analysis and, 418
   technostress, 500
   testing with, 349–353
   virtual reality, 436, 471–472
   in workspace, 467
Concurrent validity testing, 342–343
Conference training, 433
Conformity, 97
Consensus decisions, 173
Consideration behavior, 241
Construct validity, 344
Consultative decisions, 173
Content validity, 343–344
Contingency models, 88
Contingency theories of leadership, 243–253
   Fiedler's Cognitive Resource theory, 245–246
   Fiedler's contingency theory, 243–246

House's path goal theory, 248–250
   leader-member exchange model, 246–247
   Vroom and Yetton's decision-making model, 250–253
Continuing education, 414
Continuous reinforcement, 215, 421
Contrast errors, 296, 390
Control groups, 43
   in quasi experiments, 47
Controls
   affordance, 462
   compatibility, 462–463
Controls in equipment design, 461–464
Core hours, 477
Core job characteristics, 200–202
Corporate culture, gossip and, 168
Corporate social responsibility, 25–26
Correlational studies, 51–57
   correlation coefficient, 52–55
   linear and curvilinear relationships, 56
Correlation coefficient, 52–55
Criterion-related validity, 341, 342–343
Critical incidents, job analysis, 373–374
Cross-training, 414
Crystallized intelligence, 123
Cumulative frequency graphs, 64, 65
Curvilinear relationships, 56
Cutoff score, 310–311

Dairy Mart Convenience Store, 525–526
Data, visual presentation of, 63–65
Debriefing, in research, 67
Decentralized networks, 161–163
   advantages of, 163
   job satisfaction, 163
Deception, in research, 67–68
Decertification, 184
Decision making
   brainstorming, 175–176
   computer-based communication, 170
   consensus decisions, 173
   consultative decisions, 173
   democratic decisions, 173
   group decision support system, 174–175
   by groups, 173–175, 180–181
   groupthink, 176–178
   by individuals vs. groups, 173–174

by leaders, 250–253
   Vroom and Yetton's decision-making model, 250–253
Democratic decisions, 173
Democratic leadership style, 241
Dependent variable, 43
Depersonalization, 508
Descriptive statistics, 535–543
   measures of central tendency, 535–536
   measures of variability, 540–543
   normal distribution, 536–538
   skewed distribution, 539
Descriptive validity, 341, 343–344
Detroit Edison, 135
Dictionary of Occupational Titles, 374
Differential Aptitude Battery, 334
Differentiation, 91, 324
Diffusion of responsibility, 178
Digital Equipment, 194
Dime Savings Bank, 286
Directive leadership, 248
Direct market pricing, 377
Disability issues, 23, 125–130
   accommodations made, 127–128
   defined, 126
   outdoor experiential training, 433–434
   performance, 126–127
   personnel selection process, 298
Discrimination
   age discrimination, 122–125
   performance appraisal, 371
   reverse, 326
   testing and, 324–327
Disney, 98
Displays, in equipment design, 459–461
Distress, 495
Distributed practice, 422
Distributions
   forced, 388
   normal, 536–538
   skewed, 539
Diversity issues, 23
   age issues, 122–125
   Americans with Disabilities Act (ADA), 125–130
   barriers to women/minorities, 116
   benefits of diversity, 116, 117–118
   characteristics of companies that encourage diverse workforce, 116–117

cross-cultural communication and, 157

cross-cultural management, 269

disability issues, 125–130

Glass Ceiling Commission, 116–117

group cohesion and, 180

job fairs, 285

language issues, 120–122

racial and ethnic issues, 118–120

selection rations, 307–308

Diversity training, 140–143, 417

case study of, 142–143

defined, 140

legal issues, 141

problems of, 140–141

suggestions for successful, 141–142

types of, 140

Division of Industrial and Organizational Psychology, 18

Division of labor, 81–82

Double-blind control, 47

Downsizing

organizational effectiveness, 108–109

stress and, 497

Downward communication, 164

Drug abuse, 517

Drug testing, 300

Dual-career families, 475

Dynamic homeostasis, 90

Eastman Kodak, 125

Education vs. training, 411

Elderly workers. See also Age issues

performance appraisal and frame of reference errors, 391

Electronic Communications Privacy Act, 169

Electronic mail. See also Computer-based communication

as communication channel, 156

as downward communication, 164

information overload, 169

privacy, 169

rumors, 168

Electronic Performance Support System, 438

Employee Aptitude Survey, 334

Employee assistance programs, 510

Employee empowerment, 257

case study of, 258–259

Employee Polygraph Protection Act, 336

Employees

downward communication, 164

suggestions by, 257

upward communication, 164

Employment at will, 281

Employment Non-Discrimination Act, 19

Employment Reliability Inventory, 519

Engineering psychology, 455

defined, 4–5

Entitled, 205, 209

Equal Employment Opportunity Commission, 19, 325, 371, 500–501

Equal Pay Act, 377

Equifinality, 91

Equipment design, 16–17

accidents and, 514

computer workspace design, 468

controls, 461–464

displays, 459–461

to prevent accidents, 517–518

role of human factors psychologist in, 456–458

roles of people and machines in, 458–459

Equity sensitive, 205

Equity theory, 204–207

Ergonomics

computer workspace design, 468

defined, 455

workplace envelope design, 466

ERG theory, 197

Errors

central tendency errors, 389

contrast, 390

frame of reference, 390–392

fundamental attribution error, 200

halo (devil) errors, 388–389

in interviews, 296

leniency and severity errors, 389

in performance appraisal, 388–392

recency, 390

similarity, 390

Errors of commission, 158–159

Errors of omission, 158–159

Ethical Climate Questionnaire, 105

Ethical issues

charismatic leaders, 255–256

organizational climate, 106

in research, 67–69

testing, 327–328

use of influence, 263

Eupsychian Management: A Journal (Maslow), 195

Eustress, 495

Exclusion design, 518

Executive recruitment, 287

Expectancy, 208

Experimental groups, 43

in quasi experiments, 47

Experimental realism, 49–51

Experiments, 42–47

assigning subjects to groups, 45–46

defined, 42

field, 48–49

laboratory, 48–49

preventing bias, 46–47

quasi, 47–48

realism, 49–51

replication, 44

variables in, 43

Expert power, 260

Externally focused, 211

External recruitment, 283, 285–287

External validity, 61

Extinction, 215

Extraneous variable, 45

Extrinsic reinforcer, 215–216

Eyestrain, 468–469

Facet measures of job satisfaction, 223–225

Face-to-face communication, as communication channel, 156

Face validity, 344–345

Fail-safe design, 518–519

Fairness, in equity theory, 204

Family and Medical Leave Act, 19, 26, 477

Fax messages, as downward communication, 164

Feedback

in communication process, 157

in core job characteristics, 201

need to achieve theory, 198

negative, 90

performance appraisal and, 368

in performance appraisal interview, 396–398

role playing and, 431

in sensitivity training, 432

360-degree feedback, 395–396

in training program, 425

as upward communication, 165

Fidelifacts, 289
Fiedler's Cognitive Resource theory, 245–246
Fiedler's contingency theory, 243–246
Field experiments, 48–49
Field studies, 57–58
Fight-or-flight response, 498
Filtering, 159
    downward communication, 164
First impression errors, 296
Fixed interval reinforcement, 421
Fixed ratio reinforcement, 421
Flat organizations, 83
Flexibility, importance of, as work skill, 95
Flexitour, 477
Flextime, 24, 477–478
Fluid intelligence, 123
Force, in valence-instrumentality-expectancy theory, 208
Forced choice system, 385–386
Forced distribution, 388
Formal organizational communication patterns, 163–166
    downward communication, 164
    horizontal communication, 165–166
    upward communication, 164–165
Four-fifths rule, 325
Frame of reference errors, 390–392
Freedom of Information Act, 328
Free-rider theory, 178
Frequency distribution, 62–63
Frequency polygon, 64
Functional Job Analysis, 374–376
Functional turnover, 220
Fundamental attribution error, in two-factor theory, 200

Gatekeeper in communication process, 159
    in communication network, 163
Gateway, 89–90
Gender issues
    comparable worth, 376–378
    gender attitudes and stress, 502–503
    gossip, 168
    home–work balance, 23
    integrity tests, 338
    interpreting nonverbal communication, 160
    job satisfaction and, 222
    leadership and, 264–266

mentoring and, 429
performance appraisal and frame of reference errors, 390–391
physical ability tests, 299–300
power and leadership, 240
sexual harassment, 500–502
General adaptation syndrome, 498
General Aptitude Test Battery, 334, 355
General Clerical Abilities Test, 336
Generalization, in research, 61
Genetic testing, 300–301
Gilbreth, Frank, 12
Gilbreth, Lillian, 12
Glass ceiling, 267–268
Glass Ceiling Commission, 116–117
Gliding time, 477
Globalization, 24
Global measures of job satisfaction, 223, 225
Goals
    in communication process, 154
    path goal theory, 248–250
Goal-setting theories, 194, 209–214, 248
    case study of, 212–213
    characteristics of goals, 210
    factors in fluency performance, 210–211
    high performance cycle, 213–214
    job enrichment and, 226
    self-efficacy, 212
Good worker trap, 424–425
Gossip, 168
    benefits of, 168
Grapevine, 167
    managers' use of, 167
Graphic rating scales of performance appraisal, 381–383
Graphology, 303
Graphs
    curvilinear relationships, 56
    general rules for, 63–64
    labeling, 63
    linear relationships, 56
    scatterplot, 52–55
    types of, 63–65
Great man theory, 239
Grievances, as upward communication, 164
Group cohesion, 180
Group decision support system, 174–175
Group polarization, 179
Groups in experiments
    assigning subjects to groups, 45–46

autonomous work groups, 93–94
control, 43
experimental, 43
matched, 45–46
Groups in organizations, 171–182. See also Unions
    brainstorming, 175–176
    cautious shift phenomenon, 179
    decision making by, 173–175, 180–181
    formal groups, 172
    group cohesion, 180
    group polarization, 179
    groupthink, 176–178
    informal groups, 173
    matrix structures, 172
    productivity, 15
    project team, 172
    risky shift phenomenon, 179
    social inhibition, 176
    social loafing, 178–179
    team building, 136–137
    work group, 172
    work teams, 172
Groupthink, 176–178
Growth need strength, 203

Hackman, Richard, 200
Halo (devil) errors, 388–389
Hardiness, 507
Harley-Davidson, 258–259
Hawthorne studies/Hawthorne effect, 12–16, 85, 218, 241, 454
    human relations movement, 15
    in observation for job analysis, 372–373
    productivity, 14–15
    quality-of-work-life programs, 485
Headhunting, 287
Head-up display, 460
Health. See also Safety in workplace
    sick building syndrome, 515–516
    stress and, 497–498
    wellness programs, 510
Herzberg, Frederick, 199–200
Hierarchy of needs theory, 195–197
High performance cycle, 213–214
Hindsight bias, 51
Hispanic Americans, 23
    language issues and, 120–121
    leadership and, 267–269
    racial and ethnic issues in workplace diversity, 120

in top management positions, 118–119
in workforce, 115
Histogram, 64
History of I/O psychology
beginnings of, 5–9
current trends in, 20–23
future of, 23–26
Hawthorne studies, 12–16
job design, 454–455
1960's to 1980's, 18–19
testing, 323–324
trait theories of leadership, 239–240
World War I, 9–10
World War II, 16–18
between World wars, 11–16
HIV/AIDS, 128
HIV testing in personnel selection, 300–301
performance appraisal and frame of reference errors, 391–392
Homeostasis, dynamic, 90
Honesty tests, 336–339
Horizontal communication, 165–166
Human factors, defined, 4–5
Human factors psychology
computers and, 467–472
defined, 455
equipment design, 456–464
nontraditional work schedules, 475–478
objectives of, 456
quality-of-work-life programs, 484–485
robots, 472–474
workplace design, 478–484
workspace design, 465–467
Human relations movement, 15–16
Human relations structures, 85–87
advantages/disadvantages of, 86–87
Theory X, 85–86
Theory Y, 85–86
Human resource departments, performance appraisal, 394–395
Human resource planning, 24–25
Hygiene factors, 199
Hypotheses, 41–42
operational definition, 42
Hypothesis testing, 545–546

IBM, 48, 179, 356, 467
Immune system, stress and need to affiliate, 199

In-basket exercise, 305
Incident Command System, 83
Incident methods, 433
Independent variable, 43
Indoor air pollution, 515
Industrial/Organizational psychology. See also History of I/O psychology
applied vs. research, 6, 29–30
careers in, 26–28
defined, 4, 20–21
education and training requirements, 28
fields of, 26–30
history of, 5–26
importance of, 2
major specialty areas of, 4–5
new topics of, 4
percentage of people working in, 3
regulation and licensing, 28–30
traditional topics of, 4
Inequity, 204
Inferential statistics, 544–546
hypothesis testing, 545–546
meta-analysis, 546
point estimation, 544–545
significance or probability level, 546
Influence, 261–263
defined, 262
tactics of, 262
Informal groups, 173
Informal organizational communication patterns, 166–168
gossip, 168
grapevine, 167
rumors, 167–168
Information input, 90
Information overload, 159
electronic mail, 169
In-group subordinates, 246–247
Initiation of structure behavior, 241, 243
Injuries
eyestrain, 468–469
repetitive motion injury, 468–469
Instrumentality, 207–208
Integrity tests, 336–339
Intel, 414
Intelligence
aging and, 123
crystallized, 123
fluid, 123
mental ability tests, 329–331
Interactive leadership, 266
Interest inventories, 331–332
Intermittent reinforcement, 215

Internally focused, 211
Internal recruitment, 283, 285
Internal validity, 61
Internet
communication and, 169
job fairs on, 286
rumors, 168
surveys and, 58–59
Interrater reliability, 340–341
computer-based test, 349
Interviews
applicant factors for improving, 294–295
clothing for, 294–295
contrast errors, 296
for employment, 292–297
first impression errors, 296
interactive computer program for, 295–296
job analysis, 373
job-related interview, 293
legal issues, 293
negative information errors, 296
organizational factors for improving, 295–296
performance appraisal, 396–399
psychological, 293–294
similarity errors, 296
situational, 293
stress, 293–294
structured, 293–294
unstructured, 293
Intrinsic reinforcer, 215–216
Involuntary turnover, 220
Involved listening, 157
Item analysis, 346

Japan
stress and, 493, 497
use of robots, 473
Jenkins Activity Survey, 506
Job analysis, 371–378
critical incidents, 373–374
defined, 281, 371
importance of, 371
interviews, 373
job evaluation and comparable worth, 376–378
job-oriented evaluations, 371
methods of, 371–376
observation, 372–373
in personnel process, 281
structured assessment methods, 374–376

task needs analysis, 418
worker-oriented evaluation, 371
Job Applicant Medical History
    Questionnaire, 297
Job avoidance
    job satisfaction, 218
    stress, 496–497
Job Bank USA, 286
Job characteristics theory, 200–203
Job demand vs. worker capability theory,
    517
Job description, in personnel selection
    process, 282
Job Descriptive Index, 223, 224, 225
Job Descriptive Index`, 121
Job design
    computers and, 467–472
    equipment design, 456–464
    history of, 454–455
    introduction to human factors
        psychology, 455–456
    nontraditional work schedules,
        475–478
    quality-of-work-life programs,
        484–485
    robots, 472–474
    telecommuting, 480–484
    theory of motivation, 199–203
    two-factor theory, 199–200
    workplace design, 478–484
    workspace design, 465–467
Job Diagnostic Survey, 200
Job enlargement, 226
    repetitive motion injury and, 469
Job enrichment, 200, 226
Job evaluation, 376–378
Job fairs, 285
    on Internet, 286
Job in General Scale, 223, 225
Job instruction training, 427–428
Job involvement, job satisfaction, 219,
    221–222
Job-oriented evaluations, 371
Job outcome, 207
Job-related interview, 293
Job rotation, 226–227, 427, 474
    repetitive motion injury and, 469
Job satisfaction, 218–227
    absenteeism, 219, 220–221
    decentralized networks, 163
    defined, 218
    grapevine and, 167
    increasing, 225–227
    job avoidance, 218
    job involvement, 219, 221–222

job outcomes and, 218–222
job performance, 218–219
leadership style and, 243
measurement of, 223–225
motivation and, 199
organizational citizenship, 107
vs. organizational climate, 104
organizational commitment, 219,
    221
personal factors in, 222–223
relationship to motivation, 194
turnover, 219–220
unions, 182
Job sharing, 24, 478
Job specification, in personnel selection
    process, 282
JOBTRAK, 286
Journal of Applied Psychology, 9

Karoshi, 497
Kennedy, J. F., 260
Kenworth, 414
Keyboard design, 463–464
Kuder Personal Preference Record, 331,
    332

Laboratory experiments, 48–49
Laissez-faire leaders, 257
Landscaped offices, 479
Language issues
    diversity issues, 120–122
    goal of common language, 121
Leader Behavior Description
    Questionnaire, 242
Leaderless discussion group, 305
Leader Match Training, 244–245
Leader-member exchange model, 246–247
Leader-member relations, 244
Leader Opinion Questionnaire, 242
Leader position power, 244
Leadership
    achievement-oriented leadership,
        248–249
    attribution bias, 263–264
    authoritarian, 241
    behavioral theory of, 241–243
    case study of, 258–259
    charismatic leaders, 254–256
    consideration behavior, 241
    contingency theories of, 243–253
    cross-cultural management, 269
    decision making by leaders,
        250–253

definitions of, 237
democratic leadership style, 241
directive, 248
effective leaders, 269–270
gender roles in, 264–266
initiation of structure behavior,
    241, 243
interactive leaders, 266
laissez-faire leaders, 257
Leader Match Training, 244–245
Least Preferred Co-Worker (LPC)
    scale, 243–245
managers vs. leaders, 237–238
participative, 248
power and, 259–264
racial issues and, 266–269
substitutes for leadership theory,
    257
supportive, 248
theories of, 238–256
trait theories of, 238–241
transformational leaders, 254
Leadership Grid program, 242–243
Leadership motive pattern, 240–241
Learning, 420–426
    active practice, 422
    cognitive learning, 423
    distributed practice, 422
    Internet-based learning, 444
    massed practice, 422
    readiness and motivation,
        423–424
    role of trainer, 424–426
    schedules of reinforcement, 421
    transfer of training, 421–422
    whole and part learning, 422
Learning criteria, 440
Least Preferred Co-Worker (LPC) scale,
    243–245
Lectures as training, 430
Legal issues
    age discrimination, 122–125
    Americans with Disabilities Act
        (ADA), 125–130
    background and reference checks,
        301–302
    biodata form, 292
    comparable worth, 376–378
    cutoff score, 310–311
    disability issues, 125–130
    diversity training, 141
    fairness of performance appraisal,
        370–371
    genetic testing, 300–301
    history of I/O psychology, 18–19

HIV testing, 300–301
integrity tests, 338
internal recruitment, 284
interviews, 293
medical conditions and personnel
  selection, 298
performance appraisal, 397
physical ability tests, 298–299
regulation and licensing of I/O
  psychologists, 28–30
testing, 324–327
Legitimate power, 259
Leisure, 21
Leniency errors, 389
Letters, as downward communication,
  164
Liberty Mutual Insurance, 377
Lighting levels, 513–514
Linear programs, 437
Linear relationships, 56
Line graph, 64
Listening
  active, 157
  in communication process,
    157–158
  involved, 157
  passive, 157
Literacy, workplace literacy, 412–413
Lone Star Steel, 413

MacQuarrie Test for Mechanical Ability,
  335
Magnavox, 413
Maids International, 8
Management. *See also* Leadership;
  Supervisors
  assessment centers for, 304
  consideration behavior, 241
  downward communication, 164
  grapevine, 167
  initiation of structure behavior,
    241, 243
  managers vs. leaders, 237–238
  organizational culture and, 99
  performance appraisal done by
    immediate supervisor,
    392–393
  racial issues of, 266–269
  satisfaction with bureaucracy and,
    84
  Theory X assumptions, 85–86
  Theory Y assumptions, 86
  upward communication, 164

Management by objectives, 212–213,
  379–380
Managerial Grid, 243
Mapping, 459–460
Maritz, Inc., 165
Maslach Burnout Scale, 508–509
Maslow, Abraham, 195–197
Massed practice, 422
Mass psychogenic illness, 515–516
Matched groups, 45–46
Matrix structures, 172
Mayo, Elton, 12, 14
McClelland, David, 197–198
McDonald, Charles, 184–185
McDonald's, 125
McGregor, Douglas, 85–86
Mean, 536
  in normal distribution, 538
  in skewed distribution, 539
Measures of variability, 540–543
Median, 535, 536
  in normal distribution, 538
  in skewed distribution, 539
Medical examinations, 297–298
Medical insurance coverage, Americans
  with Disabilities Act (ADA), 128,
  129–130
Memos, as downward communication,
  164
Men. *See* Gender issues
Mental ability tests, 329–331, 356
Mentally ill employees, Americans with
  Disabilities Act (ADA), 128–129
Mental Measurements Yearbook, 329,
  336
Mental Measurement Yearbook, 337, 354
Mentoring, 429
Merit-based employment, 82
Merrill Lynch & Company, 481–482
Message, in communication process, 155
Meta-analysis, 66–67, 546
  organizational development, 146
Metropolitan Life Insurance, 194
Micronite, Inc., 468
Milgram, Stanley, 50
Military
  classification, 9–10, 16
  history of I/O psychology, 9–10,
    16–18
Military Equal Opportunity Climate sur-
  vey, 105
Military Outplacement, 286
Miniature Punch Press Test, 336, 349
Minnesota Clerical Test, 347

Minnesota Form Board Test, 351,
  352–353
Minnesota Multiphasic Personality
  Inventory, 332, 351
Minnesota Satisfaction Questionnaire,
  223, 224–225
Minorities. *See also* Diversity issues;
  Racial issues
  affirmative action, 327
  apprenticeship programs, 429
  barriers in workplace, 116
  leadership issues and, 266–269
  mental ability tests, 329–330
  mentoring and, 429
  race norming, 326
  racial and ethnic issues in work-
    place diversity, 118–120
  testing of, and legal issues of, 325
  in top management positions,
    118–119
  in workforce, 115
Mixed standard scale, 386
Mode, 535, 536
  in normal distribution, 538
  in skewed distribution, 539
Mohrman, Susan, 95
Mommy track, 502
Moonlighting, 476
Motivating potential score, 201
Motivation
  affectively based outcomes,
    441–442
  behavioral theories of, 214–217
  case study of, 212–213
  cognitive theories of motivation,
    203–214
  defined, 193–194
  emerging theory of, 217
  equity theory, 204–207
  ERG theory, 197
  goal-setting theory, 209–214
  hierarchy of needs theory,
    195–197
  job satisfaction, 199
  in learning, 423–424
  need theories of motivation,
    195–199
  need to achieve theory, 197–199
  organizational behavior modifica-
    tion, 216
  reinforcement theory, 214–216
  relationship to job satisfaction,
    194
  theories of, 195–217

two-factor theory, 199–200
valence-instrumentality-expectancy
theory, 207–209
Motivator factors, 199–200
Motorola, 89–90
Movement compatibility, 462
Multiple aptitude batteries, 334
Multiple cutoff model, 310–311
Multiple hurdle model, 311–312
Multiple regression model, 310
MUM effect, 159
Mundane realism, 49
Münsterberg, Hugo, 6

National Referencing Corporation, 302
National Test of Basic Skills, 336
Need theories of motivation, 195–199
ERG theory, 197
need to achieve theory, 197–199
Need to achieve theory, 197–199
Negative affectivity, 506
Negative entropy, 89–90
Negative feedback, 90
Negative information errors, 296
Negative reinforcer, 215
Negligent hiring, 302
Negligent referrals, 302
New-employee orientation, 413–414
Noise level, 513
Nokia, 90
Nonfunctional turnover, 220
Nontraditional work schedules, 475–478
Nonverbal communication, 159–161
defined, 159–161
job interview and, 295
role of, 161
types and uses of, 160
Normal curve, 536–538
Norms, 346–347
Northeast Texas Community College, 413
Notebaert, Richard, 117
Nova Corporation, 415
Nufield Hospitals System, 402

Observation
job analysis, 372–373
self-observation, 373
Occupational Safety and Health
Administration, 19, 23, 469, 511, 523
O'Connor Finger Dexterity Test, 335
Office Depot, 121
Offices. See Workplace design

Off-the-job-site training, 430–439
audiovisual training, 434–435
behavior modeling, 431
business games, 437
case studies, 432–433
computer-assisted instruction,
438–439
conference training, 433
incident methods, 433
lectures, 430
outdoor experiential training,
433–434
programmed instruction,
437–438
role playing, 430–431
sensitivity training, 431–432
simulation training, 435–437
Oldham, Gary, 200
Olfactory displays, 461
Omni Hotels, 220
On-site training, 426–429
apprentice training, 427–429
job instruction training, 427–428
job rotation, 427
mentoring, 429
on-the-job training, 426–427
vestibule training, 427
Open offices, 479–480
Open systems, characteristics of, 88–91
Operant conditioning, 420–421
behavioral theories of motivation,
214–217
programmed instruction,
437–438
Operational definition, 42
Organizational behavior modification,
216
Organizational citizenship, 106–107
job satisfaction, 107
Organizational climate
defined, 95
ethical issues, 106
examples of, 96
vs. job satisfaction, 104
measurement of, 104–105
questionnaires for, 105
uses of, 106
Organizational commitment, job satisfaction, 219, 221
Organizational culture
case study of change in, 102
changing, 101–104
creation of, 99–101
defined, 95

examples of, 96
levels of, 96–98
measurement of, 98–99
person-organization fit, 99
team building, 103
uses of, 106
values in, 98
Organizational development, 130–146
action method of planned organizational change, 133–134
change agent, 132
components of, 130–132
defined, 130
diversity training, 140–143
evaluating, 145–146
motivations for, 130
organizational transformation,
143–145
process consultation, 137–139
resistance to change, 132–133
survey feedback method, 135–136
team building, 136–137
Organizational effectiveness, 107–109
downsizing, 108–109
facets of, 108
Organizational needs analysis, 417
Organizational psychology, defined, 4
Organizational results criteria, 440
Organizational structure, 80–95
bureaucratic structures, 81–85
flat organizations, 83
human relations structures,
85–87
sociotechnical system structure,
92–95
systems theory structures, 87–91
tall organizations, 83
Organizational target variables, 131
Organizational transformation, 143–145
Organization Man, The (Whyte), 356
Orientation, new-employee orientation,
413–414
Outcome-based methods of performance
appraisal, 378–381
computerized performance
appraisal, 380–381
management by objectives,
379–380
personnel data methods, 379
quantity and quality of work, 379
Outdoor experiential training, 433–434
Out-group subordinates, 246–247
Overpayment, 204–205

Paired comparisons in performance appraisal, 387–388
Paper and pencil exercises, 306
Paralanguage, use of, as nonverbal communication, 160
Parallel forms, 340
Participative leadership, 248
Path goal theory, 248–250
Pay. *See* Compensation
Peer evaluation, 393
PeopleSoft, Inc., 92–93
Percentile, 542
Performance appraisal, 367–402
    absolute standard methods, 381–386
    age discrimination, 124
    assessment centers, 394–395
    behavioral rating scales, 383–384
    case study of, 396
    checklists, 384
    computerized performance appraisal, 380–381
    defined, 367
    discrimination and, 371
    errors in, 388–392
    evaluating, 400–402
    fairness of, 370–371
    forced choice system, 385–386
    forced distribution, 388
    gender/racial issues and frame of reference errors, 390–391
    graphic rating scales of performance appraisal, 381–383
    human resource departments, 394–395
    by immediate supervisor, 392–393
    improving, 399–400
    individual purposes for, 368–369
    interviews, 396–399
    job analysis, 371–378
    legal issues of, 370–371, 397
    management by objectives, 379–380
    mixed standard scale, 386
    multiple raters for, 395–396
    multiple raters in, 400
    organizational purposes, 369–370
    outcome-based methods, 378–381
    paired comparisons, 387–388
    peer evaluation, 393
    personnel data methods, 379
    purposes of, 368–370
    quantity and quality of work, 379

ranking, 387
relative comparisons methods, 387–388
reverse, 165
self-evaluation, 394
subordinate appraisal, 393
as upward communication, 164, 165
Personality
    hardiness, 507
    job satisfaction, 222–223
    negative affectivity, 506
    stress and, 505–507
    of trainers, 425
    Type A, 505–507
    Type B, 505–507
Personality tests, 332–334, 357
Personal power, 259
Person-machine systems, 456–459
    controls, 461–464
    displays, 459–461
    steps in designing, 457
Person needs analysis, 418–419
Personnel placement, 281
Personnel psychology, 4
    defined, 4
Personnel screening, 281
Personnel selection, 280–313
    accident reduction and, 519
    application blanks, 289–290
    assessment centers, 303–307
    background and reference checks, 301–302
    biodata form, 290–292
    case study of, 286
    defined, 280
    diversity issues and selection ratios, 307–308
    Employment Reliability Inventory, 519
    graphology and miscellaneous selection methods, 303
    importance of, 280–281
    interviews, 292–297
    length of time for, 281
    multiple cutoff model, 310–311
    multiple hurdle model, 311–312
    multiple regression model, 310
    physical examinations, 297–301
    realistic job preview, 287
    recruitment, 283–288
    résumé, 290
    simple regression model, 308–310
    utility test, 313

Personnel Selection Inventory Test, 339
Pet Incorporated, 402
PhotoDisc, 396
Physical ability tests, 298–300
    legal issues of, 298–299
Physical examinations
    drug testing, 300
    genetic testing, 300–301
    HIV testing, 300–301
    medical examinations, 297–298
    physical ability tests, 298–300
Pie chart, 64, 65
Placebo effect, 46
Pluralistic ignorance, 51
Point estimation, 544–545
Polygraph, 336–337
Polyphasic, 505
Position Analysis Questionnaire, 374, 388
Position power, 259
Positive reinforcer, 215
Posttest-only design, 442
Power
    bases of, 259–260
    charismatic leaders, 256
    coercive, 259
    expert, 260
    of followers, 263–264
    leader position power, 244
    leadership, 259–264
    in leadership motive pattern, 240–241
    legitimate, 259
    need to, 197–199
    personal, 259
    position, 259
    presidents and, 259
    referent, 260
    reward, 259
    use of influence, 261–263
Preemployment drug testing, 300
Pregnancy Sex-Discrimination Prohibition Act, 19, 477
Presidents, U. S.
    as charismatic leaders, 255
    power and, 259
Pretest–posttest design, 442–443
Prevention design, 518
Principles of Scientific Management (Taylor), 7
Privacy, electronic mail, 169
Probability level, 546
Process consultation, 137–139
    assumptions of, 138
    example of, 138–139

Proctor & Gamble, 96, 98
Productivity
        group cohesiveness, 180
        groups, 15
        Hawthorne studies, 14–15
        human relations structures, 87
        management by objectives, 380
        stress, 494–496
        telecommuting, 482
        worker satisfaction, 14–15
Programmed instruction, 437–438
Programmer Aptitude Test, 356
Project team, 172
Psychological interview, 293–294
Psychology
        defined, 3
        specialization areas in, 3–4
Psychology and Industrial Efficiency
        (Münsterberg), 6
Psychology of Everyday Things, The.
        (Norman), 456
Punishment, 215
Purdue Pegboard, 335

Quality-of-work-life programs, 484–485
Quantity and quality of work measures,
        379
Quasi experiments, 47–48
Questionnaires, for organizational cli-
        mate, 105

Race norming, 326
Racial issues. *See also* Minorities
        job satisfaction and, 222
        leadership, 266–269
        mental ability tests, 329–330
        norms and, 346–347
        performance appraisal and frame
                of reference errors, 390–391
Random assignment, 45
Range, 540
Ranking, in performance appraisal, 387
Ratings, 399
Rating scales
        behavioral, 383–384
        graphic, 381–383
Reactions criteria, 439–440
Realism, 49–51
        simulation studies, 58
Realistic job preview, 287
Receiver, in communication process,
        156–157

Recency errors, 390
Recruitment, 283–288
        college, 285
        external, 283, 285–287
        factors that influence, 287–288
        internal, 283, 285
        on Internet, 286
        legal issues, 284
        methods of, 283–287
Red Lion Hotels and Motels, 300
Reference checks, 301–302
Referent power, 260
Referrals, negligent, 302
Reinforcement theory, 214–216
        schedules of, 215, 421
        types of reinforcement, 215
Reinforcers, defined, 420
Relative comparisons methods of perfor-
        mance appraisal, 387–388
        forced distribution, 388
Reliability, 339–341
        defined, 339
        interrater, 340–341
        parallel forms, 340
        in research, 61–62
        split halves method, 340
        test-retest, 339–340
Repetitive motion injury, 468–469, 514
Replication, 44
Research
        analysis and presentation of data,
                62–67
        applied, 40
        basic, 40
        case studies, 60
        correlational studies, 51–57
        ethics in, 67–69
        experiments, 42–47
        field experiments, 48–49
        field studies, 57–58
        generalization, 61
        hindsight bias, 51
        laboratory experiments, 48–49
        meta-analysis, 66–67
        pluralistic ignorance, 51
        purpose of, 40
        quasi experiments, 47–48
        realism, 49–51
        reliability, 61–62
        replication, 44
        requirements of good, 60–62
        scientific method, 40–42
        simulation studies, 58
        statistical significance, 66

        statistics and, 66–67
        surveys, 58–59
        validity, 60–61
        visual presentation of data, 63–65
Résumé, 290
Retirement planning, 416
Retraining, 414
Reverse discrimination, 326
Reverse performance appraisals, as
        upward communication, 164, 165
Reward power, 259
Right Stuff, The. (Wolfe), 465
Risky shift phenomenon, 179
Robotics, production line and, 93–94
Robots, 472–474
Role ambiguity, 499
Role conflict, 499–500
Role playing as training, 430–431
Role reversal, 430
Rorschach Inkblot Test, 333, 341
Rosenbluth International Travel Services,
        86
Rules, in bureaucratic structures, 82, 84
Rumors, 167–168
        electronic mail, 168
        Internet, 168
        stopping, 168

Safety in workplace, 511–527
        accidents, injuries and illness,
                512–517
        defining accidents, 512
        physical environment and,
                513–514
        reducing and preventing accidents
                and injuries, 517–522
        safety programs, 520–522
        sick building syndrome, 515–516
        workplace violence, 522–527
Sandia National Laboratories, 142–143
Scatterplot, 52–55
Schedules of reinforcement, 215–216
        training and, 421
Scholastic Aptitude Test, 340
Scientific management
        case study of, 8–9
        early applications of, 7–8
        fundamental principles of, 7
Scientific method, 40–42
        hypotheses, 41–42
        principles of, 41
        theories, 42
Score banding, 326

Scott, Walter Dill, 5–6, 10, 11, 29, 323
Sears, Roebuck and Company, 106, 127
Selection. *See* Personnel selection
Selection rate, 325
Selection ratio, 307–308
Self-actualization, 195
Self-assessment, in needs analysis, 418
Self-efficacy, 424, 425
    goal-setting theory, 212
Self-esteem, self-evaluation and, 394
Self-evaluation, in performance appraisal, 394
Selye, Hans, 498
Sensitivity training, 431–432
ServiceMaster Corporation, 522
Severity errors, 389
Sexual harassment, 500–502
    types of, 501
Shift work, 475–476
    accidents, 514–515
Sick building syndrome, 515–516
Significance level, 546
Similarity errors, 296, 390
Simple regression model, 308–310
Simulations, 305
Simulation studies, 58
Simulation training, 435–437
Single-blind control, 46
Situational interview, 293
Skewed distribution, 539
Skill-based learning outcomes, 441
Skill variety, 200, 202
Skinner, B. F., 19
Small Business Administration, 23
S.M.A.R.T. system, 377
Social inhibition, 176
Social loafing, 178–179
Sociotechnical system structure, 92–95
    advantages/disadvantages of, 94–95
    autonomous work groups, 93–94
Solomon Four-Group Design, 443–444
Space, use of, as nonverbal communication, 160
Span of control, 83
Spatial compatibility, 462
Split halves method, 340
Stakeholders, 108
Standard deviation, 540–542
Standardization, 7
Standardization of testing, 347
Standardization sample, 346
Stanton Survey, 339
Starbucks Coffee, 283, 526

State Farm, 350
Statistical significance, 66, 545
Statistics
    correlation coefficient, 52–55
    descriptive, 535–543
    frequency distribution, 62–63
    hypothesis testing, 545–546
    inferential, 544–546
    item analysis, 346
    measures of central tendency, 535–536
    measures of variability, 540–543
    meta-analysis, 66–67, 546
    normal distribution, 536–538
    norms, 346–347
    percentile, 542
    point estimation, 544–545
    reliability, 339–341
    significance or probability level, 546
    skewed distribution, 539
    standard deviation, 540–542
    statistical significance, 66, 545
    validity, 341–346
    Z-scores, 542–543
Steady state, 90
Stereotypes, knowledge stereotypes of older workers, 123–125
Stress
    absenteeism, 496
    burnout, 507
    cost of, 494
    defined, 494
    demands of work, 499–500
    Downsizing, 497
    employee assistance programs, 510
    fight-or-flight response, 498
    gender attitudes, 502–503
    general adaptation syndrome, 498
    hardiness, 507
    health and, 497–498
    job avoidance, 496–497
    life changes, 503–505
    need to affiliate and immune system, 199
    organizational consequences of, 496–497
    organizational contributors to, 499–503
    personal consequences of, 497–498
    personal contributors to, 503–509
    productivity, 494–496
    repetitive motion injury, 468–469

    sexual harassment, 500–502
    stress management programs at work, 509–511
    tardiness, 496
    technostress, 500
    Type A/Type B personality, 505–507
Stress interview, 293–294
Stressors, 495
Strong Vocational Interest Blank/Strong-Campbell Interest Inventory, 331, 332
Structured assessment methods, job analysis, 374–376
Structured interviews, 293–294
Subordinate appraisal, 393
Substance abusers, Americans with Disabilities Act (ADA), 128
Substitutes for leadership theory, 257
Sucker-effect theory, 178
Suggestion boxes, as upward communication, 164–165
Sun Microsystems, 414
Supervisors. *See also* Management
    leadership style and productivity, 15
    performance appraisal done by immediate, 392–393
    Theory X assumptions, 85–86
    Theory Y assumptions, 86
Supportive leadership, 248
Survey feedback method, 135–136
Surveys, 58–59
    of employees, as upward communication, 164, 165
    Internet and, 58–59
Systems theory model, 87–91
    advantages/disadvantages of, 91
    closed system, 88
    contingency models, 88
    open systems, 88–91
    organizational climate, 104
    organizational culture change, 101
    organizational development, 132

Tactile displays, 461
Tall organizations, 83
Tardiness, 379
    stress, 496
Task identity, 200–201, 202
Task needs analysis, 417–418
Task orientation, gender differences and leadership, 265

Task significance, 201–202
Task structure, 244
Taylor, Frederick, 7, 454
Team building, 136–137
    organizational culture, 103
Technology, 21–22
    sociotechnical system structure, 92–95
Technostress, 500
Telecenter, 480–481
Telecommuting, 24, 480–484
    case studies, 48
    case study of, 481–482
    productivity, 482
Telephone communication
    as communication channel, 156
    as downward communication, 164
Terman, Lewis, 11
Termination
    cost of, 281
    employment at will, 281
Testing, 29, 322–357
    advantages of, 355–356
    aptitude and achievement test, 334–336
    case study of, 350
    classification of, 347–353
    computerized testing, 349–353
    disadvantages of, 356–357
    discrimination, 324–327
    ethical issues of, 327–328
    future of, 357
    history of, 323–324
    individual vs. group, 348
    integrity (honesty) tests, 336–339
    intelligence, 10
    interest inventories, 331–332
    item analysis, 346
    language vs. nonlanguage, 349
    legal requirements of, 324–327
    mental ability tests, 329–331
    norms, 346–347
    objective vs. subjective, 348
    paper and pencil vs. performance, 348
    personality tests, 332–334
    physical ability tests, 298–300
    power vs. speed, 347
    purpose of, 322
    race norming, 326
    reliability, 339–341
    score banding, 326
    standardization, 347
    test utility, 354–355

U. S. Army and classifying recruits, 9–10
U. S Army and, 16–17
validity, 341–346
vocational interests, 11
Test-retest method, 339–340
Test utility, 354–355
Texaco, 136, 145
Texas Instruments, 106, 107, 226
Thematic Apperception Test (TAT), 198, 333
Theories, 42
Theory X, 85–86, 98
Theory Y, 85–86, 98
Thorndike, Edward, 11
360-degree feedback, 395–396
Three Mile Island nuclear plant, 461
Time, use of, as nonverbal communication, 160
Titchener, Edward, 11
Training
    accident reduction, 519–520
    case study of, 444
    diversity training, 140–143
    training culture, 424
Training assessment
    affectively based outcomes, 441–442
    cognitive learning outcomes, 440–441
    cost of, 444–445
    criteria for, 439–440
    posttest-only design, 442
    pretest–posttest design, 442–443
    skill-based learning outcomes, 441
    Solomon Four-Group Design, 443–444
Training/development. See also Training assessment
    assessment of needs, 416–419
    career development, 415–416
    classical conditioning, 420–421
    continuing education, 414
    cross-training, 414
    defined, 411
    diversity training, 417
    vs. education, 411
    evaluation on, 439–445
    guidelines for effective training program, 425
    new-employee orientation, 413–414
    objectives for, 419–420
    off-the-job-site training, 430–439

on-site, 426–429
operant conditioning, 420–421
organizational needs analysis, 417
person needs analysis, 418–419
principles of learning, 420–426
resistance to training, 423
retirement planning, 416
retraining, 414
role of trainer, 424–426
schedules of reinforcement, 421
steps in, 426
task needs analysis, 417–418
transfer of training, 421–422
workplace literacy, 412–413
Trait theories of leadership, 238–241
    historical and current, 239–240
    leadership motive pattern, 240–241
Transfer of training, 421–422
Transformational leaders, 254
Turner, Clair, 14
Turnover
    job satisfaction, 219–220
    new-employee orientation, 413–414
    training as way to reduce, 417
Tweezer Dexterity Test, 335
Two-factor theory, 199–200
Type A personality, 505–507
Type B personality, 505–507

U. S Army, testing, 16–17
Underpayment, 204–205
Uniform Guidelines for Employee Selection Procedures, 325
Unions, 18, 182–185
    changes in union membership, 182–183
    comparison with nonunion employees, 183
    decertification, 184
    job satisfaction, 182
    lack of involvement of I/O psychologists, 183
    organizational transformation, 145
    reasons for joining, 182
    ways to use I/O psychologists to rebuild, 183–185
United Parcel Service, 8–9
Unstructured interviews, 293
Upward communication, 164–165
Utility test, 313

Valence, 207–208
Valence-instrumentality-expectancy theory, 207–209, 248
Validity, 60–61, 341–346
    concurrent validity testing, 342–343
    construct, 344
    content, 343–344
    criterion-related, 341, 342–343
    defined, 60, 341
    descriptive, 341, 343–344
    external, 61
    face, 344–345
    internal, 61
    validity generalization, 345–346
Values, in organizational culture, 98
Variability, measures of, 540–543
Variable interval reinforcement, 421
Variable ratio reinforcement, 421
Variables
    defined, 43
    dependent, 43
    extraneous, 45
    independent, 43
    organizational target, 131
Vestibule training, 427
Videoconferencing, 483
Video Display terminal, 514
Video display terminal, 468, 469, 470
Violence in workplace
    case study of, 525–526
    crisis teams, 526–527
    prevention, 523–526
    workplace violence, 522–527
Virtual office, 480
Virtual reality, 436, 471–472
Visual displays, 459–460
Voice mail, as downward communication, 164
Voluntary turnover, 220

Wallace Company, 445
Wal-Mart, 101

Walton, Sam, 101
Watson, John, 11
Weber, Max, 81
Wechsler Adult Intelligence Scale-Revised, 330, 331, 348, 349
Weighted application blank, 290
Wellness, 25
Wellness programs, 510
Westech Job Fair, 286
Western Electric Company, 12–16
Whirlpool Corporation, 171
Whole and part learning, 422
Wolfe, Tom, 465
Women. *See also* Gender issues
    barriers in workplace, 116
    in workforce, 17, 23
Wonderlic Personnel Test, 329, 340, 348, 356
Word Processor Assessment Battery, 336
Worker Adjustment and Retraining Notification Act (WARN), 414
Worker-oriented evaluation, 371
    Position Analysis Questionnaire, 374
Worker satisfaction, productivity, 14–15
Workforce
    changing structure of, 115–116
    demographics of, 21, 23
    manufacturing-based vs. knowledge based, 25
Work groups, 172
    autonomous work groups, 93–94
    team building, 136–137
Work-home balance, 24, 47, 48
    gender attitudes and stress, 502–503
    nontraditional work schedules, 475–478
    telecommuting, 480–484
Working conditions
    computers and, 467–472
    equipment design, 456–464
    nontraditional work schedules, 475–478

quality-of-work-life programs, 484–485
    stress, 493–511
    telecommuting, 480–484
    workplace design, 478–484
    workspace design, 465–467
Work motivation. See Motivation
Work overload, 499
Workplace, defined, 479
Workplace design, 478–484
    open offices, 479–480
Workplace envelope, 465–467
Workplace literacy, 412–413
Work schedules
    compressed workweek, 476–477
    flextime, 477–478
    job sharing, 478
    nontraditional work schedules, 475–478
    shift work, 475–476
Workspace design, 465–467
    computer workspace design, 468
    problems in computer workspace, 468–469
    psychological factors in, 465
    workplace envelope, 465–467
Work teams, 172
Work underload, 499
World War I, 9–10
World War II, 16–18
Written communication, as communication channel, 156
Wundt, Wilhelm, 5

Xerox Corporation, 126, 129

Yerkes, Robert M., 9

Z-scores, 542–543